ON NOT DEFENDINC

Sidney's *Defence of Poesy*—the foundational text of ~~~~~~~~~~~~ ~~~~~lly taken to present a model of poetry as ideal: the ┤ ~~~~~~ ideals of human conduct and readers are inspired to imitate them. Catherine Bates sets out to challenge this received view. Attending very closely to Sidney's text, she identifies within it a model of poetry that is markedly at variance from the one presumed, and shows Sidney's text to be feeling its way towards a quite different—indeed, a *de*-idealist—poetics. Following key theorists of the new economic criticism, *On Not Defending Poetry* shows how idealist poetics, like the idealist philosophy on which it draws, is complicit with the money form and with the specific ills that attend upon it: among them commodification, fetishism, and the abuse of power. Against culturally approved models of poetry as profitable—as benefiting the individual and the state, as providing (in the form of intellectual, moral, and social capital) a quantifiable yield—the *Defence* reveals an unexpected counter-argument: one in which poetry is modelled, rather, as pure expenditure, a free gift, a net loss. Where a supposedly idealist *Defence* sits oddly with Sidney's literary writings— which depict human behaviour that is very far from ideal—a de-idealist *Defence* does not. In its radical reading of the *Defence*, this book thus makes a decisive intervention in the field of early modern studies, while raising larger questions about a culture determined to quantify the 'value' of the humanities and to defend the arts on those grounds alone.

Catherine Bates is Research Professor at the Centre for the Study of the Renaissance at the University of Warwick. She studied English at Oxford and was Fellow of Balliol College, Oxford, and of Peterhouse, Cambridge, before moving to Warwick in 1995. She has been awarded a number of fellowships, including a Solmsen Fellowship at the University of Wisconsin-Madison and a Mellon Fellowship at the Huntington Library; and has also won a number of prizes, including the British Academy Rose Mary Crawshay Prize for *Masculinity and the Hunt: Wyatt to Spenser* (OUP, 2013).

On Not Defending Poetry

Defence and Indefensibility in Sidney's *Defence of Poesy*

CATHERINE BATES

OXFORD
UNIVERSITY PRESS

OXFORD
UNIVERSITY PRESS

Great Clarendon Street, Oxford, OX2 6DP,
United Kingdom

Oxford University Press is a department of the University of Oxford.
It furthers the University's objective of excellence in research, scholarship,
and education by publishing worldwide. Oxford is a registered trade mark of
Oxford University Press in the UK and in certain other countries

First published 2017
First published in paperback 2021

Published in the United States of America by Oxford University Press
198 Madison Avenue, New York, NY 10016, United States of America

British Library Cataloguing in Publication Data
Data available

Library of Congress Cataloging in Publication Data
Data available

ISBN 978–0–19–879377–9 (Hbk.)
ISBN 978–0–19–285634–0 (Pbk.)

for the poets

Preface

This book offers a radically new reading of Philip Sidney's *Defence of Poesy* (1595), the foundational text of English poetics. The prevailing view—long held—is that Sidney's text articulates a model of poetry as ideal. Working from an '*Idea* or fore-conceit' in his mind, the poet imitates ideals of human conduct that, in turn, inspire readers to imitate them. Poetry thus profits both the individual and the commonwealth to which he or she belongs by promoting ethical ideals of heroic love and political action. This understanding of Sidney's treatise has remained the consensus—among critics of quite different theoretical persuasions—for many years. One consequence of this orthodoxy, however, has been a tendency to treat Sidney's treatise as the classic articulation of a traditional, idealist Renaissance poetics against which other texts—by Gascoigne, Marlowe, Nashe, Shakespeare, Spenser, Donne, and others—can be measured as contrastingly critical, experimental, and divergent. The effect has been twofold: to deny those qualities to Sidney's writing, and to consign the *Defence* to the status of doctrine. While its tenets are repeatedly asserted, the actual text of Sidney's treatise is rarely subjected to systematic textual analysis. As a result, it risks ending up in a critical backwater, as if it had been interpretatively exhausted and there were nothing 'new' to be said about it.

This book sets out to change that. It attends very closely to the text of the *Defence* in order to identify within it a model of poetry that is markedly at variance from the idealist one generally presumed. Indeed, it argues that Sidney's text is feeling its way towards a model of poetry that is *de*-idealist: that is to say, positively hostile to and critical of 'idealist' poetics. It does this by performing an 'economic' analysis of the treatise which shows the idealist model of poetry to be one that essentially promotes profitability: the 'profit' that—in terms of intellectual, moral, and spiritual capital—poetry is understood to yield. Following key theorists of the new economic criticism, especially Marc Shell and Jean-Joseph Goux, the book identifies this idealist poetics with the idealist philosophy that, starting with Plato, emerged as a result of and in response to the advent of the money form. This philosophy, and the poetics that emerged from it, participated in the abstraction of value that the money form made possible, and in the myriad social, political, sexual, and material subordinations that, as general equivalent, the money form brought in its wake. Viewed in this light, poetry's 'ideal' profitability comes to be seen as complicit with the specific ills that the money form effectuated: among them, commodification, fetishism, and the abuse of power.

Many readers of the *Defence* have commented on the layeredness of Sidney's text: the sense that more than one 'voice' is speaking and that the various polemical positions taken are inconsistent or at odds with one another. None, however, has suggested that one of these 'voices' is directly contravening—indeed, terminally disrupting—the argument for an idealist aesthetic that the treatise officially makes. This book suggests exactly that. The alternative model of poetry that the *Defence* sketches out—one in which idealism and profitability are rejected on grounds of their complicity with 'money thought'—is never stated openly, as in a radical manifesto. It is evident throughout the treatise, however, in the textual irregularities to which this book attends—ideals that are not ideal, examples that do not exemplify, rhetorical questions that go unanswered, positives that are expressed as double negatives—and that might be read as symptomatic of resistance and denial.

One of the things to have discouraged such a reading of the *Defence* in the past is the element of self-interest at work in promoting an 'idealist' model of poetry (since the argument that poetry is 'profitable' obviously reflects well on those who have a professional investment in saying so) and the consequent lack of any incentive for arguing the reverse. As Richard Helgerson wrote, many years ago, '[i]n making Sidney the answer to their exculpating dream of a gentleman-poet, his contemporaries necessarily ignored any second thoughts that he may himself have had. They found in him an unquestionable hero who was also a gentleman, a poet, and a defender of poetry. Why look any closer? And modern critics . . . have been equally unwilling to consider his work as anything less than a triumphant embodiment of a nobly pure aesthetic—even if Sidney thought otherwise'.[1] There are clearly risks in looking closer and thinking otherwise, and indeed one might draw up a 'risk register' of readings of the *Defence* to date in order to locate the precise level of risk to which the more adventurous critics have hitherto been prepared to go. At the safest, most risk-averse end are those readings that essentially defend the *Defence* (repeat and endorse its promotion of idealist poetics). At the next level are those—like Helgerson's—that identify the high degree of defensiveness evident within Sidney's text (being more willing to concede the many inconsistencies, weaknesses, and ironies within it). At the far end—which is where the present book seeks to situate itself—would be readings that see Sidney's text as scoping out a model of poetry that, according to idealist criteria, could only be described as indefensible (profitless, masochistic, perverse).

The book is organized around the three charges against poetry that the *Defence* ostensibly takes it upon itself to refute: namely, that poetry is profitless, that poetry lies, and that poetry abuses. These charges had been put by Stephen Gosson's *School of Abuse* (1579)—dedicated to Sidney and to which the *Defence* was quite possibly written in response—although they were also well-rehearsed arguments within the antipoetic tradition. These accusations—and the ways in which Sidney responds to them—are addressed in Parts I, II, and III in turn. Each Part is subdivided into a number of sections in which the context of the charge in question and the complexity of Sidney's response to it is explored in detail.

Part I shows how the logical response to the charge that poetry is profitless—the counter-assertion that poetry is profitable—commits Sidney to a specific economic praxis: one that might, in a historicist analysis, be identified as that of an emergent bourgeois, mercantile class. As Weberian models of turning a profit (the mechanical reproduction of 'many Cyruses' from a single prototype, for example) compete with

---

[1] Helgerson 1976 (127).

a fantasized 'golden world' of infinite credit that is destined (as it did for Sidney as for so many others of his class) to run out, so the *Defence* is shown to play the pleasures of accumulation and consumption against one another. At first glance, this difference appears oriented along class lines, as an instructional, instrumentalist, and 'bankable' model of poetry competes with a delirious bankruptcy or *dépense* on the part of a courtly class whose debts would remain forever unpaid. On analysis, however, the latter position is shown to be less courtly than oppositional: a way of expressing misgivings about a model in which poetry is justified only according to the value it provides, and of fielding instead an alternative aesthetic in which poetry is autonomous—not obliged to endorse the agendas of profit and power implicit within idealism—and 'courtly' only insofar as it represents everything the bourgeois ethic of growth, productivity, and functionality is not.

Part II takes apart the charge that poetry lies and shows it to elicit a more complex and, ultimately, self-defeating response than the one that precedes it. In defending poetry against this second charge, Sidney finds himself in the position of having to argue that lies are profitable: in effect, that 'idealist' poetry is ideology and its defender an apologist for power. It shows that the *Defence* does not—indeed, cannot—defend against this charge, thereby evacuating its self-proclaimed status to be a juridical oration or counsel for the defence. It considers the interpretative possibilities to which this gives rise, including that of different forms of jurisprudence that, by 'idealist' standards, might seem to arrive at judgements—of behaviour, of literature—that are quite un-ideal. It suggests that the *Defence* is not so much a defence as an example (or would-be example) of paradoxical praise, and that, as such, it puts paid to any straightforward claims regarding poetry's profitability and pleasure, and, in their place, floats the possibility of quite different measures of 'value'. As in Part I, it shows how closely the *Defence* is aligned with Thomas More's *Utopia*.

Part III considers the charge that poetry abuses its readers, luring them to immorality, and tempting them to vice. It unpacks the various meanings and implications of good use, bad use, usefulness, utility, uselessness, abuse, and the relative moralizations of each. It shows how, like Shakespeare's *Sonnets*, the *Defence* also ponders the question of whether poetic production is 'natural' (in the sense that it makes use of things already provided by Nature, as in household management) or 'unnatural' (in the sense that it artificially creates an infinite number of man-made representations, as usury 'makes' gold). It maps these two options onto the alternatives the *Defence* proposes between a poetry that makes Nature 'better' (that is, makes use of it) and a poetry that makes things 'anew' (and that is therefore abusive, usurious). It examines this problematic to ask whether *poesis* is 'natural' or 'unnatural', 'good' or 'bad', 'useful' or 'abusive', 'profitable' or 'pleasurable', or whether any of these binaries, in fact, do justice to the alternative model of poetry that Sidney envisions.

This book thus addresses the 'problem' that an idealist *Defence of Poesy* does not sit easily with Sidney's literary texts, in which the loves and wars represented are very far from ideal. This problem has been dealt with in various ways: by claiming a discrepancy between theory and practice, for example, or by suggesting that un-ideal conduct in *Astrophil and Stella* or the *Arcadia* represents a negative example and therefore remains consonant with the idealist agenda to the extent that it still promises to teach and delight. By arguing that the *Defence* makes the case for a poetry that is non-idealist—or at least explores such a possibility—this book shows that it is entirely consistent with Sidney's other literary writings and, indeed, that it shares their dark and complex vision of human motivation and desire.

This book is not, therefore, a comparative study of Renaissance poetics: ground that has been very well covered elsewhere but that has generally found Sidney's text to be saying what it is expected to say. Rather, it is an analysis of the aesthetic struggles and preoccupations of one of the period's most important and serious poets, and demonstrates that this work, which has had so long and strong an influence on the English literary and critical traditions, is saying something more complex, surprising, and interesting than first appears. It suggests that the *Defence* brings into view what Gavin Alexander has called 'the suppressed subtext of Renaissance poetics'—'what Renaissance defenders of poetry did not dare to admit, and how Renaissance poets expected to be read'—and argues that failing to attend to that subtext risks perpetuating an idealist aesthetic in which no one, least of all the artist, really believes: a recipe for bad faith.[2] By arguing against poetry, literature, and art that is only deemed defensible when 'profitable', more-over, this book also makes a powerful intervention in current debates about the value of the humanities. It suggests that to ask 'what is the value of the humanities?' is to ask the wrong question, or to ask a leading question the answer to which is a given when a certain economic mindset is presupposed. It suggests that to defend poetry or the humanities on those terms is to behave as if that mindset constituted the sum total of all possible artistic and creative endeavour. It suggests that the kind of art that is defensible on those terms alone—as ideal, as profitable, as serving the interests of capitalist ideology whether knowingly or otherwise—is not actually the kind of art we want, respect, or admire, any more than it was the kind of poetry that Sidney actually wrote.

There is a danger, of course, that the alternative aesthetic this book attributes to Sidney—one that resists economic or utilitarian concepts of value—might too closely resemble what a twenty-first century academic reader would be expected to desire, and that stressing Sidney's 'radicalism' in this way risks making him look (as Ben Saunders writes of similar readings of Donne) 'rather like a politically sensitive contemporary professor of English'.[3] As Saunders goes on to suggest, however, this is an argument for appealing not to protocols of disinterest and objectivity but rather to the very desire that is implicit within all interpretative practice: 'we can at least ask [the] critic to acknowledge and understand his or her own stakes in the practice, the purpose, the pleasure-pain of literary analysis, and perhaps use this acknowledgement and understanding to reach a position of still greater insight' (32). Such readerly identification is to be acknowledged, that is, not denied.

---

[2] Alexander, ed. 2013 (xlviii).   [3] Saunders 2006 (30).

This book is to a large extent written in response to the new historicist methodologies that have dominated the discipline since the 1980s, when those theorists who studied relations within a given power structure (principally Foucault) were favoured over those whose more deconstructive methodologies aimed at critiquing power structures per se (such as Bataille, Barthes, Derrida, Lacan, Goux). Insofar as this book has a polemical edge, it is to suggest that the mode of criticism which sees the politics of literature and culture as its central concern might at times be more aware of—if not willing, on occasion, to resist—the sometimes regressive politics implicit within its methodologies. Many new historicist critics, for example, analyse Renaissance texts with the same tools of economic criticism invoked here. This book, however, takes a different approach. Where new historicist modes of analysis are typically dialectical—exploring resistance and the power it invokes—a more deconstructionist approach seeks to critique dialectical thinking per se. Where new historicist modes of analysis typically explore resistances *within* a system—capitalism, for example—a more deconstructionist approach looks to resist the system itself, at least to the extent that dialectical thinking (as formulated in idealist philosophy, for example) can at times be complicit with it. This book owes more to the work of Fredric Jameson than to that of Stephen Greenblatt, therefore, and hopes thereby to contribute to the lively aeration of the larger field of early modern studies that is currently in play.

It is quite right, therefore, to raise the question of readings that reflect back an idealized image of the critic's own face. One of the difficulties this book has with idealist poetics—and with idealist readings that perpetuate it—is precisely the self-interest it entails (usually at the expense of riskier readings). It is to this narcissism, therefore, that its deconstructive method is largely directed. The aim, however, is not to prevent readers from engaging personally and intimately with texts but rather, like Saunders, to encourage a greater degree of self-awareness and above all a willingness to see that the reflection in the mirror is not ideal. Self-love is not the same as self-interest—indeed, they are diametrically opposed—and yet, as Sidney suggests in the opening paragraph of the *Defence*, the former is what he proposes to follow. Richard Strier takes issue with readings of Renaissance texts that reflect back an image of the period as over-controlled, conformist, and risk-averse on the grounds that they say more about the readers than they do about a period he regards as altogether 'more bumptious, full-throated, and perhaps perverse'.[4] Any reading will reflect back an image of the critic's face, that is, but the question is how far that projection does justice to the period in question and what it leaves out. My image of a radical, 'queer', aesthetic Sidney is, of course, just as much a projection as the model, Protestant, pedagogical Sidney of idealist readings, but it aims to re-balance the picture: to draw attention to those aspects of the *Defence* which the latter omit, and to reveal a side of Sidney which is not otherwise much discussed. I seek to resurrect the Sidney whom Jonathan Crewe described as figuring not only 'a losing politics (though perhaps that too) [but] a problematic and recurrent

---

[4] Strier 2011 (2).

quixotry which like so many other things ("folly," "picaro," "utopia," Machiavel") is invented, named and embodied in this fabulously energized, strongly "poetic" time'.[5] At the same time, this book also makes a substantive point about the _Defence_: namely, that it intuits—even anticipates—an aesthetic that was not to be fully philosophized for nearly two hundred years; or, to put it the other way round (and taking a cue, in this respect, from the recent resurgence of interest in the Renaissance sublime), that elements of a post-Kantian aesthetic can indeed be traced back, possibly via Bacon, to Sidney.

This book is provocative, therefore, on a number of fronts. It follows previous books in which I have similarly explored radical and alternative formations in early modern English literature: male-authored lyric poems that—in cultivating abject, masochistic, melancholic, and lesbian forms—deviate dramatically from culturally approved modes of masculine subjectivity; or images of the hunter (from archaeological times a symbol of masculine prowess) that become—in the hunter–hunted figure of literature and myth—an occasion for self-sabotage and failure.[6] Such positions of negativity and loss have not always been well served by the critical orthodoxies of the day which can sublate antithetical positions within a larger ideological structure: a move that often proves totalizing in its effects when virtually any oppositional stance is taken to be doing ideology's work. This critical manoeuvre has accorded less space to positions that challenge or operate outside this dialectic but that, when attended to, restore a sense of the period as more uncooperative, maverick, and refractory than has sometimes been allowed.

---

[5] Crewe 1986 (89).   [6] Bates 2007, 2013.

Acknowledgements

This is not the book I was planning to write. It began as the introductory chapter to a book on the *Arcadia*—a project for which I had been given a Solmsen Fellowship at the Institute for Research in the Humanities in the University of Wisconsin, Madison—but after about 60,000 words it became obvious that it was a book and not a chapter that wanted to be written. My first thanks, therefore, go to Susan Friedman, Director of the IRH, for embodying the intellectual generosity of that enlightened institution in allowing the project to go in this new and unexpected direction. The year I spent at the IRH was one of the most stimulating and productive of my career and this book would quite possibly never have come into being without the profound and sparkling wit—in all senses of that word—of the colleagues I met there. I owe a debt of gratitude to the entire year group, whose work—drawn from across the humanities—made for truly interdisciplinary conversations and debates, but in particular I would like to thank the people who made the year such a special experience for me: Jim Bromley, Christelle Fischer-Bovet, Victor Goldgel-Carballo, Ann Harris, Max Harris, Bethany Moreton, Lucy Traverse, Scott Trudell, Pamela Voekel, and Eliza Zingesser. Their presence is everywhere in the pages of this book. Nor would the year have been what it was without the intellectual and social hospitality of the University of Wisconsin colleagues I met, especially Joshua Calhoun, Stephanie Elsky, and Nandini Pandey. David Loewenstein—still, then, at Wisconsin—comes into a category of his own for his long-standing support and encouragement of my work. I would not be where I am today without him. I would also like to thank the students and faculty of the English Department at Penn State, who heard a part of this project in its early iteration and gave me the confidence to continue: especially Claire Colebrook, Bob Edwards, Marcy North, and Garrett Sullivan. Again, Patrick Cheney has his own special place in my thanks for his boundless generosity and encouragement even (or perhaps especially) when my work takes an unconventional or dissident turn. Two thirds of this book was written in Madison and the remainder finished in Cambridge. I am most grateful to the Master and Fellows of Churchill College for granting me a Visiting By-Fellowship in which to complete the project, and especially to Andrew Taylor who was my sponsor and host in the College for the year. It has been a privilege to be involved again with the early modern community at Cambridge and to take part in its many events, including the lively Renaissance Research Workshop and Renaissance Graduate Seminar. Special thanks go to the organizers of these series—Raphael Lyne, Sophie Read, and Hester Lees-Jeffries—for their invitations to present parts of this book, and to the students and staff of the English Faculty for their helpful suggestions and overall welcome, including Hero Chalmers, Helen Cooper, David Hillman, Joe Moshenska, Jason Scott-Warren, Lizzie Swann, and Andrew Zurcher. In particular, I would like to thank Micha Lazarus for sharing with me his wonderful article on poetry and horseplay in

Sidney's *Defence* prior to its publication, and my former student, Vladimir Brljak, now at Trinity Hall, for teaching me far more than I ever taught him (not least the art of the discursive footnote). It has also been a huge pleasure to share thoughts about books and poetry with Gavin Alexander. I have greatly enjoyed meeting or re-meeting friends and colleagues who have been in Cambridge on sabbatical—in particular, Tess Grant, Jane Grogan, Michael Schoenfeldt, and Regina Schwartz—who have shared and made easier the ups and downs of the writing life while being on research leave, and who have, I hope, benefited as much as I have. It has been wonderful to see Mike again after a long period when we were both busy with big administrative jobs, and he too must be singled out for special thanks as a colleague whose ongoing support and encouragement has been a blessing since the beginning of my career. I am most grateful to staff and students at the University of Oslo for the invitation to present a part of this project there, and especially to Tina Skouen for her welcome, generosity, not to mention organizational genius. A special tribute also goes to my colleague, Paul Botley, for sharing his astonishing erudition with me. This book would not be in the shape it is now without the insights of the two anonymous OUP readers who looked into the soul of the project and weighed its merits and demerits with an unwavering eye. No failing could hide from their penetrating vision and those that remain are my own. Finally, thanks go to Jacqueline Norton for her receptiveness to a project that may have seemed out of kilter with the OUP list and her willingness to take it on. Risk is one of the things this book is about, and if the gamble pays off the rewards are entirely hers.

Contents

List of Abbreviations　　　　　　　　　　　　　　　　　　　xvii

I. THE POET'S GOLDEN WORLD

I. Poetry Is Profitless　　　　　　　　　　　　　　　　3
II. Poetry Is Profitable　　　　　　　　　　　　　　　33
III. Poetry Is Profitless　　　　　　　　　　　　　　47

II. THE COUNTERFEITER

I. Poetry Lies　　　　　　　　　　　　　　　　　　83
II. Lies Are Profitable　　　　　　　　　　　　　103
III. Lies Are Profitless　　　　　　　　　　　　　115
IV. Poetry Is Profitless　　　　　　　　　　　　131
V. Poetry Is Free　　　　　　　　　　　　　　157

III. THE EMPTY CHEST

I. Poetry Abuses　　　　　　　　　　　　　　179
II. Poetry Is Useful　　　　　　　　　　　　195
III. Poetry Is Abused　　　　　　　　　　　233

Bibliography　　　　　　　　　　　　　　　　　275
Index　　　　　　　　　　　　　　　　　　　293

List of Abbreviations

Alexander	'The Defence of Poesy', in *Sidney's 'The Defence of Poesy' and Selected Renaissance Literary Criticism*, ed. Gavin Alexander (Harmondsworth: Penguin, 2004).
APGRD	*Archive of Performances of Greek and Roman Drama* <http://www.apgrd.ox.ac.uk>.
AS	*Astrophil and Stella*, in *The Poems of Sir Philip Sidney*, ed. W. A. Ringler, Jr (Oxford: Clarendon Press, 1962).
Correspondence	*The Correspondence of Sir Philip Sidney*, ed. Roger Kuin, 2 vols. (Oxford: Clarendon Press, 2012).
Duncan-Jones	'The Defence of Poesy', in *The Oxford Authors: Sir Philip Sidney*, ed. Katherine Duncan-Jones (Oxford: Oxford University Press, 1989).
Liddell and Scott	*A Greek-English Lexicon*, Henry George Liddell and Robert Scott, revised Sir Henry Stuart Jones et al. (Oxford: Clarendon Press, 9th edn., 1996).
Maslen	*An Apology for Poetry, or The Defence of Poesy*, ed. Geoffrey Shepherd, revised with a new introduction by R. W. Maslen (Manchester: University of Manchester Press, 3rd edn., 2002).
NA	*The Countess of Pembroke's Arcadia (The New Arcadia)*, ed. Victor Skretkowicz (Oxford: Clarendon Press, 1987).
OA	*The Countess of Pembroke's Arcadia (The Old Arcadia)*, ed. Jean Robertson (Oxford: Clarendon Press, 1973).
OED	*Oxford English Dictionary* <http://www.oed.com>.
Shepherd	*An Apology for Poetry, or The Defence of Poesy*, ed. Geoffrey Shepherd (Manchester: Manchester University Press, 2nd edn., 1973).
Smith	'An Apology for Poetry', in *Elizabethan Critical Essays*, ed. G. Gregory Smith, 2 vols. (Oxford: Oxford University Press, 1904).
Tilley	*A Dictionary of the Proverbs in England in the Sixteenth and Seventeenth Centuries* (Ann Arbor, MI: University of Michigan Press, 1950).
van Dorsten	*A Defence of Poetry*, in *Miscellaneous Prose of Sir Philip Sidney*, ed. Jan van Dorsten and Katherine Duncan-Jones (Oxford: Clarendon Press, 1973).

PART I

THE POET'S GOLDEN WORLD

I

Poetry Is Profitless

Summarizing the various charges against poetry that have prompted him to write the *Defence of Poesy*, Sidney lists as 'First' the imputation that, 'there being many other more fruitful knowledges, a man might better spend his time in them than in this'.[1] This accusation—that the reading or writing of poetry constitutes an illegitimate expense because it nets the investor an insufficient yield (or the wrong kind of yield) for his or her outlay of time; that it qualifies as a poor transaction (if a transaction at all) because it fails to match the expenditure, let alone provide a more substantial return; that it performs badly in comparison with other 'more fruitful' investments; that it is not worthwhile; essentially, that it fails to turn a profit—had a long history in the tradition of antipoetic sentiment. Of this, Sidney would no doubt have been aware; but it had also received extensive treatment in a text that, as it was dedicated to Sidney, may well have provided him with a contemporary articulation of the issue that served to bring it to his attention and to prompt if not to focus his mind. That text, of course, was Stephen Gosson's *Schoole of Abuse* (1579), the chief 'disprayse' of which is that 'Poets, dwelleth longest in those pointes, that profite least'.[2] For Gosson it follows as night follows day that if an activity is profitless it is indefensible, and to this end he structures the argument of the *Schoole* around an apparently straightforward binary—profit and pleasure—onto which he also closely maps another: use and abuse. This binary is announced from the title page, which offers a 'plesaunt inuectiue'—a discourse 'as pleasaunt for Gentlemen that fauour learning, as profitable for all that wyll follow vertue'—adding a quotation from Cicero to the effect that the writer who fails to express himself clearly or to please his reader makes an unpardonable abuse of his pen.[3] It is not just that the content of what follows will pronounce on profit and pleasure, that is, or on use and abuse, but that the volume as a whole promises to exemplify those ideals, much as, in his dedicatory letter, Gosson invites Sidney to enter his *Schoole* 'for your pleasure . . . [to] see what I teach' (73/☞5ᵛ). This Horatian profit-and-pleasure

---

[1] Maslen (102.20–23). References give page number followed by line number. All references to the *Defence* to this edition.

[2] Gosson 1579, in Kinney, ed. 1974 (76/A1ᵛ). References give page number in the modern edition followed by original signature. All references to Gosson will follow this format.

[3] Cicero 1927, *Tusculan Disputations*, I.iii.6: '*sed mandare quemquam litteris cogitationes suas, qui eas nec disponere nec illustrare possit nec delectatione aliqua adlicere lectorem, hominis est intemperanter abutentis et otio et litteris*' [but to commit one's reflections to writing, without being able to arrange or express them clearly or attract the reader by some sort of charm, indicates a man who makes an unpardonable misuse of leisure and pen].

formula—which first appears on the title pages of pedagogical works printed in England in the 1540s and becomes an established convention in the prefatory matter of English printed books from the 1560s on—symptomized the profit-driven conception of education that characterized the humanist new learning.[4] According to this new conception, pleasure was defensible only if it could be turned to good account—positivized, made to yield a profit, both to the individual reader and, ideally, to the larger commonwealth of which he or she was a part—much as proponents of the new learning such as Erasmus, Sir Thomas Elyot, and Roger Ascham urged that enjoying good quality literary works made them better instruments of learning and thus maximized their pedagogic potential. For Gosson, too, what, for the avoidance of any ambiguity, he qualifies as the proper, commendable, or *right* use of poetry is precisely its capacity to effect this transaction—to convert or exchange pleasure into profit—rather as the 'right vse of auncient Poetrie' (82/A7ᵛ), such as the praise of famous men, inspired emulation and so was permitted to remain within Plato's Republic. Probing this 'right vse' as that which turns a profit reveals a distinct economic praxis or business model, and while the profit in question is emphatically for the greater good as opposed to merely private profiteering—we are reminded that man does not use this reason 'to his owne profite' (100/D1ᵛ)— nonetheless, space is very carefully made not to exclude the possibility of personal gain: 'No man is borne to seeke priuate profite: parte for his countrie, parte for his friendes, parte for himselfe' (108/E2ᵛ).[5] Over and against this ideal model in which pleasure yields to profit, however, Gosson holds up a repeatedly negativized scenario in which pleasure leads not upwards, through learning to virtue and the intellectual and spiritual capital that benefits all concerned, but rather—as if in a kind of perverse *gradatio*—downwards to sin and death, or worse: 'from Pyping to playing, from play to pleasure, from pleasure to slouth, from slouth too sleepe, from sleepe too sinne, from sinne to death, from death to the deuill' (81/A6ᵛ–A7).[6] Not sharing the

---

[4] The formula first appears in England on the title pages of Erasmus 1542 and Ascham 1545. As Finkelstein 2006 (4) notes, despite 'tirades against profit-seeking, it must have sometimes seemed as though being *profitable* was the highest praise the age could offer' (emphasis original). Fraser 1970 attributes the antipoetic sentiment of the sixteenth and seventeenth centuries entirely to the rise of a profit-driven, industrious, utilitarian ethos that came with the transition from feudalism to capitalism. For him, Gosson and the other criticizers of poetry symptomize a new class whose pragmatic, mercantile values made them impatient with artistic activities they regarded as fundamentally unproductive and which they associated with an effete, decadent, courtly world that theirs was fast overtaking. For them (as, it appears, for Fraser), 'Gain is the integer of value', although this extends from purely financial gain to include other, symbolic forms of capital such as education, spiritual salvation, and so forth (92).

[5] Gosson is alluding to Cicero 1913, *De Officiis*, I.viii.25: '*Nec vero rei familiaris amplificatio nemini nocens vituperanda est, sed fugienda semper iniuria est*' [Still, I do not mean to find fault with the accumulation of property, provided it hurts nobody, but unjust acquisition of it is always to be avoided]. Gosson's position might be identified with the 'commonwealth discourse' of the early to mid-sixteenth century, in which the polity was modelled—on ethical, broadly Aristotelian lines—as a programme of mutual enrichment and prosperity in which private gain was ideally regulated by and subordinated to the general good, although not always successfully: see Landreth 2012 (21–33, 227–38).

[6] Elsewhere, poetry, piping, and playing are said to be 'all three chayned in linkes of abuse' (85/B3); together with feasting and dancing, these 'may win vs to pleasure, or rocke vs a sleepe' (91/B8ᵛ); they 'bringe vs too pleasure, slouth, sleepe, sinne, and without repentaunce to death and the Deuill' (99/D1).

humanists' optimism in the reliability of the pleasure/profit exchange, Gosson fears that poetry's pleasure will all too often lead in the opposite direction. On those occasions where such activities do *not* translate into profit, therefore (which amounts to more or less all of them), they are to be expelled, and on good precedent: '*Plato* when he sawe the doctrine of these Teachers [i.e. poets], neither for profite, necessary, nor to be wished for pleasure, gaue them all Drum*m*es entertainment, not suffering the*m* once to shew their faces in a reformed com*m*on wealth' (78–9/A4).

It is in the introductory *narratio* or statement of the case that Sidney first takes it upon himself to answer this charge, resolving to defend 'poor Poetry' (81.30) and to restore the 'credit' (82.2) that, unlike other arts such as horsemanship, it has lost (we will return to the *exordium* and its anecdote about Pugliano in Part II). Given this newly announced direction, Sidney logically embarks on a disquisition that will focus on poetry's credibility and profitability, and from the outset claims for the precedence of poetry are inextricably bound up with its use-value. Educative, didactic, and the foundation of all later knowledge and learning or *scientia*, poetry is said to be the 'first light-giver to ignorance' (82.8). Poetry was the 'first nurse' that enabled men to feed afterwards on 'tougher knowledges' (82.8, 9–10), and it is 'the first' ancient poets who delivered knowledge to posterity as 'fathers in learning' (82.17, 19): as models of nurture that are as parental (motherly and fatherly) as they are pedagogical (schoolmasterly), these are heavily positivized as teleological. Similarly, just as Italian was 'the first' (82.25) language to dignify the vernacular as learned speech, so, encouraged by the 'excellent fore-going' (82.28) of Chaucer and Gower—themselves following Dante, Boccaccio, and Petrarch in this regard—contemporary English poets might also find in their native tongue a suitable vehicle for such learning. In both cases, Sidney's metaphors show the practice of poetry as leading inexorably to the accumulation of learning, something he strikingly figures in terms of the accumulation of cultural and intellectual *wealth*: such learning, he says, will make the English vernacular 'a treasure-house of science' (82.25–6).[7] That is to say, the development that leads from an original or preliminary learning towards a great store of it is unselfconsciously presented as a narrative of progress in which not only does that which is 'first' or 'before' (82.8, 17, 20) lead naturally to what comes 'afterwards' (82.9)—or 'priority' (82.19) to 'posterity' (82.18)—but

---

[7] Sidney repeats the phrase in his letter to Edward Denny dated 22 May 1580 in which he refers to Latin and Greek as 'the tresure howses of learninge': *Correspondence* (981). This humanist conception of language as a treasury or store (from Greek θησαυρός) is a commonplace: see e.g. the titles of Robert Estienne 1543, *Dictionarium, seu Latinae linguae thesaurus* and Thomas Cooper 1565, *Thesaurus linguae Romanae & Britannicae*. On the imagery of language as a treasury capable both of enriching the nation and of being defrauded or robbed, see Blank 1996 (33–68). For Hadfield 1994 (134), the development of a national language leads not only to the development of cultural wealth but also to the development of a sense of national identity: Sidney's phrase at the beginning of this sentence in the *narratio*—'the noblest nations and languages' (82.7)—indicating the 'syntactic and logical connection drawn up between knowledge, national identity and poetry'. According to this logic, poetry would, could, and should come to be seen as a national treasure. Landreth 2012 (37) cites the *Defence* as affirming that the 'poet's role is to mediate particular and otherwise contrary forms of knowledge into a continuous and capacious discourse that, in creating "in effect another Nature [85.18–19]," can wholly account for the present world in its own idealist unity'. The poet's project is thus both cause and effect of the development of such a 'ramifying model of knowledge production' (36).

that outcome is presented and celebrated as resulting in a hefty reserve or deposit in the national bank.

The first paragraph of the *narratio* thus constitutes the beginning of the 'more available [i.e. valid, powerful] proofs' (82.1–2) that Sidney will wield in making his defence, launching his 'just cause' (81.30) with a counter-challenge which 'may justly be objected' (82.6): namely, that those beneficiaries of learning who impugn the educative profitability of poetry are guilty of gross ingratitude.[8] All seems set, therefore, for poetry's profitability to be proved. However, the fact that all may not be well with this optimistic humanistic project is hinted at in Sidney's initiatory 'And first, truly' (82.5), this being, as his editor Robert Maslen points out, 'Sidney's favourite word' ('truly' occurs thirty-three times in Olney's text, and thirty-five times in Ponsonby's), and one that he 'invariably uses . . . to signal the contingent status of truth, to announce the approach of a particularly contentious or opinionated utterance'.[9] As the argument proceeds, various resistances will come to give Sidney's stated confidence the lie. His next proof, for example, is that, following on from their poetic progenitors (Musaeus, Hesiod, and Homer), ancient philosophers used poetry too: the Presocratics first and then Plato. As we shall see, the idea that philosophy *is* poetry—that it shares in poetry's defining quality of fictiveness—will in the long run prove one of the most far-reaching views of the *Defence*, and, even if it does not entirely break through to consciousness as yet, a hint of it is suggested in the various ructions and illogicalities that serve to disturb or crease the otherwise smooth surface of the argument. It is with these disturbances, therefore—as they appear in the *narratio*, in the first instance—that the following discussion will for the time being concern itself. Thus, two difficulties come to light. First, Sidney is uncertain whether these ancient philosophers were merely *using* poetry (that is, simply masquerading as poets) or whether they actually *were* poets. Second, he is uncertain about what constitutes 'poetry' as such: that is, whether the term should be used in the highly restricted sense of speech or writing in verse, or whether poetry might be defined more expansively as the use of feigning, fables, or fiction. In both cases, the attempt to keep apart definitions that otherwise have a tendency to collapse into one another can be read as a defensive manoeuvre. Taking the first of the two difficulties in turn: to keep poets and philosophers apart—to stress their intrinsic difference such that the latter only appeared 'under the masks of poets' (82.31)—serves to maintain the traditional view that philosophy constitutes the hard core of thought, the serious, inner, substantive *res*, while its poetic expression is surface, dressing, mere *verba*.[10] Thus, in Plato's 'body of . . . work', the 'inside and strength' constitutes the philosophy

---

[8] This is a charge later repeated with respect to philosophers who, in criticizing poets, behave like 'ungrateful prentices' (106.26) to their former masters.

[9] Maslen (4); 'Sidney's term "truly"', he comments later, 'invariably occurs at moments when he is at his most controversial, when the truth of his claims is self-evidently in dispute' (60). 'Truth' occurs thirteen times in Olney's edition of the treatise; sixteen times in Ponsonby's; 'true' twenty-one times in each.

[10] See also the references to Plato and Boethius who 'made mistress Philosophy very often borrow the masking raiment of Poesy' (96.2–3); and to Plutarch who 'trimmeth both [his histories' and philosophy's] garments with guards [borders, decorative trimmings] of Poesy' (108.7–8).

per se while its 'skin as it were and beauty' consists in the poetry (82.40, 41). Against this highly traditional view of philosophy, however,—and we sense there is going to be a 'however' because Plato is introduced with an 'And truly' (82.39)— jostles a rather different one in which philosophers do not simply borrow poetry (assume its external form in order to transmit their content more expeditiously) but actually communicate *as* poets: 'or rather they, *being poets*, did exercise their delightful vein in those points of highest knowledge, which before them lay hid to the world' (82.34–6, my emphasis). The illustration provided, moreover, is not—as it could have been—some transcendent Idea that the philosopher has unveiled and revealed to the world, but rather a *fable*: 'wise Solon *was directly a poet*... having written in verse the notable fable of the Atlantic island, which was continued by Plato' (82.36–8, my emphasis). Similarly, the Plato whose poetic effusions were characterized as the mere 'skin' covering the 'inside and strength' of his philosophy, is now presented, like Solon, as the originator of poetic fictions: as in the dialogues in which he 'feigneth' (82.42) Athenian contemporaries—their conversations, banquets, walks, and so forth—as well as 'mere tales' (83.2) such as that of Gyges' Ring. The tale of Gyges' ring—dropped in here casually and apparently only in passing—will turn out to be highly consequential in Sidney's soon-to-be-developed account of the 'golden' world. At this stage, however, what this passage sets in conflict are two quite different and possibly incompatible portraits of the philosopher. Either the philosopher is a thinker who uses poetic form merely to mask or clothe the content of his thoughts or 'moral counsels' (82.33), or the philosopher is a thinker (more accurately, a writer) who creates fictions, composes fables, feigns dialogues, and tells tales, all of which bear a much less secure relation to any content that might be presumed to be probable, real, or true.

This uncertainty, in turn, feeds into the second of the two difficulties mentioned above: namely, whether poetry should be defined merely as versification or by this more expanded understanding of the fictive. If the former, it is easier to maintain the traditional view of philosophers insofar as they can present their thoughts in verse without there being any suggestion that those thoughts lack substance.[11] If the latter, this is precisely the danger risked. The weak point, again, is Solon, whose being 'directly a poet' is demonstrated conclusively by his having written 'in verse' a 'fable' (the categories, that is to say, collapse), but the potential danger extends to Plato as well: all the more so, in fact, since the 'versification' get-out does not apply in his case. It will be one of the arguments of this book that the *Defence* as a whole constitutes a major conversation if not confrontation with Plato on just this point. At this stage, however, floating the idea that poetry might be defined narrowly as versification alone might be taken as a means to shore up the traditional view of philosophy and fend off a more radical one. That the narrow definition will shortly be dismissed, however, suggests that the battle may be a losing one, just as Sidney's

---

[11] This view would also be consistent with those humanists who harboured a more sceptical attitude towards poetry's ability to teach, such as Juan Luis Vives. While Vives excoriates the immoral content of much poetry, he finds himself able to praise its purely formal properties, including the use of verse: see Vives 1913 (126).

hesitancies and qualifications—'or rather' (82.34), 'as it were' (82.41), those give-away 'And truly's' (82.5, 39)—also hint at discordances within.[12]

The debate is next applied, albeit in more condensed form, to historians, who have also strayed into the fictive by describing events and feelings 'which no man could affirm', including 'long orations put in the mouths of great kings and captains, which it is certain they never pronounced' (83.10–12). Just as Plato attributed speeches to his fellow Athenians that, had they been 'set on the rack, they would never have confessed' (82.43–4), so in this designation both philosophers and historians look ahead to the famous description of the poet who also 'never affirmeth' (103.13): none of them, that is, affirm (or deny) what was neither confessed nor pronounced. Indeed, this comes close to the account Sidney gives, in a letter to his brother Robert, of the true historian as opposed to mere historiographer or chronicler: a figure who 'makes himselfe . . . an Orator, yea *Poet*' by fabricating details 'of a Poeticall vaine . . . for though perchance they were not so, yet it is enough they might be so'.[13] The fear that, 'although their lips sound of things done, and verity be written in their foreheads' (83.5–6), historians might simply be making things up—as expressed later in the charge that their accounts are based on 'the notable foundation of hearsay' (89.11)—is the same fear that philosophers might not be telling the truth but rather 'mere tales'. Sidney appears to grant the historians greater license at this point (although not later): perhaps there is less at stake.[14] All the same, similar illogicalities manifest themselves here as in the discussion about philosophers. On the one hand, there is the same move to shore up the truth-content of the subject in hand: not by resorting to the 'versification' argument, admittedly, but by asserting the intrinsic difference between historians and poets. Thus, just as philosophers merely masqueraded as poets, so historians, too, simply 'borrow[ed]' (83.6)—'stole or usurped' (83.9)—from poetry, temporarily and expediently making use of what was essentially an alien form: they took poetry's 'passport' (83.15). On the other hand, hesitancy creeps in—heralded by a 'So that truly' right on cue (83.13)—as if the temptation to collapse these categories were just too great. Thus, historians are said to borrow 'both [the] fashion and perchance weight of poets' (83.6–7): that is to say, both form *and* content. Briefly, the spectacle looms that the cherished truths of philosophy and history might in theory be entirely fictitious, a heady prospect, the attractiveness and risk of which is registered, as before, in Sidney's symptomatic protestations and choppy prose: 'perchance' (83.7), 'if that be denied me' (83.11), 'So that truly' (83.13).

---

[12] See: 'the greatest part of poets have apparelled their poetical inventions in that numbrous kind of writing which is called verse—indeed but apparelled, verse being but an ornament and no cause to Poetry, since there have been many most excellent poets that never versified, and now swarm many versifiers that need never answer to the name of poets' (87.24–9); 'One may be a poet without versing, and a versifier without poetry' (101.25–6).

[13] 18 October 1580: *Correspondence* (1007).

[14] Later, the risk that historians' reliability and veracity in reporting actual events—'what men have done' (85.9), 'what is' (90.18), the '*was*' (92.44, emphasis original), or 'bare *was*' (93.6, emphasis original)—might be compromised by such flights of fancy fatally damages any faith one might have that they faithfully report things 'such as indeed were done, and not such as fantastically or falsely may be suggested to have been done' (92.10–11).

CR

Insofar as it answers challenges that have already been put, a gauntlet already thrown down, the *Defence* is necessarily secondary—prompted, reactive—and this regardless of whether it is seen as responding directly to Gosson alone or to the tradition of antipoetic sentiment more generally. If the standing charge is that poetry is profitless, then to defend poetry as profitable makes, on the face of it, perfect sense. Indeed, for many (perhaps most) readers of the *Defence*, Sidney's aim if not achievement consists of nothing less. It is an entirely logical response, and one might well ask what else a defender of poetry might be expected to do. The claim that poetry conveys intellectual and moral knowledge (self-knowledge) of the highest order is taken to be the glory of the *Defence* and a major justification for continuing to read, study, and teach it. It also provides a major justification for continuing to read, study, and teach literature, since it defines literature as instructional, instrumentalist, and awards it value on those grounds. As this brief account of the first few paragraphs of the *narratio* suggests, however, arguing in favour of poetry's profitability—its ability to stock the nation's 'treasure-house of science' (82.26)—may not add up to the whole story, for the discrepancies in Sidney's logic that have been touched on so far suggest the possibility of an internal conflict—a resistance or irresolution of some kind—as if something not always or even necessarily acknowledged were nonetheless interrupting or in some way disturbing the otherwise logical defence, set out at the beginning of the *narratio*, that poetry is not a waste of time. As we proceed through Sidney's text, these discrepancies need somehow to be accounted for.[15] The fact that examples will routinely contradict, counter, undermine, even demolish the ostensible argument, or at least nudge it in a different direction from the one in which it is supposedly trying to go, opens up the possibility that poetry might be conceived of in a quite different way, even if this is not (possibly, could not be) openly articulated as such or even admitted fully to consciousness. The strategy of most 'idealist' readings of the *Defence* is to ignore these troubling reminders—often in the name of preserving harmony, synthesis, and serenity (at the level of form) and morality, virtue, and goodness (at the level of content)—while readings that are more willing to dispense with such ideals and to acknowledge the existence of inconsistency and irony within Sidney's text are, by contrast, that much more open to them. One way of explaining their undeniable existence within the *Defence*, therefore, might be to revive the old idea, first mooted by O. B. Hardison, that the text is carrying 'two voices'.[16] Not, however, in the sense that Hardison meant (namely, that Sidney wrote different parts of the treatise at different times), but rather in the sense that

---

[15] And preferably not by resorting to the expedient of De Neef 1980 (158), who seeks to demonstrate internal consistency by 'ascrib[ing] logical consequences to Sidney's statements, even where there appears to be little explicit textual support'.

[16] Hardison 1972. For other critics who approach the 'voice' of the *Defence* as double if not multiple, see e.g. Barnes 1971; Ferguson 1983 (151); Levao 1985 (101); and Hager 1991 (9). Critics who seek to restore the synthesis that Hardison questions include Craig 1980; Raitiere 1981; Ulreich 1982; and Hunt 1987.

there is an 'official' voice—one that articulates what is expected and what had been articulated by other defenders of poetry (Julius Caesar Scaliger, Sir Thomas Elyot, Roger Ascham, Richard Wills, Henry Dethick, Thomas Lodge, and so on)—and an 'unofficial' voice: one that is probably more of an undertone than a voice, more of a Freudian slip than a full-blown analysis, and quite possibly not much more than a register of the dissatisfaction felt at the 'official' argument and a groping towards a newer, more radical conception of poetry that is, for all that, very far from fully formed.

It is in an attempt to seek out the political and economic 'unconscious' of the *Defence*, therefore, that in what follows my model will be the relation between manifest and latent content.[17] Moreover, no matter how obviously imprecise the nomenclature, I will henceforth refer to the treatise's 'official' voice as that of Sidney's 'speaker', insofar as the latter has been designated with putting forward a defence of poetry that is for the most part entirely typical of the period and that, whatever its particular insights, conforms to standard views on the subject that had been voiced by others, and does not, therefore, altogether surprise. By contrast, I will refer to the 'unofficial' voice of the *Defence* as that of 'Sidney', not to fall foul of any intentionalist fallacy but, on the contrary, to suggest that the latter is precisely *not* a simple, unified subject or ideal ego—making pronouncements that can be taken at face value—but rather the self-doubting, self-contradicting, and self-divided creature who appears so often within the fictions that bear this signature: a creature thwarted by 'daemonic' forces that can be guaranteed to undo or countermand his best interests and best intentions. As I use them here, therefore, 'Sidney' and the 'speaker' should be taken throughout as a *façon de parler*: a means of disentangling—for the purposes of the argument and in the interests of clarity—contrasting positions that are the *product* of self-division.[18] As I hope to show in the pages that follow, the conflict between these two voices accounts for much of the 'layeredness' of the *Defence*: its unevenness and restlessness, its notorious resistance to summary explanation. To those who still hold out for a model of harmonious synthesis, therefore, I should say now that I regard the *Defence* as a text terminally in conflict with itself. It is confused—and a record of that confusion—but as such it makes claims about poetry that in my view genuinely do have the power to surprise. I should also say that, for the purposes of the argument, I will in what follows be talking 'up' this unofficial voice, if for no other reason than to give it a hearing, since it has so often not been heard. As a result, it may sometimes appear as if I am attributing to Sidney fully rationalized and conscious views that, were he (or many of his readers) to be confronted with them directly, he (and they) would quite

---

[17] In homage, of course, to Jameson 1981.

[18] I am aware that this may cause some confusion on those occasions when I refer to Sidney as a biographical subject (as, for example, when citing his correspondence). However, I would caution against treating the latter as any more unified an entity. In this respect, I seek to distance myself from readings that see the *Defence* as the expression of Sidney's 'whole person', Berry 1998 (142); that 'a renowned, uniquely accomplished, and truly noble person in his own voice employed his keen wit, vast learning, and deep love of virtue to praise, defend, and nurture poetry', Coogan 1981 (261); or that Sidney impresses us as 'honest, passionate, witty, civilized, and, above all, fully human', Hamilton 1977 (111).

probably deny. As already mentioned, it is entirely possible that this other 'voice' remained largely below the level of Sidney's consciousness and manifested only in the pesky tendency of his argument to go awry. Such symptomatic presentations, however, are always saying something, and if the rhetorical strategy of giving them a voice runs the risk of over-simplification, I trust that the price for this will not be too high.

C3

To pick up where we left off, therefore, the suggestion that Sidney is not, in fact, wholly committed to his speaker's earnest defence of a content-filled, profitable—one might say 'bankable'—model of learned poetry appears in the next paragraph of the *narratio*, where the speaker reverts to the argument about poetry's precedence. He presents a series of representatively barbarous countries (Turkey, Ireland, the New World, Wales) where 'learning flourisheth not' (83.16) in order to demonstrate that these places nevertheless all have poets. This, however, is hardly demonstrable proof that poetry nurtures learning. If anything, it shows that it is possible to have plenty of poetry—and for inordinate periods of time—with no 'learning' whatsoever. In the case of the most deprived group, for example—the 'simple Indians' (83.21), who lack even writing—the presumed connection between poetry and learning, as was apparently demonstrated in ancient Greece, is left hanging like the proverbial missing link. The speaker is forced to create that presumption, floating the suggestion, as a 'sufficient probability' (83.23), that

> if ever learning come among them, it must be by having their hard dull wits softened and sharpened with the sweet delights of Poetry; for until they find a pleasure in the exercises of the mind, great promises of much knowledge will little persuade them that know not the fruits of knowledge. (83.24–8)

This, however, only begs the question. Where is that learning going to come from if not from poetry? Since, as far as the speaker is concerned, such learning has evidently not come to the Indians from their own poetry—'songs, which they call *areytos*, both of their ancestors' deeds and praises of their gods' (83.22–3; exactly the kind of 'right' poetry that Plato had endorsed and permitted within the Republic)—it must follow that poetry in itself does not necessarily cultivate or produce learning, or at least not as the speaker understands it. The speaker's presumption, once ironed out, is that the Indians will only acquire this from *someone else's* poetry: that is, from the already learned poetry of the colonizers. Thus, until they have the 'fruits of knowledge' (83.27–8), the speaker contends, the Indians will not be persuaded by 'great promises of much knowledge' (83.26–7). The otherwise official law of epistemological increase and progress, that is to say, is not an inevitable process: the colonizers first have to plant their own culture and poetry—so that its 'fruit' will grow—in order to produce more of it, on the approved industrial model. That the Indians would ever have (quite apart from want) such 'knowledge' remains open to question, however, as does the optimistic humanist belief that poetry might be the means of delivering it. We get an early glimpse here, in other words, of an alternative form of poetry—one that is unlearned, pre-monetary, pre-capitalist, *not* committed to stocking the 'treasure-house of science', and yet (perhaps for that reason) heroic and greatly reverenced by its practitioners—that will have an important bearing on the later image of the poet's golden world.

It is interesting, moreover, to compare the Indians with the example that immediately follows them: the Welsh. The Welsh, we are told, for a 'long time ... had poets' (83.29) and continue to do so, in spite of waves of conquest and colonization on the part of Romans, Saxons, Danes, and Normans that sought to 'ruin all memory of learning from among them' (83.31–2). According to the ostensible logic of the argument, the miraculous survival of the Welsh bards should make Wales the pinnacle of learning, and—as they are the 'true remnant of the ancient Britons' (83.28)—an absolutely authentic and pristine repository of the cultural memory and knowledge-bank.[19] Sidney's speaker is clearly not intending to say this, of course, but as with the Indians another glimpse emerges of a pre-colonized if not resistant heroic poetry that does not confirm the theory that poetry in itself leads naturally to humanistic learning.[20] If the idea was that the colonists would provide the Indians with learned poetry in order to grow more learning, then the heroic and successful resistance of the Welsh against colonial rule provides a destabilizing counter-narrative. From their (British) point of view, colonization was experienced as an aggressive destruction—not a planting—of learning: and this refers not only to the barbarous Saxons and Danes but also to the Romans, guardians of classical learning and the very people who, in the next paragraph, are reverentially credited with being 'the authors of most of our sciences' (83.34).

Since the beginning of the *narratio*, then, the speaker has been defending poetry's profitability on the grounds of its learning: poetry inaugurated learning

---

[19] For Hadfield 1994 (134), 'Poetry stands as the originating foundation of *Ur*-knowledge in the particular community of the nation: logically, it must also be the first form of knowledge of that nation so that "tougher knowledges" [82.9–10] are *ipso facto* offshoots of this literary nationalism'. However, it is clear that for Hadfield Wales does not qualify as either a 'particular community' or a 'nation'—any more than the other places where 'learning flourisheth not' (83.16)—which are presented, rather, as a 'counter-genealogy' of barbarous countries (136). Thus the Welsh, Irish, Indians, and Turks are understood to stand in contrast to the development of a positivized—i.e. civilized, aristocratic, militarized, imperial, and colonial—'national' English culture, the imposition of which on others is presumed to be a natural ('offshoots') and welcome development. My view, by contrast, is that—while this may indeed be part of the speaker's 'official' argument—it is not necessarily shared by Sidney: or, at least, that the contradictions within the text betray an alertness to the oppressions of colonial rule (which include the destruction of 'national' cultures) and an awareness that the 'originating foundation of *Ur*-knowledge' of a particular community might in fact provide an alternative model of poetry that was politically not to say ethically preferable. Kennedy 2003 (169) suggests that—although, in his *Discourse on Irish Affairs* (1577), Sidney sees the imposition of the English language as a means by which to 'tame and conquer the unruly passions of persons and of nations'—he 'neglects to mention that his argument may also lead to the opposite conclusion', and that (as in his own poetry) English 'can also unleash ambiguity and confusion'.

[20] See the mockery with which Hubert Languet and Sidney treat a history of ancient Britain written by Humphrey Lhuyd (Sir Henry Sidney's protégé and an ardent Welsh nationalist) in an exchange of letters between 28 January and 26 February 1574. Languet laughs at Lhuyd's theories that the Saxons from whom the English are descended were so many pirates and robbers, that one Brennus (in fact, the conflation of two Celtic chieftains of the third and fourth centuries BC) was a Welshman, and other such 'idiocies' [*ineptiis*] and 'arrant nonsense' [*insigniter ineptire*]. For his part, Sidney jokingly attempts to 'lighten the reputation of stupidity [*stultitia*] which you have given good old Lhuyd': *Correspondence* (103, 100; 128, 125; 115, 113).

at the dawn of human civilization, it grows more learning, and that learning is a solid, substantive, accumulable thing. What his examples have actually demonstrated, however, is that poetry is indeed original, and that it has a great following (including philosophers and historians of great renown), but that its learning might quite possibly constitute nothing more substantial than 'mere tales', and that it is esteemed everywhere including places where 'learning flourisheth not'.[21] Having opened up the possibility of poetry without learning (or without learning recognized as such)—its adherents safely cordoned off as barbarous yet at the same time sneakily attractive in their resistance and warlikeness—the speaker beats a hasty retreat and returns to more familiar territory: 'But since the authors of most our sciences were the Romans, and before them the Greeks, let us a little stand upon their authorities' (83.34–5). If this is a bid to get his argument back on track, however, the attempt proves no more successful than before, and for the same reason: namely, the examples he chooses have an uncanny way of derailing the thesis he is trying to defend. Thus, he lights with relief on the Romans' name for poet—*vates*—adding five explanatory glosses for emphasis: six, if one counts his observation that they bestowed this 'heavenly . . . title' (83.40) on the poet on account of his 'heart-ravishing knowledge' (83.41). Like learning, however, knowledge has in the preceding paragraphs become something of an awkward commodity, and it does not cease to be so as the speaker attempts to identify just what this 'knowledge' might consist of. The first example he gives is of readers hitting upon meanings by pure chance, opening Virgil at random and interpreting their futures and fates in whatever they happen to find. This is a very odd example to choose if your aim is to demonstrate that poets are holy prophets, speaking on behalf of the sacred Logos and revealing otherwise hidden but divine truths. The meanings that these spot-readers of Virgil hit upon seem highly foolish—vacuous projections, the product, no doubt, of self-love—rather than anything that might be described as 'heart-ravishing knowledge'. The speaker seems momentarily to realize this, hastily collecting and correcting himself so as to condemn this practice as a 'very vain and godless superstition' (84.6–7), but he does not thereby recover the seriousness and *gravitas* of the knowledge that poetry is supposed to communicate. On the contrary, he comes up with the suggestion that such magical 'charms' (84.8)— from the Latin word for songs, *carmina*—might very precisely determine what poetry is (Roman nomenclature again taking his argument in a different direction from the one in which it was supposed to be heading). As before, the speaker comes perilously close to admitting that the apparently serious content of poetry might not in fact constitute anything more substantial. All the example proves, in fact, is that poetry was held in 'great reverence' (84.9) by such people, regardless of the vain use to which they put it and the foolish knowledge they derived from it, just as

---

[21] Hutson 2007 (121) notes that in 'classical judicial oratory a *narratio* was defined as a preliminary exposition, designed to be persuasive, of the facts in dispute', and gives as an example the circumstantial case that Philanax makes against Pyrocles and Musidorus in the *Old Arcadia* (*OA* 386–91). Here as there, however, the *narratio* proves to be erroneous and, for all its apparent credibility, turns out not to carry the day.

poetry was held in 'devout reverence' (83.20) by the barbarous Irish, despite the fact that in their country 'truly learning goeth very bare' (83.19–20).

The examples the speaker cites in this and the preceding paragraph, therefore, effectively undo the optimistic opening of the *narratio* in which he had trotted out the humanist commonplace that the first poets (Orpheus, Amphion, and so forth) had drawn 'with their charming sweetness the wild untamed wits to an admiration of knowledge' (82.21–2). This progressivist, expansionist, and colonialist cultural myth is systematically undermined by the examples that follow which rather conclusively demonstrate the opposite. First, that the 'charming sweetness' of this pedagogic poetry might in fact be nothing more than mere charms (*carmina*); second, that this 'admiration of knowledge' might equate to the 'admiration' (83.42) the Romans had for the highly dubious knowledge they derived from their spot-readings of Virgil; and third, that distinctly 'untamed wits'—indeed, foolish, barbarous, vain, godless, superstitious, and unchristian wits—might in fact have had and continue to have poetry, might enjoy and greatly reverence it, without any appreciable sign of what would officially pass for 'knowledge' in learned circles, and often with a respect for and belief in things that no self-respecting Protestant, humanist professor of learning could ever knowingly put his or her name to.

From the perspective of someone trying to argue on behalf of the latter and to uphold their view of poetry as profitable (serious, weighty, educative, and so forth), things go from bad to worse as the speaker's next example illustrating the poet as *vates*—the ancient oracles—fares no more happily than the last. His appeal to the 'versification' argument—that the oracles constitute poetry on the ground that their prophecies were delivered 'in verses' and observed 'number and measure' (84.11, 12), as usual, an attempt to distinguish their truthful content from mere external poetic form—slides straight into the concession that, in their case, the 'high flying liberty of conceit proper to the poet, did seem to have some divine force in it' (84.13–14). Like the philosophers and historians before them, that is, the oracles also turn out to produce poetry in both form *and* content. This is an astonishing claim, for the stakes here are a whole lot higher: not only might the cherished truths of philosophy and history fall within the domain of the poet—the fiction-maker, feigner of fables, teller of 'mere tales'—but the very utterances of the gods themselves. This is the first point, although not the last, at which Sidney comes close to entertaining a possibility that the *Defence* circles around several times: that the poet might exercise godlike powers.[22] Such a poet does not merely ventriloquize or

---

[22] For Shepherd (156) Sidney 'makes no such claim' and is 'more discreet' in this respect than Scaliger, on whose *Poetices libri septem* (1561) he otherwise draws closely: 'it is only poetry which includes everything of this kind, excelling those other arts in this, that while they . . . represent things just as they are . . . the poet depicts quite another sort of nature, and a variety of fortunes; in fact, by so doing, he transforms himself almost into a second deity. Of those things which the Maker of all framed, the other sciences are, as it were, overseers; but since poetry fashions images of those things which are not, as well as images more beautiful than life of those things which are, it seems unlike other literary forms, such as history, which confine themselves to actual events, and rather to be another god, and to create': see Scaliger 1905 (7–8). Sidney's speaker also appears to go less far in such claims than Puttenham 2007 (94) would: 'if [poets] be able to devise and make all these things of themselves, without any subject of verity . . . they be (by manner of speech) as creating gods.'

mouth the speeches of the gods (a person's fate, from Latin *fatum*, is literally 'that which is spoken') by dressing them in poetic form but may, rather, be responsible for originating, conjuring, creating them him- or herself. As the 'heavenly' title of *vates* slid into a 'very vain and godless superstition' within the space of two sentences, so divine revelation threatens to slide into profanity, heresy, and blasphemy equally quickly, as the definition of the poet that is ventured effectively evacuates the gods/ God and puts poets in their/His place. Indeed, it is an indication that the hierarchies sacred to the logocentric, patristic, and patriarchal order are here in jeopardy that, under this new dispensation, 'poet' can evidently extend to include the sibyls and the priestesses of Delphos, so far has the Protestant humanist pedagogic view of the poet (as scholarly and male) been superseded and overgone.

Perhaps this is the reason why David is brought in to rescue the situation, the Psalms serving as indisputable testimony to the divine, vatic, and revelatory poetry—communicating the highest and most transcendent truths—that the speaker has thus far proved unable securely to identify. Surely the Psalms fit this description, testifying to 'that unspeakable and everlasting beauty to be seen by the eyes of the mind, only cleared by faith' (84.26–8)? Yet the speaker's diffidence and his increasingly familiar dodges are evident even here. The versification argument appears, for example—the Psalms are 'fully written in metre' (84.20)—but with a half-heartedness that seems virtually self-cancelling: 'although the rules be not yet fully found' (84.20–1). As was the case with the ancient oracles, the appeal to form seems incapable of holding back the irresistible slide towards content (the 'conceit proper to the poet'), as the sentence proceeds directly to the assertion that David's handling of his prophecy was 'merely poetical' (84.22). Editors gloss 'merely' as 'entirely' or 'exclusively' so as to remove any sense that the Psalms might *only* be poetical, even though the tautological appeal to etymology with which the sentence begins—'even the name psalms . . . being interpreted, is nothing but songs' (84.18–19)—does not in itself prove that they are anything more.[23] The speaker lists a series of rhetorical features and figures (invocation, voice, personification, the pathetic fallacy, and so forth) as evidence that the Psalms constitute a 'heavenly poesy' (84.25): 'poesy' (the first time this term is used in the body of the *Defence*) in the specific sense of the act or art of making, possibly suggested by the way David is said to '*maketh* you, as it were, see God coming in His majesty' (84.24, my emphasis) and anticipating the discussion of *poesis* in the following paragraph. That is to say, David approximates here to the ancient oracles whose poetic utterances may not merely have been transmitting the messages of the gods but

---

[23] 'wholly', Smith (385); 'entirely', van Dorsten (189) and Alexander (7); 'exclusively', Shepherd (152) and Maslen (132). The other use of 'merely' in the *Defence*—'poets . . . do merely make to imitate, and imitate both to delight and teach' (87.13–15)—is similarly glossed as 'exclusively' by Shepherd (163) and Maslen (147). Maslen (127) glosses the 'mere tales' (83.2) that Plato tells, including the story of Gyges' ring, as 'obvious fictions'. Such editorial interventions serve to shore up the suggestion that these poetic productions must be more substantive than the qualifying adverb/ adjective would potentially admit. Shepherd (151) notes, on the other hand, that while the Church Fathers believed that David composed the Psalms through the direct inspiration of God, it was Petrarch who reasserted their poetic character: one result being that Psalm-translation came to occupy a special place in the development of the vernaculars of Renaissance Europe. On this, see also Prescott 1989.

may also have been of their own composition: their 'conceit . . . did seem to have some divine force in it' (84.13–14).[24] The hesitancy of that 'did seem' is analogous to the way David is said 'almost' (84.26) to express himself in the same possessed and transported mode.[25]

That the speaker is getting perilously close again to the position that such effusions might be of the poet's own devising—and that this making or 'poesy' carries a divine force all its own—is signalled by another of his hasty retreats and attempts at recovery. As the 'heavenly' title of *vates* rapidly shifted to a 'very vain and godless superstition', so the hint that David may have been the author of the Psalms himself is quickly retracted: 'I fear me I seem to profane that holy name' (84.28–9). Again, however, the speaker's abrupt turnaround lacks conviction (the sentence is introduced by a 'But truly . . . ', 84.28), for the supposed profanity turns out to arise not from the suggestion that David as opposed to God might have had a hand in authoring the Psalms but rather from associating them with poetry in its currently denigrated state: from applying David's 'holy name' to 'Poetry, which is among us thrown down to so ridiculous an estimation' (84.29–30). The true profanity, in other words, consists in the throwing down of poetry, in denying and depriving it of its own true power—the 'divine force' that is evident in the transport of the ancient oracles—which is what Sidney if not his speaker seems really to want to say.[26] The inhibitions against saying such a thing manifest in the speaker's circular logic and faulty reasoning which, as if in spite of itself, ends up arguing the opposite anyway (namely, that if it is 'profane' to associate David with something 'ridiculous', then it must be acceptable to associate him with something revered, in which case that which is 'merely poetical', like 'mere tales', seems to qualify).[27] The crucial question—which has come up before when the speaker's

---

[24] It is not impossible that 'divine' is here being used in the weaker sense: see *OED* divine *adj.* 5b: 'of things: of surpassing beauty, perfection, excellence, etc.' (current from the late fifteenth century). See in particular the citation from Calvin 1561 (E1ᵛ): 'I graunte in dede that oftentimes a thing is called Diuine or of God, that is notable by any singular excellence.' As Refini 2012 (39) notes, the notion that such divine force might originate in the poet him/herself—rather than in some sort of 'external inspiration coming from the gods or other superior spiritual beings'—belonged to the theory of the sublime, newly revived from the mid-sixteenth century, if not before, by the circulation and translation of Longinus' treatise on the subject.

[25] *Pace* Shepherd (152) and Maslen (133) who gloss 'almost' here as an intensive—as 'indeed'— rather than as a qualifier.

[26] I owe this formulation, as so much, to Crewe 1986 (82) who asks: '*did* Sidney want what he knew he should want? Did he know what he wanted?' (emphasis original), adding, 'It depends, of course, on what one means by "know" and "want"' (165n).

[27] van Dorsten (188) describes the use of David as the second example to illustrate the *vates* theme (after that of the ancient oracles) as 'Logically . . . disconnected' since it belongs to the '"inspired" literary tradition, which [Sidney] rejects'. 'Characteristically', he continues, 'each time an "enthusiastic" topic of current literary debate is approached, the obvious occult implications are omitted.' Like many critics, he picks up here on the sense that Sidney's position on the issue of the 'heroic frenzy' seems to be contradictory or at least unresolved, for the fact that David is introduced here as a 'passionate lover' (84.26) would suggest that the Psalms in fact bear all the hallmarks of the *furor poeticus*. One way of resolving the issue might be to suggest that this contradiction arises directly from a conflict within Sidney's thinking and manifests in the prevarications of his speaker. If so, this conflict could be described as that between (1) what Sidney finds himself officially committed to saying but does not really want to say, and (2) what he wants to say but feels inhibited or intimidated about saying. The

faulty logic similarly betrays a conflict with and within his author (as in the case of the barbarous Irish and foolish Romans)—is what the Psalms, or songs or oracles or poetry, for that matter, should be revered *for*. In what, exactly, does their content—their 'knowledge'—consist?

As if to address this question, the discussion moves on to consider the Greek name for poet—literally, 'maker'—and here what Sidney really wants to say about poetry is given its first and, so far, most thorough airing. The speaker's argument in this section organizes itself around a binary that at first glance seems to invite a reading along distinctly social if not class lines. Thus, like the 'heavenly . . . title' (83.40) of *vates*, so 'maker' or 'poet' is also presented as a 'high and incomparable . . . title' (84.39), its incomparable eminence being immediately demonstrated by means of a comparison: here, with the practitioners of 'other sciences' (84.40), who necessarily emerge as inferior or lower in status. The qualities that are said to characterize those who practise these other sciences and arts are those of dependence and subjection, with a hint even of subservience: they are also referred to as the 'serving sciences' (88.23; 89.36). They are essentially functionaries in that they do not lead but *follow*: they 'follow Nature' (85.7), taking their lead from her. Like clerks or notaries, they merely take dictation or copy out what someone else has written, as they 'setteth down' (85.2) what Nature has 'set forth' (85.1). Like 'actors and players' (84.43) they merely recite lines that someone else has scripted. In following Nature they are like huntsmen who similarly follow leads, track down prey: an increasingly popular image in the sixteenth century for the pursuit of knowledge and development of natural science by means of deductive reasoning.[28] In this sense, their following is not unlike that of the English poets who were earlier said to 'have followed' (82.28) Chaucer and Gower—the latter in turn following Dante, Boccaccio, and Petrarch—in making their native language a 'treasure-house of science'. That is to say, these other sciences and arts are worthy enough: they fit the approved model of humanist learning in following the authorities, or Nature, or the authorities that advise the following of Nature (Aristotle, mainly, but also the Stoics), with a view to increasing the sum of human knowledge and so 'build[ing] upon the depth of Nature' (85.16). But there is a strong sense of their secondariness (Nature provides the foundations upon which they build) as well as their limitations. What a natural scientist might

---

first of these would correspond to the position that poetry is necessarily logocentric, i.e. that language is structured so as to reveal a transcendent signified, a God-given Truth, by means of the Logos or Word. This is the Augustinian position that Freccero 1986 (21) designates by the 'fig tree'. It was also close to that of the Florentine Neoplatonists, and the suggestion that Sidney may not have been wholly committed to it is hinted at in the uncertainty surrounding his reception and appreciation of *De gli eroici furori* (1585), dedicated to him by Giordano Bruno: on this see Waller 1972. The second view— what Sidney wants to but dare not say—would correspond to the position that poetry is entirely man-made, that the poet thereby does indeed exercise god-like creative powers, and that his (or her) effusions and transports thus have their own 'divine force' without being dependent upon or grounded in a prior metaphysics and without, therefore, being 'ideal'. This is the position that Freccero identifies with the 'laurel': 'a totally autonomous portrait of the artist, devoid of any ontological claim' (21). For conflicted and conflicting views on the notion of the *furor poeticus* in Sidney's writings and in the period more generally, see: Farley-Hills 1991; Kinney 2008; Moore 2010; and Alexander, ed. 2013 (xliv).

[28] See Bates 2013 (238–9).

have presented as the heroic pursuit, hunting down, and capture of knowledge is here damned with faint praise as the speaker offers—ostensibly to avert the charge of his own personal bias or 'partial allegation' (84.40)—to demonstrate his point by 'marking [their] scope' (84.40): a hunting term (from Greek *skopos*) that designates a target or mark for shooting at, but that also implies that these 'other sciences' are something he can easily take within his purview—take in at a glance, set his sights at, get the measure of—as if their terrain were circumscribed, confined, easy to map or track. The same sense of the confinement or boundedness of these other sciences and arts is expressed in the image of the rules of logic being 'compassed within the circle of a question' (85.12).

Against these qualities of secondariness and limitation, the speaker—or now, perhaps one should rather say, Sidney—contrasts the poet. The latter emphatically does *not* follow. On the contrary, he either leads or flies away. Where making Nature their 'principal object' (84.42) had led naturally to the other sciences' 'subjection' to her, the poet 'disdain[s] to be tied' (85.17) to any such thing, and is instead elevated to great heights: 'lifted up with the vigour of his own invention' (85.17–18), neither tied down nor 'enclosed within the narrow warrant of her gifts' (85.22–3). He is proudly answerable to none: neither master, mistress, nor any other higher authority. He is not bound by Nature's copy-text but able to originate and write his own, 'making things either better than Nature . . . or, quite anew' (85.19–20).[29] In this respect, Sidney does not follow the followers, busy building up the knowledge bank, but—more like the historians who 'followed' Herodotus (83.9) in his extemporizing, improvising, and making up of things 'which no man could affirm' (83.10–11)—he goes with them into the limitless realm of that which can be imagined: the fictional. Indeed, just as the speaker had demeaned the scientists' pursuit of knowledge by implying that the latter was something whose 'scope' he could mark, so here Sidney appropriates the hunt motif for his own purposes, identifying the poet not with the hunters or followers but rather with the creatures that elude them: 'freely ranging only within the zodiac of his own wit' (85.23), like wild deer that, neither immured or imparked nor tracked down and captured, are owned by no one, not even the prince (according to Forest Law, even in royal forests such animals were strictly ownerless until they were killed); or like the soaring falcon that also disdains ownership, since being vigorously 'lifted up' by his own invention suggests an analogy with the 'high flying liberty of conceit proper to the poet' (84.13).[30] In the *Schoole of Abuse*, Gosson had compared the profitless poet to the 'wanton whelpe, [that] leaueth the game, to runne riot' (76/A1ᵛ),

---

[29] Later in the *Defence*, Sidney coins a new word, 'to poetize' (108.41), the turning of the Greek *poiein* into an English verb being a suitably active example of a maker's making of 'making'. The poet's freedom to invent—by comparison with the other sciences and arts—reappears in the discussion of tragedy: 'a tragedy is tied to the laws of Poesy, and not of History; not bound to follow the story, but, having liberty either to feign a quite new matter, or to frame the history to the most tragical conveniency' (111.21–4).

[30] The verb 'range' is especially associated with the behaviour of wild animals: see *OED* range *v*[1]: *intr.* I.1.a: 'especially of a person or animal: to traverse or move in all directions over a comparatively large area; to rove, roam, wander.' See Bates 2013 (205–36) on the general disparagement of hunters—and identification with the hunted—that characterizes Sidney's writings.

implicitly contrasting the profitable purveyor of learning who presumably bags the prey as part of his service to the common good.[31] Sidney's poet, by contrast, is less interested in catching anything than in identifying with the animals that refuse to play this game: the wanton whelp, the freely ranging deer, the high flying birds.[32]

As noted above, Sidney's presentation of the poet here could be read in distinctly class terms, as spatial images of intellectual elevation—being lifted up, flying high—effortlessly move across to images of social eminence: the 'high . . . title' enjoyed by the poet-maker who disdains any form of subjection (perhaps the same 'title of a poet' into which Sidney has himself slipped in his 'not old years and idlest times', 81.26, 25). Comparison with the practitioners of 'other sciences'—worthy but dull, honest labourers who work to build up the treasure-house of science for the collective good—allows the poet to emerge as a contrastingly aristocratic figure, glamorously free from such mundane concerns and 'freely ranging' where he would. Indeed, much of this social connotation is contained in this word that might otherwise be passed over but that, in the context, proves highly loaded. Originally a status word denoting a person who is not—or is no longer—in servitude or subjection to another, 'free' quickly assumed a secondary, social-ethical sense that attributed certain qualities to persons so classified, such as 'of noble birth, breeding, or appearance', and 'noble, honourable, generous, magnanimous'.[33] The poet-maker's disdain for 'subjection' of any kind thus fits with both the original and the earliest meanings of this word—as well as with the idea of high flying liberty[34]—but it also extends to those secondary senses that connoted typically 'aristocratic' qualities, above all that of generosity: to be 'free' came to include the sense of being open-handed, 'ready in giving', such gifts being given out of generosity 'and not in return for something else', since they were provided 'without charge'.[35] Sidney's 'freely ranging' poet, therefore, connotes not only the wild deer, exhilaratingly untrammelled, unencumbered by ownership or capture, but also the imputed generosity of the free-born aristocrat—even monarch or god—who can afford to give, and be seen to give, 'for nothing' and without thought of recompense or repayment, with the result that such giving, gifting, or gifts thus appear 'free' to those who receive them.[36] In Sidney's designation, therefore, the

---

[31] Where Gosson *does* identify the profitless poet with the hunter-figure, it is in a predictably negative sense. It is as such that the deceitful poet lures, traps, and snares the unwary reader: 'The Fowlers whistle [is], the birdes death: The wholesome bayte, the fishes bane' (77/A2).

[32] Cf. Agrippa 1569 (A1) who claims, in his attack on learning, to 'chalenge into the fielde all theese moste hardie hunters of Artes and Sciences'.

[33] See *OED* free *adj.* I.i.a: 'not or no longer in servitude' (current from early Old English); I.i.3a: 'free-born; of noble birth, breeding, or appearance' (current from Old English); I.i.3b: 'noble, honourable, generous, magnanimous' (current from the late fourteenth century). See also the discussion of this word in Lewis 1967 (111–32).

[34] See *OED* free *adj.* II.6.b: 'of an animal: not kept shut up, fenced in, or on a restraint; allowed to roam or range at will' (current from the turn of the fifteenth century).

[35] See *OED* free *adj.* III.17.a: 'ready in giving; generous' (from early to mid-thirteenth century); III.17.b: 'of a gift: given out of generosity and not in return for something else' (current from the early fifteenth century); IV.24.a: 'given or provided without charge' (current from the early thirteenth century).

[36] As Lewis 1967 (117) notes, the English word thereby conflates senses for which the classical languages had separate words (*dorean* in Greek and *gratis* in Latin signify 'costing nothing'): 'Thus

poet-maker emerges not only as free from subjection but as the munificent
dispenser of largesse.[37]

○○

The *Defence*'s famous section on *poesis*, then, seems to give Sidney a free rein, so to
speak, to set out and indulge his views on the fundamental aboriginality and
creativity of the poet when the latter's art is defined as the making of fiction.
Here Sidney dares to say what he wants to say. This section is not without its
contradictions, however, not the least of which is the way in which this image of the
beneficent courtly if not royal poet is so obviously a fantasy. Take, for example, the
statement that, unlike the plodding 'other sciences' that patiently follow Nature,
the poet is 'not enclosed within the narrow warrant of her gifts' (85.22–3): a phrase
editors gloss as 'not dependent on her restricted patronage or authorization ("warrant")'.[38] It is difficult, in the circumstances, not to see Queen Elizabeth lurking
behind Dame Nature here, nor to misread Sidney's denial as anything other than a
fantasized escape from what was, in reality, his utter dependence upon her favour.
Behind the imagined bounty of the poet-maker's free gift rather pointedly stands
the real (indeed, notorious) stinginess of the Queen's 'gifts' (and an opportunity,
not to be missed, for Sidney to remind his readers of it). Sidney's correspondence is
full of begging letters—complaints of his 'neede', 'necessitie', 'wante', 'discom-
fortes', 'pouerty' (he is 'almost to the bottome of my pursse'), of his debts (the
'vsury and other combres' entailed by his creditors), of the 'meanenes of my
fortune'—and equally full of 'suits' to Sussex, Leicester, Burghley, and Hatton,
to all of whom he remains 'much bownd', to intercede for the Queen's favour on
his behalf, whether in the form of immediate relief (hard cash), 'impropriations'
(the granting of the benefice and tithes of a church or other ecclesiastical property to
a layman), or the security of government office.[39] On occasion, Sidney's 'present
case' is desperate enough for him to consider the humiliation of suing the Queen
directly for relief: 'I will even ~~shamefully~~ shamelessly once in my lief, bringe it her
ma*je*stie my selfe: neede obayes no *l*awe, and forgett*es* blusshinge'.[40] Elizabeth's

---

dorean is rendered as *freely* in the Authorised Version; "freely ye have received", and, earlier, in the
Wycliffite translation, *freli*.'

[37] Thus the Earl of Surrey's lyrics are said to be indicative of 'a noble birth, and worthy of a noble
mind' (110.17). This also perhaps puts a new gloss on the title that Puttenham 2007 (148, 149) would
bestow on the poet, namely, that of the 'courtly maker'. In his own 'Briefe Apologie of Poetrie', which
prefaces his translation of the *Orlando Furioso* (1591) and which follows Sidney's *Defence* closely, Sir
John Harington—who credits Puttenham with having 'christened' the poet with this name—in the
next breath puts him down by making a point of distinguishing between his *Art of Poesy* and Sidney's
Defence of Poesy. In the former, Harington notes condescendingly, 'the poore gentleman laboreth
greatly' to prove what in the latter Sidney demonstrates effortlessly—namely, that poetry is 'a gift and
not an art'—'I say he proueth it, because making himselfe and manie others so cunning in the art, yet
he sheweth himself so slender a gift in it': see Harington 1904 (196, 197).

[38] Maslen (138), following Shepherd (156); Alexander (9) glosses 'warrant' as 'licence, permission'.

[39] See *Correspondence* (15, 798, 990, 991, 1034, 1040, 1042, 1046, 1047, 1049, 1050, 1058).
With the exception of the first two references—which relate to letters dated 1573 and 1577
respectively—all the others relate to the period between August 1580 and January 1582 when
Sidney is likely to have been composing the *Defence*.

[40] From a letter to Hatton dated 14 November 1581: *Correspondence* (1042).

prevarication with respect to this particular suit (despite Sidney's urgency and frequent promptings) left him complaining to Leicester that 'haue I both shame and skorne', that is, that he lacked both the financial support and, equally important, the visible signs of favour that were crucial to a courtier's credibility and credit.[41] All this puts a rather different gloss on the image of the free and debonair courtly maker who 'disdain[s] to be tied to any such subjection' (85.17). For all the kingly fantasy of this figure going 'hand in hand with [Queen] Nature' (85.22)—unlike those poor mortals who remain enclosed within the narrow warrant of her gifts—the poet as exemplified by Sidney falls entirely within the scope of the latter group and is in reality no less subservient than they.[42]

Just as the speaker's categories had an uncanny way of collapsing, suggesting that the arguments he and Sidney were promoting were somehow at odds with one another, it now appears that the categories Sidney himself seems set on rending asunder are no less prone, as the independent king, leader, master, and poet appears to dissolve into the dependent courtier, follower, servant, and maker before our very eyes. Indeed, it is worth pausing over this word 'maker' for a moment because, for all the speaker's efforts to endow the word with social status—to grant it so 'high and incomparable a title' (84.39)—historically and regionally, the term lacked dignity. Although from the outset the word was used to designate God as man's Maker, in its human application the primary sense denoted a manufacturer, and where used of writers it originally meant a person who physically composes a book or draws up a document.[43] As editors note, while the word is common in fifteenth- and sixteenth-century Northern English and Scots to indicate someone who composes in verse, in Southern Middle English it lacked status: Chaucer, for example, uses 'make' and 'making' to refer to compositions in the vernacular, including his own, modestly reserving 'poet' and 'poesy' for the same activity in the more culturally esteemed classical languages or Italian.[44] In the passage from the *Poetices* that Sidney otherwise follows closely in this section, moreover, Scaliger, noting the poet's fundamentally creative, godlike capabilities, comments that, while the name 'maker' was furnished 'not by the agreement of men, but by the provident wisdom of nature', as in the case of 'the learned Greeks', he is

---

[41] From a letter to Leicester dated 28 December 1581: *Correspondence* (1049). See also the importance of receiving 'some tokne *that* my frendes might see I had not vtterly lost my time' regarding another suit that turned out to be unsuccessful, from a letter to Burghley dated 10 October 1581: *Correspondence* (1040).

[42] As Maslen notes (70): 'Sidney's allusions to the aristocratic ancestry of the poet and the princeliness of his qualities have often been taken simply as an expression of his class interests—a carefully rationalized snobbery.' See e.g. Myrick 1935 (217): 'For the courtier fettered by poverty and empty duties there must have been an irresistible appeal in the poet's glorious exercise of free power.'

[43] See *OED* maker *n.* 1.a.: 'a person who fashions, constructs, prepares for use, or manufactures something; a manufacturer' (current from the late fourteenth century); 2.a.: 'used of God as the Creator of the universe' (current from the mid-fourteenth century); 3.a.: 'a person who composes a book, draws up a document, frames a law, or the like' (current from the mid-fourteenth century).

[44] Chaucer, for example, uses 'poet' and 'poetry' of Dante (*Wife of Bath's Tale*, line 1125), Petrarch (*Clerk's Prologue*, line 31), Homer, Virgil, and Lucan (*House of Fame*, lines 1478, 1483, 1499); and 'making', 'make', etc., of his own, vernacular productions (e.g. *Troilus and Criseyde*, Book 5, line 1789, and the *Legend of Good Women*, Text F, lines 483, 562, 579, 618): see Chaucer 1987.

nonetheless surprised that 'our ancestors should be so unfair to themselves as to limit the term to candle-makers, for though usage has sanctioned this practice, etymologically it is absurd'.[45] While Sidney's claim not to know 'whether [it is] by luck or wisdom' (84.37) that the English, like the Greeks, happily hit upon the same name of 'maker' for poet seems to echo the first part of Scaliger's comment, it is symptomatic that he suppresses the second part, as if he were trying to hide or deny the low-status connotations the word had in English and other languages, and to head off any suggestion that the poet was not so much a courtly maker as a humble if useful artisan and dealer in commodities.

Much the same insecurity about status might also be seen to manifest in the period's conceptualization of labour. As Marc Shell writes, 'Poetics is about production (*poiēsis*). There can be no analysis of the form or content of production without a theory of labor'.[46] One such theory is that put forward—very vigorously—by Stephen Gosson: namely, that poetry represents labour's exact opposite. For Gosson, poets are definitively *not* makers and that is the whole problem. They are the very antithesis of the honest workers whose 'iuste labour' (99/C8ᵛ) is a model of probity, productiveness, and profitability, like that of the industrious bees who return to the hive with the 'fruites of their labour' (100/D2).[47] While such 'Labourers' work together to advance the commonwealth—as the different parts of the body, from 'the top to the toe' serve under 'one head' (107/E2, E1ᵛ)—the poet, by contrast, 'labors wᵗʰ Mountaines to bring foorth Mise' (78/A3ᵛ). As citizens, poets are manifestly idle, unproductive, and unprofitable. Worse, they are beggars who batten upon society and drain it dry, and who—as in a perverse economy—produce nothing other than replications of their sorry selves: thus, theatres 'doe make more trewandes [i.e. vagrants], and ill husbands [i.e. bad husbandmen], then if open Schooles of vnthrifts & Vagabounds were kept' (99/C8ᵛ), the very opposite of gainful employment.[48] In defending poets and poetry against these charges—by asserting that 'maker' is a high title and denying its low-status

[45] Scaliger 1905 (8). Scaliger's joke here is that in Italian the term *fattojano* (if not *fattore*) meant 'oil-presser'.

[46] Shell 1978 (9). See also Ellinghausen 2008 (5) on the way writing came to be conceived as an act of labour in this period and the class implications of this development: 'why does labor become such a common way of imagining writing in this period . . . why are non-aristocratic writers identifying with the "fourth sort" [i.e. manual labourers]?' By way of answer, she suggests that profiting both themselves ('Economic self-interest') and the commonwealth ('an ideal of civic service') is largely what motivated non-courtly writers in their self-presentations (12). Note that, on those occasions when Sidney is mentioned (1, 45, 59n), he is treated as a courtly foil to such labouring writers.

[47] See also the worthy Spartans who 'with labour and trauell [travail] . . . whette their stomackes to their meate' (79/A4), and who are the epitome of 'thrift and husbandry' (104/D6ᵛ): 'The *Spartans* are all steele, fashioned out of tougher mettall, free in minde, valiaunt in hart, seruile to none, accustoming their flesh to stripes, their bodyes to labour, their feete to hunting, their handes to fighting' (104/D6ᵛ–D7).

[48] See also: 'Wee haue infinite Poets, and Pipers, and suche peeuishe cattel among vs in Englande, that liue by merrie begging, mainteyned by almes, and priuily encroch vppon euerie mans purse' (84/B1). Similar charges appear in Gosson, *Playes Confuted in fiue Actions* (1582), where the typical stage-player is considered 'little better than a vagrant' (141/☞7– ☞7ᵛ); 'Most of the Players haue bene eyther men of occupations, which they haue forsaken to lyue by playing, or common minstrels, or trayned vp from theire childehoode to this abhominable exercise & haue now no other way to gete theire liuinge' (195/G6ᵛ).

connotations—Sidney runs the risk of making the free, magnanimous, liberally dispensing aristocratic poet look very much like the beggarly, vagabond player-poets whom Gosson condemns. Pointless, and a drain on society to which they have nothing to contribute, the courtier and the beggar—the idle rich and idle poor—threaten to merge into one another, rather as Edgar and Poor Tom become one on the heath in *King Lear*. The free-born aristocrat who proudly acknowledges no master comes to look uncannily like that type treated with such incomprehension, fear, and vitriol in Elizabethan England: that of the masterless man.[49]

Spenser famously comments that, in dedicating the *Schoole of Abuse* to Sidney, Gosson was 'for hys labor scorned': as much, perhaps, for his theory of labour—against which Sidney takes it upon himself to defend the poet—as for any effort he may have taken in writing the treatise in the first place.[50] This courtly scorn, however, evidently proves something of a liability—the scorner himself is scorned if or when he fails to secure a visible token of favour—which could be one of the reasons why Spenser quickly qualifies his remark ('if at leaste it be in the goodnesse of that nature to scorne') and also why some doubt has always remained over whether Sidney actually scorned Gosson or not.[51] Indeed, it may be that Sidney was all too aware of what his speaker in this section of the *Defence* seems not to be: namely, that the courtly maker could in reality no more afford to disdain subjection than he could afford to scorn labour.[52] If defending poets against the charge of profitlessness threatens to take Sidney down the blind alley of making them look very like the idlers Gosson condemns, then the obvious route that remains open to him is precisely that of the humanist pedagogues—the purveyors of learning and learned poetry—whose worthy labour does its bit to contribute to the common good. If this ends up undermining the image of the courtly maker as pure fantasy—and so undoing the difference between the poet with his 'high . . . title' (84.39) and the 'other' (84.40) serving sciences—so be it. The tale of the belly attributed to Menenius Agrippa, for example, that appears later in the *confirmatio* could be seen to pick up on Gosson's bodily metaphor of idealized labour—in which the limbs work cooperatively under one head—as a way of demonstrating that the courtly

---

[49] See the discussions of this phenomenon in Halpern 1991 (61–100); and Finkelstein 2006 (163–6).

[50] Spenser 1580 (G3ᵛ).

[51] Ibid. Gosson dedicated *The ephemerides of Phialo*—to which he appends his 'Apologie of the *Schoole of Abuse*' (1579a)—to Sidney, writing in the dedicatory epistle that 'I can not but acknowledge my safetie, in your Worships patronage' (244/☞3), and offering this second book as 'a manifest pledge of my thankfull heart' (244/☞3ᵛ). I agree with Maslen (26) that this suggests 'Gosson had received at least some sort of reward or encouragement for his earlier dedication'.

[52] Such courtly 'scorn' could in fact be cynically manufactured by printers with no other end in view than to heighten the rarity value of their product and so raise its price: a well-known tactic and one employed by Richard Tottel, among others, in claiming to bring otherwise secreted courtly materials to a hungry reading public, its appetite duly whetted. The same strategy is exploited by Henry Olney, who published the first edition of the *Defence* in 1595. On the title page Olney quotes on Sidney's behalf the well-known tag from Horace 2004, *Odes*, III.i.1—'*Odi profanum vulgus et arceo*' [I shun the uninitiated crowd and keep it at a distance]—effectively ventriloquizing his author and thus manufacturing courtly scorn in order to trade on it. Printers clearly profited materially from producing copies of Sidney's texts. In 1586 Fulke Greville referred to the threatened publication of the *Old Arcadia* as a 'mercenary book', and damned the errors and carelessness of such 'mercenary printing': quoted in Woudhuysen 1996 (416).

class is, in fact, wholly integral to the smooth functioning of the commonweal and not the 'unprofitable . . . spender' (96.23–4), wantonly consuming the 'labour' (96.23) of others, that it may have appeared to be.[53] Indeed, conceptions of labour serve as the classic site for negotiating the difference—and changing relation—between humanist and courtly values.[54] Writing earlier in the century, for example, Sir Thomas Elyot had found himself having to fend off scornful charges on the part of his peers—to the effect that, as a courtier, he had no business writing or publishing books—by appealing to exactly the same humanist justification: that his 'labour' in doing so was of direct profit to the state.[55] For Gosson, too, the advice was to 'Set your talents a worke . . . so shall you please God, profite your country, honor your prince, discharge your duetie, giue vp a good account of your stewardship' (109/E3ᵛ). If Sidney were likewise to adopt this humanist, pedagogic guise—and ditch the poet's pretensions to 'high . . . title'—then the poet-maker in the *Defence* might take his rightful place among a worthy crowd, redeeming any 'low' connotations that may still have lingered around the word 'maker' by giving it a new dignity, and offering his services to prince and people as an honest labourer among the rest.[56] His beloved freedom, after all, could convert all too easily into

---

[53] For Matz 2000 (64–6) the anecdote of the belly appears to serve Sidney's purpose—in that it works to reconcile the humanist values of profit with the courtly values of pleasure—although the attempt at synthesis ultimately fails. Ferguson 1983 (140–2, 161–2) offers a similar reading. I return to this anecdote in Part III, section II.

[54] Sidney's speaker would thus join Gosson in articulating the position of the 'commonwealths men', i.e. the model of the polity as harmonious, ethically regulated, and mutually beneficial: an 'idealist unity' as Landreth 2012 (37) calls it. For Ferguson 1983 and Matz 2000 the conflict that plays out within the *Defence* is between the opposing values of humanism and courtliness. Sinfield 1992 (80–94) reads this as the central tension within the *Arcadia*, thus making for a deconstructive reading of that text, i.e. as opposed to the 'perfect reconcilement' (96.28–9) which the anecdote of the belly achieves in the *Defence*, rebellions in the *New Arcadia* result in division, disintegration, and ruin. However, he curiously attributes a different conflict to *Defence*—that between humanist and Protestant values—as a result of which his reading of the latter (181–213) is altogether more conservative. Much the same is true of Herman 1996 (61–93).

[55] See Elyot 1533 (A2): 'to the desire of knowlege . . . I haue ioyned a constant intent to profyte therby . . . my natural countrey'; 1541a (A2): 'why shuld I be greuyd with reproches, wherewith some of my countray do recompence me, for my labours taken without hope of temporall rewarde, onely for the feruent affectyon whiche I haue euer borne toward the publike weale of my countray'; and 1541b (a2ᵛ): 'diuerse there be which do not thankfully esteme my labours, dispraysinge my studies as vayne and vnprofitable'; 'some ingrate persons with ille reporte or mockes requite yl my labours' (a3ᵛ). Maslen (71) suggests that Sidney drew from Elyot the idea that nobility 'originated as a meritocracy'. For a discussion of Elyot as an intermediary between courtly and humanist positions, see Matz 2000 (25–55).

[56] As Maslen (69) notes: 'for Sidney being born a poet is not enough; one must work to cultivate one's poetic status, just as aristocrats must work to make themselves worthy of their aristocratic "title" or inheritance.' It is clear that the profit presented by Elyot as benefiting the state is that of the cultural or intellectual capital that derives from the acquisition and growth of knowledge (that is, from the use-value of humanistic education) rather than any immediate financial reward that might accrue to the individual from printing and publishing such material (its mere exchange-value). Nevertheless, as noted above, the profits to be made by the latter (more, admittedly, by printers rather than by authors themselves) could be considerable: the *Schoole of Abuse*, for example, had an initial print run of 3,000 (six times the normal size). Williams 2009 (640–1) suggests that Gosson may have stirred up outrage so as to sell more copies of his tract. Sidney, of course, did not have the *Defence* printed: as Woudhuysen 1996 (211) notes, even as a manuscript text the *Defence* was 'kept on a tight rein' as 'it does not appear that Sidney wanted it to circulate widely' (234). By the same token, the speaker

that of the 'free sciences' or liberal arts—so called because they are studied for their own sake with no ulterior purpose in mind—and all of which are included among the 'other sciences' that Sidney lists.[57] In relation to these, the art of poetry no longer looks so very different after all.

◌෴

It might seem, therefore, as if the poet-maker's claim to 'high' title and courtly status is wholly spurious, and that any effort made to distinguish his art from these other, more industrious and serviceable forms thus doomed to failure.[58] In this case, the speaker's avowed aim, as expressed at the beginning of the *narratio*—to defend poetry for the solid contributions it makes to the nation's 'treasure-house of science'—could be seen to get back on track after a somewhat shaky start. However, the fact that the image of the 'freely ranging' courtly maker is manifestly a social fantasy does not invalidate the case being put forward—openly in the section on *poesis* and more covertly in the examples of the preceding paragraphs—for an alternative conception of poetry: one that does not see profitability as the sole criterion of value, that values 'value' differently if at all, and that sees poetry as neither a bankable commodity nor a transaction to be held to account. Deconstructing the credentials of the courtly maker does not discredit this vision, and that for two reasons. First, because in this alternative model the poet is being defined

takes it upon himself to scorn those hack writers who do profit financially in this way: they are 'base men with servile wits . . . who think it enough if they can be rewarded of the printer' (109.11–12), as opposed to presumably worthier types who disdain to be 'accounted knights of the same order' (109.23). Such low types are still designated 'knights', however, and any presumed irony or social condescension falls rather flat when one recalls that Sidney's own knighthood was bestowed for purely expedient reasons (how 'high' a title, in fact, was it?). On Sidney's sensitivity to title, see Berry 1998 (149–51, 159); Maslen (5–6, 8–9, 69, 71); and Part III, section III, note 177.

[57] The seven liberal arts were astronomy, geometry, arithmetic, music, grammar, rhetoric, and logic. The practitioners of Sidney's 'other sciences' include 'the astronomer', 'the geometrician and arithmetician', 'the musician', 'The grammarian', 'the rhetorician and logician' (85.1–10). On the use of the word 'free' to designate the liberal arts—originally, writings and studies 'worthy of or suitable for one of noble birth'—see *OED* free *adj.* I.4 (current from Old English); and Lewis 1967 (129–30).

[58] Such is the reading put forward by Fraser 1970, for whom the model of the courtly maker was definitively over by the end of the sixteenth century—challenged and ultimately defeated by the meritocratic world ushered in by the mercantilist values and social mobility of the 'new' men—in relation to which Sidney's *Defence* represents an antiquated throwback to outdated feudal values and a hopelessly rearguard action. Low 1993 (12–30) makes much the same argument with respect to *Astrophil and Stella*. Warley 2005 (72–100) presents a more sophisticated version of this thesis, reading Sidney's sonnet sequence as playing out unresolved tensions between status (static and heritable, belonging to birthright and the bloodline, and associated formally with lyric) and class (mobile and dynamic, belonging to cash or moveable capital, and associated formally with narrative). In Astrophil's case, status is shown to be dependent upon and undermined by his possession or otherwise of wealth, material goods, capital in circulation (i.e. class), and it is therefore articulated, very precisely, as the desire for something he lacks and can never possess: Lady Rich. In this reading, the aspirant, 'noble' figure of Sidney's dreams (and those of many idealist critics) emerges as nothing more than wish fulfilment on the part of that 'other' Sidney: the impoverished, debt-ridden, compromised, would-be court servant. By extension, the highly titled poet of the *Defence* could also be read as a fantasy projection on the part of the earnest, hard-working, honestly labouring, Protestant humanist pedagogue and professor of learning. See also Kennedy 2016 (20) who traces a shift from a 'Platonic poetics of *fureur* to an Aristotelian poetics of craftsmanship and skill' in the period that can readily be conceived in class terms.

and defended as a creator of *fictions*, someone who makes things up 'such as never were in Nature' (85.20). In this context, the fantasy of the poet freely dispensing largesse—the product less of labour or hard graft than of a divinely inspired heroic frenzy or *furor poeticus*—might easily take its rightful place among the other mythical creatures there listed: 'Heroes, Demigods, Cyclops, Chimeras, Furies, and such like' (85.20–1). Indeed, a fantasized image of the poet might be said to support the argument rather than to contradict it: to be the perfect illustration of poetry's status as fiction, while, quite properly, never affirming it for true (the best illustration of all, of course, would be to write more fiction: that a product of the imagination should defend other products of the imagination is a trick that Astrophil would pull off, after all).[59] From the point of view of someone wishing to promote a definition of the poet as a creator of fictions, arguably, the more fantastical that image, the better. Second, deconstructing this fantasy does not deconstruct the sense that a difference *in kind* exists between the two types of poet that are here being compared: the poet as creator of fictions as against the poet as producer and depositor of profitable knowledge and learning. That difference remains, even though it has been expressed, perhaps ill-advisedly, in terms of *degree*: the highly titled poet as opposed to those who labour for profit. That this was a false binary in practice does not obviate the fact that a binary is here being scoped—groped towards, sketched out—between two alternative, entirely different, and incommensurable conceptions of poetry: one that very insistently presents itself in terms of profitability, and one that presents itself, in reaction, as opposed to those terms in every way. In this working out, rough, even crude social stereotypes come to stand in for and mark out these two different conceptions. The more 'courtly' dispensation—that which gravitates towards the set of ideas historically connoted by a complex word like 'free'—emerges as a way of signalling, however vaguely or gesturally, its absolute difference from everything it perceived itself as not: that is, from a contrastingly 'mercantile' dispensation that it characterized if not caricatured as profit-driven and identified with certain distinct values and aims (discipline, industry, frugality, thrift, service, progress, wealth-getting, self-advancement, and capital accumulation). As the image of the courtly maker is a fantasy, so the contrast between the courtly maker and the labourer for profit is a metaphor: the vehicle (a differentiation expressed in social or class terms) communicating the tenor (two alternative models of poetic production). Like any metaphor, it can be deconstructed—shown not to tally with the realities of the period's highly complex and rapidly changing social and economic scene—but the point of the metaphor is to distinguish between two very different ways of thinking about poetry, not to give a subtle or even accurate account of that scene.[60]

---

[59] *AS* 45: 'Alas, if Fancy drawne by imag'd things, / Though false, yet with free scope more grace doth breed / Then servant's wracke, where new doubts honor brings; / Then thinke my deare, that you in me do reed / Of Lover's ruine some sad Tragedie: / I am not I, pitie the tale of me.'

[60] For this one might turn to the exemplary studies of Lawrence Stone which reveal a distinctly mixed picture. On the one hand, there was a basic absence of profit-mindedness among the nobility during this period. See e.g. Stone 1965 (279): 'The spread of double-entry book-keeping had not the slightest effect upon the landed classes'; and Stone 1973 (xvi): 'the maximization of profits was far from

As such, courtly 'scorn' could therefore be read less as a record of personal condescension or snobbishness on the part of Sidney than as a vehicle for articulating any sense of discomfort he may have had with—discontent or dislike for— what might be called 'profit-mindedness'. No matter that such scorn could prove a highly labile commodity in practice: that it was hardly tenable at court, for example, or could be cynically manufactured by jobbing printers in order to boost their sales. As an attitude, stance, position, or gesture, it could serve as a way of mobilizing any concerns that may have been held about the costs of this 'costing' mentality. Sidney need not have scorned Gosson personally to scorn the model of poetry as bankable (indeed, in this respect, he and Gosson were halfway in agreement). Rather, for someone who might have found himself harbouring profound misgivings and reservations about this model—taking exception to it, even holding it in contempt—such scorn served as a conveniently emotional mode of response. It allowed such a person to resort intuitively to older 'feudal' models that he knew perfectly well were nostalgic, antiquated, and long out of date, as a means of feeling his way towards an alternative understanding of poetry—as *not* for profit, even profitless—that might not have seemed in need of defending had it not been for the increasing pressure and vociferousness of the competing model.[61] Moreover, seeing the more 'courtly' dispensation as a way of registering scruples against the 'bankable' model—rather than as a way of associating poetic production with and/or reserving it for a courtly class—makes it possible to see that the issue has, in fact, nothing to do with courtliness at all. That is to say, the class binary that Sidney mobilizes here is a means to an end but having served its purpose it can ultimately be kicked away. For the alternative, not-for-profit, non-bankable model of poetry

being in the forefront of the minds of many of the leading members of this highly restricted group.' On the other hand, some members of this class operated as what can only be described as venture capitalists. See e.g. Stone 1965 (375–6): 'In the Elizabethan period the most active entrepreneur in the country was not some busy merchant or thrusting member of the new gentry, but a peer of ancient stock, George Talbot, 9th Earl of Shrewsbury . . . The nearest rival to Shrewsbury in the range of his operations was Robert Dudley, Earl of Leicester.' For Sidney's own (invariably abortive) forays into such speculative ventures, see notes 81, 87, and 90.

[61] Leinwand 1999 (12) explores the 'affective economies' of the period, i.e. the gamut of feelings and emotions associated with different economic activities and positions: 'Before early modern English people could rationalize profit, they had a lively sense of what it felt like, or at least of what they thought it ought to feel like.' Warley 2005 also sees the articulation of class consciousness in intuitive terms: e.g. Drayton 'does not know what he is writing even though he has a feel for how it ought to look' (9); Henry Lok 'reiterates a sense of social change and an uncomfortable groping about for conceptual categories with which to explain his existence' (17). Warley stresses that this intuitive response is largely unconscious: that in their sonnet sequences Sidney, Spenser, and Shakespeare express class fantasies 'without the cooperation, or possibly even the awareness, of their speakers' (6), and that these speakers want to 'reinforce an aristocratic social imaginary, not start a revolution' (14). Suggesting that Sidney was perfectly aware that the older feudal models of courtly largesse to which he gestures were largely obsolete by the late sixteenth century accords him greater credit than Fraser 1970 (151–3), who effectively writes him off as a courtly dodo. As Spufford 1988 (240–63) shows, the feudal economy had effectively come to a close with the commercial revolution of the 'long' thirteenth century, by the end of which all the recognizable features of a capitalist economy—bills of exchange, lending at interest, foreign exchange, commercial accounting, wage labour, the development of national 'capital' cities, etc.—were being developed within Europe, albeit at different rates.

turns out to be profoundly un- if not anti-economic—radical, revolutionary, even anarchic—and in this respect it cannot really be said to be 'courtly' in any way.[62]

We get a better sense of this if we shift our sights for a moment away from the specifics of the sixteenth century—and its particular position along the fraught and much-debated road from feudalism to capitalism—to take what is, in historical terms, a much longer view: if we go back, that is, to the origins of the money form itself and to the particular way of thinking—what Marx calls the '*money* of the mind'—to which it gave rise.[63] It is generally recognized that the introduction of coinage in Lydia around 600 BC inaugurated a 'new *order*' or 'new logic' in western thought, of which Greek philosophy—as both a product of and response to this paradigm-breaking moment—gave the first systematic articulation.[64] Economism, that is to say, marked the inception of a mode of thinking that would be characterized thereafter as 'logical', 'rational', as philosophy, if not as thought itself: 'The economics of thought, set down by Greek dialecticians at the origin of critical thinking, has not ceased to influence us'.[65] What the money form revolutionized, of course, was the understanding of exchange. As exchange is predicated on substitution (one commodity for another), so it raises the question of equivalence (is the substitution of equal value to what it replaces?), thereby creating the notion of value. What money does for the first time is provide a means of measuring that value. Uniquely, it effects the symbolization and thus the abstraction of value, and it does this by acting as the common denominator or general equivalent: as one commodity singled out and set apart to measure the value of all the others. Where a simple barter situation involves the exchange of one commodity for another, the money form introduces a third term: a commodity that is functionally different from the other two in that it alone is capable of measuring not only their relative values but those of all other commodities as well. As general equivalent, the money form therefore assumes a position of exteriority, exclusivity, and privilege in relation to that which it measures: it dominates what it denominates. These characteristics of the money form gave rise to fears that found early articulation in fable and myth. The fear that, in merely representing or symbolizing wealth, money effectively

---

[62] It might be helpful at this point to differentiate my position from that of Landreth 2012. First, the 'idealist' (37) stance that he attributes to Sidney I attribute to the *speaker* on grounds that it represents only one part of the *Defence*'s argument and never goes uncontested. Second, Landreth explores resistances to the 'commonwealth' model that, in his view, show the latter to be increasingly inadequate for explaining actual economic conditions on the ground (e.g. inflation) and thus register the passing of an older 'ethical' paradigm and emergence of a new one (contrastingly unethical and 'scandalous') that would come to be articulated as 'political economics' in the seventeenth century. At first glance, it might seem as if the resistances I have been identifying within the *Defence* are doing the same thing. I should clarify, therefore, that I am not suggesting this. My position is that Sidney is resisting profit (and profit-mindedness) whether the latter is accounted for 'ethically' or not. This difference marks a rather decisive parting of the ways, methodologically speaking, with new-historicist practice focusing on resistances *within* a given system, and deconstructionist practice (or at least the kind I will be pursuing here) focusing more on resistance *to* a given system. On this see Correll 2003 (61): 'when the New Economic Criticism tries to silence hard questions of power and signification and reduces its terrain to one of historicist orthodoxy it fleeces the political and robs us by concealing critique'.

[63] Marx 1963 (200, emphasis original).

[64] Goux 1990 (92, emphasis original); Shell 1978 (11).   [65] Shell 1978 (62).

'disappeared' the wealth that, in a pre-monetary economy, had depended on being seen to be believed—on being displayed before a duly impressed community (as, for example, in the Homeric world)—is expressed, for example, in the tale of Gyges where the folk motif of the magic ring narrativizes such an abstraction of value as a rendering invisible. The fear that this development would entail the loss of 'real' wealth, that the mere representation of that now abstracted, disappeared, or invisible wealth (that is, money itself) would come to be valued in its place (fetishism), and that this in turn would be the precondition for the abuse of power—for tyranny, in a word—is likewise narrativized in Gyges' murder of the king and appropriation of his wife and wealth for himself. In this respect, the tyrant assumes for his own purposes the key feature of the money form—as the privileged element that is set above and apart from all others yet able to regulate them— anticipating the centralization of power and absolute monarchies that, in the later but logical development of the money form, would come to characterize capitalism. 'The term *capitalism* might be applied with all its etymological weight to this centralization of value and values. The general equivalent functions as head and capital of a divided territory from which it is barred as empty, omnipotent center'.[66]

In Marc Shell's analysis, Plato was distrustful if not profoundly suspicious of the money form and sensitive to the dangers it posed. Indeed, in Shell's view, Platonic philosophy emerged largely as a response to these fears and constituted an attempt to stave them off by offering, through philosophy, something higher and better— truth, the Good, the Ideas—that was no less abstract or invisible yet for all that more valuable, more 'real'. For Plato, the quantification of value that the money form made possible was dangerously infiltrating the thinking of his contemporaries, the Sophists in the first instance (whom he accused of selling their wares, exchanging wisdom for money and prioritizing rhetoric and persuasion over truth), but also Socrates, who conceived of his own dialectical practice in monetary terms: a hypothesis corresponding logically to a *hypothēkē* (deposit, pledge, mortgage; literally, a 'putting down'), that was deposited in him as principal and from which he, as the 'banker-philosopher', drew and dispensed knowledge as *tokos* (offspring, but also interest).[67] Plato's response, argues Shell, was that the dialectician should properly shed such hypotheses as he proceeded towards a higher, more abstract level of thought, his strategy being, effectively, to play money's abstraction of value at its own game. Although Socrates was no wage-earning Sophist, he still incorporated money thought into his philosophical method. Sensing the possible contradiction between his teacher's reliance on hypothesization and his attack on making money, Plato made his Socrates in the *Republic* appeal 'powerfully from hypothesis and dialectic to the Ideas, which are supposed to rise above hypotheses'.[68] The result was idealist philosophy. Prompted by the feared loss (of substance, wealth, 'real' value) that money's abstraction of that value threatened, Plato countered it with a philosophical abstraction that was 'higher' and 'better' in that it

---

[66] Goux 1990 (44, emphasis original).
[67] Shell 1978 (45n, 46), referencing Plato 2013, *Republic*, 507a.
[68] Shell 1978 (47).

promised to obviate that loss. And it did this by refusing to separate the Ideas from the sensible world, or value from material things, rather making the one immanent within the other: the Idea of the Good, for example, is 'at once visible and invisible, unreal and real'.[69] As such, value was not something that was *represented* but something that *inhered*, just as meaning was not something that language merely conveyed (thereby laying it open to the same charge as money) but something that language, as Logos, embodied and lucently revealed. If meaning inhered within language and value within things, then the risk of idolatry or fetishism—the misplaced valuation of the representation alone—was reduced. In this reading, Plato's idealist philosophy thus worked to fend off the illusory valuations and false consciousness of money thought by seeking to bypass the operations of representation altogether (hence the logical expulsion of the poets from the ideal city). Debating the relative desirability of wealth or philosophy, this provided Plato with a powerful argument in favour of the latter. It is in the context of such a debate in the *Republic* that the tale of Gyges is told and the conclusion ultimately reached that the ideal, purified state of the human soul—as evident in its love of wisdom and performance of virtue—constitutes its true nature and is its true reward, regardless of any powers that might be granted by the magic invisibility-ring.[70]

Returning to the *Defence*, we might now suspect that the tale of Gyges' ring to which Sidney refers (83.2) carries greater resonance than its apparently casual mention seems at first to suggest: indeed, that it serves as shorthand for Plato's complex response to the money form and for Sidney's no less complex response to it. In particular, Gyges' ring could be seen to inform the key image with which the section on *poesis* now culminates, that of the poet's golden world:

> Nature never set forth the earth in so rich tapestry as divers poets have done; neither with pleasant rivers, fruitful trees, sweet-smelling flowers, nor whatsoever else may make the too much loved earth more lovely. Her world is brazen, the poets only deliver a golden. (85.24–7)

It is not an accident that, in gesturing towards his ideal—the ability of the poet to create a whole fictional world *ex nihilo*—Sidney should think in terms of Plato's idealist philosophy, nor endow that ideal with the highest possible value, one that transcends the earthly as absolutely as wisdom transcends wealth. This transcendence is of a piece with the trajectory of the 'high' (84.39) titled poet and the 'high flying liberty of conceit' (84.13), or the ascent from labourer to leader, from bound to free. The Golden Age to which Sidney's golden world alludes was classically, of course, the age of perfection: a prehistory of bounty that need not be laboured for, an original plenitude or primary sufficiency that could be taken as a free gift with no need of payment. In the sentence immediately preceding the one quoted, Sidney describes how the poet 'doth grow in effect *into* another nature' (85.18–19, my emphasis), as if, in the very act of creating such a world, the poet could transcend his own humanity (nature here in the sense of 'human nature', and especially a

---

[69] Ibid. (41).   [70] *Republic*, 359d–360d, 611c–612b.

person's 'better nature'). That, however, is the reading of only one of the extant versions of the *Defence* (that printed by Ponsonby). All other versions, including manuscript copies, read 'doth grow in effect another nature', as if—following the implications of the horticultural metaphor—the poet, Godlike, grows a whole new nature: plants a whole new Eden (nature here in the sense of 'the phenomena of the physical world collectively, especially plants, animals, and other features and products of the earth itself, as opposed to humans and human creations').[71] One might recall at this point the world of the 'simple Indians' whom Sidney described a page or two earlier, where not only 'no writing is' (83.21) but, to the fascination of the Renaissance world—a fascination registered very early on by Thomas More's *Utopia* (1516), published only a generation after Columbus' discovery of America—no money either.[72] This absence is what allowed More—and, arguably, Sidney as well—to see the money form as a distinct phenomenon: to isolate it, defamiliarize it, make it strange, as a way of analysing its effects on society and of imagining what society might be like without it. As a result, as Fredric Jameson writes, 'this strange foreign body as which money and gold momentarily present themselves, can at one and the same time be fantasized as the very root of all evil and the source of all social ills and as something that can be utterly eliminated from the new Utopian social formation'.[73] The world of which Sidney's speaker had then sneaked a fleeting glimpse—a world that had a praiseworthy poetry, and a praiseworthy reverence for the same, but was as yet free from the dubious import of 'profitable' learned poetry with all its ruinous colonialist oppressions, and thus ignorant of the 'fruits of knowledge' (83.27–8)—might now, perhaps, look very like this golden world: a prelapsarian paradise restored, a second Eden whose

---

[71] See *OED* nature *n*. III.7.b, and IV.11.a respectively. Only Maslen (138) comments on this textual crux, and that to the effect that the meaning of the metaphor is 'a little obscure'. It is curious that, while he and Shepherd (without comment) import Ponsonby's 'into' into the Olney version they are otherwise using as their copy-text, van Dorsten and Duncan-Jones—who, conversely, use Ponsonby as their copy-text—remove it in favour of Olney's reading (again, without comment). Maslen's note that, for all its obscurity, the drift of Sidney's metaphor is 'clear enough' belies the sense, I think, that the meaning of 'nature' is being subjected here to a new, unfamiliar, and potentially radical evaluation—one, essentially, that denies the Fall—and that this is symptomatically registered in the textual crux.

[72] It is worth mentioning, perhaps, that the Arthurian world—chosen by Spenser as the locale for faerie land—was also, as Landreth 2012 (60) notes, 'innocent of the gold economy by virtue of predating it'; or, more precisely, represented the period between the collapse of the Roman empire in the fifth century and establishment of the Anglo-Saxon kingdoms in the seventh during which time Britain was without a money economy of any kind: see also Spufford 1988 (9, 41, 379). This may provide an additional reason for Sidney's association of the ancient Britons—as represented by the Celtic remnant of the Welsh—with the moneyless Indians. In the Proem to Book II of *The Faerie Queene* Spenser also, of course, tropes the New World as what Landreth calls a 'prehistory in the present' (60).

[73] Jameson 2005 (17), adding that 'despite the commercial bustle of More's London the money form is still relatively isolated and sporadic in the agricultural world that surrounds it (enclosure will be the essential step that opens this older world up to wage labor). We may thus posit the money form as leading a kind of enclave existence within More's historical moment . . . in this still largely medieval moment of "early modernity", money and commerce will have remained episodic, embodied in the decorative ostentation of gold on the one hand or the excitement of the great fairs on the other: but this enclave status of money is precisely what allows More to fantasize its removal from social life in his new Utopian vision' (16–17). On this see also Spufford 1988 (385).

'fruitful trees' (85.25) have gone as yet untasted.[74] The world of the Indians has no money, no writing, no representation, no abstraction of value, and yet it has poetry—a poetry that is clearly capable of being free from profit-mindedness— much as Plato's philosophy seemed capable of transcending money thought and overcoming the power of Gyges' ring.

---

[74] The Golden Age was classically the first and best age—see Ovid 1916, *Metamorphoses*, I.89–112—but also a future age when 'a golden race' [*gens aurea*] of human beings would return to perfection and become immortal: see Virgil 2001, *Eclogues*, IV.9. Compare Shell 1982 (24–46) on the Grail legend of medieval romance: for him the Grail serves as a similar fantasy of the idealized 'free gift'—the idea that God gives and forgives infinitely—and was developed by the medieval nobility to symptomize and work through the transition from feudalism to capitalism.

II

Poetry Is Profitable

Things are never that simple, however, and for all its promise of innocence and freedom, Sidney's golden world turns out, on closer analysis, to be no less compromised by profit-mindedness than Plato's Ideas. I should clarify, therefore, that for the purposes of the argument I have thus far somewhat misrepresented Shell's reading of Plato as the philosopher's principled rejection of money thought and determination to provide an alternative. As Shell goes on to show, however, in the long run Plato fails in this attempt, for his very promotion of dialectic as a means of sublimating provisional, lesser, or 'lower' positions (hypotheses) in order to arrive at 'higher', better ones—a purer, more abstract, more valuable version of the truth—is in itself wholly symptomatic of that way of thinking and testimony to the degree with which, like it or not, he too had internalized it. Conceptions of comparison, of relative value, of how the latter might be measured or quantified: they are all there. Thus, while Shell sees Plato as intuitively uncomfortable with money thought but unable, in the final analysis, to escape it, Jean-Joseph Goux sees Plato—and the entire tradition of idealist philosophy that extends from him to Hegel—as blindly complicit with money thought: indeed, as guilty of enshrining it as *the* logic, mentality, and philosophy that for good or ill was to become the dominant way of thinking in the West. 'It is impossible not to relate this movement of sublimation and idealization—inherent in the very process of exchange, in the dialectical logic of the process of social exchange—to the history of philosophical idealism'; from this *ideal measure of values* [constituted by money or the general equivalent] could be derived all of Platonism'.[75] Where Shell argues that—unlike later idealist philosophers, who would radically separate ideal from real, or value from the material world—Plato stressed the immanence of the one within the other, Goux contends that idealist philosophy developed and precisely systematized this split: 'The most elementary exchange contains the germ of idealism, which first culminates when the symbolization process attains the form of the general equivalent. The split between matter and value then becomes manifest in that an object fundamentally represents value, whereas its existence as matter is *secondary*' (98, emphasis original). Far from ridding philosophy of the invidious hierarchies and subordinations

---

[75] Goux 1990 (50, 93, emphasis original). On the difference between Shell and Goux see Correll 2003 (61–2): '[it] is not a matter of historicism but rather a difference between Shell's structural functionalism . . . and a more politically invested post-structuralism that does not lose sight of the relationships between signifying practices and social relations, or between structures of power and manifestations of resistance.'

that come with the money form and its concomitant propensity to enact and enable the abuse of power, for Goux Plato's philosophy institutionalizes it, thus bringing the question of class right back in: 'Plato perceives the relations between the universal equivalent and the relative form *from the standpoint of* the universal equivalent, that is, from that of the class that wields economic and political power' (95, emphasis original), as a result of which, 'idealism, which affirms the primacy of idea, consciousness, and mind . . . and the subordination of matter, will become the philosophical ideology of the dominant classes' (98). Far from obviating the idolatrous, fetishized overvaluation of the sign, Plato's philosophy elevates that fetishistic thinking to the highest possible level: 'the relation between Platonic forms (models, ideal standards) and the concrete world is the displaced yet faithful philosophical parallel of the relation between (fetishized) general equivalents and relative forms, as perceived by the dominant ideology' (94); 'the fetishism of the general equivalent . . . leads to the decisive reversal of matter and reflection which is at the very core of idealism' (95).

Much the same fetishistic thinking could be said to operate with respect to Sidney's metaphor of the poet's golden world. What is that metaphor if not a postlapsarian symbol projected back, after the event, to name and quantify prelapsarian values? There was no labour in that fantasized period of origin, of course, no mining, no metalwork, and so no gold (or brass, for that matter): men had not yet learned to ravage the bowels of the earth. The Golden Age can only be named as such recursively, from the perspective of a later, fallen Age, by which time gold had become the signifier of value. In Book VIII of the *Aeneid*, for example, Aeneas walks on the still wild and forested hills that, a thousand years later—at the time when Virgil was writing his epic—would be crowned with an urban, imperial Rome. That distant golden age—those 'golden ages' [*aurea saecula*] that extend back even beyond Aeneas—can only meaningfully be named as such from the vantage point of the poet's resplendent, capitalized capital (and Capitol) that is 'golden now' [*aurea nunc*].[76] The inhabitants of the Golden Age, had they ever existed, would never have called it by that name. It can only be called that—and nostalgically *re*called as a past of innocence and bliss—by those who judge their present time to be marred and corrupted by the cursed hunger for war and gain. Using 'golden' as their adjective of value, however, only shows how trapped they remain in the capitalized culture they apparently deplore. For 'golden' to mean 'innocent', therefore, must always be a contradiction in terms. In the parallel case of Sidney's 'simple Indians', who might have been seen as the miraculously still living, embodied inhabitants of this golden world, it now appears that (whatever kind of 'nature' the poet doth grow) there is no Eden without (a tree of) knowledge preplanted in it. For the poet's world to be described as golden—and for that to be a

[76] Virgil 2001, *Aeneid*, VIII.324–5, 348. See also Landreth 2012 (67) on the mythos of the Golden Age in Ovid and Spenser: 'Even in Guyon's account of the golden age, the vice of gold is already present, working its way to the surface for its own realization'; 'money is never simply discovered at some time or place; rather, it discovers itself to have been there—in Ovid's fable, in the mountains of the Andes—all along, so that the golden age recedes indefinitely before the age of gold'.

term of praise—its 'fruitful trees' (85.25) must necessarily have already been tasted. As a result, the fantasy briefly glimpsed of a poetic world that might exist *without* knowledge, learning, or profit promptly evaporates. Unlike the world of the Indians (to which Sidney did not apply this epithet), the poet's 'golden' world is thus capitalized—monetarized—from the outset. The poet (like the philosopher) finds himself committed to those values after all, as if, in order for them to be 'values' at all, they can only be valued in this particular, monetary way. There is no innocence, no sinlessness, no freedom, no world before or without profit-mindedness, no escape from the money of the mind. The Fall intervenes, or rather the monetary relation to God that it represents (economism invading theology), as redemption becomes the payback for the accursed (short)fall of Adam, a divine forgiveness for the debt that humanity has incurred simply by virtue (if that is the right word) of being human.

That Sidney's image of the poet's golden world is shot through with and deeply compromised by money thought becomes evident if the metaphor is looked at a little more closely, for it is 'economic' not merely in its content but also in its structure or form. 'Literary works', comments Shell, 'are composed of small tropic exchanges or metaphors, some of which can be analyzed in terms of signified economic content and all of which can be analyzed in terms of economic form'.[77] Sidney's metaphor can be analysed on both counts, and, although justly famous and the subject of much critical attention and debate, it has not, I suggest, been considered in these terms before. In the first instance, then, we might say that the metaphor—'Her [Nature's] world is brazen, the poets only deliver a golden' (85.27)—transacts an exchange between two objects: Nature's brazen world and the poet's golden one. At this level, the exchange is presented as an impressive trading up—a spectacularly good deal—in order to communicate the comparative superiority and all-round excellence of the poets' product. The component parts of this exchange, however, can in turn be broken down into two further parallel exchanges in which Nature's world is exchanged for brass, and in which the poets' world is exchanged for gold. At this level, an interesting complexity begins to enter into the equation, for one way of looking at these exchanges is to say that, prior to their exchange one with another, the worlds of Nature and the poets have already been bought and sold: that is to say, each has been traded for a metal that is then used to signify its value. Instead of simply exchanging Nature's world and the poets' world directly (as, for example, in a straightforward barter arrangement), Sidney's metaphor of the metals introduces a third term in each case: mediating

---

[77] Shell 1978 (7). See also Shell 1982 (4): 'This participation of economic form in literature and philosophy ... is defined neither by what literature and philosophy talk about (sometimes money, sometimes not), nor by why they talk about it (sometimes for money, sometimes not) but rather by the tropic interaction between economic and linguistic symbolization and production.' This mode of interpretation is named 'critical' or 'poetic economics' to distinguish it from other forms of economic criticism: see Woodmansee and Osteen 1999 (22, 28). Against what she sees as the structuralist bias of Shell and Goux, Anderson 2005 (172–3) offers a thoroughly historicized account of the processes involved in such tropic exchange, although one consequence of this is to effect a thorough depoliticizing of their readings in the process.

materials that are exchanged for the two commodities before they can be exchanged for one another. The point of the metaphor, clearly, is to signal a striking difference in value—with gold at one end and brass at the other—and this, I think, might be thought about in three different ways. First, it could be seen in terms of the difference between gold and so-called 'white money': that is to say, the silver coins that, since the re-introduction of gold coins England in the mid-fourteenth century, had been used for the smaller denominations that were most practical for such local transactions as wages, rents, and taxes. This difference was exacerbated to crisis levels during the 'Great Debasement' of the English currency from 1541 to 1562, during which the silver content of the smaller denominations was drastically reduced in relation to the base metals within the alloy, such that, as William Harrison wrote in his *An historicall description of the Iland of Britaine* (1587), 'our siluer coine [was turned] vnto brasse & copper monies'.[78] This debasement, naturally, had the effect of increasing the difference between a still fine gold coinage, on the one hand, and an increasingly adulterated, 'brazen' sterling, on the other, and dramatically reducing the value of the latter in relation to gold.[79] Second, it could be seen in terms of the difference between gold and so-called 'black money': that is to say, the still smaller denominations or small change that increasingly came to be necessary for facilitating the small-scale, personal transactions of urban daily life. The brass or copper coins that came to serve this purpose first appeared (in Naples) in the late fifteenth century, but, although they were not introduced elsewhere in much of Europe until later (and, in England, not until well after Sidney's lifetime), the need for such black money was nonetheless met by the use of tokens. Lead tokens, worth the equivalent of one, one half, or one third of a farthing, for example, were used in sixteenth-century London, while outside England, such tokens although initially made of lead, were later more frequently made of copper or brass.[80] Given his extensive travels, Sidney may well have been familiar with these, in which case his metaphor would clearly be gesturing towards what Peter Spufford calls 'the immense distances that separated the three types of coinage, gold, good silver and black money' (332).

In both of these scenarios, the brass and gold of Sidney's metaphor would be understood as representing units of differing value within a currency: as if to say, a gold coin was equivalent to—could be exchanged for or 'buy'—many 'brazen' coins

---

[78] Harrison 1587, in Holinshed 1587 (T6ᵛ). English medieval kings had maintained the quality of sterling and (unlike many of their European counterparts) had not on the whole succumbed to the temptation to debase their currency to raise a quick profit. Henry VIII, by contrast, found such opportunities impossible to resist. It is no small part of the *Chronicle*'s ideological purpose to praise Elizabeth's policy of reversing this decline in the quality of sterling: she 'did finish the matter wholie, vtterly abolishing the vse of copper and brasen coine, and conuerting the same into guns and great ordinance, she restored sundrie coines of fine siluer' (T6ᵛ), although this policy did not in itself relieve the economic problems of the period. On the Great Debasement, see: Challis 1978 (81–112); Mayhew 1999 (44–52); Wrightson 2000 (118–19); Deng 2011 (87–102); and Landreth 2012 (15–30).

[79] The adjective 'brazen' developed the moralized (and implicitly sexualized) sense it has today— 'hardened in effrontery, shameless'—in this period (see *OED* brazen *adj.* 3): *OED*'s first citation (1573) is from Gabriel Harvey.

[80] On the production and use of tokens in the period, see: Challis 1978 (205–10); Spufford 1988 (332); and Deng 2011 (99, 110, 165, 172, 174).

or a very great many brass tokens. This would maintain the superiority of gold, although it would rule out any sense that a profit was being made. Equally, the exchange could go in either direction—that is to say, given brass enough and time, Nature could theoretically 'buy' gold with the lower denomination—although, again, there would be no profit to be made in doing so (just the convenience of having a single valuable coin rather than mountains of small change). The third way in which the difference between brass and gold could be thought of, by contrast, would be to say that the two metals here do *not* share the same symbolizing function: that is to say, gold remains the money form—the general equivalent that measures and thereby represents and abstracts value—whereas brass is a mere, 'dumb' commodity, the relative value (and price fluctuations) of which only gold can determine. In this scenario, Nature's world has not previously been bought or sold for (and thus represented by) brass, but simply 'is' brazen. Indeed, the verb deployed by Sidney's metaphor would suggest exactly this—downplaying the potentially symbolic or representational function of brass here—while the poet's world, by contrast, is said to be 'deliver[ed]', infusing gold with the active, executive, transformative function typical of the money form. Similarly, the poet's world has not previously been bought or sold for (and thus represented by) gold, either. Rather, in this model, the poet, his world, and gold are commensurate and occupy the same high, commanding position of the general equivalent. Nature, by contrast,—and here gender- and eco-politics as well as economics enter into the picture—exists only in relation to the latter and is thus subordinated to them, as female to male, to be traded off, commodified, and exploited. Here, the poet does not so much trade with Nature—exchanging her many less valuable coins or virtually worthless tokens for his single, valuable, 'strong' one—as buy and sell *her*, on the model of the commodity trade: buying up brass cheaply and selling it for a profit on the market in order to make more gold.[81] Where the other two scenarios involved no financial profit, therefore, this one entails exactly that: the poet takes brass and makes gold out of it. In which case, what the poet-maker 'makes' is money. He delivers the goods, comes up with the cash, as a result of which his world is more 'rich' (85.24) than Nature's, 'more lovely' (85.26–7) than hers.

All the same, there is a price to be paid, of sorts. If the metaphor of the golden world is intended to promote the poet's ideal world of creative fiction over Nature's brazen world of brute fact, then the comparison only works if gold is taken to be superior to brass, regardless of whether the latter is treated as a unit of currency or as

---

[81] That Sidney dabbled in such ventures himself is suggested by Greville 1986 (70) who describes a plan on Sidney's part to encourage investment in a colony on the Panama isthmus, his earlier attempt to join Drake's expedition in the autumn of 1585 having been aborted: 'to incite those that tarried at home to adventure, he propounded the hope of a sure and rich return ... to the ingeniously industrious, variety of natural richesses for new mysteries and manufactures to work upon; to the merchant ... a fertile and unexhausted earth', concluding that 'generally, the word "gold" was an attractive adamant to make men venture that which they have in hope to grow rich by that which they have not'. Greville's witness cannot always be relied upon for its accuracy or objectivity, however, and if this plan was indeed hatched (his editor finds no evidence either to support or refute it) it never came to fruition; see Duncan-Jones 1991 (280). On Sidney's abiding interest in New World ventures, see also Greene 1999 (171–93).

a commodity. As general equivalent, gold certainly occupies the superior position as the one element historically set apart from and able to regulate all the others. To imply that this makes gold itself 'worth' more, however, is to impute to it an intrinsic value which—if it were purely an instrument for measuring value—it strictly would not have.[82] It is to attribute value not to the material object of any exchange but rather to what *represents* that value and thus mediates that exchange: it is to fall prey, in other words, to money-fetishism. In this respect, treating brass and gold as alternative denominations or units within a currency (as in scenarios one and two) goes some way towards mitigating this danger, since it keeps the decision about which material is selected to serve as general equivalent—or the purely representational function of money's token value—in open view. Treating gold as something capable of buying commodities such as brass, on the other hand (as in scenario three), makes it harder to resist investing it with a mysterious power—an 'abstract potentiality' or buying power—and an essential, intrinsic value in its own right (not to mention an ability to make profits and thus to 'grow').[83] While it is possible to read Sidney's golden world in terms of all three scenarios—and they certainly play off against one another—I think on balance that the general direction of the metaphor is tending, whether Sidney likes it or not, towards the third. One might, perhaps, compare another example used later in the *Defence* where, once again, what is being defended is the use of a representational fiction: 'What child is there that, coming to a play, and seeing *Thebes* written in great letters upon an old door, doth believe that it is Thebes?' (103.23–5). The rhetorical question that would appear to invite a resounding 'none!', however, might have elicited a no less resounding affirmative had it been phrased somewhat differently—'What person is there that seeing the word "pound" inscribed upon a gold coin doth believe that it is worth a pound?' (gold coins representing the value of a pound were first minted by Henry VII)—for here is a representation that commands near-universal credit.[84]

---

[82] See Landreth 2012 (12–13) for a good exposition of the ways in which the bullion coin—which operates quite differently from electronic or paper money—uniquely combines intrinsic with extrinsic value by means of the authorizing princely face/name stamped upon it: 'Renaissance coins measured their own value as a quantum of precious metal, but the ideal relation of the mineral ("intrinsic") value to the face value of the coin in exchange could never be fixed: not only might different coin series vary greatly in their purity, but the intrinsic value of an individual coin was itself subject to the daily fluctuations of price in the international market for precious metals. To compensate for this variability, the coin was understood to manifest a second, "extrinsic," value, which made up the difference between its metal price and its face value and kept the face value stable by fluctuating inversely to the price of metal. While the intrinsic value was defined by the dynamics of the market, the extrinsic value was produced by the authority of the state. The royal stamp of the coin's face yoked together three kinds of value—intrinsic, extrinsic, and exchange value—in order to enable the simplest everyday cash transactions.' The experience of inflation, however, put this 'ideal relation' under immense if not intolerable strain. The question of whether the money form had a purely extrinsic value or combined intrinsic with extrinsic value, went back to Plato and Aristotle: see Goux 1990 (95–6). These two value theories remained in tension throughout the sixteenth and seventeenth centuries: see e.g. Anderson 2005 (196–8, 202, 204); and Deng 2011 (1, 3, 10–18, 92–100).

[83] Landreth 2012 (57).

[84] On Henry VII's 'sovereign', first minted in 1489, see Challis 1978 (46–52); and Deng 2011 (56–7). Shakespeare 1997 also famously relates this issue of the believability of theatrical representations to the money form: see the Prologue to *Henry V*, where 'a crooked figure may / Attest in little place a

In practice, everyone behaves as if coins have value in their own right.[85] In the case of both *Thebes* and the golden world, I would argue, Sidney stops short of exposing the strictly fictional nature of the money form (in this respect, More's *Utopia* goes further), and to that extent his metaphors betray an unavoidable complicity with money thought.[86]

If the world of the 'simple Indians' had shown that poetry does not necessarily lead to profit, then the poet's golden world shows that profitability can entail subordination and exploitation of the most invidious kind. What lies behind both images, I suggest—what constitutes their economic 'unconscious', if you will—is the money form itself. In the first example, the money form is conspicuous by its absence: the world of the Indians presents a fantasy in which the money form does not exist. In the second example, the money form is omnipresent: indeed, the poet's 'golden' world reifies the money form and behaves exactly like it, creating fictional representations that are highly valued (idealized, fetishized) and reproducing more of the same. Here, the fantasy is not of a world without profit but of profitability on a grand scale (the equivalent fantasy would be Astrophil winning Lady Rich and making more riches), except that it turns out to be less of a fantasy and more of a nightmare. For, while he sets out to praise the poets' world by calling it 'golden', the speaker thereby *quantifies* its value. He effectively tells us what it is 'worth' (something the simple Indians would presumably never have needed to do). That is to say, according to the logic of the golden-world metaphor, for us to value the poet's golden world over Nature's brazen one is not—or not primarily—to value creative fiction over banal fact but rather to value *gold*. It is to value not the thing itself (poetry) but what *represents its value*, much as the miser values his money over what it can actually buy.[87] Everything the poet touches can turn to

million' (lines 15–16), and where, in representing the battle of Agincourt, his few actors will serve as 'ciphers to this great accompt' (line 17).

[85] As Hawkes 2001 (37) notes, as a result of inflation it 'penetrated the mind of the simplest peasant that the value of gold fluctuated . . . It took a long time for the lesson to sink in, but it was clear enough: Gold was not the literal embodiment of value, but its *sign*' (emphasis original). 'By the end of this period we find economists making the innovative, and to conservative contemporaries astonishingly counterintuitive, argument that, although financial value was admittedly (indeed undeniably) imaginary, *it was nonetheless real for that*' (40, emphasis original). In classical economics, money as pure representation thus blurs the distinction between fiction and reality: 'If money is a fiction, then surely fiction is real' (45).

[86] For Anderson 2005 this is a feature embedded in theorizations of metaphor itself. By providing a term that is needed but otherwise absent, metaphor fills a gap—'borrows' a term from one discourse to use it in another—thereby producing a 'usurious surplus' (20) or yield of some kind (of pleasure, of a word's increased expressive potential or constructive capacity) which serves as a form of 'payoff' (133) or 'mutual gain' (142).

[87] See Languet's admonitory response to Sidney's apparent excitement at the discovery—false, as it turned out—of gold-bearing ore by Martin Frobisher on his second voyage to North America between May and September 1577. Calling gold 'the most harmful and destructive thing Nature has ever offered mankind, the desire and greed for which drive most men mad' [*quo nihil nocentius & humano generi perniciosius natura protulit, cujus tamen desiderio & cupiditate ita insaniunt plerique*], Languet cites *Aeneid*, III.57 to warn his protégé against it in no uncertain terms: 'Beware, I beg you, or (as the Poet says) that execrable hunger for gold will creep into your soul, into which so far you have admitted nothing but the love of virtue' [*Cave obsecro, ne illa (ut ait Poëta) auri sacra fames irrepat in animum tuum, in quem nihil hactenus admisisti, præter amorem virtutis*]; 'if those golden islands have perchance

gold (this is the fantasy), but that condemns him—and us if we buy into this logic—to the fetishism of Midas (this is the nightmare). For Shell, such money-fetishism is what Plato feared but ultimately could not avoid. For Goux, it is what Plato and the entire tradition of idealist philosophy that followed him permanently enshrined: 'The value of gold, absolutely guaranteed, becomes a metaphor for the transcendental guarantee of meaning. Gold fetishism, concept fetishism: what is the Platonic *idea*, if not *the fetishized meaning of a word*?' (103, emphasis original).

Even though Sidney uses one form of representation (gold) to represent another form of representation (creative fiction), the fetishistic power of the money form—gold in its capacity as general equivalent—proves, in the end, all but irresistible. Gold is good, valuable, 'worthy' in itself, and to have it is to be 'rich', end of story. And if poetry is 'golden', then to read it is to accrue intellectual, moral, and spiritual capital, and thus to accumulate treasure, to make a 'profit'. The discourse of profitability—which, in Sidney's metaphor, the poet's golden world speaks to and represents—is, therefore, idealist, bullionist, and fetishistic: it rests on the philosophical idea (Idea) that value, like meaning, *inheres*, and on the faith and belief that it will continue to do so. Consciously or unconsciously, Sidney thus identifies the weak spot—the Achilles' heel—in Plato's philosophy, for he locates very precisely the point of contradiction within idealism's bid to distance itself from the taint of money thought and the evil power of Gyges' ring. In attempting to elevate the truth, the Good, the Logos to a plane above and beyond representation—where they are not to be read or interpreted like texts but rather to be silently intuited, apprehended, *seen* (*idein*, to see) in the Ideas where they lie immanent—idealist philosophy simply replicates the fetishistic logic that imputes the same mystified, essential value to the money form. In playing the abstraction of value at its own game, Plato was bound to lose insofar as he was playing money's game. To this extent, money-mindedness wins: its logic is triumphant; it is the only game in town.[88] And this is no less true for Sidney who, in the hope of escaping from such money thought, understandably but perhaps ill-advisedly follows Plato, only to find himself, like the idealist philosopher, back where he started. Profit-mindedness proves all-pervasive, and the poet's golden world—Sidney's bid to free himself from the bankable model of poetry—depressingly collapses into so many payments made to the national treasure-house after all.

The collapse of this vision—registering similar contortions and self-contradictions within idealist philosophy itself—is symptomized in the two paragraphs that follow and that bring the *narratio* to a hasty and undignified exit. That these are among the densest and most confused passages within the *Defence* strongly indicates that the

---

too deeply possessed your mind, you may exorcize them thence before they take you over completely' [*si forte insulæ illæ aureæ altius in animo tuo insederint, eas inde deturbes, antequam te plane expugnaverint*], from a letter dated 28 November 1577: *Correspondence* (792, 787; 793, 788; 793, 788).

[88] Discussing Plato's banishment of the poets later in the *Defence*, the speaker considers the charge that, as a philosopher, Plato might have been a 'natural enemy of poets' (106.21). Here (as at 82.10–12), philosophers are set up as 'ungrateful prentices' (106.26), taking from poets and then rejecting them, so as to 'set up shops for themselves' and thereby to 'discredit their masters' (106. 26, 27). Although he comes to reject this charge as it applies to Plato himself, this suggests that the speaker is capable of entertaining the idea of the 'banker-philosopher' in principle.

theoretical argument is undergoing some kind of crisis. Seeking to salvage an idealism that finds itself to be tainted—fearing, for example, that such idealism might be dismissed, 'jestingly' (85.33), as a mere escapist fantasy or 'fiction' (the first time this word is used in the *Defence*)—Sidney makes a last-ditch appeal to the Platonic '*Idea* or fore-conceit' (85.35) as that which is *not* mediated by representation. At first glance, this is a bid to restore the material value of things before they 'fall' or become mere objects or commodities for exchange: to bypass representation and the fetishizing of representation that seems otherwise invariably to follow. In not being party to representation, the Platonic Idea is thus said, quite properly, to exist in the mind of the poet-maker: his 'skill' (85.35) lies precisely in conceiving this ideal rather than in creating 'the work itself' (85.36), since the representation he makes is necessarily at two or more removes from it. However—and here the contradiction within idealist philosophy that the golden-world metaphor located very precisely surfaces again— the fact that the poet has the Idea in the first place is made 'manifest' (85.37) where else but in the work itself, in the representations he has made? The Idea is nothing other than a representation, and a highly fetishized one at that. For all his attempt to extricate himself from money thought, Sidney lands his poet more deeply in it, for what the poet is praised for 'delivering forth' (85.37, 38)—twice within two lines—is exactly what he was said to 'deliver' in the preceding paragraph: namely, gold. More of it, in fact, since Plato's bid to avoid the fetishism of money thought had led to the desperate expedient of shutting down representation altogether by banishing poetry from the ideal Republic, while here it is poetry that Sidney is supposed to be defending and precisely representations that he is claiming to value. Sidney's poet positively gushes with gold, therefore, brokering Nature's product (man) for multiple better, improved versions in the heroes (truer, more constant, valiant, and so forth) of literary fiction. Such productions, moreover, are explicitly said *not* to be fictions— they are 'not wholly imaginative' like 'castles in the air' (85.38, 39)—but substantial and real, as the poet is said to make, out of one individual, historical Cyrus, 'many Cyruses' more (85.42).[89] This is the first time in the *Defence* that the notion of poetry inspiring its readers to imitative action is mooted, looking ahead to much of what is to follow from the *propositio* on, yet nothing could be designed to commodify poetry more effectively. For, in a model that strikingly anticipates that of capitalist mass-production, poetry is here conceived as a mechanism for producing fetishized commodities on a grand scale (all those Cyruses). Fiction paradoxically becomes the means by which the fictionality of representation comes to be disavowed, exactly as in the case of *Thebes*. It is as if Sidney's poet just cannot help himself.[90] Like a

---

[89] For Halpern 1991 (33), the poet thus described thereby conforms to the humanist pedagogic project which constituted a 'well-nigh global process for the ideological (imaginary) production of social subjects'.

[90] Indeed, Sidney appears to have remained interested in the possibility of lucrative New World ventures, regardless of Languet's admonitions of November 1577. See his comment that 'I am starting to contemplate something in the Indies' [*aliquid iam Indicum mecum Meditor*], in a letter to Languet dated 10 March 1578: *Correspondence* (821, 820), this being the first mention of any possible participation in such an expedition. See also his comment in a letter to Robert in a letter dated 18 October 1580 that Drake had arrived back from his circumnavigation of the globe and that 'riche he is returned': *Correspondence* (1009). On 22 October 1580 Languet writes to encourage Sidney to make friends with

financial wizard or trader on a lucky streak, he keeps on clocking up the profits, committed to making money thought, and plenty of it.

We can almost witness Sidney's thought process in action—see his connecting thoughts laid bare—in the desperation that arises from trying to rescue an argument that seems intent on going its own stubborn way (Sidney now experiencing what his speaker had experienced before, albeit in the opposite direction). The Platonic Idea having failed him, Sidney's mind turns to the next best thing: religion, or more specifically the Protestant religion that emerged from the period's own particular struggles with the same philosophical conundrum. Sidney thus makes one last appeal to a source of value that might finally transcend all others, by giving

> right honour to the heavenly Maker of that maker, who having made man to His own likeness, set him beyond and over all the works of that second nature: which in nothing he showeth so much as in Poetry, when with the force of a divine breath he bringeth things forth far surpassing her doings . . .   (86.2–6)

At one level, this sentence presents a series of makers—God makes Nature makes man—the first and last of which assume a position of priority and superiority over the second. That is to say, Nature is not just 'second' in the series but also second in the sense of being secondary, lower in relation to the other two.[91] Insofar as she mediates between two male parties, who reflect each other in being powerful and set up 'beyond and over' all her other works and herself, Nature here occupies the position of woman in the classic homosocial triangle.[92] At another level, the logic of Sidney's sentence also presents a ratio or simultaneous equation: as God is to man, so man is to Nature. Here it is man who occupies the second, middle position, but he is not 'second' in the same way that Nature was (that is, subordinate; as female, of course, Nature retains this position). Rather, what is emphasized is his god-likeness, his power: as God rules over him, so he rules over Nature (his subordinate position to God is thereby discreetly passed over). Insofar as he reflects the image of God—constitutes the latter's 'likeness'—man's position is more that of a mirror than a mediator, as it was for Nature (indeed, she almost drops out of the picture as an active agent, since God is explicitly credited with making that prime creature, man, while she is merely responsible for making everything else, 'that second

---

Drake but only on the basis of the latter's 'intelligence, virtue and capacity for hard work' [*esse ingenii, virtutis, & industriæ*]—and because he performed a great 'deed that will redound not only to his own glory but to that of your whole nation' [*Perpetravit facinus, quod non solum ipsi, sed etiam toti vestræ genti erit gloriosum*]—and not on account of the great wealth he brought back with him: *Correspondence* (1014–15, 1012). See also Sidney's later, unsuccessful attempt to join Drake's expedition in 1585.

[91] The earlier claim that the poet 'doth grow in effect [into] another nature' (85.18–19)—which draws on the comment in Scaliger 1905 (8) that the poet produces 'another sort of nature, and . . . by so doing, he transforms himself almost into a second deity' as if he were creating another Eden—is not to be confused with the 'second nature' mentioned here which refers to the phenomenal, material world, imperfect since the Fall, and which is therefore inferior to the ideal created worlds of God and the poet.

[92] This set of relations might be seen to correspond with scenarios one and two outlined above in which Nature's brass and the poet's gold are still units within a given currency, albeit ones that command different values. This brazen Nature/coin/token is a member of the same species (human/currency) but, in relation to the golden poet/coin, a weak if not virtually worthless one. On the homosocial triangle, see Sedgwick 1985 (1–27).

nature'—including women, presumably—over which both God and man rule).[93] This special relation between God and man, moreover, is said to appear nowhere more clearly than in poetry, where man assumes his optimal form as maker with his Godlike ability to create whole worlds from nothing and to people them with the 'force of a divine breath'. The idealized 'high flying liberty of conceit' that was 'proper to the poet' (84.13) in the earlier discussion of the oracles—and in which, as sibyls and priestesses, women were also credited with the same power, the same 'divine force' (84.14)—thus returns here in full patriarchal guise. The male poet resumes his commanding position 'beyond and over' Nature, converting her lower world into his higher one, her brass into his gold. Only now he does so with divine sanction. If Protestantism sought to avoid the same pitfalls of idolatrous, fetishistic thinking that Plato had feared but could not avoid, by determinedly moving in the opposite direction from him—stripping the divine Logos of its aura and celebrating the plain, bare, naked truth in its place—then it fails in its objective no less than he. Like idealist philosophy, Protestantism winds up faithfully reflecting the money thought it originally sought to avoid. And if Protestantism systematizes this unavoidable fall into representation, commodification, and fetishistic thinking as the inevitability of the Fall—as Sidney's train of thought would seem to suggest: 'with no small argument to the incredulous of that first accursed fall of Adam' (86.6–7)—then this does not avoid the problem either, but only serves to set up God as banker general, condemning humanity to an eternity of profit-mindedness to make up for the fall from an ideal innocence that constitutes, in turn, the human condition.[94]

◌

The *narratio*—in which Sidney has struggled to free poetry from the implications of this bankable, profitable model—thus ends in defeat, with the proto-capitalist logic of the money economy fully intact and all efforts to escape it having failed. As an indication that his argument has arrived at a dead end, Sidney hastily shuts it down: 'But these arguments will by few be understood, and by fewer granted. Thus much (I hope) will be given me, that the Greeks with some probability of reason gave him the name above all names of learning' (86.9–11). The highly-titled, high-flying, freely ranging, gender-neutral, ecstatic, oracular, courtly maker of creative fictions is gone, his/her bid for transcendence having failed, to be replaced once again by the capitalist, colonialist, male, Protestant, humanist, pedagogic, bourgeois banker-poet purveying learning for the profit of individual and state.

---

[93] This set of relations might be seen to correspond with scenario three discussed above in which the various parties exist in a more hierarchical relation. God is above man but only as the CEO is above the COO. Both are partners that work and cooperate together to buy the commodity—and exploit natural resources in doing so—for the overall benefit and profitability of the firm.

[94] This, of course, is the burden of Max Weber's celebrated although not uncontested thesis: see Weber 2001. On figuring redemption in financial terms, see Weiner 1978 (12–18), reaffirmed in Weiner 1990 (120–2); and Stillman 2009 (14) who sees the 'economy of God' or 'divine economy' of redemption as central to Sidney's *oeuvre* and seeks to recover from the *Defence* an account of 'the godly economy's philosophical importance to poetics' (15) in order to argue that Sidney's mobilizes it in the *New Arcadia*.

It is with the latter, I think it is fair to say, that we remain for much of what follows, and certainly for the *propositio, divisio, confirmatio,* and *refutatio* that constitute the bulk of the treatise and comprise the most sustained articulation yet of its 'official' argument: the defence of poetry's profitability. While classifying the various parts of the *Defence* according to the formal subdivisions of a rhetorical oration has always been taken to imply its overall coherence—as if its argument were carefully planned in advance and marshalled to mount smoothly and progressively towards the conclusion—a close reading seems rather to suggest that it is full of false starts, deviations, retreats, recoveries, repetitions, and revisions, as if the latter were attempting to correct wayward lines of reasoning and to bring them back into line.[95] As if turning over a new leaf, Sidney's speaker (this nomenclature appropriate again, since the profitability argument is now back in the ascendant) leaves the tormented, failed, self-contradictory *narratio* behind (his contemplations of Platonic philosophy having got him nowhere), to embark afresh on a 'more ordinary opening' (86.12), which will hopefully set the argument back on track and which (appealing this time to the precepts of Aristotle, Horace, and Plutarch) defends poetry on the apparently incontrovertible grounds that it is an imitation or 'representing' (86.18) whose aim is 'to teach and delight' (86.20). Exhilarating glimpses that had flashed briefly in the *narratio* of the 'high flying liberty of conceit proper to the poet' (84.13) or the poet 'freely ranging only within the zodiac of his own wit' (85.23) are here firmly circumscribed or tied down, as poets are now said to be those which '*most properly* do imitate to teach and delight' (87.8, my emphasis) and to 'range, *only reined* with learned discretion' (87.9–10, my emphasis). Such and no other are now said to be 'right poets' (86.44), and it is under this dispensation of the 'right'—a powerfully corrective not to say coercive word—that they remain for much of the rest of the treatise.

The model of inspired, oracular poetry, capable of extending to include the female voice, is henceforth firmly re-requisitioned as the proper domain of the educated—indeed, militarized—male, as the 'laurel crown [set] upon the poet as victorious' (94.21–2) is equally appropriate for 'triumphing' (100.34) and 'triumphant captains' (108.18). With this model of the muscular poet who labours to serve his country, the old contradistinction between aristocrat and worker once again collapses, as those who have a 'most just title to be princes over all the rest' (88.32–3)—those, indeed, who possess 'nobleness' (88.34), who are 'waited on' (87.12), who are 'peerless' (90.22), and who are like a 'monarch' (95.9) to whom others, such as historians, are 'subject' (93.25) and their 'underling' (108.8)—are at the same time civil servants or qualified literary professionals who have 'attained to

---

[95] As Hulse 2000 (33) usefully reminds us, Tudor aesthetic discourse differs from 'the more abstracted discourse of modern and postmodern literary theory' insofar as—written at a time when the status of literature was 'in continual crisis' (34) and before the formalization of aesthetics in Enlightenment philosophy—it proceeds not so much in linear fashion as in a 'series of dialogues and interplays of discourses' (37). With its opening anecdote of the dialogue between the speaker and Pugliano, the *Defence* is initially argued to typify this dialogic nature of Tudor aesthetic theory, although ultimately Hulse's reading of Sidney's text remains a conservative one: Sidney 'returns in the body of his *Defence* to the project that had failed at the outset in his conversation with Pugliano' (57–9), a corrective move in which the 'new ideal' that Sidney fashions, modelled on Cyrus, is said to be that of the 'armored male body' (57).

the high top of their profession' (91.28–9). As 'virtue is the most excellent resting place for all worldly learning', the speaker concludes, 'so Poetry, being . . . most princely to move towards it, in the most excellent work is the most excellent workman' (96.41–4). Under this dispensation, the princely courtier and the humanist workman labour together as one as the poet assumes his approved function as pedagogue. 'Commonwealth discourse' is thus resumed. Henceforth, 'right poets' are those who 'merely make . . . to delight and teach' (87.14–15)—this being the sole official purpose of poetry, its 'very end' (110.33)—for such poetry is as instrumental as it is instructional.[96] 'Learning' and 'knowledge' are repeatedly invoked as self-evident goods, referring not simply to such intellectual know-how or to scientific and technological advances as boost the nation's knowledge economy but to 'the mistress-knowledge, by the Greeks called *architectonike*, which stands . . . in the knowledge of a man's self . . . with the end of well-doing and not of well-knowing only' (88.24–7), or to 'moral doctrine, the chief of all knowledges' (100.27).[97] Such knowledge yields still greater moral and spiritual capital, and the poetry that teaches it is therefore described as 'doctrinable' (92.28), 'profitable' (102.38; 103.31), 'fruitful' (100.7)—indeed, as an explicitly 'more fruitful knowledge' (102.41) than the supposedly 'fruitful knowledges' (102.22) to which the antipoetic tradition had unfavourably compared it (history, for example, is 'a less fruitful doctrine', 90.20–1)—and as working 'more effectually' than any other art (96.40). Such poetry finds its quintessential expression in 'instructing parables' (91.43), since it is difficult to compete with the most illustrious practitioner of this form, and comes to be defined as 'a representation of whatsoever is most worthy to be learned' (98.42). The glimpse, briefly snatched in the *narratio*, of pre-monetary nations that had managed to possess a poetry that was *not* so learned and therefore profitable, is here firmly corrected and put straight once and for all: 'never was the Albion nation without poetry' (105.6–7), and to suggest any such thing is 'a chainshot against all learning, or bookishness, as they commonly term it' (105.8–9), making such a thought, obviously, unconscionable.[98]

As a result of purveying this culturally valued and valuable commodity, poets are said to be 'in price' (105.1), and, where they are not, they should be awarded the laurel crown precisely in order to show the world how valuable they are to the economy and 'the price they ought to be had in' (108.19). Since learning is defined, among other things, as the 'enriching of memory' (88.4)—memory being described, in turn, as something the philosopher 'replenisheth . . . with many infallible grounds of wisdom' (90.39–40), even though these lie dark without the

---

[96] See also: the 'final end is to lead and draw us to as high a perfection as our degenerate souls . . . can be capable of' (88.7–9); 'the end of well-doing and not of well-knowing only' (88.27), 'the ending end of all earthly learning being virtuous action' (88.31–2); 'virtue is the most excellent resting place for all worldly learning to make his end of' (96.41–2) and poetry the prime means to that end; *Gorboduc* 'doth most delightfully teach, and so obtain the very end of Poesy' (110.33); 'that delightful teaching which is the end of Poesy' (112.43).

[97] See also: the poet excels the historian 'not only in furnishing the mind with knowledge, but in setting it forward to that which deserveth to be called and accounted good: which setting forward, and moving to well-doing, indeed setteth the laurel crown upon the poet as victorious, not only of the historian, but over the philosopher' (94.18–22).

[98] See also: 'For heretofore poets have in England also flourished' (109.2–3).

illuminations of poetry—and as 'the only treasurer of knowledge' (101.37), so poetry's contributions to both are again conceived in terms of furnishing the nation's knowledge bank. For all the speaker's fresh-start appeal to the poetics of Aristotle, Horace, and Plutarch—as if to rescue his argument from the contradictions and pitfalls deeply embedded within the idealist philosophy of Plato—the latter is still very much in evidence, not least in the repeated references to its characteristically visual or specular aesthetic. Thus, poetry is a 'speaking picture' (86.19; 90.42) which presents the ideal as that which 'is fittest for the eye to see' (87.4), such that one may 'see Ulysses' (91.1; 93.39), for example, as an emblem of patience or magnanimity, human actions being thus 'laid to the view' by the poet so that we may seem 'clearly to see through them' (91.16–17). Such seeing—or 'insight' (91.6)—is testimony to the 'inward light each mind hath in itself', which is 'as good as a philosopher's book' (95.2–3) and which demonstrates that the ideal is immanent within existence and waiting only to be recognized and revealed. The trap of fetishistic thinking or money thought is here repressed, denied, or conveniently forgotten, for such ideals of conduct as are represented by the literary heroes are said to convey, even to an ignorant reader, 'an apparent shining' (91.10), such that Ulysses' virtues (to continue that example) may 'shine the more' (93.41), and the examples of magnanimity and justice illustrated by Achilles, Cyrus, Aeneas, and the rest, may 'shine throughout all misty fearfulness and foggy desires' (99.31–2).[99] The poet's golden world is gold, indeed, and it glisters and glimmers accordingly.

This remains the case for the bulk of the *Defence* from the end of the *narratio* on, certainly as far as the *digressio* if not the *peroratio* itself, where poets are said to be the 'ancient treasurers of the Grecians' divinity' (116.25) in the sense, presumably, of keeping them alive in—and so stocking—the cultural memory.[100] Nowhere in these pages are the exhilarating glimpses of a poetry that is *not* learned, *not* under the sway of the profit-motive allowed to break cover or to puncture the surface narrative that is solemnly arguing for and defending the opposite. This does not mean, however, that the profitability argument 'wins' or that hints of a radically different conception of poetry—one that opposes the latter in every way—are terminally closed down, routed, and righted by the superior polemic of the opponent. On the contrary, the sense that there might be an alternative to the bankable model remains very much in evidence, manifesting as before in the textual disturbances and logical contradictions that constitute classic signs of resistance. Such disturbances—the use of rhetorical questions, of conditionals ('ifs' and 'supposes'), of those tell-tale 'truly's, of non-exemplary examples, of the speaker's tic-like hesitations and prevarications— are everywhere apparent. And they appear nowhere more illustratively than at those points where the official argument finds itself contemplating two texts that, in their own use of deconstructive irony and wit are, I suggest, the true intellectual forebears of the *Defence*: namely, the *Utopia* and the *Praise of Folly*.

---

[99] The speaker's observation here prompts a citation from Plato 1914, *Phaedrus*, 250D-E, to the effect that 'who could see virtue would be wonderfully ravished with the love of her beauty', the poet being the one that represents such virtue 'to the eye' (99.33–4, 35). See Robinson 1972 (97–136) for a classic study of the *Defence* as an articulation of this specular and idealist aesthetic.

[100] Although, like so much in the *peroratio*, this reference does not in fact stand up to scrutiny: see note 127.

III

Poetry Is Profitless

The discussion of the *Utopia*—the only time More's text is explicitly mentioned in the *Defence*, even though it is, in my view, subliminally present on every page—follows immediately after the account of the way the poet, in delivering forth his speaking pictures, reveals idealized images of virtue that manifest themselves to his readers in the form of an 'apparent shining' (91.10). Arguing, not for the first time, that this demonstrates the superiority of the poet's teaching-power over that of the philosopher, Sidney's speaker turns his mind to examples that, to prove the point, would illustrate the supreme embodiment of such teaching, the ultimate aim of the humanist pedagogical project and endpoint, indeed, of all its training: the dispensing of advice to princes. '[W]hat philosopher's counsel can so readily direct a prince', the speaker asks rhetorically, as the 'feigned' (91.18–19) Cyrus in Xenophon or Aeneas in Virgil (tried and tested examples that will be cited, in total, sixteen times in the course of the *Defence*), or, citing his third and, as it turns out, less obvious example: the feigning of 'a whole commonwealth, as the way of Sir Thomas More's *Utopia*?' (91.21).[101] The speaker hereby situates More's text within the well-known genre of humanist advice literature as an exemplary instruction manual or guide for princes. As other readers in the period were also known to do, that is, the speaker presents the *Utopia* as an *idealist* text—all known variants of the *Defence*, for example, including manuscript versions, spell the title '*Eutopia*', or 'good place'—and it is as such that the speaker introduces it to illustrate the 'shining': the visual aesthetic and moralized objectives that are typical of idealist philosophy.[102] That More's text can also be read as a radical exposé of that philosophy and the fetishistic thinking or money thought to which it gives rise, however—something Sidney's speaker (wilfully?) represses or denies—manifests in the characteristic about-turns that proceed to disturb his text and that betray nothing so clearly as a theoretical argument under strain. 'I say the way', the speaker finds himself needing to interject—meaning, presumably, More's method

---

[101] Cyrus is mentioned eight times (85.32–43; 87.31; 91.19; 92.28–9, 35; 95.26; 99.28; 103.42), as is Aeneas (91.20; 92.29–30, 35; 95.26, 36–8; 99.29, 41–100.6; 103.42).

[102] The alternative spelling of 'Eutopia' first appears in English in Wilson 1553 (Dd2), although it was preceded by a play on the meanings of 'Utopia' and 'Eutopia' in Latin verses prefacing the text and attributed to one 'Anemolius' (Greek, 'windy'): see More 1995 (18, 19). On the use of this spelling in all known versions of the *Defence*, see van Dorsten (195). In *The Model of Poesy* (1599), William Scott also treats the *Utopia* as a straightforwardly idealist text concerned with the 'praise or celebrating [of] praiseworthy things', without any sense of the text's irony or status as a mock encomium: see Scott 2013 (19). He, too, spells it 'Eutopia' (see Scott 2013, old spelling version, 10ᵛ).

of feigning in the *Utopia*—'because where [he] erred, it was the fault of the man and not of the poet, for that way of patterning a commonwealth was most absolute, though he perchance hath not so absolutely performed it' (91.21–5).[103] This leads to the observation that the 'feigned image of poesy' (91.25) may not in fact outdo the 'regular instruction of philosophy' (91.26) after all, and that if philosophers thereby prove themselves to have operated more 'rightly' (91.27) than poets, then this is not to indict the latter in general but simply to show that, in this particular instance—and whatever his good intentions—Thomas More did not succeed in delivering his ideas entirely satisfactorily.

As in previous cases, therefore, the example turns out not to be exemplary, or not in the way the speaker intended it to be: the *Utopia* does *not* illustrate the ostensible point about poetry's ability to teach the prince and citizens and yield a profit to the commonwealth in doing so. Quite the reverse: Sidney's painstaking differentiation between the poet as an excellent teacher and the philosopher as a poor one—to which several discussions within the *Defence* are devoted—here rather suddenly deconstructs. Unlike the philosophers who, in providing 'regular instruction', do what philosophers do and so act 'rightly', More, it transpires, does not. That is to say, he 'feigns', like the poet, but he does not teach as he is supposed to, or he does not teach the right thing. In this respect, in fact, he is the very antithesis of the 'right poet' (86.44): he is perverse, goes awry.[104] Yet, having upended the speaker's argument, the 'example' of More's *Utopia* is nonetheless allowed to stand. Sidney does not scrub it out as, on reflection, a counterproductive illustration that undermines the point his speaker is trying to make; and the reason for this, I suggest, is that his sympathies largely lie with More's devastating critique of money thought and the tyranny that invariably accompanies it. For all the speaker's efforts first to redeem More's text—to preserve idealist philosophy (and the '*Eutopia*' with it) as that which promotes and teaches 'goodness' (91.18), and then, having realized his mistake, to distance himself from it with some serious back-pedalling—the fact that, as 'no place', More's *Utopia* can be read as terminally deconstructive of that philosophy, registers powerfully in the logical and syntactical twists and turns that disturb the surface of the speaker's prose. Those disturbances are allowed to remain, the residual yet permanent record of an argument at war with itself. When the speaker accuses More of having 'erred', for example, I suspect

---

[103] Evans 1996 (7) describes this commendation of the work but not the man as 'problematic'—as an 'enigma' (7), 'intriguing in its complex ambiguity' (8)—and finds it 'surprising' that Sidney should choose to praise 'a work that criticized or mocked much of what an Elizabethan aristocrat held dear' (29). Nevertheless, he minimizes any possibility that Sidney might have sympathized with More's radical agenda and insists that the *Utopia* is co-opted to support an idealist poetics.

[104] More thus conforms to type. See Jameson 2005 (10): 'The Utopians, whether political, textual or hermeneutic, have always been maniacs and oddballs: a deformation readily enough explained by the fallen societies in which they had to fulfill their vocation. Indeed, I want us to understand Utopianism, not as some unlocking of the political, returning to its rightful centrality as in the Greek city-states; but rather as a whole distinct process in its own right ... [What Machiavelli and Carl Schmitt] dared to enunciate publicly, in a heroism indissociable from cynicism, our Utopians grasp more furtively, in forms more redolent of perversion than of paranoia, and with that passionate sense of mission or calling from which *jouissance* is never absent.'

that this does not refer, or not only, to the fact that More opposed Henry VIII's break with Rome and was executed for doing so (the view of the *Defence*'s editors), but rather to the fact the *Utopia* exposes the tyrannical logic that inheres within capital, instead of celebrating it: More's text, that is, is moving in the opposite direction—an errant direction—from the one the speaker assumes for it.[105] The 'error', in other words, is not More's but the speaker's, and it stands as testimony to the bad faith that arises when Sidney attempts, by means of the latter, to repress or deny something that he wants to say but dare not (again, More goes further in this respect: he took the ultimate risk). By the same token, when the speaker describes the patterning of the commonwealth in the *Utopia* as 'absolute'—even though More may not have presented or executed his plan 'absolutely' (91.24)—it is difficult in the circumstances not to pause over the speaker's choice of word. Editors gloss 'absolute' here as 'perfect', 'consummate', 'complete'.[106] But could the *Utopia* not be described as 'most absolute' because it is, most absolutely, an attack on absolutism? And could More not be said to have failed to execute the latter 'absolutely' because he was, as it happens, executed by just such an exercise of absolute power? That is to say, I do not think we can necessarily assume on Sidney's part a sectarian dislike for More's Catholicism, or, if this is in evidence, then it should be counterbalanced by the fact that More stood up to tyranny and suffered the ultimate penalty for doing so.[107] In the politics of the *Defence* (not to mention Sidney's other writings), this is not a bad thing. Indeed, if there is one place (no place? good place?) where Sidney and his speaker are consistent—in accord, for once, and not in conflict with one another—it is on the subject of tyranny. Tyrants are barely mentioned in the *Defence* except to be shamed, reproved, reformed,

---

[105] Shepherd (174), Maslen (165), van Dorsten (195), and Duncan-Jones (377, although see note 107), all concur on this point. In the dedication to his translation of the *Utopia*, Ralph Robinson criticizes More on the grounds that he refused to see the 'shining light of godes holy truthe' (the Protestant version of it, that is): see More 1551 (+3ᵛ). It may have been clear to Sidney, if it was not to Robinson, that such an appeal to idealist philosophy and theology did not always take the thinker or believer where he or she expected.

[106] Shepherd (174); Maslen (165); Alexander (17); Duncan-Jones (377). While it is true that Sidney uses the adjective and adverb in this sense elsewhere in the *Defence*—e.g. describing the *Cyropaedia* as 'an absolute heroical poem' (87.31–2), or English, unlike other languages, as observing the accent in rhyme words 'absolutely' (116.3)—the political sense of the word, 'of authority: free from all external restraint or interference; unrestricted, unlimited' (see *OED* absolute *adj.* I.4.a) was available from 1475; and the sense 'of a ruler, government, etc.: having uninhibited authority or power' (I.4.b) from 1567. The development of these meanings under the Tudors is telling in itself.

[107] Duncan-Jones (377) notes that George More—a kinsman (although not blood relation) of Thomas More and the future father-in-law of John Donne—travelled with Sidney on his 1577 embassy and was the occasion, at a social gathering in Nuremberg in late March of that year, of a laudatory account of More to which Sidney was a witness. As Höltgen 1981 (68) elaborates, given the 'obvious Protestant bias' of the works in which this anecdote is recorded—Philip Camerarius' *Operae horarum succisivarum sive meditationes historicae* (Nuremberg, 1591), and its German translation by Georg Maier, *Historischer Lustgarten* (Leipzig, 1631)—'it is remarkable to find . . . a eulogistic account of Thomas Morus'. More is referred to, for example, as another John the Baptist, i.e. implicitly as the victim of another tyrannous, corrupt, and adulterous king. 'Humanists like Camerarius and Maier obviously admired Sir Thomas More's moral integrity and constancy'; 'A common humanistic ideal has triumphed over narrow sectarianism and has brought together, in this historical work, the Catholic martyr and the Protestant champion' (69). On Sidney's association with prominent Catholics on the continent, see also Evans 1996 (22, 24).

punished, or killed; and neither are their victims, except to be heroized or pitied.[108] Moreover, poetry has a special part to play in bringing such absolutists to book, devising 'new punishments in hell for tyrants' (94.13–14) and, in the case of tragedy, making 'kings fear to be tyrants' (98.27). In this context, I suggest, the explicit introduction of More's *Utopia* into the argument of the *Defence* serves as a powerful counter-statement that has the effect of disrupting if not overturning the 'official' argument in favour of fetishized, golden, 'shining' but politically suspect ideals, by slipping in, guerrilla-wise, the potential for a radical alternative.

Similar—and similarly symptomatic—textual contortions arise a few pages later, when the speaker gives his first direct response to the antipoetic arguments of Gosson and others: the point that formally announces the beginning of the *refutatio* and that leads, in turn, to a discussion of Erasmus' *Praise of Folly*. Again, the issue arises from Sidney's efforts, by means of his speaker, to repress or deny readings of texts that, at some level, articulate what he wishes to say and whose 'side' he is really on. Thus, the speaker strangely and obliquely chooses to approach Gosson's *Schoole of Abuse* as if the latter were a mock encomium or example of paradoxical praise: 'First, truly I note not only in these *mysomousoi*, poet-haters, but in all that kind of people who seek a praise by dispraising others, that they do prodigally spend a great many wandering words in quips and scoffs' (100.41–101.1) and 'are full of very idle easiness' (101.4). This serves as a way of turning Gosson's charges against the vanity and errancy of poetry very neatly against him. If, in dispraising poetry and poets, Gosson sought only 'a praise' for himself, then this makes him a legitimate target for the speaker's correctively deflationary satire, allowing him self-righteously to mock the mocker, scoff at the scoffer, and 'instead of laughing at the jest, to laugh at the jester' (101.6–7). This train of thought leads, in turn, to a consideration of other jesting dispraises of good things—Agrippa's *De incertitudine et vanitate scientarum et artium* (first published in 1527 and translated into English by J. Sandford as *Of the vanitie and uncertaintie of artes and sciences* in 1569)—and, while he is at it, jesting praises of bad things (asses, debt, the plague), culminating in Erasmus' *Folly* (first published as the *Moriae encomium* in 1511 and translated into English by Sir Thomas Chaloner as *The praise of folie* in 1549). This way of approaching Gosson seems strange and oblique, however, because it imputes to the *Schoole of Abuse* an irony and wit that are conspicuous by their absence. Rather as, a paragraph or two later, the speaker assumes that, while not strictly essential to poetry, versification is nonetheless so useful as a memory-aid that it could never be criticized except 'in jest' (102.18), so here too he appears to assume that Gosson could not *really* have been attacking poetry, any more than Agrippa, in attacking its abuses, was really attacking learning itself.[109] The situation arises because the speaker has effectively bundled together Agrippa, Gosson, and other '*mysomousoi*' as

---

[108] For references in the *Defence* to tyrants who are, in one way or another, called to account, see: David (96.30), Alexander Pheraeus (98.34–8), Hiero (106.35), and Polymnestor (111.35). For their victims as heroized or pitied, see Lucretia (87.5), Sylla (94.10), and the 'people under hard lords' (97.18).

[109] On the mixed reception of Agrippa's text in the period—in the sense that it was interpreted as both serious and paradoxical—see Hamilton 1956 (152); Ferguson 1983 (157); and Maslen (196, 197).

the antipoetic authors on whom he draws, for charges and refutations, throughout the *Defence*, and then bundled these together, in turn, with a series of quite unrelated texts and authors—'all that kind of people' (100.42)—whose only point of comparison is that, along with Agrippa, they too use the paradox of praise.[110] That Gosson does not belong within this latter group, however, and that the *Schoole of Abuse* can by no stretch of the imagination be considered a humanist jest or be categorized with the 'weighty humanist literature of sustained paradox', as Maslen calls it (196), requires the speaker rapidly to backtrack and withdraw the parallel his associative thinking has perhaps over-hastily made: 'But for Erasmus and Agrippa, they had another foundation, than the superficial part would promise' (101.15–16). They were clearly doing something different from what they appeared to be doing, in which case laughing at *them* would be an inappropriate and ignorant response that only reflected badly on the uncomprehending reader. In praising folly and dispraising learning, Erasmus and Agrippa were not seeking 'a praise' (100.42) for themselves, but rather seeking to puncture pretension and teach their readers the virtues of humility and self-knowledge. Their irony and wit is thereby recuperated since, in both cases, their use of paradoxical praise or dispraise serves the higher purpose of inculcating virtue, identifying true wisdom, and so teaching their readers a profitable lesson. In this context, the method the speaker proposes—'instead of laughing at the jest, to laugh at the jester'—would therefore be exactly the wrong way round, for the appropriate and intelligent response would be to admire the jesters for their cleverness and wit and, in getting their jokes, correctly to apply their lessons to oneself. Such, indeed, is the process the speaker had described only a few pages earlier in his discussion of satire—in which the reader, in laughing at folly, learns, at length ashamed, 'to laugh at himself, which he cannot avoid, without avoiding the folly' (97.38–9)—and which, given the way ideas seem to suggest themselves and set trains of thought in motion in the *Defence*, may well have prompted the discussion of Erasmus' *Folly* that, even though not strictly relevant to the argument, then follows.[111]

Where, then, does this leave the *Schoole of Abuse* that Sidney's speaker is supposed to be refuting? Having realized or remembered that Gosson is *not* a second Agrippa or Erasmus—whose texts both rest upon 'another foundation' (101.15)—the speaker relegates him to another vague category: that of 'these other pleasant fault-finders' (101.16–17). But what is this 'other' of 'another'? If this group does not comprise the writers of witty humanist paradox, from which Gosson has just been excluded—the whole discussion of such 'playing wit' (101.7) having proved, in the event, a red herring—then the (still large) category of texts

---

[110] Cf. Harington 1904 (200) who condemns Agrippa 'for a generall libeller' and presents his own defence of poetry as a direct refutation of his arguments, although as we shall see it remains distinctly possible that Harington was not deaf to Agrippa's satire and is therefore only pretending to take his attacks seriously.

[111] Maslen (185) is the only editor to make this connection, even though the speaker's train of thought in the earlier discussion—'works in commendation or dispraise must ever hold an high authority' (97.2), Heraclitus 'surely is to be praised' (97.31) for his portrayals of human weakness—would seem to anticipate the later one.

that manage to jest without being paradoxical cannot be said to accommodate the *Schoole of Abuse* either. That is to say, Gosson not only fails to be 'as merry in showing the vanity' of poetry as Agrippa was of science (101.12–13): he fails to be merry, period. There is nothing 'witty' (nor, despite the claims of its title page, particularly 'pleasant') about Gosson's dispraise of poetry. There is no jest and thus no jester, leaving the speaker's proposed method of dealing with such antipoetic literature high and dry. If the option 'instead of laughing at the jest, to laugh at the jester' was back to front in the case of Erasmus and Agrippa, it is not applicable to Gosson either, whether that way or in reverse. Why the confusion? Why all the false starts, retreats, non sequiturs? There seems to be a considerable degree of logical and syntactical dodging going on that it is difficult not to read symptomatically, nor, as in the similarly tortuous reading of the *Utopia*, as a classic sign of resistance, conscious or otherwise. For what the persistent but ultimately unsustainable attempts to associate Gosson with jesting, paradox, and wit seem to suggest is a reluctance to accept the case that he was, in fact, very much in earnest. Just as, over the page, 'it must be in jest' (102.18) that anyone would speak against versification, so here there seems to be a powerful resistance to the idea that someone might actually criticize poetry *without* intending the opposite: that they might dispraise poetry without either praising it paradoxically (as a 'playing wit') or appearing to dispraise it in jest (as the 'pleasant fault-finders'). What the faltering logic and syntax of this paragraph suggests, rather, is a dawning realization that Gosson is a more formidable opponent than he first appeared and his line of argument strangely resistant to refutation. For if this fluster of activity on the page indicates nothing so clearly than the speaker's defensive tactics in disarray, it also suggests the force of the argument—evidently not to be laughed out of court—that poetry is, without any gainsaying, profitless indeed.

Since this goes to the heart of the present investigation, it warrants a little further probing. Consider again the sentence that begins this paragraph in the *Defence*, and especially its broad-brush categorization of all those who 'seek a praise by dispraising others' (100.42). How does this relate to Gosson? The praise he seeks by dispraising poetry and stage-plays so systematically is not, I suggest—or not primarily—for himself but rather for the entire modus vivendi that he opposes to poetry and poetic production in general: that is, for the economic model, articulated as 'commonwealth discourse', that prioritizes profit and profitability, with all its associated values of thrift, hard work, industry, productivity, and business. *These* are praiseworthy. The binaries on which the *Schoole of Abuse* is structured hammer home the contrast between the two worlds relentlessly: the profitability, and thus exemplarity, of this set of values is made manifest in the countless comparisons with the profitlessness that characterizes all forms of artistic production. Where discipline, application, and the accumulation of capital (financial, intellectual, and spiritual) within the nation's treasure-house are signalled as being most useful to the state and its citizens, poetry and stage-plays do nothing but abuse them. The qualities that Gosson values, however, are the very things to which Sidney—I have been suggesting—took exception: even if, in the first instance, that distaste took the form of an intuitive, instinctive, and emotional response (articulated, for example, in simplistic class terms as a courtier's 'scorn' for mercantile values), rather than a logical or economic critique; even if that distaste was for the tendencies towards fetishistic thinking that he sensed in Plato's philosophy, rather than their logical culmination in the market economics of capitalism, something of which he, understandably, may only have had the dimmest grasp at the time; and even if that distaste arose largely in reaction to reading a text like Gosson's, which bore home to him exactly what he did not like, rather than being a fully formulated position with an anti-capitalist agenda that he had already worked out in advance. It is just such an instinctive, 'gut' reaction against the qualities that Gosson positivizes, in my view, that explains or at least accounts for the symptomatic disturbances of Sidney's text, especially here where he first takes Gosson on head to head.[112] For if Gosson is promoting the virtues of profitability—and if the profitable, bankable model is what, in its commodification of poetry, Sidney at some level detests—then Sidney's sympathies would most logically lie with what Gosson excoriates: profitlessness. A close reading of the *Defence* and the contradictions that routinely disrupt the surface of its 'official' argument—that poetry is profitable—indicates to me that this is exactly where Sidney's sympathies lay, whether he (or subsequent readers of the *Defence*) admitted that fully to consciousness or not. It also shows the liabilities that Sidney brought upon himself by setting out to defend poetry against such accusations, thereby committing himself—or his speaker—to a position that he could not wholeheartedly defend. It is this bad faith that registers in the paradoxical reasoning that this paragraph (like so many others) reveals.

According to this reading, the profit-mindedness that is praiseworthy for Gosson would be anathema to Sidney, or at least alien and strange to him—a modus operandi that belonged to a different class, another 'kind of people' (100.42)—and this regardless of Sidney's personal debt crisis or desperation for cash that a little profit-mindedness might, in practical terms, have gone a long way towards alleviating. Such profit-mindedness was not his people's way of doing things, even if it was increasingly having to become so, and even if their own self-identification with 'courtly' values and a 'feudal' mode of operation took shape only recursively, in reaction to the appearance (I will not say 'rise') of a recognizably different class: the so-called 'new' men who in their view were possessed of a quite different economic praxis and mentality.[113] In defending poetry against Gosson's charge of profitlessness,

---

[112] This might be the moment for a timely reminder that by 'Sidney' I am not referring to an embodied, autobiographical subject but rather to a polemical position, to be distinguished from that of the 'speaker'. In both cases, the nomenclature remains a way of distinguishing between alternative positions as they can be seen to collide within the argument of the *Defence*.

[113] As discussed by Warley 2005. Leinwand 1999 (13–41) gives a detailed discussion of such 'recursion' in *The Merchant of Venice* and *Timon of Athens*, in which the eponymous characters of these plays attempt in various ways to revert to older, nostalgic, more primitive economies—e.g. the gift economy—as a means of resisting their interpellation within the otherwise all-encompassing credit economies of Venice and Athens. Heinzelman 1980 (14) notes the semantic shifts that symptomized this period of intense economic change in the sixteenth century: 'Already, by Jonson's time, the concept of "value" had bifurcated . . . "value" in respect to one's physical and spiritual well-being is not the same "value" as represented by one's monetary or economic wealth . . . Words which had earlier signified the bonds of feudal loyalty lost their ethical overtones, their invocation of an ethos. "Price" no longer meant esteem. "Fee" no longer meant an estate held by homage, and "in fee" no longer signified

Sidney sets out to refute his argument by turning the tables and arguing the reverse. This apparently logical move, however, represses or denies the fact that what is positive for Gosson is negative for Sidney, with the result that, when it comes down to it, Sidney finds himself—or his speaker—defending the one thing it turns out he hates most of all. What he should have done, had this surfaced fully to consciousness or had he felt able to—but what the logical and textual disturbances of the *Defence* effectively do for him anyway—is to take a third way: namely, neither (1) that poetry is profitless (Gosson's position), nor (2) that poetry is profitable (the official argument of the *Defence* and the speaker's position), but rather (3) that profitlessness is, at least as far as poetry is concerned, a good thing. Here, Gosson and Sidney would effectively be on the same side, insofar as they both agree that poetry is profitless.[114] The difference is that what for Gosson and the whole ethos of profitability represents that absolute negation of value turns out to be, for Sidney, his highest possible aim. That is to say, it is not *poetry* that has shifted position (from profitless to profitable) but *profitlessness* that has shifted position (from undesirable to desirable). While the latter might disturb the otherwise serene surface of its 'official' argument, it is in fact entirely consistent with what I have been seeking to excavate as the *Defence*'s 'other' argument: its resistance to any model of poetry as commodified, fetishized, transactable, or bankable, and its plea, instead, for an understanding and appreciation of creative fiction as, in every sense of that word, 'free'. It is also consistent with the radical rethinking of value that this process of turning profitlessness into a *desideratum* requires: for it entails an understanding of value that, by definition, does *not* conceive it in terms of accumulable capital but that rather seeks to opt out of—to deconstruct and terminally refute—that kind of thinking or 'logic' altogether.[115] In the same way, saying that aspiring towards such an empty, contentless re-evaluation of value is Sidney's 'highest' possible aim is not merely to re-fetishize transcendence (the trap into which Plato's idealist philosophy falls) but rather to opt out of dialectical, hierarchical thinking, and the many tyrannies that attend it, for good: or at least to

---

a relationship subject to feudal obligation. "Fynaunce" no longer meant to take as ransom, nor did "mortgage" mean security, or "purchase" endeavor, or "thrift" luck, or "commodity" advantage. These words, among others, acquired a singularly commercial, fiduciary significance'.

[114] Critics have long noted affinities between Sidney's and Gosson's positions: see e.g. Kinney 1972; Kinney, ed. 1974 (44); Herman 1996 (14, 61–93); Maslen (23–31); and Williams 2009 (643–4).

[115] It might be apposite here to reconfirm my difference from Landreth 2012 for whom what registers as 'scandalous' (5, 36) in the texts he explores does so because it transgresses the ethical codes of commonwealth discourse to show that practices the latter deplored (e.g. waste, prodigality, spending, etc.) would—in terms of the new discourse of political economy to be developed in the seventeenth century—come to be seen as profitable for the state: thereby proving capitalism's mantra that, essentially, greed is good. For him, the authors he examines anticipate (without, of course, necessarily endorsing) the fully capitalist economy that was to come. The epistemic break they announce, therefore, is *into* capitalism. For my part, what is 'scandalous' about Sidney's position— by which I mean the 'unofficial' position of the *Defence*—is that it rejects profit-mindedness itself, regardless of whether it is formulated 'ethically' or not. The epistemic break that Sidney announces, therefore (although 'announces' is the wrong word), is not from one iteration of profit-mindedness into another (commonwealth to capital, as it were), but rather out of profit-mindedness altogether: out of money thought and the entire *mentalité* that the money form brought with it, as formulated in dialectical thinking and idealist philosophy from Plato on.

do so in and by means of creative fiction.[116] This paradox—that profitlessness is something to be desired, and that such value cannot therefore be 'value' as it is conceived by a capitalist, monetary ideology—registers here in the otherwise illogical drift of Sidney's thinking towards paradoxical texts (that praise by dispraise and vice versa) and in his own paradoxical and highly symptomatic response to them.

The speaker's odd approach to Gosson—setting him up initially as a playful wit only to risk having the laugh turned on himself for getting Gosson's earnest dispraise so wrong—could thus be explained in the following terms. First, it tries to deflect the fact that Gosson is indeed in earnest: that is, that poetry is not praiseworthy and should not therefore be praised; or rather that praising poetry as profitable entails certain unacceptable costs of its own (commodification, fetishism, tyranny, and ultimately capitalism), which would strongly suggest that it should not be praised in those terms. Second, it tries to deflect the fact that the paradox is therefore *Sidney*'s, not Gosson's: that is, where Gosson 'logically' praises profitability and dispraises poetry as profitless (this being 'logical' according to money thought, which sees everything in terms of business), Sidney 'illogically' and paradoxically finds himself wanting to dispraise poetry as profitable and praise it as profitless. In other words, it is the *Defence* and not the *Schoole* that belongs to the tradition of paradoxical praise, should its author allow it to. In the event, the *Defence* belongs to the tradition of Agrippa and Erasmus, but it does so only unofficially. It is the text's 'unconscious'—its secret, disruptive, counter-voice— that feels its way towards a new, radical, and alternative conception of poetry: one that undermines the official argument which the speaker is trying, with a decreasing measure of success, to prosecute, and that problematizes the latter's status as a defence, insofar as what Sidney really wants to defend is, according to his speaker, indefensible. Thus, to return for a moment to the idea of a 'third way' outlined above, another way of presenting this would be as follows. The speaker behaves as if he has two options before him: either (1) that poetry is justified and defensible only if it turns a profit (if it is learned, if it teaches and so moves to virtue, the 'ending end of all earthly learning being virtuous action', 88.31–2); or conversely (2) that poetry is *not* justified or is indefensible when it fails to turn a profit (as, for example, when even its virtuous lessons can be twisted to vicious effect: a liability which, since it cannot be ruled out, would argue for poetry's complete abolition). These are the terms of the argument that Gosson sets out in the *Schoole of Abuse* and within which the speaker continues to operate. An alternative position, however,— unthinkable both to Gosson and to the speaker, but present at some level within

---

[116] For all her generous engagement with poststructuralist theory, Anderson 2005 (142) ultimately resists such a prospect, her general direction of travel being towards the 'constructive' rather than the 'deconstructive': 'the positive exchange and positive production' of Roman conceptions of metaphor rather than 'the exclusively negative emphasis on rupture' in some of Derrida's writing. The *Defence* is invoked in this context: Quintilian's understanding of metaphor as both natural and unnatural (see Quintilian 2002, *Institutio Oratoria*, VIII.vi.4) is said to find an analogy in 'Sidney's argument that the poetic making (art, fiction) that exceeds Nature is not in a deeper sense unnatural since God made the poetic maker; indeed, in traditional terms, He did so through His agent Nature' (141). Sidney's naturalizing of metaphor's perverse or tropic character also serves to naturalize certain hierarchies of gender and power here.

Sidney's consciousness—would be (3): a conception of poetry that can be thought of as free from the entire nexus of profitability, no matter how all-encompassing, 'logical', or self-evident the latter might appear to be. A poetry, indeed, that like the *Utopia* might show that nexus for the ideological construction that it is.

Staying for the moment with the paragraph that launches the *refutatio*, then, and looking at it again with this in mind, one could argue that—just as in the equally tortuous passage around the golden-world metaphor, with its extraordinary density of negatives, 'never' (85.20), 'not' (85.22), 'never' (85.24), 'neither' (85.25), 'nor' (85.26), 'Neither' (85.33), 'not' (85.36, 38, 40), 'Neither' (85.44), 'nothing' (86.4), 'no' (86.6)—so a similar level of denial is in evidence here too. Everything that is officially negativized begins to look increasingly like the self-characterization of the courtly class whose 'free' modus vivendi Sidney mentally opposes to the costing mentality of the bankable one. Thus, there is a 'kind of people' (100.42) who 'do prodigally spend' (101.1), who are 'full of very idle easiness' (101.4), who even 'praise . . . the comfortableness of being in debt' (101.7–8), this being the perennial condition of the Elizabethan aristocracy, many of whom took full advantage of the credit economy (that is, did not repay their debts).[117] By the same token, everything that is officially positivized begins to look like a characterization of mercantile practice: beholding 'the worthiness of the subject' (101.3), for example,—here poetry—subjects the latter to the commodification and quantification typical of the money economy (it asks what it is 'worth': something that would never have occurred to the 'simple Indians'). In such a world, that paradoxically praises 'the jolly commodity of being sick of the plague' (101.8–9), the 'jolly commodity'—duly fetishized—might well be thought of as a plague wherever capitalist practice takes hold. In the line from the *Ars amatoria* that the speaker cites to make the point that everything can be turned to a profit, Ovid advises that, in order to speed up and secure the seduction process, the poet-lover should turn his mistress' shortcomings to good effect—if she is short, call her petite, if fat, curvaceous, and so on—thus may 'good lie hid in nearness of the evil' (101.12, the speaker's translation of '*Ut lateat virtus proximitate mali*', 101.11). Just as this is the sales trick of the classified ads, so what Ovid is proposing here is a transaction (essentially a purchase and sale), and the speaker cites this line in order to make a roughly similar point: namely, that in appearing to undersell a good product (learning) or oversell a bad one (folly), Agrippa and Erasmus actually deliver a truly valuable one (wisdom, self-knowledge, and so forth). This would be in line with the ostensible argument in favour of profitability: that is, irony is stabilized and paradox redeemed as a temporary jest—light, airy, empty, free—can reassuringly be filed away as a profitable lesson to be learned, much as More's *Utopia* was redeemed as *Eutopia*, its empty space as no place filled with something good. Yet, in offering to 'turn' (101.10) Ovid's verse so as to turn a profit

---

[117] Commenting on Sidney's last will and testament (which effectively bankrupted his father-in-law, Sir Francis Walsingham) Duncan-Jones, ed. 1973 (144) notes that 'Sidney seems . . . to have lived beyond his means throughout his life; but so did most of Elizabeth's courtiers'. Also referring to Sidney, Alsop 1997 (471) notes that '[s]ystematic tax evasion by some leading members of the court aristocracy was a not uncommon feature of the late Tudor period'.

from it (good from bad, seduction from possible failure), the speaker ends up misquoting it by reversing its terms: for the original reads '*Et lateat vitium proximitate boni*' [let its nearness to a virtue conceal a fault].[118] As Shepherd puts it, Sidney 'adapts the verse to his purpose by replacing *vitium* by *virtus*, and *boni* by *mali*' (195), and, where they comment on this line, the *Defence*'s other editors agree. Yet this is to assume that Sidney's 'purpose' was consistent with that of his speaker. I would suggest, by contrast, that whatever his presumed intention, Sidney's swap of good for bad and bad for good is a classic example of what Freud calls 'representation by the opposite', and that it passes silent comment on the supposed values and virtues of profitability, salesmanship, and its innumerable trades.[119]

Such a reading also opens up the possibility (and this really would be counted a plus) of a more searching and radical account of Erasmus' *Praise of Folly*—not to mention More's *Utopia*—in which these texts are recognized for their potential to critique and indict the ideology of profitability rather than co-opted in support of it. It would enable a reading of More, for example, that contrary to the one half-heartedly proposed in the *Defence*, felt able to embrace the *Utopia*'s radical exposure of the money form and the political evils that follow on from it.[120] And it would enable a reading of Erasmus that did not tamely dispose of folly as a roundabout means of delivering wisdom, but rather cultivated the role of the holy fool—as innocent of profitable learning as the 'simple Indians'—whose stance, while naturally deemed foolish, ignorant, barbarous, stupid, illogical, perverse, and mad by the 'other' side, is deemed those things precisely because it opts out entirely from the latter's pseudo-logic and so presents the best possible riposte to and ultimate refutation of the *homo economicus* and professor of bankable learning whose logic this is. Addressing the 'other pleasant fault-finders' (101.16–17), among whose company Gosson is not but Sidney, I suspect, is, the speaker tries fearsomely to beat them down with the charge that 'scoffing cometh not of wisdom' (101.19) and that the 'best title' (101.19–20) they deserve is 'to be called good fools' (101.20–1). According to the paradoxical counter-argument of the *Defence* that runs beneath the official one and disrupts it throughout this paragraph, however, being called the good, innocent, holy fool might indeed be the optimal title for the poet who seeks to free himself from the trials of money thought. Indeed, it could be as 'high and

---

[118] Ovid 1929, *Ars Amatoria*, II.662.

[119] See Freud 1905 (70–4, 88–9, 173–4), where 'representation by the opposite' is a key feature of how jokes (and dreams) work. Ferguson 1983 (157) comes closest to identifying that this is really what is going on here when she describes Sidney's misquotation of Ovid as 'a complex example' in which the logical expectations raised by his offer to 'turn' Ovid's verse are, in turn, 'turned to nothing'. Ultimately, however, this glimpse of a radical, new poetics is firmly closed down, insofar as Sidney's attribution to Agrippa and Erasmus of 'another foundation' (101.15) offers him (and Ferguson) an 'escape' from such potentially endless, unstable, and unredeemed irony, i.e. 'the Christian escape . . . the Word whose true promise the reader must find beneath the false promises of human words' (158).

[120] As Strier 2011 (13), who argues that the *Utopia*—'the most sustained attempt in the period, serious or not, to imagine "alternative modes" of social, religious, and psychological organization'— should be 'fully acknowledged and appreciated' as such.

incomparable a title' (84.39) as that of poet or 'maker' itself.[121] A few lines later, the argument apparently having moved on to a new topic but these ideas still, clearly, very much in Sidney's mind, the speaker avers, as 'undoubtedly true', that 'if reading be foolish without remembering' (101.36–7) then versification, which aids the latter, can only be praised. The speaker's conditional, however, suggests that something quite different is being said, for the force of his argument rests upon 'memory being the only treasurer of knowledge' (101.37). If memory is thereby co-opted to the bankable model with its 'treasure-house of science', then ignorance might indeed be bliss, and foolish laughter and forgetting preferable.

When, a few pages after these paragraphs that launch the *refutatio*, the speaker again finds himself circling back to the supposed value of learning and knowledge— saying that those who glorify an earlier age when men fought battles rather than wrote poetry are simply cultivating ignorance and so firing 'a chainshot against all learning, or bookishness, as they commonly term it' (105.8–9)—this actually rather attractive prospect rears its head once more, and again by means of the symptomatic 'turning' of a Roman poet's verse. To such as would dare to cultivate ignorance, the speaker threatens, he would answer as Horace does, and proceeds to quote from the latter's *Satires* that in the original read '*iubeas miserum esse, libenter / quatenus id facit*' [Bid him be miserable, since that is his whim], but that Sidney's speaker alters to read: '*jubeo stultum esse libenter*' [I willingly tell him to be a fool].[122] The *Defence*'s editors comment only that Sidney 'adapts' Horace here, but in the circumstances it seems to me that inserting a fool in the place of a miserable man is a telling substitution: for the fool, by definition, is not unhappy (in Horace's satire, the truly unhappy man is compared to the miser who gloats over his gold but thinks he can never have enough). Much as the truant Astrophil would resist the schoolmasterly lessons of virtue at every turn—and urges those who are not moved by poetry, or who would call it vain, to 'learne in wonder's schooles, / To be (in things past bounds of wit) fooles, if they be not fooles'—it is just such a good fool that Sidney would like to, and secretly does, identify himself.[123] In the *digressio*, he presents contemporary poets (including himself) as having taken it upon themselves to be poets 'in despite of Pallas' (109.26–7), that is, as ignorant, foolish, and *un*beholden to the dictates of learning, knowledge, or wisdom.[124] When the schoolroom is remembered in the *Defence* it is rarely fondly or with reverence, and clearly 'bookishness, as they commonly term it' is

---

[121] Cf. Landreth 2012 (178–83) and what, in his reading of *The Merchant of Venice*, he formulates as 'fool's money'. Here folly represents the faux 'niceness' and bourgeois politeness that makes the world go round and that Aragon's choice of the silver casket (for which he receives a fool's head in return) mobilizes: '[Aragon's] passport through the commonwealth of fools is money [silver], the "common drudge 'tween man and man" [*MV* III.ii.103]—through which we all make fools of ourselves in order to participate in making fools of each other, without for a moment fooling anybody' (183). For my part, folly is precisely opting out of—refusing to 'participate' in—this monetarized commonwealth, by acting foolishly *according to its rules*, i.e. by renouncing rational self-interest and taking the masochistic path towards depletion and absolute loss.

[122] Horace 1926, *Satires*, I.i.63–4.   [123] *AS* vii, lines 5–6.

[124] Thereby flouting the dictum of Horace 1926, *Ars Poetica* (line 385), that the ideal poet whom he addresses 'will say nothing and do nothing against Minerva's will' [*Tu nihil invita dices faciesve Minerva*]. This statement of subversion on Sidney's part is one that the (typically idealist) Scott 2013 (9) will seek to restore: 'I say, with Horace, nothing can be done *invita Minerva*.'

not an understanding of true wisdom that Sidney shares.[125] From this perspective, the 'doctrine of ignorance, and many words sometimes I have heard spent in it' (105.16–17) that the speaker takes it upon himself to reprove (and which should include, logically, his own not inconsiderable contribution to those many words, and no less profitlessly spent) is, truth be told, what the counter-argument of the *Defence* finds itself promoting loud and clear.[126] As so often when this happens, the speaker hastily attempts to close things down:

> but because this reason is generally against all learning, as well as Poetry, or rather, all learning but Poetry; because it were too large a digression to handle, or at least too superfluous (since it is manifest that all government of action is to be gotten by knowledge, and knowledge best by gathering many knowledges, which is reading), I only, with Horace, to him that is of that opinion, *jubeo stultum esse libenter*.
> (105.17–23)

As also happens so often, however, the attempted shut-down fails, as the speaker's prose—jerky with repetitions ('learning', 'knowledge'), qualifications ('or rather', 'or at least'), redundancies ('too superfluous'), and apparent statements of the obvious ('it is manifest that')—is clearly protesting too much. It is the counter-argument that ends up having the last word when, in the *peroratio*—by which stage it may well have appeared to him that he had nothing left to lose—Sidney calls upon the readers

---

[125] See, for example: if men were to learn virtue from philosophy alone, 'they would swear they be brought to school again' (95.29); there are some for whom virtue is purely 'a school name' (96.4); 'Who is that ever was a scholar that doth not carry away some verses of Virgil, Horace, or Cato, which in his youth he learned, and even to his old age serve him for hourly lessons?' (102.8–11) as the Olney text has it; the Ponsonby version, however, adds the following far from flattering examples (and none from Virgil or Cato): from Horace 1926, *Epistles*, I.xviii.69: '*percontatorem fugito, nam garrulus idem est*' [Avoid a questioner, for he is also a tattler] (102.12); and from Ovid 1929, *Remedia Amoris* (line 686): '*Dum sibi quisque placet, credula turba sumus*' [while each of us flatters himself, we are a believing crew] (102.13). See also: 'Alexander left his schoolmaster, living Aristotle, behind him, but took dead Homer with him' (105.36–7); philosophers made 'a school-art of that which the poets did only teach by a divine delightfulness' (106.24–5); the schoolmasterly Daedalus with neither whose 'artificial rules nor imitative patterns, we much cumber ourselves withal' (109.43–110.1); the comic archetype of the 'self-wise-seeming schoolmaster' (113.9); 'I have found in divers smally learned courtiers a more sound style than in some professors of learning' (114.42–4); and it would be 'a piece of the Tower of Babylon's curse, that a man should be put to school to learn his mother-tongue' (115.19–20). Together with frequent references to truancy, to reading or learning the wrong things, and to bad or inappropriate schoolmasters or -mistresses in *Astrophil and Stella* (e.g. *AS* 1, 11, 16, 42, 46, 56, 61, 71, 73, 79, 90, 102; v, line 35, and vii, lines 11–12), not to mention the pedantic schoolmaster, Rombus, in *The Lady of May*, I think it would be fair to say that Sidney's references to the schoolroom do not exactly exude respect or gratitude.

[126] In the *peroratio*, Sidney finally situates himself among the company of those paradoxical praisers who 'do prodigally spend a great many wandering words' (101.1), thereby illustrating rather than countering the antipoetic charge that 'a man might better spend his time' (102.22–3, 33). Note that in all these cases, words and time are *spent* rather than exchanged for something: i.e. the figure is not of a profitable transaction (trade, purchase, or sale) but rather a giving away (for nothing? for free?). Related to this is the way poetry's supposed delivery of teaching is figured as *stealing*: e.g. Aesop's allegories 'stealing under the formal tales of beasts' (92.5–6); the poet is a 'good-fellow' (i.e. thief) whose promise of entertainment will move even the hard-hearted to 'steal to see the form of goodness' (96.7, 8) before they are aware of it. Although in both cases stealing is used in the sense of covertly entering, there remains a residual sense, as Maslen (180) notes, of '"steal" meaning to obtain unlawfully'. As prodigal or thief, the poet or poetry does not figure as the sober bourgeois shopkeeper or banker.

of the *Defence* 'no more to laugh at the name of poets, as though they were next inheritors to fools' (116.22–3). He had never, I suggest, more sincerely meant what he said in the *Defence*, even if he could only get away with saying it as a joke.[127]

∞

If the poet's golden world is to be more than a merely capitalist venture, then— more than a means of transacting those exchanges or commodity trades—perhaps it can only do so if it is thought of in terms of *fool's gold*: as that which exposes—and so evacuates, empties out—the lure, fascination, and power of a fetishized metal. Such might be the poetry that (in the form of tragedy) shows 'upon how weak foundations gilden roofs are builded' (98.29–30) or (in the form of paradoxical praise) how 'self-love is better than any gilding to make that seem gorgeous wherein ourselves are parties' (81.21–2).[128] From the bankers' point of view, to opt for fool's gold over the 'real' thing is naturally to make an idiotic and irrational choice, yet it is also to align with those traditions that have sought to oppose the supremacy of their 'logical' thought from Longinus on.[129] In the case of More, and arguably Erasmus and Sidney as well, it is to anticipate those modes of thinking that, as Goux characterizes them, would seek an 'exit'—a 'passage beyond'—the logic of a capitalist economy that was becoming increasingly entrenched, not to say global-ized.[130] As the 'possibility of superseding the general equivalent structure loomed

---

[127] Equally ironic is the invitation to believe, 'with Aristotle', that poets were the 'treasurers of the Grecians' divinity' (116.24–5), i.e. that they kept the gods of antiquity alive in the collective memory bank (for this figuration of memory, see also 88.4; 90.39; and 101.37; and contrast the violent conquests of Britain that sought to 'ruin all memory of learning', 83.31, i.e. to ransack the bank rather than stock or replenish it). The reference quickly unravels, however, since it alludes to a discussion in Aristotle 1935, *Metaphysics*, 1000a—in which the school of Hesiod 'and all the cosmologists [θεολόγοι]' are said to have attributed first principles to the gods or things generated from gods— that was subsequently misinterpreted by Boccaccio as a statement to the effect that 'the first poets were theologians': see Boccaccio 1930 (46, 163n). The irony in the *peroratio* is directed not at poets' godlike powers of creation but rather at their co-opted role as culture's treasurers, just as those who treat them as such are ironically destined to be 'most fair, most rich, most wise, most all' (116.40).

[128] Asserting her happy superiority over the philosophers whose insistence on learning has been a bane to mankind and made them miserable, Erasmus' Folly blithely contrasts 'the good simple people of the olde *golden worlde*, [who] without any disciplines at all, liued onely as Nature taught, and instincted theim': see Erasmus 1549 (F3ᵛ, italics original). A few lines earlier she similarly praised the felicity of animals in their natural state: 'as an horse, who can [i.e. knows] not his grammer, is not wretched, no more a man for his Folie is myserable, because it agreeth so aptly with his nature' (F3). It is as just such a horse, perhaps, that Sidney might 'have wished myself' (81.20) at the beginning of the *Defence*. Of poets, Folly notes that their study is 'naught els, than to fede fooles eares with mere trifles and foolisshe fables' (L1), and to them 'more than to any other, bothe *Selfeloue*, and *Adulacion* are annexed familiarly, and of no kynde of men am I obserued more plainly, nor more constantly' (L1–L1ᵛ, italics original).

[129] See Derrida 1992 (35) on the 'madness' of that which opposes or flouts the logic of economy— such as the gift—and its concomitant resistance to theorization or even nomination: as something that exceeds such economic logic, it has no place—is '*atopos*'—and thus constitutes 'the extraordinary, the unusual, the strange, the extravagant, the absurd, the mad', and is, specifically, a '*utopic* madness' (emphasis original). See also Adorno 2005 (73) on the 'fool's truth' as the only thing capable of mitigating 'the sickness implacably dictated by the healthy common sense of the rest'.

[130] Goux 1990 (5). See also Goux's paraphrase of Bataille's thinking with respect to the theoretical and political extremity required to think outside of money thought: 'in theory—*beyond* the principle of centralization and not hunkering *within its limits* as does every anarchist or confederalist regression—

with increasing pervasiveness and complexity', Goux notes, so critiques of the idealist philosophy that lay at its heart would prompt assaults from numerous quarters, the 'reversal of idealism' proposed by Nietzsche and Marx, and the 'departure from metaphysics' by Heidegger and Derrida, among them (4, 5). In Sidney's case (as in More's) the 'simple' Indians with their pre-monetary economy may well have prompted thoughts of how money thought, gold-fetishism, and the capitalist rapacities and tyrannies that otherwise stood to dominate the early modern world might—even if only in creative fiction—be opted out of or defied. In Sidney's case (as in Erasmus'), the foolish, lazy, idle, ignorant, unlearned, self-loving, happy reader may well have shown, in a kind of *via negativa*, a way of countering the dialectic of idealist philosophy and its relentlessly positive thinking, by simply 'unthinking' it.[131] If Sidney found himself harbouring a distaste for, not to say a growing aversion towards the model of poetry as profitable, bankable, dependable, and defensible that was increasingly coming to dominate cultural discourse—even if only reactively and (quite possibly) to his own surprise—he would already have been out of step with the times: already querying the 'logic' of the general equivalent and resisting its sway. Since a dislike of profitability would already have been 'illogical' anyway, cultivating a preference for the unprofitable need not have been anything other than the intuitive and emotional development described earlier on.[132] Indeed, precisely because such a response would have been instinctive, 'unthinking', affective, felt, there was nothing to prevent it—and

the very thought of the general equivalent (which finds its theory in idealist philosophy) would have to be *decapitated* to pave the way for a polymorphic, acephelous social organization that would challenge the monopolies on representation' (46–7, emphases original). For Goux, one of the more theoretically promising ways of achieving such a 'transcendence of the sociosymbolic system governed by the logic of general equivalents' (6) is by studying 'Utopian fiction and its significant predilection, since Thomas More, for economic exchange without money, as well as for religion without images' (7). For Jameson 1991 (206), likewise, thinking beyond capitalism poses the same theoretical challenge: 'we are *inside* the culture of the market and . . . the inner dynamic of the culture of consumption is an infernal machine from which one does not escape by the taking of thought (or moralizing positions), an infinite propagation and replication of "desire" that feeds on itself and has no outside and no fulfillment' (emphasis original). Like Goux, he, too, looks to the Utopian by way of an answer, although with the crucial proviso that 'Utopia' is not idealized or positivized in the process: what Utopian writers aim for is 'something rather different from achieved positivity' (208). Rather, they demonstrate, 'for their own time and culture, the *impossibility* of imagining Utopia. It is thus the limits, the systemic restrictions and repressions, or empty places, in the Utopian blueprint that are the most interesting, for these alone testify to the ways a culture or a system marks the most visionary mind and contains its movement toward transcendence. But such limits, which can also be discussed in terms of ideological restriction, are concrete and articulated in the great Utopian visions: they do not become visible except in the desperate attempt to imagine something else' (208, emphasis original).

[131] See also Agrippa 1569 (Aaa3ᵛ), the conclusion of whose treatise Sidney seems to echo in his *peroratio*: 'it is better therefore and more profitable to be Idiotes, and knowe nothinge to beleue by Faithe and charitee, and to become next vnto God, the*n* being lofty & prowde through the subtilties of sciences to fall into the possession of the Serpente'; 'there is no beaste so able to receiue diuinitee as the Asse, into whome if yee shall not be tourned, yee shall not be able to carrie the diuine misteries' (Bbb1).

[132] On the complex affective economies of the period, Leinwand 1999 (140–1) concludes: 'The early modern English economy, considerably less theorized than our own, must certainly have operated according to a blend of cognition and affect.' 'No master trope, even an implicitly affective trope premised upon a transition from passions to interests, is adequate to the multiplicity of men's and women's affective engagements with a changing economy' (142–3).

everything to encourage it—being taken to the furthest possible extreme: this preference for the unprofitable becoming, in turn, a downright cult of the profitless, of expenditure without income, of prodigality without forgiveness, of sacrifice without redemption.

A number of critics have identified in Sidney and other Renaissance writers the draw and appeal of this otherwise perverse cult of *dépense*: of expenditure, gambling, debt, loss, waste, bankruptcy, insolvency, dissolution, suicide, and self-destruction. Robert Matz, for example, notes that the *Defence* evokes 'a golden world of pleasure rather than labor . . . the freedom to play rather than to work'— this signifying the courtly world of conspicuous consumption with its prodigy houses, extravagant parks and gardens, entertainments and masques, fine food and expensive clothes—and that, as such, it 'negotiates Sidney's ambivalence about profitability itself'.[133] Indeed, 'unprofitability returns in the *Defence* as an embarrassing waste' (68), the foregrounded act of writing defying the end of well-doing only and becoming, instead, mere 'excess, straying, and waste' (76). On those occasions when the ending end of all earthly learning really *is* virtuous action, moreover—when it culminates in that apogee of heroic action which is military service in support of the state—this turns out to be no less wasteful either, death on the battlefield (including Sidney's own particularly pointless and unproductive one) being the ultimate form of aristocratic expenditure: 'Spending without reserve, the gentleman enjoys a privileged freedom to destroy even himself' (84). Matz's explicit model here is Richard Halpern's celebrated reading of *King Lear* as a systematic portrayal of this courtly tendency towards self-destruction: '*Dépense* resembles aristocratic expense', Halpern writes, 'but perfects it . . . by refusing to recoup its losses through the cultural capital of the consumption sign. It moves beyond mere luxury or display to the realm of the gamble, the challenge, suicide, madness'.[134] In Lear's self-divestiture of kingdom and power it is not 'the magnitude of the display but the intensity of loss that counts' (264–5). 'Any scale will do, as long as it admits of total depletion' (265). Some question remains in this reading, however, over whether such a passage 'beyond' consumption is really possible or such a totality of loss achievable, for is *something* not recouped in these grand gestures of self-annihilation? This courtly self-divestiture, for example, is characterized as a contest in which Cordelia, in renouncing her own kingdom and patrimony, effectively outbids her father's 'aggressive generosity' (249) with a calculated act of still greater self-denial and so wins the 'game' (250). Similarly, *dépense* is said to offer a tragic 'but ennobling' (266) alternative to mere display, a 'more heroic form of expense' (267), the critic's language of comparison—of 'more'—hinting that, for all their frantic nostalgia for contrastingly 'feudal' values that are being steadily eroded by capitalist ones—Shakespeare's aristocrats are unable entirely to escape from the invidious and all-pervasive logic of the latter.

---

[133] Matz 2000 (67, 68). Matz thus develops Rudenstine 1967 (46–52) who argues that the lures of courtly leisure, love, and play which Sidney indulges elsewhere in his life and art—in particular in the writing and contents of the *Old Arcadia*—are suppressed in the *Defence*.

[134] Halpern 1991 (264).

Some form of capital is still retained, even in the 'maddest' moments of self-obliteration: a transaction still takes place, as life is exchanged for winning the game, for one last glorious flare of transcendent power before the light goes out.[135] This lingering doubt over whether it is possible to theorize absolute loss—a loss that is *not* recouped as symbolic capital in some way—is something that registers in Halpern's conclusion, where he admits that this 'cultural redemption entails a complex relation with the material economies of consumption' (267).[136] Thus, *dépense* is said to be 'enabled' by and 'able to feed on' the destruction of symbolic values—that is, it is still capable of positivizing loss—even though it does not aim at self-reproduction since its very basis is 'a suicidal exhaustion of value' (267). '*Dépense* cannot extend or transcend the limits of its material; it simply reverses course and rushes towards implosion rather than conserve or dilute itself. Turning loss into a positive value, it chooses a catastrophic and tragic end over slow depletion' (267–8). Halpern's language here—of the material and of reversal—captures very precisely, I think, the critic's dilemma: the difficulty he faces in practice—even when theorizing extreme loss and an aristocratic 'defiance' of capitalist values—of finally escaping from the ambient logic of capital that seems able to re-appear ghost-like and to re-insinuate itself in even the darkest moments of tragic desperation. The problem Halpern's conclusion points to, in other words, is that challenging the idealist philosophy behind the logic of capital by means of a materialist critique runs the risk—in simply reversing the terms and so valuing, fetishizing the material instead—of keeping the structural logic of capital, and with it of the general equivalent, intact. While such a move has historically, celebratedly, been an essential step in the struggle against idealism and capitalist hegemony, it does not in itself constitute the terminal overthrow on which any escape from that logic would ultimately depend.[137]

One critic who is especially sensitive to the difficulties of theorizing scenes of wilful self-destruction in Renaissance texts without, in one way or another, recouping or capitalizing them is Jonathan Crewe: his reading of the 'suicidal poetics' of the Earl of Surrey—a figure who sets a 'stellar precedent' for Sidney in numerous

[135] Poetry remains similarly capitalized in Matz 2000 (75)—it is 'an alternative form of capital: a particular form of cultural capital'—even if Sidney remains ambivalent about its value. For Matz, 'understanding the uncertain value of poetry during the period requires understanding the uncertain cultural values to which this poetry responded' (17). While Leinwand 1999 goes further than either Halpern or Matz in acknowledging the presence of the death drive behind economically self-destructive or suicidal behaviours, he too concludes that such tragic bids to escape from the logic of self-interest ultimately fail and/or are balanced by comedic moves towards recovery: as in his two readings, alternately 'tragic' and 'comic', of the *Merchant of Venice* (13–23, 113–20).

[136] See also Landreth 2012 (185) for whom waste—'most disruptive to the paradigms of...commonwealth discourse'—is similarly theorized/dialecticized as being *really* 'productive', culturally and financially speaking.

[137] See Goux 1990 (6): 'Even if this "materialist" direction may be considered as a simple turnabout that leaves the oppositional structure intact, it is situated in a strategy that challenges the logic of general equivalents by reinstating what the metaphysics of *value* and *idea* (that is, metaphysics period) was obliged to eliminate in the course of its development' (emphasis original). For a further discussion of Nietzsche's (ultimately unsuccessful) attempt to terminate such discourse and Marx's (more successful) one, see ibid. (88–111).

ways—being a case in point.[138] For Crewe, the story Surrey tells about himself is one in which 'a "poetics of suicide" is elaborated, and it is therefore irreducibly a story of willfully embraced failure or defeat' (51). Surrey's problem, however, is just how easily his suicidal bids—which include, for example, repeated moves to flaunt the superiority of his name and claim over those of the King—can end up by 'suiciding' themselves in their recuperation of capital of some kind: whether in an 'aggressive-defensive self-construction' (51), an heroically re-asserted masculinity, or the killer move in a deadly game of courtly one-upmanship. In the sonnet about the suicide of Sardanapalus, for instance,—in which Surrey 'suicidally' appears to implicate Henry VIII in the unnaturalness and degeneracy of the Assyrian king— Surrey's action can still be recuperated as either the morally logical end of a lifetime of unmanly dissipation or as promoting a contrastingly manly *virtus*. The Roman tradition of stoic, heroic, anti-degenerate suicide is always going to be capable of recouping this '"sick," "Assyrian" ending' (56), with the result that a position of absolute loss—unrecuperable and fully masochistic—effectively becomes an impossibility: 'no gesture that Surrey ever makes towards establishing an openly death-*wishing*, perverse, or Teutonic Petrarchanism is thus ever likely to succeed' (57, emphasis original). Elsewhere, however, Crewe suggests that, where this recuperative 'logic' lies primarily in critical strategies, rather than in the Renaissance texts to which these get applied, there is a better hope—once those strategies are put to one side—of finding in those texts just such scenes of extreme possibility.[139] Impatient with reductively 'careerist' readings of Spenser, for example,—and with the critical strategies they exemplify which attempt to contain the wildness, exuberance, violence, vandalism, surprise, and scandal of the 'illogical' as it appears in the period's literature—Crewe asks whether the earth-born, 'Dionysiac' Red Crosse Knight can really be said to represent an ideal of sixteenth-century Protestantism without also invoking its '"imaginative" madness'. 'Does this almost unbridled fantasy of the clownish, lowborn "knight" . . . ultimately reconstructed as the patron saint of the kingdom, constitute an authoritative ideal . . . or a symptomatic delirium of the imperialistic English sixteenth century'?[140] (Much the same might be asked of More's Utopians, Erasmus' Folly, or Sidney's 'simple Indians'.) Suspicious of the critical move that unduly tames or domesticates erotic fantasies by inserting them into 'a benign dialectic of cultural production in which forms of irrational excess either disappear or get absorbed', Crewe makes the case that such cultural production remains bound to 'forms of potentially destructive irrationality ("madness")', and that to understand or appreciate the role of those fantasies cannot be to 'settle for "work" or "production" alone' (92).

---

[138] Crewe 1990 (62). Cf. Hadfield 1994 (135–6, 142–8) who similarly links Sidney with Surrey but does so in order to shore up the presumptively 'courtly' values of social superiority, the will to power, and militant, masculine imperialism.

[139] Strier 1995 (5–6) is similarly sympathetic to this type of inquiry: the 'notion of "unthinkability" seems to me a very dangerous one', he comments, 'It is another sort of a priori. It makes it necessary for a critic or scholar to explain away—or simply not see—moments in texts where the "unthinkable" is actually thought'.

[140] Crewe 1986 (91).

This willingness to defy the Protestant work ethic—and the whole capitalist agenda of productivity and profitability that goes with it—is a refreshing example of the willingness to question the apparently automatic and self-evident nature of its 'logic'. Applying this to Sidney, however, seems to encounter a considerable degree of resistance, as if the Establishment's poster boy for a legitimate and defensible professional literary criticism somehow exerts a kind of force-field around himself to discourage even the most willing critic and to ward off any thoughts he or she might have of deconstructing it. In Crewe's first book, for example, Sidney appears as the (golden?) foil to Thomas Nashe, whose 'scandalous' authorship, by contrast, promotes an excess of style over content that, in defiance of all logocentric proprieties, is 'not economically proportioned to it'.[141] Nashe's praise of the red herring in *Lenten Stuffe* (1599) is read as a mock encomium, but not Sidney's *Defence* which, by way of comparison, is routinely upheld as the classic articulation of idealist values and the 'redeemed', logocentric, metaphysical poetics they sponsor.[142] The closest Crewe comes to deconstructing the latter is in the essay in *Hidden Designs* that mentions the *Defence* briefly before proceeding to a similarly 'scandalous' reading of *Astrophil and Stella*. As impatient here as in the Spenser essay with reductively careerist readings of Sidney, Crewe presents his own reading in terms of an alternative economy in which the (self-)'interest' of a critical profession that insists on seeing in Sidney's sonnet sequence a mirror-image of its own ambition and career-management is replaced by 'another and perhaps more exciting interest' (72) which does not simply reflect back to the literary critic a flattering portrait of him- or herself. The *Defence* gets only a passing mention here (as if that gilded mirror were still resistant to shattering), but it is one that indicates the way forward most precisely. That is to say, Crewe identifies the apparent idealism of Sidney's text as the *problem*—not the solution—to its interpretation. As he notes, new historicist critics also pick up on this, showing an observable preference for the *Art of English Poesy* over the *Defence*, presumably on account of its greater materialism: 'for the dislodgment of Sidney to have been effected it was also necessary for a sustained, general critique of critical "idealism" and/or "essentialism" to have occurred' (71). But, as the example of Halpern would suggest, turning to a materialist critique does not necessarily counter idealist thinking nor the logic of productivity that goes with it (indeed, Puttenham's demystification of poetry as 'really' doing political work commits it to capitalist enterprise wholeheartedly). Getting behind or 'beyond' idealist thinking requires, rather, a different kind of thinking altogether, one that does not have to turn every loss into a gain—the 'logic' of turning a profit—but is willing to look illogicality in the eye and to follow its lead into surprising places.

---

[141] Crewe 1982 (2).

[142] Ibid. (47, 52, 67). This tendency to treat Sidney as a foil to writers who can afford to be identified as radical or subversive is a common one. See e.g. Fineman 1986 and Hulse 2000, with respect to Shakespeare; Low 1993, with respect to Donne, Herbert, Crashaw, Carew, and Milton; Maslen 2003, with respect to Gascoigne; Ellinghausen 2008, with respect to Nashe and Jonson; Correll 2008, with respect to Donne; Landreth 2012, with respect to Spenser, Marlowe, Shakespeare, Nashe, and Donne; and Nicholson 2014, with respect to Lyly, Spenser, and Marlowe.

∞

One way of doing this might be to follow the example set by Freud when he comes to theorize masochism, a phenomenon that immediately strikes the observer as illogical and strange insofar as—in seeking out situations of suffering, pain, or loss—it appears to be at considerable variance from any form of rational self-interest. This is what Freud means, in the 1924 essay of that title, by 'the economic problem of masochism': masochism is 'mysterious from the economic point of view', because, as a practice that aims neither to ameliorate nor to optimize things but actively to make them worse, it is profoundly *un-* if not *anti*-economic.[143] Freud's thinking in this late (indeed, last) essay on the subject goes further than previous discussions because it draws closely on the text that first introduces 'an "economic" point of view into our work': 'economic' being inserted between scare quotes to suggest that, again, it is fundamentally *un*economic processes that will be under review.[144] That text, of course, is *Beyond the Pleasure Principle* (1920), the essay in which Freud traces his own passage beyond the realm of what might otherwise be considered normal or axiomatic economic thinking, and with it beyond one of the key axioms of his theory to date: namely, that wish fulfilment and the pursuit of pleasure constitute a guiding principle in all human action and motivation, unconscious as well as conscious. Staying on familiar territory to begin with, Freud considers activities that, in the first instance, appear to obey the *'economic* motive' insofar as they result in a 'yield of pleasure'.[145] His examples are children's play and works of literature that represent and repeat unpleasant experiences so as to take command of them aesthetically: the payback or profitable gain of pleasure the transaction yields in such cases—the recuperation or cancellation of unpleasure with interest—being the 'instinct for mastery' (16) to which they give rise.[146] Such reflections, however, are quickly left behind, as being 'of no use for *our* purposes', since they remain firmly inside economic thinking and so fail to forge a passage that goes '*beyond* the pleasure principle' (17, emphasis original). To do this, Freud reconsiders a phenomenon that illustrates the 'mysterious masochistic trends of the ego' (14) and that had remained as strangely resistant to theorization as it did to treatment: namely, the compulsion to repeat. In the form of flashbacks or nightmares that take trauma victims back to the scene of their ordeal, or the seemingly fateful, 'daemonic' force that causes some individuals to repeat unresolved oedipal dilemmas throughout their lives in the recurrence of distressing situations and self-destructive behaviours, often with startling exactitude, the compulsion to

---

[143] Freud 1924 (159). This essay forms the culmination of a series of earlier attempts to theorize masochism: in the *Three Essays on the Theory of Sexuality* (1905), 'Instincts and their Vicissitudes' (1915), and '"A Child is Being Beaten"' (1919).

[144] Freud 1920 (7). The scare quotes are Strachey's.

[145] Ibid. (14). Note that Strachey puts *'economic'* in italics when the word is intended to convey what is understood as the *'normal'* (also italicized) sense of the term, i.e. as tending towards profitability.

[146] The child in Freud's famous example is thus said to have 'compensated himself' for the unpleasure of his mother's absences by means of the *'fort, da!'* game, his renunciation of instinctual satisfaction signifying his 'great cultural achievement': Ibid. (15).

repeat flatly defies the pleasure principle in that it recalls and re-enacts experiences from the past 'which include no possibility of pleasure, and which can never, even long ago, have brought satisfaction even to instinctual impulses which have since been repressed' (20). No 'lesson has been learnt' from these old experiences that led only to unpleasure, and yet they find themselves being repeated 'under pressure of a compulsion' (21).

As Freud pursues this line of thought, he speculates about ways in which the mental apparatus might be understood to deal with quantities of energy, stimulus, or excitation that come to it both from the external world without and from its own internal processes within. In this scenario, a functioning or economic model would be one in which those energies are successfully 'bound'—that is, contained, defused, and kept to a minimum—pleasure being defined as the reduction or control of these otherwise unwanted, unpleasurable, and disruptive elements by means of regulating, cancelling, or in a word 'mastering' (30) them. A dysfunctional or uneconomic model, by contrast—that causes 'economic disturbances comparable with traumatic neuroses' (34)—would be one in which those energies are *not* so mastered, turned, or recuperated but permitted, rather, to flood the organism destructively with an unpleasant excess of stimuli. These speculations, in turn, lead Freud to a famous—or infamous—but either way 'strange' (36) conclusion: namely, that if pleasure consists in *reducing* the quantity of excitation, then its ultimate aim would logically be to eliminate such excitation altogether and to deliver the organism back to the condition of maximal quietude and stillness from which it came: the inorganic state. More primitive, elementary, and instinctual than the pleasure principle, the death drive moves into a position of logical and chronological priority to it, so that, paradoxically, the aim of all life becomes death, and the ultimate pleasure, extinction. (Such would be the 'openly death-*wishing*, perverse, or Teutonic Petrarchanism' that Crewe attributes to the Earl of Surrey.) As a form of 'primary masochism' (55), the death drive thus allows Freud finally to theorize the otherwise baffling masochistic tendencies that direct the human subject towards the definitively uneconomic goals of absolute negativity and unrecuperable loss.[147] One consequence of this is that the life-instincts emerge as highly deceptive—in the way they appear to promote survival and self-preservation— since 'in fact they are merely seeking to reach an ancient goal by paths alike old and new' (38). Seen in this new light, 'the theoretical importance of the instincts of self-preservation, of self-assertion and of mastery greatly diminishes. They are component instincts whose function it is to assure that the organism shall follow its own path to death' (39). Indeed, the life-instincts begin to behave rather like the reality principle here—in the way they, too, postpone ultimate satisfaction and promote the toleration of unpleasure on the 'long indirect road to pleasure' (10)—and thereby to resemble (although this is not a connection Freud makes) the prudent bourgeois who has learned to delay gratification, to hold something in reserve, and

---

[147] Where Freud's earlier essays on masochism had derived it from a previous or existing sadism, the 1924 essay, following *Beyond the Pleasure Principle*, rejects this dialectical model and firmly posits the existence of a 'primary' or 'original' masochism: Freud 1924 (162, 164).

to keep money in the bank. Like the pleasure principle, however, the life-instincts remain subordinate to the death drive whose function they serve—the thrifty, economical banker in service to the 'foolish', uneconomic spendthrift who is nonetheless master—and that marks the end of that circuitous path that leads fools the way to dusty death: the terminal point at which all will be spent, in one last breath, for the final pleasure of nothing, of silence.

If I set out Freud's modelling of the masochistic tendency at some length here, it is because it is one on which other critics writing on courtly *dépense*, and indeed on Sidney's *Defence*, have also drawn. Richard Halpern, for example, considers the question of pleasure in More's *Utopia* and concludes that, for the Utopians, pleasure corresponds to the regulated, 'economic' model of the organism as described above: its flows of excitation fully mastered and 'bound', any surpluses or depletions being carefully balanced out, so as to lead to the calm, peaceful existence, undisturbed by any disorder, that for Halpern represents the 'economy of the zero degree'.[148] The critic is explicit in attributing this model to Freud's theorizations in *Beyond the Pleasure Principle*. What he does not do, however, is take full cognizance of the death drive: that is, acknowledge that such regulation, control, and minimizing of excitation only serves the purposes of the latter— extinction or a return to the inanimate state being the pleasure to end all pleasures—and that, in holding off or postponing the latter, the economic virtues of regulation and balance do not strictly constitute pleasure at all.[149] By conflating the calm, regulated body with a return to the zero level—a state of complete rest—Halpern in effect collapses the primary processes into the secondary ones, for the death drive is not equivalent to an 'economy of the zero degree' (that is just an optimally efficient economy). The death drive represents, rather, a passage beyond economism altogether, to a place (no place?) where there is no 'economic' thinking at all, no economy, period: zero economy. The critic's reluctance to acknowledge the death drive, however, effectively rules out any possibility that his own argument—or those of the texts he writes about—might also escape, or seek to escape, from the money thought that is otherwise assumed to be all-encompassing, any alternative 'beyond' it being reduced to the unthinkable. Instead, Halpern condemns himself to remaining within the parameters of that presumptively universal logic, one consequence of which is that his account of the *Utopia* forecloses any potentially radical reading to which that text might lend itself. Thus, the critic ends up reading More's text as one in which the Utopian

---

[148] Halpern 1991 (172).

[149] Allowances could be made for Halpern's oversight on the grounds that the term Freud uses in *Beyond the Pleasure Principle* is the 'Nirvana principle': see Freud 1920 (56). The 'death drive' was more fully elaborated, and first named as such—*Todestrieb*—in *The Ego and the Id*: see Freud 1923 (40) ('drive' now accepted as the preferred translation of *Trieb*, rather than Strachey's controversial 'instinct'). The 'Nirvana principle' could be thought to connote a sense of peacefulness rather than one of non-existence. However, when Halpern 1991 (172) describes Freud's metapsychology as a version of 'essentialism', and claims that the economy of the zero degree, apparently naturalized by Freud, is 'frequently refuted by social practice' (173), it becomes clear that the 'Freud' he refers to is the foundationalist Freud of ego-psychology rather than the anti-foundationalist and other-centred Freud of Lacan, Laplanche, and the French school.

system is finally exploded or deconstructed by the underlying logic of the general equivalent (commodity–fetishism, class domination, conspicuous consumption, and all the rest) which, as the repressed returned, inescapably bursts through from below. The surface appearance of a utopian socialist society is thus found to conceal 'an "interior" realm whose primal fantasy and pleasurable substance turn out to be—the logic of capital itself' (141). Pleasure is thereby co-opted by capitalism as, for Halpern, the real, secret pleasure of More's text turns out to be not its exposure of the latter but rather its liberating explosion of the Utopians' pseudo-pleasure and a joyous release into free market economics. His prize example being the golden chamber pots which symptomatically manifest the very fetishism which the Utopians' ritual debasement of the metal had sought to deny, Halpern's strategy here explicitly follows that of Stephen Greenblatt who similarly reads proscriptions within the *Utopia* as indications of repressed desire.[150] In readings of this kind, the idea that More might be relentlessly satirizing capitalist logic—excoriating the voracious landlords, the evils of enclosures, and the human costs of a nascent capitalist economy that he was able to apprehend with a piercingly clear eye—is, however politely acknowledged, severely compromised. Instead, More emerges as the unwitting agent of a capitalist logic that finally overpowers any attempt he might have made to think outside of it. With the type of reversal that characterizes arguments of this kind, Halpern locates, behind what the *Utopia*'s narrator, Hythlodaeus, identifies as the real social problem in sixteenth-century England—the lack of subsistence—a 'corresponding term' (159), namely, *excess*. This excess manifests in the insatiable gluttony of the enclosing landlords who throw tenants off their property so as to maximize their profits; yet within the logic of the argument, this quality of excess quickly slides across from gluttony, greed, and the accursed hunger for gold, to a mobilization of *desire*. Excess becomes a guilty pleasure, a secret vice, and since 'the desire to accumulate is infinite' (160), it can accordingly know of no solution, no reform. The capitalist presuppositions of Halpern's argument, that is, prevent him from theorizing negativity as such (it is invariably an opportunity for turning a profit). Thus, greed, hunger, and desire are not conceived of as negativities—as a want or lack (of, for example, subsistence)—but, as the 'corresponding term', they are positivized, exactly as, in his reading of *King Lear*, *dépense* is recouped as symbolic capital: as the conspicuous consumption that such extravagant behaviour pays for and buys, with no other end in view than coming out on top and winning the

---

[150] See Greenblatt 1980 (33–58). Deng 2011 (70–86) reads the *Utopia* in a similar way, his charge that More 'has difficulty thinking beyond monetary systems' (71) being perhaps more applicable to his own set of assumptions than to More's. Such interpretations of More's text characterize the new-historicist mode of analysis as critiqued by Jameson 1991: i.e. that such discussions of money thought and its economic logic can end up by presupposing that 'logic', thereby naturalizing and replicating it rather than submitting it to rigorous analysis or deconstruction. Much the same applies, I would suggest, to those readings of the *Defence* that, as Matz 2000 (3, 8) argues, unconsciously repeat rather than analyse the humanist construction of literature as pedagogic, profitable, and productive, not least because it is in the interests of a literary critical profession to do so. Equally indicative is the tendency of Landreth 2012 (236) to treat dialectical thinking as thought per se, with a corresponding dismissal of what he calls 'escapist, nostalgic-utopian fantasies on the part of capital's critics in the present'.

game of power.[151] What is absent here is any sense that such expenditure might *not* buy anything, might get *nothing* in return: that is, that *dépense* comes under the sign of nullity, of an absolute negativity that, according to the logic of capital, can only appear masochistic, death-wishing, and perverse. Since the argument has firmly relegated the latter to the realm of the unthinkable, it naturally does not appear in Halpern's book, but that does not mean to say that this paradoxical counter-logic—this ability to think otherwise—does not exist elsewhere: in Freud, for example, or Goux, or Bataille, or Sidney, or Shakespeare, or Erasmus, or More.[152]

A similarly partial reading of *Beyond the Pleasure Principle*—which yields similarly partial results—occurs in Margaret Ferguson's book on Renaissance defences of poetry, Sidney's among them. Freud's discussion of the organism's ability or otherwise to 'bind' excitatory stimuli is here taken to model the processes of psychic defence that Ferguson sees as underlying all literary defences of poetry, including academic literary criticism itself. Citing Freud's observation that the organism seeks to master or bind stimuli that arise from within, as well as from without—by bringing a protective shield into operation against these as well—Ferguson describes this as a 'metapsychological *prise de position*' and uses it as the foundation for the analyses that follow.[153] As Freud makes clear in the next sentence, however, while these preliminary discussions serve to clarify the operations of the pleasure principle—the various means by which the organism seeks to reduce or control an otherwise unpleasurable amount of stimuli—they have as yet failed to deliver him to the point where his investigations are heading, that is, *beyond* the pleasure principle: to do that, it is necessary to 'go a step further'.[154] This step—towards the recognition that there are cases where the defence fails, where the defensive shield is inadequate or absent, where unpleasure is allowed to flood the organism, and where such traumatic experiences are compulsively repeated in a way that is powerfully resistant to cure—is not one that Ferguson takes. Moreover, she has a

---

[151] Applying Bataille's theory to *King Lear*, Halpern 1991 (164) describes his account of 'destructive expenditure' as a functional version of 'recouping apparent sacrifice for a surplus of prestige and political power'. Matz 2000 (84n), who follows Halpern in his reading of Sidney's *Defence*, misreads Bataille in a similar way. For Bataille, however, excess is explicitly *not* greed, conspicuous consumption, or surplus. Rather, it is waste—the excremental, the unproductive—his entire project being to theorize such unrecuperable loss and thereby to 'decapitate' capitalism: to argue that 'the possibilities of human existence can as of now be located *beyond* the formation of monocephalous societies', *Acéphale* 2 (1937), quoted by Goux 1990 (46, emphasis original); a point emphasized by Derrida 1978 (317–50).

[152] The *Utopia* can mount a critique of idealist thinking (the logic of the general equivalent) without presenting the Utopian system as an ideal. Insofar as the latter shows itself to be prone to that logic—in its weakness for those golden chamber pots, for example—it is no less prone to attack than any other economic system. The purpose of More's text is less to propose an alternative economic system (which is more or less a contradiction in terms) than to propose an alternative kind of thought. A simple reversal of idealist logic (such as that effected by materialist critique) does not necessarily arrive at this, since for the most part it keeps the structure of the general equivalent intact. What is required is to show that the logic of the general equivalent is just that—*a logic*—not an immutable law but just one way of thinking that need not exclude others: i.e. that idealism is an ideology, not the truth. The notion that the *Utopia*—as '*Eutopia*'—represents an ideal of some kind has led many readers astray. On this see also Jameson 1991 (208–9) and 2005 (12).

[153] Ferguson 1983 (15).   [154] Freud 1920 (29).

tendency to refer to the organism—what Freud figures illustratively as living matter in its simplest possible form, 'an undifferentiated vesicle of a substance that is susceptible to stimulation'—as the *ego*, which is by no means the same thing.[155] The approximation nonetheless licenses her to imagine the latter as a homunculus in various defensive positions, and to base her account of Renaissance defences of poetry on this model accordingly: Sidney's *Defence*, for example, is captioned 'The Egoistic Project' (138). Notwithstanding the complexity of Freud's various and changing models of the mental topography—and his admittedly confusing treatment in *Beyond the Pleasure Principle* of the so-called 'ego-instincts'—Ferguson's reading of Freud here evinces the same curious blindness to the death drive that Halpern's did, and a distinct unwillingness (also like the latter) to follow Freud in his reflections on what he called 'the mysterious masochistic trends of the ego'. On the contrary, Ferguson presents the defences of poetry examined in her book as advocating 'what we might call the claims of the ego' (12), proceeding to quote Sidney on the self-love that is better than any gilding in order to conjure an essentially narcissistic scene of self-interest, self-promotion, and self-advancement. Even if they have to redeem their fallen natures to do so, Sidney and other defenders of poetry (including literary critics) are said to 'all long for a golden world in which the poet would be master of his own territory' (17). That this golden world is clearly an idealized not to say idealist one becomes evident (although its masculinist, capitalist, and colonialist implications remain unexamined) in Ferguson's account of the 'economy' (146) of Sidney's *Defence*: a discussion that begins with Menenius Agrippa's fable of the mutinous body.[156] For Ferguson, Sidney uses this story to show poetry as a 'beneficent power, a power which masters only in order to serve the general good' (140), the subduing of the rebellious limbs against the 'unprofitable' belly serving to mend a breach, recover the status quo, and restore balance: 'to reestablish a balance of power in the body of culture' (141). This restoration—figured as both a kind of bodily homeostasis and an economic turning of the unprofitable back into profit again—is presented as a return to the normal state of things. Similarly, within the ideal economy of the *Defence* as a whole, 'weakness on one front is strength on another' (146), suggesting that the game of one-upmanship is evidently still in full swing and that, on balance, power—or 'strength'—is destined to come out on top. Business as usual, then. The only point at which Ferguson entertains the possibility that Sidney may have sought something beyond this all-enveloping and apparently self-evident picture of normality is when she considers his use of irony. For a brief moment, the self-undercutting irony of, for example, the 'better than any gilding' statement—which effectively 'denies us the pleasure of deconstructing the text because it has already been deconstructed' (153)—is permitted to destabilize the otherwise relentless ascent of the argument's dialectic, putting all Sidney's claims for poetry 'into radical

---

[155] Ibid. (26).
[156] See also Stillman 2008 (120): 'The tales of [Menenius] Agrippa and Nathan are introduced at an especially crucial juncture in the methodically designed economy of Sidney's argument' as a final 'demonstration' or 'proof' of poetry's ultimately salvific function.

question' (153), much as the tradition of paradoxical praise also destabilizes knowledge so as to leave the ironist suspended, hovering in a vertiginous, permanently self-doubting state of unknowing: 'here signifiers truly float' (157).[157] This heady prospect, however, having been briefly floated, is rapidly shut down and the usual defensive arsenal brought into play: morality, virtue, pedagogy, learning ('the educational role of self-love', 155), faith ('one *must* accept, on faith, the claim Sidney makes for the ideal poet', 156, my emphasis), redemption, the Logos, the Platonic and Christian 'foundation' (159), and so on.[158] This is what it takes to keep 'right' poetry on track and to ensure that—like the literary critical profession which has an interest in defending it—both remain thoroughly defensible to the end. If, at the close, Ferguson allows herself to question the ultimate success of Sidney's 'Egoistic Project' as a bid for mastery (all things—including his troubled relations with Elizabeth and lack of any real influence or power at court—being considered), it is nevertheless the case that the *Defence* has been co-opted to speak on behalf of a very particular—that is, profitable—model of poetry. The alternative—the possibility of a poetry that might not conform to this ideal economy, that might not be bankable, and that is, according to these criteria, thus quite indefensible—is banished from view, rather as Freud's theory of the death drive and its strangely irresistible, overpowering lure is, likewise, symptomatically blanked.

◌

To see this alternative, there is no better place to look, strangely enough, than Stephen Gosson, for the *Schoole of Abuse*—which has no interest in defending poetry—gives a very thorough and refreshingly un-conflicted picture of exactly this. The idea that poetry is fundamentally uneconomic—a bad bargain—is reiterated constantly throughout his text. Any wit, learning, or understanding that might be extracted from poetry is 'dearly bought' (77/A2), as poets, like so many con-men, 'sette theyr trumperie too sale without suspect' (77/A2–A2ᵛ). There is a strong sense of *caveat emptor* in the way the unwary, innocent reader is liable to be mis-sold fake, fraudulent, or counterfeit goods; to be cozened or defrauded into paying too high a price; to be subjected to daylight robbery.[159] Gosson presents himself as the 'Clarke of the market' (110/E4ᵛ) whose job it is to ensure equitable sales by

---

[157] Ferguson 1983 (11) suggests that the *Defence* has a close 'kinship' with this tradition, but in neither case is irony allowed to stand. Rather, epideixis is redeemed by virtue of its serious (i.e. self-interested) functions—moving, persuading, showing off—with a view to winning praise and fame for the poet himself. What drops out of the picture, in other words, is the notion of *paradox*: the idea—which Fineman 1986 explores at greater length—that the poet might choose to praise something that is *not ideal.*

[158] As above, the possibility of a motive for writing other than self-interest is ruled out (somewhat coercively) by means of a (somewhat coercive) reading of Kenneth Burke. Although he is said to have found it 'morally disturbing, to be sure', Burke 'nevertheless insists' on a phenomenon 'that the critic, and everyone else, *must* accept as a truth: all discourse is to some degree "motivated" by the author's desire for personal advantage, economic, political, or sexual': Ferguson 1983 (9, my emphasis), referencing Burke 1950 (268–9).

[159] See also 'An Apologie of the *Schoole of Abuse*' (130/L7ᵛ–L8): 'A theefe is a shrewde member in a common wealth, he empties our bagges by force, these [players] ransacke our purses by permission; he spoileth vs secretly; these rifle vs openly.'

confiscating vendors' scales when they are faulty and forfeiting their weights when they are false.[160] Against satisfying images of capital accumulated within the treasure-house—'Little Chestes may holde greate Treasure' (72/☞4)—poets are presented as the stark opposite, especially 'amarous Poets [who] dwelleth longest in those pointes, that profite least' (76/A1ᵛ) and who are duly expelled from Plato's *Republic* as 'vnprofitable members' (77/A3). Against satisfying accounts of mercantile wealth—'a fewe Cyphers contayne the sub*sta*nce of a rich Merchant' (73/☞4)—the number of good poets comprises a sorry roll-call: if the authorities 'shoulde call an acco*m*pt to see how many *Chirons, Terpandri,* and *Homers* are heere, they might cast the summe without pen, or counters, and sit downe with *Racha*, to weepe for her Children, because they were not' (84/B1ᵛ–B2). Its lack of substance or content, of course, justifies the ubiquitous charge of poetry's 'vanitie' (77/A2ᵛ, 78/A3, 81/A6, etc.). Against images of proper eating (an image cluster that Gosson returns to many times)—in which the models are those of nourishment (the wisdom of choosing what 'doth nourish best', 76/A1ᵛ) and sustenance (as in the 'pleasaunt banquet' as that which 'sustaineth the body', 88/B6)—poetry offers but poor nutrition: 'Alas here is fat feeding, & leane beasts' (85/B2). To try to find moral instruction in stage-plays is to 'gather Grapes among thistles', and to 'seeke for this foode at Theaters, we shall haue a harde pyttaunce, and come to shorte commons' (89/B6). Interestingly, however, this grim picture of nutritional poverty turns out to look rather like another ideal of proper eating: the model of sufficiency. These 'shorte commons', for example, are surprisingly similar to those of the impressively hardy English soldiers of earlier times who 'fed vppon rootes and barkes of trees . . . would stand vp to the chin many dayes in marishes without victualles: and they had a kind of sustenaunce in time of neede, of which if they had take*n* but the quantitie of a beane, or the weight of a pease, they did neyther gape after meate, nor long for the cuppe, a great while after' (91/B8ᵛ).[161] In other words, when *sufficiency* is positivized as modelling the best and most rational form of economic behaviour, then its opposite is no longer dearth—which, by comparison, begins to look rather thrifty, heroic, and soldierly—but, rather, surfeit: superfluity and excess. This, indeed, is exactly where the *Schoole* begins, with Pindar unable to choose which topic to write about in his poetry on account of the infinite number of possibilities open to him, comparable to the abundance of a Syracusan banquet. Poets are thus likened to Mithecus, the

---

[160] Plato 1926 similarly emphasizes the regulatory role of market stewards in the *Laws*, 849A–850A. Gosson describes the theatre as a 'Market of Bawdrie' (92/C2) on account of the negotiating for sexual favours that goes on there. Along with the moral outrage, however, comes the weary acknowledgement that it is a buyers' market: 'Were not we so foolish to taste euery drugge, and buy euery trifle, Players would shut in their shoppes, and carry their trashe to some other Countrie' (101/D3). Note also that for Gosson credit is frequently presented in sexual terms, as those women who 'for theyr credite, be shut from Theaters' (87/B4ᵛ) and who are encouraged, rather, to seek pastimes that 'shall yeelde you most profite & greatest credite' (117/F3ᵛ). Poets, by contrast, 'discredit themselues' (76/A1ᵛ).

[161] See also Gosson's humble offering of the *Schoole* to Sidney, which in the dedicatory epistle he compares to the simple meal a farmer offered to Philip of Macedon: not 'a feast fit for the curious taste of a perfect Courtier' (73–4/☞5ᵛ), but one that shall 'for this time suffice your selfe & a great many moe' (74/☞6).

'excellent Cooke . . . honored for his confections' (79/A4) who was banished from Sparta because his gastronomic pleasures won 'the body fro*m* labor' (79/A4ᵛ)—that is, induced idleness—while a similar lesson is to be drawn from the Epicures who 'nigh burst their guts with ouer feeding' (87/B4ᵛ). 'Cookes did neuer shewe more crafte in their iunckets to vanquish the taste', Gosson observes, 'then Poets in Theaters to wounde the conscience' (89/B6ᵛ).

I stress the point because, unlike Halpern—in whose reading of the *Utopia* excess becomes positivized as gluttony and greed—Gosson here negativizes it: that is, he correctly computes that excess as emptiness, unproductiveness, pointless waste. It is quite logical, therefore—and in some ways anticipates the thinking of Bataille—that Gosson should associate poetry with the excremental.[162] Thus, just as the scarab beetle disregards the sweet flowers and 'lightes in a cowshard', or the fly leaves the 'sound places of the Horse, [to] suck at the Botch', or pigs 'forsake the fayre fieldes' to 'wallow in the myre' (76/A1ᵛ), so the poets in ancient Rome—considered 'pleasant as *Nectar* at the first beginning'—were 'cast out for lees, when their abuses were knowen' (89/B7). Conceived thus, poetry is nothing but a superfluous, useless, noxious waste product, and it is as such that it meets its fate, which is not accommodation or regulation but complete expulsion from the body politic. Whether one describes it as puritanical or not, this response is certainly purist: a bid to rid the body of this waste in the interests of health and hygiene. Where poets 'discredit themselues, and disperse their poyson through all the worlde' (76/A1ᵛ)—worse, where, like a 'deceitfull Phisition', the poet gives 'sweete Syrropes to make his poyson goe downe the smoother' (77/A2), a highly cynical take on the sugared pill motif—Gosson, by contrast, presents himself throughout the *Schoole* as the 'good Phisition' (73/☞5, 88/B5ᵛ, 108/E2ᵛ) who seeks, by means of purgation, to effect this purist cure.[163] Where the 'foole' coming into a garden, merely sticks flowers in his cap, such a 'Phisition' will, rather, judge their health-giving properties and stick them in the pot: 'in the one they wither without profite; in the other they serue to the health of the bodie' (108/E2ᵛ). For Gosson, no less than for Plato, this phobic intolerance—as to a toxic pathogen—arises from a perception that strikes at the heart of any optimistic humanist claim on behalf of poetry's profitability: namely, that even in those cases where poetry *might* be

---

[162] As Stoekl, ed. 1985 (xi) notes, André Breton described Bataille as an 'excremental philosopher' on the basis of such works as his surrealist essay, 'The Solar Anus' (1927). Bataille's effort was directed to countering idealistic thinking, i.e. toward theorizing negativity without fetishizing the latter into an alternative, 'perverse' ideal. Bataille does not therefore privilege a 'new object (excrement, flies, ruptured eyes, the rotten sun, etc.) over the old one (the head, the king, spirit, mind, vision, the sun of reason, etc.)' (xiii), as that would simply perpetuate the fetishized and hierarchical thinking he seeks to deconstruct. Bataille's mission—the final success of which remains open to debate—is the difficult one of theorizing an absolute negativity: 'Thus filth does not "replace" God; there is no new system of values, no new hierarchy' (xiv). I am not, of course, suggesting that Gosson attempts anything of this kind, but rather that his 'logical' association of the profitless with the excremental could have opened up—for one to whom the whole 'logic' and ethos of profitability was becoming increasingly execrable—a potentially new way of thinking.

[163] See also 'An Apologie' (124/L2): 'If I giue [my readers] a Pil to purge their humor, they neuer leaue belking till it bee vp, wherein you may perceiue what vnruly patientes I deale withall, howe vnwilling they are to receiue remedy, when their disease hath gotten the vpper hande.'

praised—*might* be admitted to teach, delight, move to virtue, and so forth—its positive effects can never be entirely guaranteed.[164] It runs into the insuperability of what might, after Ovid's heroine, be called the 'Medea problem'.[165] This blow to the pedagogical, profitable model of poetry is one to which Gosson adverts on several occasions, pointing out that even those poems and plays (including his own) that set out to reform manners and morals—and that might seek to be justified on those terms—do not necessarily do so, and in practice often have the opposite effect. He admits, for example, that contemporary plays do not (as Old Comedy did) depict the gods in what Marlowe might call 'heady riots, incest, rapes', but rather (as in New Comedy), depict 'wooing allowed by assurance of wedding; priuie meetinges of bachelours and maidens on the stage, not as murderers . . . but as those that desire to bee made one in hearte' (87–8/B5).[166] On the face of it, this scenario might seem innocent enough, if not socially curative: 'Nowe are the abuses of the worlde reuealed, euery man in a play may see his owne faultes, and learne by this glasse, to amende his manners' (88/B5), a humanist commonplace. In Gosson's book, however, any hope or expectation that such a vision of imperfection will automatically lead to amendment is replaced by a much more realistic assessment of audience response: '*Curculio* [a parasite in Plautus' play of that name] may chatte til his heart ake, ere any be offended with his gyrdes' (88/B5). That is to say, a negative example does not necessarily carry any force—its requisite 'offence' is in no way guaranteed—thereby dealing a major blow to the humanist faith in education, self-improvement, and reformation.[167] Rather, 'Deformities are checked in ieast, and mated in earnest' (88/B5). The 'pleasure of sportes, temper the bitternesse of rebukes', such that 'this exercise shoulde not be suffered as a profitable recreation' (88/B5–B5ᵛ): precisely, that is, because pleasure *cannot*, in the event, reliably be turned to good effect.[168] For all their pedagogical pretensions, poets are *bad*

---

[164] As Kinney, ed. 1974 (28) notes, for all Gosson's debt to humanistic thinking and its emphasis on education and self-improvement, his use of it in the *Schoole* is 'inverted, for he cites his authorities to deny [the] efficacy of art—as the true humanist never would'. Gosson's 'strict and anti-humanist applications' of otherwise humanist axioms are thus 'surprising, for they strain poetry out of man's culture' (34).

[165] Ovid 1916, *Metamorphoses*, VII.20–1: '*video meliora proboque, / deteriora sequor*' [I see the better and approve it, but I follow the worse]. The Medea problem was a crux in seventeenth-century philosophical discussions of the passions and the freedom of the will: see James 1997 (256–7, 264, 271–6); and Steinvorth 2009 (29–31).

[166] Marlowe 2006, *Hero and Leander*, line 144.

[167] For Halpern 1991 (56) the idea that a literary education could inculcate the ideal, virtuous, self-fashioned subject was humanism's 'great wager'. Like a number of other critics who similarly throw doubt on the ability of this great pedagogical regime actually to deliver, Halpern notes that in practice poetry revealed 'a subject that is fundamentally less governable or trainable than the humanist one . . . Poetic imagination was felt to be an outlaw faculty . . . Its dangers lay in its autonomy and automatism, which resisted instrumental control and thus threw a shadow on humanist optimism' (56–7). For a similarly sceptical take on schoolmasterly prescription, see Enterline 2012; Nicholson 2014; and (specifically in relation to the *Defence*) Lamb 1994.

[168] See also Gosson's reference in the *Schoole* to a play of his own, on the subject of Catiline's conspiracies, in which his whole aim had been 'too showe the rewarde of traytors . . . and the necessary gouernment of learned men' (97/C7) but in which, having failed to do either, he 'lost bothe my time and my trauell [i.e. labour]' (97/C7ᵛ).

teachers.[169] If even worthy, well-intentioned, learned, pedagogical, 'right' poetry may not teach, nor its examples exemplify, then the poet-banker may not always—or ever—be able to turn a profit, after all. He is effectively out of business.

It becomes easier to see, therefore, why Sidney and Gosson come into such close alignment, for while they differ over whether profitability should be a *desideratum* in itself, they are both agreed (whatever Sidney's speaker may say to the contrary) that poetry is unable to deliver it.[170] While they disagree on whether—in the definition and practice of poetry—this is necessarily a bad thing, they are both agreed that poetry does not guaranteeably obey or take part in the profit-motive. While they are on opposing sides with respect to the defensibility of this position, they are as one on poetry's fundamental profitlessness. This explains why, in the *digressio*, where Sidney discusses the state of English poetry in his own time, he comes very close to assuming Gosson's position a number of times. This is not, however, as other critics have suggested, because he is inconsistent or because he wrote this part of the *Defence* at a later, more 'mature' (read crabbed) period of his life, but because he is no longer struggling with a speaker whom he has committed to putting forward the official, humanist, pedagogical view. In the *digressio* Sidney can afford to cast some doubt upon the latter because he is no longer—or not so pointedly—in conflict with his speaker and so not having to deal with so acute a conflict of interests. Insofar as they are (or in Gosson's case, were) both poets, the two of them are/were both, as Sidney puts it, 'sick among the rest', presenting with 'one or two spots of the common infection grown among the most part of writers' (115.9–11). As a former playwright—a position he now formally recants—Gosson offers to 'wipe the blot from my forhead' (98/C7ᵛ), but although in his role as 'Phisition' he had promised to thrust 'the corruption out in the face' (73/☞5), by the end of the *Schoole* he is so overcome by the modesty topos that he confesses himself still to have 'more spots in my body then the Leopard' (111/E5). Sidney's own confession of sickness—'acknowledging ourselves somewhat awry'—is, he concedes, intended that 'we may bend to the right use' (115.11–12). But the possibility of making that turn in the future or in the past—by means of poetry, at least—has been thoroughly thrown into doubt. The same is true for Gosson, too, for although, as a repentant prodigal (a narrative which he repeatedly invokes), he regrets 'misspending my time' (74/☞6ᵛ)—and, in an earlier work, for having, as a poet, sometimes 'trod awry'—by the close of the *Schoole*, the forgiveness of the prodigal's debts and his re-entry into adulthood on the approved economic model is, again, held up to question: 'And because I accuse other for treading awry, which

---

[169] It is, of course, the purpose of Gosson's presiding metaphor to indict poets as bad teachers: as 'euer the head Maisters' (80/A5ᵛ) in the school of abuse, like Ovid, 'the Amarous Scholemaister' (86/B4), or players, 'the very scholmaisters of these abuses' (94/C3ᵛ).

[170] According to Greville 1986 (11) Sidney may ultimately have shared Gosson's scepticism about the ability of poetry to teach virtue. Calling to mind his writings on his deathbed, he is said to have 'discovered not only the imperfection, but vanity, of these shadows, how daintily soever limned: as seeing that even beauty itself, in all earthly complexions, was more apt to allure men to evil than to fashion any goodness in them', as a result of which he bid the unfinished *New Arcadia*—'this unpolished embryo'—be consigned to the fire.

since I was borne neuer went right . . . shut vp the Schoole, and get you home. FINIS' (110–11/E5).[171] When it comes down to it, the absolute distinction that Sidney and Gosson both draw between going 'aright' and going 'awry' proves all too traversable in the end.

What lies behind both texts—and both writers—is a fundamental acknowledgement of the power of art: an acceptance that, for every injunction towards temperance or self-restraint, art may or may not deliver the goods but, either way, it cannot be forced or guaranteed to do so, and is just as likely to have the opposite effect. While they may differ on what to do about it, Sidney and Gosson are in agreement on poetry's potentially disruptive power: its refusal, practicably speaking, to be tied to any profitable purpose.[172] Notwithstanding human sense, wit, reason, and understanding, Gosson complains, we are 'euer ouerlashing, passing our boundes, going beyond our limites, neuer keeping our selues within compasse' (100/D1ᵛ–D2). It is into just this 'beyonde', however, that I suggest Sidney and the true—that is, the wrong, awry, un-ideal, or in any case not 'right'— poet would seek to go, impatient with the logic that remains 'compassed within the circle of a question' (85.12). In Gosson's idealized scenario of cultural activity— ushered in to counter this possibility—absolutely nothing is in danger of happening. Wayward human affections are held in check—indeed, in permanent lockdown—as the 'Arrowe, which getting lybertie, with winges is carryed beyonde our reach' is instead 'kepte in the Quiuer' where 'it is still at commaundement', or the dog, lest it let slip, is kept on the leash, and the colt, lest it 'flinges about', under the bridle (101/D2ᵛ, D3). It would be for Sidney to set these free, to imagine the poet 'not enclosed . . . but freely ranging within the zodiac of his own wit' (*Defence*,

---

[171] The earlier work referred to is a congratulatory poem that Gosson wrote on behalf of one T. N., the translator of Francisco Lépez de Gómara's *The pleasant historie of the conquest of the VVeast India* 1578 (b2): 'The Poet which sometimes hath trod awry, / And song in verse the force of fyry loue, / When he beholdes his lute with carefull eye, / Thinkes on the dumpes that he was wonte to proue. / His groning spright yprickt with tender ruth, / Calles then to minde the follies of his youth'. On Gosson's other self-references to the prodigal son story, see *Schoole* (73/☞4ᵛ, 81/A6ᵛ, 91/C1, 97–8/C7ᵛ); 'An Apologie' (247/☞6; translated 249); and *Playes confuted* (167/D3ᵛ). For what it is worth, when Sidney gives his own personal response to the 'instructing parable' (91.43) of the prodigal son in the *Defence*, the lesson he seems to draw from it is more one of prodigality than of repentance and forgiveness: 'Truly, for myself, me seems I see before my eyes the lost child's disdainful prodigality, turned to envy a swine's dinner' (91.40–2). If one were to grant a subliminal distaste for the greed associated with capitalism—and given what has already been noted about courtly 'scorn' or disdain, and about Sidney's potential identification with those who 'do prodigally spend' (101.1)—the swine's dinner might well have been perversely preferable to the fatted calf and the submission to paternal approval it represents.

[172] For Dollimore 2004 (xxiv) the 'case for saying that literature all the time violates the humanist imperative could proceed by invoking the views of those who have wanted to censor art, from Plato, through the anti-theatrical prejudices, to advocates of modern state censorship'. Such 'enemies of art . . . are not as philistine as some would claim' (xxiv), for those 'who love art the most also censor the most' (xxviii). Contrast the self-proclaimed lovers of art who value high culture for its supposedly civilizing function: 'Such an attitude not only fails to take art seriously enough, but rests on a prior process of pro-art censorship more effective than anti-art state censorship. Their defence *of* art is more often than not a defence *against* art, and an exaggerated respect for it becomes a way of not engaging with it' (xxviii, emphases original). In Dollimore's view, this attitude characterizes 'the obsolete, complacent and self-serving clichés of the heritage culture industry, the Arts establishment, and a market-driven humanities education system' (xxii).

85.22–3), like a courtly huntsman, or better still like the still wild, uncaught, freely roaming animal, masterless and owned by none. Gosson's alternative, by contrast, is to 'shut vppe our eares to Poets . . . pull our feete back from resort to Theaters, and turne away our eyes from beholding of vanitie' (101/D3), rather as he enjoins the women of London to 'Close vp your eyes, stoppe your eares, tye vp your tongues' (118/F4ᵛ), as if he, too, were heading unconsciously towards the death drive, just by a more direct route.[173] '*If* Players can promise in woordes, and performe it in deedes, proclame it in their Billes, and make it good in Theaters; that there is nothing there noysome too the body, nor hurtfull to the soule: and that euerye one which comes to buye their Iestes, shall haue an honest neighbour', Gosson concedes—his conditional made ironic by the impossibility of such a likelihood—then his reader may 'goe thither and spare not, otherwise I aduise you to keepe you thence' (101/D3–D3ᵛ, my emphasis).[174] It is Gosson's ironic conditional here that Sidney will repeatedly appropriate in a series of equally ironic and rhetorical 'ifs' of his own that extend throughout the course of the *Defence* and whose implicit question—'and what if *not*?'—always goes unanswered.[175] In this way, Sidney will come not to defend poetry against Gosson, calling his bluff, but rather to undermine that dutiful project, and reach instead towards a radical and new conception of poetry that can accept this assessment of its own power—its ability to operate outside the profit-motive—without resorting to its control or its expulsion.

◌

If an acknowledgement of art's power is ultimately what lies behind Gosson's *Schoole* and Sidney's *Defence*, then behind them both looms the figure of Plato. Where that power is mortally feared, the only expedient is, indeed, complete eradication and total shutdown. But to such as might, on occasion, entertain doubts as to whether profitability does or should constitute the be-all and end-all of human existence—or consider whether, as a form of thought, it might entail unacceptable costs of its own—acknowledging the power of art to disrupt or disobey the profit-motive can open up a space in which the poet, artist, philosopher, or theorist might

---

[173] See also the conclusion of *Playes Confuted* in which Gosson addresses his readers as 'louers of the Gospel, haters of libertie' (197/G8–G8ᵛ).

[174] Gosson repeats this strategy of wielding rhetorical 'ifs' in order conclusively to demonstrate the opposite in *Playes confuted* (169/D5ᵛ, 170/D6ᵛ), with a last flourish on the penultimate page (197/G8).

[175] See e.g. 'if Pugliano's strong affection and weak arguments will not satisfy you' (81.23–4); 'if I handle with more good will than good reasons' (81.27–8); 'if ever learning come among [the simple Indians]' (83.24); 'if [readers] will learn aright why and how that maker made him' (85.42–3); 'if we can, show we the poet's nobleness' (88.34); 'if [the poet] go beyond [the philosopher and the historian]' (89.38); 'if the question be for your own use and learning' (92.25–6); 'If the poet do his part aright' (92.34); 'if severed they be good' (97.11); 'if the saying of Plato and Tully be true' (99.32–3); 'if anything be already said in the defence of sweet Poetry' (99.36–7); 'if *oratio* next to *ratio* . . . be the greatest gift bestowed upon mortality' (101.28–9); 'if reading be foolish without remembering' (101.36–7); 'if there be much truth in it' (102.32); 'if it be, as I affirm' (102.34–5); 'if to a slight conjecture a conjecture may be opposed' (105.30); 'if I knew, I should have mended myself' (109.28); 'if they be inclinable unto it' (109.33); '*Si quid mea carmina possunt*' [If my poetry has any power] (116.43), citing *Aeneid*, IX.446.

speculate freely without being obliged to make a return on their investment or have a bankable deposit to file in the national treasure-house of science, as if that were the only thing worth defending. If Marc Shell is right in attributing to Plato a distrust of the (then, relatively new) money form that was deeply sensed—even if its internal logic of symbolization would end up being enshrined within his philosophy of the Ideas—then Gosson's rant against the profitlessness of poetry may well have given Sidney the prompt he needed: may have served as the spark that led him to locate that deep distrust within Plato, too, and to identify the same within himself. Gosson need not have shared the same distrust himself in order to serve as the catalyst here (on the contrary, while he roundly castigates poetry as profitless, he is not against profitability in general, and is indeed, in every other respect, its greatest advocate). Perhaps this is why, whatever Spenser may have said to the contrary, Sidney most probably did not scorn Gosson. Without the *Schoole of Abuse*, quite possibly, Sidney might never have been moved to produce the very deep engagement with Plato's philosophy that—along with many other critics, although for different reasons—I think the *Defence* is. At a level that may have been intuitive for both of them—rather than being thrashed out and fully theorized in the clear light of rational day—Sidney and Plato (and perhaps More, too) share the same scruples, misgivings, and unease about money thought and the places it has a tendency to end up: with commodification, fetishism, tyranny, inequity, the abuse of power, the cursed hunger for war and gain. Although nearly two thousand years separate them; although the various phases through which the money form passes on its inexorable way towards capitalism intervene; although they remain on opposite sides over whether poetry should be banished or not, Sidney and Plato (and More, too) share the same resort, the expedient of expedients. They all turn to what comes from nothing, what can represent non-existent places or things, and what can be given and taken for free, namely, fiction.[176] If it is as a banker-philosopher that Plato is Sidney's enemy, it is as a poet-philosopher that he is Sidney's friend (and More's, too). It is to the topic of fiction, therefore, that Part II will turn.

---

[176] See Barish 1981 (5) who considers the 'conflict' within Plato at some length (5–31), and suggests that Sidney deals with this unresolved tension between the philosopher/critic and the poet/artist by resorting to those aspects that are present within Plato's philosophy but marginalized there, especially the *furor poeticus* and fiction (12n, 94, 112, 142).

PART II

THE COUNTERFEITER

I

Poetry Lies

The second imputation that Sidney's speaker takes it upon himself formally to refute is the charge that poetry lies: specifically, that poetry is 'the mother of lies' (102.23) and that poets are 'the principal liars' (102.42). Put thus, the accusation implies a scene of monstrous generation: not only that poetry spawns untruths like some Spenserian embodiment of error but also that the poet himself somehow gives birth to this grotesque material in a preposterous reversal of the natural order.[1] Later, in the *digressio*, where Sidney is more open to such charges and more willing to accept their validity in respect of himself and the poets of his generation, he admits that, although the poet is born not made (109.38–9), he and his fellow poets are guilty of operating 'very fore-backwardly' (110.1–2) when it comes to their relation to poetic matter. Where, properly speaking, they should 'exercise to know' (110.2) by actively seeking out the truth, instead they 'exercise as having known' (110.2–3) by producing what is already in their heads—implicitly, material that is fantastical, imaginary, and consequently untrue—with the result that 'our brain [is] delivered of much matter which never was begotten by knowledge' (110.3–4). The son gives birth to matter (*mater*) that in turn generates further falsehoods, apparently without any intervention from a knowledge-bearing, paternal third term. Summarizing this position at the end of the *digressio*, Sidney confesses that it is this specific abuse of matter that has made him 'sick among the rest' (115.9) and blighted him with the same 'common infection' (115.10) that afflicts most if not all writers of imaginative literature.

The charge that 'poets tell many a lie' was an old one—Aristotle traces it as far back as Solon (fifth century BC)—and it had been exhaustively debated, *pro* and *contra*, by philosophers, theologians, and poets ever since.[2] It most likely came to Sidney mediated via contemporary sources, however, in particular Agrippa's *Of the Vanitie and Uncertaintie of artes and sciences* and Gosson's *Schoole of Abuse*. Agrippa, for example,—or, more precisely, his English translator—also castigates poetry as 'the mother of lies [*mendaciorum parentem*]' (D4ᵛ) on the grounds that it makes poets spend their study not on good things but rather 'disceitefullie to deuise all things vpon a matter of nothinge' (D4ᵛ). For the same reason, he argues, 'shee dothe deserue to be called the principall Authoure of lies [*architectrix mendaciorum*], and the maintainer of peruerse opinions' (D3), for Poetry disseminates a 'venemous eloquence' (D3ᵛ) that 'dothe not onlie deceiue & infecte' her contemporary readers

---

[1] On the 'preposterous', see Parker 2007.
[2] Aristotle 1935, *Metaphysics*, 983a, referencing Solon 1999, fragment 29.

but posterity as well, insofar as later generations imbibe the same 'furious venims' and are thus 'infect[ed] with her doctrine & lies' (D4), even at a historical distance. For his part, Gosson brands poets 'the fathers of lyes' (78/A3), this accusation heading up his three-pronged attack against poetry, the other two charges being that poets are 'Pipes of vanitie, & Schooles of Abuse' (78/A3), a charge-sheet he would repeat verbatim in the 'Apologie of the *Schoole of Abuse*' a few months later (125/L3).[3]

Such are the three 'most important imputations' (102.20) that Sidney's speaker also lists, changing only the order so as to put the charge that poetry lies second, after the charge that it is profitless or 'vain'. Although in both cases this presentation implies that the accusations are equal and interchangeable, however, the same equivalence does not apply to their refutations. That is to say, refuting the charge that poetry lies is more complex than refuting the charge that poetry is profitless. The latter is, structurally speaking, a comparatively simple affair since, as we saw in Part I, it maps onto a simple binary and merely involves mobilizing the counter-charge that poetry is profitable. At first glance, at least, the two terms can easily be moralized, so that—whatever their different positions on poetry itself—Sidney's speaker and Gosson could be seen to share a common ethical code in which profitlessness is judged to be as negative for the individual and state (wasteful, irresponsible, criminal, and so on) as profitability is judged positive (rational, rewarding, patriotic, and so forth). On the face of it, such a position is logical, self-evident, and quite irrefutable, especially when it has a powerful humanist literature on the value of knowledge and learning in the acquisition and growth of intellectual and moral capital on which to draw. Although, in the event, refuting this charge turned out to be less simple than first appeared (the first of many deceptions)—with Sidney thinking outside its 'logic' so as to grasp at a quite different conceptualization of poetry, thereby terminally undermining the speaker's position, whether knowingly or otherwise—in its opening premise, at least, the latter's position was eminently plausible. It was simply a question of showing that the features Gosson had positivized but denied to poetry—the qualities of good, goal-oriented labour that, whether in reading, writing, or performing, led to the exercise of goodness and godliness in the form of virtuous action—were entirely poetry's domain, and the case was made. Poetry was demonstrably profitable and clearly, therefore, worthy not only of reading, writing, and performing but also (while doing all three) of defending.

In the present case, however, defending poetry against the charge of lying involves a more intricate and multi-staged approach, in the first place because, unlike the last, this refutation is barred from drawing on any straightforward binary. Although the speaker concedes that, on those rare occasions where such a simple binary *does* present itself, the choice is obvious—'if the question were whether it

---

[3] Sidney's speaker repeats this formulation when he refers to the charge that poets are 'the fathers of lies' (104.42–3). One of the very few who read the *Defence* before it was published, Harington 1904 (199) uses the appellation 'nurse of lies' in his own 'Briefe Apologie', listing the other charges against poetry as 'a pleaser of fooles, a breeder of dangerous errors, and an inticer to wantonnes'.

were better to have a particular act truly or falsely set down, there is no doubt which is to be chosen, no more than whether you had rather have Vespasian's picture right as he was, or . . . nothing resembling' (92.22–5)—this eventuality is quickly dismissed as purely academic, a mere point of departure for the more sophisticated analysis that follows. Indeed, the proposition that poetry might be taken for true is scoffed at with the degree of scorn more normally reserved for the poet-haters. Any simpleton who believes that Aesop wrote his animal fables 'for actually true were well worthy to have his name chronicled among the beasts he writeth of' (103.22–3), while not even a child, 'coming to a play, and seeing *Thebes* written in great letters upon an old door, doth believe that it is Thebes' (103.24–5), and only a fool or 'a very partial champion of truth' could say we lied for giving a chesspiece 'the reverend title of a bishop' (103.40–2). Since, as an effective counterargument, this route is obviously closed to him, the speaker is forced into taking a more indirect if not oblique approach to the problem, and he does this by breaking his refutation down into two parts. The first part, in fact, is not a refutation at all but rather an affirmation, although an affirmation arrived at by means of the negation of a negation: the outright denial of the charge that poetry is true (or that it does not lie). The original charge that poetry lies is upheld, therefore— poetry does not tell the truth, or poetry does not 'not lie'—albeit by means of the kind of tricky logic that would come to characterize Astrophil's witty justification for desire ('That in one speech two Negatives affirme').[4] This, in turn, leads to the refutation's second part, a modification that effectively works to turn 'lying' from a negative into a positive term. Thus, the things that the poet recounts as 'not true' (103.18) and that he tells 'not for true' (103.18–19) are nevertheless justified— whether they are called lies, fables, fictions, tales, parables, or whatever—when they can be shown to be profitable, and where that profitability is measurable in terms of its effects. In this respect, the speaker's refutation could be seen to expand the brief 'defence of Poetes' that Sir Thomas Elyot makes in *The boke named the Gouernour* (1531), where he undertakes to demonstrate 'what profite may be taken by the diligent reding of auncient poetes, contrary to the false opinion that nowe rayneth of them that suppose, that in the warkes of poetes is contayned nothynge but baudry (suche is their foule worde of reproche) and vnprofitable leasinges'.[5] In the course of his own defence of poets, Sidney's speaker will follow Elyot's strategy of turning the tables on the accusers (it is their charges that poetry lies that are 'false') and of appropriating their arguments for the opposing side—poetry *is* 'profytable' (F7ᵛ) and yields 'fruite' (F7ᵛ, G2) and 'commoditie to the diligent reders' (G2)— in order to mount an extensive case that poetry's undeniable lack of truth-content is no bar to its profitability. On the contrary, by inspiring its readers to emulate the examples of virtuous action it depicts, 'fiction' is said to become the ground-plot or seedbed of a 'profitable invention' (103.30–2).[6] This riposte has the effect of

---

[4] *AS* 63. [5] Elyot 1531 (G1ᵛ).
[6] See Alexander (342): what Sidney means here is 'not "treat the story as a mental outline of a useful plot" . . . but rather "make use of the story in building in your own mind the foundations of some useful idea or course of action". We become poets of our own lives in this dense metaphor'.

producing a virtuous cycle—or, better still, a model of exponentially profitable growth—whereby the poet's original 'invention' or act of creativity comes, in turn, to generate on the part of the reader further 'invention' in the form of acts of virtue. That is to say, the latter's good or heroic life, inspired by such poetic fictions, itself becomes a kind of living poem—poetry in action, poetry in the world—which will presumably be capable of inspiring a potentially infinite number of others (many Cyruses) who are witness to it on either the stage or the page of history. One thinks of the careful fabrication of the Sidney legend by his family and friends after his death, and the heroism that, in some quarters, it still is held to inspire. Needless to say, this polemical strategy on the part of the refuter is designed to reverse the vicious cycle produced by the illegitimate and perverse model of poetic generation that the poet-haters had laid at his door with the charge that the poet's offspring is the 'mother of lies'.

One corollary of this argument is that it becomes possible to distinguish between two types of lie, each moralized accordingly. Thus, on the one hand there are 'bad' lies, bad in the sense that they are negative in their effects: in a word, they are profitless. These are the lies against which Agrippa fulminates on the grounds that they 'deceiue mens mindes' (D3) and 'hinder true histories' (D4) by being baseless, empty of content, and founded 'vpon a matter of nothinge' (D4^v). They are the lies to which Gosson takes exception on the grounds that they are 'dearly bought' (77/A2) and deceive the consumer by failing to deliver the goods they promise: 'Many good sentences are . . . written by Poets, as ornamentes to beautifye their woorkes, and sette theyr trumperie too sale without suspect' (77/A2–A2^v). 'Good' lies, on the other hand, are those that are contrastingly positive in their effects, profitable alike to individual and state (to bypass any negative connotations, 'lying' is here generally replaced with different words or formulations). Such, for example, might be the 'honest dissimulation' (93.21) by means of which Zopyrus and Abradatas, faithful servants of Darius and Cyrus, respectively, deceived their masters' enemies and so ensured their masters' military success. Such might also be the 'honest fraud' which Harington—whose 'Briefe Apologie of Poetrie' follows Sidney's closely, and makes its own answer to Agrippa—attributes to the poet who sugars the pill and thus deceives the reader into imbibing wholesome doctrine that he or she might otherwise have shunned: 'he that is deceiued is wiser than he that is not deceiued, & he that doth deceiue is honester than he that doth not deceiue'.[7] For Sidney's speaker, likewise, the poet effects the same benign deception and 'pretending no more, doth intend the winning of the mind from wickedness to virtue: even as the child is often brought to take most wholesome things by hiding them in such other as have a pleasant taste' (95.19–22), and as even the most 'hard-hearted evil men' (96.4) can be made to take in goodness under the cover of a

---

[7] Harington 1904 (199). Harington sources this claim in Plutarch 2004, *Moralia*, 'How The Young Man Should Study Poetry', 15D. It is repeated in a discussion on tragedy in *Moralia*, 'Were the Athenians More Famous in War or in Wisdom?', 348C, with the additional comment that 'he who deceives is more honest, because he has done what he promised to do; and he who is deceived is wiser, because the mind which is not insensible to fine perceptions is easily enthralled by the delights of language'. On both occasions, Plutarch attributes the saying to the Sophist, Gorgias.

'medicine of cherries' (96.10); indeed, this is the only means by which the latter can be induced to do so. Such beneficial pretence, judged by its effects, similarly characterizes the great orators who, like Cicero, performed 'that artificially which we see men do ... naturally' (114.15), or who, like Antonius and Crassus, either 'pretended not to know art' (114.35) or to use it in their speeches because the appearance of plainness won the 'credit of popular ears; which credit is the nearest step to persuasion' (114.37).

By the same token, it also becomes possible to distinguish between two types of truth, also moralized accordingly. Thus, there is 'bad' truth, bad because profitless or negative in its effects. Such is the 'truth of a foolish world' (94.1) which, in his fidelity to the facts, the historian is bound to relate, regardless of the moral consequences of seeing that tyranny is routinely rewarded in the historical record and virtue just as routinely crushed underfoot. Indeed, there is a hint that, in being 'captived' (94.1) to this foolish truth, the historian is in some way complicit with the evil men whom, in tragic drama, poets make sure to leave the stage 'manacled' (93.43) and so duly punished for their crimes. By presenting in his work a kind of tyrants' handbook—not to mention a glaring illustration of the fact that minimal rewards are to be had, in practice, for choosing the virtuous life—the historian is implicitly no less of an object lesson, and no less worthy of punishment, than they.[8] 'Good' truth, by contrast, since its 'goodness' is measured by means of its positive or beneficial effects for all concerned, is essentially indistinguishable from 'good' lies. Truth becomes an ethical as opposed to an empirical category and, since this thereby detaches it from any necessary relation to actuality or fact, that which is not strictly true according to those criteria—such as fiction—can nevertheless claim to be so according to these new, ethical ones. Indeed, fiction can be 'more' true than mere fact according to the comparably larger amount of profit it is capable of generating. Thus, in inspiring its readers to the kind of virtuous and heroic conduct that will advance them and their country and win glory for both, for example, epic poetry 'doth not only teach and move to a truth, but teacheth and moveth to the most high and excellent truth' (99.29–31).

By such means, Sidney's speaker is able to arrive at the triumphant conclusion—with which he rounds off the *refutatio*—that poetry is not 'an art of lies, but of true doctrine' (108. 14), as a result of which it should be prized and valued as a cultural treasure, and poets fêted and championed as national heroes. However, if his blithe claim that the excellence of poetry can thus be proved 'so easily and so justly' (108.12)—and the charges against it refuted 'so soon' (108.13)—suppresses the tortuous reasoning he has had to deploy in order to get to this apparently counter-intuitive statement that 'lies' are in fact 'true', that twisty logic is nevertheless all too evident in the argument it has taken him to get there. Indeed, it is announced in the speaker's opening gambit when, to the charge that poets are liars, he answers

---

[8] A knowledge of history 'can afford [invaluable information to] your Cypselus, Periander, Phalaris, Dionysius [all notorious dictators and tyrants of the ancient past], and I know not how many more of the same kennel, that speed well enough in their abominable injustice or usurpation' (94.15–18); whence, 'in History looking for truth, [readers] go away full fraught with falsehood' (103.29–30).

'paradoxically, but truly, I think truly, that of all writers under the sun the poet is the least liar' (103.1–2). Although always tricky, 'truly' is used here (as Maslen notes) 'most trickily of all'.[9] For in solemnly proceeding to affirm for true that the poet never affirms for true, the speaker's statement seems to be a contradiction in terms—is this the kind of thing that can be affirmed?—and leaves us scrambling for the tone (serious? facetious?) in an effort to identify the veracity of both the statement and the person who is making it.[10] When unpacked and taken to its logical conclusion, however, the speaker's reasoning threatens to have fairly terminal consequences for the project in hand, for it leaves open to question—and ultimately indeterminable—the two necessities that would be crucial to its success: namely, his ability to be believed, and his ability to defend. His paradoxical answer, that is, puts in doubt the two kinds of truth distinguished above—truth as an empirical category and truth as an ethical one—and although much of the ensuing difficulty arises from the confusion between the two and (as usually happens with the speaker's binaries) their categorical collapse—for the purposes of the present argument, we shall deal with them separately and in turn.

◌

While the whole direction of the speaker's defence of poetry consists in subordinating empirical to ethical truth, then—the one is 'foolish' (94.1), the other 'high and excellent' (99.30–1)—it is far from clear that, in his role as *defender*, he personally is free to dispense with the rigours of mere accuracy, fact, and logical deduction in quite so cavalier a fashion, or at least not to the detriment of the case he has undertaken. If winning that case is paramount, then the freedoms he makes available to the poet are presumably unavailable to him—or for the time being and in the present text, at any rate—for the credibility of his argument depends upon maintaining a clear distinction between those texts that do not affirm (such as the fictions he is writing about) and those that do (such as the current treatise, written in propositional prose, that sets out to affirm exactly that). The proof that, by the end of the *refutatio*, he judges 'confirmed' (108.12–13), rests on a series of claims—that the poet 'nothing affirms, and therefore never lieth' (103.8–9), that he 'never affirmeth' (103.13) and thus 'never . . . conjure[s] you to believe for true what he writes' (103.13–14), that he recounts things 'not true' and 'not for true' and so 'lieth not' (103.18–19)—all of which are presented as affirmative statements. To accept them as such—to take them seriously, to believe them for true, to find them credible and plausible, and thus to be persuaded by them as a valid defence of

---

[9] Maslen (4), adding that the sentence 'reaches giddy heights of complexity, especially if we remember that the man who writes this is himself a poet, and therefore scarcely the most trustworthy witness as to the poet's trustworthiness'. Later, he comments that this sentence is Sidney's 'most striking instance of this usage' and comprises 'an extraordinary blend of assertiveness and caution' (60).

[10] It similarly does nothing to inspire confidence in the statement made only five sentences earlier: 'for if it be, as I affirm, that no learning is so good as that which teacheth and moveth to virtue, and that none can both teach and move thereto so much as Poetry, then is the conclusion manifest that ink and paper cannot be to a more profitable purpose employed' (102.34–8). For a good account of this dilemma see Levao 1985 (153–4).

poetry (all of which the conclusion of the *refutatio* presumes)—is to act on the assumption that, while he might be defending poets on their behalf, the speaker is not a poet himself, or at least is not for current purposes writing *as* a poet. In the case of a metadiscourse such as poetics or literary criticism, this distinction is elementary and taken for granted—it would be impossible to write academic prose about imaginative literature otherwise—and identifying the speaker or defender as a distinct 'voice' within the *Defence*, quite separate from the generic poet he writes about is—however artificial it might seem in the case of a writer like Sidney, and no matter how often the speaker confuses the issue by referring to his 'unelected vocation' (81.27) as poet, and his self-identification with other such 'paper-blurrers' (109.25)—nonetheless a necessary move for all those who see the text as making serious statements about the essential nature of poetry. One effect of this necessary distance, moreover, is to situate poetics or literary criticism among the group of 'other sciences' (84.40) that earlier, in the *narratio*, the speaker had characterized precisely by their *not* being poetry: *unlike* the poet, who is free to make things up 'such as never were in Nature' (85.20), the practitioners of these other sciences are bound to follow her 'order' (85.2), which includes, presumably, taking into consideration things like empirical reality and testable truth. When, in the *refutatio*, the speaker comes to address the charge that poetry lies, he returns to this group—naming four of the original list (the astronomer, geometrician, physician, and historian) but referring to the remainder as 'other artists' (103.10)—again to demonstrate how entirely different they are, in terms of methodology and praxis, from the poet.[11] In relation to the latter, these scientists and artists must always be 'other', since the polemical point is to show how the poet's special licence with the truth is unique, but the effect is to confirm that, while the poet might be free to substitute ethical truth for the empirical variety—the routine business of investigating, explaining, and understanding phenomena—the others are not, and if poetics is going to be a bona fide disciplinary field then the same must apply to it, too.

The problem, of course, is that in his enthusiasm for demonstrating the many excellencies of poetry, the speaker positivizes the kind of truth that the poet manifests at the expense of the kind of truth that he—in the very process of defending the latter—is necessarily engaged in himself. If the poet's truth is high and excellent, then simply to be able to affirm that statement—to comment on it, to trace the historical and philosophical antecedents of such an idea, to consider its practice in classical and contemporary poetry, to cite examples, and so forth—the defender's truth must necessarily be humdrum, hidebound, tied to the laws of logical proof and demonstration. While he does not, or not openly, apply the

---

[11] The others are: the arithmetician, musician, natural philosopher, moral philosopher, lawyer, grammarian, rhetorician, logician, and metaphysician. The defender of poetry might be seen to have things in common with at least the last six. See Blasing 2007 (4) on the incommensurability of propositional prose—including that which defends poetry—and poetry itself: 'Disciplinary discourse inaugurates itself as "not poetry".' Defences of poetry 'confirm the precedence—and reinscribe the authority—of a "normal", "rational", instrumental language'. They also 'often defend something else—something that poetry might be useful for' (19n).

criticism to himself (as in all justice he should) the speaker never stops complaining of how, when practised by these 'other' professionals, what passes for empirical truth is, when pressed, more often than not a mere sham. In affirming for true many things that, 'in the cloudy knowledge of mankind' (103.11–12), turn out to be false, the astronomer, geometrician, physician, historian (and, implicitly, all the rest) do 'lie' (103.5): an eventuality that, at least theoretically, must also be applicable in the present case, unless by some miracle the speaker has managed to exempt himself from the human condition. In fact, as counsel for the defence, he has no doubt availed himself of the dissembling tactics of the great orators—pretending passion or artlessness, for example, in order the better to persuade the jury—and if so is already on the way to that tempering of the strict truth according to its ultimate effectiveness that is the hallmark of the poet (a temptation not unknown, presumably, to the other professionals, either). In earlier sections of the *Defence*, indeed, some of these other arts were argued to be at their best precisely when they shed the constraints of this low-level, error-prone, and impure truth, and took the poet's leap into imaginative fiction: the philosophers who wrote 'fable[s]' (82.38) and 'mere tales' (83.2), and the 'poetical' historians (92.37; 93.8) who fabricated speeches and other details 'which no man could affirm' (83.10–11). All of this would suggest that the speaker's poetics, too, aspires to the condition of poetry, and that, given half a chance, he would willingly be released from the liabilities of the propositional and exchange the false, foolish, lying kind of pseudo-empirical truth, to which his project condemns him, for the boundless, unchanging, heaven-reaching kind of ethical truth that is the poet's special domain.

That the best way of demonstrating the excellence of poetry would be to write it rather than defend it was something touched on in Part I, in the context of the speaker's vision of the poet's mystical, quasi-supernatural powers being a kind of imaginative fiction in its own right, and worthy to be included among the supernatural beings (heroes, demigods, and such like) that a poet himself might create. If the *Defence* aspires to be the poem that, so long as it remains a treatise on poetics, it can never be, then the *Arcadia* has suggested itself to many as the text that best illustrates the precepts the treatise puts forward, although that is to presume that those precepts have a stable, exemplary, and applicable quality quite unaffected by the logical shenanigans we are tracing here, and also to presume things about the exemplary nature of the *Arcadia* that would require a separate study to consider in the detail they deserve. A more compact but in some ways more appropriate analogy might be the opening sonnet of *Astrophil and Stella* which, like the *Defence*, also presents itself as a false start—a rough sketch, a preliminary draft, a to-do list—for the ideal poem it aspires to be but infinitely postpones. However, if finding a way to take the speaker of the *Defence* at his word is still the aim in view, then whether we choose to take him as a defender, a poet, or something in between, ultimately makes no difference. The problem of establishing whether what he says can be believed, taken seriously, or deemed in any way true remains unsolved, for he is veridically challenged either way. As a defender and practiser of poetics he is forced to make statements that may turn out to be false; as a poet and practiser of poetry he makes no statements at all. If he affirms, he lies; and if he does not lie, he does not affirm. Moreover, the fact that we only have *his* word for all this—that we have arrived at this indeterminate position by following the speaker's own logic if not his own admission—adds only another dimension to the problem, for it deposits us firmly within the disputed territory (no place?) of the liar's paradox, where every claim is self-cancelling and even claims to untruth have to be doubted.[12] In case we miss the point, the speaker makes a direct allusion to this paradox towards the end of the *refutatio*, by which stage his credibility might be considered strained, to say the least, but which this allusion does nothing to restore. In the context of arguing (somewhat disingenuously, it has to be said) that in banishing poets from the Republic Plato was in fact banishing the abuses of poetry, not poetry itself, the speaker compares a parallel warning issued by St Paul against the abuse of philosophy. In a parenthesis, however, the speaker cannot resist referring to the four occasions on which the Apostle cites, quotes, or otherwise makes mention of poetry, and the poet given the most extended treatment—and whom St Paul is proudly said to have singled out 'by the name of a prophet' (107.6)—is none other than Epimenides of Crete, a famous poet of the sixth century BC and, as the eponymous Cretan Liar, legendary originator of the paradox in question.[13] The speaker ostensibly inserts this passage so as to provide heavy-weight support for his defence of poetry: St Paul's references were made 'for the credit of poets' (107.5), he notes, and they were frequently mobilized in the period to justify the Christian use of pagan literature. In the circumstances, however, it is difficult to close the door on the unsettling possibilities that this reference opens up. If no less an authority than St Paul could call a 'prophet' one whose assertions of truth are set in perpetual and deliberate free-fall, then what implications might this have for other poets so named, for all those worthy of the title *vates*? The exhilarating prospect glimpsed at earlier in the *narratio* of the oracular poet creating poems entirely of his or her own devising— producing what, in reference to Petrarch, John Freccero calls 'an autonomous universe of autoreflexive signs without reference to an anterior logos'—thus makes

---

[12] For Colie 1966 (6) the logical contradiction that the liar's paradox poses characterizes the literature of paradoxical praise: 'In more than one sense, paradox equivocates. It lies, and it doesn't. It tells the truth, and it doesn't. The Liar paradox is a perfect example of equivocation in still another sense, since its negative and positive meanings are so balanced that one meaning can never outweigh the other, though weighed to eternity. The one meaning must always be taken with respect to the other—so that the Liar paradox is, literally, speculative, its meanings infinitely mirrored, infinitely reflected, in each other.'

[13] The reference is to St Paul's Epistle to Titus, 1:12: 'One of them selues, *euen* one of their owne prophetes said, The Cretians *are* alwaies lyars, euil beastes, slowe belyes' (Geneva Bible). The context is St Paul's advice to Titus on continuing his ministry in Crete, and in particular on dealing with troublesome individuals—'vaine talkers and deceiuers of mindes' (1:10)—who are threatening it. St Paul (who seems to be suffering from an acute sense of humour failure here) takes Epimenides' low estimation of his countrymen at face value: 'This witnes is true' (1:13). A marginal gloss notes that Paul calls him a prophet 'because the Cretia[n]s so estemed him: & . . . sacrificed vnto him as to a God, forasmuche as he had a marueilous gift to vnderstand things to come: w[hich] thing Satan by the permission of God hathe opened to the infideles from time to time, but it turneth to their greater condemnation'. While Epimenides is traditionally credited as originating the paradox, there is no reason why Solon—to whom the proverb that poets lie was attributed by Aristotle—could not also have been indulging it a century or so later, especially if he is taken (as he is in the *Defence*) to have been 'directly a poet' (82.37).

a fleeting appearance once again.[14] In the context of trying to establish the truth-content of the *Defence* as a serious statement on poetics, however, or of trying to take the speaker at his word and to establish his 'credit' once and for all, this intervention might be considered problematic, for in effect it undermines any attempt at—or appeal to—any authoritative statement whatever. No solution is to be found by referring back to Agrippa, either, as one of the instigators of this refutation, for the potentially self-cancelling irony of *his* text—with its statements that poetry (indeed all sciences and arts) generates lies—makes the truth of those statements, and the speaker who makes them, no less undecided and indeterminable.[15] At the beginning of the *refutatio*, apparently in recognition of the paradoxical nature of Agrippa's text, Sidney's speaker had attributed to him 'another foundation, than the super-ficial part would promise' (101.15–16). Critics who would seek to arrest the endless cycle of self-denying statements in order to stabilize the argument of the *Defence* once and for all—in order to preserve not only its ability to make true statements about poetry but that of poetics and literary criticism in general—take this as an opportunity to make that foundation a solid one: calling it 'Christian and Platonic', for example, and re-introducing the Logos as the guar-antee of truth and meaning that alone can stabilize such irony and put paradox to rest.[16] The alternative, however,—a possibility which the speaker leaves open and with which the *Defence* will, therefore, always be haunted—would be an infinite regress of lying liars extending in both directions: one way, back to Agrippa, Solon, Epimenides, and beyond, and the other, forward to other defences of the *Defence* and other defences of poetry and other defences of those defences, without end.

☙

So much for empirical truth. The speaker's appeal to poetry's ethical truth, however, does not fare much better. Indeed, the whole argument about the nature of fiction—the two-part structure by means of which this refutation argues first that poetry lies and second that those 'lies' (or fictions, fables, parables, stories, tales, dissimulations, and so forth) inspire readers to virtue and are therefore good,

---

[14] Freccero 1986 (27). This may be the reason why, although present in Olney and in all manuscript versions of the *Defence*, the parenthesis in question is absent from the Ponsonby edition—the 'official' version of the text that was authorized by the Sidney family and formed the basis for the text included in the 1598 folio of Sidney's works. It may have been felt that even the hint of such possibilities was a step too far and, in the interests of preserving the Sidney legend, a risk not worth taking.

[15] As noted earlier, Agrippa's text had a mixed reception in the period, with some readers taking it satirically and others not. These positions need not be mutually exclusive, however: that is to say, where paradox is in the offing, it is always possible to doubt the sincerity of a response. It is difficult to say for sure, for example, whether Harington 1904 (200) is being entirely serious where he claims to lock horns with Agrippa—'for that he writeth against Poetrie, I meane to speake a word or two in refuting thereof'—when he later confesses to finding scurrilous poetry 'too delightfull' (209) (referring to the figure of the chaste matron who reads erotic literature behind her husband's back), and when he takes the trouble to enumerate the lascivious passages in Ariosto that he would ostensibly have his readers avoid: 'yea, me thinks, I see some of you searching already for these places of the booke, and you are halfe offended that I haue not made some directions that you might finde out and read them immediatly' (214).

[16] Ferguson 1983 (159); see also Hamilton 1956 (153, 156).

profitable, defensible, and so ethically 'true'—could be seen as a giant red herring: a deviation that serves to distract the reader from the one truly serious charge that has been levelled against poetry, and allows the speaker tactically to dodge a question he does not and cannot answer.[17] This becomes more apparent, perhaps, if we return to Gosson's articulation of the problem, for his objection to poetry is not that it tells of humans and creatures that never existed or of events that never occurred—not, that is to say, that it is fiction—but rather that it *deceives*: it appears to offer its readers something good when in fact it only corrupts them.[18] Poetry is not just poisonous because it becomes an enticement to immorality, wanton behaviour, and so forth. It is doubly treacherous because, on top of doing that, it also appears—so often and so plausibly—to be doing the opposite, to be promising its consumers something wholesome and good but that turns out to be deadly: 'The deceitfull Phisition giueth sweete Syrropes to make his poyson goe downe the smoother' (77/A2).[19] Responding to Gosson's charge by surreptitiously turning an accusation of deceit into an accusation of lying—and then, once he has firm hold of the 'fiction' theme, running with it as far as he can (effectively using the empirical argument to arrive at an ethical defence of poetry by roundabout means)—Sidney's speaker manages to circumvent the original ethical charge altogether.[20] Like other

---

[17] As noted by Bronowski 1939 (21–2), also calling it a 'spoiling tactic' (21). For similar views, see Shepherd (72); Kinney 1972 (12); Kinney, ed. 1974 (47–8); Webster, ed. 1984 (31–3); and Webster 1985 (318–19).

[18] The distinction is less clear in Agrippa whose objection against poetry *is*, for the most part, that it represents the counterfactual (his examples are mainly drawn from classical fable and myth), and that this is indeed what constitutes its chief deception: poetry 'deceiue[s] mens mindes with the delectation of fables' (D3). In depicting the immorality of the pagan gods, for example, classical poetry 'dothe . . . deceiue & infecte' its readers with 'venims' (D4) by encouraging wantonness and vice, but its primary deception is an empirical one. This is because, unlike Gosson, Agrippa is less willing to concede that poetry even claims to offer good things, however deceptively so (he does not deploy the sugared pill motif, for example). He comes closer to this position when, having discussed poetry, he moves on to the question of history: a discourse that *does* present itself as 'verie profitable' (E1ᵛ) and where not only mere errors or factual inaccuracies but the deliberate distortion of the historical record for political purposes therefore constitutes deception indeed. The same is true of his views on medicine, for which see notes 23 and 25.

[19] Thus poets 'disperse their poyson through all the worlde' (76/A1ᵛ). The metaphor is the medical equivalent of Gosson's charge that poetry presents a false transaction or bad bargain: that its ostensible lesson or 'wit' is 'dearly bought' (77/A2) because the reader is essentially mis-sold a fraudulent product or counterfeit goods. He or she is not only corrupted but cozened: 'Many good sentences are spoken by *Dauus* [the scheming servant in Terence's play, *Andria*], to shadowe his knauery: and written by Poets, as ornamentes to beautifye theyr woorkes, and sette theyr trumperie too sale without suspect' (77/A2–A2ᵛ). See also *Playes Confuted* where, in response to playwrights' claims that their 'matter is good, simple, sweete, and honest', Gosson replies: 'that as no man, which desireth to giue you a deadly poyson will temper the same with gaull, and *Elleborus*, or any thing that is bitter, and vnpleasaunt; but with sweete & holsome confections: So the Deuill, at Playes, wil bring the comfortable worde of God, which, because it norisheth of nature is very conuenient to carry the poyson into our vaines' (169/D5ᵛ–D6).

[20] As noted by William Temple, the Cambridge-educated logician who was appointed Sidney's secretary in late 1585 and was one of the earliest readers of the *Defence*, recording his response in a careful and detailed analysis. Being a trained logician Temple 1984 (137) was rightly suspicious of the speaker's refutation of the lying charge which demoted empirical truth as a first step before promoting ethical truth as a second: 'Your Proposition here fails to deal with the most general level of argument' [*Propositio non est* καθόλου πρῶτον], he comments, meaning that the 'ethically' true should properly be derived from first principles, i.e. logically deduced by rational thought and above all

such defenders of poetry, he wilfully attributes to Gosson (and other such attackers) a naïvely literalistic understanding of poetry—that it 'lies' because it tells things 'not true'—because, as a strategy, this so easily mobilizes the superficially more sophisticated counter-argument that poetry conceals good things under the cover of its fables: that poetry is always 'allegorically and figuratively written' (103.28–9) and that the poet thereby administers 'wholesome things' (95.21) under the appearance of sweetness so that readers will 'take their physic' (95.23).[21] The move serves to turn deceitfulness from a negative into a positive term—yes, poets deceive, but theirs is an 'honest fraud', these are 'good' lies—but it also assumes that the physician is always good. It does nothing to address the specific case in question, which is that of the physician who is 'deceitfull': whose fraud is not honest, nor his lies good, nor his bitter 'medicine' wholesome.[22] The speaker simply blanks the possibility of such a thing, passes over it in silence as 'unthinkable'.

Dividing his refutation into two parts so as to make the case that poetry lies but that lies are profitable allows the speaker to fall back on the profitability argument: on the face of it, one easy enough to marshal and difficult enough to refute (who is going to deny that profitability is a good thing?). But it also allows him to duck the standing charge—much more difficult to deny—that the appearance of profitability can be deceptive. Indeed, the speaker's very defence that poetry is morally

dialectic. There is no distinction between empirical and ethical truth, in other words: if a statement can be made that satisfies the most rigorous demands of the former, then it will necessarily meet the criteria of the latter. Whether a text is a 'fiction' or not is a side-issue if not irrelevant as far as Temple is concerned, because if they are derived by logical inference from first principles, then the poet's exempla will represent ideals and therefore universal truths, regardless of whether they exist empirically in the world or not. As an idealist reading of the *Defence*, Temple's 'Analysis' is committed to showing how Sidney's text could make a stronger case for the claim that poetry imparts ethical truths and is therefore defensible. Temple never entertains the possibility, as Gosson does, that while it might appear to impart such ideals, and indeed claim to do so, poetry (let alone the *Defence*) still retains the power to deceive.

[21] The same strategy is deployed by Thomas Lodge when, in his own response to Gosson, he accuses the latter of being over-literal and of thus failing to understand that poets 'like good Phisitions . . . so frame their potions that they might be appliable to the quesie stomaks of their werish patients': see Lodge 1904 (66). Harington 1904 (201) similarly finds 'this obiection of lyes . . . the chief' of Agrippa's charges against poetry, responding that 'a good and honest and wholesome Allegorie is hidden in a pleasaunt and pretie fiction' (206) and that in poetry 'is both goodnesse and sweetnesse, Rubarb and Sugercandie, the pleasaunt and the profitable' (207–8). In Harington's case, however, this response does not necessarily restore poetry's honesty, as it may appear to do (see note 24), not least because he later deploys it in his mock praise of the privy where he claims to 'allegorise' his homely subject and to show his reader what 'prety pils you haue swallowed in your pleasant quadlings, & what wholsome wormewood was enclosed in these raisins of the sunne': see Harington 1596 (K2, I7). A similar wariness should also be extended to the suggestion in Borris 2000 (112) that the *Defence* straightforwardly promotes this allegorical understanding of poetry—and that 'Sidney assumes the importance of profit or utility as a criterion of literary value and justification of literature'—insofar as this reading takes the speaker's position at face value.

[22] For his part, Gosson anticipates and thoroughly deconstructs this move on the part of the defenders of poetry in his explicit critique—and, indeed, mockery—of allegory and scornful dismissal of allegoresis as something that can be marshalled in poetry's defence: see, for example, *Schoole* (78/A3–A4) and 'An Apologie' (127/L5). As Brljak 2015 (93) points out, however, the defenders of poetry 'consistently omit any mention' of this, presumably because they are unwilling or unable to countenance the possibility that the hidden kernel of poetry might *not* be wholesome and that its attractive surface might therefore be nothing but a lure. The defenders' collective silence on this matter is eloquent testimony to the fact that idealist readings and defences of poetry have no answer to this charge.

wholesome—that by means of its exemplary characters (Cyrus and the like) it teaches 'true doctrine' (108.14) and moves its readers to virtuous and heroic action—could be seen to be complicit with that deception. The sweeter the syrup—the more virtuous-seeming the poem—the more readily the poison will be swallowed. For, although Gosson's sinister take on the sugared pill motif could be seen to imply a *deliberate* will on the part of poets to deceive (making them sociopaths on a grand scale), intention is not, in fact, necessary for the harm to be done. The doctor *could* be simply evil (the well-poisoning type of the morality tradition), but he could also be merely ignorant, negligent, or badly trained (inadvertently making errors), or he could be thoroughly well-intentioned—'pretending no more, doth intend the winning of the mind from wickedness to virtue' (95.19–20)—and convinced of the beneficial properties of the remedies he administers to achieve that desired end (only to be proved, with hindsight, sadly wrong). Whether murder, manslaughter, or accidental death, however, the outcome for the patient is the same.[23] Poets and their defenders might both believe—and in good faith—that their works are morally justified, but that does not absolve them (or their readers) of the ability to be deceived. As noted in Part I, this is the weak point of an idealistic, optimistic, humanist poetics: the simple fact, all too observable in everyday life, that not even writing that claims to be morally uplifting can be guaranteed to have the desired effect. This is what Gosson puts his finger on with unerring accuracy, and what his image of the sugared poison—indistinguishable from the sugared pill—so neatly encapsulates. The sweetness seems to be the same, the bitterness seems to be the same, but while one kind of bitterness can cure, the other kind can kill, and, since there is no guarantee of the first, then it is safest to assume the second.[24] Poetry as

---

[23] For Agrippa, likewise, 'Phisicke . . . is a certaine Arte of manslaughter' (Nn4), and 'being very well skilled in makinge poisons, [physicians] mighte easely be moued with hatred, ambition, or gaine, to minister poyson in steede of Medecine' (Qq1ᵛ). Whether their motivations are bad or good, however, the results are the same: 'it maketh no matter, whether thorow wante of knowledge, or negligence, folly, or malice, vncarefully, or diligently, the Phisition in steede of medicine, hath ministred poyson, and brought man in daunger of his life' (Qq2). To be clear, however, Agrippa is referring to *physicians* here, not to poets: it is Gosson who makes the metaphorical link.

[24] Harington, whose 'Briefe Apologie', as we have seen, bears an indeterminate relation to Agrippa—now appearing seriously to refute his charges, now evincing a knowing and self-undercutting irony—illustrates the liability (and lability) of the sugared pill motif particularly well. When ostensibly warning his readers against the more lascivious passages in the *Orlando Furioso*, for example—'read them as my author ment them, to breed detestation and not delectation'—Harington reverses the normal arrangement whereby an attractive exterior conceals a hard moral lesson by proposing that, in such cases, 'sweet meate wil haue sowre sawce' (214). This begs the question, however, of why—if a moralistic reading were really what the poet was after—he should hide it under such an unsavoury covering at all: a question Harington evidently finds difficult to answer, and in the end can only crave 'pardon' (214, 215) for Ariosto and other such ribald writers. The unspoken conclusion, that would only have confirmed Gosson's worst fears, is that poets do indeed poison their readers, in this case without even pretending to do otherwise: and, worse, that there is nothing to prevent readers from swallowing that poison with the greatest enthusiasm where the sour sauce (sexual licence) is sweet (delectable), nor from rejecting its supposedly healing properties when the sweet meat (moral instruction) is sour (detestable). For Harington, that is, readers will swallow the poet's sweet syrup/sour sauce even when they know perfectly well it is bad for them. For a similar slippage, see the quotation cited in note 21—poetry 'is both goodnesse and sweetnesse, Rubarb and Sugercandie, the

Russian roulette. 'How often, think you', Sidney's speaker asks rhetorically, 'do the physicians lie, when they aver things good for sicknesses, which afterwards send Charon a great number of souls drowned in a potion before they come to his ferry?' (103.5–7).[25] The aim of the question, of course, is to contrast the poet, whom he affirms 'never lieth' (103.9) on the way to averring that, unlike physic, poetry *is* good for sickness and conducive to spiritual health. For the benefit of his readers, that is, the poet dispenses bitter but medicinal potions under the cover of sweetness, rather as Nathan cured David of his blind desire by means of a simple parable. Although the speaker refuses to see its applicability to himself, however, and here suppresses the connection between physician and poet that he makes elsewhere, does his question not pose another? What if, as Gosson suggests, the poet/doctor might, unbeknownst to his reader/patients—and even to himself—unwittingly dispense something that does them harm? And, if that is the case, then to prevent the trail of self-deception from going any further, should this good doctor, for one, not first examine, know, and so heal himself?[26]

ॐ

The speaker's strategy in this refutation, then, might be said rather spectacularly to backfire: for his initial move—to take the lying charge as an empirical issue (that poetry depicts things not 'true' in that sense)—gives rise to a number of consequences that seriously undermine the case in hand. First, it makes it difficult to believe for true anything he (as either poet or defender) says. Second, it dodges the real charge, which is not that poetry is empirically false but that it is ethically false:

pleasaunt and the profitable' (207–8)—in which the bitter emetic rhubarb comes to be aligned not, as expected, with the harsh but medicinal moral lesson ('the profitable') but rather with 'the pleasant', i.e. the sour comes to be conflated with the sweet again. Where Gosson assumes that any sane person would avoid the immorality that spells spiritual death, Harington hints that people are perversely likely to seek it out, consequences be damned, or at least that there is no stopping them from doing so. Not for the first time, when an idealist poetics is subjected to pressure it seems to lead back to masochism.

[25] For the image of the lying physician, see also Agrippa: 'euery one is beleued yᵗ professeth him self a Phisition, whereas there is no greater daunger in any leesing' (Oo2ᵛ), 'Phisitions be . . . the falsest men of al other', 'all their promises be vaine trifles, and mere lyes', making '*thou liest like a Phisition*' a common proverb (Oo4, italics original). The saying is not listed in Tilley, or in Hassell 1982, but it seems to have been current in Italy. Petrarch cites it—'*Mentiris ut medicus*' [You lie like a physician]— in the first of his four *Invectives against a Physician* (1355) which pit poetry against medicine as part of the wider humanist debate about the relative value of the arts and the sciences: see Petrarch 2003 (30, 31). Petrarch cites the saying in the context of a defence of poetry in which the poet's 'good' lies are contrasted favourably with the physician's 'bad' ones (i.e. the former are mysteries or metaphors that minister to the soul, while the latter are falsehoods that are directed at—and generally destructive of— the body). On this see the discussions in Trone 1997; and Singer 2011 (65–8). It is not clear whether Sidney is alluding to Petrarch's *Invective* here, but the contrast his speaker draws between the poet and the physician certainly allows him to take the same position. Gosson's metaphor neatly anticipates and overturns this line of defence, however, by presenting the poet *as* a physician who lies.

[26] Gosson, of course, presents himself as the 'good Phisition' throughout the *Schoole* (73/☞5, 88/B5ᵛ, 108/E2ᵛ, 118/F4ᵛ), 'An Apologie' (124/L2–L2ᵛ), and *Playes Confuted* (141/☞7), *his* cure being a strong dose of demystification: i.e. to expose the claims of those pseudo-physicians, the poets and their defenders, whose promises of moral instruction are deceptive. This makes him the Physician of physicians. As patron deity of the Petrarchan tradition, by contrast, the love-struck Apollo—the 'God of musicke, phisicke, poetry, and shooting' (Cooper 1565) who is unable to cure his own wounds—might serve as the mythic prototype of the perverse, non-idealist poet.

that its apparently 'good sentences' can 'shadowe . . . knauery', and that, instead of promoting the health and well-being of his readers, as it so often promises to do, its 'sweete Syrropes' (77/A2) might actually make them worse or even sicken the healthy, poison the well. As noted above, critics have long pointed out that the speaker has 'no defense' against this charge, his repeated assertion that poetry *is* ethical—that it teaches 'true doctrine' (*Defence*, 108.14) and moves its readers to 'the most high and excellent truth' (99.30–1), the refutation's second move—constituting 'not so much counterargument as counter-statement'.[27] 'But I list not to defend Poesy with the help of her underling Historiography' (108.8–9), the speaker disarmingly asserts, immediately before the 'triumphant' conclusion of the *refutatio*: 'Let it suffice that it is a fit soil for praise to dwell upon; and what dispraise may set upon it, is either easily overcome, or transformed into just commendation' (108.9–11), a startling example of question-begging and wishful thinking. Even if the speaker had not already predisposed us to doubt him and undermined his own ability to affirm such statements for true, in any case, his inability to mount a reasoned argument here—to take apart his opponent's charge and offer a coherent rebuttal in its place—represents a serious problem. It means, in effect, that this defence of poetry cannot really be called a 'defence' at all, since it does not do its job. Third, this pseudo-defence is itself implicated in the deceptiveness with which poetry has been charged. That is to say, the sweet syrup that entices readers and draws them in need not be restricted to the appeal of entertainment or easy listening, like the 'tale which holdeth children from play, and old men from the chimney corner' (95.18–19). It might also extend, as Gosson implies, to the appeal of its own 'good sentences' themselves: its very promise of wholesome teaching and the offer to move its readers to moral health and spiritual salvation. If that is the case, then this must logically extend to a text like the *Defence*, insofar as it, too, offers good sentences, its whole project being to promote the essential goodness of poetry for the same virtuous ends as it claims for poetry itself. But the *Defence* does not—indeed, cannot—dodge the charge of deception, since according to the latter the more innocent a text seems, the more treacherous it might be: the sweeter the syrup, the greater the suspicion of 'knauery'.[28] The speaker's ethical case for poetry rests on giving its 'good' lies (empirical falsehoods or fictions) the same status as 'good' truth (true doctrine or ethical truth) such that, judged by their effects, they are all but indistinguishable from one another. But he has no answer to Gosson's charge that supposedly 'good' lies are the very worst kind of all: that these are the most dangerous and deadly in *their* effects precisely because their appearance and

[27] Kinney 1972 (12), repeated Kinney, ed. 1974 (48). See also Bronowski 1939 (22) who argues that Sidney 'does not answer' but rather 'shirk[s]' Gosson's charge; and Webster 1985 (322) that 'to this more sophisticated charge . . . Sidney provides no very good reply'.

[28] To the objection that Gosson's text is equally open to this charge—given that it, too, promises to teach its readers a moral lesson—the response might be that the *Schoole* proposes as *its* remedy the elimination of all such texts (including itself, if necessary) in favour of the one text the truth or goodness of which is doctrinally guaranteed (i.e. the Bible), in which, he notes, 'if people will bee instructed, (God be thanked) wee haue Diuines enough to discharge that' (88/B5ᵛ). The *Schoole* 'wins' the argument, that is, first by being an attack not a defence, and second by offering to disabuse readers of the abusive/deceptive tactics deployed by poets and their defenders alike.

promise of goodness is what expedites their sale and hastens their consumption. Nor does he have any answer to its logical corollary that the same must apply to himself and that his own worthy sentences are in no way exempt (good faith makes no difference except to deepen the deception, and, as we have seen, self-deception is no defence). Far from escaping the charge of deception or making it go away, the speaker's ruse—appealing to the empirical question in order to avoid the ethical one—only lands him more deeply in it, effectively catching him in his own trap. He is not only vulnerable to Gosson's attack, in other words, but to the very strategy with which he chooses to 'defend' himself against it, since, on examination, the latter turns out to undermine his argument, weaken his case, and make his own position a whole lot worse than if he had never attempted a defence of poetry in the first place (which is more or less where the *peroratio* ends up). The bottom line is that his chosen strategy leaves the speaker unable to persuade his readers to believe him, unable to defend poetry, and, on both counts, unable to defend himself.

As a result of the speaker's tricky operations, then, the second refutation—of the charge that poetry lies—ends up on much less secure ground than the first: the refutation of the charge that poetry is profitless. That profitability is a good thing was—as a general principle, at least—relatively easy to defend and cultural discourses readily available to support it. By arguing in favour of poetry on those grounds the speaker was in a comparatively strong position. By the same token, Sidney's attempts to counter that position—to count the costs of its 'costing' mentality and to experiment with the intuitively felt but logically counterintuitive view that poetry's profitlessness might not in fact be such a bad thing after all—was correspondingly difficult. Where this did occur, it was evident for the most part not in affirmative statements to that effect so much as in resistances that registered from the margins and between the lines. The comparative strength and weakness of those positions made it possible, therefore, to extrapolate them onto a rough class binary—the humanist who labours for profit as against the courtly maker who does not—and to differentiate between the speaker and Sidney accordingly. Although artificial in many ways, this distinction served a useful purpose in making it possible to fillet out objections to the former's position on the part of the latter that may not have been identifiable, or even thinkable, any other way. In the present case, however, where the speaker's position rests on the shakiest of premises and on ironic, parodic, or paradoxical statements that are unstable not to say self-destabilizing, it is much more difficult to draw the distinction between a strong argument and a weaker one, or between a culturally endorsed, 'official' line that the speaker takes, on the one hand, and attempts by Sidney to disrupt it, on the other. The speaker is still in favour of profit here, but he now finds himself trying to argue that *lies* are profitable: a statement he proves, in the event, unable either to affirm or defend. It is an impossible case. Where the speaker's position is so weak—so self-sabotaged that I think we are justified in judging it close to collapse—it is harder to maintain, first, the view that it represents anything resembling an 'official' position, and, second, that Sidney's resistant, nay-saying position is so very different from it.[29] Although I have been

---

[29] When discussing the first, 'empirical' move of this refutation above, I noted the difficulty in practice of differentiating between the speaker's roles as defender and as poet (the one committed to

referring to the 'speaker' throughout, therefore, the collapse of his position here robs him of any distinctive function and I will henceforth use this designation only on those occasions when it is still useful to discuss the view—which many continue to hold, after all—that the *Defence* does indeed have a logical argument and mount a coherent defence of poetry. In general, however, as the speaker's chaotic position comes into closer alignment with Sidney's unorthodox one, it is hoped that the case I have been making for the latter will be strengthened, and that it will become easier to appreciate the alternative and radically different understanding of poetry that Sidney is feeling his way towards. This position—that poetry might enjoy an autonomous existence independent of any profit that might be gained from it or accumulable 'knowledge' it might convey—may still have been identifiable only as that which an official, culturally sanctioned discourse was *unable* to say: that is, it might still be evident only in resistances that register from the margins and between the lines. But it is given much greater leeway—thinkability, scope, and room for development—when the opposing 'official' discourse is presented in such theoretical disarray, and shown, very graphically, to be unable to say the things it is supposed to be able to say.

The trickiness of this refutation has other consequences too. If, in spite of its comparatively more secure grounding, the first refutation—its argument for the profitability of poetry initially so plausible, so self-evident—could prove, in the long run, vulnerable to deconstruction and capable, as it turned out, of coming apart, then the fate of the present one—its argument for the profitability of lies from the outset so vaporous, so self-contradictory—hardly inspires confidence. Where an apparently irrefutable defence could, in the course of things, come asunder, what hope can there be for one that is not only so paradoxical as never really to get off the ground, but, in ducking the charge, is not strictly speaking a defence at all, and, indeed, ends up turning on and deconstructing itself? This doubt about its success or even status as a defence suggests, therefore, that the text's self-presentation as a formal juridical oration, framed on the model of a counsel for the defence, might be in line for a little re-examination. The *Defence* is certainly structured like such an oration, its design conforming to the prescribed division of parts (*exordium, narratio, propositio, divisio, confirmatio, refutatio*, and so on), and in this respect it bears affinity with academic orations in defence of poetry written in the 1570s.[30] But the weakness of its case—its lack of a case, its paradoxical negation

affirming things, the other not). On the face of it, this might seem to anticipate the present situation, i.e. the difficulty in practice of differentiating between the speaker and Sidney. However obvious it might seem at first, however, I would caution against making too hasty an equation between the 'poet' and 'Sidney' here, if only because the former would not have tried to affirm anything—i.e. would have written a poem instead, and never attempted a defence of poetry—whereas for good or ill the latter did undertake this impossible, self-contradictory task. The roles of defender and poet are as contradictory for Sidney, that is, as they were for his speaker, and where the latter collapses into the former, as here, he simply passes that unresolved and unresolvable contradiction on.

[30] In particular, Richard Wills, *De re poetica* (1573; see Fowler, ed. 1958), but also the *Oratio in laudem poëseos* (*c.*1572–76), a version of which was attributed to John Rainolds (see Ringler, ed. 1940) but subsequently re-attributed to Henry Dethick (see Binns 1975, and Binns, ed. 1999). Wills writes in defence of poetry, as Sidney's speaker would do, while Dethick writes more in praise of his chosen subject. I will return to the difference between defence and praise below, to suggest that the latter—at

of a case—would seem to suggest that, rather than an earnest plea directed to the
bench and aimed at demolishing the opposition, the *Defence* has, like other trials in
Sidney's writing, two very different judges and juries: on the one hand, an 'official'
jurisprudence, if not always male then always identified with authority, and, on the
other, an alternative jurisprudence, if not always female then always identified with
a private world of family and friends.[31] In *The Lady of May* and the *Old Arcadia*, for
example, a case is presented for deliberation to a princely judge (Elizabeth and
Euarchus, respectively) whose judgement in both cases is absolute but in neither
case final or interpretatively binding. Elizabeth's controversial choice of the shepherd in the masque has long been felt to be the 'wrong' one, and Euarchus' sentence
against the lovers in the romance evaporates in the twist of the plot's comedic
ending and never gets to be carried out. In both cases, but especially the latter, there
is a strong sense that, for all the stagey appeal to figures in authority, it is a different
audience that is making the final judgement call. This different audience might
consist of the sister to whom Sidney dedicates the *Old Arcadia*, perhaps, and the
female readers whom he addresses throughout it: characters who, like those who
presided over the medieval 'courts of love', might arbitrate the *questioni d'amore*
they are presented with *not* according to the tenets of criminal law, or even rational
self-interest, but by different criteria altogether, and take into consideration such
things as passion, paradox, and play.[32] In the same way, while the *Defence* has all
the accoutrements of a formal juridical oration and thus may well appeal for a just
hearing to a learned, trained, and specialized audience—as, indeed, it has been
received by the scholarly community from William Temple on—that does not
necessarily exhaust all the interpretative possibilities to which it is open. Harington's
use of the *Defence* in his own 'Briefe Apologie', for example—on inspection, no less
difficult to pin firmly to a 'profitable' or moralistic agenda than its predecessor and, in
spirit, just as tricky—could be held alongside Temple's 'Analysis' as a way of showing
how Sidney's defence-that-is-not-a-defence might alternatively be received, read,

---

least in the peculiar sub-form of paradoxical praise—constitutes the model that Sidney (as opposed to
his speaker) follows in the *Defence*. Myrick 1935 (46–83) was the first to point out that the *Defence* is
structured like a juridical oration. As noted earlier, in this book I use the divisions (*narratio, refutatio*,
etc.) to pinpoint sections of argument within the *Defence*, rather than to imply any progressive
marshalling of its argument.

[31] Ferguson 1983 (137–8)—who sets her reading of the *Defence* entirely within the context of
Sidney's 'lifelong concern with trials in which young men who resemble their creator find themselves
accused of crime by social authorities or by the "voice of reason" in their own minds'—sees the text as
directed principally, and in self-justificatory fashion, to Elizabeth, or at least to 'a court in which the
Queen played the role of chief judge', a view with which Maslen (39–40) concurs. Hager 1991 (104),
by contrast, sees the *Defence*'s speaker as an Astrophil-figure—a 'would-be love-poet intentionally
failing to defend himself'—and suggests that the audience addressed by the *Defence* is a 'coterie,
primarily ladies' (110), a view with which Matz 2000 (74) concurs.

[32] I take the idea of the alternative jurisprudence from Goodrich 1996 and 2001. That Sidney
seems to have restricted the circulation of manuscripts of the *Defence* to a very close circle of family and
friends (his siblings, Temple, Harington, possibly Penelope Rich) is noted by Woudhuysen 1996
(234). Critics who connect the *Defence* with the *Old Arcadia* as a way of showing how, in both, Sidney
queries and performatively subverts the patriarchal rule of law as it applies both to conduct and to
writing include Dickson 1992 and Williams 2009.

and judged. Able to countenance the deleterious impact that (if anything can be guaranteed) desire can be guaranteed to have on the best of intentions and the most perfectly formulated and rational of arguments, including his own, Harington is much more open to the possibility that an idealist reading of the *Defence* is not the only one available, and, indeed, not necessarily the one best able to do justice to its subtlety, intelligence, and wit.

Starting from *this* premise, moreover,—that, as readers, we might better appreciate the *Defence* if we, too, were to range within if not beyond the zodiac of our own wit and, for once, *not* be reined with learned discretion (or at least be aware of the limitations such reining entails)—makes it possible to see that Sidney's mock trial here is not only playful but also *perverse*. That is to say, Sidney does not only fail to defend poetry. He positively lays himself open to attack: to the unanswerable charges of the poet-haters, and especially of Gosson. Indeed, like Astrophil beating himself for spite, he even turns on and attacks himself. Where a psychological model of defence classically involves the living organism deploying a 'shield' to secure protection from the flood of stimuli that would otherwise overwhelm it, the defensive 'shield' that Sidney mobilizes on the part of his speaker is so weak, self-destructing, and non-existent that it lets the tide of traumatic stimuli come flooding in. A defence of poetry is a non-starter—trying to demonstrate the excellences of poetry in propositional prose is a contradiction in terms—and Sidney, who seems to have been (or become) more aware of this than most, gives in his *Defence of Poesy* a performance of that contradiction that is quite on a par with those of his most tormented, conflicted, and self-divided literary characters. He did not have to do such a thing—he was not, so far as we know, asked to defend poetry—and a rational person who had neither time nor reputation to spare might well have taken one look at the project and sensibly walked away. Sidney, however, claims to have been 'overmastered by some thoughts' and so 'yielded an inky tribute unto them' (109.30–1), a part of that inky tribute being just such a confession of the masochistic and frankly irrational 'rationale' of the work in hand. Rational self-interest does not come into it, or does not tell the whole story, and to recognize this is at least to cede the possibility that profit—in the form of personal advancement, or the gain of intellectual, moral, personal, and spiritual capital—need not constitute the outermost parameters of the zodiac of wit. As Jonathan Crewe asks (in response to those who read the defensive postures that Sidney variously strikes in his life and works as in some way careerist or self-justificatory), is Sidney really 'to be understood in terms of a prima facie commitment to self-advancement, public life, etc.?'[33] Might the power relays not rather be 'more complex than they seem, the forms of indirection more subtle, the circuit not quite so short' (82)? Might

---

[33] Crewe 1986 (82). In *AS* 23, Astrophil rejects the interpretation, imputed to him by others, that ambition is what 'Holds my young braine captiv'd in golden cage'. This is not, of course, to attribute any naïve biographical meaning to the statement but rather to note the metaphor here deployed: i.e. ambition, self-advancement, self-interest, etc., is characterized as an entrapment—specifically an entrapment within gold-fetishism or money thought—that Astrophil would abjure were it not for the fact that he remains masochistically fixated on the beauty of Lady Rich (and the impossibility of obtaining it/her).

they not include, in fact, the possibility of abnegating profit altogether (whether experimentally or decisively), of choosing to enter into if not embrace the experience of loss—of losing face, losing the argument—and of wilfully undertaking actions that are likely if not sure to lead to reprimand or rustication?[34] If, according to the standards of strictly logical argument, Sidney's defence of poetry is flawed (as even Temple politely points out)—in pieces, in ruins, quite as much as the shattered masochistic subject who declines the idealist illusions of wholeness and plenitude—then it is, for all that, a project self-sought and self-chosen: the record of an unwinnable case that Sidney could easily have avoided had he wanted to, but that he voluntarily imposes upon himself.[35]

Despite the collapse of its arguments, however, the *Defence* has been and still is taken by many of its readers to be the defence of poetry it purports to be: its rousing thesis about the ability of poetry to inspire heroic conduct and political action living on, in the words of one of its editors, 'even in its perversions'.[36] For these, perhaps the majority of readers, the idea that poetry's fictions or 'good' lies are capable of promoting in the individual and the state profit of the highest moral order remains the beauty of the *Defence* and the most obvious justification for continuing to read, study, and teach it. Since the profitability argument lives on, therefore, and constitutes the generally accepted if not orthodox reading of the *Defence*, it will be necessary to stay with it a little longer, and to consider the speaker's arguments to that effect in the following section.

[34] Such as the tennis-court quarrel with the Earl of Oxford (1579) and Sidney's letter to Elizabeth objecting to her proposed marriage to the Duke of Alençon (1579–80?). As Crewe 1986 (82) hints, Sidney may well have used such means to engineer his rustication from court, since his 'literary career . . . was facilitated by his expulsion from public life'. On reading Sidney's New Year's gift to Elizabeth of a jewelled whip in 1581 as an overtly masochistic gesture of submission, see Loewenstein 1985 (132) and Bates 2007 (38).

[35] Temple, of course, is trying to correct the logical flaws he detects in the *Defence* in order to make it more rather than less ideal. He nonetheless sees it as his duty to point out occasions where the argument goes awry or 'strays from the truth' [*aberrat a Veritate*]: see Temple 1984 (89). On the shattered masochistic subject, see Bersani 1986 (29–50), and, specifically in relation to Renaissance texts, Marshall 2002.

[36] Shepherd (1).

II

Lies Are Profitable

Before his paradoxical statements in the *refutatio* come to complicate the issue—some two thirds of the way through the *Defence*—the speaker has, after all, been making the case that poetry's 'lies' are profitable for quite some time: most directly, from the *propositio* where he first introduces the idea that poetry is an art of imitation: 'for so Aristotle termeth it in his word *mimesis*, that is to say, a representing, counterfeiting, or figuring forth...with this end, to teach and delight' (86.17–20). Repeated three paragraphs later—'it is that feigning notable images of virtues, vices, or what else, with that delightful teaching, which must be the right describing note to know a poet by' (87.37–9)—this definition remains the set theme through the *divisio* and *confirmatio* which, together with the *propositio*, form the polemical heart of the *Defence* and constitute some forty per cent of the treatise as a whole. After the 'failure' of the *narratio*—where his attempts to idealize poetry had effectively been compromised by Sidney's intimation of the costs such idealism entails—it is entirely understandable that the speaker should cut his losses and re-launch his argument afresh by putting Plato firmly behind him and announcing Aristotle as the new guiding spirit of his argument.[37] This 'more ordinary opening' (86.12) appears, therefore, as a rescue attempt: an effort on the part of the speaker to get his defence of poetry back on track. If Plato had argued that poetry misrepresents the ideal and is, therefore, *un*-ideal (an argument that, in the event, had proved difficult to deny), then Aristotle—whom the speaker invokes as arguing, in his theory of mimesis, that poetry represents the real—seems to offer a promising alternative. Aristotle's name signals a shift, in other words, from the abstract and quasi-mystical speculations of Plato's philosophy and its Neoplatonic iterations to much more practical, grounded, and down-to-earth considerations of how poetry might have useful applications—pragmatic effects, positive outcomes—in the real world. According to this new *telos*, poetry is understood as having 'the end of well-doing and not of well-knowing only' (88.27) for, 'as Aristotle saith, it is not *gnosis* but *praxis* must be the fruit' (94.33–4).[38] In such a poetics, Plato's other-worldly idealism is harnessed and put to work so as to translate ideals into practice and reproduce them for the benefit of the real world and its human inhabitants. This

---

[37] As Reisner 2010 (334) notes, 'one would indeed expect Sidney to invoke Aristotle at this stage of his argument'. It is noticeable that Scott 2013 (6) begins his *Model of Poesy* squarely with the position that Sidney's speaker only belatedly takes—i.e. that poetry is 'an art of imitation...with delight to teach and to move us to good'—effectively skipping the problematic *narratio* and demonstrating, as his editor notes, 'a fundamental sympathy with Aristotle that Sidney lacks' (xlv).

[38] Referencing Aristotle 1926, *Nicomachean Ethics*, 1095a.

shift maps conveniently onto the Renaissance valuation of the active over the contemplative life—poetry becomes the 'active deployment of that scheme in everyday affairs', as one critic writes—and, for him as for others, onto confessional affiliations as well: 'To achieve this activist aim, [poetry] must be more experiential than meditational . . . less an exercise in ritual worship and more an instrument of politics.' As such, it forms the basis for a distinctly Protestant poetics: Sidney needed such a definition of poetry 'to effect his plan for Protestant renewal'.[39]

The speaker's particular take on Aristotelian mimesis is most evident in his discussions of history. For, should it be asked what the object of this imitation is— what it is that the poet is supposed to be imitating—then it is nothing so obvious as this real world which his poetic productions are supposed to be influencing so profoundly: neither the natural, physical world nor the things that might be or happen in it. That is the domain of the historian, or, more accurately, of the mere historiographer, who simply chronicles those things in the order in which they occurred. However, 'although their lips sound of things done, and verity be written in their foreheads' (83.5–6), the historiographers' commitment to actuality and factuality does not earn them any credit for the truth-value of their writing. On the contrary, it is denigrated on both counts, as full of lies and of little worth.[40] In his 1580 letter to Robert, Sidney distinguishes between the historiographer's 'Story', which is 'nothing but a *Narration* of thinges done', and the historian's 'treatise', which 'besides that addeth many thinges for profite and Ornament'.[41] The true historian has the edge over the mere historiographer, that is, because—by putting great speeches into the mouths of his historical protagonists and fabricating details for dramatic effect—he behaves like a poet: 'for though perchance [such things] were not so, yet it is enough they might be so.' This makes him—like the right poet but unlike the historiographer—'a discourser for profite'.[42] Such profit clearly derives, therefore, from *adding* something to the simple representation of things as they are or were: to 'what men have done' (85.9), 'what is' (90.18), 'things as things were' (92.37), 'that *was*' (92.44), the 'bare *was*' (93.6), and so on. As a result

---

[39] Heninger 1989 (223, 224); for an earlier iteration of these views, see Heninger 1984. See also Stillman 2008 (30): Sidney 'locates his discourse not in relation to a history of poetics . . . and still less in relation to an abstract philosophical question . . . but instead he fashions his defense much more pragmatically by comparing poetry as a species of knowledge to rival sciences'; 'Audaciously and without precedent, Sidney argues . . . for poetry as the "princely" science for promoting virtuous action within the always interconnected spheres of personal and political governance. In the space where politics reigns for Aristotle, Sidney inserts poetry'.

[40] As the speaker notes, the practitioners of all the 'other' (i.e. non-poetic) arts are prone to falsehood, but 'especially the historian, [who] affirming many things, can, in the cloudy knowledge of mankind, hardly escape from many lies' (103.10–12). Agrippa agrees that 'Historiographers doo so mutche disagree emonge them selues, and doo write so variabe [*sic*] and diuers thinges of one matter, that it is impossible, but that a number of them shoulde be verie Liers' (E2).

[41] 18 October 1580: *Correspondence* (1006).

[42] Ibid. (1007). The speaker exhibits some uncertainty over whether the 'historical' (86.37–8) kind of poet such as Lucan belongs to the second type he delineates or to the third, i.e. that of the 'right poets' (86.44). The question hinges on the matter of invention and the degree to which historians deploy it. The speaker defers this doubt, 'whether they properly be poets or no' (86.42–3), to the grammarians to determine, although it is fairly clear that, for the purposes of his argument, the more 'poetical' the historian, the better.

of which, one might say that the mimesis the speaker presents is more properly a kind of 'mimesis-plus', and that it is profitable to the degree to which it aggregates this additional x-factor to its representation of life and the world as they appear to us.[43] If it is to achieve any profitable effect, that is, mimesis must imitate phenomena not simply in their particular, concrete instantiations, as communicated to us by our sense data and experience, but rather in their optimal manifestations, their full potential, as communicated to us by our intellect. For Aristotle, while the former might constitute the 'actual', the latter constitutes the 'real', and it is this optimized reality that is the proper object of poetic imitation.[44] The historian might claim to present 'images of true matters, such as indeed were done' (92.10)—as opposed to the poet who might simply make things up 'fantastically or falsely' (92.11)—but 'Truly', the speaker asserts, citing the *Poetics*, 'Aristotle himself... plainly determineth this question, saying that Poetry is ... more studiously serious than history' because it deals with '*katholou* ... the universal consideration', and history with '*kathekaston*, the particular' (92.11–17): and where the former 'weighs what is fit to be said or done', the latter marks only whether a particular individual 'did, or suffered, this or that' (92.17–20).[45] Profit is to be derived from—and so true value accorded to—those texts that concern themselves with the former, by representing 'what may be and should be' (87.10–11): what 'should be' (92.27), 'that which deserveth to be called and accounted good' (94.19–20), 'not ... what is or is not, but what should or should not be' (103.16–17), 'pictures [of] what should be, and not stories [of] what have been' (103.26–7), 'what men ... should do' (103.43), and so on. Thus, to the extent that a historian remains tied to 'what is, to the particular truth of things and not to the general reason of things' (90.18–19), his will remain the 'less fruitful doctrine' (90.20–1), while the extent to which the poet (or the 'poetical' historian, 92.37; 93.8) depicts what might be or should have been, his, conversely, emerges as the 'more fruitful knowledge' (102.41) of the two.

Although the speaker does not spell it out, his model of mimesis thus operates on at least two levels. First, the poet (or poetical historian) imitates optimized scenarios

---

[43] See Fineman 1986 (3) on the celebrated definition of *epideixis* as 'what happens when mimesis and metaphor meet ... With metaphor added to it, mimesis becomes more than merely lifeless imitation, just as metaphor, grounded by mimetic reference, is more than extravagant ornamentation'. Although he acknowledges the potential ambiguity of metaphor in its role as supplement here, Fineman nevertheless situates Sidney's *Defence* squarely within this tradition of idealist, humanist poetics: 'In traditional rhetorical and poetic theory there is of course no real suspicion regarding the truth of poetic figure, not if figure is handled properly. Quite the contrary, as in Sidney, the colors of rhetoric are the means whereby the poet manifests and actualizes his "Idea"' (96). See also Ferguson 1983 (10) on the three types of oration distinguished by Aristotle—forensic, deliberative, and epideictic—in which the last, uniquely, has the added factor of aiming 'not only to persuade, but to delight an audience'; it also 'pleases the speaker, who seeks to win praise for his own eloquence as well as for his subject'.

[44] Referencing Aristotle 1995, *Poetics*, 1460b–1461a.

[45] Ibid. 1451b. For similar statements, see Scott 2013 (11, 33, 57). Curtright 2003 (110) suggests that Sidney drew as much on Aristotle's discussion of character, *ethos*, and persuasion in the *Art of Rhetoric* as on the *Poetics*: 'As his modification of Aristotle's teaching on mimesis allowed Sidney to rebut the challenge that poets misrepresent nature, Sidney's addition of Aristotelian *ethos* allows him to maintain that poets persuade audiences toward moral living', referencing Aristotle 1926, *Art of Rhetoric*, 1356a, 1377b–1378a. 'As a result', he concludes, 'the Ideas might be called idealized universals' (112).

of human conduct in action. He does this by apprehending this conduct at its very best, its most fully realized (hence, 'real'): that is, by having a 'fore-conceit' (85.35) of what such heroic action might look like, and then making it manifest by 'delivering [it] forth' (85.37, 38) in his writing. As the speaker's favourite example of such exemplary poetics, one might cite Xenophon whose fictionalized biography of Cyrus presents the latter as 'so right a prince' (85.31–2) that his 'feigned' account of the hero 'certainly is more doctrinable... than the true Cyrus in Justin' (92.27–9).[46] Consequently, nothing else 'can so readily direct a prince' (91.19) in determining his own course of action than Xenophon's text. Second, uplifted and inspired by this material, the reader will, in turn, imitate the poet's (or poetical historian's) imitation. In this particular case, the results are dramatic for, in being a poetical history, Xenophon's text is not 'wholly imaginative, as we are wont to say by them that build castles in the air; but so far substantially it worketh, not only to make a Cyrus... but to bestow a Cyrus upon the world to make many Cyruses' (85.38–42). That is to say, the *Cyropaedia* does not only represent human heroism at its most 'real', most 'true'. By inspiring readers to act likewise, it actualizes that potential in the real world—realizes it, brings it into being—with very real ('substantial') social outcomes and beneficial political effects. Moreover, as noted earlier, this series of imitations need not end there, for the reader so motivated by Xenophon's text might go on to perform deeds that will then inspire imitation in others, especially if, as the speaker suggests, that reader is a public figure like a prince (this being the optimal example). As individuals might be moved to imitate such a reader/prince, and/or poets (or poetical historians) to represent his (or their) actions so that others still might be further inspired, and so on, so Xenophon's primary act of imitation gives rise to a potentially infinite series of imitations of imitations of imitations. While the beneficial effects of such mimesis might ideally manifest themselves in actual events—actual heroics on actual battlefields, for example—it is important to register how crucial the poetic intervention is to this process. For in this model imitation is almost never unmediated. Models and exempla are not, for the most part, taken directly from life, and even if they are based on actual, historical figures as Cyrus was, in order to *be* models and exempla they must have been thoroughly worked over first: enhanced by the poet's tools which take the 'bare *was*' and, by giving it the make-over of a lifetime and turning it into what might have been, render it worthy of imitation.[47] It is important to register, in other words, the extent to which the speaker's model of imitation is *necessarily* a

---

[46] I.e. Marcus Junianus Justinus (second or third century AD), whose *Historiarum Philippicarum libri XLIV*—an abridgement of the *Historiae Philippicae* of the Augustan historian Trogus Pompeius (now lost)—was translated into English by Arthur Golding in 1564. Editors agree that Justinus' account of Cyrus is in fact 'no more historical than Xenophon's but lacks the fictive purpose of the *Cyropaedia*': Alexander (331). See also Shepherd (176), Maslen (168), and van Dorsten (196).

[47] Heninger 1989 (291) gives a good summary of this process: 'Sidney progresses ... from a poetics of re-presenting what the poet has observed in nature to a poetics of metaphorically figuring forth ideas that exist only in his mind. Although the poet must begin with his own "stuff" [100.23], he puts it through a process of generalization and "represents" it as Aristotelian universals ... Sidney expands the basis of his poetics from empiricism to idealism.' On the dubious gender implications of this model of poetics-as-cosmetics, see Dolan 1993.

literary one: the object of imitation, that is to say, is not Nature in the first instance but rather other *texts*. The process of imitation might eventuate in actual heroics—the doings of all those Cyruses—but the primary scene is one of readers and writers imitating other, older writers, much as the humanist pedagogical system pre-scribed.[48] There would be no heroics at all, real or imaginary, without that first, literary, poetical, imitative step.

Such is the theory of imitative action and inspired emulation that the speaker introduces with his model of mimesis and supports by invoking the authority of Aristotle. For many readers, this theory—set out most fully in the *propositio, divisio,* and *confirmatio*—constitutes the main body of the *Defence* (earlier and later sections are deemed extraneous if not supernumerary and often ignored) and one of the most eloquent (and, in English, earliest) articulations of a genuinely Renaissance poetics.[49] After the shaky start of the *narratio*—which did not always seem entirely clear where it was going and where arguments and examples tended to clash confusingly with one another—this central section, by contrast, promises relatively plain sailing, its argument clear, confident, and on course, which may account in large part for its readerly appeal. If this was the means by which the speaker had hoped to put the problems of the *narratio* behind him, however—finally to put to rest those doubts that had been troubling his otherwise serene vision of the poet's idealized, golden world—then his confidence in this strategy proves sadly mis-taken.[50] For, as will have become obvious during the preceding discussion, not-withstanding his invocation of Aristotle and promise of a pragmatic, empirical poetics grounded in and justified by real-world political activism, the theory of mimesis the speaker sets out is, in conception and execution, entirely idealist. Drawing on Aristotle's distinction between actual, particular instantiations of things (things as they are or were) and real, general, universal exemplifications of them (things as they ought to be), the speaker arrives—as the proper object of imitation—at what critics have variously described as a 'high realism', a 'meta-reality', a

---

[48] Although Ascham 1967 (114) notes in *The Schoolmaster* that 'all the works of nature in a manner be examples for art to follow', he specifies that the imitation of classical authors is his particular pedagogical purpose and that following them is the method he recommends for his ideal school. This would confirm the speaker's assumption in the *narratio* that learned poetry will automatically go on to grow more learned poetry and that—in order for the 'simple Indians' (83.21) to acquire knowledge—they must first be given learned (i.e. European) models to imitate. That the Indians had for many centuries clearly developed a robust heroic poetry of their own without such a literary intervention provides, of course, a counter-example to the mimetic model of poetry that the speaker is here trying to defend. See also Miller 2001 (411), who notes that in the *Defence* 'Sidney proposes that proper imitation results in the internalization and personal possession of what is imitated'—as, for example, the great orators imitate the appearance of an emotion such as anger so as to induce the same in their hearers—leading to a potentially infinite series of 'imitated' actions, ever further removed from a notionally authentic or foundational point of origin. On the theory and practice of imitation in the Renaissance, see Greene 1982.

[49] E.g. Fineman 1986 (91): 'This is one reason why the poetry of praise so readily becomes the praise of poetry as a whole, because this is the generic explanation or "apologie" of poetic "profit and delight." As Sidney says... "Poesie... is an arte of imitation... to teache and delight" [86.17–20]'.

[50] The quotation cited in note 37 above should now be given in full to make its qualification clear: 'While one would indeed expect Sidney to invoke Aristotle at this stage of his argument, it is all too often missed just how misleading this reference to the *Poetics* actually is': Reisner 2010 (334).

'representation of the real *through* the ideal', that bears an uncanny resemblance to the Platonic Idea.[51] Even when those critics try to differentiate the speaker's 'Aristotelianized' version of this Idea—as, for example, by suggesting that it 'avoids the tenuousness and elusiveness of a philosophical essence by being a concrete instance, a verbalized image'—the distinction is not always easy to maintain.[52] In the case of one such verbalized image, for instance (that of Cyrus), Platonic and Aristotelian imperatives are found to exist in complementary and chiastic relation: 'poetic idealization of the real [is] at the same time a realization of the ideal.'[53] Such mimesis is, in effect, Platonic in all but name: 'The imitation thus produced follows the ideal behind nature rather than the actual in nature which has been warped by fortune and circumstance.'[54]

That the speaker should announce his departure from such a Platonic paradigm in the *propositio* only to land squarely back in it is an irony not lost on critics, even those who are sympathetic to his enterprise and willing to give him, and Sidney, the benefit of the doubt. Recent scholarship has decisively overturned the old view that Sidney encountered Aristotle only via secondary texts—commentaries and redactions—rather than directly, and his careful reading of the *Poetics* can no longer, therefore, be in doubt.[55] Nevertheless, although the *propositio* cites only Aristotle by name when launching its 'more ordinary opening', it is clearly importing Horatian poetics wholesale into the discussion as well, the formula that poetry's end is 'to teach and delight' (86.20) being so commonplace as to need no attribution.[56] The effect of this import on the *Defence*, however, is to infuse its model of Aristotelian mimesis with a powerfully ethical directive that is not necessarily present in the original (or not compellingly so), but the net result of which is to produce a typically humanist conception of poetry as 'morally

---

[51] In order: Shepherd (55); Heninger 1989 (248); Fineman 1986 (91, emphasis original). See also McIntyre 1962 (359): 'in the Renaissance ethos this ideal world, identified with the divine ideas, is more real than the domain of empirical fact.'

[52] Heninger 1989 (255). See also Stillman 2008 (110): 'poetry does not shadow forth transcendent realities behind a fictive veil...Instead, Ideas are realized by substantive images exemplified paradigmatically as pictures of the poet's making.'

[53] Fineman 1986 (95). See also Robinson 1972 (103): 'The idealized images of heroic poetry . . . teach by setting forth a moral abstraction that can be viewed by the mind's eye, and they delight . . . by making the abstraction concrete in the lofty image of some worthy, also viewed by the inner eye.'

[54] Shepherd (61). See also Raiger 1998 (36): 'This is why Sidney's "right poet" is a Platonist and not an Aristotelian.'

[55] See Lazarus 2015a and 2015b.

[56] On the mediation of Aristotle's *Poetics* via Horace's *Ars Poetica* in the period, see Herrick 1946. See also Shepherd (48): 'When the art of letters fell into the clutches of the schoolmasters of the Roman world, a much looser and broader notion of imitation becomes current. Horace usually thinks of imitation as copying what is already created (the common analogy for poetry is with the copy that painting or sculpture makes of a visible object).' Defined in this way, imitation tends to be understood as the imitation of other imitations (as opposed to imitations of life), i.e. to be dependent on the literary—or at least 'poetic' in the sense of artistic, creative—intervention that is necessary to set the imitative series in motion. This is not necessarily a model of mimesis that Aristotle would have recognized or even signed up to. The *propositio* also silently imports Plutarchian poetics into the discussion, its reference to poetry as a 'speaking picture' (86.19) alluding to *Moralia*, 'How the Young Man Should Study Poetry', 18a, and 'Were the Athenians More Famous in War or in Wisdom?', 346F.

mimetic'.[57] As Noam Reisner puts it, Sidney 'is writing in the Italian tradition of Scaliger, Minturno, and probably Castelvetro as well, which fused the moral didacticism of Horace's *Ars Poetica* with Aristotelian classifications and Platonic idealism'. Aristotle is thus 'read through Horace to arrive, ironically, at a Platonic ideal'.[58]

Responses to this typically Renaissance medley—which puts quite incompatible if not contradictory theoretical positions together—are themselves mixed. To cite three typical examples, Heninger claims that, by combining Plato and Aristotle in this way, Sidney 'sought nothing less than the amalgamation of all the previous systems into one compendious poetics that would make poetry the supreme achievement of the human intellect'.[59] Bronowski, who is generally more critical—the argument for mimesis being in his view 'not of a piece with Sidney's theory', 'counter' to it, and 'not a deep reading of Aristotle'—nonetheless takes this as a challenge: an opportunity to solve the problem heroically by means of 'the Renaissance search to hold together, almost by force, the contradiction between the actual and the ideal'.[60] Reisner, who sees the tension and oscillation between these two positions as mutually contradictory if not irreconcilable, suggests that Sidney resolves the issue by means of his Protestant poetics, in which all idealisms— whether achievable by humans (including poets) or not—are ultimately referred to and grounded in God: 'After all the rhetorical dust is allowed to settle, it appears Sidney's shaky ground remains a firmly Protestant one: he must depend on faith for the clarity of his mimetic vision.'[61] While they take different approaches, however, all three responses are heading in the same general direction. Whether they see the 'Platonizing' of Aristotle as a sublime synthesis, a hard-won compromise, or the submission to a higher power, one way or another they all work to preserve, protect, and if necessary recuperate the idealist poetics of the *Defence*. To keep in play, that is, the idea that poetic imitations or fictions ('lies') are at some fundamental level 'true': good, real, worthy, profitable, and thus defensible. What none of them ventures to suggest is that this idealist poetics might be a problem: *the* problem, in fact, that had all but wrecked the logical and textual composure of the *narratio*, and

---

[57] Fineman 1986 (90).   [58] Reisner 2010 (335).

[59] Heninger 1989 (301). For similar formulations, see ibid. (231); Heninger 1984 (8, 15); and Fineman 1986 (92).

[60] Bronowski 1939 (44, 45, 49).

[61] Reisner 2010 (338); see also Ferguson 1983 (156, 158, 159). In some respects, Reisner comes closer to my own position insofar as he sees the stance that Sidney takes in the *narratio* (from which he quotes more than any other section in the *Defence*) as glimpsing the radical possibilities of an aesthetic in which the poet, godlike, is able to create whole new worlds without reference to a prior Logos. Where we part company, however, is: (1) in his attribution of this vision to the image of the golden world (which goes unanalysed); (2) in his association of Aristotelian mimesis with the *narratio* (when it is introduced after the latter); and (3) in his claim that Sidney could not make 'such radical claims without being deeply embarrassed about them from a religious point of view' (335). My position is not that Sidney's Protestantism was embarrassed by his poetry and poetic theory but the other way round. Sidney's poetry and poetic theory were embarrassed—held back and strained to breaking point—by the speaker's self-imposed requirement that these be 'reined with learned discretion' (87.9–10) and made to fit a model of poetry—as 'studiously serious' (92.14)—that only philosophers and pedagogues could possibly have come up with (no poet worthy the name would have dreamt up such a thing). Reisner and I both see Sidney as recoiling, therefore, but from diametrically opposed things.

that the speaker did his best to put behind him with his brave new 'opening', but that—still unresolved at some deep, intuitive, and quite possibly unconscious level—he (or now, rather, Sidney) finds himself continually drawn back to, like a moth to a flame.

Having seen what happened in the *narratio*—where, as shining idol of that idealist poetics, the golden world triggered not exactly a crisis of conscience but at least a stirring of doubts that proved fatal to its defence—the failure of that argument in the *propositio, divisio,* and *confirmatio,* since it is exactly the same argument, is entirely predictable, and its eventual collapse in the tricky, paradoxical, self-destructing *refutatio* (which symptomizes nothing so clearly as an argument foundering on bad conscience) only a matter of time. It should be said, of course, that even if Sidney *had* made a thoroughly materialist use of Aristotle in order to counter Platonic idealism (had he been fully aware that that was what he wanted to do), he would still most likely have failed since, in simply reversing the priorities, a materialist critique can often end up fetishizing the actual and so keeping the idealist structure intact (it simply provides another ideal).[62] However, despite the fact that the introduction of Aristotle may have seemed at first to promise such a move, Sidney does not do this (he is quite uninterested in the question of verisimilitude, for example): he does not (and, to be fair, most probably could not) take this promising detour, even though it might eventually have returned him to the same place. Instead, his speaker goes straight back to—compulsively repeats—the same problem he had encountered in the *narratio*: the inability, for all his best efforts and intentions, to make the golden world stand up. As a result, his idealist poetics runs into difficulty all over again. Swayed no doubt by the heavy filters of Horace and humanism that gave a very particular angle on Aristotle's *Poetics* in the period, Sidney's speaker takes the passage on the universal ('*katholou*', 92.15) and the particular ('*kathekaston*', 92.16) in order to reconstruct—or try to reconstruct—the kind of idealist poetics that would conform entirely to the humanist expectations of his time: defending a poetry that will inspire its readers to virtue, and so on. Such poetry does not represent the actual—what actually happened or happens, like the fact that tyranny routinely triumphs over virtue— since, as the naked truth or 'bare *was*' (93.6), this has no moral value whatsoever and might as well be a lie. Rather, such poetry represents the real (i.e. the 'ideal' or ideal 'realized')—what *should* happen—which, in having the requisite moral value, is thereby true. Of course such poetic representations are not believed 'for actually true' (103.22): 'What child is there that, coming to a play, and seeing *Thebes* written in great letters upon an old door, doth believe that it is Thebes?'

---

[62] See Goux 1990 (95–6): 'Plato's and Aristotle's divergent conceptions of money can be systematically linked to their respective philosophies. The different ideas of these two philosophers with regard to the relation between market *value* and the monetary *matter* that embodies this value can be linked to different degrees of adherence to the spiritualist and idealist approach . . . For Plato, currency is only "a token for purposes of exchange" [*Republic*, 371b]. In contrast, Aristotle . . . maintains that money is not without an intrinsic value, that it is marked with the sign of its value . . . [Plato] points skyward, while [Aristotle] reaches down below to measure, to *ponder* the Platonist elevation, to gather it to earthly limits without, however, completely reversing it' (emphases original).

(103.23–5). However, everyone *does* believe in those representations—or should do, according to this idealist poetics—enough to be moved, stirred into action, and morally edified by them: as by the sight of the tyrant leaving the stage if not 'manacled' (93.43) then self-punished and blinded by his own hand, if the tragedy of Oedipus is what '*Thebes*' is here alluding to.[63] The playgoer returns home with a valuable lesson in hand (that tyranny comes to a bad end): something most profitable to learn and definitely a good return on the outlay of his or her time and money at the theatre. Such knowledge can be banked, added to, accumulated, filed away for future use. No one believes that these representations are actually, empirically true—and no one is pretending that they are—but everyone must believe that they are *ethically* true: that they represent ideal actions, situations, outcomes. The speaker's whole theory of imitative action and inspired emulation depends upon this, and his model of poetry as 'morally mimetic' would be meaningless without it. If readers and playgoers do not believe in the poetic representations they read about or see sufficiently to be moved by them (moved to love, to horror, to pity, to fear), so as to learn from them and apply what they have learned to their individual and collective lives, then the entire justification of poetry as profitable—moral, didactic, uplifting, virtuous, heroic, and all the rest—promptly collapses.

To explain why that is exactly what happens, let us take another look at this poetic representation that makes no attempt to disguise the fact that it is a representation: a fiction, a feigning, a figuration, pure and simple (a point on which the *propositio* is

---

[63] Editors do not venture to guess which play, if any, the Thebes reference may allude to. The *Defence* refers to 'the remorse of conscience in Oedipus' (91.10–11) and 'the violence of ambition in the two Theban brothers [Eteocles and Polynices]' (91.12–13), i.e. to Sophocles' *Oedipus Tyrannos*, and Aeschylus' *Seven Against Thebes* (or Euripides' *Phoenissae*, which is concerned with the same events). With the exception of George Gascoigne's *Jocasta* (based on *Phoenissae* via an Italian translation), which was performed at the Inns of Court in 1566, none of these plays, nor any of the other Greek tragedies set in or related to events set in Thebes, were performed in England in Sidney's lifetime: see *APGRD*. Seneca's Theban dramas, however, based on the Greek tragedies, were performed at the Universities in the 1550s, 1560s, and 1580s. *Oedipus Rex* was performed in Latin at Trinity College, Cambridge, in 1559 and possibly a version of his *Thebais* by Thomas Browne at King's College, Cambridge, in 1561–62: see Nelson 1989 (208, 933, 969). A play entitled *The Destruction of Thebes*, recounting the Eteocles and Polynices story, was prepared if not performed at Oxford in 1568–69: see Elliott et al. 2004 (150, 848). William Gager's Senecan drama, *Oedipus*, may have been performed at Magdalen College, Oxford, in 1582: see ibid. (178, 645, 816, 848, 992). The first English version of a 'Theban' play to be published was *The lamentable tragedie of Oedipus the sonne of Laius Kyng of Thebes* (1563), a translation of Seneca's play by Alexander Neville. In his 'Preface to the Reader', Neville certainly presents the play as teaching a moral lesson, claiming to have translated it 'for thy profit' (a5) and urging readers to 'Marke thou rather what is ment by the whole course of the Historie: and frame thy lyfe free from suche mischiefs, wherwith the worlde at this present is vniuersally ouerwhelmed' (a5–a5ᵛ): 'Onely wysh I all men by this Tragicall Historie (for to that entent was it written) to beware of Synne: the ende wherof is shamefull and miserable' (a6). It has been argued that Neville's translation may have been performed in a coterie setting in Cambridge or at the Inns of Court in the 1560s: see Winston 2006 (48–9). Seneca's *Thebais* was translated by Thomas Newton and published for the first time in his collection, *Seneca his tenne tragedies* (1581), which also included Neville's *Oedipus*. While the reference in the *Defence* to 'a play . . . [with] *Thebes* written in great letters upon an old door' (103.24–5) probably refers to a generic or imagined performance, then, rather than to one that Sidney may actually have seen, it most likely refers to some version of the tragedy of Oedipus and its aftermath.

explicit). Yet it is a representation that is highly valued. Indeed, it is infused with as much value as a defender of poetry can muster. As the imitation of what the greatest authorities assure us is an ideal reality, this representation positively glimmers— glows—with value, and is all but fetishized for it. Its characteristic feature is to 'shine' (91.10; 93.41; 99.31–2). And precisely because it is presented as something so valued, so valuable, this representation is more or less universally believed in. Everyone understands intellectually that a representation is *all* it is, of course, but all the same they believe in it enough to be moved, changed, transformed by it (always for the better, that is the promise). Indeed, this highly valued, valuable, shiny thing— that is nothing more than a representation—is said to be capable of moving people like nothing else (this is the defence of poetry). It motivates them, drives them, directs their lives, makes them do things they would not otherwise do. It inspires them to improve themselves, to profit themselves, to accrue personal, intellectual, moral, and spiritual capital on a potentially unlimited scale. If this is all sounding rather familiar then it is because, in this generic 'representation', the speaker comes face to face again with the same silent presence that he met with in his image of the golden world. What else but the money form? What else but the abstraction and commodification of value that the money form effectuates?[64] And, in reproducing itself and setting in motion imitative series that lead to the exponential growth of more of the same—as Xenophon's Cyrus yields many Cyruses, and they more still— what else is this poetic representation but the money form in its most capitalist, or at least usurious, manifestation?

This is the kind of poetry that the speaker is trying to defend, and that many critics (the defenders of the *Defence*) would have us believe that Sidney is trying to defend too. Defined as profitable—and defended for it—poetry naturally emerges as something of value. When the most important thing becomes what poetry is *worth*, then the kind of poetry (like epic) in which 'the lofty image of such worthies most inflameth the mind with desire to be worthy, and informs with counsel how to be worthy' (99.39–41) will be deemed the most valuable and summoned in poetry's defence. To have such poetry is not only to be worthy—to be worth something, to be intellectually and morally rich—but, through education and the acquisition of 'learning', to be given the opportunity to be worth still more: to

[64] Cf. 'I know very well, but all the same' [*Je sais bien, mais quand-même*], Octave Mannoni's famous characterization of the process of disavowal (Freud's *Verleugnung*): a process that the logic of fetishism makes particularly visible. The fetishist knows perfectly well, rationally and intellectually speaking, that the woman does not possess the phallus but substitutes a fetish object by means of which that knowledge might be disavowed. This process of disavowal has ramifications that extend far beyond the particularities of psychological perversion, for, as Mannoni 2003 (76) suggests, 'belief in the presence of the maternal phallus is the first belief that one disavows and the paradigm for all other acts of disavowal'; i.e. it 'opens up paths of all sorts: the use of misinformation to propagandistic ends, even if it must later be admitted that the information given out was false; hollow promises; the psychology of the practical joke; and the psychology of imposters' (82). For the purposes of the present argument, a belief in the value of money—a fetish object if ever there was one—serves as a quintessential example of such disavowal: the willingness to invest special, precious, 'magical' properties in something that, rationally and intellectually speaking, one knows perfectly well is simply a means of abstracting and representing the value of other things. See also Žižek 1989, and Žižek 1991 (241–53) on the ways in which ideology mobilizes the same process of disavowal.

become intellectually and morally even richer. Indeed, it is not merely the individual but the state—the world—that will be enriched thereby (infinite progress: who
could possibly not want that?). Acquire this property, this precious commodity—
this golden world—and you will gain immeasurably by it. Buy this product and be
absolutely confident that you will get your money's worth and more, for it will
grant you an ideal world that you could gain access to no other way. Believe in those
poetic representations: they are ideals, models, examples you must follow to the
benefit of others and yourself. Believe the speaker when he says that the real is ideal,
that the poet's lies are true, that they are good because they are profitable. Believe
him when he says that poetry can deliver, that it will always do what it promises,
and that as a reader or playgoer you will reap the rewards.[65] If, as he assures us, the
poet's lies are profitable, then it follows that the speaker's can be profitable too.
After all, the orators lie: they say things they do not mean and perform things they
do not feel in order to win the 'credit of popular ears; which credit is the nearest step
to persuasion' (114.37). Where persuasion is the measure of success, what matters
is that lies are believed, and this holds as much for the counsel who seeks to
persuade the jury of poetry's value as it does for the poet who seeks to inspire virtue
with his golden world, or for the orator who seeks to persuade with his golden
chain. In defending poetry, the speaker sets himself the task of restoring the
'deserved credit' (82.2; 89.30) that other arts, like horsemanship or history, still
have but that poetry has lost, and that other arts, like philosophy, have sought all
means 'to discredit' (106.27). He even calls on St Paul who, 'for the credit of poets'
(107.5), mentions them four times in his sayings and his Epistles.[66] Whether we
choose to extend our credit to Sidney's speaker, however, is up to us.[67] And since
one of those poets (alluded to only obliquely but, in the tricksy *refutatio*, very much
there in spirit) is Epimenides the Cretan liar, we may choose to reserve our

---

[65] It may now become clearer why, in the *peroratio*, Sidney ironically resorts to a similar series of
commands to 'believe' (116.24, 26, 27, 28, 32, 34, 36), as a result of which, if readers do so, they will
miraculously become 'most fair, most rich, most wise, most all' (116.40).

[66] Acts 17:28; Titus 1:12; and I Corinthians 15:33.

[67] The financial sense of *creditum* (loan or debt), from the past participle of *credere* (to trust, to
believe), was available in classical Latin, as in Italian from the mid-fourteenth century, and French from
the mid-fifteenth. The noun reached the English language relatively late and initially in the general
sense of 'favourable estimation, good name or standing' (*OED* credit *n.* I.1.a). The earliest citation in
OED and EEBO is Thomas More *A dyaloge . . . Wherin be treated dyuers maters* (1529): 'The temporal
man . . . was a good worshypfull man, and for hys trouthe and worshyp was in grete credyte' (Q3ᵛ). The
noun then developed the specifically financial sense of 'trust or confidence in a customer's ability to pay
at some future time, shown by allowing money or goods to be taken, or services to be used without
payment' (*OED* credit *n.* II.9.a) in 1542/43. In the case of the verb, it was the other way round, the
financial sense—'to trust or allow [someone] to take money or goods, or to use services, without
immediate payment' (*OED* credit *v.* I.1)—coming first, in 1541, and no doubt giving rise to the
financial sense of the noun. This then developed the more general sense—'to accept as true or truthful,
give credence to, believe' (*OED* credit *v.* II.4.a)—in 1547. When this relatively recent addition to the
lexicon appears in the *Defence*, therefore, its financial and general senses were already inextricably
entwined. By encouraging readers to believe that poets' 'lies' are true—that they represent ideals it will
profit them to follow—Sidney's speaker is effectively asking readers to extend credit to the poet: to
believe on trust that the service promised (the accrual of virtue, learning, and so forth) will be
forthcoming. Gosson's attitude to such salesman's tactics is altogether more astute. On the credit
economy in the period generally, see Muldrew 1998.

judgement and to hold out for an understanding of poetry that does not have to be conceptualized in such credit-worthy, commercial, or bankable terms. That does not have to be defended—advertised—and commodified, fetishized, in the process. There is always the option of *not* believing, of not being persuaded, of wanting to resist the idealist model that is being foisted upon us, of sensing a disconnect between what the speaker is arguing for (not very well, it has to be said) and the alternative that, in the very weakness of his case, Sidney allows us every now and then to glimpse. Not for the first time, it may be Stephen Gosson who holds the key. By advising *his* readers to be wary of poets and their defenders—*not* to believe that their 'good sentences' are true or 'sweete Syrropes' wholesome (77/A2)— Gosson opens up the possibility that a profound suspicion might be exercised towards anything that appears or presents or sells itself as precious, valuable, good, and true: poetry and idealist poetics included. It is a bad sell. Gosson does not, it is true, extend this suspicion (as Thomas More did) as far as that idealist fiction to end all idealist fictions: the money form itself. He is too wedded to the principles of thrift, profit, and good business practice for that, and his objections are directed purely at poets (and playwrights) insofar as they fail to conform to that practice. But, by way of suggesting that poetry is profitless and valueless—its golden promises empty and illusory—it may have been he who indicated to Sidney a promising way forward: a way out of and beyond the otherwise all-encompassing logic of the money form and its myths of rational self-interest.

III

Lies Are Profitless

That an idealist poetics should share the underlying structure and rationale of idealist philosophy is no cause for surprise. That it should faithfully reproduce the logical developments of that structure and rationale should not, therefore, be a cause for surprise either. As discussed in Part I, economic critics like Marc Shell and Jean-Joseph Goux see idealist philosophy, starting with Plato, as systematizing the new frame of reference or new 'logic' that the introduction of the money form ushered in. As the latter made it possible to abstract, measure, and quantify the value of things for the first time, so idealist philosophy came to accord a higher degree of truth or 'reality' to things in their valued, abstracted, idealized form, as opposed to their merely secondary existence in the fallen, phenomenal world. The actual, material existence of things was but a poor imitation—a second-hand copy, an insubstantial simulacrum, emanating only a weak, moony, reflected light—by comparison with their real, true, essential, unchanging, eternal, and ideal value: the concept of which—in the Ideas or Ideal Forms that allowed such value to radiate and shine, sun-like, forth, to be lucently apprehended by the philosopher— was fetishized accordingly. Its *value* thus came to be idealized as a commodity's abstract, etherealized, and permanent quality or worth, as opposed to its crude, brute, empirical, contingent existence, a development that quite logically led to a division— or, more properly, a hierarchy—being introduced between the two: 'What becomes apparent for the first time . . . is the division between a plural relative form in a subordinate position and a general equivalent form that dominates and governs it.'[68] The infinite relativity, multiplicity, and heterogeneity of things as they exist in the world thus comes to be regulated, reduced to order, the concept of value being the organizing principle that relates—or, rather, relegates—them to a single, abstract, mystified, yet unanimously agreed-upon standard that measures that value. This subordination of the particular (concrete, material, diverse) to the general (ideal, central, transcendent) extends, in turn, to all the subordinations that characterize the ideology of the West: matter to mind, female to male, mother to father, labour to capital, periphery to centre, nature to man, animal to human, sound to language, image to word, and so on. Early intimations that the money form constituted an exercise of power, and that it naturally lent itself to an abuse of that power—to tyranny—were thus entirely founded: the greater the move towards social organization along these lines, the greater the subordination of individual elements to a single

---

[68] Goux 1990 (94).

point of reference—the common denominator and agreed-upon unit of measurement—whether that be gold, the phallus, the father, God, or whatever. The structure of the general equivalent, introduced by the money form, thus instantiates the centralization of power for, as Goux writes, it 'furnishes the principle of the subjection of many to the sovereignty of one' (39):

> the established domination of the universal and normative equivalent (money, father, phallus, word) centers or anchors all products of exchange in a single point, such that their multiple, heterogeneous relations swivel around a single, unilateral fulcrum. It acts as a pivot, axle, or axis (axiomatics or axiology) at the same time that it institutes a systematic and separate monovalent perspective over the entire collectivity under its sway. The general equivalent, as standard and measure of values, having all values expressed in it, has an unobstructed (panoramic, synoptic, and detached) view over the world it regulates.   (44)

The idealist poetics of the *Defence* not only shares with idealist philosophy the structural logic of the money form, moreover. As a working example of such a poetics in which the poet's '*Idea*' (85.35, 36) is made 'manifest' (85.37) in his work, the *Defence* also *illustrates* that logic, revealing it to view with a peculiar visibility. Golden poetry (with its ability to make ideal values 'shine' through its accounts of various literary heroes) is perhaps the best example of money-fetishism yet. That same poetry's subordination of brass, Nature, and woman to its gold—not to mention its rise from an unjustly lowly position to triumph as the supreme discipline, to win the 'civil war among the Muses' (82.4), to be accorded 'the highest form in the school of learning' (89.33–4) so as to have the 'title' (89.36) over 'all other serving sciences' (89.36), to 'win the goal' (90.10), to conquer its rivals, to usurp their power, to crush them underfoot so that poets will 'have a most just title to be princes over all the rest' (88.32–3), will be 'victorious' (94.22), will be 'of all sciences . . . the monarch' (95.8–9), will be the ruler to whom others, such as historians, are 'subject' (93.25) and mere 'underling[s]' (108.8), until the poet has 'all, from Dante's heaven to his hell, under the authority of his pen' (93.29–30)—could similarly be read as a fantasized acting out of the tyranny towards which, as a reflection of the money form, an idealist poetics will invariably tend.[69]

This idea of a conquering discipline that carries all before it—such that its practitioners deserve, as 'triumphing' and 'triumphant captains' (100.34; 108.18), to be awarded the laurel crown—comes very close to what Alan Sinfield, taking exception to this sinister political development, has called 'absolute aesthetics'.[70] As

---

[69] Although Ferguson 1983 (145) initially characterizes the competition between the poet and his rivals in terms of a pastoral singing match, she goes on to draw out the aggressiveness of the poet's tactics: 'To gain recognition for poetry, Sidney shows it rising from a position of low esteem to a monarchy based on its "moving" power. In the course of this rhetorical ascent, poetry metaphorically usurps the places of the philosopher and the historian.' In a footnote she adds that this 'political drama of usurpation staged metaphorically in the *confirmatio* is in fact a revenge play whose traces are dispersed through the text' (230n). Ferguson is not, however, entirely uncritical of this imperialistic will to power and suggests that the *Defence* overall might not be uncritical of it either.

[70] Sinfield 1992 (181). The chapter on the *Defence*, from which this quotation comes, is largely a re-working of Sinfield 1984. As Braden 1999 (9) notes, Petrarch was the first to emphasize the laurel as

he points out, the proclaiming 'of ideal images in literature, with the hope that they will move the rest of us to virtue' is something the *Defence* has in common with state-sponsored art such as Soviet realism: for both 'suppose that truth, right, and goodness are organized in an ideal, universal hierarchy, that this is displayed especially in the works currently recognized as good culture, and that the role of that culture is to incite people to aspire to the ideal' (181). Sinfield uses the term 'aesthetic absolutism' because, 'like an absolutist political ideology, it posits an ultimately static model for societies and their values' (181–2), and acknowledges 'a directly propagandist function for culture': 'if societies and their values are fixed, people had better adjust themselves to their proper slots' (182). For, to say—as we have seen Sidney's speaker do, or try to do—that lies are really 'ideals', that they are 'profitable' to follow and therefore ethically 'true', is nothing other than to insinuate such an ideology, whether knowingly or otherwise, just as the *defence* of such a poetics, as of idealist philosophy more generally, is also (again, whether consciously or otherwise) nothing other than an apology for it: for a regime predicated on the subjection of the many to the few. The weight and pressure of this directive is felt most acutely in the repeated commands to *believe* those ideological lies for true, to *credit* those ideals as ideal. In the coerciveness of models and modes of operation that are routinely presented as 'right' and 'proper', assent to those ideals is if not compelled then assumed (which amounts more or less to the same thing): the reader *must* believe, *should* follow, *ought* to know what they ought to do (going 'awry' or doing the 'wrong' thing is not presented as an option). Indeed, the model of imitative action and inspired emulation by which Sidney's speaker apparently sets so much store rests on a number of assumptions, the first being that the ideal—the 'real', the exemplary, what 'should be'—is universal, the same for everyone. It is on these grounds that a poetry which depicts such things can be said to convey 'true doctrine' (108.14). The second assumption is that everyone immediately recognizes this ideal to *be* ideal according to 'the inward light each mind hath in itself' (95.2–3), so that when they 'see the form of goodness (which seen they cannot but love)' (96.8–9), even the most reprobate will be moved thereby, just as negative examples similarly cannot fail in their designed, educative function: 'little reason hath any man to say that men learn evil by seeing it so set out; since, as I said before, there is no man living but, by the force truth hath in Nature, no sooner seeth these men play their parts, but wisheth them *in pistrinum*' (98.16–20), that is, condemned to hard labour (literally, the pounding mill, normally worked by horses or donkeys, to which slaves were sent as a punishment). Recognizing ideological directives, reading them correctly and acting on them accordingly thus comes from the internalized, naturalized 'force' that characterizes the good citizen and that condemns any outlier to the category of slave or beast (send them to the gulags!). The third assumption is that, having seen and read the ideological directives correctly (which is the only thing they are permitted do), everyone will naturally, unquestioningly, and spontaneously react in the appropriate and directed manner, imitating these paragons of virtue so as to

symbol of both political/military power and poetic fame: 'the due reward of Caesars and of poets', as he described it in his coronation oration. See also Roche 1989 (12–14).

perform virtuous deeds on their own part, this being the (culturally) desired 'end of
well-doing' (88.27): 'Truly, I have known men, that even with reading *Amadis de
Gaule* . . . have found their hearts moved to the exercise of courtesy, liberality, and
especially courage. Who readeth Aeneas carrying old Anchises on his back, that
wisheth not it were his fortune to perform so excellent an act?' (95.33–8). And if the
speaker's 'truly' here threatens to give the game away, then he assures us later on that
'as the image of each action stirreth and instructeth the mind, so the lofty image of
such worthies most inflameth the mind with desire to be worthy' (99.39–41). These
three assumptions conform to what Sinfield proposes as the three principal means by
which ideology maintains its successful operation: the presentation of sectional
interests as universal ones, the denial of contradiction or opposition, and the
naturalization of the result. 'Sidney in the *Defence*', he writes, 'manifests all
three'.[71] The speaker's promotion of idealist poetics in the *Defence*, therefore, can
hardly be taken as anything other than blatantly ideological.

Critics of an idealist persuasion do not seem to be particularly concerned about
this and, indeed, are often very enthusiastic about it: 'Sidney's golden world is more
than a mere metaphor . . . it is a concept determining the structure of fictions
shaped according to specific philosophical (and pious!) assumptions—assumptions,
for instance, about the rational design of the cosmos, its transparency to interpretation, and its purposefulness', that were 'infused by confidence about the goodness
of nature', and circulating among Protestant (especially Philippist) thinkers at the
time.[72] For such critics, it is the glory of the *Defence* that in it Sidney should claim
'not that poetry does good, but that poetry is good: and more, that poetry is the
good . . . poetry is a standard of good, absolute in itself: towards which good
conduct and right thinking merely look'.[73] All human pleasure and delight is
naturally assumed to lie in the achievement of this ideal good and the ideal is
understood to be naturally desired because it is supremely rational. A poetic
example can thus exemplify the ideal because 'all life, all nature is coherent,
organised, pervaded by general reason': the poetic paradigm or example 'is a
construction controlled by reason in its conception, and working by reasonableness
in its argument, and achieving its establishing faith by relying on the rationality of
its hearer'.[74] Such faith is highly prized, and appealing to it, or evoking it in the
reader, the sine qua non of the *Defence*'s success. Sidney is said to follow Scaliger,

---

[71] Sinfield 1992 (206), referencing Giddens 1979 (193–5).

[72] Stillman 2008 (163). Goux 1990 (104) asks whether the substitution of the real by the ideal leads
to profit or loss: 'Does thought gain on this exchange?'. For materialist philosophers like Nietzsche and
Bergson it leads to *loss*: a falling away from the unique, original thing to the banalized, standardized,
generalized, clichéd, 'ideal' version of it (what is lost is originality, individuality, uniqueness, difference,
the priceless element that resists evaluation). For idealist philosophers like Hegel, on the other hand,
the substitution leads to *profit*: conceptual, abstract thought is 'richer', truer, more permanent,
universally endorsed, a distillation and crystallization of meaning and value.

[73] Bronowski 1939 (37). See also Hamilton 1990 (110), who claims that Sidney's poetic theory and
practice 'counter any humanist defense of literature as a force that confirms society's dominant
ideologies', but then affirms that they invite readers to share 'a higher vision of values held more
deeply than any ideology is in a position to formulate' (115): a good example of ideology naturalized.

[74] Shepherd (74, 75). For similar views see Bergvall 1992.

for whom 'the end of all discourse is to establish faith or belief'; and the 'faith' Sidney has that, by means of mimesis, poetry can realize the ideal, bring it to life in actual, practical, heroic and virtuous actions in the world—his 'faith . . . that poetry can be serious', in other words—is to be shared with or (if it is not there already) awakened in his readers: a faith that language means, that its God-given, God-guaranteed meaning can be recovered, that God is good, and that a good God would not deceive us.[75] *Sola fide*! 'To read allegorically, one must accept, on faith, the claim Sidney makes for the ideal poet and, implicitly, for himself: "pretending no more, [he] doth intend the winning of the mind from wickedness to virtue" [95.19–20]'.[76] Poetry achieves this desired result by means of the reader's collaboration, almost a co-creation: 'The poet's "delivering forth" [85.38] of his *"idea* or fore-conceit" [85.35] is made "substantial," [85.39–40] Sidney suggests, only insofar as the poet's word, like God's, becomes flesh: the imagination "so far substantially . . . worketh, not only to make a Cyrus, which had been but a particular excellency as nature might have done, but to bestow a Cyrus upon the world to make many Cyruses, if they will learn aright why and how that maker made him" [85.39–43]' (156).[77]

Other critics, by contrast, are altogether more cautious about the agenda this unacknowledged ideological programme is aiming to set out. The magical ability of poetry to produce 'many Cyruses', for example—so often touted as an unquestioned good and, as here, mystified to a frankly uncritical degree—might just as

[75] Quotations from Shepherd (72), and Bronowski (56), who adds: 'The faith is almost childish; and Sidney knew hardly any poems to uphold it. Yet Sidney held to the faith. Sidney was dead before his friend Spenser, with the same faith held in the same word Virtue, wrote *The Faerie Queene*. He was dead before Ben Jonson, Shakespeare, Donne, Milton, Dryden, Pope, Gray, Blake, Wordsworth, Coleridge, wrote. In them Sidney's faith came true. Only because we have their poems can we be so sure that Gosson was wrong when he held that poetry needs "dwelleth longest in those pointes, that profite least". And we owe their poems to such faith as Sidney's'. See also Stillman 2008 (110): 'Sidney's golden world is something more than a loosely constructed, rhetorically suggestive metaphor. Instead . . . it is the methodically conceived imitation, counterfeit, and figuration of the Maker's own prelapsarian creation, the world itself—one that has a maker who works by intention, one that possesses its own natural goodness and power, and one that is constructed according to a specific purpose, aim or scope.' Goux 1990 (91) notes the close connection between faith and the money form: 'Monetary capital partakes of the same social logic as divine centralization: religious centers are fulcrums of capital. A single tendency associates *credo, credence, credit*' (italics original).

[76] Ferguson 1983 (156).

[77] See also Perry 2005 (392–3): 'In Sidney's *Defence, imitatio* performs a quasi-sacramental role, reversing the trajectory of the fall and reasserting, although not fully restoring, the relationship between creature and Creator. For the Protestant Sidney, *imitatio* imbues "natural" language with supernatural significance, transforming the words of the human poet into a vehicle of divine presence analogous to the sacred Word.' Bergvall 1989 (38) concurs: 'Behind this communicative model stands the assumption that we *can* know the Logos. This may be an uncomfortable premise in the twentieth century, but given the Christian conception of an ordered universe under divine supervision, we cannot fault Sidney on philosophical grounds' (emphasis original). It should be noted that when Bergvall insists Sidney's poetics are not 'idealist' he means something entirely different from me. He uses the term to refer to the beliefs of the Florentine Neoplatonists—e.g. that, by means of heroic frenzy, the poet could achieve transcendence—a heretical view, in Bergvall's view, and something that the Protestant humanists of northern Europe, including Sidney, firmly rejected (Bergvall reads *Astrophil and Stella* and the *Arcadia* as negative examples and thus as satirical parodies of this tradition). In presenting an unapologetically logocentric reading of the *Defence*, however, it is clear that Bergvall regards Sidney's poetics as entirely idealist in the sense in which I am using the term.

easily be seen as a horrific outcome: a fantasy of the entirely logical result that a propagandist, ideologically-driven, state-sponsored art would produce if it actually worked.[78] The other side of this idealist poetics, that is—in which figures like Cyrus are held up as ideals to be followed—is a nightmare scenario of identical robots programmed to produce more of the same.[79] The ideal 'virtuous cycle', by means of which imitations of virtue come to generate more imitations of virtue in a fantasy of unbroken and exponential growth, is—when that 'ideal' and 'virtue' are looked at a little more sceptically—nothing other than the mechanism by which ideology would (hopefully, without anyone noticing too much) faithfully, virally reproduce itself. Idealist poetics thus finds its natural culmination, its home, in a world full of Cyruses (all ideal because they are doing ideology's work): the image of the conquering, imperial, authoritarian, militarized male—the ultimately disciplined subject—being the fitting and entirely logical conclusion to a poetics that is also presented as crushing its rivals (the 'other' arts and sciences) so as to claim its rightful status as an academic subject, a bona fide disciplinary field in its own right, and, indeed, *as* such, to reign supreme. Critics invested in such a model for their discipline seem neither to be aware of nor to care about the offensive nature of the tactics the speaker uses to defend it: 'offensive' in both senses of the word. Agrippa, by contrast, who has no time for the argument that lies are justified if they are said to represent the 'truth' and to promote 'ideals', has a much clearer idea of what is really going on. Many write histories, he concedes, 'not so mutche to tell the Truthe, as to delite that thei maie expresse, and depainte, the Image of a noble Prince . . . Whiche if any shal reproue for liynge, they saie, that they haue not so greate a regarde, to thinges done, as to the profite of the posteritee' (E4). Agrippa's chief example of this tendency is the *Cyropaedia*: 'Such an example hath *Xenophon* sette out of *Cyrus*, not as it was, but as it ought to be, as a resemblance and paterne, of a singular good Prince, writing a proper and trimme Historie, but without truthe' (E4). As a result, 'many apte to lyinge by nature and industrie, haue writen fained Histories' (E4–E4ᵛ) and this is the reason 'why in no parte any credite may be throughly geue*n*' to them (E4ᵛ). Readers might well be advised to take a leaf out of Agrippa's book, for, indeed, it is precisely when such credit or belief is *withheld*

---

[78] See e.g. Fineman 1986 (93) who comments of the 'many Cyruses' passage: 'Here is the high Renaissance conception of poetic vocation.' Doherty 1991 provides perhaps the most extreme example of this tendency, seeing those multiple Cyruses as the offspring of a mystical union between 'the mistress-knowledge and the poet-architect', for the 'ethical principle of a universal knowledge generates heroes in the audience' (15), leading to the creation of 'a heroic citizenry' (100), 'the moral peopling of a kingdom' (111).

[79] See Wolfley 1976 (239): 'The problem is that Sidney wants us to believe that poetic example *necessarily and invariably* inspires virtuous action on the part of a reader. The idea is absurd, since it could be true only if men were automatons. Renaissance faculty psychology has mechanistic tendencies, but it will not support any such idea as this; so Sidney has to illustrate his argument with examples [i.e. Menenius Agrippa, Nathan] that imply necessity without raising any troublesome complications. As a result, his illustrations are so simplistic that they prove nothing' (emphasis original). Wolfley is effectively challenging the ideological assumptions that the model of imitative action makes (as listed above), especially the third. He is also, therefore, conscious of the highly tendentious use Sidney makes of Aristotle's theory of mimesis: 'I think the main usefulness of Aristotle's "imitation" is for understanding what early literature typically is *not*' (219, emphasis original).

on the part of the reader that the ideological operation (otherwise masked) is laid bare to the view: 'For they whiche with wonderfull praises doo depainte *Hercules, Achilles, Hector, Theseus, Epaminondas, Lizander, Themistocles, Xerxes, Cyrus, Darius, Alexander, Pirrhus, Hannibal, Scipio, Pompei, Caesar,* what other haue they described but greate and furiouse theeues, & famouse spoilers of the worlde? I confesse that they were very good Capitanes, doubtles very wicked and naughtie men' (F1).[80]

As Sinfield notes, it is, of course, 'the project of ideology' to represent the relations between economic, political, military, and cultural power as 'harmonious and coherent', but, given the dire consequences to which crediting such a project can lead—the consequences of this blind faith that is otherwise so prized, so celebrated, so naturally assumed on our behalf, and all but compelled—we may be thankful for the fact that ideology has constantly to be *produced*: that it has to perform its own work of *poesis* by creating ideal fictions and minimizing any contradictions as might exist within or between them.[81] Thankful, because it is *as* such that those fictions can be analysed and critically read: 'Despite their power, dominant ideological formations are always, in practice, under pressure, striving to substantiate their claim to superior plausibility in the face of diverse disturbances . . . Conflict and contradiction stem from the very strategies through which ideologies strive to contain the expectations that they need to generate' (41). It is here that the inability or refusal to 'identify one's interests with the dominant may occur, and hence where dissidence may arise' (41–2). In the specific case of the *Defence*, moreover, which, on the surface at least, is all about the importance of creating, reproducing, and crediting these fictions, we get a particularly clear view of ideology in action: of how these fictions *ought* to be written and read (this is the official argument, as mounted by Sidney's speaker), but at the same time of how— if they are to decline the opportunity to abuse their powers—these fictions might also *not* be so written or read (this is the alternative, dissenting view that I have been attributing to 'Sidney', even if it is present only reactively and visible only in growing indications of the author's bad faith). The *Defence* thus furnishes a particularly good (or bad, depending on which side you are on) example of how ideology works because, as Sinfield writes, the 'unity proposed in absolutist aesthetics' is so obviously a fiction—'a chimera' (182–3)—as a result of which, 'despite the clean-cut line it cultivates, aesthetic absolutism is always disintegrating as a theory' (183).[82]

---

[80] Harington 1904 (200) purports to be scandalized by Agrippa's demystifications: 'I maruel how he durst do it, saue that I see he hath done it; he hath spared neither myters nor scepters. The courts of Princes where vertue is rewarded, iustice maintained, oppressions relieued, he cals them a Colledge of Giants, of Tyrants, of oppressors, warriors: the most noble sort of noble men he termeth cursed, bloodie, wicked, and sacrilegious persons.' As usual, it is difficult to know whether Harington can be taken entirely at his word.

[81] Sinfield 1992 (9), referencing Williams 1980 (31–49).

[82] In his own reading of the *Defence*, Sinfield 1992 locates the 'faultline' that ultimately deconstructs Sidney's absolutist aesthetics between the competing demands of Protestantism and humanism: specifically, between a hard-line Calvinist view that, as a means to educating the population in virtue, would subordinate all imaginative literature to the Bible (if not abolish it

It is that disintegration—of the proposition that lies are good, true, ideal, profitable, and hence defensible—that I have been seeking to trace here, along with other critics who are equally non-committal about an idealist poetics and the ideological programme it aspires to roll out, and who are equally prepared to countenance a Sidney who might have been also. Critics who are entirely at one with Gosson on the observable reality that, notwithstanding the assumptions outlined above, idealized representations in literature and art are, mercifully, *not* guaranteed to produce idealized behaviour in those who read or see them.[83] Critics who are alert to the hesitancies and prevarications that typically disrupt the ostensible argument of the *Defence* and that show such an assumption to be entirely conditional: the poet works 'substantially' (85.39–40), bestowing 'a Cyrus upon the world to make many Cyruses, *if* [readers] will learn aright why and how that maker made him' (85.41–3, my emphasis), and '*If* the poet do his part aright' (92.34, my emphasis), too, by showing 'in Cyrus...each thing to be followed' (92.35–6). That is a big 'if'—two big 'ifs'—rather menacing to those concerned (with its implicit threat that the reader and writer will do 'aright' or else), but at the same time, since that desired rightness is always deferred to some ideal future, opening up infinite possibilities that either reader or writer or both might, in fact, just as easily do the exact opposite.[84] The overwhelming force of reason by means of which everything is judged and before which no contradiction or deviation is allowed to stand—money thought's flattering image of itself as the *right* way of organizing thought, as the *only* way of philosophizing, indeed, as thinking per se— is also shown to be surprisingly dependent on certain key conditions being in place first: 'Nay truly, learned men have learnedly thought [always a bad start] that *where*

altogether), and a more enlightened humanist view that would extend the same educative potential to the pagan classics. Although he comes to the conclusion that both 'finally *share* the same authoritarian deep structure' (205, emphasis original), Sinfield continues to maintain a polar opposition between the two: 'each asserts an absolute notion of humanity—either sunk in spiritual degradation or blessed with godlike vision' (205–6). The view of Sidney as a hard-line Calvinist has now usefully been revised by work exploring his debt to the more ecumenical thinking of Philip Melanchthon and his followers: see e.g. Bergvall 1989, and Stillman 2008. My own view is that Protestantism and humanism were not so much opposite as contiguous—i.e. equally profit-driven—as a result of which I locate the 'faultline' not between these two directives but rather between the (Protestant humanist pedagogical) speaker, who acts as their joint spokesman, and (the courtly) Sidney who feels his way towards a conceptualization of poetry in which those directives meet with a fierce resistance.

[83] See e.g. Levao 1985 (145): 'All we know is that the "invention" [103.32] ought to be "profitable" [103.31]. We are not guaranteed a fixed unity between speaker and hearer; the most interpretation can aim for is some ethical utility.' He adds, 'Sidney would very much like to present poetry as an instrument of the moral, active life, but the very process of making the argument exposes its gaps...As Sidney's argument stands, it verges on telling us that poetry ought to be what it ought to be, and like the moral philosophers he parodies, Sidney finds his terms pointing back to themselves' (146–7). This closed circuit anticipates the flattering 'glass of reason' (109.33) to be discussed shortly below. See also Wolfley 1976 (238–9), and Williams 2009 (648).

[84] See Maslen (26): 'the pregnant "if" [92.34] that begins this sentence—one of the many conditionals that fill the *Apology*—indicates that Sidney can offer no guarantees that the poet *will* "do his part aright" [92.34]. In fact, poets very often do the opposite' (emphasis original). See also Lamb 1994 (499) who notes that poetry can elicit 'the wrong sort of pleasure'; adding that Sidney does not defend 'against the wrong kind of poetry which "trains man's wit to wanton sinfulness and lustful love" [103.44–104.1], the charges still stand' (503), referencing Helgerson 1976 (128–9).

once reason hath so much overmastered passion as that the mind hath a free desire to do well, the inward light each mind hath in itself is as good as a philosopher's book' (94.44–95.3, my emphasis).[85] Epic poetry, that details the heroics of characters like Cyrus and makes their qualities shine through, will have the desired effect '*if* the saying of Plato and Tully be true, that who could see virtue would be wonderfully ravished with the love of her beauty' (99.32–4, my emphasis). In a mind '*not* prejudiced with a prejudicating humour, [Aeneas] will be found in excellency fruitful' (100.6–7, my emphasis).[86] The 'instructions' (107.2) of philosophy and of poetry might be honoured and blessed '*so as* they be not abused' (107.3, my emphasis). An ideology that guarantees rightness *if*, *once*, and *so long as* certain conditions are met—and *not* if they are not—is an ideology ripe for deconstruction, for what emerges as the intaglio of the presumptively rational subject who is here addressed (learned, self-interested, virtue-inspired, profit-driven, and so on) is one that is in fact, or is in danger of becoming, passionate (but not passionate about virtue), prejudiced, and prone to subject all that ideological nonsense to the abuse it deserves.[87] Such bad readers and writers might

---

[85] It is not entirely clear whether the results of this overmastering of passion by reason are always favourable. In the *digressio* Sidney claims to have been 'overmastered by some thoughts' (109.30), as a result of which he penned, among other things, the *Defence*. As we shall see shortly, however, this exercise does not find him looking in the 'glass of reason' (109.33), suggesting that those 'thoughts' may have been passionate rather than strictly rational. Sidney is a curious omission from the otherwise thoroughgoing discussion of the triumph of passion over reason in Tilmouth 2007.

[86] By contrast, one wonders just what a mind that *was* 'prejudiced with a prejudicating humour' might make of Aeneas' actions, as, for example, his 'obeying the god's commandment to leave Dido, though not only all passionate kindness, but even the human consideration of virtuous gratefulness, would have craved other of him' (99.44–100.2). What might an alternative jurisprudence have made of this, as, for example, the female readership of the *Old Arcadia* or, arguably, of the trial of idealist poetics that is going on in the *Defence*? To prejudicate, in the specific sense of 'to judge beforehand; to form a prior opinion of, especially hastily or rashly; to condemn in advance', was a Sidney coinage (see *OED* prejudicate *v.* 2a *trans.*, and prejudicating *n.* and *adj.*, as opposed to the weaker, original sense, 'to affect' or 'act prejudicially', *v.* 1a and b). Sidney had also used the word in this specialized, quasi-legalistic sense in the *Old Arcadia*: when Philoclea tries to dissuade Pyrocles from killing himself after they have been discovered in bed together—to do so would be 'to prejudicate [God's] determination' about human life (*OA* 297)—and when Pyrocles reacts to the sentencing of Philoclea to life imprisonment in a nunnery for having allowed him to seduce her: 'Although this were a great prejudicating of Pyrocles' case, yet was he exceedingly joyous of it, being assured of his lady's life, and in the depth of his mind not sorry that, what end soever he had, none should obtain the after-enjoying that jewel whereon he had set his life's happiness' (*OA* 381). It is interesting that Sidney's uses of this word in the *Defence* and the *Old Arcadia*—in the specific sense of a decision that would have been rash and ill-judged had it been carried out—all centre round reactions to sexual relations that take place outside of marriage.

[87] The fact that passion is not necessarily aroused *by* virtue, nor likely to lead *to* it, is the weak point of the argument for imitative action: for passion is supposed to be both aroused by reason *and* 'overmastered' by it. The speaker claims that 'as for to move, it is clear [that poetry is superior to history], since the feigned may be tuned to the highest key of passion' (93.10–11), just as the 'poetical' historians usurped from poetry the 'passionate describing of passions' (83.9–10). It is far from clear, however, whether such passion—assuming it is aroused in the reader—will move him or her in the prescribed direction. As we have seen, contemporaries like Gosson and Harington reserved the right to be sceptical about this. Later in the *Defence*, Sidney contrasts the effectiveness of those who only 'coldly' apply their 'fiery speeches' (113.27) in poetry with those whose 'passions' are betrayed by 'forcibleness or *energia*' (113.31, 32), although, again, it is far from clear that the effectiveness he has in mind is necessarily very virtuous. *Astrophil and Stella* might be read, alongside Shakespeare's *Sonnets*, as

correctively, of course, 'look themselves in an unflattering glass of reason'
(109.32–3), but only '*if* they be inclinable unto it' (109.33, my emphasis). This
'if' can work in both directions, evidently: choosing the 'right' thing to do is just as
contingent as choosing the wrong thing. Except that, in this case, choosing the right
thing is exactly what Sidney is *not* inclined to do: 'taking upon us to be poets in
despite of Pallas'—that is, in spite of having no knowledge and learning—that
'wherein we want desert were a thankworthy labour to express; but *if* I knew,
I should have mended myself' (109.26–8, my emphasis). The glass of reason, that
is to say, is not unflattering at all. On the contrary, it is supremely complimentary,
especially to those who see themselves reflected in it. It suggests to them that
thought is rational, that their rational thought is 'ideal', and that the ideal is
therefore 'rational'.[88] It reflects back a mind that sees itself as both, and brings a
whole series of subordinations (of others, of matter, of feelings, of passions, of
intuitions, of dreams, of desire, of the counterfactual, of the contradictory, of the
incomprehensible, of the irrational, of the unconscious, of the sublime) in its wake.[89]
Sidney is not, therefore, inclined to consult it and has no intention of 'mending'
himself according to its mendacious and deeply compromising reflections.

The tension or 'faultline' between the speaker's official argument in favour of lies
and Sidney's instinctive balking at it, appears with particular visibility in the passage
in the *confirmatio* in which the clinching, definitive proof of poetry's superiority
over history is triumphantly asserted: fittingly enough, in terms of stories about
triumphant conquest. Seeking to demonstrate once and for all that 'a feigned
example hath as much force to teach as a true example' (93.9–10), the speaker
discusses a particular military stratagem, described by historians and poets alike, to
show that the reader—who, according to good humanist principle, would seek to

a meditation on just this problem: that passion can very powerfully be felt for people, actions, and
things that, according to the prevailing ideology, are most definitely not ideal.

[88] Such is the self-reflecting and fundamentally narcissistic model that Fineman 1986 (7) sees as
characterizing idealist poetry and poetics: based on the presumed homology between an idealized
object and the idealizing subject, this model is particularly evident in the visionary, specular aesthetics
of the traditional Renaissance sonnet, which is based on 'an identification guaranteed by a specific kind
of idealizing speech' and so develops 'a laudatory poetry of ideally mutual admiration'. Although
Fineman is chiefly concerned with the relation between the poetic subject and the poetic object, here,
the same essentially narcissistic mirroring can be extended to include any kind of praise relation—such
as that between a speaker and the poetry he praises (as in the *Defence*), for example, or that between
idealist critics and the *Defence* that they praise—so long as the mutually flattering and self-congratulatory
nature of that relation is always borne in mind: see Bates 2007 (230).

[89] While Lehnhof 2008 gives a fairly accommodating account of Sidney's feminism in the *Defence*,
a number of other critics have identified in it a feminine/feminized counter-discourse that runs parallel
to and disrupts if not undermines its official argument, rather as the 'nurse of abuse' (102.24)
countermands the male, martial, scholarly, disciplined defender of poetry: see e.g. Dickson 1992
(49, 50, 51); Dolan 1993 (227, 236); Lamb 1994 (499, 503, 514); Prendergast 1999 (18–25); and
Williams 2009 (647, 653–4). Wolfley 1976 (241) is also clear that in both his theory and his practice
Sidney is not hidebound to the demands of reason: 'we may be thankful that Sidney's literary practice
was no more consistent with his theory than the theory per se is consistent within itself. The sensibility
which made Sidney a creative artist dictated in turn the eclectic inconsistencies of the *Apology*, and
transcends in its genius the limitations inseparable from his own and every other merely reasoned
theory.' Amen to that.

advise his prince on similarly successful tactics—might learn it 'as well' (93.22) if not 'truly so much the better' (93.23) from the poet's fictional representation as from the historians' factual one. The stratagem in question involves the loyal retainer of a military general infiltrating the enemy—so as to deliver them straight back to the conquering hero and thus destroy them—by means of the simple expedient of getting them to believe that he has been disgraced and discharged, and therefore has every reason to go over to their side: a credibility he strengthens by making it look (through some dramatic self-mutilation) as if he has been tortured and brutalized by the superior power. In terms of historians, this story—of how the faithful Zopyrus delivered the 'rebellious Babylonians' (93.14) back to his master, Darius—is told by Herodotus and Justinus.[90] In terms of poets, a similar story—involving another such stratagem performed by Abradatas for Cyrus—is told by Xenophon.[91] The first thing to notice about this 'example' (93.9, 10)—which the speaker presents as entirely self-evident—is the difference in registers between the *action* that is described (self-mutilation with a view to deceiving the enemy) and the *descriptions* of this action by historians and poets alike. The point of the comparison between the historical and the poetical accounts is to minimize the difference between empirical and ethical truth, to reduce it virtually to vanishing point: something we have seen the speaker do, or attempt to do, many times before. For him, it makes no difference whether the action described actually happened or whether it was only 'feigned' (93.9, 10, 19), because, in terms of its teaching value, the example details a tactic that is a winner in military terms and therefore qualifies as ethically 'true' (93.9): it is, as he assures us, an 'honest dissimulation' (93.21).

If this dismissal of the merely empirically true—now so familiar a part of the speaker's repertoire—is designed to make the case for the ethically true, however, then that appeal (as should also, by now, be familiar) ultimately backfires. And it does this for two, related reasons. First, by drawing the reader's attention away from the trivial question of the example's empirical truth (whether it actually happened, as reported in history, or whether it was made up, as narrated in poetry) to its overpoweringly ethical truth (that it secured victory)—the reader's assent to which is assumed—the speaker inadvertently brings very much to our attention the fact that this 'ethical' truth applies only to one (that is, to the winning) side. The speaker is, as usual, busy with his argument that poetry has 'as much force to teach' as history (93.9), but what he in fact demonstrates is how it can be used *to teach force.*

---

[90] Herodotus 1925, *Persian Wars*, III.153–60; followed by Justinus 1564 (B4–B4ᵛ).

[91] Xenophon 1914, *Cyropaedia*, V.i.3–VII.iii.11. As editors note, however, Sidney has in fact confused Abradatas (king of Susa), who takes part in no such stratagem, with either Araspas (who pretends to desert Cyrus in order to spy for him, VI.i.39–45; iii.14–20) and/or Gadatas (who plots to help Cyrus gain an Assyrian fort by surrendering it to him, V.iii.8–21): see Shepherd (178), van Dorsten (196), Duncan-Jones (378), Maslen (171), and Alexander (332). Both Maslen (61) and Ferguson 1983 (229n) suspect that Sidney's 'confusion' here may have been deliberate, lending further credence to the idea that he effectively undermines the speaker's position. As Ferguson comments, 'Sidney's examples in the *Defence* frequently serve to complicate or undermine the points they are supposed to prove'. For her, the 'undersong of this theory and practice of power . . . is the admission that poetry's teaching may be "questionable" [94.23]—an admission obliquely dramatized in the example of the "feigning" [93.9, 10, 14, 19] that teaches "honest dissimulation" [93.21]' (145).

The whole argument about the respective claims of poetry and history is a distraction—a side-issue, for in the end there is no significant difference between them—making it all the more obvious and impossible to avoid noticing that, as Maslen puts it, 'both versions of the story are designed to teach their readers how to lie'.[92] Second, by making it difficult for the reader *not* to question the supposed ethics of this lesson, the speaker also inadvertently re-directs our attention to the very thing he had worked so hard to distract it from: namely, to the *empirical* truth, not of either the historical or the poetical accounts but, rather, of the action itself. The example is not just 'feigned' (93.9, 10, 19) by the poet, that is (nor by the historians who, as we know, were also perfectly capable of making things up). Rather, the pretence of going over to the other side was also 'feigned' (93.14) by Zopyrus, and by others who made use of the same tactic. Where, as a feigned, 'poetical' example, with force to teach, such a story does well (according to the speaker) to arouse the admiration of its readers—so as to encourage them to do likewise in imitative action (this being defined as 'well-doing', 88.27; 94.21)—as a feigned action on the part of a double-dealing and true-seeming but ultimately false and faithless friend, it arouses belief in its viewers very much to their disadvantage: Zopyrus 'feigned himself in extreme disgrace of his king: for verifying of which, he caused his own nose and ears to be cut off, and so flying to the Babylonians, was received, and for his known valour so far credited, that he did find means to deliver them over to Darius' (93.14–18).[93] To those on the ground, the consequences of 'crediting' such a fiction could hardly have been more dire, and, unlike the readers of poetry and history who are being rallied to believe in and imitate such heroic actions themselves, the Babylonians would have been much better advised to exercise some critical reading skills. *Especially* as the tactic had been repeated throughout history and poetry and, for the most part, proved reliably fatal to the credulous side (think of Sinon and the Trojans). Agrippa was right. If historical or poetical accounts of such actions teach anything at all, it is—or ought to be—that we should *not* extend them any credit whatsoever, and most certainly not imitate them.[94]

It should come as no surprise, then, that this prize example on the part of the speaker fails, like so many others, to exemplify what it is supposed to exemplify. In setting out his ethos of heroically imitative action, and in justifying it accordingly,

---

[92] Maslen (61), adding: 'in both versions of the story the definition of "truth" depends on which side you happen to favour. Abradatas's "feigning" demonstrates his "truth" to Cyrus, just as the servant's proves his loyalty to Darius; but in each case one must assume that the enemies they duped would have seen their dissimulations in quite another light. Truth here, as elsewhere in the *Apology*, is a fiercely contested concept, whose ownership is claimed with equal conviction by opposing parties in any ideological quarrel.'

[93] See also the account in Justinus 1564 (B4ᵛ): Zopyrus 'was well knowen among them all, to be a noble man, and a man of much prowesse, and as for his credite they doubted not at all, as whereof they thoughte hys woundes and wrongfull maymes to be a sufficient pledge and wytnesse. Therefore by a common consent, they made him a captayne . . . At the last being put in trust with the whole armye, he betrayed it to the kyng, and brought the cytie againe vnder his obeysance'.

[94] See Agrippa 1569 (F1): 'if a man saie to me that by the reading of Histories a singular wisedome maie be gotten, I denie it not, so that he also graunte me this, that out of the same is receaued in like manner great damage.'

what the speaker actually presents is a scenario in which believing in poetical/ethical fictions leads, 'ideally', to the triumph of military dictatorship (those Cyruses again), while believing in empirical fictions leads to resounding defeat at that dictatorship's hands. There is no reason to think that the monarchomachist, tyranny-hating Sidney would have relished either prospect, nor to doubt that—in the logical contradictions that here as elsewhere fatally disrupt the speaker's official position—Sidney may well have been signalling, whether consciously or otherwise, the withholding of his consent. Indeed, the split between Sidney and his speaker widens perceptibly here, since, on analysis, they seem to have diametrically opposed views of what it is that poetry is supposed to be teaching. For what the example shows more clearly than anything else is a basic contradiction lying at the heart of what is considered the 'ideal' outcome of things: what the 'should be' should be. Is it tyranny or the overthrow of tyranny? Is it the triumph of men like Darius and Cyrus, who, as Agrippa noted, 'were very good Capitanes, [but] doubtles very wicked and naughtie men' (F1), or is it the vanquishing of such tyrannical overlords and the defence of their duped, crushed, and helpless victims? Should you crush the rebellious Babylonians or rescue the rebellious Babylonians or, better still, be a rebellious Babylonian yourself and rise up to defend yourself against the tyrannical Persians? That you or your party might at any given time be on the side of the tyrannical overlord in question is not quite strong enough an argument to warrant entirely dismissing the dubious ethics of actions that would have looked very different had the boot, as it were, been on the other foot. Zopyrus and Abradatas are ingenuously offered by the speaker as *exempla* of how the reader might likewise 'serve your prince by such an honest dissimulation' (93.21), but on the following page acting 'honestly' is said to be the putting down of 'dishonest tyranny' (94.10–11), not the founding of it, even when carried out by notorious Roman dictators like Lucius Sylla or Julius Caesar.[95] In his determination to win his case

---

[95] Lucius Cornelius Sylla (or Sulla) (*c*.138–78 BC) abdicated his dictatorship and died in retirement a year later, after which the young Julius Caesar (*c*.100–44 BC), whose uncle, Caius (or Gaius) Marius had been Sylla's enemy and rival for power, continued to support those who had opposed Sylla's policies. The passage in question is highly ambiguous and, as such, typically marks the disjunction I have been proposing between Sidney and his speaker: 'mark but even Caesar's own words of the forenamed Sylla (who in that only did honestly, to put down his dishonest tyranny), *literas nescivit* [he was ignorant of letters], as if want of learning caused him to do well. He meant it not by Poetry, which, not content with earthly plagues, deviseth new punishments in hell for tyrants, nor yet by Philosophy, which teacheth *occidendos esse* [that they must fall]; but no doubt by skill in History, for that indeed can afford your Cypselus, Periander, Phalaris, Dionysius, and I know not how many more of the same kennel, that speed well enough in their abominable injustice or usurpation' (94.9–18). First, editors are split over whether it was *Caesar* who 'did honestly' in opposing the tyrannical policies of his predecessor—the view of Shepherd (180), van Dorsten (197), and Maslen (174)—or whether it was *Sylla* who did so in abdicating: the view of Alexander (333). Clearly, the sentence can be read either way, although in both cases notoriously 'dishonest' tyrants are described as acting 'honestly' *not* when they use 'honest dissimulation' but rather when they oppose or relinquish tyranny. Second, it is unclear precisely in what Sylla's imputed ignorance lay or in what it resulted. The reference is to Suetonius who reports Caesar as having said '*Sullam nescisse literas, qui dictaturam deposuerit*' [Sulla did not know his ABC when he laid down his dictatorship]: see Suetonius 1914, *Lives of the Caesars*, 'The Deified Julius', 1.77. We are told that his 'want of learning caused him to do well'—'well' being glossed by Maslen as 'succeed as a dictator' (174)—suggesting Caesar must have meant that Sylla was ignorant of poetry and philosophy (both of which show the comeuppance that all tyrants should expect), rather than history

and to prove poetry the outright champion of the competition with the 'other' arts, the speaker asserts its superior teaching power in setting forward 'that which deserveth to be called and accounted good' (94.19–20)—this kind of good always being something you can count and account for—as a result of which he sets 'the laurel crown upon the poet as victorious, not only of the historian, but over the philosopher' (94.21–2): a perfect re-enactment of ideological manipulation and tyrannical overlordship in action. Sidney, however, meanwhile undoes this disciplinary will to power from within, for, in *his* definition, poetry 'deviseth new punishments in hell for tyrants' (94.13–14). Since—in a spectacularly imperial gesture worthy of Cyrus and his ilk—the speaker had just claimed that the triumphant poet had 'under the authority of his pen' (93.29–30) everything that extends from 'Dante's heaven to his hell' (93.29), the latter becomes a fittingly infernal place for him to end up in: the place Sidney evidently feels, in coming full circle, that the speaker and his idealist poetics finally belong. For an understanding that would conceptualize poetry in quite different terms, this is poetic justice, indeed: and, perhaps, what the alternative (female) judges of the trial in the *Defence*—as in the *Old Arcadia*—might have determined also.[96]

The effect (gratefully) is to call a halt to the unstoppable march of the speaker's idealist poetics on its otherwise fantasized ascent towards world domination, with its triumphant captains, laurel crowns, and all the rest. Instead, we get to see very graphically that what is 'ideal'—good, true, profitable, defensible, shining, golden, and so forth—is only so to those, naturally, who profit from it: to the dominant elite that faithfully reflects the logic of the general equivalent and the money form by subordinating everyone and everything else to one measure of value, typically a single, male (heroized, deified) head. We also get to see, equally graphically, that the dissimulation that is 'honest' (93.21) as far as the latter is concerned—the lies that are 'profitable', 'good', ethically 'true', and so forth—is most definitely none of those things to anyone or anything who happens to be occupying the subordinate,

---

(which shows tyrants both succeeding and how to succeed). Sylla's doing 'well' is, therefore, ironic and of a piece with Cypselus and other dictators who are similarly said to 'speed well enough'. What the passage actually says, however, is that Caesar meant his comment *'not* by Poetry . . . *nor yet* by Philosophy' (i.e. that it was not these that Sylla was ignorant of) but rather—or *'no doubt* by'— history. In which case, Sylla's doing 'well' lay in his abdicating—not in his succeeding—as a dictator. Amid all the confusion (caused, as elsewhere in the *Defence*, by the proliferation of negatives: 'not . . . nor . . . no doubt'), it emerges that what poetry teaches—and what those who read it, including otherwise notorious tyrants, learn in no uncertain terms—is that tyranny ultimately *fails*: a position inconsistent with the speaker's glorification of Darius and Cyrus but in tune, I would argue, with Sidney's political ethics and poetical agenda.

[96] On the punishment of tyrants, see Dante 2004, *Inferno*, XII.103–8, where they are sunk up to the eyelids in blood. Dante's examples are both referenced by the *Defence*: Alexander, being either Alexander the Great (92.38; 97.23; 105.33–41; 107.41; 112.35) or Alexander Pheraeus (98.34–8), and Dionysius of Syracuse, either the Elder or the Younger, both being equally cruel (94.16; 106.36). For his part, Sinon is relegated to the tenth and lowest circle of hell, along with other fraudsters, falsifiers, and counterfeiters, *Inferno*, XXX.98. The topic of tyrannicide, urgently debated in the sixteenth century, had of course been given a recent and famous airing in *Vindiciae, contra tyrannos* (Basel, 1579), a tract associated with if not composed by two of Sidney's closest friends and confidantes, Hubert Languet and Philippe du Plessis Mornay.

relative position: in this case, the Babylonians.[97] For good measure, the speaker slips in a further illustrative example—'Much like matter doth Livy record of Tarquinius and his son' (93.18)—a reference to the stratagem by which Sextus, son of Tarquinius the Proud, deceived the citizens of Gabii into thinking he had deserted Rome so as to deliver their town captive to his father.[98] The Tarquins, of course, were also the last kings of Rome and, if *exempla* of anything, then of the exercise of power at its absolute worst, as Sidney recalls only a few pages earlier with his reference to Lucretia (87.5–7). The outrage of her rape by Sextus Tarquinius— and subsequent suicide, punishing herself for 'another's fault' (87.6)—was what precipitated the ousting of the tyrannical family and the founding of the Roman Republic.[99] What, in spite of their official function, the speaker's examples actually illustrate, then, loud and clear, is that ideal, golden fictions are under no circumstances to be credited or believed—or are at the very least to be treated with the utmost caution and to be put to the test by even the most elementary of deconstructive reading skills—by anyone who wishes not to be bamboozled, duped, defrauded, tricked, conned, betrayed, brainwashed, manipulated, bullied, coerced, controlled, conquered, defeated, colonized, subjugated, enslaved, raped, or worse.

---

[97] See also Goux 1990 (46): 'It is therefore not in vain that in all compartments of social organization we shall decipher the complex yet unmistakable shapes taken by the opposition between a general equivalent and its relative form. It is not in vain that we shall discern the consequences of the *classification* introduced by the separation between two forms of value, of which one governs and the other is governed. For we are certain thereby to unravel the class domination that constitutes the principal historical structuration of the social organism in its various separate registers' (emphasis original).

[98] Livy 1959, *History of Rome*, I.53–4.

[99] See ibid. I.57–60. On Renaissance appropriations of this story, see Donaldson 1982, and Shuger 1998.

IV

Poetry Is Profitless

Where, then, does this leave the poet? What might the poet do, who—urged to produce the kind of poetry that is defended on his behalf and noisily supported by a whole public and cultural caucus—might, Bartleby-wise, prefer not to? Or who—on finding in this poetry a legitimation if not glorification of male aggression, both physical and intellectual—might recoil in distaste and choose to renounce the privilege: actively to disengage? What about the disjunction between what Sidney found his speaker saying and—this being a strangely revelatory dissociation—what he really wanted to say? Not to mention between that and the poetry he actually wrote? As I suggested earlier, with the exception of one or two moments in the *narratio* where an alternative form of poetry briefly comes into view—ecstatic, visionary, and the province not of the scholarly male but of priestesses, sibyls, and shamans—a positive image of this other kind of poetry does not appear openly in the *Defence*. Given that presenting positive models—telling poets what they 'ought' to do—so readily gets co-opted into the ideological project, it is probably inevitable that any debunking of that project, or even questioning or doubting it, is going to get articulated obliquely: to make itself felt in ways other than the imperative and in contradistinction to the propositional. An image of that other kind of poetry can be identified, therefore—can, in fact, be fairly fully filled in and filled out—but only by extrapolating it from and inferring it as everything that the official, positivized model is not. We have seen before how the disjunction between Sidney and his speaker becomes especially visible in those passages where negatives cluster and accumulate with a density that can often prove symptomatically confusing and self-cancelling in its effects. This is a direct product of Sidney's tendency to present the speaker's positives in terms of double, qualified, or rhetorical negatives: a classic indication of disavowal or denial. We can learn to make out the traces and depths of Sidney's alternative vision of poetry, then, precisely by heeding these negatives—by learning to discern what he is saying by means of what is not being said or what is being denied—and we can do this by developing a kind of infra-red night-vision: by seeing this elusive, alternative view as the negative or reverse image of everything that the speaker would otherwise positivize.[100] Or, to use another metaphor, by

---

[100] As I note elsewhere, it is in direct response to the negativities of the *Defence* that the motif linking the disparate poems in Jonson's *Forest* is precisely what they, or their speaker, does or has *not*. The *Forest*, after all, includes an epistle addressed to Sidney's daughter, Elizabeth, Countess of Rutland, which Jonson offers her in exchange for the gold he does not have, suggesting that Jonson for one may have been well aware of the alternative argument being mounted in the *Defence*: see Bates 1992.

seeing it as the cast or mould from which a sculpture or relief is made. Or, better yet—to use a term the etymological and punning potentialities of which are difficult to resist—by seeing it as a die: the engraved stamp from which coins are struck.[101] The image (typically, that of the sovereign) that appears in incuse form on the surface of a coin is transferred—through a violent process of hammering and beating—from its mirror-image, engraved, punched, or otherwise worked on the flat surface of the cylindrical or pyramidal die. From the latter object—a mere tool used in the process of mechanical reproduction, itself routinely disregarded, over-looked, very much in the background, nothing but a means to an end, perennially worn out and discarded or replaced, the 'feminine' impress from which the prototypically 'masculine' face is formed—we might read, in its preposterous, back-to-front, intaglio surface, an alternative legend to that of the culturally valued 'golden' poetry which the speaker of the *Defence* is trying to sell us, with its inevitable and complicit debt to the structure and subordinations of the money form.[102]

In this alternative vision, poetry would renege on the expectation—the require-ment, the demand—that it be 'ideal'. It would not set itself up competitively as the premier art, the best and most valuable of the disciplines to be stocked in the treasure-house of science, against which the others are measured and, found wanting, subordinated to the position of others, servants, or slaves. It would not propose itself as inherently worthy—as worthwhile, as worth something, as worth reading, writing, teaching, or funding—or as uniquely capable of indicating the worth of other things: of making their true value 'shine'. Indeed, it would not 'propose' anything, and would never seek to explain or defend itself in anything resembling propositional prose. This poetry would not suggest that its own 'worthiness' be measured by its profitability, least of all by the promise, which idealist poetics never fails to make, that poetry will provide something over and above what it already is: some added bonus or dividend, an over-plus or expected return, that is seen and justified as what—in the form of moral, social, and intellectual capital ('learning' covers most of these)—it can be guaranteed to yield. It would not claim to add some mysterious quantum of value to real, actual, natural, material things in order to make them—or to pass them off as—ideal (the province of the ad-man). It would not insist that the ideals promoted by the

---

[101] 'Die' in this sense derives from the die (plural, dice) used in gaming (from Latin, *datum* [given]—presumably in the sense of 'that which is given or decreed') via the Old French *de* (plural *dez*): transferring the sense of a small carved/engraved object to an engraved stamp capable of impressing a design or figure onto a softer material (see *OED* die *n*.1). On English coin production in this period, see Challis 1978 (10–20). Admittedly, the term 'die' was not used in this sense until the seventeenth century, the words current in Sidney's time being 'irons' or more specifically 'trussell' and 'pile' for the dies used to produce the impress on the upper and the lower sides of the coin, respectively. 'Die' could, however, also refer to any small, cubed object, such as the square bullets (die-shot or dice-shot) used in the period. One of Sidney's men was wounded at Gravelines by 'a square die out of a field-piece', for example, according to Greville 1986 (74), so one could evidently die from a die.

[102] Appropriately enough, this object that fashions the coin is what gives it its name. The word derives from the French *coin* (wedge, corner) which came to denote the die used for stamping money or medals because the latter was often pyramidal or wedge-shaped (see *OED* coin *n*.; compare the wedge-shaped stone at the apex of an arch, now usually spelled 'quoin', and derived from the same root).

prevailing ideology are presumptively real, good, profitable, and true, and that nothing will 'sooner make you an honest man than the reading of Virgil' (116.27–8): a salesman's tactic if ever there was one (indeed, if it works at all, this alternative poetry would disabuse you of such ideological sharp practice). It would not make 'circles about your imagination' or 'conjure you to believe for true' (103.13–14) what it presents, either empirically or, more importantly, ethically. The question of whether poetic fictions are actually, empirically true is not in contention: it is a point on which the idealist poet and his alternative can agree. But what the latter would not do is pretend that those fictions are ethically true (are 'good' lies): that everyone must believe them—or already does believe them—and can therefore be guaranteed to do, unthinkingly, robotically, as ideology directs. This poetry would not tell its readers what they ought to do—any more than its poetics (were there to be such a thing) would tell poets what they ought to write— for the simple reason that it rejects the whole idea of the 'ought': of the owing, of the assumption that there is some obligatory payment to be made for some imaginary debt, some shortfall between the 'erected wit' (86.7) and the 'infected will' (86.8) that has to be redeemed.[103] That particular nexus of ideas is the product of idealism, and through the agency of idealist philosophy and poetics (not to mention religion), the means by which ideology works its spell. An indebted population is a population ready to be manipulated and controlled, and the 'ought' an unrepayable debt—a kind of eternal spiritual taxation—designed to keep everyone in order, in line: good citizens busy aspiring to be what the system ensures from the outset they can never be—discharged of their dues, 'saved'—or at least not until after they are dead (this mortgage has a very long term). Since it reneges on this transaction—indeed, on all such transactionality—an alternative, non-idealist poetry and poetics, by contrast, would not insist on what a poem/poet ought to be or that this impossible paragon is better than what a poem/poet is. The first sonnet of *Astrophil and Stella* is not the poem that it 'ought' to be, that it aspires to be, that its speaker 'faine' would write—the ideal poem by the ideal poet about the ideal Beloved—because desire intervenes decisively to collapse this fanciful and imaginary virtuous circle from the inside. Instead, the first sonnet of *Astrophil and*

---

[103] As a modal auxiliary, 'ought' expresses 'duty or obligation of any kind; originally used of moral obligation, but also in various more general senses, expressing what is proper, correct, advisable, befitting, or expected' (see *OED* ought *v.* II). In Sidney's time, 'ought' was available as the past tense of 'to owe' (current until the end of the seventeenth century), as well as the present and future tenses (still current). Interestingly, the verb 'owe' originally denoted possession as well as indebtedness: via its Indo-European root it is cognate with 'own'. Thus 'ought' could mean 'possessed, owned' *and* 'had (something) to pay', both significations being current from Old English until the late twelfth century (see *OED* owe *v.* I.1. and I.2, respectively). Thereafter, the sense of ownership became obsolete in English (although it is still current in some dialects, e.g. Scots), so that, in English, 'to owe' denoted the sense of indebtedness only—'to be required or obliged to pay or repay (money, etc.), especially in return for something received'; 'to be or feel under an obligation to render (obedience, allegiance, etc.)'—the sense it retains to this day (see *OED* owe *v.* I.3). See also Derrida 1992 (69n) on the unique quality of the gift as that which defies such owing: 'this *ought-to without owing, duty without duty* [devoir sans devoir] prescribes that the gift not only *owes* nothing, remains foreign to the circle of the debt, but must not *answer* to its own essence, must not even be what it has to be, namely, a gift' (emphasis original).

Stella is the poem that it is: preliminary, notional, experimental. Its rough jottings are but foul papers: a mere collecting of ideas and gathering of materials for the ideal poem it indefinitely postpones and thus declines—or refuses—to be. It is all the better for it.

◌

That the *Defence*, likewise, is not always doing what it is supposed to be doing or saying what it is supposed to say—that, by deviating from its official argument, it is off-message, that at some level it speaks 'otherwise'—confirms the suspicion, long held, that it belongs to the tradition of paradoxical praise. Numerous readers have found affinities not only with the illustrious examples the *Defence* cites by name (Erasmus, Agrippa, More) but with this entire modus operandi that seems to have had a particular appeal for writers in the period and that went back to classical times.[104] Nonetheless, for all this interest and attention, the particular complexity and layeredness of the paradoxical speaking in the *Defence* has not, I think, been fully appreciated or thoroughly ironed out before. How and why this should be the case thus warrants some investigation.

Those readers who engage with the paradoxical other-speaking of the *Defence* most closely certainly acknowledge the deconstructive irony to which it gives rise: 'there is no exit from the circle of irony Sidney draws around his "I" and his oration', Ferguson writes. 'The text undermines that "assumption of intelligibility" which, according to Paul de Man, makes "the mastering of the tropological displacement the very burden of understanding." How can we master an irony which allows us to be certain of no intention but the intention to hide intention?'[105] Yet, for all that, an exit *is* found: 'the Christian escape', the Logos that, as the transcendental Signified, marks the endpoint of otherwise endless trains of signifiers, guarantees meaning (the 'assumption of intelligibility'), and ultimately grounds the irony of Erasmus' and Agrippa's texts—this is the 'other foundation' (101.15) that Sidney's speaker attributes to them—and thus of Sidney's text as well.[106] As a result, 'mastery'—in the sense of the reader understanding what is going on and grasping what the writer truly means and intends—is miraculously restored. The problem with this kind of reading, however, is that the paradoxical other-speaking under investigation ends up by being 'straightened': defused, corrected, redeemed.[107] If the writer is saying the opposite of what he means (that folly

---

[104] See e.g. Hamilton 1956; Helgerson 1976 (155); Connell 1977 (5–8, 38–40); Ferguson 1983 (10–11, 153–8); Levao 1985 (134–56); Hager 1991 (11, 103–14); Duncan-Jones (381). On the tradition of paradoxical praise more generally, see Colie 1966.

[105] Ferguson 1983 (154), referencing de Man 1979 (300).

[106] Ferguson 1983 (158). For a similar move, see Barker 1964 (39–42); Helgerson 1976 (155); and Hager 1991 (9, 12, 37, 40, 103–7).

[107] By contrast, critics who stress the deconstructive power of paradoxical praise tend to see it in texts that—not protected by the aura of Protestant sainthood or taken as proxy for the literary critical profession—can afford to be read as more radical. See e.g. Fineman 1986 and Crewe 1982 (91–101) who read Shakespeare's Dark Lady sonnets and Nashe's *Lenten Stuffe*, respectively, as examples of paradoxical praise, both holding up the *Defence* as the classic articulation of an idealist poetics which these works subvert.

is praiseworthy, for example, or learning vain) then, by reversing this, the truth can be recovered and the record, happily, set straight. In effect, the texts in question cease to be paradoxical. They are 'really' educational and instructional all along since they are, in fact, teaching a valuable lesson, even if the reader arrives at it via an indirect route (in such readings, Sidney's *Defence* can thus be said to provide 'the necessarily devious route to a coherent reading of the work').[108] Indeed, the lesson is all the more valuable for having been taught heuristically, as the reader—surprised by sin—takes the perils of folly and vanity to heart by having learned to identify them within him- or herself first. This may be the model of learning that the speaker of the *Defence* proposes: in the form of satire, for example, which 'make[s] a man laugh at folly, and at length ashamed to laugh at himself, which he cannot avoid, without avoiding the folly' (97.37–9), or of comedy, in which 'nothing can more open his eyes than to find his own actions contemptibly set forth' (98.22–3). It is not, however, the model that Sidney—or anyone else who might be scoping out the possibility of an alternative, non-idealist kind of poetry—would endorse, if only because, once neutralized and cancelled out in this way, 'paradox' is simply affirming pedagogical values and so doing ideology's work.

The inconvenient truth—which cannot be stated openly but which the text's double negatives sneakily give away—is that, in practice, a negative example has no force to teach: that there is indeed nothing that can be guaranteed to open people's eyes, and they most certainly can avoid laughing at folly and applying its lessons, shamefacedly, to themselves. Gosson's charge to this effect still stands, and with it the paradoxical situation of a so-called *Defence* that is unable, finally, to defend against it. If Sidney's speaker and the critics who follow him try to close paradox down, then—by means of the tricky locutions and logical disturbances that we have come to see as characteristic of the *Defence*—Sidney opens it right back up again. The paradoxical speaking of Sidney's text—which, if heeded, fundamentally disrupts the humanist faith and optimism in poetry's ability to teach and delight—cannot so easily be righted, and to do so in the name of right reading is to 'master' the text at the expense of the subtle, surprising, complex, paradoxical, contradictory, and ultimately much more interesting argument that, beneath the surface (although not very far) is really going on. One way of explaining this might be to see it in terms of Socratic irony—the model to which all these examples of knowing and not knowing ultimately refer—insofar as it poses a question that cannot be resolved. Is the paradoxical state of knowing that you know nothing a definite 'thing to know': a practical and concrete form of knowledge that—once learned by means of a rigorous dialectical training—allows you to graduate to wisdom?[109] Or is even this

---

[108] Hager 1991 (104).

[109] Hager 1991 in particular, stresses irony's ultimately curative function: 'our cure . . . [is] having us taste our own folly' (11); Sidney's readers 'diagnose themselves' (13); his 'medicine of cherries' [96.10] aims to 'cure us of our folly' (15); Sidney sets out 'to entrap his readers in the ironies of existence, for their own benefit' (32). Hager discusses Alcibiades' description of Socrates as a Silenus-figure (a hollow statue of the ugly satyr which, when opened, has images of the gods inside) in Plato 1925, *Symposium*, 215B. For Hager, both the idea of a 'solid core' and an 'ideal nothing' (103) lying behind the ironic surface are misleading, or at least a false dichotomy. Such images invite us to mine or excavate the surface for truth

something that you cannot know, that has to be held in doubt, effectively depriving you of that 'other foundation' (101.15), and leaving you in the state of permanent suspension, hovering, or free-fall—'unrelieved *vertige*'—which is where, for Paul de Man, the true ironist ends up?[110] That this particular philosophical conundrum was a point on which idealist philosophy would come to be challenged, shows the extent to which the latter has an investment—an interest—in maintaining the view that knowledge is ultimately achievable (a final *telos* to be reached, a home to be arrived at), that dialectic leads ever upwards to more abstract forms of reasoning and higher levels of thought, and that mastery is thus finally, serenely, assured.[111] In the case of those for whom such a move towards the Absolute is not necessarily a good thing, on the other hand, unstable irony and unresolved paradox might well seem an attractive alternative, if not the only one available, and especially for writers who want to induce in their readers not knowledge but doubt, and not the half-baked school-masterly doubt that is simply designed to lead the pupil experientially towards 'enlightenment', but rather a radical, permanent doubt that is designed to see through that ideal, shining, golden light and the ideological mystifications carried out in its name.[112]

Such, I think, is the strategy Thomas More undertakes in the *Utopia*. It is noticeable that those critics who attend to the irony and paradox of the *Defence* tend to locate its model in Erasmus (putting Sidney among those who, 'for a higher ironic and curative purpose—sometimes propagandistic—[follow] the humanist praisers of folly'), and sometimes Agrippa, but less commonly More.[113] It is as if the paradoxes of Sidney's treatise—defending something that his society treats as valueless (poetry has had a 'hard welcome in England', 108.42) but that the speaker considers supremely valuable ('golden', and so forth)—can be made legible, 'intel-ligible', when they are read alongside texts that (with a view, presumably, to suggesting the opposite) also praise something their society treats as un-ideal (folly) or disparage something it treats as ideal (learning). Quite apart from the question of whether Erasmus' or Agrippa's texts should be read or were received by contemporary readers in this way—or even if they were (given that paradox breeds

---

when truth is 'literally on the surface. The truth is in the search for truth, or, shall we say, in our experience of the dialectic, the often self-contradictory *logos*, of the text itself' (104).

[110] de Man 1983 (215). The paradox of the Cretan Liar similarly resists stabilization.

[111] See Kierkegaard 1989 who presents Socratic irony as counter to Hegel's model of Absolute Knowledge. Stillman 2008 (i, 67, 70, 74, 90) exemplifies interpretations of the *Defence* that characterize the arrival at meaning or understanding as the *telos* of reading: the returning home at the end of an interpretative odyssey. This model draws on Eden 1997 (30) who argues that in classical and early modern rhetorical theory '*oikonomia* . . . takes social organization, based on the unit of the family, the *oikos* . . . as the shaping analogy for literary composition'. A contextualizing principle—and the equivalent of *decorum*—the aim of such *oikonomia* was to accommodate word and meaning so as to make the recipients of a speech or text feel familiar with it: comfortable and 'at home'. Cf. Shell 1978 (89–112) and Derrida 1992 (6–7, 158–9), both of whom re-politicize the concept of *oikonomia* in the interests of theorizing that which is radically unfamiliar or *unheimlich*: the aporia of the gift, for example, which exceeds and so disturbs the expected models of circulation, exchange, and return.

[112] On stable and unstable irony, see Booth 1974.

[113] Hager 1991 (9), although Hager discusses Sidney's relation to More (107–8) more than most. Cf. Hamilton 1956; Helgerson 1976 (155); Connell 1977 (5–8); and Ferguson 1983 (10–11, 153–8).

paradox), whether we can ever really know it for sure—the *Utopia* operates quite differently. More's text neither praises something valueless nor dispraises something valued. Rather, it takes the means by which his society values anything (money) and imagines a society without it. The *Utopia* does not dispraise something valuable (money, learning, wisdom) so as to show how valuable it 'really' is. Rather, it dispraises the whole value *system*. And it does this neither by dispraising it in so many words, nor by reversing the values (holding the valueless up to the valued, and vice versa) that, in a comfortably knowing, scholarly way can be 're-reversed' back again to render the irony of the text stable and its meaning readable, teachable. Rather, the *Utopia* creates a world in which that whole value system is absent: where it is not. This is No place before it is a Good place. Utopia is not idealized: it is not 'Eutopia'. Rather, the text shows how the categories of ideal (valuable) and non-ideal (valueless) are ideological productions—are, specifically, productions of the money form—and, for good or ill, extremely powerful in their effects. More's text does not teach what society 'ought' to be like, or how it 'ought', ideally, to be organized. If it teaches anything, then it does so negatively, disabusing the reader of the fetishisms and mystifications of the money form by depicting a world in which they and it are removed (where the 'ought' is nought). More's strategy of absenting the value system is subtly different from Erasmus' or Agrippa's strategy of reversing that system's values. In satirical terms it is much harder-hitting, however, and in political terms more radical, because in this case the paradox is much more difficult to straighten out or to redeem (clearly, proposing an alternative system of value is not an option, for that would only perpetuate the problem). This impasse is wholly appropriate, however, in a text that takes issue with a system predicated on such valuations, debts, and redemptions, and in which everyone and everything that is not identified with the general equivalent is found to come up short. The *Utopia* thus dispenses with the neat inversions and reversals by means of which a simplified version of praise paradox typically gets to be interpreted and (in ways that only confirm ideological categories) put straight. Something similar, I think, is going on in the *Defence*, the 'other', unofficial argument of which is straining towards a position that not only devalues something valued—golden poetry—as, for example, Agrippa might (potentially, a still recuperable position), but also dispraises the entire value system—idealist poetics, idealist philosophy, ideology—as, for example, More did (a much less recuperable position, for the reasons outlined above). A comparison with the *Utopia* makes this easier to see, while the tendency to pass over the connection—and to emphasize similarity with Erasmus' and Agrippa's texts instead—equally obscures it.

The paradoxical speaking of the *Defence* clearly has close affinities with More's text—more so, perhaps, than with Erasmus' and Agrippa's—but, to add a further twist to an already complicated situation, it is also unlike them all in one obvious way: it does not recognizably situate itself within the paradoxical tradition, or identify itself as such. Even though some readers were evidently capable of taking such texts at face value, for the most part clearly recognizable rhetorical figures advertised their paradoxical status beyond reasonable doubt. Sidney's speaker can refer to texts that 'praise the discretion of an ass, the comfortableness of being in debt, and the jolly commodity of being sick of the plague' (101.7–9), for example, in the knowledge that most of his readers would be able to recognize the cultural and rhetorical markers sufficiently to classify them accordingly. And even though unstable irony might then prevent those readers from reducing the texts in question to some pat pedagogical lesson or packaged wisdom—that is, from ever arriving at 'knowing' per se—they would still know it was a paradoxical text that had left them in that predicament in the first place. A good part of the difficulty that Sidney's *Defence* presents, however, is precisely that we do not know this. The question of knowing and not knowing—which the tradition of paradox has already made problematic—is thus further problematized by the possibility, even the likelihood, that Sidney may not have known (in the sense of having intended or planned ahead) that this was what he was doing. Paradox depends on recognizing other-speech so as to appreciate its ironic, satirical effects, but the speaker of the *Defence* does not 'knowingly' speak otherwise—or not in any arch or deliberate way—and neither, arguably, does Sidney. Gosson dispraised something that he and some elements of his society judged valueless and non-ideal (poetry), and the speaker responds by praising it as, in his judgement, valuable and ideal. Neither of these positions is paradoxical. Generations of readers have rightly sensed a degree of paradox within the *Defence*, however, because the speaker's case—on the face of it so logical, so non-paradoxical, so incontrovertible (how could the ideal not be an object of praise, not be defensible?)—is, for all that, somehow felt not to go smoothly. Something—some hidden hand—intervenes to upset, disturb, or interfere with it: to gainsay it. That something, I have been arguing, is Sidney's rejection of idealist philosophy and poetics, but that rejection is not (as it was for More) a conscious starting position: a point of departure from which the paradoxical other-speaking of the text is devised and signalled to the reader by means of certain well-recognized rhetorical signs in order to present a radically alternative position (whether some readers understood this or not). In Sidney's case, the rejection of idealist poetics is reactive: it arises in response to the argument he finds his speaker making, rather than anticipating that argument and framing it ironically, paradoxically, so as to undermine it from the start. To this extent, paradox follows rather than leads—it comes after the event—and is, to that extent, belated.

As I have suggested throughout this book, I do not believe that Sidney set out with a plan in mind to draft a radical, alternative, non-idealist poetics. Indeed, at the rational, cognitive level, he may well have intended to do the opposite—to answer Gosson, to defend poetry, to speak as his speaker spoke—only to find, at some visceral, semi-conscious level, as the latter's argument progressed, his gorge rise and his creative spirit revolt at the prospect. This, I think, is what is happening in the *narratio*. From the *propositio* on, the speaker redoubles his efforts and does his best to parry the internal opposition—to silence it, repress it—but, in response, the latter only redoubles its resistance. The *Defence*, caught in the crossfire, is a record of the war between the two. But the paradoxical other-speech that arises as a result—'I answer paradoxically, but truly, I think truly . . .' (102.42–103.1)—is an effect of that war, not its cause: a sign of resistance, not an opening move. Such paradox may end up undermining the official position and sabotaging it beyond repair (how can the speaker come back after a statement like that?). For all his firefighting, his denials, his protestations to the contrary, the speaker will find his argument trailing off with less and less conviction—with increasingly faint praise— to recognize by the *peroratio* that the losing battle he has been fighting has conclusively been lost. For all its official endorsement and idealist credentials, therefore, the speaker's 'erected wit' (86.7) will lose out to Sidney's 'infected will' (86.8), the guerrilla tactics of which might not win the war but certainly ensure that the other does not win it either. Even though this is where it ends up, however, the paradoxical other-speaking in the *Defence* is not a means to that end. It is not strategically deployed (as it was by More) to declare war on idealism and ideology from the outset. While aligned with the *Utopia* at the most fundamental level, therefore—in agreement with it on the evil effects of the money form and the costs of its costing mentality—the *Defence* is also unlike it in this equally fundamental way. Its paradoxical other-speech, although unmistakably there, is not there by design: is not artful, conceived in advance, calculated in its effects, or planted by means of certain rhetorical devices for the reader to recognize and understand (something that may account for why, when the *Utopia*—as '*Eutopia*'—is mentioned in the *Defence*, it is not treated, or not on the surface at least, as a paradoxical text). Rather, paradox in the *Defence* is secondary, accidental, a by-product of the 'No!' that the speaker's official project unwittingly calls into being.

This has an important bearing on the question of 'wit' in the *Defence*: a quality often invoked when the argument of the text is seen to deviate in some way from the one it is supposed to be making. Contradictions within the official, idealist argument are thereby accounted for—and frequently brushed away—by being treated as light-hearted banter: as instances of Sidney's much-touted '*sprezza-tura*'.[114] However, this not only fails to do justice to the radical possibilities of play that the *serio-ludere* tradition allows for: to the irony that destabilizes every philosophical position, including its own. It also assumes on the part of Sidney an admirable level of authorial knowing and control, as if he were in complete command of his text at all times and, starting out from a stable position and set of clear propositions, able to throw out a joke from time to time to lighten the tone, or, on the heuristic model discussed above, to use paradox in order to lead the reader back to that starting position via a roundabout route. It is not difficult to see behind this a projection of the author as ideal (that is, as scholarly, masterly), nor to see how Sidney is being recruited as a spokesman for such an author's school-masterly values or for the pedagogical mission of teaching by delight. The 'wit' of the *Defence*, however, is not at all like that. It is adventitious. It is the product of discomfort and increasing desperation. Fractious and fraught, it leaves a trail of destruction through the logic of the argument, and leaves the surface of the text potholed, scarred, and distressed. The paradoxical 'wit' of the *Defence* is not the exercise of intellectual nimbleness or display of authorial ingenuity that was most

---

[114] Myrick 1935 is a particular offender: the final chapter of his book is entitled '*Sprezzatura*' and provides a lengthy meditation on the topic. See also van Dorsten (186); Hunt 1987 (13); Miller 1987 (276); Hager 1991 (28–9); and Reisner 2010 (336), for a sampling of similar views.

commonly associated with the tradition of paradoxical praise—clever, playful, pleasing to all concerned—and it is not, therefore, *sprezzatura*, the artful artlessness that conceals art.[115] Rather, it is a genuine artlessness that, in this case, reveals a disconcerting and unexpected conception of art. It is not good-humoured banter, designed to win the reader round, but the result of a violent collision between the author and the voice that speaks on (or not, as it turns out) his behalf. And it is 'paradoxical' only in the sense, first, that it is left on record (had Sidney really wanted to promote idealist poetics, there was nothing to prevent him from consigning this particular failed attempt to the flames, as he threatened on his deathbed to suppress his literary works), and, second, that a model of idealist poetics is what, in many quarters, the *Defence* is still taken to be.[116]

This is not to say that Sidney was incapable of such paradoxical wit, of course. *Astrophil and Stella* pulls it off superbly, in particular in the opening sonnet where—though still at war with himself and still 'beating myselfe for spite'—this poet who is self-confessedly 'sick among the rest' (115.9) and spotted with 'the common infection' (115.10) finally dares to out his desirous will.[117] Here, however, paradox works not in the service of the ideal but very much at its expense: the ideal sonnet or sonnet sequence is precisely what does not get written.[118] Much the same might be said of More's *Utopia* where, again, the ideal (idealism, ideology, and the value system they represent and reproduce) is precisely what is absented, removed from the picture: what is not there (one might also say that an alternative 'ideal' society is not there either). Both texts thereby pass eloquent, silent, paradoxical comment on the invidious effects of the ideal and, conversely, on the freedoms of an imagined world—and of a poetry—that is not beholden to it. As far as proponents of that value system are concerned, these texts thus defend the indefensible. The *Defence* does not go that far. In large part it cannot: it is prevented from doing so by virtue of its form, by presenting itself as propositional rather than—like *Astrophil and Stella* or the *Utopia*—as fictional (another reminder that

[115] On the paradox of praise as an opportunity to show off the orator's rhetorical skills, see Colie 1966 (3); Fineman 1986 (5–9, 30–5); and Ferguson 1983 (10–11).
[116] On Sidney's dying wish that the *New Arcadia* be destroyed, see Greville 1986 (11); and that his poetry meet a similar fate, see Moffet 1940 (91): 'He blushed at even the most casual mention of his own Anacreontics, and once and again begged his brother, by their tie of common birth, by his right hand, by his faith in Christ, that not any of this sort of poems should come forth into the light.' Duncan-Jones 1985 (228) takes 'Anacreontics' here to refer to Sidney's secular poetry in general. On the other hand, Sidney does seem to have closely guarded the *Defence* and restricted its circulation to immediate family and friends, 'for reasons', Maslen speculates, 'we can only guess at' (9). Woudhuysen 1996 (234) comments that when the *Defence* was published, 'what to modern eyes appears to be one of his most important and brilliant works may have been passed over by contemporaries with a certain amount of puzzlement', on account, perhaps, of the complexities and paradoxes that prevent it from being read as a statement of idealist poetics in any straightforward way.
[117] See Bates 2001.
[118] This is very much Fineman's argument with respect to Shakespeare's *Sonnets*: i.e. that they, too, mark a point of irreversible rupture with idealist poetics. *Astrophil and Stella*, like the *Defence*, remains firmly within that tradition, as far as Fineman is concerned, but other readers have found the scope of Fineman's argument to extend beyond Shakespeare and to apply to other, earlier authors whom, for the purposes of his argument, he had characterized as unproblematically idealist: see e.g. Levao 1987 (816); Enterline 1995 (325n); and Warley 2005 (6).

the best way to defend poetry is to write it). The real argument of the *Defence*—what Sidney wants to say but dare not, or dare not openly, or has not yet found a means to say—is, in this text, still inhibited, still held back. The plea for a non-idealist, non-profitable, non-bankable model of poetry is still unsayable, and remains the unspoken, unofficial argument that has to be deduced, inferred, from the traces it leaves symptomatically on the page. It is the text's political, economic, ethical, and poetical unconscious, and not surprisingly, therefore, it manifests itself in slips, jokes, puns, and other paradoxical forms.[119] The *Defence* is thus a would-be paradoxical text—a paradoxical text by accident, by proxy, a paradoxical text *manqué*—and the *Utopia*, perhaps, the brave, risk-taking, paradoxical text it secretly (ideally/un-ideally) desires to be. Not yet bold enough to be that ('*Be bolde, be bolde . . . Be not too bold*'), the *Defence* still timidly presents itself as the ideal, idealist text it is 'officially' supposed to be—and many continue to read it as such—even though its tormented psychomachia ensures that it is not.[120] In sum, the *Defence* is not strictly paradoxical, in the way that the traditional exempla of paradoxical praise are: that is to say, designedly so. But neither is it straightforwardly non-paradoxical, in the way that Gosson's dispraise of something valueless is, or the speaker's praise of something valued tries to be. Rather, it lies somewhere indeterminate (no place?) between the two. It would be most accurate, perhaps, and most in keeping with its subtle, signature effects, to say that what the *Defence* is is not *not* paradoxical.

ca

It is an indication of how all-pervasive—how internalized, how naturalized—money thought is that thinking outside it should prove so tricky, and entail this kind of puzzling, teasing, looking-glass logic, liable to produce brain-ache before too long.[121] Since there is no 'overturning' of idealism that does not risk simply

---

[119] For Lacan 2002 (223) Freud's analysis of wit in *Jokes and Their Relation to the Unconscious* 'remains the most unchallengeable of his works because it is the most transparent; in it, the effect of the unconscious is demonstrated in all its subtlety. And the visage it reveals to us is that of wit [*l'esprit*] in the ambiguity conferred on it by language, where the other face of its regalian power is the witticism [*pointe*], by which the whole of its order is annihilated in an instant—the witticism, indeed, in which language's creative activity unveils its absolute gratuitousness, in which its domination of reality [*réel*] is expressed in the challenge of nonmeaning, and in which the humor, in the malicious grace of the free spirit [*esprit libre*], symbolizes a truth that does not say its last word'. 'To grant priority to the signifier over the subject is . . . to take into account the experience Freud opened up for us: the signifier plays and wins . . . before the subject is aware of it, to such an extent that in the play of *Witz* (in witticisms, for example) it may surprise the subject. What it lights up with its flash is the subject's division from himself' (712).

[120] Spenser 2007, *The Faerie Queene*, III.xi.54. One of the few points on which I disagree with Levao 1985—with whose resolutely anti-foundationalist and anti-metaphysical reading of the *Defence* I am otherwise greatly in sympathy—is in his characterization of its carelessness and playfulness as 'studied' (134).

[121] It is this all-pervasiveness that Jameson 2005 (xii) laments: 'late capitalism seems to have no natural enemies . . . Yet it is not only the invincible universality of capitalism which is at issue . . . What is crippling is . . . the universal belief, not only that this tendency is irreversible, but that the historic alternatives to capitalism have been proven unviable and impossible, and that no other socio-economic system is conceivable, let alone practically available. The Utopians not only offer to conceive of such alternate systems; Utopian form is itself a representational meditation on radical difference, radical otherness, and on the systemic nature of the social totality, to the point where one cannot imagine any

installing another system of value and so of power in its place, however, then
countering it—delaying it, disrupting it, deconstructing it—remain the only
options available: '*flectere si nequeo superos, Acheronta movebo*' [if Heaven I cannot
bend, then Hell I will arouse!].[122] Yet this, in turn, may licence us—embolden
us—to pay particular attention to the 'nots' in Sidney's *Defence* (all the more so if
their effects exceed or defy intention) and, where prompted, to seek to unravel
them. When the speaker assures us, therefore, that the poet's project of bestowing a
Cyrus upon the world to make many Cyruses is 'not wholly imaginative, as we are
wont to say by them that build castles in the air' (85.38–9), we might see—as the
alternative project being scoped out—precisely one that *is* wholly imaginative, and
building castles in the air as a pretty good description of what creative fiction is
(especially in an epic romance like the *New Arcadia*). Indeed, if the business of the
right poet's most worthy and defensible project is to ensure the optimum delivery
of maximum Cyruses, then any alternative project—one that might seek, by
contrast, to delay or disrupt this eventuality and to send its ideal outcome of
intellectual aggression and ethical tyranny, appropriately figured as a military
dictatorship, off-course or awry—would naturally choose the opposite: and, if
this were the means of doing so, then the more imaginative, fictive, and 'airy' the
better. To the poet of a non- or anti-idealist persuasion, that is, one obvious way to
counter the ideal 'reality' represented by officially sanctioned or state-sponsored art
is to move away from reality altogether and towards the counterfactual—away from
mimetic, representational art and towards the made-up, the baseless, the factitious,
precisely the 'wholly imaginative'—so as to devise things, as Agrippa put it, 'vpon a
matter of nothinge' (D4ᵛ). In this More's *Utopia* presciently led the way.[123]
'Neither let this be jestingly conceived' (85.33), Sidney's speaker insists, seeking
to forestall the objection that Nature's works are 'essential' while those of the poet
are only 'in imitation or fiction' (85.34): all part of his campaign to impress upon us
the fact that the latter *are* capable of working 'substantially' (85.39–40), but, at the
same time, an invitation to see that 'jestingly' is just how such an idea might be
received, especially if that jest is seen, in the spirit of More, as the kind of serious
joke that does not simply mock such idealism (trivially, dismissibly, reversibly) but
evacuates it, hollows it out, brings it face to face with its own vacuity. The *Defence*,

fundamental change in our social existence which has not first thrown off Utopian visions like so many
sparks from a comet.'

[122] Virgil 2001, *Aeneid*, VII.312, being Juno's resolution to thwart Jupiter's plans for Aeneas'
imperial destiny by every means at her disposal. The line was chosen by Freud as the epigraph to *The
Interpretation of Dreams* (1900), Juno figuring the disruptive power of the unconscious. See also
Dickson 1992 (42–3) on the power Sidney attributes to a specifically female disruptiveness: '*The
Defense* consistently uses woman as a metaphor for both transgressive language and poetry in general',
adding that 'the point in such gendering seems . . . to articulate a disturbingly feminized aspect of
Sidney's poetic identity' (43). Following Levao 1985 (235–49), Dickson sees this tendency as
culminating in the figure Cecropia in the *New Arcadia*: 'a nightmarish image of feminine power and
demonic creation' (50), making her 'a subversive articulation of Sidney's frustration with authority'
and of his 'unconscious preference for confusion over the linearity and clear reasoning represented in
Euarchus' (51).

[123] Jameson 2005 (xiv) sees Utopian fiction as a 'socio-economic sub-genre' of Science Fiction,
'specifically devoted to the imagination of alternative social and economic forms'.

which does not go as far as the *Utopia*, is typically divided on the issue, presenting the poet as making things 'either better than Nature bringeth forth, or, quite anew' (85.19–20). Despite their apparent similarity and continuity, these alternatives in fact map onto two quite different—indeed, diametrically opposed—positions that might be identified with those of the speaker and of Sidney respectively. Thus, the speaker is committed to making things 'better' than Nature—to improving her, outdoing her, surpassing her—while Sidney is committed to making things quite 'anew': 'forms such as never were in Nature, as the Heroes, Demigods, Cyclops, Chimeras, Furies, and such like' (85.20–1). He is committed, that is, to the counterfactual.[124] Like More, Sidney, too, would veer away from an art that claims to be a representation *of* something else, because representation so easily lends itself to the abstractions, idealizations, and fetishisms of the money form, where one ideal thing—the general equivalent—is taken to represent everything else. There is always a danger, even in counterfactual works, that this might still happen and the possibility can never be entirely ruled out (misreadings of the *Utopia* as '*Eutopia*' being a case in point), but, insofar as it minimizes the imitation of any recognizable, everyday world, the creation of an entirely fictional or fantastic one can help to guard against it and at least reduce the risk. Indeed, the further removed such fictions are from Nature, the less chance there is that they will be taken as representations or idealizations of Nature, which is why (as in much science fiction) these 'new' forms that the poet conceives so readily lend themselves to the monstrous, the unnatural.

This distinction between the speaker's official project and Sidney's alternative one also comes out in the vague phrase used to describe the poet's work (as opposed to Nature's) as 'in imitation or fiction' (85.34). Again, two terms are presented as continuous, even synonymous—as both things that the right poet might do—but, when subjected to a little interpretative pressure, they can be shown to eventuate in two quite different models of fiction. Thus, the speaker (and the right poet he defends) sees his project primarily as one of *imitation*. As we saw in section II, however, since the 'end' of this imitation is 'to teach and delight' (86.19, 20), what he imitates is not the ordinary, everyday world, but rather an idealized version of it: a heightened 'meta-reality' that is somehow supposed to be more 'real' than the poor, quotidian world that actually substitutes for it.[125] The right poet does not imitate Nature, therefore, but the (presumptively masculine) ideal that she 'ought' to be. This is what allows him to convert her brass into his gold—to make her poor world 'rich' (85.24), to supply the phallus, close the gap, eliminate the deficit, make good the shortfall, repay the debt owing and more—all in the name of an ideology whose logic (money thought) he thereby exemplifies in the fetishized representation,

---

[124] For Levao 1985 (145), Sidney eschews Platonic/Augustinian metaphysics, with their appeal to some ideal truth or Logos: 'More decisively committed to poetic feigning, he welcomes the mind's ability to create such new forms "as never were in Nature" [85.20].'

[125] Heninger 1989 (248). As Goux 1990 (94–5) notes, this reversal is typical of idealism: 'The *idealist optical illusion* consists in viewing the visible material world as the reflection of general equivalents, whereas general equivalents constitute the focused reflection, the specular image, of the visible world's multiplicity and differentiation' (emphasis original).

the 'golden' poem, that he makes. The world he creates in his art is not 'realistic', therefore—indeed, by comparison with the ordinary world, it may look pretty fictional—but this is a direct result of his commitment to making things 'better' than Nature (85.19).[126] The ideal world that he 'imitates', and self-justifyingly argues for, produces a world that—in order to teach and delight (that is, to educate the reader in the prevailing ideology's ethical 'truths')—ensures that the good end happily and the bad unhappily: Miss Prism's definition of fiction being the logical conclusion of the optimistic, humanist, pedagogical project, and she herself the logical culmination of all the schoolmasterly types who promote it.[127] The right poet's 'fiction', in other words, is the agent of ideology. It constructs and disseminates the values and ideals of that ideology and therefore operates as its vehicle. Indeed, one might say that, insofar as it does ideology's work, this fiction is continuous and coterminous with ideology: that such fiction *is* ideology. Sidney, on the other hand (or the alternative, non-idealist poet he would argue for), sees his project primarily as one of *fiction*, but of fiction in a quite different sense. This poet's fiction does not make things 'better'. It makes things 'quite anew' (85.20), a much stronger meaning of the verb and one that brings out the sense of creation or *poesis*: of bringing something into being that did not exist before, rather than simply tweaking or embellishing something that was already there.[128] This poet's fiction thus has a quite different relation to imitation from the speaker's, giving much greater force to the 'or' in 'imitation or fiction', now no longer used weakly to suggest a couple of things that the right poet (as opposed to Nature) might do—this or that—but rather two quite separate things—this *or* that—one of which the non-idealist poet will do (fiction) as opposed to the other (imitation).[129] This kind of fiction, then, does not

---

[126] Behind this one might locate what Bersani 1990 (22) characterizes as the 'culture of redemption': an idealist aesthetic in which 'art redeems the catastrophe of history' and that 'carries within it the conviction that, because of the achievements of culture, the disasters of history somehow do not matter. Everything can be made up, can be made over again, and the absolute singularity of human experience—the source of both its tragedy and its beauty—is thus dissipated in the trivializing nobility of a redemption through art'.

[127] Wilde 1989 (501): 'The good ended happily, and the bad unhappily. That is what Fiction means', from *The Importance of Being Earnest*, Act II.

[128] These are the two ways of thinking about creativity in relation to Nature that Dolan 1993 (227) identifies in Renaissance defences of poetry: a cosmetic (and implicitly misogynistic) model, in which Nature is deemed imperfect and in need of male 'improvement' through art, and a more positive, maternal model, in the form of Great Creating Nature. In Dolan's view Sidney takes the former position in the *Defence*, and although he remains vulnerable to his figuration of virtue, which is 'specifically represented as feminine'—granting it 'a potentially disturbing power over the male spectator, who is vulnerable to ravishment as well as to edification'—this remains a misogynistic reading of the *Defence* since 'virtue' is (somewhat paradoxically) characterized as a seductress. To distinguish between the speaker's desire to improve Nature and Sidney's desire to bring forth new things, by contrast, makes greater allowance for the possibility of a positive figuration of creativity as female on Sidney's part (as his extension of poetic utterance to include the ecstatic effusions of priestesses and sibyls also does), while still acknowledging the official position of the *Defence* to be that of the scholarly male (and presumptively misogynistic) poet.

[129] The same split and contradictory definition of fiction may also be said to apply to invention, as well. On the one hand 'invention' is used in the *Defence* to indicate the imitating of some ideal in order to have a beneficial effect on its readers. Thus Heliodorus represents ideal love in his 'sugared invention' (87.32), the *Aethiopica*; the tales of Menenius Agrippa and Nathan demonstrate 'the strange effects of this poetical invention' (96.11); the poet asks the Muses to inspire him to 'a good

imitate reality with some extra patina of value added to gloss it up and make it 'shine'. It is not 'mimesis-plus'. Indeed, insofar as imitation so understood shows how easily, how inevitably, the representation of something can come to be fetishized—to be valued over the thing it represents (faithfully reproducing the structure of the money form)—the non-idealist poet will consciously abjure it, choosing not to represent something else (least of all something ideal) but rather to present something non-existent: something entirely new.[130] To the extent that he or she rejects the imitation of ideals—refuses to present 'lies' as true—such a poet will move as far away from representation as possible and towards the counterfactual: to create worlds that have no basis in reality, that make no claim to represent somewhere or something else, that are totally made up, and where the poet's fictions or 'lies' are therefore *obviously* false. Both the right (idealist) poet and the wrong (non-idealist) poet produce fictions that are empirically false: that is never in dispute. But where the former claims that the empirically false is ethically true, the latter refuses to make that dog-leg turn and, in that refusal, reveals it, cancels it. This is the kind of fiction that finds its apogee in More's *Utopia*: a text that is indeed 'wholly imaginative', a mere castle in the air, but one that is, for exactly that reason, able to expose ideology's functioning: to show how its ethical 'truths'—its valued 'values'—are arrived at, how represented, how distributed, how made to seem 'real'. To show, in short, that ideology *is* fiction. The 'fiction' invoked in Sidney's *Defence*, therefore, points in two opposite directions: one kind perpetuates ideology, the other deconstructs it.[131]

---

invention . . . not labouring to tell you what is, or is not, but what should or should not be' (103.16–17); 'in Poesy looking but for fiction, [the reader] shall use the narration but as an imaginative ground-plot of a profitable invention' (103.30–2). In all these examples, 'invention' is used to bolster the official argument of the *Defence* that the purpose of poetry is to teach ideological truths. As such, 'invention' is effectively indistinguishable from imitation, since what it 'imitates' is ideals. Other usages, however, pull against this to suggest that invention is not the imitating of some notional, given, pre-existent, ideal but rather the act of *poesis*—of creating something from nothing, of making something up that is entirely new—like the poet, who, 'lifted up with the vigour of his own invention, doth grow in effect into another nature' (85.17–19), as opposed to the philosopher and historian who, by contrast, borrows poetry and thus 'takes not the course of his own invention' (86.42). It is interesting that when Sidney uses 'invention' in the latter sense of creation, the qualifying adjective he chooses is the morally neutral but personally invested 'own'. When using the word in the former sense, by contrast, he feels the need to qualify it with a positive adjective (sugared, poetical, good, profitable), as if this idealist, imitative model had to be *made* attractive.

[130] Guy-Bray 2009 (29) notes that at a time when poetry was 'expected to do more work and make more sense, to be more obviously useful . . . it was harder for Renaissance poets to focus on poetry's ability to make things different, and their struggle to imagine difference often ended in defeat. Nevertheless, for them . . . poetry could be less a way to reproduce what was than to produce something new—which is exactly what Sidney praised about the best poets in his *Defence*'. Insofar as it defies the culturally normalized models of production, fiction thus provides an opportunity for a countercultural positioning: 'texts in which poetry is celebrated for its own sake, not for what it might lead to, are one important medium for poets to protest the implications of the reproductive metaphor' (25).

[131] See also Dollimore 2004 (74), for whom the ambiguity between these two positions in the *Defence* 'remains unresolved', although he sees Sidney's portrayal of a wholly fictive, poet-made world as anticipating Bacon's theorization of poetry as a purely imaginative category. 'Sidney retains the didactic function of literature but begins to undermine the providential sanction which, in the late sixteenth century, it presupposed and depended upon. Once it is denied that the source of the didactic scheme is a reality both ultimate and more real than the phenomenal world, the scheme itself withers in the face of a world which contradicts it. And, of course, this is what Bacon, by implication, does

There is also, of course, a third option—one the *Defence* tends to pass over or play down but that still has complete artistic validity—and that is the possibility that the poet might imitate reality: not some idealized, rarefied version of it but the actual, real world that is in front of his or her face.[132] The speaker of the *Defence* acknowledges such realistic productions, but accords them a low status and associates them with practitioners other than the poet: the historian, for example, who is unable to rise above showing the 'bare *was*' (93.6), or the painter who portrays Vespasian 'right as he was' (92.25) or Canidia 'as she was . . . foul and ill favoured' (92.32–3). To the speaker, committed to his ideal reality, such warts-and-all productions have no value and are therefore of little interest: in his view, the right painter would paint 'a most sweet face' (92.31) and simply write 'Canidia' under it. For that very reason, however, they have a profound interest for the kind of artist who might be committed to turning idealist aesthetics on their head. Like Shakespeare, for instance, who sets out to do exactly that in the sonnets addressed to the Dark Lady: a love-object whom he characterizes as most definitely foul and ill favoured. This praise is 'paradoxical' only to the extent that it overgoes or speaks 'other' than the idealist tradition—with its high, golden measure of value—in order to see the unique, inimitable, heterogeneous, and non-commodified thing that has not been priced or 'valued' according to that ideal measure ('belied with false compare'), and yet that is, for that reason, the more beloved, the more desired (it is only idealism that renders the praise of such a thing paradoxical).[133] If it is an idealist 'reality' that is the object of derision, then to present a world that is not ideal is just as legitimate a move as to present a world that is not real. Non-idealist art, that is, will show something not as it 'ought' to be but either as it is (realism) or as it is not (the counterfactual). These two alternatives need not be mutually exclusive. Indeed, Shakespeare's works as a whole might be said to occupy the space between these two poles: to show how broad a span it covers, and how the 'ought' can be dispensed with pretty conclusively without anyone missing it too much. In Sidney's case, too, although the theory of the *Defence* does not endorse it, the practice of his own literary writing could be said to fill this space very amply as well. The combination of the non-ideal, on the one hand (realistic, verisimilar), and the non-real, on the other (the counterfactual, the monstrous, the un- or supernatural),

---

deny' (81). 'Thus, the ambiguity found in Sidney's *Apology* can be seen as preparing the way for Bacon's subversion of idealist mimesis' (82).

[132] The word appears in something more like this sense when Sidney writes that 'Comedy is an imitation of the common errors of our life' (98.4–5).

[133] Sonnet 130. Cf. Langer 2015 (7) on lyric poetry as a celebration of the singular and the particular as opposed to the universal, general, and ideal, 'as an object in space and time is opposed to *categories* of objects, circumstances, persons or events that imply no determination in space and time (and hence require no existence to be meaningful)' (emphasis original). Thus, contrary to Aristotle's dictum that poetry should properly deal in generalities, universals, and ideals—depicting 'what is fit to be said or done' rather than 'whether Alcibiades did, or suffered, this or that' (92.17–20), as Sidney translates *Poetics* 1451b—lyric poetry could be said to do exactly the opposite. In its obsession with the minutiae of a thoroughly subjective, private, individual, and unique experience—precisely what a particular 'I' (whether called Alcibiades or Astrophil) may have suffered or done—lyric prioritizes what Langer calls the 'radically singular': 'something or someone beyond or simply not encompassed by categories, by attributes shared' (2). On this see also Adorno 2005 (76–80).

could pretty well account for all the sexually importunate lovers, cross-dressed princes, sexually available princesses, absconding kings, adulterous queens, atheistical queens, not to mention the rebels, murderers, torturers, cheats, spies, bores, failures, fools, dragons, giants, and monsters that populate *Astrophil and Stella* and the two *Arcadia*s. As with purely counterfactual art—whose non-real fictions can, against the odds, still be taken as ideal ('*Eutopia*')—there is always the danger that the same can happen here, to the non-ideal fictions of realistic art. The possibility can never be entirely ruled out, that is, that the 'ought' will not be re-instated by the determinedly idealist reader and the text made to 'teach' something or other: that those non-ideal figurations will be redeemed, made to pay their way, to justify their existence by delivering some lesson to the reader who has invested his or her time in them, imparting some knowledge they can add to their store. But since such figures can only be made to teach by means of the weak expedient of the negative example—'See what it is to love'—the threat can fairly easily be seen off.[134]

It is in the sense of the realistic—of imitating Nature as she is, not as she ought to be—that the word 'counterfeit' is introduced in the *Defence*: first, in the *propositio*, to gloss Aristotle's '*mimesis*' as 'a representing, counterfeiting, or figuring forth' (86.18–19), and shortly after, towards the beginning of the *confirmatio*, to describe the 'meaner sort of painters, who counterfeit only such faces as are set before them' (87.2–3), this being the first example given of such simple painterly types.[135] These despised, second-order artists are compared unfavourably with the 'more excellent' (87.3), who by contrast enhance what is set before them, or ignore it altogether, in order to produce some idealized portrait and to show what 'is fittest for the eye to see' (87.4). As noted, the speaker has little time for the former and reserves all his commendations for the latter—they alone are the 'right' kind of artist (86.44) who undertake their work 'properly' (86.43; 87.8)—his example being a painter who depicts the 'outward beauty' (87.7) of a figure like Lucretia, 'whom he never saw' (87.6), so as to produce an idealized representation of Constancy.[136] The speaker would thus dismiss and downgrade the 'meaner' painters on the grounds that they do not represent ideals: they counterfeit 'only' what is in front of them. Although the speaker tries to negativize them, however, the word 'counterfeit' itself does not do so, for its negative sense—suggesting something forged, spurious, made with intent to deceive—is precisely not applicable in this case: that is exactly what these

---

[134] *AS* 107. For readings of Astrophil as a negative example, see e.g. Scanlon 1976, and Roche 1989 (193–233). Scott 2013 (12) also sets great store by the negative example: 'for evermore I hold the worsing of bad things is a kind of bettering of them, because thereby things receive perfection (as I may say) of deformity.'

[135] Alexander (10) is the only editor to note either usage, glossing the first (i.e. 'counterfeiting' as a synonym for Aristotle's mimesis) as 'imitating, making after a pattern'.

[136] Compare Scott 2013 (12): while 'the true picture of Lucretia . . . gives you more true knowledge of the person of Lucretia in such a distressful plight', 'imitating the conceit of her virtue and passion', by contrast, 'sets you out a perfecter image of the look (as it were) of constancy and desperate sorrow in an imagined beauty. So as where the one evermore makes the person more eminent and conspicuous, the other fully recompenses that by delivering an absolute form whether of good or evil to be followed or fled': a statement that illustrates the economics of the idealist aesthetic very clearly. On this see also Dundas 2007 (63–4, 231).

poor painters do not do. In spite of the speaker's best efforts to damn the latter, therefore, 'counterfeit' is not being used pejoratively here. Like the word 'fashion', it derives from the Latin *facere*, to make, and although the 'counter' (from *contra*) indicates something made in opposition or contrast, this did not in itself give the word a negative inflection. A neutral sense—of simply imitating, copying, or following something, without any implied intention to deceive—existed (in noun, adjective, and verb) alongside the pejorative sense, and would have been available to Sidney at the time.[137] The same, incidentally, is true of the word 'fiction', like 'feign' derived from the Latin *fingere*, to mould or form, where, again, a neutral sense suggesting something simply fashioned or framed existed alongside more pejorative senses suggesting something fashioned or framed with a view to deceive, dissimulate, or defraud.[138] In these neutral senses, one might see words like 'counterfeit', 'fashion', 'fiction', and 'feign' as extending the vocabulary of *poesis*: as widening the lexicon and providing Sidney with a range of terms with which he could describe the poet's eponymous act of making, without implying any moralized judgement either way. If the speaker intends to damn the non-idealist painters by saying that they 'counterfeit', therefore, then the word on this particular occasion fails to oblige.

On the other occasion that the speaker uses 'counterfeit', by contrast, it is in a would-be positive sense, for here the word is mobilized in the context of the right and proper poet who would 'serve [his] prince' (93.21)—or motivate his readers to serve theirs—by means of the 'honest dissimulation' (93.21) with which the likes of Zopyrus, Abradatas, and Sextus Tarquinius deceived their enemies by pretending to be other than they were. Although the 'counterfeit' in question (93.24) refers in the first instance to the action taken by such operatives on the ground—rather than to the action of the poet who describes it—this difference in registers ultimately collapses as the feigning of the former is used to justify the feigning of the latter, in the name of teaching readers (and princes) how to use force and how to lie. If

---

[137] See *OED* counterfeit *n.* 3; *adj.* 2; *v.* 7, 8, 9; and also Barker 1964 (39). The word 'fashion' also maintains a neutral sense of shaping, forming, moulding something (see *OED* fashion *v.*), with the exception of sense 4b: to counterfeit, pervert (the only citations given dated 1600, and both from Shakespeare). See also Fischer 1985 (60–1), and Landreth 2012 (173) on the various meanings of the word 'counterfeit' in the period.

[138] See *OED* fiction *n.*1. Interestingly, the first citation for 'fiction' in this neutral sense derives from Gosson's *Schoole of Abuse*. The context is the way in which poetry has made Englishmen weak and pusillanimous: 'If the enemy beseege vs . . . it is not Ciceroes tongue that ca*n* peerce their armour to wou*n*d the body, nor Archimedes prickes, & lines, & circles, & triangles, & Rhombus, & rifferaffe, that hath any force to driue them backe. Whilst the one chats, his throte is cut; whilest the other syttes drawing Mathematicall fictions, the enimie standes with a sworde at his breast' (106/D8). While the denunciation is clear, it is nevertheless not *literary* fictions that Gosson is damning here, confirming the sense that it is not the empirical falsity of literary fiction that is his concern. In the case of 'feign', the neutral sense of fashioning, forming, or shaping something did exist (see *OED* feign *v.* I.1), although this was admittedly less strong than the uses derived from the pejorative sense of fashioning something fictitiously or deceptively (sense II), including the relating or representing of something in fiction (sense II.3). Although not used by Sidney, 'figment' (also derived from *fingere*) similarly divides between a neutral sense (something moulded or fashioned: see *OED* figment *n.*1) and a pejorative one (the product of fictitious invention, sense 2). See also Scott 2013 (11) on 'imitation', 'feigning', 'representing', and 'counterfeiting' as key words in the vocabulary of making.

'counterfeit' would not cooperate in the speaker's attempt to negativize the non-idealist painters, therefore, then it equally fails to cooperate in his mission to positivize the idealist poet, for here the word can only be understood in its pejorative sense. First, there is no 'positive' sense of 'counterfeit'; second, the neutral sense—of making a true, faithful, un-altered copy—while applicable to the meaner painters, is precisely not applicable here, because the action described is explicitly one undertaken with intent to deceive: a calculated act of fraud. Brought in by the speaker to describe and defend the action of the right poet, 'counterfeit' just cannot be made to fit the positive spin he would put on it. Appropriately therefore, it betrays its master.[139] There is no distinguishing between a dishonest act and a heroic use of it, and, if you are going to look at the situation in the round and not just from the point of view of the winning side, there is no such thing as an 'honest' dissimulation either. What this 'counterfeit' tells us, in other words, is that idealism is a fraud. There is no getting around it. It may well be to mitigate this embarrassing contradiction that what the speaker actually says is that 'Abradatas did not counterfeit so far' (93.24): the double negative implying that there can be degrees of fraud, and Abradatas' mutilation of his ears only was thus a lesser dissimulation than that of Zopyrus who cut off his nose as well. But this only runs into the objection that the latter was thereby all the more 'heroic' for the dramatic lengths to which he was prepared to go for his prince, with the corollary that the greater the fraud, the more ideal. As discussed above, the speaker's example here backfires because the action he selects to illustrate ideal conduct is so manifestly not ideal, involving extreme deception in the name of brutal aggression that will stop at nothing to achieve absolute power. Agrippa was right, such soldiers and their masters were 'very wicked and naughtie men' (F1), and the poet who would heroize them, 'beautifying [such actions] both for further teaching, and more delighting' (93.27–8)—like the painter who would beautify Lucretia, the suicidal rape-victim of just such a man as this—is party to the same fraud: an apologist not for poetry but for power. Gosson, therefore, was right too. Such poets claim things to be ideal that are manifestly not: their 'good sentences' shadow 'knauery' as effectively as Zopyrus, Abradatas, and Sextus Tarquinius did, and the means by which they 'beautifye their woorkes' (77/A2) are therefore complicit in the same deception. Gosson sees it as his self-appointed task to expose this imposture—to bring it to light and to book—and Sidney, in defiance of his speaker, is minded to do the same.

One way of doing this would be to cultivate the kind of counterfeiting that would expose fraud rather than perpetuate it: like the kind of fiction that would deconstruct ideology rather than perpetrate it. To do this would be to go back to the options described above which offer themselves as alternatives to the kind of poetry that would represent reality in some supposedly idealized state. On the one

[139] The negative inflection of 'counterfeit' here similarly infects and complicates the uses of 'fashion' (92.30), 'fiction' (93.22), and especially 'feign' (92.28, 29; 93.9, 10, 14, 19)—including the pun on 'fain' (93.20)—in this section of the *Defence*, almost as if it were meditating on the negative turn which the neutral meaning of making or *poesis* was liable to take.

hand, to turn towards realism: to the kind of art that represents a non-ideal and non-idealized reality, like the meaner painters whom the speaker would negativize but in the end cannot (and who, if they saw Lucretia, would not turn her into some emblem of Constancy but would portray the horror that they saw). On the other hand, to turn towards the counterfactual: to the kind of art that presents the non-real, that creates anew what does not exist, that thereby absconds from representation altogether, and that, in cutting ties with Nature, can venture into the unnatural, the monstrous, the perverse (instead of portraying an actual victim, for example, such an artist might invent a monster of equal horror). Although it is fair to say that in his own art Sidney, like Shakespeare, combines the two, in the *Defence* (in its unofficial argument, at least) he tends more towards the latter—towards the kind of fiction that More had exemplified and that Spenser would go on to do—and this for the reason that it is easier to detach the counterfactual, the 'wholly imaginative', from the representational. For the radical, wrong, awry, non- or anti-idealist poet, the aim ultimately is to move beyond counterfeiting in the neutral sense—simply copying reality in its unadorned state, although this certainly makes a contribution to non-idealist art—in order to conceive a kind of counterfeiting that is somehow more active, more interventionist, more able to show the point of such non-idealist art: its deconstructive political, anti-ideological, anti-capitalist agenda. Between the speaker's failed attempts to positivize the negative (idealize fraud) or to negativize the neutral (dismiss the meaner painters), Sidney is, I think, feeling his way towards a strange, new, third sense of 'counterfeit': one that is 'positive' but only in the paradoxically negative sense that it takes something down—deconstructs money thought and the dominant ideology it serves—and does not put something else, some other ideal, some other 'ought', in its place.[140] This kind of counterfeit, non-idealist art does not, therefore, redeem anything.[141] It does not teach, except a negative lesson; and it does not delight, except, perhaps,

---

[140] Cf. the sense in which Ferguson 1983 (138) reads Sidney as a counterfeiter: 'if we grant Sidney the intelligence to be a counterfeiter rather than a blunderer, his case for poetry becomes at once more cogent as a theoretical statement and more interesting as a literary performance.' Ferguson situates the *Defence* within the context of Sidney's 'personal desires for action in the service of God and England' (160), and sees it as parallel to the letter he wrote to the Queen advising her against the Alençon marriage. The 'counterfeiting' she has in mind thus belongs to the kind of crafty dissimulation and functional ambiguity typified by *allegoria*: the quintessentially courtly figure, according to Puttenham 2007 (270–2), because used by those who say one thing to mean another. While opposed to Elizabeth's foreign policy, this kind of counterfeiting ultimately works in the interests of power, personal and political ('God and England'), rather than against it.

[141] As Lacan 2002 (434–5) notes, it was the way in which the wordplay, puns, witticisms, and jests of dreams and jokes made a mockery of the supposed function of language to communicate meaning that aroused (and arguably still arouses) the fiercest resistance to psychoanalysis, a resistance commonly manifested by an assertive re-statement, and re-instatement, of Platonism: 'It was the abyss, open to the thought that a thought might make itself heard in the abyss, that gave rise to resistance to psychoanalysis from the outset—not the emphasis on man's sexuality, as is commonly said. The latter is the object that has clearly predominated in literature throughout the ages. And the evolution of psychoanalysis has succeeded by a comical stroke of magic in turning it into a moral instance, the cradle and waiting area of oblativity and attraction. The soul's Platonic steed, now blessed and enlightened, goes straight to heaven.'

those who delight in deconstruction (the pedagogues, or those who delight in instruction, will be appalled).

The kind of counterfeit I have in mind, then, is that which wears its fraudulence on its sleeve. Like imitation jewellery, or like the gilding that makes things 'seem gorgeous' (81.22) but that no one takes to be anything else: there is no intent or attempt to deceive (indeed, what this imitation jewellery or gilding imitates is the ideal—the gold or jewels that represent value—but in a way that openly shows such 'value' to be a fiction, a deception, a device).[142] Or like fake, false, or toy money that everyone knows to be exactly that and no one in their right mind would take to be counterfeit currency or report to the authorities. The great 'value' of this valueless coin is that it cannot be exchanged for, buy, or redeem anything, except perhaps in play (the gambler can still play, even if he or she only has non-exchangeable chips with which to do so). The 'beauty' of it, by the same token, is that, since it is worthless, it cannot be fetishized. It abstracts no value so has no value. It does not represent or measure anything else. It does not set itself up as the general equivalent and subordinate everything else as relative to itself. It might look like money but it does not act like money, and so puts paid to the illusions held and upheld by the idealist poets: 'Lies are to these both golde and good'.[143] Such gilding—such pretend, 'counterfeit', fool's gold—breaks this spell, because there is nothing to believe: everyone knows it is false, a 'lie'. No one is deceived. No one believes that it is 'really' money or 'really' valuable, just as no one believes that the 'Thebes' represented in the theatre is 'really' Thebes the town. Of course, the same can be applied to 'real' money too, since that, technically, is no more than a representation either: nothing more than a convenient and socially agreed way of representing the value of other things. But the difference is that this toyful, counterfeit gold *shows* us that: reminds us of it, demonstrates beyond any shadow of a doubt that believing that money has value (treasure, riches, wealth), and acting as if it did (accumulating capital), is no more rational than believing the same of itself. This applies equally to other forms of capital too. Believing that money has value is like believing that a representation of Thebes in the theatre has pedagogic value: that it can impart important, 'valuable' lessons, and therefore dutifully stock the theatre-goer's or reader's treasure-house of knowledge, their (properly diversified) spiritual, moral, and intellectual portfolio. A counterfeit, non-idealist, non-golden art, by contrast, might disabuse them of such a gratifying notion. This 'Thebes'—if it is the Oedipus story it is referring to—might not teach, schoolbook fashion, that 'if evil men come to the stage, they ever go out . . . so manacled as

---

[142] Derrida 1992 (94) also distinguishes between counterfeit money that is not known to be such—and that therefore lies, deceives, defrauds—and counterfeit money that *is* known to be such (as, for example, by the readers of a short story by Baudelaire) and that therefore does not perform these operations: when you know that 'this fiction is a fiction, there is no phenomenon here of "counterfeit money," that is, of an abuse of trust that passes off the false for the true'. On the association of counterfeit money with other forms of social and sexual transgression in the sixteenth century, see Fisher 1999.

[143] Agrippa 1569 (E1), quoting Giannantonio Campano (1495), 'Elegiarum et Epigrammatum', III.20, line 5: '*His mendacia sunt opes et aurum*', in *Opera* (C4).

they little animate folks to follow them' (93.42–4), a lesson worthy of Miss Prism. Rather, it might suggest, as Marc Shell does, that 'Poetry is a counterfeit human production as vexing as interest', and that *Oedipus Tyrannos* is 'a study of tyranny in which is discovered not its monetary genesis, as in Plato's *Republic,* but rather its perverse sexual genesis'.[144] It might suggest that, like the *Utopia,* this text too could be a study of the money form: of interest, of credit, of the 'unnatural' reproduction of money through usury, although figured here, in sexual terms, as incest. Like so many other examples in the *Defence,* Thebes does not exemplify what it is ostensibly brought in to exemplify—what it 'ought' to exemplify—but it is also particularly over-determined. This ancient city—in myth, the creation, the making, of a poet, as 'Amphion was said to move stones with his poetry to build Thebes' (82.22–3)—is one that, in the *Defence,* puts belief to the test. Do we believe what 'was said', since it is only another poetic frame, after all? (Yes, no, it depends on the answer to the next question). Do we believe that '*Thebes*' is Thebes? (No). Do we believe that money has value? (Yes). Do we believe that the play has value, that it can tell us something 'useful'? (Yes, no, it depends on the answer to the next question). Or is this belief in the supposed, intrinsic, inherent value of money, and the consequent drive to make more of it—to put it to use, to usury—a tragedy of monstrous proportions? It is almost as if Sidney chooses the Thebes example because it quite literally *beggars* belief.

If the speaker, with his official argument in favour of idealist poetics, would advocate an art that is 'not wholly imaginative' (85.38), then Sidney counters with one that is just that: not openly in the *Defence,* it is true (there this counter-argument is submerged, although not so deeply that it is unable to disturb the surface or make some serious waves), but openly enough in his literary works. If the speaker would propose an art that works 'substantially' (85.39–40), to the benefit of the individual and the profit of the state (Cyrus Inc.), then Sidney counters with one that does neither and instead builds castles in the air.[145] An art that is baseless,

---

[144] Shell 1978 (101). Shell reads *Oedipus Tyrannos* through the lens of Aristotle 1932, *Politics,* 1257b, in which the philosopher ponders the question of whether poetic production/creation is 'natural' (in the sense that it makes use of things already provided by Nature, as in household management or *oikonomia*) or 'unnatural' (in the sense that it artificially creates an infinite number of man-made representations, as in wealth-getting or *chrēmatistikē,* i.e. the way usury 'makes' gold). These two alternatives—which Shell (following Aristotle) characterizes as the 'shuttle' (which weaves wool from the fleeces provided by nature) and the 'Golden Fleece' (a fantasy of acquired wealth)—are left purposefully ambiguous. We might map them onto the alternatives the *Defence* proposes between poetry that makes Nature 'better' and poetry that makes things 'anew'. It is this problematic—whether *poesis* is imitation or fiction, natural or unnatural, good or bad, useful or abusive—that Shakespeare ponders in the *Sonnets,* where he considers, among other things, what kind of production poetry is: a potentially infinite making from nothing (like usury) that might at the same time be empty or a debt (also like usury). On this voluminous topic, see especially: Greene 1985; Traub 1999; and Correll 2008. It is also, I think, what Sidney ponders when he addresses the third charge levelled at poetry—that it abuses—meditating on the nature of right use, usefulness, utility, wrong use, uselessness, misuse, and abuse, and the relative moralizations of each. This will be the topic of Part III.

[145] The three kinds of 'counterfeiting' I am describing thus map onto the subtle but importantly different conceptions of—and relations between—imitation and invention/fiction. (1) Idealist art seeks to imitate reality in some ideal state: it thus imitates a false reality. Such art is inventive/fictive insofar as it represents something that is not there (hence, invents it) but since it is only copying what should be there—the '*Idea* or fore-conceit' (85.35)—invention/fiction is here used only weakly and is effectively synonymous with imitation (it is mimesis-plus). Such art *falsifies with intent to deceive:* it

content-less, substance-less: empty insofar as it makes no claim to provide some other thing, some capital to be accumulated, some value to be acquired in exchange. An art that pays no debt, redeems no 'ought', but serves rather to show the valuelessness of such 'value' and the tyrannies that are perpetrated—and tragedies suffered—in its name. An art like that which Dametas finds when he goes rushing off excitedly to dig for gold only to find 'his hope of wealth turned to poor verses', and the supposed treasure he expected to find replaced by some lines of poetry telling him that such riches as he imagined do not exist—except as a purely fictitious concept—so that he ends up being 'punished in conceit, as in conceit he had erred': that is to say, his 'conceit' or conceptualization of value was wrong.[146] An art that can be appreciated and admired, loved and enjoyed, delighted in and desired for its own sake and in its own right, and not for anything extra that it can 'yield': as Astrophil loves the fiction of Stella—the 'faire text' he has made—and not for any gain he gets out of it (as he constantly tells us, this love nets him nothing, and certainly no riches, in return).[147] An art that is 'nothing but songs' (84.19)—that can enchant and charm like the *carmina* (84.8) from which those songs take their name—and not because it conjures or speaks on behalf of spirits ('a very vain and godless superstition', 84.6–7), but precisely because it dispels such spells, shows those spirits to be human productions, and either conjures you not to believe (103.13–14) or conjures you to believe only in jest (116.20–37).[148] An art

makes out that lies are 'profitable' and 'true', with a view to teaching force and forcing readers, in turn, to imitate those ideals. It is ideology. It thus aligns with 'counterfeit' in the negative sense. (2) Non-idealist art has the option of turning towards realism, i.e. of imitating reality in its actual, non-ideal state. Here imitation is distinct from invention/fiction in that it copies reality as it is, without the addition of any cosmetic touch-ups or extras that might idealize it (it is mimesis). Such art *neither falsifies nor deceives*. It therefore aligns with 'counterfeit' in the neutral sense. (3) Non-idealist art also has the option of turning towards the counterfactual, i.e. of not imitating reality at all (neither reality as it is nor some ideal version of it), but rather making the 'wholly imaginative' and 'quite anew'. Here imitation has been taken out of the picture and invention/fiction is used in the strong sense of creating something from nothing, 'making' it up, *poesis*. Such art *falsifies without intent to deceive*. It therefore aligns with 'counterfeit' in the third sense that I have been developing here.

[146] *OA* (265, 266). The verses in question are: 'Who hath his hire, hath well his labour placed; / Earth thou didst seek, and store of earth thou hast' (265). Stillman 1986 (187) comments that Sidney here draws 'a direct connection between the kinds of fictions with which the mind deceives itself and allows itself to be deceived by others, and the literary fictions of the "bad" poet'. My sense, by contrast, is that it is the so-called 'right' poet who seeks to perpetuate such ideological fictions, and such fictions that the anti-idealist poet would seek to expose and deconstruct.

[147] *AS* 67; Astrophil frequently refers to Stella as a text (see e.g. *AS* 3, 56, 71, 102). Levao 1985 (180) addresses the critical 'problem' of how the author of 'the apparently didactic *Apology*, [could] have devoted so many poems to carnal love and an ultimately unredeemed protagonist'; against those who would read Astrophil as a negative example, Levao argues that what Sidney has created in Astrophil is 'not a poetic "object lesson," but an embodiment in English verse of a poetic "subject"—complex, passionate, self-conscious, caught up, perhaps, in its own egotistical drives and self-deluding fictions, but also aware in the end that it is doing so'. See Correll 1995 and 2008 for an example of what reading poems (here Donne's *Sapho to Philaenis* and Shakespeare's sonnet 31, respectively) as being at odds with the early modern profit economy—and especially heterosexuality and reproductive sex—might look like.

[148] See Levao 1985 (139): 'Sidney's "highest point of man's wit" [86.1] is *not* a mystical *apex mentis* directly sparked by the divine. It is the faculty that creates fictions, the faculty that creates another nature and so reveals our divinity to ourselves' (emphasis original). Once again, we find ourselves in the environs of the poetic sublime.

that is 'merely poetical' (84.22): not 'entirely', 'wholly', or 'exclusively' poetical, as the editors would have it, but an art that is *only* poetical, that is poetical and nothing more (why ask for more?). An art that does not take its existence or justification from some distant and mystified deity—mouthing the latter's utterances or oracles—and that need not, therefore, be grounded in or redeemed by some given, presupposed, anterior Logos. An art, rather, that can be an autonomous universe of autoreflexive signs created, *ex nihilo*, by the poet him- or herself: 'the dream', John Freccero writes, 'of almost every poet since Petrarch'.[149] An art that is not the dress that would clothe some prior truth or existent meaning, the *verba* that would modestly, apologetically cover the *res*: not the 'masking raiment' (96.3) that philosophy would borrow, not what shows abstractions like Beauty in their 'holiday apparel' (99.35), not the 'garments' that clothe Plutarch's philosophy and history, trimmed with 'guards [borders, decorative trimmings] of Poesy' (108.7–8). An art, rather, that is nothing but such trimmings, nothing but *passementerie*, nothing but embroidery. An art that might show the earth in a more 'rich tapestry' (85.24) than Nature does, but that is still only a tapestry—a text or textile that is pure surface— and claims to be nothing more (certainly not to better, to enrich, or to idealize Nature, to make the 'too much loved earth more lovely', 85.26–7). An art that, like the purse Pamela embroiders while in prison (a supremely pointless act), could be accounted 'not as a purse for treasure, but as a treasure itself', as Cecropia would have it, or, better still, 'even as a very purse', as Pamela would have it: as nothing but a purse, and an empty one at that, decorative, pretty, and worked to while away the time by a woman who has nothing, and who has nothing better to do: the ultimate aesthetic object.[150] The speaker of the *Defence* would characteristically subordinate needle to sword (woman to man, relative form to general equivalent): 'Truly a

---

[149] Freccero 1986 (27). Bergvall 1989 (38) makes a point of disavowing this: 'Sidney is far from claiming moral autonomy for poetry, some early version of art for art's sake, but is simply reiterating the Augustinian position which "defends poets from those who say that they write lies, since a feigned fable which refers to a true *significatio* is not a lie"', referencing Robertson 1962 (59). Landreth 2012 (37) also denies that Renaissance writers saw '"literature" as an aesthetic sphere antagonistic to that of the marketplace', citing Sidney's *Defence* as evidence. Cf. Levao 1985 (139): the mind's highest capacity 'may suggest an intuitive leap to a higher unity, but it always returns us to the mind's active fashioning'; 'Sidney exploits an important feature of sonnet writing that reaches back to Petrarch: a reflexive awareness about the making of poetic fictions' (158), with a note to Freccero's article.

[150] *NA* (355, 356). Like Bergvall, Shepherd (53–4) also disavows the aesthetic, denying the possibility that Pamela's purse might be an autonomous work of art: '[Pamela] insists on thinking of things according to their true nature and use . . . The beauty of a beautiful thing is not simply aesthetic . . . The consequences of this aestheticism, as Pamela and Sidney see it, are Epicurean, libertine, atheist, and determinist . . . The discussion on beauty takes a moral turn . . . Each thing is directed to an end, even speaking and laughing, even beauty, even a purse or a poem.' For a similar reading, see Stillman 2009. Cf. Bates (forthcoming), and also Dickson 1992 (53): 'In contrast to Cecropia's atheism, which argues for autonomy and constructs her as an "unabashed epicurean," Pamela argues for natural order . . . Yet, as much as Pamela's theology presents a more harmonious world vision, it has a tinge of Euarchus' . . . rigidity, stressing the human obedience owed to divine power and law.' 'If Cecropia is indeed a figure for the fictional world of *The New Arcadia*, she is the source not only of its horrors but also of its delightful excesses, transgressions, and plots. Perhaps Cecropia is a necessary component of the fictional world that Sidney creates in his revised text and stands not only for its evil, but also for its wonderful overabundance, its fanciful repetition, its expansion, its effusiveness. In the absence of Urania, she is, perhaps, his grotesque muse' (55).

needle cannot do much hurt, and as truly (with leave of ladies be it spoken) it cannot do much good. With a sword thou mayest kill thy father, and with a sword thou mayest defend thy prince and country' (104.39–42). Really (those 'trulies' seem to be saying), if those are the options—and especially if defending your prince and country (not to mention poetry) involves the kind of subterfuge carried out by the likes of Sextus Tarquinius (and the heroizing of it by the poet)—then a spot of light sewing might, frankly, be preferable. As Robert Matz suggests, 'Rather than transcending its context of courtly leisure and consumption, the poet's pen is identified with the charming court lady's needlework'.[151] If the speaker of the *Defence* aims to produce a golden poem, then what his author actually wrote would, by his own admission, be just such a trifling thing: a 'toyfull Booke', a 'trifle, and that triflingly handled'.[152]

As promised at the end of Part I, the argument of the *Defence* thus finally returns, after a somewhat circuitous route, to Plato: for Sidney could have found a precedent—a parallel—for the tension he plays out with his speaker there. Plato, he reports, would banish the poets because they made 'light tales' (107.9) of the gods. But Plato also interlaced his own philosophy with 'mere tales' (83.2), tales, one might say, that were merely 'poetical' (82.44), that 'feigneth' (82.42) things people did not say or do, and the prime example given of which is the tale of 'Gyges' Ring' (83.2): a story that, like the saga of Thebes or like the *Utopia*, focuses with a particular scrutiny on the money form: its genesis, its structure, its effects. These tales all use fiction—the mythic, the counterfactual—to reveal the fiction of the money form for what it is: to show how money claims to represent abstract value, the supposedly ideal truth or 'real' reality of things; how believing in this can have dire consequences, long since borne out; and how fiction without belief (as in imitation jewellery, toy money, or the self-confessed 'gilding' that everyone knows not to be gold) might, therefore, be preferable. For Goux, Plato is the father of idealism, his philosophy the ultimate statement of this fiction, the official endorsement of its abstract values and ideal truths. For Shell, while this may have been the unintended, and, in the circumstances, profoundly ironic outcome of Plato's philosophy, it was nevertheless the result of an intense internal struggle: of a deeply felt dismay at the effects that this relatively new invention seemed to be capable of having on human thought, and an attempt, one way or another, to counter them. That attempt may not have succeeded so far as philosophy was concerned, for the propositional is not the best way to fight this war. But it may succeed better with the fictional: specifically, with those fictions that choose not to replicate the operations of the money form but, rather, to abjure its claims to 'representation' and to 'value' from the outset. If Shell locates this tension in Plato, then I think we can locate it in Sidney too, and infer that Sidney may, by sensing it in Plato, have

---

[151] Matz 2000 (74). See also Goldberg 1990 (137–55, esp.141); and Lamb 1994 (503).

[152] First quotation from Sidney's letter to Robert, 18 October 1580, referring to the *Old Arcadia*: *Correspondence* (1009). Second quotation—adding, 'looking for no better stuff [cloth, material] than, as in a haberdasher's shop, glasses or feathers'—from the dedicatory letter to his sister that prefaces the *Old Arcadia*: *OA* (3).

come to recognize it within himself. This would explain why the *Defence* keeps circling back to Plato, as a pseudo-opponent whom it can neither defeat nor reject and with whose own internal struggles it is actually in profound accord: circling back not to Plato the philosopher, who would banish the poets, but rather to Plato the poet, whom the former (in a moment of self-division that Sidney, I suspect, would have relished) would banish. Plato, Sidney confesses, is 'of all philosophers I have ever esteemed most worthy of reverence, and with great reason: since of all philosophers he is the most poetical' (106.16–18). Plato, Harington echoes in his 'Brief Apologie', may have rejected allegory, but he 'still preserued the fable'. He may have banished the poets from his ideal Republic, but he 'kept still that principall part of Poetrie, which is fiction and imitation', 'inuention or fiction', 'inuention or imitation'.[153]

---

[153] Harington 1904 (203, 204, 207).

V

Poetry Is Free

We might now, therefore, be in a better position to understand the figure of Pugliano: be able, perhaps, to make more sense of this negative example—this example that does not exemplify—that nonetheless leads the *Defence* and that (also nonetheless) is followed. I have deliberately held back from considering the *exordium* until now because it is only in light of the preceding discussions that these negativities that surround Pugliano might be seen as part of a larger pattern and so assume a significance beyond the merely incidental.[154] As the portal or frame through which we gain entry into the *Defence*, the Pugliano anecdote has mostly been read 'forwards': either as the witty jest or 'pleasant tale' recommended by the rhetorical handbooks as an ice-breaker to warm the hearers to the orator and incline them towards his argument—which done, having served its purpose, it can be dismissed without need of further analysis (some readings minimize the *exordium* in this way, if not ignore it altogether)—or as signalling to the reader, in the form of an antitype or counter-example, an early warning or caveat regarding the speech or text that is to follow: as, for example, that we are 'not to take theories too seriously'.[155] When read 'backwards', by contrast—'preposterously', with the beginning of the treatise seen from the perspective of its end—the Pugliano anecdote might be seen not only to anticipate internal rifts and contradictions to come but also to set the scene for the possibility of another argument, an alternative vision that is not yet visible—and that never gets to be 'posited' in any positive sense—and yet that (as it evolves and emerges in response to the argument that ensues, so as to disrupt it and send it awry) will come to be intuited, glimpsed, scoped out, and felt towards: a vision that can only be seen 'backwards', in intaglio or reverse. Seen in this way, the *exordium*—like the other paradoxical other-speaking in the *Defence*—is not 'knowing' in the sense of being pre-planned or calculated in advance. It does not set this alternative up with a view to inducing

---

[154] See also: 'not only . . . but' (81.5); 'none . . . more' (81.7–8); 'Nay, to so unbelieved a point he proceeded, as that no earthly thing bred such wonder' (81.13–14); 'if I had not been a piece of a logician' (81.18–19); 'no few words' (81.21); 'if Pugliano's strong affection and weak arguments will not satisfy you' (81.23–4); 'I know not by what mischance' (81.24–5); 'my not old years' (81.25); 'my unelected vocation' (81.27); 'if I handle with more good will than good reasons' (81.27–8).

[155] Levao 1985 (134). For similar views, see: Hager 1991 (113); Ferguson 1983 (152–3); Barnes 1971 (426); Bergvall 1989 (40); and Herman 1996 (63–4). The use of some witty jest or 'pleasaunt tale' to open an oration is recommended by Thomas Wilson in *The arte of rhetorique* 1553 (p2), following Quintilian 2002, *Institutio Oratoria*, IV.i.49, and Anon 1954, *Rhetorica ad Herennium*, I. vi.10. For critics who see the Pugliano anecdote as nothing more, see e.g. Myrick 1935 (55–7); Heninger 1989 (228); and Doherty 1991 (6–7).

certain effects: to prompt the reader to scorn Pugliano as a negative example, or even to admire him as a positive one.[156] The Pugliano anecdote is not, therefore, 'witty' or 'ironic' in this sense (the view held by the majority of critics, from the most idealist to the most sceptical). Nor does it communicate a 'lesson' of some kind (the view of those for whom it is more than mere rhetorical throat-clearing). Yet it is, for all that, a model. Pugliano is not ideal—he is not a role model in that sense—and yet he is followed. He is followed and yet he is not promoted. He is not presented as showing the right way, the way the poet 'ought' to go. Indeed, according to criteria already set out here in the *exordium*, he is presented as showing the *wrong* way, the way the poet ought *not* to go. And yet, while seeing the better, and even approving it, Sidney nonetheless chooses, Medea-like, to follow the worse. This is not 'witty', it is not a bagatelle. It is certainly not a mere opening gag, and, if it is ironic and paradoxical to the extent that it playfully suspends the seriousness of the culturally approved, official argument that ensues and even deconstructs it, then it does not do so frivolously, any more than it seeks, by such a roundabout route, to impart some 'valuable' advice. It belongs, rather, within the purview of the tragic: an irresistible tendency to *miss* the mark (*hamartia*) rather than to hit it: a 'daemonic' compulsion to do whatever it is that your society and culture, the dominant ideology, urge you not to do.[157] Insofar as the *Defence* opens up the possibility—the thinkability—of a poetry that is not beholden to the bankable model and its bourgeois values of capital growth, it holds open the possibility—the thinkability—that such a position might actually be, like Medea's, very earnestly, very passionately held, even if (or perhaps precisely because) it can only ever be, paradoxically, a negative position. The preceding discussions, that is, might make it possible to see Pugliano and his place (no place?) at the head of the *Defence* in a different way: as neither a negative example to be shunned, nor a positive example to be followed but, rather, as a negative example *that is* followed. Equivalent to the

---

[156] Berry 1998 (148) goes against the trend in seeing Pugliano as an unambiguously positive figure who exemplifies Sidney's militaristic goal to support the Protestant cause in Europe: since 'training in horsemanship carried with it a true sense of vocation', Pugliano is said to be recruited in support of Sidney's argument rather than to undermine it. See also Socolow 2012 (129), for whom the figure of Pugliano is gently mocked but the art of horsemanship similarly treated as a synecdoche for self-discipline and good governorship.

[157] As Astrophil does: 'I may, I must, I can, I will, I do / Leave following that, which it is gaine to misse . . . Soft, but here she comes' (*AS* 47), the prototype for this Medea-like behaviour being Petrarch, '*et veggio 'l meglio et al peggior m'appiglio*' [and I see the better but I lay hold on the worse]: see Petrarch 1976, *Rime Sparse*, 264, line 136. Cf. Stillman 2008 who organizes his reading of the *Defence* around the concept of the *scopus* (from Greek *skopos*): originally a hunting term denoting a target or aim, and co-opted by Aristotle in the *Art of Rhetoric* (and later by Ascham, Melanchthon, and others) as the *scopus dicendi* or aim of speech. In this entirely teleological model of rhetoric—which, for Stillman, Sidney both practises and preaches in the *Defence*—the author's 'scope' represents 'the aim or mark or target at which an archer shoots his arrow' (72), whence 'the strong teleological drive of the rhetorical art . . . toward purposeful, causally organized argumentation' (74). For a similar reading, see Hunt 1987 (9–10). Cf. Crewe 1990 (130) who observes that 'shooting straight and hitting the mark [are] unequivocal goals of a particular, gender-coded, athletic discipline' and that the 'construction of an empowered yet disciplined phallomorphic subject . . . is manifestly at stake in this pedagogy of the unerring bowman'. Crewe's reading of Gascoigne's 'Woodmanship' as countercultural because it is 'virtually all about missing the mark' (131) seems to me to be a better description of what Sidney does in the *Defence*, and, indeed, in his other literary writings: see Bates 2013 (173–236).

'third way' sketched out earlier, this would be a position in which the counterfeit, the valueless, and the empty might be embraced as the qualities of true art—or at least of a creativity that is unfettered by the demands for utility and profit—and to be valued as such, even though doing so entails a quite different conception of what 'value' might be taken to mean.

From the strange, nebulous, and surprising place where the unofficial argument of the *Defence* has left us, therefore, I think we are justified in going back to the beginning and in looking at the Pugliano anecdote a little more closely, for what the opening sentence seems set on advertising is Sidney's *courtly* credentials: 'When the right virtuous Edward Wotton and I were at the Emperor's court together, we gave ourselves to learn horsemanship of John Pietro Pugliano, one that with great commendation had the place of an esquire in his stable' (81.1–4). As secretary to the English embassy at the court of the Holy Roman Emperor, Maximilian II, Wotton was in Vienna on court business, although Sidney, at that time, was not. When he became acquainted with Wotton in 1574–75, Sidney was on his 'Grand Tour' of Europe, his own similar service (a single embassy to Prague in 1577) still being two or more years ahead of the anecdote related. Nonetheless, it is clear that both men—all three men, in fact—evidently have time on their hands and that, even for those engaged in it, court service is hardly what one would call 'labour intensive' since it evidently involves a great deal of waiting around. As Robert Matz notes, the other side of Puttenham's claim that courtiers do 'busily negotiate by color of otiation' is the truth that some courtiers 'seem very busy when they have nothing to do': the suggestion that courtiers are otiose, profitless, and idle wasters being, in the critic's view, the anxiety against which poetry's redemptively pedagogic mission to teach and delight is mobilized—not wholly successfully—to defend.[158] As if to reinforce this, such learning as Wotton and Sidney acquire from Pugliano is presumably largely supernumerary, since neither of them could be perceived as absolute beginners: aged twenty-six and twenty respectively, they would already have been thoroughly versed in the art of horsemanship, this being a central part of any sixteenth-century gentleman's education.[159] The scene on which the curtain opens, then, is one of un- or under-employed court servants wasting or at least whiling away their time by teaching something that does not strictly need to be learned or learning something that they already know: as in a kind of finishing school which merely polishes or perfects an already mastered skill. This scenario, I suggest, lends to Pugliano's speech, shortly to be reported, the status and logic of the supplement. That is to say, it both 'finishes' something, in the sense of rounding it off, completing, or perfecting it, and, at the same time, it is or can be endlessly added to: a potentially infinite series of finishing touches.[160] This would fit the special quality with which

---

[158] Puttenham 2007 (381); Matz 2000 (12–13).

[159] See e.g. Ascham 1967 (33, 53). On Sidney's own 'eponymous' love of horses and reputation for horsemanship, see: Shepherd (144); van Dorsten (186); Maslen (55, 120); Berry 1998 (142–62); Socolow 2012 (122); and Bates 2013 (206–7).

[160] See Fineman 1986 (5–6): 'This is what makes praise into extraordinary language, for, according to traditional accounts, it is through something discursively "extra," as an effect of something registered

Pugliano's 'wit' (81.4) is endowed—namely, its 'fertileness' (81.4)—its ability to stimulate growth, expansiveness, and apparently endless increase in the production of rhetorical *copia*. Although originally a biological and agricultural metaphor, this quickly transmutes into an economic one, as Pugliano is explicitly said to have wanted to 'enrich' (81.6) his hearers' minds with what he considered to be 'most precious' (81.7), this turning out (again, explicitly) to be *speech*: that is, the 'contemplations' (81.6) about horsemanship that—over and above the merely physical demonstration and dumb exercise of his art, that he could otherwise easily 'afford' them (81.5)—he thereby adds to it.[161] In going on to report Pugliano's speech, Sidney provides a brief though suitably rhetorical sample that includes *gradatio* ('He said soldiers were the noblest estate of mankind, and horsemen the noblest of soldiers', 81.10–11), comparison ('He said they were the masters of war and ornaments of peace', 81.11–12), and euphuistic alliteration ('speedy goers and strong abiders, triumphers in both camps and courts', 81.12–13), before going on, somewhat superfluously, to add to this already additive speech: 'Then would he add certain praises...' (81.16). A further list of superlatives then follows, about 'what a peerless beast a horse was, the only serviceable courtier without flattery, the beast of most beauty, faithfulness, courage, and such more' (81.16–18). As a result of this self-generating and seemingly unstoppable rhetorical performance, the ears of Pugliano's auditors (or Sidney's at any rate; we never learn what Wotton thought) come to be weighed down—'loaden' (81.8)—with this precious cargo, like a rich merchant's ships.

The other special quality with which Pugliano's 'wit' is endowed is its Italianness: indeed, the extraordinary 'fertileness' of which we are given this brief, tantalizing glimpse, is said to be the distinguishing feature of 'the Italian wit' (81.4). In sixteenth-century England, 'Italian' was itself, of course, a loaded word, especially after Ascham's lambasting of Italian culture, learning, and books in *The Schoolmaster*, giving voice to the fear that these might seduce Englishmen into an acceptance of what Maslen calls 'perverse Italian values: atheism, republicanism, intellectual sophistication, and freedom of speech'.[162] In his 1579 letter to

---

as supplementary or "epi-," that praise becomes a showy showing speech.' On the supplement, see Derrida 1976 (144–5).

[161] The senses of the verb 'afford' that would have been available to Sidney at the time of writing the *Defence* and that are relevant here are: 'to give, provide, contribute; to grant, bestow, confer (a privilege, benefit, gift, etc.)' (see *OED* afford *v. trans*, II.3.a.); 'to supply, provide, offer (something sought, or something useful or desirable)' (II.3.b); 'to put forth or exhibit naturally or characteristically' (II.4.b); 'to manage to give; to spare (time, room, money, etc.)' (III.5); 'to have the means or (financial) resources (to do something); to have enough money (to do something)' (III.6.a); and 'to manage to offer (goods) for sale at a specified price or rate while achieving an acceptable profit' (III.7).

[162] Maslen (24). Ascham 1967 (66) warns that 'overmany of our travelers into Italy do not eschew the way to Circe's court but go and ride and run and fly thither... being mules and horses before they went, [they] returned very swine and asses home again... If you think we judge amiss and write too sore against you, hear what the Italian saith of the Englishman, what the master reporteth of the scholar, who uttereth plainly what is taught by him and what is learned by you, saying *Inglese italianato è un diavolo incarnato*; that is to say, "You remain men in shape and fashion but become devils in life and condition"'. This might be an example of what Sidney's speaker would later call 'an awry-transformed traveller' (113.9).

Robert—in which he advises his brother on his own impending 'Grand Tour' and which is often cited in this context—Sidney appears to be equally negative about the Italians, in his view good for nothing but the purveying of luxury goods: 'As for Italie I knowe not what wee haue, or can haue to doe with them but to buye their silkes and wynes.'[163] Although some, he concedes, are 'excellentlye learned'—the art of 'Horshemanshypp [*sic*]' being singled out as a particular area of expertise which is 'better there, then in the other Countryes'—this nonetheless fails to redeem the otherwise general tendency of the fertile Italian wit to talk ten to the dozen, to make things up, to exaggerate, and to build great rhetorical structures on very slim foundations indeed: 'yet are they all given soe to counterfeit learninge', Sidney warns his brother, ' as a man shall learne emonge them more false groundes of thinges then in any place else that I knowe: for from a Tapster vpward they are all discoursers'.[164] As Ascham feared, such 'discourse' both falsifies true learning ('counterfeit' here being used as a verb) and offers learning that is false ('counterfeit' here being used as an adjective), and is for that reason assumed to be groundless, insubstantial, vacuous, empty, specious, showy, and worse than useless. To the extent that Pugliano's soaring rhetoric might be seen to typify the speech of one such 'discourser', it conforms to Ascham's famous characterization of the 'quick wits'—who, for all their superficial dazzle, turn out not to be 'very profitable to serve the commonwealth'—as opposed to the more tractable and teachable 'hard wits' who do and whom he therefore recommends to the attention of other schoolmasters.[165] In which case, Pugliano is being disparaged as a false and deceptive teacher, as per the humanist commonplace that deplored not only such Italian flashiness but also the tendency of the English noble class to value the men who trained their horses over the men who educated their children (paying them, on average, five times as much).[166]

While Pugliano might be negativized according to Ascham's criteria of value, however—in which the 'profitable' is the only thing that passes muster—he is not necessarily shunned for that reason. On the contrary, Pugliano is *followed*, not as a 'positive' role model but as a 'poetical' one.[167] That is to say, in his ability to

---

[163] *Correspondence* (881). For critics who cite this letter in the context of Pugliano, see e.g. Shepherd (144); Maslen (120); and Hager 1991 (112).

[164] *Correspondence* (882). In his letter to Robert of 18 October 1580, Sidney recommends three books on horsemanship, all of them by Italians: Federigo Grisone, *Degli Ordine del Cavalcare* (Naples, 1550), Claudio Corte, *Il Cavallarizzo* (Venice, 1562), and Pasqual Caracciolo, *La Gloria del Cavallo* (Venice, 1566). Sidney seems to promise that reading such materials will benefit Robert in much the same way that Pugliano's speech was ostensibly intended to benefit Wotton and himself in the *Defence*: 'withall, that yow may ioyne the through contemplation of it with the exercise, and so shall yow profite more in a Moneth, then others in a yeare': *Correspondence* (1009).

[165] Ascham 1967 (22, 24), following Plato 2013, *Republic*, 413d–e who similarly compares the training of youth to the training of horses—adding, for good measure, that children should also be tested 'more than you would test gold in the fire'—in order to prove 'who would be most useful to himself and the state'. Ascham also complains that Englishmen corrupted by Italy learn to be 'common discoursers of all matters' (74). See also Maslen's discussion of Ascham's text and Sidney's use of it (55–8, 119–20).

[166] Ascham 1967 (xxxi, 26–7, 28). For similar complaints, see Pace 1967 (23), and Heron 1579 (A8ᵛ).

[167] Sidney uses the word 'discourser' more positively in his 1580 letter to Robert, in which he describes the historian as 'a discourser for profite' on the grounds that (unlike the mere historiographer,

'counterfeit learninge' (or to proffer 'counterfeit learninge')—to give something other than or that goes beyond what passes for learned, serviceable speech without pretending to do differently or aiming to deceive—Pugliano could be said to be a poet. He is, perhaps, not unlike Hythlodaeus: the advocate in More's *Utopia*, whose name has been variously translated as 'expert in trifles', 'well-learned in nonsense', 'Nonsenso', 'merchant, purveyor of nonsense', 'nonsense peddler', 'expert in nonsense', 'distributor... of nonsense', or 'skilled in pleasant speech'.[168] Indeed, insofar as he builds spectacular castles in the air, Pugliano exemplifies the model of *poesis* that we have been tracing from the inverse, negative imprint that the official, humanist model leaves behind. His speech is superfluous and supernumerary. It is additive in the sense that new tropes and figures of speech can always be added to it, but not in the sense that it adds much or anything to his hearers' 'treasure-house' of knowledge: it simply provides an infinitely varied way of saying things they already know. It might accumulate words—impressively so—but it does not accumulate capital. It is the product of an idle hour—a mere 'tale' (95.18) like that which keeps children from play or old men from the chimney corner— told by a poet to his appreciative but otherwise unoccupied hearers who, for the time being, have nothing better or more 'productive' to do. They may have whiled away the hour, but they do not come away better informed: unless, perhaps, it is with a sense of how value might be differently conceived. Pugliano's fertile wit is infinitely generative—we get the impression that there is no end to the tropes he could come up with—but it is an airy productivity. It does not work 'substantially... to make many Cyruses' (85.39–42). Indeed, if it works at all, it is to make Sidney virtually wish himself a horse: presumably a counterproductive outcome as far as Ascham was concerned, and as clear a demonstration as any that the quick wit is most definitely not profitable to the state. To the extent that Pugliano values his 'contemplations' as 'precious' and believes that they will 'enrich' the minds of those who hear them, it is because they belong, like Italian silks and wines, to the order of luxury goods: fashioned, beautiful, intensely desired, yet strictly useless, dispensable, inessential, supplementary, and quite possibly counterfeit or fake.[169]

If Pugliano is a poet, then the kind he most closely resembles is the poet of praise. Indeed, in its very additive quality, Pugliano's 'speech in the praise of his faculty' (81.9–10) epitomizes epideictic poetry as Joel Fineman describes it, where praise consists, by definition, in the addition of something extra (metaphor) to what is

who simply records events of the past with no embellishment) he is 'an Orator, yea P*oet* sometimes for Ornament. An Orator in making excellent Orations *e re nata* [arising out of the matter] ... a Poet in painting forth the effetts, the motions, the whisperings of the people, wh*i*ch though in disputation one might say were true, yet who will marke them well shall finde them taste of a Poeticall vaine, and in that kinde are gallantly to be marked, for though perchance they were not so, yet it is enough they might be so': *Correspondence* (1007).

[168] See: More 1965a (301n); More 1965b (38); Wilson 1992 (33); More 1995 (35n); Nelson 2001 (890); and Halpern 1991 (142), respectively.

[169] Sidney is unlikely to have used 'enrich' unthinkingly, if his play on this and the word 'rich' in *Astrophil and Stella* is anything to go by: see *AS* 3, 9, 24, 35, 37, 48, 79, v (line 46), viii (line 1) and ix (line 10). On the luxury item as something that by definition flouts the principle of necessity, see Sekora 1977 (23–62).

already known (mimesis) so as to heighten, enhance, and idealize it.[170] In the traditional, idealist poetics that, in Fineman's view, Sidney thoroughly exemplifies, the 'proper' and complementary relation between metaphor and mimesis must be governed by decorum at all times. Insofar as metaphor adds to mimesis (and thus constitutes the 'plus' of what I have been calling 'mimesis-plus'), it 'must somehow augment, but in doing so it must thereby distort, its verisimilar imitation of the real' (95), the risk being that, if not so governed or controlled, metaphor might run away with itself—create images that potentially do not reflect reality or, indeed, have any appreciable bearing on it whatsoever—in other words, might lie. While this problem—'how to relate the poet's mimetic mirror to his metaphoric lamp' (96)—affects all poetry, it is particularly acute in the case of epideictic poetry because there such a 'hyperbolic amplification' (96) of reality is very much to the fore. Fineman insists that in 'traditional rhetorical and poetic theory there is of course no real suspicion regarding the truth of poetic figure, not *if* figure is handled properly' (96, my emphasis), a propriety that Sidney is seen to exemplify since, for the critic, he remains un-problematically true to this idealist aesthetic. For Fineman, Sidney's position 'reflect[s] very traditional notions of poetic decorum, namely, that mimesis and metaphor, *if* they are properly deployed by the poet, will exemplify and support each other' (97, my emphasis). My own view, by contrast, and what the preceding discussions have sought to bring out, is that letting metaphor off the leash, as it were—allowing it to run wild and free and not 'reined with learned discretion' (87.9–10)—is precisely the risk that Sidney (the 'unofficial' Sidney, Sidney the poet rather than Sidney the defender of poetry) is prepared to take, and flirts with, so far as he can, within the *Defence*, but luxuriously expands in *Astrophil and Stella* and the two *Arcadias*.[171] I have emphasized Fineman's 'ifs' in the quotations above, therefore, to show how, in replicating Sidney's own pregnant conditionals, such 'proper' handling and deployment is something that, in the imagination and in poetic practice at least, might all too easily, gratefully, joyously, and creatively be dispensed with. Where Fineman sees the *Defence* as the quintessential statement of idealist poetics—as the foil against which to set and measure Shakespeare's radical departure from that aesthetic in his *Sonnets*—I see Sidney as having got there first: as heading his treatise with an example of idealist poetry in action (Pugliano's excessive speech of praise), only to find that it need not behave 'properly', that it can call the bluff on those 'ifs', that for this horse-loving horseman there is no rein on *poesis*, no limit to where the quick, fertile, high-flying wit might range, or where metaphor might go.[172] In Pugliano, that is, whose metaphors

---

[170] See Fineman 1986 (3–4, 95–8).

[171] Lazarus 2016 suggests that Sidney's identification with the horseman here wittily alludes to the horse-man or centaur-figure that stands at the head of the *Ars Poetica* as Horace's cautionary emblem of what results when poets defy the principles of decorum: '*Humano capiti cervicem pictor equinam iungere si velit . . . risum teneatis?*' [If a painter chose to join a human head to the neck of a horse . . . could you refrain from laughing?]: see Horace 1926, *Ars Poetica*, lines 1–5. For examples of the excessive praise of a horse being satirized, see Shakespeare 1997, *Henry V*, III.vii.11–40; and *Edward III*, II.i.98.

[172] It is not impossible that Sidney might have given Shakespeare and Nashe the idea that the ideal '*Idea* or fore-conceit' (85.35) was in fact something that could—even should—be dispensed with. See Crewe 1982 (111n): 'In the "strong" version of Elizabethan poetics—that represented by Sidney's

clearly exceed both decorum and expectation—'Nay, to so unbelieved a point he proceeded...' (81.13)—the *Defence* opens with a negative example of how epideictic poetry, already a risk in its reliance on metaphor, might indeed stray beyond the bounds of propriety, and be all the more 'poetical' for doing so. In defiance of idealist poetics and the criteria that would judge this non-exemplary, Sidney follows suit, just as the scholar (or the horse) 'followeth the steps of his master' (81.29).[173] The tension between what Sidney the poet would choose to do and what the speaker—saddled with the task of defending idealist poetics—finds himself obliged to do, can probably be traced back to this point.

Apologie—ideal poetic order does not follow from ideal pastoral order, but rather constitutes it. In doing so, poetic "making" remains an image of the divine creation of a "golden world." Although the poetic act is thus nominally underwritten by divine example, a curious reversal is incipient. The mere existence of poetry, and of the creative power of the poetic "wit," begins to emerge as "no small evidence" of the actuality of a prelapsarian world, and thus of the truth of revelation. Within a skeptical world, poetry thus tends to constitute, not derive itself from, an original mythic moment of creation. Despite its fictional character, poetry becomes primary evidence of a truth for which other evidences have failed. A failure of poetry would, therefore, have profound repercussions. This point is highly pertinent to an understanding of Nashe.' In my view, the 'other' argument of the *Defence*—by analogy, the weak, feminine, non-idealist version of Elizabethan poetics—is what effects this reversal, precisely by imagining a creativity that is able to supersede and go beyond money thought with its structural (short)fall, debts, 'oughts', and redemptions. Such *poesis* is able to allow for prelapsarian possibilities— as glimpsed, for example, in the poetry of the simple Indians—and thus instantiates the potentially revolutionary repercussions that Crewe here identifies in Nashe.

173 The *Defence* is symptomatically split between 'good' and 'bad' types of following, each of which might be mapped onto the speaker and Sidney respectively. Thus, the speaker praises Gower and Chaucer, whose 'excellent fore-going, others have followed' (82.28) in making English a treasure-house of science. Similarly, the Aristotelian philosophers command that if you ' "follow Nature ... thou shalt not err" ' (85.7–8); readers are urged to 'follow St James's counsel in singing psalms when they are merry' (86.30–1); poets will show you 'each thing to be followed' (92.36), so that representations of vice and virtue in poetry (as opposed to philosophy) will teach the reader 'to follow but by your own discretion' (92.40); watching the example of evil men punished in tragedies will 'little animate folks to follow them' (93.44); learning is supposed to 'lead and draw us to as high a perfection' (88.7–8) as we are capable of, and the poet thus defeats the philosopher in his ability to 'lead a man to virtue' (88.44); poetry must follow instruction and 'the highest-flying wit have a Daedalus to guide him' (109.39–40). In all these cases, the act of following involves moving (or, more specifically, being commanded, directed, or pressured into moving) in the direction of authority-figures towards learning, science, knowledge, and virtue. Sidney, by contrast, 'followeth' Pugliano (81.29). Similarly, Herodotus 'and all the rest that followed him' (83.8–9) incorporate poetry—specifically, the 'passionate describing of passions' (83.9–10)—into their histories; the Greek philosophers ungratefully 'spurn at their guides' (106.25) the poets, when they should have followed them; the Greek poets told light tales of the gods because they 'followed according to their nature of imitation' (107.15), that is to say they followed superstition and dreams, rather as the foolish proponents of the spot-reading of Virgil found there 'great foretokens of their following fortunes' (83.43); in the case of *Troilus and Criseyde*, Sidney does not know 'whether to marvel more, either that [Chaucer] in that misty time could see so clearly, or that we in this clear age walk so stumblingly after him' (110.12–14); where the historian blindly bids you 'follow the footing of them that have gone before you' (89.23–4), the poet, by contrast, is 'not bound to follow the story, but, [has] liberty ... to feign quite new matter' (111.22); the courtier evidences more style than the professor of learning because 'following that which by practice he findeth fittest to nature ... [he] doth according to art, though not by art' (115.1–3), as opposed to the obsessively euphuistic poets who behave as if they were 'bound to follow the method of a dictionary' (113.40). In sum, 'Poesy ... must be gently led, or rather it must lead' (109.34). In all these cases, 'bad' or non-exemplary following—like Medea's '*deteriora sequor*'—nonetheless involves moving in the direction of poetry, passion, superstition, folly, dreams, love, freedom, and good style.

Looking back from the experience of how this tension comes to develop and play out as the rest of the *Defence* unfolds, we might identify early signs of it in the speculation that surrounds Pugliano's motives. He 'sought to enrich our minds with the contemplations therein which he thought most precious' (81.5–7). Why? What would motivate someone to 'enrich' others? On the premise or promise of what interest, return, or net gain? The situation is presented as something of a mystery. The alternatives floated—that Pugliano was 'either angered with slow payment, or moved with our learner-like admiration' (81.8–9)—both assume an ulterior motive on his part: that he stood to profit personally in some way and that self-interest is, thus, the only rational explanation. Pugliano sought to 'enrich' others as a way of enriching himself, either directly, in the form of hard cash ('payment') or indirectly, in the abstract form of cultural and professional capital ('admiration'). The first alternative is definitely the more demeaning of the two: it puts Pugliano in the category of the service-provider who works for immediate reward (cash in hand) and it thus gives his speech a crude exchange value. This is speech for hire, selling rhetoric for money (Plato's charge against the Sophists), like the hack writers—'base men with servile wits' (109.11)—who write only to be 'rewarded of the printer' (109.12), or like the servant who, being 'more stored with discowrces then monej', effectively has to sing for his supper.[174] This is a devalued position and such speech is not worth very much precisely because it can be measured, quantified, and, like a servant, dismissed or paid off. The second alternative—'admiration'—is a longer-term and more highly valued return. The teacher who basks in his students' satisfaction nets a higher reward—cultural approval—because his work cannot or cannot only be calculated according to crude remuneration, and his 'product' (learning), having a genuine use-value, is more highly regarded for the same reason.[175] Such work is socially more 'respectable' since it is of a higher status in class terms and its practitioners are only 'servants' in the sense that they are civil servants—they 'serve [the] prince' (93.21) or serve the commonwealth—a category large enough to accommodate aspirant humanists and courtiers alike. As Maslen notes, William Temple 'loyally supposes' in his 'Analysis' of the *Defence* that Pugliano was angry at *other* students' late payment of their bills (Wotton and Sidney being presumed guiltless of such an oversight), but it might, alternatively, have been supremely insulting for a minor embassy official and his friend to give the Emperor's equerry money in return for his bestowal of time and attention upon them, just as no self-respecting courtier

---

[174] In a letter dated 17 December 1581, Sidney begs Sir Francis Walsingham to recompense the family servant (probably Harry White or possibly his nephew, Roland White) who had brought him the missive: 'fauor this bearer, that he maj haue som consideration for the packet he brought, becawse belonging to my brother Robert, a yonger brother of so yongeli a fortuned familj as the sidneis, I am sure at least haue very vehement coniectures *that* he is more stored with discowrces then monej': *Correspondence* (1044). On Plato and the Sophists, see Shell 1978 (36–9), referencing Plato 2013, *Republic*, 337d; and Plato 1924, *Meno*, 91B, 91D; and *Protagoras*, 349A.

[175] Arendt 1958 considers the different cultural valuations of the 'labour' of *homo laborans* (endless, repetitive, of low status, the work of the manual labourer or the housewife, the labour of childbirth) as against the higher status 'work' of *homo faber*: work that is not mere maintenance but the working towards some defined end as in the production of an 'opus'.

would stoop to selling his poetry for cash.[176] Behind this higher estimation of Pugliano's speech, art, and motives, perhaps, may also lie Ascham's piqued concession that, although horse-trainers commanded considerably higher salaries than schoolmasters (in England, at any rate), they were in some ways the better teachers and their methods (which stressed the pleasure, delight, and freedom of their art and so obviated the necessity of beating their students into submission) something from which pedagogues could usefully learn.[177] Nevertheless, even though the second alternative grants Pugliano a more honourable motivation, it remains for all that a self-interested one. His students' 'learner-like admiration' may be beyond price and not to be enumerated, but it is deemed sufficiently self-pleasing to warrant the outlay of his energy and time. In this estimation, admiration for the praised object (horses and horsemanship) reflects back positively on the praising subject (the horseman) in the way that typifies epideixis: 'the rhetorical magnification praise accords its object also rebounds back upon itself, drawing attention . . . to its own grandiloquent rhetoricity', as Fineman writes; 'praise is an objective showing that is essentially subjective showing off'.[178] In this sense, Pugliano is not only a masterly teacher, who gains the wonder of his students, but also the epideictic poet par excellence who makes a powerful impression on those who hear him. We know that this great praiser has been praised before since it was with 'great commendation' (81.3) that he secured his position at the Emperor's court. Like the poet who garners praise, therefore, Pugliano gains—in the admiration he earns—something infinitely more valuable than mere payment (late or otherwise): symbolic capital in the form of celebrity and fame, like the laurel crown (*lauro*), or the reputational gold (*l'auro*) that compensated Petrarch for the lack and loss of his Laura.

So much for the motives that are explicitly attributed to Pugliano in the *exordium* and offered us by way of explanation. With hindsight, however—given the way that positions come to develop and bifurcate within the course of the *Defence*—I think both these explanations might justly be identified with the character I have been differentiating as the 'speaker'. That Pugliano should ultimately be (could only be) motivated by self-interest—that his speech should essentially be transactional and aimed at eliciting a return of some kind, whether paltry or prized, and that this mode of thinking (money thought) should be considered self-evident,

---

[176] Maslen (120, emphasis original), referencing Temple 1984 (63).

[177] See Ascham 1967 (32–3): 'Fond schoolmasters neither can understand nor will follow this good counsel of Socrates, but wise riders [i.e. horse-trainers], in their office, can and will do both; which is the only cause that commonly the young gentlemen of England go so unwillingly to school and run so fast to the stable. For in very deed fond schoolmasters, by fear, do beat into them the hatred of learning, and wise riders, by gentle allurements, do breed up in them the love of riding. They find fear and bondage in schools; they feel liberty and freedom in stables; which causeth them utterly to abhor the one and most gladly to haunt the other . . . If ten gentlemen be asked why they forget so soon in court that which they were learning so long in school, eight of them, or let me be blamed, will lay the fault on their ill-handling by their schoolmasters.' 'Cuspinian', he adds—referencing Cuspinianus 1561 (602–3)—'doth report that that noble Emperor Maximilian would lament very oft his misfortune herein' (33), suggesting one reason why the Emperor may have held his equerry, Pugliano, in particular estimation.

[178] Fineman 1986 (5, 6).

self-explanatory, natural, 'rational', and the only kind available—would entirely fit the mindset of the defender of poetry: officious, righteous, at times sanctimonious, on the side of the Protestant, humanist, pedagogic, profitable, bankable model of poetry, and thus self-appointed spokesman for the prevailing ideology.[179] The trouble with his explanations, however, is that they do not really account for what Pugliano chooses to do. They would make more sense if Pugliano came away from the encounter with Sidney and Wotton with something positive to show for it (ideally admiration, but failing that a tip), but he does not. While wholly logical so far as the speaker is concerned, such self-interested motivations do not cover every eventuality and do not, therefore, entirely satisfy. More to the point, they are not what actually happens. The possibility remains, therefore, that Pugliano might be motivated by something else, by some other, different reason: one that may not necessarily be rational, and that is certainly not stated openly, but that might (in ways we have come to see as typical of the *Defence*) be inferred from what is hinted at or left unsaid, from actions that are taken, or not taken, but that nonetheless speak louder than words. This alternative explanation, I suggest, might justly be identified with the character I have been differentiating as 'Sidney'. For Pugliano does not, after all, earn any payment from Sidney or Wotton (that much is clear), and, ultimately, he does not earn their admiration either. Whatever 'wonder' (81.14) he may have aroused in them during the course of his speech gives way, by the end, to an amused doubt: at least, it does so on the part of the recipient who finds himself nearly persuaded 'to have wished myself a horse' (81.20), Wotton's response, again, goes unrecorded. Pugliano has clearly got carried away, gone overboard on his praises, proceeded to 'so unbelieved a point' (81.13) that any initial wonder finds itself shading into disbelief or worse: scepticism, dissent, disrespect, ridicule, even rebuke. In his excitement he has evidently overstepped the mark and this costs him anything he might have earned, large or small. He is manifestly not the ideal idealist poet, not the model of epideixis in action who stays within bounds, aims at and hits the mark, maintains decorum and the 'proper' balance between metaphor and mimesis. Quite the reverse. It is one thing for a star-lover to love his star—a scenario that allows for at least some semblance of idealism to be maintained—but quite another for a horse-lover to love his horse. The very thing that the question of motives was called upon to explain, namely, the sheer excessiveness of Pugliano's speech—the fact that Sidney's ears were never 'more loaden, than when (either angered with slow payment, or moved with our learner-like admiration) he exercised his speech in the praise of his faculty' (81.8–10)—is finally what renders the two explanations offered null and void: what ensures that

---

[179] For Heinzelman 1980 (38) this mode of thought finds itself embodied in Spenser's figure of Mammon: 'The basis of Mammon's art is his metaphysical assumption that commerce is the only imaginative structure which explains where we live and what we live for. His art prefigures, therefore, the later metaphysical claims made for economics.' For similar formulations, see Landreth 2012 (7, 41, 43, 67, 89, 151, 234, 237). One could argue that Mammon's cave is where the poet's 'golden' world, as promoted by the speaker in the *Defence*, finds its logical conclusion: the 'hell' (93.29; 94.13) to which Sidney would also end up consigning his ambitious, tyrannical speaker, or the 'golden cage' (*AS* 23) from which Astrophil seeks to escape.

Pugliano ends up with neither. His *copia* forfeits both, for, like Narcissus, his very plenty is what makes him poor.[180] Pugliano comes away with nothing for his pains. Indeed, he comes away with less than nothing, with less than he started out with: with a wasted hour and a formerly illustrious reputation far from intact. Having given more than he could 'afford' (81.5), Pugliano overspends himself and, in capital terms, ends up out of pocket.

'Wherein', Sidney continues, 'if Pugliano's strong affection and weak arguments will not satisfy you, I will give you a nearer example of myself' (81.23–4). Logically (where 'logically' means following the self-interested rationale of the speaker), what Sidney should do at this point is reject Pugliano's example out of hand and, in his own oration, proceed with less affection and considerably stronger arguments. The implication is that Pugliano's speech was not ultimately successful and that it will not 'satisfy' the reader who has just been given a précis of it any more than it satisfied Sidney (or Wotton?) when they first heard it in full. If Sidney, by contrast, is to satisfy *his* readers—persuade them, convince them, enhance the credibility of himself and his subject so as to earn their respect and remuneration (as Pugliano did not)—then he would be well advised to learn his lesson: to tone down the excited rhetoric, argue disinterestedly, and offset the charge that he might have a 'partial allegation' (84.40) by minimizing any personal interest, investment, or stake he has in the topic at hand. Or at least convince his audience that this is the case, for this ideal of disinterested, objective inquiry only masks the self-interest—the desire to win the argument, the bays, and possibly more besides—that is assumed to be the motive underlying all human action.[181] Sidney, however, does not do this. Illogically (where 'illogically' means not following the self-interested rationale of the speaker), Sidney elects to follow Pugliano—chooses to go awry—his own 'more good will than good reasons' (81.28) mapping directly onto the 'strong affection and weak arguments' of his predecessor. If Pugliano's excessive, ecstatic, enthusiastic speech yields him nothing and costs him dear, then by following it and repeating his error, Sidney's, by extrapolation, risks doing the same. He thus makes a non-exemplary 'example' (81.24) of himself.

What I am suggesting is that, in defiance of the speaker and the apparent 'logic' of his position, Sidney chooses not self-interest but, rather, self-love. Superficially, these might appear to be rather similar—looking out for yourself, doing right by yourself, doing what is best for yourself—but on inspection they turn out to be very different: indeed, to be diametrically opposed. Self-interest will do whatever it takes (including trying to appear 'disinterested') in order to satisfy the reader or hearer

---

[180] '*inopem me copia fecit*': see Ovid 1916, *Metamorphoses*, III.466.

[181] For Ferguson 1983 (9) 'all discourse is to some degree "motivated" by the author's desire for personal advantage, economic, political, or sexual': i.e. she conflates self-interest with self-love and, effectively, the speaker with Sidney. See also Warley 2014 (68–70), for whom the pose of disinterestedness (even or especially in literary criticism) only denies the economic self-interest otherwise omnipresent and thus masks the interest of a particular class position. My own view is that, while this might be true of the speaker in the *Defence*, it is not necessarily true of Sidney who (along with Surrey and the Shakespeare of the 'Young Man' sonnets or of *King Lear*) attempts to find some way to conceptualize the anti-economic and—only insofar as it is not bourgeois—codes the 'courtly' as such.

(the customer) and to elicit something from them in return (admiration or pay). Self-love, by contrast, makes no attempt to be disinterested or to deny its interest in the topic at hand. It is very interested in its subject indeed, even passionate about it, willing to argue for it with the strongest of affections—with the most 'infected will' (86.8), if necessary—to be utterly partisan and quite incapable of denying its 'partial allegation'.[182] It therefore forfeits any serious consideration, gains nothing, and, like Narcissus, risks losing all. To love your subject—to be a self-loving subject in that sense—is not in your own 'best' interests. It is to risk losing 'interest' in the sense of some capital return on your outlay of energy and time. It is—as the period's best known spokeswoman of this paradox points out—to risk being taken for mad, irrational, and a fool.[183] It is to swap payment (real money, real gold) for counterfeit gold, fool's gold. It is to opt for what is 'better than any gilding' (81.21–2), and to choose the illusory self-love that promises to 'make that seem gorgeous wherein ourselves are parties' (81.22). Yet this is exactly how Sidney proceeds, and such 'mak[ing] ... gorgeous' constitutes the very first act of *poesis* in the *Defence*. Pugliano is a foolish figure. There is no denying it and Sidney does not attempt to do so: he knows very well, but he follows all the same, and in doing so he sketches out how limited, how passionless, how predictable, how boring, how bleak, how uncreative—frankly, how unartistic—the speaker's alternative position ultimately is. Self-interest is professional, polite, rational, risk-averse, and irremediably bourgeois. It is the preserve of the philosophers and the pedagogues. It leads to 'proper' idealist poetry (should such a thing exist) and to a 'proper' idealist poetics: a treatise in propositional prose, a 'defence of poor Poetry' (81.30) that seeks to make it valuable again—'rich' (85.24)—and to restore its lost 'credit' (82.2). Self-love, conversely, is paradoxical, passionate, partial, and partisan. Whatever else it is, it is not bourgeois—it takes its definition from everything the latter is not—which is why it appears here as contrastingly 'courtly': not as some nostalgic throwback, a futile attempt to turn back the rising tide of capitalism and revert to some imaginary feudal idyll, but as an attempt to imagine and conceive a world in which these bourgeois criteria of value are not the only ones available, a no place similar to More's Utopia and, like it, a thought experiment no less radical. It leads neither to poetics nor to some idealized, speaking picture of what poetry 'ought' to be, but rather to non-idealist poetry: 'ideally/non-ideally' to rhetorically excessive and/or counterfactual poetic fictions that do not just turn idealism on its head but deconstruct it altogether, show the costs of its costing mentality, the

---

[182] For Maslen (28), any poetry that derived from such an infected source—as from the 'common infection' (115.10) that Sidney claims afflicts contemporary poets, including himself—would be 'a textually transmitted disease'. Aligning Sidney with Gosson here, Maslen argues that the *Defence* 'presents itself as a cure for England's poetic sickness'. My point, by contrast, is that the sickness is the cure, and vice versa.
[183] See Erasmus 1549 (L1): '*Poetes* are somewhat lesse beholding vnto me [i.e. Folly], notwithstandyng, euin by theyr profession they shew theim selues to be of my secte, a free kynde of men, that lyke peincters maie feigne what they list, whose studie tendeth naught els, than to fede fooles eares with mere trifles and foolisshe fables.' See also Agrippa 1569 (D3): poetry was devised 'to no other ende, but to please the eares of foolishe men', 'to delite the eares of fooles' (D4ᵛ), and to work 'to the delite of fooles' (E1).

unacceptable price it demands. If self-interest is about gaining something or winning, self-love is not only about *not* gaining or winning anything (leaving you in a neutral position, as it were, neither better off nor worse) but about risking or losing everything: achieving a net loss, an absolute loss, an unredeemable loss, as in the 'suicidal poetics' of the Earl of Surrey, or the ending of *King Lear*.

Pugliano serves as Sidney's model, I would suggest, because his speech is entirely gratuitous: supernumerary, superfluous, extra, unnecessary, something that Sidney and Wotton could easily have done without, and would not have missed if they had. It is spontaneously given (it was not asked for) and it asks for nothing in return. It does not seek the gratification of Pugliano's ego (as if he were the showy orator showing off his skill), nor the gratitude of his hearers (their admiration, wonder, or satisfaction), nor even a gratuity from them. It is nothing of great importance—it is, as Agrippa might say, 'a matter of nothinge' (D4ᵛ)—and Pugliano gives it for nothing and gets nothing for it. It is *gratis*. Since he 'sought to enrich' others without the presumed requirement that he enrich himself in the process, one might say that his is an act of pure giving: not part of some 'gift economy' in which decorous delay and a pretence of disconnection masks what is always the reciprocating gesture of the return gift—which is how that 'slow payment' (81.8) might be interpreted—but something given in the full knowledge that it will net no payback, no return at all, and will indeed entail a net loss, a loss of things, like reputation and time, that can never be recovered.[184] Similarly, Sidney and Wotton do not buy Pugliano's services: they do not sign up for his tuition and expect to get billed for it. Instead, they 'gave' (81.2) themselves to learn horsemanship from him. They, too, freely give up their time and attention for something they do not strictly need and for which they get very little in return. Except, perhaps, a lesson in how not every encounter need necessarily be a transactional one; in how people might choose to do things at their own expense, at whatever the personal cost to themselves; in how profit—whatever particular form it takes—need not constitute the sum total, the *ne plus ultra*, of all human action and motivation; in how there may be more things in heaven and earth than idealist philosophy can dream of (like dreams, for example); in how there may be 'things past bounds of wit' that it is worth being called a 'foole' for seeking out or defending; and in how there may be a place, no place, that lies outside self-interest's 'golden cage'.[185] Here there is no negotiation to be transacted, no business to be exchanged: the situation is entirely 'courtly', otiose. Pugliano's speech is valueless both to the man who gives it and to those who receive it, if positivity and profit are taken to be the sole criteria of value. At 'best' it offers

---

[184] See Derrida 1992 (13) on the true gift as that which interrupts or overruns the normal yet self-cancelling circuits of economic exchange: 'Even though all the anthropologies, indeed the metaphysics of the gift have, *quite rightly and justifiably*, treated *together*, as a system, the gift and the debt, the gift and the cycle of restitution, the gift and the loan, the gift and credit, the gift and the countergift, we are here *departing*, in a peremptory and distinct fashion, from this tradition. That is to say, from tradition itself. We will take our point of departure in the dissociation, in the overwhelming evidence of this other axiom: There is gift, if there is any, only in what interrupts the system as well as the symbol, in a partition without return and without division [*répartition*]' (emphases original).

[185] *AS*, vii, line 6; sonnet 23.

something strictly unnecessary, supplementary, surplus to requirement (an idle hour passed, a little extra polish acquired) rather than any substantive, packaged knowledge: something that its pupils need and that it will profit them and their country to know. At 'worst' it offers a negative lesson, teaching its pupils to unlearn what they thought they knew: to challenge apparent certainties, received ideas, the pseudo-logic of rational self-interest; to test the limits of what passes for the thinkable and to see it for the ideological programme that it is; not to perpetuate or prop up the latter's patterns of thought but to move beyond them into new, unexplored, un-thought territory and to make something truly creative, radical, and 'anew'. This is *poesis*. And it is not well served by an 'economic' logic with its checks and balances, its ideal measures, its general equivalents, its idealized golden worlds. For such poetry—the product of such *poesis*—is free in every sense of that word: free from the demands of ideology, free from its 'ideals', free from the necessity of reproducing those ideals, free from the necessity of production, period (no more Cyruses, thank you). And it is free in that it is given for nothing and received for nothing. It is not a transaction, not a quid pro quo. It does not provide a valuable cultural service that has been or will be paid for. It does not supply learning that can be accumulated, or knowledge that can be banked. It does not turn a profit on any investment, and it should not be expected to do so.

Looking back at the *exordium* with the rest of the *Defence* behind us, it is, perhaps, easier to see how, at even this earliest point, a divergence is marked: a parting of the ways. On the one hand, there is the path identified, signalled, and taken by the speaker. As noted, it is professional in tone and pedagogic in nature. It makes an entirely rational argument for the profit and purpose of poetry, a wholly logical case for its positive value—for the important contribution poetry can make to the individual, the state, the economy—and it operates on the assumption that whatever works 'substantially' to the greater good must in and of itself therefore be *a* good (and, hence, merchandisable goods). This path is clearly signed as 'right' and 'proper'. It has a clear destination, target, and scope—the 'ending end of all earthly learning being virtuous action' (88.31–2)—which mostly means going to war, preferably under the banner of religion (the Protestant religion, that is). It is as straight as the orator's sure-fire arrow, that heat-seeking missile that is guaranteed to hit its target and 'persuade' whoever happens to be on the receiving end of it. This is the path, I think it is fair to say, that professional readers of the *Defence* have for the most part chosen to follow. On the other hand, there is the path I have sought to identify as that which is—or would be—taken by Sidney. As noted, it is the opposite of professional, and in unguarded moments it betrays a singular lack of respect for the pedagogue or for those who have, in the business of teaching or instruction, 'attained to the high top of their profession' (91.28–9). It rejects the rationale of self-interest as the explanatory logic that accounts for everything—or for poetry, at any rate—and thus opens up a space in which poets are not motivated or incentivized to write (as if by tax breaks), so much as 'overmastered' (95.1; 109.30) to do so: compelled, driven, inspired by some overwhelming 'passion' (95.1) and by some uncontrollable 'force' (84.14) within them, as the sibyls and the priestesses at Delphos were (they did not go to war). It opens up a space for the irrational, for the unconscious, for the mysterious masochistic trends of the ego, for the possibility that human beings—or poets, at any rate—might go out of their way to disadvantage themselves, to impoverish themselves, to work against their own best interests, to risk being taken as frenzied lovers (self-lovers), madmen (or madwomen), and fools, if necessary: if that is what it takes to show that there is a place beyond the pleasure principle, no place, where its logic no longer applies.[186] This path is not signed at all. It is deviant and dark. It does not have a clear destination, except, perhaps, to lose, confuse, and disorient those who are (or who want to be) on the straight one. It is as crooked as the poet's arrow that, if it can be guaranteed to do anything, it is to miss the mark and tragically to go awry (in the case of the lyric poet, it finds itself embedded permanently in his or her own heart). It sees the better but follows the worse. It abandons the schoolmaster and goes with his nemesis, the 'good horseman', instead.[187] Indeed, much of the ensuing struggle within the *Defence* might be seen as the tension that arises between a pedagogic speaker who would keep to the straight and narrow and an errant horse-lover who, like virtually every Spenserian knight, finds it impossible not to stray from the path. Sidney leaves the speaker and chooses to follow Pugliano, and in doing so he becomes just like him: a horseman who does not fight, who in the end does not and cannot defend what he is supposed to defend, and who terminally sabotages the defensive mission of his other half, especially when that involves the kind of poetry

---

[186] One might revisit here the split position in the *Defence* with respect to the *furor poeticus*. In his enthusiasm, Pugliano might be seen to resemble the foolish Cuddy in the October eclogue of *The Shepheardes Calender* (1579), who exemplifies the position Spenser is said to have taken in his own defence of poetry (the lost *English Poete*): namely, that it is 'even amongst the most barbarous alwayes of singular accounpt [*sic*] and honor . . . indede so worthy and commendable an arte: or rather no arte, but a divine gift and heavenly instinct not to bee gotten by labour and learning, but adorned with both: and poured into the witte by a certain ἐνθουσιασμὸς and celestial inspiration': see Spenser 1989 (170). Cuddy's effusions—which qualify him as 'the perfect paterne of a Poete'—also put one in mind of the poetry of the simple Indians and the oracles of Delphos and of the sibyls: all types of poetry that fail to conform to the 'laboure and learning' that characterizes the scholarly, male understanding of what 'right' and 'proper' poetry ought to look like. For similar iterations, see: Elyot 1531 (G1ᵛ); Lodge 1904 (71–2); Webbe 1904 (231–2); Puttenham 2007 (94); and Chapman 1598 (A2ᵛ). From this point of view, that is, heroic frenzy need not be thought of as 'ideal'. Instead of being conflated with Neoplatonic idealism, the *furor poeticus* might also be seen to extend to the Longinian sublime which precipitates an extinction of category (beyond good and evil, as it were) rather than a vision of the Ideal. On this see Shell 1978 (102–3): 'Longinus argues that sublimity (*hypsos*) is the polar opposite of economy and that the effect of sublime language is transport, while the effect of economy is persuasion' ('economy' here being used in the rhetorical sense of *dispositio* or *decorum*). 'Longinus's polar opposition of economy to sublimity implies a corresponding opposition of work (resistance) to beauty' (104). For the recent resurgence of critical interest in the Renaissance poetic sublime, see e.g. Sedley 2005; Dundas 2007 (227–33); Cheney 2009, 2017; Costelloe, ed. 2012; Refini 2012; and Langer 2015 (125–50). Not unrelated is the similar revival of interest in the conceptualization of genius: e.g. McMahon 2013; Jefferson 2014; and Grayling 2016.

[187] Ascham 1967 (26, 28). As Raber and Tucker 2005 (9) note, the Italian rediscovery of Xenophon's *On the Art of Horsemanship* and *The Cavalry Commander* (both published in Florence in 1516 in an edition of Xenophon's works) 'ushered in a renaissance in horsemanship in sixteenth-century Italy' which included the establishment of famous riding academies in Naples and Ferrara in the 1530s. Where Pugliano's school of horsemanship might have been expected (like these) to teach the latest thinking on the art, however, in fact it divulges a quite different lesson and in so doing proves to be not so much a counter to as another variant on the school of abuse.

that urges you to 'defend thy prince and country' (104.42).[188] Sidney is not, like the speaker, 'provoked to say something... in the defence of that my unelected vocation' (81.26–7): a prompt that, when all is said and done, eventually produces but a 'pitiful defence' (81.30).[189] He is, rather, moved like Pugliano to '[exercise] his speech in the praise of his faculty' (81.9–10): to praise his art—to practise his art—and to do so by the most effective means available: which is, like Pugliano, but also like Erasmus, More, and Agrippa before him, and like Harington, Nashe, and Shakespeare after, to produce a work of paradoxical praise. One that, in precisely *not* meeting expectations—in the shock and surprise of exceeding or falling short of them—is better able to show the value of what otherwise goes unvalued and the importance of knowing what otherwise goes unknown: even if such knowing entails a quite different way of thinking about value. And even if such praise paradoxically abjures its own praise: the prize of the laurel crown that, if the speaker had his way, would 'show the price [poets] ought to be had in' (108.19).[190]

The Pugliano anecdote, then, is more than just a 'pleasaunt tale', as dismissible as the opening gambit of an after-dinner speech; and it is more than mere irony, where that is taken to mean speaking 'otherwise' so as to enable your auditors, in a clubbable and self-congratulatory kind of way, to understand what you 'really' intend, thereby comfortably affirming what everyone already thought that they knew, and already knew that they thought. It is not *sprezzatura*, and nor is it *serio ludere*, where that is taken to mean temporarily reversing things—turning them, as if in 'play', upside down or inside out—so as ultimately to revert to and restore the status quo.[191] Pugliano's speech has the effect, rather, of causing its first 'scholar'

---

[188] See Matz 2000 (76): 'Instead of an "end" in "well-doing" [88.27], in which writing cancels itself in warrior service, Sidney's text ends by foregrounding writing as an act—of the poet and of the critic who evaluates him. Thus foregrounded, writing seems to have no end, but becomes instead excess, straying, and waste.' As an 'ornamental' horseman, Pugliano embodies these contradictions: 'Such ornamentality suggests not the knight's traditional social role, but links the courtier instead to the unprofitable pleasure that Sidney would displace onto the court lady and the "ornaments of peace" [81.12] her needle creates' (80).

[189] As Maslen notes (122), 'pitiful' may mean 'either that he is defending poetry out of pity or that his defence is a wretched one'.

[190] The words price, praise, and prize are cognate. See *OED* price *n.*, derived from Anglo-Norman *price, priese, pris, prise* and Old/Middle French *pris*, French *prix* (sum of money for which anything is bought or sold), in turn derived from classical Latin *pretium* (money for which anything is bought or sold, price, cost, pay, fee, compensation, reward, recompense, prize, penalty, advantage, ransom, bribe, value, worth, rank, esteem, precious possession, expensive article). In branches I (praise, honour) and III (superiority), price *n.* came to be superseded by praise *n.* and prize *n.*[1] respectively.

[191] While Berger 1988 (7) distinguishes between the 'idealist' and the 'true poet', and sees the *Defence* as the '*locus classicus* of the true poet's credo' with its emphasis on the '*counterfactual* nature of fiction' (8, emphasis original), he nonetheless insists that this 'is only a first moment, and if there were nothing more than this in the species of Renaissance poetics exemplified by Sidney, it would be thin and fanciful business indeed. What makes it worth attention is that this withdrawal from life to fiction is seen as fulfilled in a return to life which has two aspects: a return to the image of life within the play world of art and a return to life itself at the end of the fictional experience' (8). This move leads naturally to the metaphor of the sugared pill—'the enlightened Renaissance understanding of the metaphor is *profit inside pleasure*' (9, emphasis original)—for, conceived thus, Renaissance fiction-making remains essentially instructional. See also Shepherd (72): 'of course the whole treatment of imitation and the "other nature" would be a superfluity, all moonshine and self-deception, if no logical relation at all were to be established between the fiction and reality.' Both examples illustrate the critics'

(81.28), and anyone who might think of following after him, to unlearn what they already thought that they knew, to unthink what they already knew that they thought (where that is money thought), and to affirm nothing at all. It gives nothing, gains nothing, and affirms nothing. It is a 'mere tale' (83.2) in the same way that Plato's reporting of the tale of Gyges' Ring is: something interlaced, supplementary, and non-propositional—a mere add-on, not philosophy 'proper', where Plato is at his most 'poetical' (106.18)—and yet ruthlessly incisive as to its target and potentially devastating in its effects.[192] It does not induce the kind of positive knowledge that can be accumulated, gratifyingly stashed in the national knowledge bank or added to the knowledge economy, built up towards ever higher levels as if to some grand Absolute. Rather, it induces the negative, self-doubting, self-cancelling, self-evacuating kind of knowing that leaves the ironist in no 'position' at all but, instead, hovering on a cloud, suspended, high and dry. It is the irony of Aristophanes' Socrates or of Epimenides the Cretan Liar, and it gives an infinitely more radical inflection to the idea of play. No longer a mere break from the schoolroom—an hour's recreation before returning, refreshed, to the world of the philosopher, the pedagogue, and the 'theoretical man' that, by this means, is made to seem contrastingly 'serious' and 'real'—*this* kind of play has no end.[193] It

interest in restoring 'reality', the 'logical', the 'serious', and so on, and their resistance to the idea that these in themselves might be poetic fictions and that 'fancy', 'superfluity', 'moonshine', and 'self-deception' could be precisely where the unofficial argument of the *Defence* ends up. Cf. Lamb 1994 (515): 'The exclusion of the amoral poets who offer pleasure without instruction—the writers of love poetry or (even worse) the lower-class, female narrators of fairy tales—finally grants to them the considerable power of very bad dreams. Hovering in the moonlit spaces around and between the words of the text, these ghostly presences assume silent control of the central arguments of the *Apology*.'

[192] The discussion in Halpern 1991 (142) on the name of More's Hythlodaeus is apposite here. While Plato certainly uses the word *hythlos* pejoratively to mean 'idle talk' or 'nonsense', he also uses the term to refer to 'old wives' chatter' (see Plato 1921, *Theaetatus*, 176b) or to poetry (see Plato 1925, *Lysis*, 221d). 'In neither case', comments Halpern, 'does *hythlos* designate that which is false within the sphere of philosophical discourse. Rather, it designates nonphilosophical speech, the gossip of old women or poetry spun out for its own sake. The word seems to describe speech that aims at pleasure rather than knowledge. Plato uses it consistently to denote the *evasion* of dialectic (for example, Plato 2013, *Republic*, 336d). Similarly, *daios*, the second half of Hythlodaeus, does not mean "learned," in a philosophical or a scholarly sense, but "experienced," "cunning," "skilled" as an artisan might be skilled at his craft. A better translation of "Hythlodaeus" might be "skilled in pleasant speech"'. In the same way, the tale of Gyges in Plato's *Republic* might also be seen as an example of explicitly non-philosophical, non-propositional, non-dialectical, non-learned speech, something not false but fictional, and the preserve therefore of women and poets, as opposed to 'serious', 'scholarly', or 'learned' men. In which case, Pugliano/Sidney would find himself in good company along with Hythlodaeus and Folly, not to mention other representatives of such unlearned speech (Spenser's Cuddy, the 'simple Indians', the female oracles, etc.).

[193] Nietzsche 2000 (81). As Dollimore 2004 (xxxi) comments, the fact that art is fundamentally threatening to the social order largely explains why 'in defences of literature, both [in the Renaissance] and later, *knowledge* was often tied restrictively to the idea of *instruction*' (emphases original). While the 'rationalist might regard the accumulation of knowledge as a progressive and irreversible consolidation of civilisation', however, 'Nietzsche is speaking of another kind of knowledge . . . the knowledge that civilisation itself is at heart illusory': a perception that tends towards deconstruction rather than instruction and is grasped in the terrible play (*in ludere*) of tragedy (for a fuller discussion of this, see Bates 1999). See also Derrida 1992 (29): 'This gap between, on the one hand, thought, language, and desire and, on the other hand, knowledge, philosophy, science, and the order of presence is also a gap between gift and economy.'

shows that there is no such 'world' to return to—it shows the costs and compromises entailed in thinking (or being made to think) that there is—and it thus puts the *serio* back into *serio ludere*. For this kind of play is not teleological. Like Pugliano, it does not play to win but will endlessly repeat the experience of loss, of coming away empty-handed. There is no redemption, neither a jackpot to be won nor a final paying off of the gambler's debts. For this kind of play is purely aleatory, and, like the gambler's die that gives its name to the tool used for making coins, it represents a quite different kind of making—one profitless, risky, and truly creative—and it thus represents a radical alternative to the otherwise self-evident 'world' of coins, gold, profit, production, credit, money, and money thought.

PART III

THE EMPTY CHEST

I

Poetry Abuses

Given poetry's ability to confound the most cherished systems of value and orders of thought, it is not surprising that those with an interest in maintaining the same—the self-appointed guardians of the status quo—should charge it with abuse. 'Abuse', Gosson's title word, conveys a sense of active malevolence much more powerfully than the charges that poetry is profitless or that it lies. With its suggestion of an entity that is capable of intruding into human lives and interfering with them in a highly deleterious way, the word conjures the image of poetry as fraudster-figure: a confidence trickster that robs its victims, royally fleeces them, and relieves them not only of their hard-earned cash—although there are several references to this in Gosson—but also of something much more precious and, once lost, all but irrecoverable, their innocence and good faith. Poetry's sinister operation, moreover, is the more effective for being subtle. It does not bludgeon its targets so much as sidle up to them, inveigle them, and play on their susceptibilities, whispering sweet nothings so as to win their trust: 'by the priuie entries of the eare, [poets] slip downe into the hart, & with gunshotte of affection gaule the minde, where reason and vertue should rule the roste' (89/B7). It is not just poetry's appeal to the senses that makes it so dangerous, however. Infinitely worse is the false promise it makes to deliver moral instruction: the pretence that it offers 'good sentences' (77/A2), and the claim (made by poets and their defenders alike) that poetry really teaches virtue and shows vice only in order to rebuke and so amend it.[1] It is poetry's appeal not to the sensual appetite but to the good conscience that, in Gosson's eyes, is what makes it truly diabolical: taking advantage of what is the very best in people—their earnest desire for goodness and reformation—in order to pervert it and turn it against them. In protesting that they mean no ill and have purged their works of wanton speeches, for example, playwrights simply serve as the Devil's instruments: 'There is more in them then we perceiue, the Deuill standes at our elbowe when we see not, speaks, when we heare him not, strikes when wee feele not' (94/C4). Gosson's word for this monstrous deception is 'juggling': as the 'Iuggler casteth a myst to worke the

---

[1] See *Schoole* (88/B5): claims that in comedy 'the abuses of the worlde [are] reuealed, euery man in a play may see his owne faultes, and learne by this glasse, to amende his manners' prove to be deceptive, and those who make them—as Lodge 1904 (81) would, predictably defending comedy as '*speculum consuetudinis*' in his response to Gosson—thus refuse to see that such plays are in no way a 'profitable recreation' (88/B5ᵛ). Gosson reiterates the point in *Playes Confuted* (163–5/C8–D1ᵛ) to ridicule the argument that comedy is a '*Glasse of behauiour*' (163/C8).

closer' (77/A2), so the poet works his mischief. In *Playes Confuted* (1582), 'it is the iuglinge of the deuill, to turne himelfe sometimes to an Angel of light, to deceiue vs the sooner' (161/C5ᵛ), and any claims as to the corrective power of comedy are 'but the iugglinge of the deuill, who perceyuing his comedies begin to stinke, giueth vs a graine or two in the weight of the cause, to make vp his market' (170/D6ᵛ).

Whatever its form—whether dramatic, epic, or lyric—poetry thus proves capable of exploiting the human will to goodness and of working its way into the deepest recesses of the conscience so as to corrupt it the more entirely, affecting not only readers and playgoers for the worse but poets and playwrights themselves: sneaking up behind them unawares and, as Gosson knew from personal experience, making a mockery of their honest intentions to write morally uplifting works.[2] Poetry's ability to abuse men's wit is, as a result, all the more difficult to counter. Although Gosson makes great show in the *Schoole* of confronting the enemy head on—unfurling the 'Flagge of Defiance' (69/title page; 72/☞3ᵛ), 'ouerthrowing [the poets'] Bulwarkes' (69/title page), striking up the 'drumme' (72/☞3ᵛ), and firing a 'volley of prophane writers to beginne the skirmishe' (99/D1)—such military tactics are, for all their bravado, quite useless for tackling the problem in hand, which is essentially one of infiltration: of a secret, silent, deadly foe operating everywhere and invisibly from within. Gosson's images elsewhere give a much clearer assessment of the problem that he—along with all those who take it upon themselves to deal with the threat poetry poses—really faces. Poetry is a Trojan horse, and no city safe that 'strikes downe her Percollices [i.e. portcullises], rammes vp her gates' but 'suffereth the enimie to enter the posterne' (89/B6ᵛ).[3] 'In those thinges, that we least mistrust, the greatest daunger dooth often lurke', he warns: 'The Countryeman is more affrayde of the Serpente that is hid in the grasse, then the wilde beaste that openly feeds vpon the mountains . . . There is more perill . . . in secret ambushe, then maine battels; in vndermining, then playne assaulting' (94/C4–C4ᵛ).[4] There is no fighting such an enemy in open combat, no offensive strategy that will face him off. In the circumstances, the only remedy is complete avoidance: either the utter expulsion of all poetry and drama from the city, or, since it is never possible to know for certain whether the threat has been entirely eliminated, a still more desperate policy of internal withdrawal. As if dealing with a lethal virus or poison cloud, citizens are advised to stay indoors and to keep their windows—not to mention their ears, eyes, and mouths—tightly shut,

---

[2] Sidney's speaker acknowledges that the charge of abuse extends from comedy to lyric and epic: 'They say the Comedies rather teach than reprehend amorous conceits. They say the Lyric is larded with passionate sonnets, the Elegiac weeps the want of his mistress, and that even to the Heroical Cupid hath ambitiously climbed' (104.2–5).

[3] For images of poetry as a Trojan horse, see *Schoole* (77/A2ᵛ): 'if you looke well too *Epaeus* horse, you shall finde in his bowels the destruction of *Troy*'; and *Playes Confuted* (152/B5): 'we are so asotted with these delightes . . . that greedely we flocke together, and with our brainesicke assemblies not vnlyke to the Troyanes hale in the horse.'

[4] See also *Playes Confuted* (153/B5ᵛ–B6), where the Devil works like Pyrrhus to 'winne that with vndermininge, which open assalt could neuer get'.

until such time as the danger is, if not overthrown as originally hoped, then at least 'ouerblowen' (101/D3).[5]

It is all this—a sense of innocence lost, of a fatal yet irresistible seduction (suitably misogynized), of diabolical practice, of an enemy against whom the normal skills of the fighting man are all but redundant—that Sidney's speaker sets out to capture when he comes, in the *refutatio*, to address this, the third of the imputations against poetry:

> that it is the nurse of abuse, infecting us with many pestilent desires, with a siren's sweetness drawing the mind to the serpent's tale of sinful fancy—and herein, especially, comedies give the largest field to ear [plough] (as Chaucer saith); how both in other nations and in ours, before poets did soften us, we were full of courage, given to martial exercises, the pillars of manlike liberty, and not lulled asleep in shady idleness with poets' pastimes. (102.24–30)

Dense as it is, the summary of this charge is considerably more expansive than either of the other two—especially the noticeably laconic 'that it is the mother of lies' (102.23)—as if the speaker were registering that the 'argument of abuse' (98.3; 104.43; or 'arguments' as Ponsonby has the first of these) contains more than meets the eye and extends well beyond any merely hysterical tirade or vitriolic accusation. When he comes formally to refute the charge, moreover, he uses 'abuse'—a word that Gosson overwhelmingly deploys as a (predominantly plural) noun—as a transitive verb, thereby emphasizing poetry's active, interventionist operation. To say that poetry 'abuseth men's wit' (103.44) is not just to say that it is a bad influence or something generally undesirable but, specifically, that it *works* on people: it practises on them, corners them, collars them, acts decisively on its objects so as to despoil or denude them in some critical way.[6] It is to invest poetry with a singular degree of agency or power: to recognize it as a force to be reckoned with, albeit as a force for ill. The specific object that poetry abuses, furthermore, is men's 'wit': not the sensual appetites that are infected with pestilent desires anyway—the 'infected will' (86.8)—but, far more problematically, the 'erected wit' (86.7), the one precious, fragile, saving spark of goodness still surviving in the human soul.[7] The effect is to emphasize both the force poetry has in acting negatively on its objects, and, by extension, the force of the argument (or arguments) against it. Although the last of the 'imputations laid to the poor poets' (102.20–1), therefore, the charge of abuse is by no means the least—as Harington admits, this 'last reproofe [of] lightnes & wantonnes ... is indeed an Obiection of some importaunce'—and its refutation, as its summary formulation, will engage

---

[5] *Schoole* (101/D3): 'Let vs but shut vppe our eares to Poets, Pypers and Players ... and turne away our eyes from beholding of vanitie'; and compare Gosson's advice to the Gentlewomen citizens of London: 'Close vp your eyes, stoppe your eares, tye vp youre tongues' (118/F4ᵛ).

[6] See *Schoole* (82/A7ᵛ; 85/B3; and 96/C6, twice) for Gosson's few uses of the verbal form.

[7] See *Schoole* (77/A2): although 'Poets are the whetstones of wit ... that wit is dearly bought'; they 'cut off the rase [i.e. race] of toward wittes' (77/A2ᵛ), obstructing them and sending them astray; and are also said to draw 'the mind from vertue, and confoundeth wit' (79/A4ᵛ).

the speaker for longer, and take up considerably greater word-space, than either of the other two.[8]

Length alone, of course, is no indication of an argument's strength. In this case, indeed, the refutation is as weak as the accusation is strong, and not only for the reason that Gosson anticipates—the near impossibility, in practice, of differentiating between true-seeming and false—but also because of the circumstances peculiar to the authorship and composition of Sidney's text. Since the accusation cedes to poetry an extraordinary agency, the defender of poetry has two options by way of reply. Either he can argue that poetry's agency is not inimical to the commonwealth but, rather, supportive of it: that is to say, poetry is not abusive but useful, not a force for ill but a force for good. Or he can argue that poetry does not have agency at all but is, rather, acted upon (shameless writers being the rogue agents here): that is to say, poetry is not abusive but abused. In the course of the *Defence*, Sidney's speaker will present both these arguments. Since each entails a major diminution of poetry's power, however, it may well be that any practising poet worthy the name would take exception to them, or at least not commit to the compromises they demand without some demur. In which case, the fractures between the speaker and Sidney—indeed, the three-way split between Gosson, the speaker, and Sidney— that I have been tracing throughout this book will be just as much in evidence here: more so, in fact, since it is here that the 'alternative' model of poetry really bares its face. The situation might, therefore, be formulated as follows. The opening position is that of Gosson. He sees poetry as a real threat. He is like the censors and philistines who, as has been noted, recognize the destructive power of art and thus respect it—take it more seriously—than those who do not.[9] These are the people whom Sidney's speaker calls the '*mysomousoi*' or poet-haters (100.41), but who might more accurately be called the poet-*fearers*. For them, the beast is dangerous and for safety's sake must be shut out, kept well outside the city gates. This, therefore, is the position of those who would *banish* poetry. The second position is that of Sidney's speaker. He does not fear the power of poetry but sees it, rather, as something to be managed and trained. He insists that poetry is not the city's enemy but its friend. He would tame the beast: neuter it, muzzle it, bring it within the city walls, and put it to use as a service animal to maintain good order and discipline among the citizenry. This is the position of those whom Socrates calls the '*philopoieitai*' or poet-lovers: the champions of poetry he invites to challenge him and to make a case for the poets he has just argued should be expelled.[10] It is the position, therefore, of those who would *defend* poetry. The third position is the one I have been identifying with Sidney. Like Gosson, he too recognizes the destructive power of art, and he takes poetry very seriously indeed.

---

[8] Harington 1904 (209). The speaker's refutation of the charge that poetry abuses is nearly four times the length of the refutation that it lies, and nearly nineteen times the refutation that it is profitless.

[9] See Dollimore 2004 (xxiv, xxviii).

[10] 'And I'm sure we'd grant [poetry's] champions, not those who are actual poets [ποιητικοί], but lovers of poetry [φιλοποιηταί], the right to make a defense on her behalf in prose': see Plato 2013, *Republic*, 607d.

He respects the beast and riles at the prospect of domesticating it or reining it in with learned discretion, despising the kind of poetry that results and declining to have anything to do with it in his own creative work. For him, the so-called '*philopoieitai*' might more accurately be called the '*mysomousoi*', since they seem so willing to accept this drastic curtailing of poetry's power: this trivialization, this cutting down to size, this reduction of art to a merely municipal function. Indeed, to prove his point and put paid to any such diminution, he would either throw the city gates wide open and welcome the beast within or, if it is inside the city already, then free it from its harness and let it do its worst. This is the position of those whom Socrates explicitly does *not* invite to come to poetry's defence, but who might, for that reason, be called the real poet-lovers: the '*poieitikoi*' or actual poets themselves. It is the position, that is to say, of those would *write* poetry.

Seen in this way, the speaker looks weaker than ever, wedged as he is between two positions, one of which is able to deconstruct all his objections in advance, while the other would reject them out of hand, and both of which accord poetry a far greater agency—and so take it more seriously—than he does. He is effectively fighting a battle on two fronts, facing an external opponent in Gosson—a difficult enough challenge in itself—and an internal one in Sidney: it is this that really hampers his efforts and effectively scotches his defence. By admitting poetry into the city and trusting faithfully in its tractability—its ability to do good—the speaker's strategy (given the cautionary example of the Trojans) is a risky one to say the least, if not a hostage to fortune, a disaster waiting to happen. He is, in effect, defending what should be defended *against*: shielding a potential foe that, like some Spenserian monster, might break free at any moment and go on the rampage. The stronger that foe turns out to be—something Gosson and Sidney both have an interest in maintaining—the more certain the defences will be breached. This seeming friend, harboured at the heart of the argument, not only weakens the speaker's case, therefore, but also serves as a fitting emblem of the dissensions and splits between the different voices or positions within the *Defence*. If the charge of abuse is the strongest of the accusations against poetry, then its refutation is arguably the most riven, self-divided, and so self-defeating of the three.

ରଞ୍

The first thing to clear up, then, is that 'abuse' does not simply mean 'wantonness', as Sidney's speaker would try to suggest when he glosses the charge that poetry 'abuseth men's wit' as 'training it to wanton sinfulness and lustful love', adding, somewhat disingenuously, 'for indeed that is the principal, if not the only, abuse I can hear alleged' (103.44–104.2). In fact, wantonness stands as mere shorthand for an entire nexus of thought, although as such it can admittedly prove quite useful and serve the purposes of both the attackers and the defenders of poetry rather well. As a *strategic* reduction, it allows the former to sensationalize their argument by tapping reliably into their readers' sense of moral outrage, and the latter both to minimize the charge and to accuse the accusers of gross generalization and over-simplification. In both cases, however, 'abuse' means much more than the arousal of sexual desire, and how it does so—how it comes to stand in as proxy for a much

larger and more serious scenario of potential economic crisis and social collapse—
therefore warrants some consideration.

Insofar as literature *is* capable of impacting physically on the bodies and senses of
its recipients, Gosson details a whole psychology of enticement and incitement
whereby those poems and plays that touch on the subjects of love, sex, and desire
are variously said to tickle, prick, sting, ravish, or whet the appetites of those who
read and see them.[11] In *Playes Confuted* he gives a graphic example of 'What force
there is' (193/G4ᵛ) in plays to titillate their audiences by reporting the performance
of a love-scene between Bacchus and Ariadne at which the spectators were so
inflamed that the married 'posted home to their wiues' (193/G5) and the single
'vowed very solemly, to be wedded' (194/G5).[12] For the most part, however,
Gosson's concern with wantonness focuses less on the content of poems and
plays than on their occasion, above all on the theatre as a place of public assembly
where 'multitudes' are 'drawne in so narowe roome' (*Schoole*, 94/C4) and the sexes
permitted to mingle freely in a way that is simply asking for trouble: 'In our
assemblies at plays in *London*, you shall see suche heuing, and shoouing, suche
ytching and shouldring, too sitte by women . . . Such ticking, such toying, such
smiling, such winking, and such manning them home, when the sportes are ended,
that it is a right Comedie, to marke behauiour' (92/C1ᵛ).[13] In contemporary
London, as in Ovid's Rome, lovers resort to theatres to scout for talent, making
the playhouse little better than a brothel's vestibule: 'euery knaue and his queane,
are there first acquainted & cheapen [bargain for] the Merchandise in that place,
which they pay for elsewhere' (92/C2), either going 'home to theire houses on small
acquaintance, or slip[ping] into tauerns when yᵉ plaies are done' (*Playes Confuted*,
195/G6). As a result, the theatre would be better named a 'Market of Bawdrie'
(*Schoole*, 92/C2). What really exercises Gosson, however, is not so much the second
of these two terms (that he should condemn sexual immorality goes without saying)

---

[11] See *Schoole* (85/B3): musical consorts in theatres 'rather effeminate the minde, as pricks vnto
vice'; 'Poets in Theaters . . . set they abroche straunge consortes of melody, to tickle the eare; costly
apparel, to flatter the sight; effeminate gesture, to rauish the sence; and wanton speache, to whet desire
too inordinate lust' (89/B6ᵛ); and *Playes Confuted* (172/D8ᵛ): 'the sweete numbers of *Poetrie* flowing in
verse, do wonderfully tickle the hearers eares'; their use of rhyme 'carrieth a stinge into the eares of the
common people' (181/F1); 'sense is tickled, desire pricked, & those impressions of mind are secretly
conueyed ouer to yᵉ gazers' (192–3/G4).

[12] Gosson's example is drawn from Xenophon 2013, *Symposium*, 9.5–6, although it is used there to
illustrate lifelike acting rather than salaciousness: 'The onlookers saw a Dionysus truly handsome, an
Ariadne truly fair, not presenting a burlesque but offering genuine kisses with their lips; and all watched
with heightened excitement . . . [the audience] would have jointly sworn that the boy and the girl were
surely in love with each other. Theirs was the appearance not of performers who had been taught their
moves but of people now permitted to satisfy their long-cherished desires.'

[13] On theatres as especially dangerous for female honour, see *Schoole* (86/B3): '*Ouid* the high
martial of *Venus* fielde planteth his maine battell in publique assemblies, sendeth his scoutes too
Theaters to descry the enimie'; 'the abuse of such places was so great' that any 'gentlewomen that
tender their name & honor' were forbidden 'to come to Theaters' (86, 87/B4); simply to attend the
theatre is 'too bee assaulted' (89/B6ᵛ); and, addressing the Gentlewomen Citizens of London, 'Looking
eyes, haue lyking hartes, liking harts may burne in lust . . . If you doe but . . . ioyne lookes with an
amorous Gazer, you haue already made your selues assaultable, & yelded your Cities to be sacked'
(116/F2–F2ᵛ).

but the first: the fact that, by such means, prostitutes, their pimps, and their customers, create a deviant economy: a kind of black market in which people who neither work hard for a living nor produce anything of substance to sell nonetheless end up making a great deal of money.[14] For Gosson, such behaviour both jeopardizes the proper functioning of the market and puts the social order at risk:[15]

> Euery Vawter in one blinde Tauerne or other, is Tenant at will, to which shee tolleth resorte, and playes the stale to vtter their victualls, and helpe them to emptie their mustie caskes. There is she so intreated with wordes, and receiued with curtesie, that euery back roome in the house is at her commaundement. (*Schoole*, 92–3/C2–C2ᵛ)

Unpacked, Gosson's dense prose here describes a scene of purposeful deception if not organized crime in which landlords and prostitutes collude to the benefit—and upward mobility—of each other, but very much at the expense of all those whose faith in the market rests on fair transactions and honest trades.[16] Such is the sharp practice or 'Ledgerdemayne' of those who 'haue neither land to maintaine them, nor good occupation to get their breade, desirous to strowt it with the beste, yet disdayning too liue by the sweate of their browes' (93/C2ᵛ). And yet—Gosson's sense of outrage rising here—such people 'drink of the best, they sit rente free, they haue their owne Table spreade to their handes, without wearing the strings of their pursse, or any thing else, but housholde and honestie' (93/C2ᵛ–C3).

This kind of malpractice may seem to have little directly to do with poetry, but it is consonant with another of Gosson's repeated alarms: the fact that 'We haue infinite Poets, and Pipers... that liue by merrie begging... and priuily encroch vppon euerie mans purse' (84/B1), not to mention players who rob and spoil the people of 'all their Treasure' (98/C8) and 'emptie their purses for thriuing to[o] fast' (98/C8ᵛ); who 'ransacke our purses by permission' and 'rifle vs openly' (*Apologie*, 130/L8). In all cases, the point Gosson is making is the same: namely,

---

[14] See also 'An Apologie' (125/L3), where Gosson again rails against prostitution (here in the context of representations of the gods in classical poetry): '*Venus* a notorious strumpet... taught the women in *Cyprus* to set vp a Stewes, too hyre out them selues as hackneies, for gaine'; likewise, '*Flora* [was] a curtezan that got infinite summes of money by sinne' (127/L4ᵛ).

[15] In *Playes Confuted* (194/G5ᵛ), Gosson reiterates the charge that theatres are 'markets of bawdry', glossing the phrase as 'where choise wᵗout shame hath bene as free, as it is for your money in the royall exchaung, to take a short stocke, or a longe, a falling band, or a french ruffe', i.e. where money is not invested for profit but rather spent carelessly and on mere trifles such as the latest articles of fashion (a 'falling band' was a collar worn flat round the neck and fashionable at the turn of the seventeenth century). Discussing Gosson's comment, Bruster 1992 (6) suggests that Gosson 'drew strong connections between the theater and the market, in one place characterizing the Royal Exchange as an institution where transactions similar to those taking place in the theater could be found... Gosson's emphasis on "choice w[i]thout shame" stresses the commodity function of the Renaissance theater, a place where money can buy the fantasy of one's choosing'. Hawkes 2001 (80–1) and 2015 (75–6) makes a similar point. What Gosson is criticizing here, however, is not the theatre as a commercial venture but the theatre as an illicit market for the trade of sex.

[16] A 'Vawter' is one who vaults or leaps, here used figuratively to suggest a sense of social mobility. A 'Tenant at will' is a tenant who holds at the will or pleasure of the lessor, i.e. does not pay rent. That she 'tolleth resorte' means that she brings in customers, as does the phrase 'playes the stale'. To 'vtter' victuals means to put them up for sale or barter in the market.

that good money is being turned over for something that has no substance or value, and this is as true for the compositions the poet writes as it is for the dramas the player performs, the music the piper plays, or the services the prostitute provides. In the 'Apologie of the *Schoole of Abuse*', for example, he reports an anecdote in which Dionysius of Syracuse offered a harper a talent for his labour but, when the musician presented himself the next day to receive his payment, told him he had already received it: 'For, said hee, thou diddest but tickle mine eares with an emptie sounde, and I did the like againe to thee, promising that which I meane not to giue, delighting thee as much with hope of my coyne, as my selfe was pleased with the sounde of thy instrument' (128/L6).[17] Nothing will come of nothing. In another example, this time describing those less canny than the Syracusan despot, Gosson notes that 'wee whiche carrie our money too Players too feede theyr pride, may be wel compared to the Bath keepers Asse which bringeth him woode too make his fire, and contenteth himself with the smell of the smoke' (132/M1ᵛ).[18] They might just as well put their money straight on the fire. That idle folk and racketeers, the purveyors of such airy nothings, should profit—and profit handsomely—from these false transactions is an outrage that calls for divine retribution: 'the litle thrift that followeth theire great gaine, is a manifest token that God hath cursed it' (*Playes Confuted*, 196/G7ᵛ). The real scandal, therefore—what lies behind the charge that money is being squandered and the good citizens of London conned—is that poetry is essentially empty. It does not *contain* anything, and it can have, therefore, no intrinsic value or worth: it lacks the weight, heft, or content that would justify its sale and consumption, let alone production. Poetry is nothing but smoke and mirrors. Like music, it is but an empty sound that floats away on the air leaving nothing behind but an empty purse and a sense that the talent might have been better spent. Like an assignation at the whorehouse, it is enjoyed no sooner but despised straight, leaving nothing behind but an expense of spirit in a waste of shame. For Gosson, poetry is pure surface, the more deceptive for its attractive exterior and above all for its false offer of value within: its empty promises to yield the investor some kind of capital (intellectual, moral, and spiritual). Behind the charge of wantonness, therefore, lies the old argument that poetry is vain:

> open the sepulchre of *Semyramis*, whose Title promiseth suche wealth to the Kinges of *Persia*, you shall see nothing but deade bones: Rippe vp the golden Ball, that *Nero* consecrated to *Iupiter Capitollinus*, you shall haue it stuffed with the shauinges of his

[17] Gosson takes the anecdote from Plutarch 2004, *Moralia*, 'On the Fortune or the Virtue of Alexander', 334A, although in the original context Dionysius serves as a negative example with which to contrast Alexander's generous patronage of the arts.

[18] On this occasion, the example appears to be Gosson's own. Gosson's worst fears would be confirmed by the reading Derrida 1992 (102) gives of Baudelaire's short story, *La fausse monnaie*: namely, that in beginning outside a tobacconist's shop it marks 'that absolute dissemination that destines the text to depart in ashes or go up in smoke', thus defying bourgeois demands that literature deliver some solid, profitable return. See also Fisher 1999 (7) on the smoking of tobacco—a luxury new to the sixteenth century—as an 'expense that provides absolutely no material return: it was, quite literally, money going up in smoke': a behaviour equivalent, in its defiance of productivity, to sodomy or the counterfeiting of coins.

Beard: pul off the visard that Poets maske in, you shall disclose their reproch, bewray their vanitie, loth their wantonnesse, lament their follie. (*Schoole*, 77/A2ᵛ)

It is to counter such fraud that Gosson opposes his own writing as bona fide. Unlike the wispy imaginative literature that he condemns, his propositional prose has something concrete to offer, a heavy-duty lesson to impart. 'The title of my book doth promise much', he writes in the prefatory letter to Sidney, and although 'the volume you see is very little' (72/☞3ᵛ) it nonetheless contains, in the author's estimation, material of great worth. There follows a list of physically small things that nevertheless contain substance and value within them—as 'Little Chestes may holde greate Treasure' (72/☞4), for example—or within which value might be said to inhere, as in the representation of value—'a fewe Cyphers contayne the substance of a rich Merchant' (73/☞4)—or, which amounts to the same thing, the money form: 'a Kings picture in a pennie' (72/☞4).[19] What makes these particular metaphors so interesting is the way they clarify the thoroughly metaphysical model on which Gosson is operating. That is to say, he is clearly working on the assumption that, properly speaking, something substantive, real, ideal, and true lies behind the superficial appearance of things, just as abstract value exists behind individual instantiations, or true meaning behind fallen words. This belief in 'presence', the baseline, of course, of idealist philosophy, manifests in other familiar metaphors—such as the naked truth clothed with words, the kernel within the shell, or the medicine inside the sugared pill (as properly administered)—which similarly insist that something healthful, precious, good, and true exists 'beyond', 'beneath', 'inside', or 'within'. As Russell Fraser puts it, the attack on poetry mounted by Gosson and others in the period represented a new 'impulse to essentiality'—an urgent desire to apprehend '*Nuda veritas*', the truth behind appearances—the other side of which was a growing impatience with and intolerance of superfices, and in particular with the shadowy second- or third-order representations created by poets.[20] For Gosson, as for Plato, 'the artist, who venerates the surface, is driven from the commonwealth' (39–40) for, as state formations the world over (and not only dictatorships) have long recognized, a fundamental incompatibility exists between ideology and creative art, especially

---

[19] Gosson reiterates the point in the letters that preface *The Ephemerides of Phialo* (1579) to which 'An Apologie' is appended. Addressing Sidney first, he modestly hopes that even if the 'value' of the *Schoole* fails to answer Sidney's expectation, the latter will nonetheless accept that he has done his best: 'little children, that drawe but a hazel sticke, thinke they performe as much as he, that shootes . . . a bowe of steele' (244/F3ᵛ). In the Letter to the Reader, he insists that his product has value and that, in a market that otherwise caters indiscriminately for all—'infinite wares in one fayre, where the Souldier approcheth to cheapen [i.e. trade] a Swoorde, the wanton inquireth for a glasse'—he remains a purveyor of quality goods: 'my desire is, to seeke out meate for manly stomackes' (250–1/☞–☞ᵛ). He also explains that he has resisted advice to 'encrease my volume' on the grounds that, although 'the Countrieman casteth his seede very thin, [he] yet findeth his barnes to be filled by them' (251/☞). His antipoetic tracts are all the more precious and substance-rich, that is, for being small. In the Letter to the Mayor of London that appends the *Schoole*, Gosson signs off 'least I seeme one of those idle Mates, which hauing nothing to buy at home, and lesse too sell in the market abrode, stand at a boothe, if it be but to gase' (114/E8ᵛ), but the value and quality of his wares is what stands as their own justification, and his confidence that he has demonstrated this is what underwrites his modesty topos.

[20] Fraser 1970 (37).

the kind of art that makes (*poieīn*) representations, because what the latter whispers is that—no matter how abstracted, rarefied, mystified, elevated, exalted, deified, or declared un-representable such ideals may be—they are, in the end, but representations like any other, fashioned by human hands. It is not only that poetry *is* essentially empty, that is to say, but that—consonant with its proactive capabilities—poetry has the power *to* empty: to hint that the pre-existent ideals and values that form the metaphysical basis of cosmological and social order might, at bottom, be man-made. Such an emptying or hollowing out—such a potential undermining of the belief in presence—spells, for Gosson, the end of civilization as we know it and is therefore to be prevented at all costs: it cannot be allowed to happen. This, and not mere wantonness, is what he means by 'abuse', his anxiety sharpened by the developing cult of the useful—of that which is fruitful, beneficial, and profitable to society at large—that was, for Fraser, becoming the new mantra in the sixteenth century. For the critic, 'utility, very amply construed, is the master motive informing the judgment of poetry and the theatre', and a 'new psychology' developing that was 'utilitarian', although not in the 'narrow sense of self-aggrandizement' (5). What was crucial, rather, was 'the impulse to refine or to rationalize: to come to the kernel . . . an apprehending of the plenary truth' (5–6): a process he identifies with the rise of mercantile values, and characterizes in terms of a class war between the industrious, pragmatic, and purposive 'new men' and what they perceived to be the effete, superficial, and wasteful productions of the privileged. This is the 'economic motive' (54), broadly conceived, that in his view, prompted the outpouring of antipoetic sentiment in the period.[21]

To put presence back where it seems to be absent, or to protect it where it seems to be threatened—both of which Gosson aims to do—is, therefore, not only a corrective but a profoundly salvific act. As an image of such happy restitution, one might return for a moment to his image of the full chest—'Little Chestes may holde greate Treasure'—for this metaphor represents not only Gosson's own value-bearing book but also the ideal state that his book systematically sets up in contrast to the sorry state of things he otherwise sees everywhere around him: namely, the 'reformed' (79/A4), 'perfect' (79/A4ᵛ), and 'well gouerned' (83/A8ᵛ) commonwealth that he, like Plato, is seeking to restore. Elizabeth, for example, is described as 'filling her chests with the fruites of peace' (96/C5ᵛ), and while such praise could no doubt be described as tactical on Gosson's part, it nonetheless clearly aligns the commonwealth the Queen would, in an ideal world, rule—'ministring iustice by order of law, reforming abuses with great regarde' (96/C5ᵛ)—with Plato's ideal Republic, also characterized by having 'good laws established . . . and all maner of abuses thoroughly purged' (79/A4ᵛ).[22] At the same time, the image of the full chest

---

[21] With respect to Gosson, for example, Fraser 1970 (72) notes the unusually large print run of the *Schoole of Abuse*, commenting that it is 'not religious fervour . . . that inspires the publishers to undertake this extraordinary issue' but rather a collective interest, on the part of the authorities and citizens of London, in legitimizing and justifying this economic motive. Lodge's reply to Gosson, by contrast, was denied a licence, printed privately, and immediately withdrawn.

[22] As Gosson's letter to the Mayor of London in the *Schoole of Abuse* makes clear, he is concerned not only with the commonwealth as a general category but specifically with the city: the maintenance

here has a domestic—almost a homely—feel to it, putting Elizabeth on a par with the good gentlewomen citizens of London who also keep 'peace in your houses, and plentie in your Coafers' (117/F3ᵛ), as if her good governance were basically a scaled up version of their good housekeeping and maternal plenitude. Iconic—indeed, almost folkloric in its simplicity—this image of the full chest could, then, be said to represent at the most basic and crudely apprehended of levels the idea of 'fullness' that lies at the heart of far more esoteric philosophical deliberations about presence. The job of the good housewife is to keep that chest full, replete.[23] To feed the family, she needs to maintain supplies: to conserve them, to replenish them through those cyclical processes of production and reproduction that ensure a steady turnover and so maintain whatever minimum is necessary to keep everyone alive and ensure continuity down the generations. The contentment to which this scenario gives rise derives, etymologically, from the fact that the chest *contains* something—has contents—just as satisfaction derives from the sense of having enough. The good housewife may also, of course, seek to increase those supplies: to boost growth, expand her operations, and bring in more, so as to fill the chest to overflowing, evoking scenes of plenty and increasing contentment or satisfaction to higher levels of wealth and well-being. Behind the larger-scale models of the ideal city or commonwealth, that is, we might discern the bases of early Greek *oikonomia*: the business, in the first instance, of the *oikos* rather than the *polis*, concerned primarily with the biological and agricultural rather than the strictly 'economic' in the modern sense, and involving the world of the household, the small business, and the family farm with their small-scale but exemplary models of good stewardship, husbandry, and thrift.[24] As such, the reassuring image of the full chest might be seen to lie—as if at a foundational level—not only below images of the ideal city

of civic order and sweeping away of the abuses he saw as rampant in contemporary London. 'If your Honour desire too see the Citie well gouerned, you must . . . sette to your hand to thrust out abuses' (114/E8ᵛ). To emphasize Elizabeth's success in keeping her chests metaphorically full, Gosson adverts to the 'prosperity' (105/D7ᵛ) of the time and 'these golden dayes' (106/E1), although he does so, admittedly, in the context of warning citizens not to be complacent. The good housewives of London are similarly credited with having created 'ease and prosperitie' (117/F3ᵛ), while also being reminded not to take their blessings for granted.

[23] As is that of the householder. Gosson includes several examples of the model householder, including a small number of players who bucked the trend and were 'sober, discreete, properly learned honest housholders and Citizens well thought on amonge their neighbours at home' (96/C6–C6ᵛ). See also the legendary figure of Miso who was found 'well gouerning his house, looking to his grounde, instructing his children, teaching his family, making of marriages among his acquayntance' (108/E3), and judged to be the wisest of men: '*Miso* can reade you such a lecture of Philosophie, as *Aristotle* neuer dreamed on' (109/E3). In *Playes Confuted* (162/C6ᵛ) Gosson notes a Persian law 'that yong men should euer after be taught simply as housholders vse to instruct their families'. In focusing on the housewife here, that is, I am not suggesting that a woman's place is in the home.

[24] On the model of stewardship, see Gosson's praise for those who serve the commonwealth through hard work: 'so shall you please God, profite your country, honor your prince, discharge your duetie, giue vp a good account of your stewardship, and leaue no sinne vntouched, no abuse vnrebuked, no fault vnpunished', *Schoole* (109/E3ᵛ). He also praises the Mayor and magistrates of London as 'the very Stewards of her Maiestie within your liberties' (112/E6–E6ᵛ). See Singer 1958 on the etymology and semantic development of the word *oikonomia* in ancient Greece and beyond; and Finkelstein 2006 (70–5) on its ready application to sixteenth-century understandings of economic activity.

or state but beyond these to still more abstract metaphysical speculations about the Ideas: about the need to ensure that the truth, meaning, or God is trustably, reliably there, and that there is always something good existing 'inside' or 'within'.

Where this is in place all else follows. Only where there is meaning in words and value in things do exchanges—verbal and commercial—become possible. The conceptualizations of idealist philosophy thus form the essential bedrock of an ordered society in which everything works: both in the sense that the normal transactions of everyday life can function because everyone knows and trusts that something of substance and value is being exchanged; and in the sense that its many members, each with different functions as 'the eye to see, the eare to heare, the nose to smell, the tongue to taste', and so forth, all labour together for the sake of the 'whole body of the common wealth' (107/E1ᵛ). Glimpses of such a functional society appear in Gosson's images of thrift and husbandry as it should be and at its best: people occupied, busy, and industrious, and a market regulated against fraud.[25] The only time Gosson demotes the arts of 'thrift and husbandry' (104/D6ᵛ) is when he compares them to the more glorious arts of war, for house-holders and farmers pale into insignificance beside soldiers (according to Homer, the sons of Jupiter, images of God, shepherds of the people, and so on): 'When the *Aegyptians* were most busy in their husbandry, the *Scythians* ouerran them: when the *Assyrians* were looking to their thrift, the *Persians* were in armes & ouercam them' (105/D7ᵛ). The point, however, is not to belittle thrift and husbandry but to emphasize the crucial role military force plays in protecting it. In preserving the commonwealth, ensuring its survival and continuity, even expanding and growing it through conquest and empire, the soldier performs a similar function to the housewife, even though he gets more glory for it. He saves the city and state from destruction so that she can save money and supplies—he keeps the savings safe—a good example of the way in which the different members of the collective ideally work together to 'saue that, which must be the suretie of vs all' (107/E1ᵛ).

For Gosson, the creative and recreative arts threaten all of this. Especially poetry, for—with its creations, its fictions, its representations of false and made-up things—poetry threatens to evacuate the Ideas and to void the God-given truths that supposedly lie beyond any such man-made constructions and thus to violate the whole metaphysical surety of the 'fullness' on which so much depends. Poetry's making reveals the made-ness of what is taken as given and thereby risks unmaking it. Poetry threatens not only to deprive people of whatever they may have paid at the bookseller's stall or the theatre door—in context, a relatively trivial loss and one easily enough written off—but, much more seriously, to unsettle their faith in

---

[25] As the 'Clarke of the market' who 'come[s] to our stall, and reprooue[s] our ballance when they are faultie, or forfaite[s] our weights, when they are false' (110/E4ᵛ). For images of the properly functioning body of the commonwealth, see also *Playes Confuted* (195/G6ᵛ): 'A common weale is likened to the body . . . if any part be idle . . . the damage redoundeth to the whole'; 'if priuat men be suffered to forsake theire calling because they desire to walke gentlemanlike in sattine & veluet . . . proportion is so broken, vnitie dissolued, harmony confounded, yᵗ the whole body must be dismembred' (196/G7). See also the 'perfecte harmony' of such an ideally ordered society, *Schoole* (83/A8ᵛ). On the 'organic analogy', see Finkelstein 2006 (137–66).

presence, their trust that meaning and value inhere within words and things, and, at the far end, to undermine their belief in the entire order that derives from this reassurance: a positively existential loss.[26] Insinuating that ideals are neither necessarily ideal nor values intrinsically valuable but both only nominally so, poetry has the power not only to disillusion the individual—to stretch his or her credulity— but to bring the entire social edifice down. This is the real reason why poetry is so feared, the root cause from which all the other related 'abuse' charges—that it demeans the gods, threatens the social fabric, fosters sexual immorality, debilitates the fighting man, and so forth—follow as secondary effects.[27] Poetry lifts the curtain not on metaphysical certainties but on a *horror vacui* that, for the ideologues, is not to be borne. The housewife and the soldier might seek increase—to enlarge the holdings of the household or the state—but at the very least they must preserve what they already have, even if only at the most basic level necessary for survival, replenishing supplies and safeguarding them from depredation or attack. They might make more or they might make the same but the one thing they must not do is make less. They cannot *deplete* the chest, so to speak: put it at risk, see its supplies emptied out, exhausted, consumed, poured away, or run dry with no hope of recovery or replacement. To do that is to conjure nightmare scenarios not only of dearth but of whole generations stopped in their tracks, of termination, annihilation, extinction: 'There was neuer fort so stro*n*g, but it might be battered, neuer grou*n*d so fruitful, but it might be barre*n*: neuer cou*n*trie so populous, but it might be wast' (106/E1). It is to submit the life-instincts—the business and busyness of staying alive—to the absolute nullity of the death drive. That, however, is effectively what poetry does. It threatens to worm its way into people's most basic understanding of how the world works and to destroy their confidence in the system from the inside: whence Gosson's image, no less sinister for being homely, of poets as 'Caterpillers of a Com*m*onwelth' (69/title page), quietly but devastatingly eating it up from within.[28] One reason why poetry might be said to 'abuse',

[26] It might be apposite here to differentiate my position from that of Hawkes 2001 (81) whose thesis is ostensibly similar to mine insofar as he traces a genealogy of the 'concept of "abuse"' to show how it came to describe 'the psychological consequences of large-scale commodity exchange'. Hawkes focuses on the theatre as a commercial venture. In charging admission, the theatre was 'designed with the primary end of making money' (86), but since (according to Aristotle and Augustine) this was not the proper *telos* of art—which should be the pursuit of virtue—stage-plays thus constituted bad art or the 'abuse' of art. For Hawkes, an antitheatricalist like Gosson thus fears that commerce threatens ('abuses') art. For me, by contrast, Gosson fears that art threatens ('abuses') the commercial world of ordinary, everyday life. Hawkes harks back to a model of *oikonomia* he regards as all but lost in the sixteenth century, while I am suggesting that for Gosson it is just this model of *oikonomia* that poetry puts at risk. In Hawkes 2010 (9–12, 49, 90, 167), the critic again appeals to essentialist and logocentric positions in order to critique capitalism, strangely viewing the deconstructive method as being complicit with the latter instead of a radical attempt to think and theorize outside it. See Correll 2003 (53) for a corrective to this 'tacitly antipolitical historicism'.
[27] In the *Republic* it is clear that—although the charges that poetry demeans the gods (II.377e–383c) and induces drunkenness, effeminacy, and idleness through its seductive use of metre (III.398e) appear earlier in the discussion—they are in fact subordinate to the main philosophical charge, which is that poetry is at two or more removes from the truth (X.595a–604c).
[28] See also: 'Such are the abuses [of players] that I reade of in *Rome*: such are the Caterpillers that haue deuoured and blasted the fruite of *Aegypt*' (90/B8). Compare Agrippa 1569 (E1ᵛ), who describes

then, is that it is seen to *use things up*—to squander them, to waste them (all senses present in the etymon of the word, both verb and noun)—emptying the chest and leaving nothing, or less than nothing, behind.[29] Poetry does not 'use' things properly—moderately, carefully, sustainably—so as to conserve them, grow them, and ensure they are there for future use. It could be said, rather, to use them excessively, repeatedly, habitually, until they are all eaten up, consumed, worn out—deteriorated, damaged, destroyed through over-use (again, all senses that are present in the word and its etymons, both verb and noun).[30]

When one approaches the charge of abuse by going back to its originating cause, then, it becomes easier to understand why 'wantonness' should be one of its effects. Poems and plays still remain capable of arousing sexual desire, of course, and can continue to be condemned for doing so, but where the real anxiety is that they are empty trades—that, in taking something for nothing, they empty out the metaphorical 'chest' and so undermine the very foundations on which society rests—it makes sense that this should be figured as the model of thrift and husbandry under threat. It is logical that such a fear should be represented in terms of a disruption to the productive and reproductive roles that, under normal circumstances, ensure the survival and continuity of the family and household. Good husbandry covers the cultivation of the soil and the rearing of livestock so as to ensure the food supply and make provision for the future, as well as the legitimate making of new human beings and orderly transfer of property and goods down the generations.[31] 'Wantonness', by contrast—certainly as it is envisaged by Gosson, with its casual sexual encounters and undermining of marriage—profoundly threatens this. The prostitutes and their pimps might live it up on their ill-gotten gains 'without wearing the strings of their pursse' (93/C2ᵛ) or spending a penny of their own money, but the one thing they *do* wear out is 'housholde and honestie' (93/C2ᵛ–C3): that is, the picture of how things ought to be, the guarantee of fair trade and proper exchange that is necessary for society to function. Poetry and plays, idle and

poetry as 'An Arte that is alwaies hungrie, and eatinge vp other mens breade like mise'. In 'An Apologie' (130/L8) Gosson likens players to 'a consuming fier ... nourished stil with our decay'; and in *Playes Confuted* (174/E2) he compares plays to 'Ratsbane'. In the *Schoole* (102/D4) he describes bowling alleys as 'priuy Mothes, that eate vppe the credite of many idle Citizens'.

[29] See *OED* abuse *v.*, from classical Latin *abusus*, past participle of *abuti* 'to use up, to squander, waste, to make full use of, utilize, to take advantage of, exploit, to put to wrong use, to misinterpret, to misuse (language)'; and abuse *n.* from classical Latin *abusus*: 'misuse, wasting'.

[30] See *OED* use *n.* I.1.b, 'the action of consuming something' (current from the late fourteenth century), from Anglo-Norman, Old and Middle French *us* connoting 'wear and tear' (thirteenth century); use *v.* II.12: 'to consume, expend (a commodity, a resource, etc.) ... to exhaust, wear out' (current from the late fourteenth century), from Anglo-Norman, Old and Middle French *user*, which includes the senses 'to deteriorate, wear out, to eat, consume (food)' (twelfth century), 'to wear (something) out, damage (something) through use' (thirteenth century); and use *n.*, from Anglo-Norman, Old and Middle French *us*, which includes the sense 'wear and tear' (thirteenth century). As we shall see, not the least of the difficulties Sidney's speaker has in refuting the charge of abuse is the fact that its opposing term contains these negative meanings within it.

[31] See *OED* husband *n.*, originally the male head of a household (from the early eleventh century) and derived from Old Norse *bóndi*, a peasant owning his own house and land, freeholder, franklin, yeoman. In English the word came to denote a cultivator, farmer, or tiller of the soil (from the early thirteenth century), and a man joined to a woman by marriage (from the late thirteenth century).

unproductive as they are, similarly turn the whole notion of thrift and husbandry on its head: they make 'more trewandes, and ill husbands, then if open Schooles of vnthrifts & Vagabounds were kept' (99/C8ᵛ).[32] The charge of effeminacy, moreover, might also be said to stand as an effect of the larger cause—the anxiety that the *oikos* and the *polis* are at risk—for, as a school of abuse, poetry contrasts with the ideal kind of school that should properly teach military discipline.[33] Gosson's favourite example of this is the education received by the Roman general, Gaius Marius (157–86 BC), who was 'taught' to lie on the ground, suffer all weathers, lead men, strike foes, and so on, who 'neuer learned the Greeke tongue' nor 'ment to be instructed in it', who did not look for 'learning beyond the fielde', and who was suspicious of 'the abuses of those Schooles, where Poets were euer the head Maisters' (80/A5ᵛ).[34] Such, says Gosson, used to be 'the olde discipline of Englande' also, but 'howe woonderfully wee haue beene chaunged, since wee were schooled with these abuses' (90/B8): the former strength, endurance, and physical exercise of Englishmen now being given over to 'banqueting, playing, pipyng, and dauncing, and all suche delightes as may win vs to pleasure, or rocke vs a sleepe' (91/B8ᵛ), transforming them into the foppish 'Gallantes' (105/D7) of the present day. The precise mechanism by which poetry is capable of enervating the fighting man in this way is left rather generalized and vague (akin, presumably, to the ways in which poetry can arouse sexual desire), but two clear ideas stand out. First, that, in the form of manpower, some vital energy or force—a resource essential to the flourishing and well-being of the commonwealth—is somehow being emptied out, drained away, or siphoned off without being replenished, to the danger and detriment of all. And second that the roles traditionally played by men in the (sexual) reproduction and the (military) protection and expansion of the commonwealth are somehow being imperilled, halted, and diverted from their proper course: the image of the effeminate soldier neatly combining these various threats.

Taking on board the full extent of the charge of abuse, therefore—appreciating what is really at stake and understanding that, when Sidney's speaker paraphrases it

---

[32] See also Gosson's (unintentionally comic?) suggestion in 'An Apologie' (125/L3ᵛ) that the gods as represented in classical poetry should be made to conform to models of thrift and husbandry: 'What stuffe is this? wantons in heauen? & a double diuinitie of he gods, & she gods? If it be so, I hope they will graunt me, that in that place nothing ought to bee vayne; if nothing be vaine, they must liue together by couples like man and wife... If they liue together in lawfull marriage, giue them houses... if they haue houses, let them haue landes... & if they haue lande, either lette it bee fruitfull of it selfe, or giue them whippes in their handes, and sende them like swaynes to plough and carte.'

[33] Model schools are held up in contrast to schools of abuse throughout Gosson's text: see the academy or 'Schoole' (77/A3) from which Plato banished poets; the fabled 'Schooles of Poetrie in *Scythia*' that were said to be 'without vice' (79/A4ᵛ); the preachers who teach virtue, 'if people will bee instructed' (88/B5ᵛ) and when 'we shoulde haue an instructer at our elbowes to feede the soule' (89/B6); and the ancient 'Schooles of Defence' (102/D4ᵛ) in which the arts of swordsmanship were taught. Such schools are clearly ideal because they are ideological, i.e. support the order and values of the status quo.

[34] Marius is invoked for the same reason in *Playes Confuted* (173–4/E1ᵛ–E2). Marius' military successes were largely the result of his reorganization of the Roman army. By reforming it from a patrician to a professional force, he solved the long-standing problem of insufficient manpower and thus laid the foundations for Rome's future success as an imperial power.

as 'wanton sinfulness and lustful love', he is making a highly summary (if tactical) formulation of a much larger argument—will make more sense of his defence of poetry and the measure (or otherwise) of its success. As noted earlier, in refuting this charge, the speaker employs two key strategies: denial and reversal. This two-pronged defence does not strengthen his cause, of course, since (typical of such kettle-logic) it raises the question of how poetry can be useful if it is abused, effectively leaving the speaker with the argument that poetry is useful only on those rare occasions when it is not abused: a vanishingly narrow window, as it turns out.[35] As might be expected, moreover, such contradictions exist not only between these two positions but also within them. Although they are intertwined throughout the *Defence*, therefore, I shall for the purposes of the argument separate them out and consider them individually and in turn. Section II thus considers the various ways in which the speaker sets out to deny the charge of abuse by mounting the case that poetry is, conversely, useful. His claim to that effect falls into three parts—that poetry is fruitful, that poetry is delightful, and that poetry is forceful—and section II is, therefore, organized accordingly.

[35] I owe the inspired phrase 'kettle-logic' to Matz 2000 (13), who uses it in relation to George Puttenham.

II

Poetry Is Useful

In countering the accusation that poetry abuses, the speaker's first line of argument is to deny the charge and to insist that poetry is useful, much as Harington would 'shew you what good vse there is of Poetrie' and the 'many good vses to be had of it'.[36] Having established that 'abuse' denotes a threat to the *oikonomia*, it becomes clearer that, if he is to demonstrate poetry's usefulness, Sidney's speaker has to show that poetry is not empty but full, and above all that it *does* not empty but, rather, actively fills: that, far from depleting the collective treasure-chest (literal and metaphorical), poetry on the contrary produces and provides. Looking again at his dense summary of the charge in the *refutatio*, we can make out—behind his characterizations of poetry as a 'nurse of abuse' (102.24) who infects her charges, and of comedy as giving poetry's accusers 'the largest field to ear' (102.26)—a converse scenario in which nurses and mothers provide, and farmers produce (plough, sow, and reap) food that is, as it should be, nourishing and sustaining. This scenario of model housekeeping and good husbandry is a prerequisite for survival, the health and wellness of individual and state being measured by their physical and spiritual hardiness and resistance to infection, sin, and doubt. As an ideal, moreover, it is not restricted to the *refutatio* but appears throughout the *Defence*, and from very early on: at the opening of the *narratio*, for example, where poetry is the 'first nurse, whose milk by little and little enabled [men] to feed afterwards of tougher knowledges' (82.8–10).[37] In this respect, the speaker's strategy of denial repeats that of Elyot, who, in his own defence of poets, similarly refutes the charge that poetry contains 'nothynge but baudry' or 'nothyng . . . but incitation to lechery' by asserting its profitability and fruitfulness.[38] There is much overlap, that is to say, between the denial that poetry abuses and the denial that poetry is profitless—the claim that, contrary to the charge that there are 'many other more fruitful knowledges' (102.22), there is in fact no 'more fruitful know-ledge' (102.41) than poetry—making it unnecessary to go over old ground. It may be worth pointing out, however, that the baseline notion of poetry as something that fills (nourishes, feeds)—and that thereby models the very system of economic production that its accusers claimed it threatened to destroy—makes the apparently dead metaphor of its 'fruitfulness' not, perhaps, so dead after all.

---

[36] Harington 1904 (196, 197).

[37] See also: poetry is 'the sweet food of sweetly uttered knowledge' (86.39–40); 'food for the tenderest stomachs' (92.3–4).

[38] Elyot 1531 (G1ᵛ, G2).

The connection between poetry's usefulness and its fruitfulness calls, therefore, for some examination.

The first example the speaker gives of poetry being properly used appears at the beginning of the *divisio*, which opens with a discussion of divine poetry: 'this poesy must be used by whosoever will follow St James's counsel in singing psalms when they are merry' (86.301). Using the poetical parts of Scripture in this way is presented as an exemplary practice and an instance of the kind of good following that the speaker recommends (or differentiates from bad following) throughout the *Defence*.[39] In the context of excoriating the rich—who have, among other things, failed to pay the labourers who reap their fields—the Apostle encourages the faithful to be patient and to wait for the coming of Christ as the husbandman waits patiently for the fruit of the earth to grow: if they are afflicted in the meantime, they should pray; if merry, sing psalms.[40] Sidney's speaker not only urges that such poetry *should* be used in this way, moreover, but reassures us that when it is it reaps the promised spiritual rewards: 'I know [it] is used with the fruit of comfort by some, when, in sorrowful pangs of their death-bringing sins, they find the consolation of the never-leaving goodness' (86.31–4). On both occasions, the speaker appears to be deploying the verb 'use' in its older liturgical sense, either meaning to celebrate a religious rite—specifically, to partake of the Eucharist—or, if that smacks too much of Catholic practice, to follow an accepted custom, psalm-singing being an increasingly common form of Protestant devotion in the period.[41] Either way, following St James' counsel and using divine poetry in this way brings great spiritual harvest and provides the reader with the soul food—what the speaker later calls 'heavenly fruit' (113.20)—that he or she craves.[42]

For the most part, however, the word 'use' (noun and verb) appears in the *Defence* in its more common instrumental sense of purposive employment or application. In the discussion about the relative superiority of the feigned over the true in the *confirmatio*, for example—the question of whether the poet or painter should depict an ideal beauty or the ugly truth—the speaker assures us that 'if the question be for your own use and learning' (92.25–6) then it is incomparably better to have something represented as it should be rather than as it is, since this will inspire you to virtuous action, the ending end of all earthly learning. Clearly

[39] On the exemplary use of Scripture as 'poetical', no more illustrious example than Christ himself 'vouchsafed to use the flowers of it' (100.31–2).

[40] James 5:1–7, 13. The Geneva Bible is unusual among early modern English biblical translations in dropping the specific injunction that the merry should sing psalms (advising them simply to 'sing').

[41] See *OED* use *v.* I.1.a: 'to celebrate, keep, or observe (a religious rite); specifically to partake of or receive (the Eucharist)' (current from the mid-thirteenth century); II.9.a: 'to consume by eating or drinking . . . (in early use) specifically to partake of Christ's flesh and blood) in the Eucharist' (current from the early fourteenth century; citations from the Reformation period often use the verb in this sense to describe specifically Catholic practice); I.2.a: 'to observe (a custom, a traditional practice or rule of conduct, etc.); to pursue or follow as a custom or accepted practice' (current from the early fourteenth century). Sidney's commitment to psalm-singing is witnessed, of course, in his translation of the Psalter, completed by his sister. On psalm-singing as a Protestant devotional practice in the period, see Zim 1987; and Hamlin 2004.

[42] Such fruit—'fruits' in Ponsonby—to be derived from 'singing the praises' of God (113.21).

'use' is being deployed here in the sense of putting something to work in order to achieve a desired end or purpose.[43] The word, moreover, is paired with 'learning' where, as the speaker's comparatives indicate, the latter is taken to be something that, like capital, can be enlarged upon, increased, and grown: such idealist art is thus said to be incomparably 'better' (92.26), 'more doctrinable' (92.27–8) and will 'more benefit' (92.31) the investor than its alternative. In this scenario of proper use, that is, idealist poetry is put to work like a good tool or financial instrument in order to produce a given outcome or yield.[44] At the individual level, this is the intellectual, cultural, social, moral, and spiritual profit that 'you' stand to gain as a result. At the collective level, it is the whole ideology of value (the notion that an abstracted or represented ideal has value in itself, and more value than the bare, actual, material thing it represents) and the logic of increase that accompanies it (the natural desirability of 'better', 'more'). Returning to the question of the feigned versus the true in the *refutatio*—here couched in terms of the relative superiority of poetry over history—the speaker similarly assures us that, where readers of history (looking for truth) will take away only falsehood, readers of poetry (looking only for fiction) will 'use the narration but as an imaginative ground-plot of a profitable invention' (103.31–2). They will come away from the experience, that is, inspired by the poet's representations of ideal conduct and moved to emulate them in their own lives, to the benefit of themselves and everyone around them. Again, 'use' is clearly being deployed in the instrumental sense.[45] This dense passage, furthermore, also draws out the horticultural and agricultural metaphors implicit in this model of growth. For if, as Maslen notes, a 'ground-plot' can be taken to denote a 'plot of land ripe for development' and 'suitable for cultivation', then readers who 'use' poetry in this way are like successful gardeners or farmers who grow in the sense both that they produce (they grow plants and crops) and that they increase (their store of produce grows): a scenario that models husbandry or *oikonomia* at

---

[43] As Plutarch, similarly, 'teacheth the use to be gathered of [poets]' (108.5). See *OED* use *n.* I.1.a: 'the act of putting something to work, or employing or applying a thing, for any (especially a beneficial or productive) purpose; the fact, state, or condition of being put to work, employed, or applied in this way; utilization or appropriation, especially in order to achieve an end or pursue one's purpose' (current from the early thirteenth century). See also III.13, 15, 16: all senses relating to the beneficial purpose of an action (current from the mid-fourteenth century). Compare Scott 2013 (12), for whom an ideal representation is also 'of more direct use and availableness than the straight imitating true, real examples'.

[44] 'Use' in the sense of 'using money borrowed or lent at interest' developed from this instrumental meaning of the noun in the mid-fifteenth century (see *OED* use *n.* I.5.a) and may, therefore, possibly be included among the penumbra of meanings that surround the phrase 'for your own use'. As Fischer 1985 (133) notes, 'use' was a 'rich word for economic puns'.

[45] See *OED* use *v.* II: 'to put to practical or effective use; to make use of, employ, especially habitually'; and in particular senses: 8: 'to put (an instrument, implement) to practical use' (current from the early fourteenth century); 10: 'to make use or take advantage . . . as a means of accomplishing or achieving something' (current from the mid-fourteenth century); 14: 'to employ or put to use . . . in some function or capacity' (current from the late fourteenth century); and 15: 'to put to practical or effective use, especially as a material resource; to utilize' (current from the early fifteenth century). Note, however, the Dictionary's warning that from the twentieth century some senses of the verb 'have increasingly been understood instrumentally as implying particular ends or purposes, even when there is no explicit context of that kind'.

its best.[46] Where readers of history come away empty-handed, cheated, and 'full fraught with falsehood' (103.30), readers of poetry fruitfully till this fertile soil—they work the ground of the 'narration' or the story they read for everything they can get out of it ('plot' doing a lot of work here)—and so come away, by contrast and by implication, with their hands, bellies, persons, purses, chests, and barns metaphorically full.[47] There is no more powerful argument that 'use' is profitable, that profit is something that can be grown, and that poetry is the best means of delivering it.

Where there is nothing or the threat of nothing—the fear that something promised might be absent, denied, or taken away—the good poet thus provides and ensures that there is always something there: something wholesome and good that will not only feed and nourish those who consume it but help them grow to their full potential and achieve the supreme self-knowledge that results in well-doing and not well-knowing only. The poet's job, in other words, is 'to take naughtiness away and plant goodness even in the secretest cabinet of our souls' (90.5–6). The noun 'naughtiness' first appears in the sixteenth century, connoting badness of various forms, and in its moral sense of wickedness or sinfulness it certainly fits the logic of the speaker's argument here; but there might also, perhaps, be a hint of the original and etymological meaning of 'naughty' as possessing nothing or having naught.[48] The word appears in something closer to this sense in du Plessis Mornay's *A vvoorke concerning the trewnesse of the Christian religion*, in the context of a discussion about the existence of evil: 'And therefore S. *Austine* sayth, that the *Latins* terme an euill man *Nequam,* and an euillnesse *Nequitiam,* that is to say, *Naughtie* and *Naughtinesse.* Now, like as of rightnought there needeth no beginner; so also is there none to bee sought of naughtinesse or euill.'[49] 'Naughtiness' here captures the sense of emptiness or loss that characterizes the Christian—and specifically Augustinian—conceptualization of evil. Since Christian belief posits the primacy and goodness of God, evil can have no ontological existence

---

[46] Maslen (205, 206), drawing on Sidney's other uses of the phrase in the *Old Arcadia* (*OA*, 92, 215). See also Elyot 1531 (G5) who compares the process of productive learning in a child to 'a delicate tree, that cometh of a kernell' which must very carefully be cultivated, otherwise 'no frute cometh of it . . . or els the frute that cometh of it, leseth his verdure and taste, and finally his estimation'. References to the 'frute' (G2ᵛ) to be gathered from comedies, 'holsome herbes', 'good herbes' (G3ᵛ), 'frute and commoditie' (G4ᵛ) from poets in Elyot's defence of poetry show how thoroughly entrenched the vegetative metaphor is.

[47] Shepherd (201) glosses ground-plot as the 'seat of argument' (from various definitions of 'argument' in Quintilian 2002, *Institutio Oratoria*, V.x.1–12); Alexander (342) as 'foundation' or 'ground-plan'. Scott 2013 (31) is similarly emphatic about the use to which this ground-plot (which he regards as the moral argument of a fiction) is to be put if it is to be useful: 'we must first see that this ground and argument be of use and substantial . . . For how can that tree bear good fruit whose poisoned root spreads vicious nourishment into every branch?' Originally denoting a piece of ground, 'plot' came to refer to a plan, sketch, outline—and especially the synopsis of a literary work—in the mid-sixteenth century (although it did not develop the sense of storyline until the early seventeenth century; see *OED* plot *n.*).

[48] See *OED* naughty *adj*.: the shift from sense 1—'having or possessing nothing; poor, needy'—to later senses (all connoting badness of some kind) seems to have occurred in the mid-fifteenth century; the noun first appears in the early sixteenth century (see *OED* naughtiness *n.*).

[49] Mornay 1587 (B5ᵛ).

and must, therefore, necessarily be secondary: a privation of or diminishment in the pre-supposed, pre-existent, and ontologically prior good. As Dennis Danielson puts it, the translation of Mornay's '*neantise*' by 'naughtiness' in this passage 'brilliantly exploits an English word that must have seemed ready-made to bear the metaphysical freight that the meonic tradition [from Greek μη ον, "non-being"] threw up . . . the English *naughty* appears naturally and almost single-handedly to confirm the relationship between moral evil and metaphysical nothingness'.[50] Essentially, Augustine's doctrine of *privatio boni* denies nothingness in the name of presence. For the Christian, there is no nothingness but only a diminution in something already there: a goodness and truth presumed always to be present and to be recovered, as far as is possible, from the dire effects of the fall. The speaker's right poet thus endeavours to 'take naughtiness away'—to cancel the effects of sin and so restore this plenitude, so far as he is able—and the goodness that he plants will be more productive in achieving this end than either the 'thorny' (90.12) philosophy or the 'less fruitful' (90.20–1) history.

There is some justification, then, in saying that the metaphor of poetry as fruit or food is doing more work than the empty cliché it might at first seem, at least in the context of the present discussion. Poetry can be defended as useful, that is, to the extent that it fills—intellectually, morally, and spiritually—and thereby reverses the effects of anything that, at any or all of these levels, might be seen to empty or abuse. Against the accusers' loaded charge that poetry draws the mind to 'the serpent's tale of sinful fancy' (102.25–6), the speaker offers counter-examples of tales that are not so cunningly forked in their telling nor so punningly sinister in their effects. One of these is the homely 'tale' (95.17, 18, 26) that holds children from play and old men from the chimney corner, and that intends nothing more nor less than the drawing of the mind from wickedness to virtue. To counteract the effects of that forbidden fruit which on eating turned all to dust, the right poet provides his listeners with a veritable cornucopia—of 'grapes' (95.12), 'aloes' (95.22), 'rhubarb' (95.23), 'cherries' (96.10)—that not only fill the metaphorical belly but also serve as classic images of metaphysical fullness themselves: of the truth hidden behind appearances, of the goodness contained within.[51] Another such 'tale' (96.21, 24, 25), and told in quick succession, is that of Menenius Agrippa, which also ends with the image of a full and contented belly. Not only are the rebellious limbs persuaded to continue feeding this central organ, in his parable of the body at war with itself, but the point of the example is to show how extraordinarily efficacious the moral of the story—its inner, allegorical meaning—was. In perfectly reconciling the warring parties, this 'wrought such effect', the speaker comments, 'as I never read that ever words brought forth' (96.26–7), thus providing demonstrable '[proof] of the strange effects of this poetical invention' (96.11). Like

[50] Danielson 1984 (271, italics original). Danielson credits this felicitous translation to Sidney, although it might, of course, be Arthur Golding's or the result of a collaboration between the two.

[51] Both the Edenic fruit and the apples of the Dead Sea or Sodom that, when eaten by the serpent, turned to ashes: referred to by Gosson, *Schoole* (90/B8), and later by Milton 2007, *Paradise Lost*, 10.520–8. For another punning 'tale' that has sinful connotations, see *AS* 45: 'I am not I, pitie the tale of me.'

the fruits full of goodness, so the belly full of fruits becomes a metonym for the entire ideological superstructure that eventuates, at the far end, in the most abstruse metaphysical and theological reflections on presence. Menenius Agrippa deliberately approaches his listeners not with 'farfetched maxims of Philosophy' (96.17–18), however, but rather as a 'homely and familiar poet' (96.20): adjectives that might equally be applied to the tale that draws children from play and old men from the chimney corner. For, as with the image of the full chest, such personal and domestic reference—metaphors of the body, family, and home—serve to bring those abstract reflections, with all their larger social, political, and religious implications, back down to the simpler, smaller level of the *oikonomia*. They are effective because they ground this ideology of truth and value in the experience of ordinary, everyday life—in the day-to-day business of household management—making sense, in an immediate and directly graspable way, of a system that everyone believes in without necessarily knowing why.

A more suspicious listener, on the other hand, might be inclined to subject this particular tale—and the story of its marvellous effectiveness—to a somewhat more critical analysis: one that considered the cost of that 'perfect reconcilement' (96.28–9), for example, and asked whether the price to be paid for it might not, in some cases, be too high. It is at this point, therefore, that the case for poetry's usefulness will be pressed a little harder so as to stress-test those places where it might be found wanting. For what Menenius Agrippa's tale miraculously restores—and confirms as order, normality, and business as usual—is of, course, the rule of 'the whole people of Rome' (96.14) by 'the senate' (96.14–15): the rule of the many, that is, by the few. The tale works entirely in the service of the latter, reinforcing all the subordinations, sexual as well as social, that follow from the subordination of relative forms to the general equivalent and thus that characterize the money economy, no matter how disguised that might be by sentimental appeals to the more homely and familiar *oikonomia*. The image of the body as fully functional—as working properly, efficiently, and as it should do—when the full belly (i.e. the powerful few) equitably re-distributes nourishment for the good of the whole (the labouring many) represents nothing so clearly as ideology natural-ized so as to discourage the rebellious listeners from taking too close a look. In the classical histories that recount the telling of this tale, moreover, the people's revolt that precipitates it is not against social injustice in general but against a specifically economic practice. Their complaint, that is to say, is directed against *money-lenders*: wealthy creditors who have reneged on promises to be lenient with regard to debts and repayments, especially in the case of soldiers who are returning from war (far from being treated lightly or given more time to settle their accounts, the latter are stripped of all they had or imprisoned for debt).[52] Menenius Agrippa's tale does not solve this structural problem: it just makes the people happy to put up with it, duly persuaded to accept a system which keeps them subordinated, exploited, and (one might very well say) abused. He offers them the strategically appealing image of the

---

[52] See the accounts in Plutarch 1926, *Lives: Caius Marcius Coriolanus*, 215–16; and Livy 1959, *History of Rome*, II.31–3.

full belly in return for their own bellies remaining empty. To that extent, he does not take naughtiness away—replace emptiness with fullness—or at least he does not do so for them. The money-lenders remain assured of their profits—their chests (and bellies, presumably) are still full—and the ideal system thus remains happily intact, but only at the expense of the people to whom they lend at extortionate rates. The outcome of Menenius Agrippa's tale is most satisfactory, therefore (and to that extent might be said to be fruitful) to the powers that be, but the underlying situation—in which the 'fruits of [the people's] labour' (96.23) are devoured by the wealthy few so as to leave the former destitute—remains fundamentally unchanged. The full belly by means of which image the people are reconciled is not their belly, in other words, while the voracious, hungry belly which their retaliatory rebellion had intended to 'starve' (96.24) ends up being their own. One might recall Thomas More's analysis of the chronic lack of subsistence in England that followed enclosures from the middle of the fifteenth century—or that, before it came to mean bad or wicked (at more or less the same time), 'naughty' meant needy, poor—suggest that the speaker's case for the usefulness of poetry might here come up against an alternative position in which what is presented as being so very full and fruitful may not necessarily be so for everyone, nor the money economy that such use (and usury) reflects and serves an unalleviated good for all.

The sense that the tale Menenius Agrippa tells may not in the end work as the speaker intends it to work—that it may actually demonstrate the power of poetry to do harm rather than good—is strengthened by considering its placement within the larger argument as a whole. For it is situated at the hinge between the two halves of the *confirmatio* which set out the 'anatomies' (88.3) of poetry's 'works' and 'parts' (88.2) respectively. The long discussion of poetry's works considers its effectiveness—the way it operates—by comparison with its competitors, mainly philosophy and history, and triumphantly concludes by declaring that the poet 'in the most excellent work is the most excellent workman' (96.43–4).[53] Menenius Agrippa's tale of the body that works—both functions and labours—provides the culminating example of this discussion. If his shrewd anatomy of the political situation by means of an anatomy of the body serves as an appropriate reminder of the speaker's larger forensic examination of the subject in hand, however, it may begin to come apart as the discussion moves, in its second half, to consider poetry's parts. For the first example the speaker provides, to demonstrate the 'right use' (97.14) of poetry in its various kinds and genres, is pastoral: a form characterized if not defined by its ability to 'show the misery of people under hard lords' (97.17–18) and 'what blessedness is derived to them that lie lowest from the goodness of them that sit highest' (97.19–20). Here, that is, sympathy seems to lie rather with the downtrodden than with their overlords. In his exposure and critique of tyranny, the writer of pastoral sides with the people rather than with

---

[53] This part of the *confirmatio* thus serves to demonstrate what the speaker had earlier laid down as the 'end and working of [poetry]' (84.31); and that 'so far substantially it worketh, not only to make a Cyrus ... [but] to make many Cyruses' (85.39–42).

their rulers—with the hard-working limbs rather than the devouring belly—as opposed to Menenius Agrippa with his apparently exemplary tale of hierarchy restored and the status quo intact. As such, pastoral offers an alternative configuration of the latter's serene vision of social harmony, by revealing what it actually costs the members of the collective body and thus the commonwealth at large. Moreover, where the tale of the body was presented as exemplary for the goodness it contained inside—the moral kernel hidden beneath its simple exterior that 'wrought such effect in the people' (96.26–7)—in the case of pastoral what lies beneath an exterior just as simple is nothing so comfortable, or not for the elite whom the likes of Menenius Agrippa would serve, for 'under the pretty tales of wolves and sheep, [it] can include the whole considerations of wrong-doing and patience' (97.20–2).[54] The inner moral of pastoral, that is, proves just as efficacious—it works just as well—but the effect it wreaks is not on the ruled (with a view to bringing them back into line) but rather on the rulers, whom it calls to account in no uncertain terms. If the moral of pastoral is fruitful and bursting with goodness, then it is so to the former and at the expense of the latter, reversing the priorities of Menenius and the speaker and, quite possibly, correcting them (especially if one reads an acid irony in 'the goodness' of those who sit highest, from which the poor are said to derive their blessedness). Much the same might be said, incidentally, of the next example but one—iambic—which is said to shame villainy with 'bold and open crying out against naughtiness' (97.34–5). Here 'naughtiness' clearly refers to the moral turpitude of the individuals whom this particular kind of personalized satire singles out for attack, but in the context one may also see it as an appropriate term for the crimes of those who would fill their own bellies and coffers by stripping others down to nothing (or, alternatively, that the 'bold and open crying out' is against the destitute condition of their victims). Set against these examples—that follow so hard upon its heels that it is difficult to avoid the comparison—the tale of Menenius Agrippa looks increasingly like becoming another example that fails to exemplify: another place where the official and unofficial arguments of the *Defence*, or where the speaker and Sidney, might be seen to diverge.[55]

The speaker's 'anatomies', moreover, could be shown to deconstruct in other unintended ways too. It is clear, for example, that the body of poetry he sets out to dissect—'his works' (88.2; 97.1), 'his parts' (88.2; 97.3, 5–6)—is conceived as male. The speaker's aim, of course, is to demonstrate that if poetry can be found commendable in its particulars then it can be commended as a whole, and to that

---

[54] Compare the tales of Aesop, 'whose pretty allegories, stealing under the formal tales of beasts, make many, more beastly than beasts, begin to hear the sound of virtue from these dumb speakers' (92.5–7).

[55] Ferguson 1983 (161–2) comes close to suggesting this, i.e. that, while the tale is supposed to prove the effectiveness of poetry, it fails to do so in the end since the *Defence* itself, being altogether more contradictory and ambivalent, lacks any such gratifyingly persuasive power. Compare Matz 2000 (64–6), who sees Sidney as using the tale in order to defend the elite, couching courtly pleasure in the language of Protestant, humanist service. For my part, this is the *speaker's* position, while Sidney is more inclined to reject the rhetoric of use and profit (pleasurable or otherwise) in favour of the naughty, in all meanings of that word.

end he promises to examine that body most 'narrowly' (97.3) in order to determine the case: 'though all together may carry a presence full of majesty and beauty, perchance in some one defectious piece we may find a blemish' (97.3–5). Notwithstanding these claims to scientific impartiality, however, there is little disguising the speaker's bias. His assumption that 'if severed they be good, the conjunction cannot be hurtful' (97.11), for example, predisposes the outcome from the outset and leaves us with little faith that—for all his promise to 'see what faults may be found' (97.14)—he will actually find any. Indeed, in the anatomy of parts that follows the evidence is so suppressed or skewed as to minimize if not deny the existence of any blemishes or defects whatsoever, particularly in the highly selective definitions of elegy and lyric which all but eliminate any mention of love or desire.[56] The result of this tendentious inquiry, unsurprisingly, is to find a wholeness, harmony, and perfection in the body poetic quite as naturally as Menenius did in the body politic, allowing the speaker to conclude the *confirmatio* with an image of poet and poetry as an optimal male body at its physical peak: triumphant and wreathed, like a winning captain, with the 'laurel crown' (100.34). The 'severed dissections' (100.33) that the speaker had laid to view in the preceding discussions were never intended to end up anywhere else, nor do anything other than affirm that this body was possessed of majestic and beautiful 'presence' all along. In this fantasy of wholeness—of a body fully equipped and phallically endowed—it is not very difficult to make out the masculine imaginary and its concomitant denial of castration.

Seen in this light, the speaker's defence of poetry begins to look somewhat defensive and, as a consequence, considerably less persuasive. Naturally poetry looks ideal when it is presented as whole, full, filling, fulfilling, fruitful, useful, and so on (a self-reflecting tautology), but the case for its usefulness rests from the outset on denial: on denying the charge that poetry abuses, that it is 'naughty', that it is empty of and empties out metaphysical truths. The speaker remains determined to negate this threatened nothingness—to take naughtiness away by all and any means at his disposal—but the repressed, as always, returns: above all in the *digressio*, where the 'defectious piece[s]' passed over in the earlier anatomies are subjected, at last, to a more thoroughgoing examination.[57] To the discomfort of his speaker (and many critics of an idealist persuasion), Sidney will there count himself among those who are 'wanting' (109.26), include a franker discussion of lyric, and even consider its songs and sonnets from the perspective of a female reader—'But truly many of such writings as come under the banner of unresistible love; if I were a mistress, would never persuade me they were in love' (113.25–7)—displaying

---

[56] Maslen (184) puts it mildly when he describes (1) the speaker's presentation of elegy as a poem of lament (with complete silence on the subject of Roman love elegy) as 'rather narrow'; and (2) his characterization of lyric as song of soldierly valour sung to the lyre (with complete silence on the subject of amorous desire) as 'traditional [and] learned' (190). The speaker's definitions are so doctored as to discredit any claim he might make to disinterested inquiry: here, his promise to examine poetry's parts 'narrowly' (97.3) *means* narrowly.

[57] I shall be considering the *digressio* in further detail in section III.

(unlike his speaker but more, perhaps, like the hero of the *Arcadia*), a willingness to identify with a body that is lacking in 'parts'.

When, therefore, to return to the end of the *confirmatio*, the speaker defends his model of poetry—that ideal male body of his—by sarcastically comparing his opponents with a hypochondriacal and implicitly hysterical female body—'But truly I imagine it falleth out with these poet-whippers, as with some good women, who are often sick, but in faith they cannot tell where' (100.10–12)—there may be some grounds for scepticism. For misogynistic statements of this kind serve as another symptomatic place where the positions of the speaker and of Sidney might be said to part company, and these closing moments of the *confirmatio* prove no exception. Immediately before this attempted put-down of put-downs, for example, the speaker has been discussing epic, the last and greatest of poetry's 'parts' and the obvious point, therefore, at which to round off his anatomy: 'if anything be already said in the defence of sweet Poetry, all concurreth to the maintaining the Heroical, which is not only a kind, but the best and most accomplished kind of Poetry' (99.36–8). Aeneas is introduced for the umpteenth time as the exemplar of exemplars. Except in one important respect, for at this point Sidney's voice seems to intervene, to slip in and make allowance for the fact that there may be some readers who would beg to differ: specifically with regard to Aeneas' obedience to the divine command to abandon Dido, even 'though not only all passionate kindness, but even the human consideration of virtuous gratefulness, would have craved other of him' (100.1–2). In his determination that Aeneas remain ideal at all costs, the speaker tries to see off this unwelcome possibility by pronouncing it as a condition that, 'in a mind not prejudiced with a prejudicating humour, he will be found in excellency fruitful' (100.6–7).[58] In order for poetry to be useful, that is, and 'fruitful' in the prescribed manner, the speaker must deny the alternative, embodied here in a female or female-sympathetic reader who might not find the hero's course of action particularly exemplary, and who might well have craved other behaviour of him (not to mention another example from the poet). In the same vein—and making a further effort to shore up his weakening case by silencing this troublesome voice yet again—the speaker goes on to cite a fragment from Horace: '*melius Chrysippo et Crantore*'. Left floating as it is, the phrase invites the reader to remember or go back to the source: the epistle in which Horace finds Homer better than Chrysippus or Crantor (a Stoic philosopher and commentator on Plato, respectively) in the context of urging his young addressee to study poetry rather than philosophy. That this should come to the speaker's mind as he rounds off his argument to the same effect in the *confirmatio* is not particularly surprising. What might be, however, is what he leaves out: for the point Horace is making is that Homer is a better teacher than the philosophers precisely because he does *not*

---

[58] Scott 2013 (70) remains loyal to the speaker's position here, noting that epic should properly exclude any 'mention of love, dalliance, and courtship . . . which doth womanize a man', quoting the lecture against love that Musidorus delivers to Pyrocles in Book I of the *New Arcadia* (*NA* 72). Scott is apparently deaf to Sidney's irony, however, since, shortly after delivering this speech, Musidorus promptly falls in love himself.

represent ideals alone. The poet tells us, rather, 'what is fair, what is foul, what is helpful, what not' [*quid pulchrum, quid turpe, quid utile, quid non*], and it is specifically this that he presents 'more plainly [or fully] and better than Chrysippus or Crantor' [*planius* [or *plenius*] *ac melius Chrysippo et Crantore dicit*]. The narration in the *Iliad*, for example, does not idealize the protagonists but rather 'embraces the passions of foolish kings and peoples' [*stultorum regum et populorum continet aestus*].[59] In his bid to prove poetry useful and fruitful, the speaker cannot afford to admit of such imperfections. Ironically, therefore, he can maintain his model of poetry as full, whole, defensible, and ideal only by cutting something out: by omitting any reference to the naughty, defectious, abusive alternative.[60] His poetry can only be *utile*, that is, where that *quid non* is repressed. It is not a very strong position.

◌R

The invocation of Horatian *utilitas* proves something of a liability in other ways too. Although, as noted earlier, the speaker can present his proposition that poetry aims 'to teach and delight' (86.20) as a commonplace in need of no attribution, the way in which he appropriates Horace's famous phrase—'*omne tulit punctum qui miscuit utile dulci*' [he has won every vote who has blended profit and pleasure]— nonetheless invites a closer look.[61] The phrase comes, of course, at the end of a dense ten-line passage in which Horace has been making the same point through a wide range of terms. Poets, he says, aim either to benefit ['*prodesse*'] or to amuse ['*delectare*'] or to utter words that are both pleasing ['*iucunda*'] and helpful ['*idonea*'] to life; they both instruct ['*praecipie*[*nt*]'] and write fictions that are intended to please ['*voluptatis causa*']; some readers reject what is unprofitable ['*expertia frugis*'], while others reject what is unpleasurable ['*austera*']; the poet who blends the useful with the sweet ['*utile dulci*'] does so, therefore, by both delighting ['*delectando*'] and instructing ['*monendo*'] the reader at the same time.[62] It is noticeable how this wider range of reference comes to be narrowed down in the *Defence* to the speaker's favourite formulation that the aim of poetry is 'to teach and delight' (87.8; 100.26; or 'to delight and teach', 87.14–15; or to combine 'teaching, and . . . delighting', 93.28) as if—and in keeping with his pedagogic principles—other forms of benefit, profit, or utility were naturally to be subsumed under the general business of instruction.[63] In joining teaching with delight, the speaker follows the third of

---

[59] Horace 1926, *Epistles*, I.ii.3, 4, 8.

[60] Compare Socrates' systematic expunging, deleting, and striking out of any passages in epic poetry that might fail to represent ideals of behaviour in the heroes or gods and so fail to inspire readers to virtuous action (or, conversely, encourage them to emulate the wrong things): see Plato 2013, *Republic*, III.386a–392c. By the time he has finished, there is not a lot left: such epic as remains might be high-minded and propagandistic but it is a poor, eviscerated, and probably unreadable thing.

[61] Horace 1926, *Ars Poetica*, line 343, although as Matz 2000 (137n) notes, this translation 'oddly picks up the phrase "profit and pleasure" here—where one would expect something like "sweetness and utility"'.

[62] *Ars Poetica*, lines 333, 334, 335, 338, 341, 342, 343, 344.

[63] Thus the speaker favours the teach-and-delight formula over the alternative profit-and-pleasure duo which, by contrast, appears nowhere in the *Defence*, although Harington 1904 (208) evidently

the options the *Ars Poetica* presents (either to profit, or to please, or to do both at the same time), and the one Horace recommends since it appeals to the largest constituency and is thereby most likely to win the competition, election, or vote. Nonetheless—since it entails the mixing of otherwise opposing positions (*'miscuit utile dulci'*) and the yoking together of terms whose antithetical meanings remain intact (*'simul et iucunda et idonea'* [at once both pleasing and helpful], *'delectando pariterque monendo'* [at once delighting and instructing])—the making of such an oxymoron remains a difficult task and one that requires the greatest skill if the poet is to avoid the grotesque indecorum of mixed forms with which Horace's treatise famously opens and which it mocks and condemns.[64] When, therefore, Sidney's speaker claims that poetry does not only teach *and* delight but offers 'delightful teaching' (87.38; 112.43) and 'teaching delightfulness' (113.11), that it 'doth most delightfully teach' (110.33) and 'teach by a divine delightfulness' (106.24–5), we can take it that, in his view, this difficult task has been successfully achieved. The right poet, that is, does not simply join the contradictory elements together—as if attaching a human head to a horse's neck—but seamlessly incorporates them so that the two terms effectively become one.[65] One might say, indeed, that this represents an advance on the recommended mingling of profit with pleasure, since these are no longer treated as separate, discrete entities—to be used either in isolation (profit or pleasure) or in combination (profit and pleasure)—but are rather made, through mutual identification, to lose their contradictory character altogether. They are merged into a single element, that is, with the result that teaching *is* delightful, and profit (the moral profit that poetry provides and yields) pleasurable in itself. This is the ideal: so much so that—to advertise his text as being 'as pleasaunt for Gentlemen that fauour learning, as [it is] profitable for all that wyll follow vertue'—Gosson himself can say, on the very title page of the *Schoole of Abuse*, that failing to attract the reader with some kind of delight [*'delectatione aliqua a[d]licere Lectorem'*] would constitute, on the part of the writer, an unforgivable abuse [*'abutentis'*].[66]

Under this dispensation, the delightful is useful by definition: *dulce utile est.* It is incumbent upon all serious writers to arouse delight in their readers since nothing else engages the latter so powerfully or serves the ultimate purpose of moral instruction, which is to convert well-knowing into well-doing, *gnosis* into

---

considers it a suitable synonym for *utile dulci* since he uses it twice within four lines in his own gloss of Horace's line. If other forms of profit get subsumed beneath teaching, however, the speaker's language of sweetness and delight throughout the *Defence* remains more faithful to the Horatian original.

[64] *Ars Poetica*, lines 343, 334, 344.

[65] The *Defence* is full of such happy conjunctions: early poets drew 'with their charming sweetness the wild untamed wits to an admiration of knowledge' and 'did exercise their delightful vein in those points of highest knowledge' (82.21–2, 35–6); 'learning [comes] . . . with the sweet delights of Poetry', which is a 'heart-ravishing knowledge' (83.24–5, 41); 'Poesy is full of virtue-breeding delightfulness' (116.15–16). On the grotesque combinations that are akin to putting a human head on a horse's body or a fish's tail on a woman's body, see *Ars Poetica*, lines 1 and 4.

[66] *Schoole* (69/tp), quoting from Cicero 1927, *Tusculan Disputations*, I.iii.6. The melding of profit and pleasure or use and abuse here is all the more striking since, as Tilmouth 2007 (18) notes, Cicero's text was 'perhaps the most celebrated guide to Stoic philosophy in the sixteenth century'.

praxis.[67] Delight, as a result, remains integral to idealist readings of the *Defence*, both as a didactic treatise and as a defence of didacticism in literature.[68] Delight is effective because it appeals directly to the feelings, affections, and emotions. Indeed, for Susan James Sidney led the way in promoting the positive contribution the passions make to the learning process. As she notes, citing the *Defence*, it was 'simply a mistake to believe, as many learned men have done, "that where [once] reason hath so much over-mastered passion, as that the mind hath a free desire to do well" [95.1–2], there the light of nature will shine'.[69] In her account, Sidney rejects this Stoic model for an alternative Aristotelian and Thomist one in which the passions are not ruthlessly repressed or crushed, as in some interminable psychomachia, but rather cultivated—even indulged—so as to be harnessed by reason and put to good use. For passions provide the necessary emotion—and thus motivation—without which the reader would never be moved to virtuous action at all: poets 'delight [in order] to move men to take that goodness in hand, which without delight they would fly as from a stranger' (87.15–16).[70] As seventeenth-century thinkers began to realize, James continues, if philosophy was to achieve the same end it had to join its purely intelligible ideas with sensible ones, and the best way of doing this was to follow Sidney and 'borrow the tools of the Poet, who "doth not only show the way, but giveth so sweet a prospect into the way as will entice any man to enter [into] it" [95.9–11]' (216). If philosophy was to get its message across, that is, its theorems and propositions—otherwise so arid and impenetrable—had to be 'represented by images that arouse appropriate passions such as love and desire for knowledge' (223). As envisaged under this model, delight represents just such an appropriate passion, and is taken to be the love that arises from the 'sensitive, reasonable, or intellectual apprehension of good, [and] is the common root that gives force and quickening to the disposition in us'.[71] 'Delight is made up of a recognition of harmony, perfection, goodness, success', as Shepherd notes (68), and it thus names the innate pleasure human beings find in truth, virtue, and justice. It is the natural human 'appetite for

[67] Writers would typically arouse such delight in the reader through their use of stylistic figures and rhetorical tropes. For Puttenham 2007 (238), 'As figures be the instruments of ornament in every language, so be they also in a sort abuses, or rather trespasses, in speech, because they pass the ordinary limits of common utterance . . . whereby our talk is the more guileful and abusing'. For Scott 2013 (53) likewise, tropes constitute 'a certain kind of comely abuse and sweet indirectness'; while figures are 'a tolerable erring in word and phrase from the common and direct use' (58). When *dulce utile est*, in other words, abuse becomes a term of praise.

[68] See e.g. Shepherd (67): Sidney's 'whole treatise and argument hang on the usefulness he finds in poetry. The delight we have in poetry is real and substantial, but it is instrumental to the major end. Poetry has a supreme advantage as a teaching discipline because it can make the discipline a pleasure'; and Fineman 1986 (92): 'Sidney is quite emphatic with regard to the ethical importance of "delight".'

[69] James 1997 (215). See also the parody of the philosophers who insist that their discipline teaches virtue best by delineating vice and its 'cumbersome servant, passion, which must be mastered' (89.3–4).

[70] Tilmouth 2007 (23) traces the same shift—under this model, he notes, 'the passions, if commensurate with reason, become the very manifestations of a virtuous soul'—although Sidney does not form a part of his discussion.

[71] Scott 2013 (15), adding: 'To the delight of a reasonable creature there must be something agreeable to the reasonable part, and therefore the poet promiseth to enrich the understanding with knowledge, to conduct the will, that noble part of the soul, to the pursuit of virtue and good' (31).

'goodness' to which the speaker's ubiquitous metaphors of poetry as food appeal.[72] Drawing on this Aristotelian and Thomist model, the *Defence* proposes that 'all delight derives from the conscious attainment of some good that is suitable to ourselves', a happy recognition of the goodness with which we have a natural affinity or accord, the speaker's own word for this being 'conveniency': 'for delight we scarcely do but in things that have a conveniency to ourselves or to the general nature' (112.21–2).[73] For critics of this persuasion, passion thus relates to reason as delight to teaching, or pleasure to profit, or sweetness to utility: an ideal conjunction in which the first term does not undermine or rebel against the second but rather enhances it, works in tandem with it for the greater good (making us passionate about reason, delighted in its teachings, pleased with the moral profit it provides, its sweet utility, and so on). As one critic puts it, 'Sidneian poesie entices and seduces for the good. It yokes pleasure to the desire for virtue'.[74] Delight may be subordinate to teaching but, since teaching would be nothing without it, their relation is more like a marriage, a mutually supporting, reciprocal, and harmonious concord.

As said, that is the ideal. The notion that teaching is intrinsically delightful and learning the greatest pleasure known to man is one proposed, naturally enough, by philosophers and pedagogues, and it is easy to see why it might appeal to literary critics (who are engaged in a similar business, after all), and how this might lead, in turn, to the idealist reading of an idealist text.[75] Robert Matz, by contrast, is among those who are more alert to the circularities embedded within this position, and to the self-interest to which this 'both/and' model clearly speaks since it combines the best of both worlds and lets you have your fruitfulness and eat it too. At the general level, the profit-and-pleasure combo admirably serves to shore up the once sacrosanct but increasingly embattled values of a liberal education and, as a corollary, to defend the profession of literary criticism 'against real declines in the status of literary studies'.[76] At a more specific level, it characterizes those readings of Renaissance texts that routinely turn pleasure into profit and lead to instrumentalist or careerist readings—of sonnets, for example, or of Puttenham—in which love is not love but a means to an end and poetry not play but work, the exercise of a writer's agency and power. For Matz, as for others, the problem with these essentially idealist readings is that they 'unconsciously repeat sixteenth-century

[72] Stillman 2008 (112); and see the poetical fruit that is 'full of that taste' and has a 'pleasant taste' (95.12–13, 22) so that even bad men will 'content to be delighted' with 'a medicine of cherries' (96.7, 10).

[73] Devereux 1982 (96). Whence the natural delight that we find in mimesis: for the 'imitation whereof Poetry is, hath the most conveniency to Nature of all other, insomuch that, as Aristotle saith, those things which in themselves are horrible, as cruel battles, unnatural monsters, are made in poetical imitation delightful' (95.30–3), referencing Aristotle 1995, *Poetics*, 1448b.

[74] Doherty 1991 (11); the idea of the mystical marriage is the presiding metaphor in Doherty's book.

[75] For the definitive statement that learning is a pleasure in itself, for ordinary people as well as for philosophers, see Aristotle 1995, *Poetics*, 1448b; also Aristotle 1926, *Art of Rhetoric*, 1371a–b.

[76] Matz 2000 (15). For similar views, see Guillory 1993; in relation to new historicist readings of Renaissance texts, see Crewe 1986 (1–18) and 1990 (1–22); and in relation to Sidney's *Defence*, specifically, see Helgerson 1976 (127); Ferguson 1983 (12, 17, 162); and Moore 1999 (152–3).

anxieties about the place of literature, especially in relationship to the "political"' (3). It is not that the values of a liberal and literary education should be left to fend for themselves, but rather that the literary texts in question run the risk of being misread if they are appropriated in this way and made to serve some ulterior purpose, especially if unwittingly so. If we are to 'analyze rather than repeat Renaissance claims about the pleasure or profitability of literary texts', Matz cautions, 'we need to understand the ambivalent value "pleasure" and "profit" had within sixteenth-century culture' (8). And the best way of doing this is to situate those terms within their social context, an approach that helps to demystify the ideological work that the Horatian poetics of *utile et dulce* can be made to do not only in contemporary critical practice but, more to the point, in that of sixteenth-century appropriations of it, Sidney's *Defence* included. As Matz notes, a whole lot is going on in that bland little 'and' that would present profit and pleasure as the happy couple, joined at the hip, for it effaces what—if viewed in social terms—represented in the sixteenth century quite divergent if not incompatible positions. For if profit was identified with the class-interests of the Protestant humanist 'new men' and their values of utility, frugality, thrift, and accumulation, then pleasure, by contrast, was identified with the class-interests of the courtly elite and its values of leisure, play, and conspicuous consumption: all signifiers of status and a means of maintaining a distance and difference from 'the largely subordinate social groups' (21) from which the former notions were seen to originate. As Matz notes, the claim that poetry can both teach *and* delight 'would mask this conflict—strategically—within that "and"' (1) in a bid to force these two constituencies together, to deny the contradictions between them, and above all to deny any suggestion that courtly recreation might be useless, frivolous, and purely otiose, by insisting instead that it, too, had value and something substantial to offer. Seen thus, the doctrine of *utile et dulce*—commonplace, received, and self-evident as it seems—serves discreetly to veil the faultline I have been tracing throughout this book: between a model of poetry as useful, profitable, bankable, and 'bourgeois', on the one hand (identified with Sidney's speaker), and, on the other, one that is 'courtly' simply by virtue of *not* being that (identified with Sidney). It is in the interests of the speaker and idealist critics alike to insist that poetry both teaches and delights—or better still, that its teaching is delightful—and to reassure the powers that be that pleasure really is profitable, valuable, hard-working, industrious, productive, and so forth, but in the sixteenth century the formula more obviously papers over the cracks and strives to hold together a relation that is an incongruous match at the best of times, and can look less like marital bliss than an uncomfortable misalliance if not an acrimonious divorce.

Reading the *Defence* in class terms, Matz thus sees *utile et dulce* as pulling in opposite directions—courtly pleasure proving resistant to the speaker's attempts to co-opt it to the bourgeois ideology of profit—a split that effectively deconstructs that ideology or at least exposes the fissures internal to it, making it difficult, as a result, to take the idealist fantasy of 'delightful teaching' at face value. The speaker might strain to keep the two together but their union remains something more desired than achieved: which has the effect of taking us back to Horace. For, idealist appropriations aside, profit and pleasure do not form a natural pair in the *Ars Poetica*, where they retain their antithetical tendencies and where the oxymoron of profitable pleasure is liable to look less like one flesh than the monstrosity of a man's head (profit, teaching, reason) tacked onto a horse's body (pleasure, delight, the passions). In the first place, the conjunction of *utile et dulce* is not presented as an absolute—the choices Horace provides, after all, are *either* 'either/or' *or* 'both/and' ['*Aut prodesse . . . aut delectare . . . / aut simul et iucunda et idonea dicere vitae*']— making the latter merely one option among many, an alternative the poet might take or leave, and putting the disjunctive 'or' in the majority over the combinatory 'and' at a ratio of four to one.[77] In the second place, even where it does exist the conjunction of *utile et dulce* is not necessarily presented as ideal, for Horace has a much more expansive and arguably realistic idea of the things to which profit and pleasure might extend and does not (*pace* Sidney's speaker) see them as reducible to moral profit—and to pleasure in the same—alone. As Matz notes, a social analysis of *utile et dulce* need not be restricted to its sixteenth-century appropriations, for the terms prove no less contested in Horace—where the passage under consideration emerges from 'a specifically identified social context' (2)—and recognizing this makes their idealization by Sidney's speaker all the more apparent. For Horace sets his discussion in the context of an unfavourable comparison between the Greeks—who are said to be greedy for nothing but glory ['*praeter laudem nullius avaris*']—and his fellow Romans who, by contrast, are greedy for nothing but gain. To illustrate the latter, he provides a vignette of Roman education in which what his compatriots see fit to teach their young is how to do their sums, with the clear aim that they will thereafter be able to look after their means ['*rem poteris servare*'].[78] Horace might deplore these material values—once the soul is tainted with such a corrosive concern for petty gain ['*aerugo et cura peculi*'], he asks, what hope can there be for the appreciation of worthy poetry?—but all the same he advises the poet to appeal to as many readers as possible: in which case, as Matz notes, it 'may be that Horace links the benefit of poetry ["*prodesse*"] to the Romans concerned only with material benefits' (2). By the same token, it may also be that he links the *pleasure* of poetry ['*delectare*'] to the Romans so inclined, for although it seems to be moral as opposed to pecuniary profit that is referred to a few lines later when the senior members of Roman society are said to reject any poems that do not yield fruit ['*expertia frugis*'], their juniors—who conversely reject any poems that do not yield pleasure ['*austera*']—may very well be these younger men who have been trained to

---

[77] The first decision the poet is confronted with is the choice between 'either/or' or 'both/and'. If he or she chooses the latter, no further options open up. If he or she chooses the former, however, three more options make themselves available: either to profit, or to please, or to do neither. Four options— the poet can choose (1) 'either/or'; (2) 'either profit'; (3) 'or pleasure'; (4) 'or neither'—thus outweigh one: the poet can choose 'both/and'.

[78] *Ars Poetica*, lines 324, 329, the following quotation line 330. Brink 1971 (347) describes this as a 'satiric sketch of Roman tuition in arithmetic' that contrasts the Greek ideal of poetry with the 'Roman concern for property built into their education'. On the phrase '*rem poteris servare*' as expressing Horace's scorn for commercial values, Brink compares Horace 1926, *Epistles*, I.i.65–6: '*rem facias, rem, / si possis, recte, si non, quocumque modo, rem*' [make money, money by fair means if you can, if not, by any means money].

value material gain above all things and whom Matz calls the 'putatively business-minded' members of Roman society (2).[79] It might, in other words, be precisely pecuniary profit in which the latter take pleasure, so the poet who wins their votes ['*tulit punctum*'] is the one who appeals to exactly that interest—with poems that might praise or defend it, for example—so that these readers might enjoy both kinds of appreciation.[80] Horace might critique such materialism—idealism's nemesis—but he is still prepared to appeal to it if that is what it takes to succeed. Spenser, moreover, reads Horace in a similarly non-idealist way, when—in a poem written at more or less exactly the time Sidney was composing the *Defence* or at least digesting Gosson's *Schoole of Abuse*—he quotes Horace's famous phrase in order to illustrate the fact that the poet who would combine *utile et dulce* must both personally enjoy worldly pleasures (including money and gold) and appeal to those who do, even if that means playing the fool ['*stultire*'] and sharing the gross delights of the multitude.[81] *Omne tulit punctum qui miscuit utile dulci*, that is to say, is not an idealist doctrine: it might represent a compromise between extremes, but it leaves any idealism deeply compromised.

Matz's analysis of the *Defence* is one with which I am greatly in sympathy. His reading of Sidney's text in class terms; his identification of the fracture between humanist and courtly positions as explaining the discrepancy between the idealist poetics the text tries to be and the mess it actually is; his inclination to see Sidney as self-divided; his alertness to the way in which idealist poetics can serve the interests of the contemporary academy and so militate against reading the *Defence* in any

[79] For Brink 1971 (357) Horace here 'obtains a double grouping that serves his purpose of a humorously overstated contrast...between...strait-laced bourgeois and young men of fashion'. Both, that is, might be equally concerned with material gain.

[80] The idea that material things might be both used and enjoyed existed in the long-established legal principle of *usufructus*. In English law, 'usufruit' denoted 'the right of temporary possession, use, or enjoyment of the advantages of property belonging to another, so far as may be had without causing damage or prejudice to this' (current from the late fifteenth century, the Latin term replacing it from the mid-seventeenth century onwards: see *OED* usufruit *n.*). That pleasure and profit might be a false binary when it comes to material things is also suggested by the fact that *fructus* [fruit] and *frugalis* [frugal, economical, useful], both derive from *fruī* [to enjoy].

[81] The Latin poem, addressed to Gabriel Harvey, appears in *Tvvo other, very commendable letters*, appended to *Three proper, and wittie, familiar letters* (1580), H1–H2ᵛ, and is dated 5 October 1579. The same letter describes Spenser's friendly relations with Sidney, whom 'I thanke his good Worship, hath required [news] of me' (H2ᵛ), while the preceding letter (dated 15 October 1579) refers to Gosson's dedication of *The Schoole of Abuse* to Sidney and the dubious reception it received: see Spenser 1580. It is, of course, impossible to ascertain whether any conversations about poetic profit and delight took place between the two men in the aftermath of the *Schoole*'s publication in the summer of 1579, but noticeable nonetheless that, in being closer to Horace, Spenser's take on *utile et dulce* is so different from that of Sidney's speaker: on this see Matz 2000 (2, 138n). In the poem, Spenser self-deprecatingly depicts Harvey and himself as representing the opposite extremes of *utile* and *dulce*, respectively, but urges his more severe friend to enjoy more worldly pleasures—including getting a wife and receiving gifts of gold ('*Aurum*', H2)—and to appeal to those who worship lucrative lands, property, and money ('*nummos*', H1, H1ᵛ), for without doing so he does not deserve the name of poet ('*Nec...Nomen honorati sacrum mereare Poëtae*', H1ᵛ). The word '*stultire*' (H1ᵛ) and the quotation of Horace's line (H2) are the only sections of the poem to be italicized. Harington 1904 (207) also connects *utile et dulce* with folly—citing Horace's phrase in the context of defending poetry against the charge that it pleases fools: 'I would thinke this an article of prayse not of rebuke'—although, in his view, the rich man remains impervious to poetry's profit or pleasure.

other way: these are all things with which I am in wholehearted agreement. All the same, the case can, I think, be pressed a little further. For Matz's assumption is that a mediation between the competing courtly and humanist positions is something *sought*—something devoutly to be wished—even if it is not achieved. In his argument, Sidney's failed attempt to mediate between these contradictory social positions is invariably characterized in terms of frustration, disappointment, and above all anxiety: the fear that the courtly values of pleasure and display might, after all that, still be considered—and dismissed as—mere trifles. There is no sense here of any active disengagement, or that idealist values—expressed in terms of the accruing of benefits, profit, or capital of some kind—might be something that at some level Sidney could or would reject. No sense that Sidney might not only seek to keep his distance from the socially subordinate 'new men' with whom such values were identified, but also harbour a distaste for those values: a visceral repugnance for the commodification and the tyrannies large and small that the money form and its 'logic' of profit-mindedness seemed necessarily to bring in their wake. No sense that resistance to or rebellion against such values might be a viable or even a thinkable position.[82] Matz presents the contradictions within the *Defence* as those obtaining between different forms of capital—intellectual, social, cultural, moral, spiritual—which, because incommensurate, unequal, and unevenly distributed, raise the problem of their relative valuation.[83] Was it better to train one's son 'in courtly graces', he asks, 'or according to Protestant-humanist precepts that emphasized discipline and industry?' (19); and, by extension, was poetry necessarily more profitable than the latter (where they led to a good education, a successful career) or more pleasurable than the former (why choose poetry over other forms of courtly recreation, after all)? How did poetry's value as cultural capital compare with other forms of capital, cultural or otherwise? These are entirely legitimate questions and they account, I agree, for much of the unresolved tension within the *Defence*. If left there, however, the argument is in danger of remaining capitalized, still contained within the logic of rational self-interest: the idea that, even if they are differentially valued and problematically compared, profit and pleasure nevertheless remain things that are naturally to be desired, attained, and preferably increased, so much so that the failure to do so induces frustration, anxiety, and distress.

My view, by contrast, is that while this certainly marks the edge or scope of the speaker's thinking, Sidney (by which locution I have been designating the text's 'unconscious') strives to press beyond this limit, as he feels his way towards the possibility of a paradoxical place (no place) that might exist outside the profit-motive and on the far side of the pleasure principle. That edge or limit might be conceived as a kind of mental membrane which these illogical and irrational possibilities nonetheless press up against, stretch, and at times puncture or break

---

[82] Cf. Strier 1995 (7): it 'seems important to acknowledge the possibilities in [early modern] culture for thinking as well as enacting resistance'. See also Greene 2010 for the suggestion that Sidney was thinking through various forms of resistance (political, emotional, and psychological) in the *Arcadia*: an argument influenced by Quint 1993 (8), who proposes that romance is the '[epic] of the defeated, a defeated whose resistance contains the germ of a broader republican or antimonarchical politics'.

[83] Drawing on Bourdieu 1984.

through, making it a site of particular sensitivity: liable to flare-ups that draw the analyst's attention in the same way that a hysterical symptom does. The question of pleasure—especially in its relation (or otherwise) to profit or utility—thus becomes a particularly acute site for such an analysis: another place at which the speaker and Sidney might be seen to diverge as they pursue alternative desiderata and pleasures that are not necessarily compatible or even commensurate with one another. To probe this pleasure a little further, therefore—and the possibility that it could take different forms—one might consider for a moment the distinction Roland Barthes makes, in *The Pleasure of the Text*, between the text of pleasure and the text of bliss:

> Text of pleasure [*plaisir*]: the text that contents, fills, grants euphoria; the text that comes from culture and does not break with it, is linked to a *comfortable* practice of reading. Text of bliss [*jouissance*]: the text that imposes a state of loss, the text that discomforts (perhaps to the point of a certain boredom), unsettles the reader's historical, cultural, psychological assumptions, the consistency of his tastes, values, memories, brings to a crisis his relation with language.[84]

Synonyms for *plaisir* include 'contentment' (the feeling that comes when things are contained, when a receptacle, literal or metaphorical, is full of contents) and 'satisfaction' (the feeling that comes from having enough), pointing up the way in which this pleasure has all the metaphysical and logocentric connotations of the full chest discussed in the previous section: consoling notions that there is truth within words, meaning within language, value within things, profit within pleasure, and so on. Barthes' aim is to distinguish this sense of fulfilment—this 'feeling of repletion'—from the 'shock, disturbance, even loss, which are proper to ecstasy, to bliss' (19). For *jouissance* marks the refusal of that ideology of 'fullness': a renunciation of the petty bourgeois pleasures of material self-advancement and moral gain for pleasure of an altogether different order of magnitude: the orgiastic surrender, bliss, and extinction of the death drive.[85] The text of pleasure is thus the 'readerly' text: the text that is classic, mimetic, tidy, and easy to follow; it contains some moral lesson which readers can readily grasp and take away with them; it confirms their worldview as familiar, natural, the way things are; it is banal; it prattles and repeats; it is an agent of ideology. The text of bliss, by contrast, is the 'writerly' text: the text that is uncomfortable, difficult, perplexing, shocking, surprising, and destructive of readerly complacency (including that of literary critics); it is empty of content and so not a 'good buy' or a 'good read'; it yields no profit, issue, or yield, and does not compensate for the loss (of faith, of confidence) that it brings about; in the text of bliss 'nothing is reconstituted, nothing recuperated'; it is 'absolutely intransitive' (52). Where *plaisir* is bourgeois, self-satisfied, and solvent, *jouissance* is anarchic, self-annihilating, and dissolute. Where *plaisir* belongs with the pleasure principle and approximates, in economic terms, with capital accumulation and growth, *jouissance* goes beyond the pleasure

---

[84] Barthes 1975 (14, emphasis original).

[85] As Gallop 2012 (565) notes, in theorizing reading as perversion, Barthes' text 'might represent the most successful instance of a queer theory of literature, a queer *literary* theory' (emphasis original).

principle, defies the logic of the profit-motive, and approximates, rather, to the magnificent giveaway, to bankruptcy, ruination, and absolute loss.

I am not suggesting that Sidney's *Defence* is a text of bliss, although it is perfectly capable of disrupting readerly complacency if permitted to—if acknowledgement is duly given to the illogicalities that everywhere fracture its propositions—the reluctance to do this being a strong indication of the way in which it has doggedly been read, for so long and by so many, as a text of pleasure: one that repeats and confirms the value of literature and the value of teaching it, thus fulfilling those readers' dearest wishes. What I am suggesting, however, is that, where such acknowledgement is given, the *Defence* opens up a space that allows for at least the conceptualization of something different. It makes thinkable—even if only by showing (consciously or otherwise) the limits of the alternative—the possibility of a text of bliss: a text that might *not* say what it is expected to say or do what it is expected to do, that might not prattle, and the reading of which might not be reducible to the readerly accumulation of moral or material wealth. Naturally, there is going to be a lot of resistance to such a thing—that is the point of the text of bliss—and it is this resistance that I have largely been tracing in this book, starting with the conflict internal to Sidney and radiating out to the moral, social, and latterly institutional and professional resistance that makes itself manifest in readings of his text. If the *Defence* is not necessarily a text of bliss itself, however, then it is straining, almost in spite of itself, towards a poetics that would allow for the possibility of a text of bliss: that could accommodate an alternative to the officially recognized, approved, and sanctioned text of pleasure (the morally improving text, written by the 'right' poet, from which anything not conducive to readerly morale is monitored by the authorities and removed). And, in those terms, the resistance the *Defence* calls into being could be taken as a measure of its success: its achievement in at least mooting the idea, counterintuitive at first, that pleasure in virtue and goodness is not necessarily something (or not the only thing) to be sought out or desired. The idea that such pleasure, however 'natural', might have unacceptable costs of its own, might demand too high a price, and might therefore be something to be resisted: rejected in favour of an alternative that—in defying and demolishing the comforts of the former—is very far from 'pleasurable' as such, and yet an experience to which the human subject is perversely, irresistibly drawn, and the overwhelming nature of which knocks those pale little pleasures definitively into the shade. Pleasure as *plaisir*, that is, does not exhaust all possibilities, does not represent the sum total of desired experience, for unpleasure in the form of *jouissance* can prove equally if not more compelling.

In the *Defence*, therefore, *plaisir* and *jouissance* could be seen, however programmatically, to map onto the positions of the speaker and Sidney respectively, and descriptions of pleasure—or of 'delight', which is the preferred term in the text—to be places where their competing tendencies are made particularly apparent.[86] The

---

[86] While 'delight' and its cognates occurs forty-six times within the *Defence*, and 'sweetness' and its cognates nineteen times (including the 'sour-sweetness of revenge in Medea', 91.13), 'pleasure' and its cognates occurs only nine times.

reader of poetry, for example, is imagined as being subjected to an overpowering force that he or she nevertheless seeks out, prolongs, and repeats, and it is no exaggeration to say that it is the burden of the *Defence* to recommend, praise, and defend this experience as being thoroughly delightful: 'the poet, with that same hand of delight, doth draw the mind more effectually than any other art doth' (96.39–40; the verb 'to draw'—meaning 'to attract by moral force'—is repeatedly used to describe the impactful action poetry has on its recipients).[87] Poetry possesses a 'sweet charming force, [that] can do more hurt than any other army of words' (104.28–9); it has the 'force of delight' (106.27–8) that philosophy lacks. The speaker's aim, of course, is to co-opt this experience for the purposes of teaching—'that delightful teaching, which must be the right describing note to know a poet by' (87.37–9) and is 'the end of Poesy' (112.43)—so that the reader will be inspired to emulation by it. Such poetry—epic above all—'inflameth the mind with desire to be worthy' (99.40–1), so that the reader will be moved to action, spurred into becoming another Cyrus. Yet this soldierly model of reception illustrates very clearly the difference between the speaker's position and that of Sidney—the way in which an image can be pulled in opposite directions and stretched to breaking point—for in order to become this ideally hard, soldier-like figure at the far end of the process, the reader has first to be invaded by poetry, moved to the core by it, and physically struck to the soul: philosophy is ineffective because it does not 'strike, pierce, nor possess the sight of the soul' (90.27–8) in the same way that poetry does. In order to become this ideally heroic, militarized, and conquering Cyrus-type, that is, the reader has to be conquered, defeated, and wounded first. Indeed, the experience of reading or listening to poetry is figured throughout the *Defence* as an all-out assault in which the mind is—or should be—variously pene-trated, beaten, pulverized, pared, agitated, wounded, and burned: all experiences which it is, at the same time, to find thrilling and delightful.[88] For the speaker (or idealist critic) to claim that this is all to the good—intended only to the spiritual, moral, intellectual, social, and cultural profit of the reader, and of the common-wealth to which he or she belongs—is just the point at which an analyst might detect something afoot: a pretty patent denial of what unmistakably has libidinal and

---

[87] See *OED* draw *v.* II.26a. Thus, ancient poets used to 'draw with their charming sweetness the wild untamed wits to an admiration of knowledge' (82.20–2); poetry's 'final end is to lead and draw us to as high a perfection as our degenerate souls . . . can be capable of' (88.7–9); the historian's example, by contrast, 'draweth no necessary consequence, and [is] therefore a less fruitful doctrine' (90.20–1); epic 'draweth with it' (99.28) great champions; poetry's detractors accuse poetry of 'drawing the mind to the serpent's tale of sinful fancy' (102.25–6).

[88] Thus Pugliano's words 'drave into me' (81.21); by borrowing of poetry philosophers and historians 'entered into the gates of popular judgments' (83.14); the simple Indians must have their wits 'softened and sharpened with the sweet delights of Poetry' (83.25); tragedy 'openeth the greatest wounds' (98.25–6), thereby 'stirring the affects' (98.28), and exerts a 'sweet violence' (98.37–8); epic 'stirreth and instructeth' and 'most inflameth the mind' (99.39). Even music, to which some are drawn by 'an admirable delight' (88.14–15), is described as 'the most divine striker of the senses' (101.35), and poetry, since it shares the same aesthetic pleasure in form—especially in verse and rhyme (95.16–17; 101.41)—therefore 'striketh a certain music to the ear; and . . . doth delight' (115.34–5).

masochistic content.[89] As far as poetry's reception is concerned, there is not a whole lot of difference, experientially speaking, between those images that inflame the mind with desire to be worthy, and those 'fiery speeches' (113.27) with which love poets persuade their readers that 'in truth they feel those passions' (113.31): the 'passionate sonnets' (104.3–4) which the poet-haters accuse them of writing. The acid test here is validated by an identification with the typically female recipient and addressee of such poems: 'if I were a mistress, [these poets] would never persuade me they were in love' (113.26–7), unless they demonstrated the same 'forcibleness or *energia*' (113.32) in their lyrics. The speaker—identifying with the male writer and arguing for *plaisir*—would have this be 'a sufficient though short note, that we miss the right use of the material point of Poesy' (113.33–4), namely, that for a poet to lack such forcibleness is to be deficient in the poetic virtue of *energia*: the clarity of expression that serves to get his point (so to speak) across. Sidney, meanwhile—identifying with the female reader and arguing for *jouissance*—enacts his openness to such masculine persuasive force and willingness to be so inflamed, persuaded, and penetrated by it. He thereby enters into the masochistic position par excellence since, as Freud noted, the masochist desires to be put in a 'characteristically female situation . . . that is, being castrated, or copulated with, or giving birth to a baby'.[90]

With this distinction between a perverse 'I' that can imagine himself a mistress and a compliant 'we' concerned only with poetry's right use, Sidney and his speaker turn out (my locutions notwithstanding) not to be all that far apart, and are liable—as here, where the one is very efficaciously penetrated by the other—to a trembling collapse. As this last example might suggest, moreover, it is not only the reader who is imagined as being subjected to poetry's great forcibleness—and thus as occupying this prone, feminine position—but the writer also. Especially when (as in the *narratio*) the poet is envisaged in a state of transport: the heroic frenzy of the oracular poet or poetess who is infused with some mysterious 'divine force' (84.14), or so inspired 'with the force of a divine breath' (86.5) as to be able to outperform Nature. Indeed, like delight, the *furor poeticus* marks another of those symptomatic divergences between Sidney and his speaker, for while the latter professes himself sceptical of the concept and distances himself from Plato who 'attributeth unto Poesy more than myself do, namely, to be a very inspiring of a divine force, far above man's wit' (107.36–8), Sidney, by contrast, seems altogether more sympathetic to the possibility and open to the idea of being overmastered, ravished, and possessed.[91] When discussing the Roman name for poet as *vates*, 'a diviner, foreseer, or prophet' (83.39), for example (also in the *narratio*), Sidney coins the

[89] See Bates 2007 (29–31, 73–6) for an earlier discussion of masochism in the *Defence*. Marshall 2002 (10) analyses the way masochistic tendencies within Renaissance texts illustrate 'the fundamentally paradoxical nature of pleasure', although Sidney is not among the authors discussed.

[90] Freud 1924 (162).

[91] As Sidney confesses in the *digressio*, his own poetry (and quite possibly the *Defence* as well) is the product of having been so 'overmastered by some thoughts' as to yield 'an inky tribute unto them' (109.30–1). As usual, Scott 2013 (7) takes the position of the speaker on this matter, being equally cautious about the idea that poetry might be divinely inspired: 'I ask, then, is this instinct, fury, influence, or what else you list to call it, is this, I say, divine seed infused and conceived in the mind of man in despite of nature and reason, as you would say by rape?'

compound epithet 'heart-ravishing' (83.41) to describe the esoteric knowledge to which the poet, in that capacity, has access. As Shepherd notes, the coinage alludes to the ancient etymology—originating in Varro—that derives *vates* from '*vi mentis*' or 'with violence of mind', *vis* [power, strength, assault] suggesting the force with which that divine knowledge floods the poet, as it were, from above.[92] In this state of sublime transport, akin to *jouissance*, the poet is no longer presumptively male (as he is for the speaker) but equally capable of being a Delphic oracle or prophetic Sybil, or of crossing gender lines as Pyrocles chooses to do in the *Arcadia*. Likewise, the passions—no longer in compliant, wifely relation to reason and so producing lots of little virtues as a result—are divorced from reason entirely and powerful enough to extinguish it altogether in an ecstatic moment of Longinian bliss. Such is the 'high flying liberty of conceit proper to the poet' (84.13)—although not necessarily proper to the 'right' poet—with which Sidney repeatedly identifies in the *Defence*, as well as in his own literary practice, opting for passion over reason whenever given the choice, for *jouissance* over *plaisir* every time, preferring to be 'lifted up with the vigour of his own invention . . . freely ranging only within the zodiac of his own wit' (85.17–18, 23). As Richard Halpern notes, this 'self-vaulting moment . . . seems designed to recall Phaeton's disastrous ride in the chariot of Helios, thus invoking the fear of imagination's power to usurp and destroy cultural authority'.[93] Yet that is exactly what Sidney chooses to do: to fly and fall rather than to do the 'right' thing, the thing that is expected of him as a writer or as a man. What Halpern sees as a 'fear', therefore, could alternatively be seen as a wish: a fantasized refusal to submit to 'cultural authority' and the dictates of the philosophers, pedagogues, elders, and fathers who represent it. Elsewhere in the *Defence* Sidney again identifies with a vaulting son over a careful father, for—although the speaker insists that 'as the fertilest ground must be manured, so must the highest-flying wit have a Daedalus to guide him' (109.39–40)—Sidney nonetheless abjures such paternal solicitude and schoolmasterly advice in order to count himself among those fallen, wayward, and far-from-ideal contemporary poets who, while they might acknowledge such well-meaning instruction, are nonetheless unwilling to 'cumber ourselves withal' (110.1). As with the example of 'forcible' lyric poetry, so the split between the speaker and Sidney opens up only to collapse once again into what it has been all along: an internal split, the self-division of a writer terminally at war with himself. For while the speaker expresses regret at the failures of the young poets of today (he speaks more in sorrow than in anger), Sidney opts to be an Icarus regardless, choosing to be carried up and away with his own wit (as fertile, perhaps, as Pugliano's) and to fly as high as he can, even if that means, ultimately, that he is destined to crash and burn.[94]

---

[92] Shepherd (151); for the reference to Varro see Isidore of Seville 2006 (180).

[93] Halpern 1991 (58).

[94] This identification with Icarus follows the injunction towards the beginning of the *digressio* that 'they that delight in Poesy itself should seek to know what they do, and how they do; and especially look themselves in an unflattering glass of reason, if they be inclinable unto it' (109.31–3). When the paternalistic and pedagogic speaker looks in that mirror what he sees is the wayward son and pupil, the poet Sidney.

It is noticeable, then, returning to Matz's reading of the *Defence* for a moment, that his account does not make more of such fatal, shattering, libidinal delight. It is interesting, for example, to compare his catalogue of the many things to which pleasurable courtly expenditure might be thought to extend, with Bataille's list of similarly unproductive forms of *dépense*—'luxury, mourning, war, cults, the construction of sumptuary monuments, games, spectacles, arts, perverse sexual activity'—for it overlaps with all these terms except the last.[95] The reason for this omission, I suspect, is that such perverse sexuality—in being a definitively unproductive expenditure (it is, as Bataille adds, 'deflected from genital finality')—is less easy to quantify and thus more difficult to convert into alternative forms of capital: it is indeed an expense of spirit in a waste of shame. One of the limitations of Matz's otherwise penetrating analysis is its tendency to confuse waste with conspicuous consumption, which—because it *is* capable of buying a different kind of capital and thus of 'turning' a profit—is, as far as Bataille is concerned, the diametric opposite of waste. As Bataille's editor puts it, both the 'noble, and even more hypocritically, the bourgeois, use this "destruction" . . . simply to reaffirm their position in the hierarchy' (xvi).[96] Even Sidney's death on the battlefield is converted into a kind of posthumous capital: the heroism of a name and reputation that is still in play to this day. While Matz certainly considers the fluidity of gender roles in the *Defence*, therefore, he again tends to see this in terms of anxiety: the worry this might evince on Sidney's part that his text was indeed no more profitable than a lady's embroidery.[97] Matz sees Sidney's gender-bending in terms of anxiety in much the same way that Halpern sees the poet's self-vaunting in terms of fear, when both might be conceived, rather, in terms of *jouissance*. For the figure of the cross-dressed Hercules 'spinning at Omphale's commandment' (112.38)—with whom Sidney, similarly involved in textile/textual production, clearly identifies—is said to inspire 'delight' (112.38) because 'the representing of so strange a power in love procureth delight' (112.39–40). Being on the receiving end of such an overpowering, overmastering, gender-blurring, and masculinity-melting force, in other words, is considered the ultimate joy. Taking libidinal pleasures into account thus lifts the curtain on the perverse and paradoxical experience to be found in those 'queer' positions that actively denounce productivity, renounce the logic of the profit motif, and defy the rationale of the pleasure principle.

Starting out with Horace's *utile dulci*, then, I have considered profit and pleasure in an ideal relation (profit *and* pleasure), an antithetical relation (profit *or* pleasure), as ideal (both profit and pleasure are moral), and as non-ideal (both profit and pleasure are worldly): all possibilities that Horace's ample and generous formula allows for. But beyond that I have also tried to scope an alternative kind of pleasure, differentiated as *jouissance*, that is not in a relation of any kind with profit but is,

---

[95] Bataille 1985 (118). Cf. Matz 2000 (14) whose catalogue extends to the 'pageantry of the tilt, the hospitality of the manor, the sartorial splendor of the court, the superior physical mien of the soldier, the possession of land and the right to hunt on it'; 'building, food, clothing, courting, gambling, funerals, and tombs' (18); 'prodigy houses and elaborately formal parks and gardens' (67).

[96] Matz is not alone in this confusion, which Halpern also shares.

[97] See Matz 2000 (66–9).

rather, its nemesis—an experience that destroys *plaisir* and annihilates everything it stands for—and that might, in this capacity, be seen to approximate to Sidney's undeniably libidinous 'delight'. In 'The Notion of Expenditure', Bataille critiques the principle of 'classical utility' (116)—the notion that material goods are to be used and enjoyed (but only moderately, sustainably) in the forms of production and reproduction—in order, like Freud, to account for otherwise irrational but nonetheless all too observable human behaviours: in particular, for 'the illogical and irresistible impulse to reject material or moral goods that it would have been possible to utilize rationally (in conformity with the balancing of accounts)' (128). There is more to life than the balancing of accounts, in other words, material or moral, and in Bataille's notion of poetry as the ultimate expression of a state of loss—and therefore as 'synonymous with expenditure' (120)—one might find a model in which poetry need not be limited to *utile et dulce* but capable of venturing past them altogether and out into that strange utopic beyond:

> Every time the meaning of a discussion depends on the fundamental value of the word *useful*... it is possible to affirm that the debate is necessarily warped and that the fundamental question is eluded. In fact... there is nothing that permits one to define what is useful to man... it is constantly necessary to return, in the most unjustifiable way, to principles that one would like to situate beyond utility and pleasure.[98]

☙

The speaker's attempts to deny the charge of abuse by asserting poetry's usefulness—its fruitfulness, its delightfulness, and so on—thus have an uncanny way of affirming the opposite, and his would-be defence of devolving into a civil war: the ceaseless struggle with a counterforce that is as undefeatable as it is indefensible because an insurgency within. For all his efforts, the speaker finds himself not so much scourging poetry's enemies as, like Astrophil, 'beating my selfe for spite': playing the exasperated schoolmaster to his own naughty pupil who will not only always evade his strictures but even find a libidinous delight in those blows.[99] As I have suggested elsewhere, this image of the self-divided and self-scourging subject can be found throughout Sidney's literary writings, and it is not surprising, therefore, that it should show up here in the *Defence*.[100] I will conclude this section, then, by considering ways in which the invocation of poetry's 'force' ends up by attacking speaker's most cherished notions of poetry as learned and as a source of learning, most especially in his attempt to answer the effeminacy charge (as we have seen, a subset of the charge that poetry abuses). Before that, however, I will briefly consider the several forces that are at play within Sidney's text: for, as in some elementary physics lesson, once identified and distinguished from one another, these different forces come into conflict and, more often than not, cancel each other out.

---

[98] Bataille 1985 (116, emphasis original). Blood 2002 (844) proposes that 'Beyond the Utility Principle' might be a suitable subtitle to Bataille's essay.

[99] *AS* 1. See Halpern 1991 (26) on the rigours of the Tudor schoolroom as being 'sadistic, arbitrary, sometimes explicitly sexual'; also Lamb 1994 (504–5); and Enterline 2012 (48–61).

[100] Bates 2007 (28–135) and 2013 (173–236).

The first of these is the force of truth. In the anatomy of poetry's 'parts' that forms the second half of the *confirmatio*, the speaker considers a form that 'naughty' (98.2) playwrights have brought into disrepute and that gives the poet-haters particular cause for concern: namely, comedy. While claiming to postpone his full answer to the latter's 'argument of abuse' (98.3) in respect of comedy until the *refutatio*, the speaker nonetheless takes the opportunity here to deny the charge ahead of time. For the possibility that spectators might imitate the representations of bad practice and skulduggery they witness on stage is declared 'impossible' (98.6), on the grounds that such representations of evil serve only as a 'foil' (98.10) to set off virtue's beauty the more powerfully. To prove the point, the speaker refers back to an earlier discussion—on the 'inward light each mind hath in itself' (95.2–3) that steers the subject unerringly towards virtuous action, 'seeing in Nature we know it is well to do well' (95.3–4)—so as to assume such a state of ethical clarity on the part of all. Thus, there is none that, 'by the force truth hath in Nature' (98.18–19), will fail, on seeing evil, to shun it.[101] However, if that were really the case, people would need no such foil (since they can presumably see the beauty of virtue already), nor any ethical teaching either, whether philosophy or poetry (since they are supposedly moved to virtuous action naturally). In practice, that is to say, the force of truth turns out not to be very forceful after all, for that supposedly natural virtue is only operable under certain key conditions: namely, 'where once reason hath so much overmastered passion as that the mind hath a free desire to do well' (95.1–2). Where that is *not* the case, which is pretty much all of the time, the force of truth needs an additional boost from elsewhere—another source of energy—and this promptly presents itself in the form of a second force: the force to teach. It is a large part of the speaker's defence, of course, that the latter is precisely what poetry provides: poetry has 'more force in teaching' (91.26) than philosophy and 'as much force to teach' (93.9) as history. However, in and of itself, this second force also turns out to be insufficient at times and less forceful than it needs to be, for philosophy and history indisputably teach, just not very effectively. The force of teaching, then, also requires some extra input if it is to be truly effectual in achieving the desired end of well-doing, and it derives this, in turn, from a third source. This is the force to move, possession of which, for the speaker, is what gives poetry the decisive edge over its rivals. The fact that poetry has as much or more force 'to move' than history, for example, 'is clear, since the feigned may be tuned to the highest key of passion' (93.10–11), rather as Herodotus and other ancient historians succeeded in getting through to their readers by borrowing from poets their 'passionate describing of passions' (83.9–10). As for philosophy, no one would 'compare the philosopher in moving with the poet' (94.27–8), for, as philosophers 'scorn to delight, so must they be content little to move' (95.42–3).[102]

---

[101] To this one might add 'the force love of our country hath in us' (90.44).

[102] See also: poets 'delight to move men to take that goodness in hand . . . and teach, to make them know that goodness whereunto they are moved' (87.15–16); poetry is 'the most familiar to teach [virtue], and most princely to move towards it' (96.42–3); epic 'doth not only teach and move to a truth, but teacheth and moveth to the most high and excellent truth' (99.29–31); 'if it be, as I affirm, that no learning is so good as that which teacheth and moveth to virtue, and that none can both teach

The ability to move thus emerges as the most powerful of the forces in play, being stronger than either of the other two. However, it remains, for all that, something of a liability, as suggested by the dodges that characterize the speaker's similar conclusion that 'moving is of a higher degree than teaching' (94.29). For, grounding this claim on the fact that moving constitutes both 'the cause and the effect of teaching' (94.30), he proceeds to demonstrate the first by asking 'who will be taught, if he be not moved with desire to be taught?' (94.30–1), and the second by asking 'what so much good doth that teaching bring forth (I speak still of moral doctrine) as that it moveth one to do that which it doth teach?' (94.31–3). If such rhetorical questions demonstrate anything, however, it is only the speaker's circular (not to mention wishful) thinking—that of the eternally optimistic humanist pedagogue with his faith in the natural willingness of his pupils to be taught and belief that such learning will naturally lead them to the practice of goodness—for, of course, they beg rather than answer the questions posed. What of those who are *not* moved with desire to be taught: like Astrophil, for example, or like Icarus, or (*contra* the speaker) like the numerous other cases of resistance to schoolmasters and to the schoolroom that Sidney evinces throughout the *Defence*?[103] And what of teaching that does *not*, in the event, eventuate in virtuous action? The speaker invokes Aristotle's dictum that '*praxis* must be the fruit' (94.34), but what of those occasions where it is not?[104] As Richard Halpern notes, the belief that the pleasures of poetry could be 'recuperated or "trained" in the end'—so as to produce the indoctrinated, ideology-compliant, and self-disciplining subjects that a sixteenth-century grammar school education was designed to turn out—constituted 'humanism's great wager', but it did not always pay off.[105] 'Poetry's subject matter is pleasure itself, or what conduces to pleasure, without reference to social utility or seriousness' (52), making it 'an outlaw faculty that, even if it did not coherently oppose the laws of moral or political reason, worked in blind indifference to them. Its dangers lay in its autonomy and automatism, which resisted instrumental control and thus threw a shadow on humanist optimism' (56–7). It is significant, I think, that the speaker finds it necessary to remind us in parenthesis that 'I speak still of moral doctrine', as if an education in literature did not always or everywhere end up by teaching that. As Maslen notes (207), the Privy Council tried in 1582 to replace 'such lascivious poets' as were on the grammar school curriculum with

---

and move thereto so much as Poetry, then is the conclusion manifest that ink and paper cannot be to a more profitable purpose employed' (102.34–8).

[103] On Astrophil as the unwilling schoolboy, see Bates 2007 (49–61) and 2013 (186–7).

[104] As in the case of the tyrant, Alexander Pheraeus, who 'could not resist the sweet violence of a tragedy' but this 'wrought no further good in him' (98.37–9) than to make him stop watching tragedies: i.e. it did not reform his behaviour or move him to virtue in the slightest. This example also overturns earlier claims that 'even those hard-hearted evil men who think virtue a school name . . . and feel not the inward reason they stand upon, yet will be content to be delighted . . . and so steal to see the form of goodness (which seen they cannot but love) ere themselves be aware' (96.3–4, 6–9). Indeed, one might say that such reprobate characters remain unmoved and continue to 'steal' in the other sense of that word (see Part I, section III, note 126), not unlike the money-lenders and their senator-supporters in Menenius Agrippa's tale.

[105] Halpern 1991 (56).

poetic texts that, by contrast, were 'heroicall and of good instruction', but this did not necessarily always pay off either. The speaker might hold with the received pedagogical wisdom that nothing can 'sooner make you an honest man than the reading of Virgil' (116.27–8) but, as Lynn Enterline has shown, those schoolboys who went on to become writers in the 1590s—although thoroughly drilled in the *Aeneid*—rarely followed its example and preferred, rather, 'to imitate the voices of loving nymphs, goddesses, and women with a loss to mourn'; and, when they did invoke the Roman epic, 'the voice they were inclined to recall was that of Dido', much as Sidney identifies with her position, or one sympathetic to it, in the *Defence*. 'Such a literary history suggests', she concludes, 'that school training in imitation may well have released identifications and emotions in its *pueri* that were at some distance from their masters' declared purpose'.[106] Teaching, that is to say, is not necessarily the same thing as learning. You can take a horse to water but you cannot make it drink, any more than you can take a naughty horse-lover to culture and make him think what he is supposed to think.[107]

The force to move is a liability precisely *because* it appeals to the passions, and in this respect it reveals a basic contradiction in the speaker's logic. The force of truth proves to be insufficiently forceful on its own because, for the most part, reason has not overmastered the passions: rather, the passions overmaster reason and thus impede, block, and get in the way both of reason's operations and of the free and natural desire to do well. The force of teaching, in turn, also proves to be insufficiently forceful on its own because (as in the case of philosophy, especially) it fails to appeal to the passions and so fails to delight. The force to move thus wins the ticket because it does appeal to the passions and so delight the reader, but (and here's the rub) it does not necessarily move the passions in the right direction: there is no guarantee that, once readers are aroused, they will be passionate about the correct things or that their desire will automatically or only be for beauty, virtue, and truth. On the contrary, the passions having been moved and the emotions mobilized, they might very well lead elsewhere: indeed, they are arguably more likely to do so. In its very appeal to the passions, the force to move (powerful as it is) is in danger of being appropriated and misdirected by a higher power still—a fourth force that is capable of swallowing up all the others in its own grand vortex—namely, the 'force of delight' (106.27–8).[108] The speaker attempts to rescue his argument from this non sequitur by reverting to the claim that moving is both the effect and the cause of

---

[106] Enterline 2012 (87).

[107] See Salman 1979 (332): 'The orator-poet can lead and draw a reader to holiness and virtue by means of delight and instruction, but he cannot ultimately compel him.' The proverb was current in Sidney's time (see Tilley M262, first citation 1546), although not of course Dorothy Parker's inspired re-make.

[108] Tilmouth 2007 (5) traces the development of a third and very different model of the relation between passion and reason which supersedes both the Stoic model (reason overmasters passion) and the Aristotelian/Thomist one (reason harnesses passion) by putting passion in the ascendant and demoting reason to the merely instrumental role of calculating 'the optimal means of satisfying the passions' interests'. Hobbes is the chief proponent of this idea, which eventuates (via the vulgarization of his philosophy known as Hobbism) in the libertine ethic that characterized the Caroline period in particular.

good literary teaching—'to be moved to do that which we know, or to be moved with desire to know, *hoc opus, hic labor est*' (95.6–7)—but, as the tag from the *Aeneid* suggests, this is a haunting, daunting, and rarely achieved task.[109] Thus, David might qualify as a vatic poet because he 'showeth himself a passionate lover of that unspeakable and everlasting beauty to be seen by the eyes of the mind, only cleared by faith' (84.26–8), but he was also a passionate lover of Bathsheba, leading to the adultery, murder, and 'filthiness' (96.36) that necessitated Nathan's admonitory tale and led to his subsequent repentance and composition of the penitential psalms. Epic might move its readers to heroic action, but the speaker's statement to this effect is strangely qualified by a conditional—'*if* the saying of Plato and Tully be true, that who could see virtue would be wonderfully ravished with the love of her beauty' (99.32–4, my emphasis)—as if that might not always be the case. Indeed, in practice the reading of epic might very well 'inflameth the mind with desire' (99.40) before it 'inflameth the mind with desire to be worthy' (99.40–1): for, as Enterline suggests, it could (and evidently did) arouse the kind of 'passionate kindness' (100.1) that would prefer to see Aeneas return to Dido rather than leave her. Similarly, one might be 'ravished with delight to see a fair woman' (112.25–6), the speaker here differentiating such delight from the 'scornful tickling' (112.25) that is mere laughter, but not differentiating the possibility that one might equally be ravished by more than her beauty and virtue alone: that one is just as likely to be ravished with the desire to ravish her, as the experiences of Astrophil, Pyrocles, and Musidorus all testify (not to mention the desire to *be* ravished like her). At the beginning of the *confirmatio*, the speaker discusses the various ends to which learning might lead, differentiating the 'immediate end' (88.6), the 'private end' (88.23), and the 'next end' (88.28), on the one hand, from the 'final end' (88.7), the 'highest end' (88.24), the 'ending end' (88.31), on the other. The context is the various goals towards which the ancillary or serving sciences are directed (a knowledge of astronomy, natural science, music, mathematics, and so on) as against the ultimate aim to which all this knowledge should finally be directed: the 'end of well-doing and not of well-knowing only' (88.27).[110] The example given is that of the saddler who aims to make a good saddle, in the first instance, but whose 'farther end' (88.28) is to serve the art of horsemanship, the horseman's to serve soldiery, and the soldier to achieve heroic and virtuous action. All the same, the speaker's acknowledgement of

---

[109] Virgil 2001, *Aeneid*, VI.129: the words are spoken by the Cumaean Sybil to warn Aeneas of the difficulties of returning to the world of the living having once descended into the world of the dead. In Freudian terms, one might read this as the power of the death drive relative to the life-instincts. Given Sidney's identification in the *Defence* with 'the oracles of Delphos and Sibylla's prophecies' (84.10–11), it is significant that the Sibyl should issue her warning here immediately after her '*furor*' (line 102), i.e. her rapturous delivery of the oracle foretelling Aeneas' fate.

[110] See also Sidney's 1579 letter to Robert in which he advises his brother to read the *Nicomachean Ethics*, Aristotle teaching 'the good ende to whiche euerye man doth or ought to bende his smaleste and greatest actions'. The advice, however, comes in the context of his own failings in this regard: 'For you thinke that my experience growes of the good thinges I haue learned, but I knowe the only experience I haue gotten is to finde howe much I might haue learned, and howe much indeed I haue myssed for want of hauinge directed my course to the right endes and by the right meanes': see *Correspondence* (878).

alternative ends also admits the possibility of ends that might not necessarily follow the approved route upwards: of wayward paths, of careers that might perversely stop short at their intermediary aims or might meet them but then veer off in unwarranted directions, notably downwards. As the mathematician might draw a straight line with 'a crooked heart' (88.21), or the philosopher look for the truth though 'blind in himself' (88.20), so another naughty star-lover might 'fall into a ditch' (88.19–20) while gazing at his star and end up desiring a whole lot more than Stella's virtuous self: 'Let *Vertue* have that *Stella*'s selfe; yet thus, / That *Vertue* but that body graunt to us.'[111] When Musidorus asks Pyrocles what he proposes as 'the end' of his newly declared love for Philoclea, the latter replies immediately: 'Enjoying'.[112] The speaker's example of the ideal, well-saddled soldier-horseman in the *Defence* thus fails (as usual) to exemplify, for the moving that is supposed to produce soldiers and heroes—to 'make many Cyruses' (85.42), ideally—is just as liable to produce other, quite unforeseen outcomes, and the passions it evokes to go off in unwanted and unwonted directions, like the unruly horses that brought Phaeton down. As Roger Ascham warned, the schoolboy was more likely to find his pleasure and learning in the stable than in the classroom, and as Horace intimated, the horse's body could end up ruling the human head that was attached, only very precariously, to it.[113]

The speaker's attempt to claim that poetry is a force for good backfires, therefore, overwhelmed by the superior firepower of delight and of the passions: as a result of which poetry remains a force for ill, at least as far as the integrity of his defence is concerned. A particularly interesting example of the way in which this internal clash works out—the way these various forces end up working against one another— appears in the denial of the effeminacy charge: the culmination of the speaker's response to the argument of abuse in the *refutatio*, and, indeed, of the three 'imputations laid to the poor poets' (102.20–1) that he has been considering throughout the *Defence*. The effeminacy charge, of course, accuses poetry of having softened and weakened a formerly warlike nation: a narrative that Gosson presents in terms of a decline—'mark what we were before, & what we are now' (90/B8)— and that he illustrates by means of some dramatic comparisons. Against formerly impressive feats of endurance, exercise, and martial discipline—when 'english men could suffer watching and labor, hunger & thirst, and beare of al storms wᵗ hed and shoulders, they vsed slender weapons, went naked, and were good soldiours, they fed vppon rootes and barkes of trees, they would stand vp to the chin many dayes in marishes' (90–1/B8–B8ᵛ)—their contemporaries cut a sorry figure: 'Our wreastling at armes, is turned to wallowyng in Ladies laps, our courage, to cowardice, our running to ryot' (91/B8ᵛ–C1). Re-stating the allegation in order to refute it, Sidney's

---

[111] *AS* 52.   [112] *NA* (75).

[113] Ascham 1967 (32–3); see also Gosson's advice on the control of 'our affection': if 'to a Colte, [you] giue him the bridle, [he] flinges about; raine him hard, & you may rule him', *Schoole* (101/D2ᵛ– D3). Behind all these types stands Plato's classic image of the human soul as 'a pair of winged horses and a charioteer', in which 'one of the horses is noble and of noble breed, but the other quite the opposite in breed and character'; 'the horse of evil nature weighs the chariot down, making it heavy and pulling toward the earth the charioteer whose horse is not well trained', as a result of which 'the utmost toil and struggle await the soul': see Plato 1914, *Phaedrus*, 246A–B, 247B.

speaker presents it in much the same way: 'before poets began to be in price our nation hath set their hearts' delight upon action, and not upon imagination, rather doing things worthy to be written, than writing things fit to be done' (105.1–4).

To deny the charge, the speaker insists that there was no such 'beforetime' (105.4)—that poetry has been in evidence from the beginning and that 'never was the Albion nation without poetry' (105.6–7)—thereby remobilizing the 'precedence' (105.5) argument that was rehearsed earlier in the *narratio*: the claim that poetry inaugurates learning and thus stands as nothing less than the origin of human civilization. As noted earlier, moreover, he also correctly diagnoses the charge of effeminacy as being a fundamentally economic question rather than, as might at first seem, a sexual one.[114] Poetry, that is to say, is charged with draining the *oikos* and the *polis* of a vital resource in the form of manpower. A surefire symptom of this disastrous using up/abuse of resources is that men are no longer able to perform the productive and reproductive roles traditionally expected of them: the first of which is to provide for the household and nation, to fill the metaphorical chest (with more people, food, supplies, and goods both material and immaterial), to save, accumulate, and grow these things; and the second, to safeguard them, to protect them from enemy attack, and to enlarge, expand, and grow the fields of domestic and national operation. Hence Gosson's illustration of the charge of abuse by means of dramatic images of male uselessness. To counter the charge, the speaker mounts a two-pronged defence, as if intending to defeat his opponents by means of a deadly pincer movement. First, he claims that poetry *provides*, most obviously in the way it promotes learning and knowledge and thus fills the national 'treasure-house of science'; and second, that it *protects and increases* this provision, most obviously in the way it inspires heroic deeds and thus fills the nation with 'many Cyruses' who are primed both to secure the national borders and to embark, like their namesake, on missions of spectacular imperial expansion. Poetry's force to teach serves the first objective, and the fact that—in the form of its best epic exemplars—it teaches force serves the second. Poetry, therefore, is useful twice over—a force for good that ensures national prosperity and growth—leading the speaker to the triumphant conclusion that it is an art 'not of effeminateness, but of notable stirring of courage; not of abusing man's wit, but of strengthening man's wit' (108.14–16).

As we keep seeing, however, such forces have a way not of reinforcing each other so much as cancelling each other out, and the problem repeats itself here: for these two lines of defence also end up clashing, to the wholesale rout, ultimately, of the speaker's argument. This happens, I suggest, because the speaker does not start with the second of his two advances (that poetry inspires heroic deeds)—even though the denial that poetry effeminizes might have made this seem like the most logical move—but, rather, with the first (that poetry fills the national treasure-chest with learning), this being his correct identification of what is primarily at stake, namely

---

[114] Cf. Maslen (206), for whom Sidney 'restricts himself to a rebuttal of the charges that poetry encourages (1) sexual immorality . . . and (2) "effeminacy"—that it weakens men by luring them away from the traditionally masculine arts of war'. In fact, the speaker expands the charge from these sexual imputations to the economic ones they really represent.

provision. However, he mounts this advance obliquely, not saying that poetry is the source of knowledge directly, as he did in the *narratio*, but rather implying it: using this as an opportunity to take a swipe at his opponents by claiming that—in their nostalgia for a mythical period of heroism that existed before poetry—their argument, while it might be 'levelled against poetry' (105.7–8), is in reality an attack or a 'chainshot against all learning' (105.8). He goes on to press the point by means of a striking analogy:

> Of such mind were certain Goths, of whom it is written that, having in the spoil of a famous city taken a fair library, one hangman (belike fit to execute the fruits of their wits who had murdered a great number of bodies), would have set fire on it. 'No,' said another very gravely, 'take heed what you do, for while they are busy about these toys, we shall with more leisure conquer their countries'.   (105.9–15)

The speaker clearly means to illustrate the ignorance of the poetry-haters here by comparing them with the barbarous, philistine, and library-burning Goths, the 'fruits of [whose] wits'—their great idea—was to destroy the fruits of the wits of a great civilization (along with much of its population), in this case by burning down the library of Athens (the anecdote refers to the sacking of the city in 267 AD).[115] The speaker's bid to demolish his enemies by means of this move, however, goes somewhat awry when said Goths end up making the strategic decision *not* to put the library to the flame after all, but to allow that treasure-house of science to stand, on the grounds that—far from strengthening the *polis*—it fatally weakens it: the Greeks being so caught up in their learning, and distracted with its theoretical issues and academic debates, as to leave their city wide open to attack. This idle work of theirs, which absorbs them in abstract and inessential things, ironically grants their enemies the 'leisure' to put them to the sword. While the speaker seeks to pour scorn on the poetry-haters by sarcastically equating them with the Goths, therefore, his example inadvertently makes the latter look rather heroic—triumphant and empire-building (the 'fruits of their wits' now not, perhaps, so ironic after all)—and makes learning (now reduced to mere 'toys') look, by comparison, weak, vulnerable, helpless, and defenceless: virtually an invitation to let the marauding hordes come pouring in. This puts the speaker's defence of poetry as the source and provider of learning at a distinct disadvantage: first, in relation to the poetry-haters (he is a Greek to their Goths), and second, to his parallel defence of poetry as the source and inspirer of heroic deeds. That is to say, military conquest (the very thing that, under the second part of his two-pronged assault, poetry is praised and defended for inspiring) can turn out to prove quite inimical to learning (the very thing that, under the first, poetry is praised and defended for providing). The two columns of the speaker's defence, that is, end up fighting one another, and the twin benefits of poetry—which he tries to present as a team, as mutually supportive—are

---

[115] In stark contrast to the 'fruits of knowledge' (83.27–8) that are earlier called upon to civilize 'the most barbarous and simple Indians' (83.20–1). A page or so after the example of the Goths, the speaker quotes Scaliger to the effect that poetry-haters are '*barbari . . . atque hispidi*' [barbarous and uncouth men] (107.23–4): referencing Scaliger 1905 (14).

shown by this example to be anything but. The force *that* poetry teaches is evidently capable of overpowering its force *to* teach.

It is an indication of how far the speaker recognizes the problem that, in the next two paragraphs, he should bluster and backtrack in a desperate (though ultimately unsuccessful) effort to recover the position he has all but ceded.[116] Thus, he suddenly seems uncertain whether poetry is learned after all—the poet-haters' attack is 'against all learning, *as well as* Poetry, *or rather*, all learning *but* Poetry' (105.18, my emphases)—leaving it unclear whether poetry is learned or not. Is poetry to be included in the poet-haters' attack on learning or might it be in some way exempt? Where learning in general might remain open to the charge that it demilitarizes men and so puts the security of city or nation at risk, poetry somehow does not—it is 'freest from this objection' (105.24), the speaker decides—but logically this would mean that poetry is *un*learned, putting it on a par with the rampaging barbarians not to mention the poetry-haters. It all gets very confused, and indeed much of this and the following paragraph consist in abortive attempts on the speaker's part to solder the two parts of his now broken defence back together, while a disruptive, internal force keeps casting them asunder.[117] For the speaker, knowledge and action *must* form a pair—'it is manifest that all government of action is to be gotten by knowledge, and knowledge best by gathering many knowledges, which is reading' (105.20–2), this being the kind of reading up on military strategy that Sidney recommends in letters to Robert and to Edward Denny—and yet the (clearly brilliant) military strategy of leaving one's enemies' libraries standing so that one might the more effectively slaughter them while they are busy with such reading only demonstrates the circularity of the argument.[118] As

---

[116] The argument the speaker has been trying to make gets repeated verbatim, for example, as if saying the same thing again and louder will cover up the contradictions he has just exposed: 'this argument . . . [is] a chainshot against all learning' thus reappears as 'this reason is generally against all learning' (105.17–18).

[117] The confusion might be traced back to Gosson, for to make his case that poetry has fatally effeminized the nation Gosson presents the terrifying scenario of enemies storming a city, and indeed uses this as a call to arms: 'Let gunns to gouns, & bucklers yeeld to bookes. If the enemy beseege vs, cut off our victuals, preuent forrain aide, girt in the city, & bring the Ram*m*e to ye walles, it is not *Ciceroes* tongue that ca*n* peerce their armour to wou*n*d the body, nor *Archimedes* prickes, & lines . . . that hath any force to driue them backe. Whilst the one chats, his throte is cut; whilest the other syttes drawing Mathematicall fictions, the enimie standes with a sworde at his breast' (106/D8). Gosson was no enemy to learning, of course—on the contrary, as Kinney, ed. 1974 (34) notes, he believed 'that learning was not simply vital, but all that was necessary'—but in presenting the learned as so utterly weak, defenceless, and lacking in 'force' here, he allows Sidney's speaker to accuse him and his kind of hating not only poetry but learning in general. As we shall see, this confusion does nothing for the coherence of the speaker's argument but ends up being a gift to Sidney.

[118] See the letter to Denny, dated 22 May 1580, in which Sidney advises his friend—'that with good reason bend your selfe to souldiery'—to read 'books *that* profess the arte, & . . . historyes. The firste shewes what should be done, the other what hath bene done. Of the first sorte is Langeai in french, and Machiavell in Italian . . . if you will studdy them, it shall be necessary for you to exercise your hande in setting downe what you reed, as in descriptions of battaillons, camps and marches', although he says no more of such books since 'I am witness of myne owne ignoraunce': *Correspondence* (982). See also the letter to Robert, dated 18 October 1580, in which he advises the reading of history so as to learn about 'the entrings, and endings of Warrs and therin the Stratagems against the *Enimy*, and the Discipline vpon the Soldiour': *Correspondence* (1007).

if in acknowledgement of this, the next thing we hear is that poetry belongs with action *as opposed* to knowledge—'the quiddity of *ens* and *prima materia* will hardly agree with a corslet' (105.26–7)—the old distinction between philosophy and poetry being wheeled in to try and save the day by tarring the former with all the accusations of being useless, abstract, and impractical so as to leave the latter looking contrastingly manly, military, and heroic. '[A]s I said in the beginning', the speaker adds—referring back to the fantasies of an unlearned and heroic poetry that Sidney had entertained in the *narratio* with the '*areytos*' (83.22) of the simple Indians and the poems of the Welsh bards—'even Turks and Tartars are delighted with poets' (105.28–9). Admitting this, however, comes perilously close to suggesting that the barbarian Goths might have done so too: that they, likewise, might have delighted in a thoroughly unlearned (and knowledge-destroying) epic poetry of their own, in the name of which they carry out very effective raids on enemy territory and a corresponding expansion of their own. To retreat from this embarrassing possibility, the speaker makes a final effort to repair the breach—a last ditch attempt to bring action and knowledge back together again—this time in the figure of Homer whose poetry, he insists, inspired both. Since Homer flourished 'before' Greece did (105.29), the precedence argument is here mobilized again to restore poetry's function as both inaugurator *and* defender/extender of civilization: 'And if to a slight conjecture [i.e. the poetry-haters' hypothesis that poetry effeminizes] a conjecture may be opposed, truly it may seem, that as by [Homer] their learned men took almost their first light of knowledge, so their active men received their first motions of courage' (105.29–32). The speaker's conditionals, hesitations, and qualifications, however, suggest that the game is up, for the benign 'both/and' he has been striving to maintain again splits apart into the antagonistic 'either/or' it has been all along, as knowledge and action are again shown to exist not in an equal but a conflicted relation. True, Homer's poetry gave rise to two different types of men, but it does not bridge the gap between the two so much as widen it, for the 'active men' reject the 'learned men', as 'Alexander left his schoolmaster, living Aristotle, behind him, but took dead Homer with him' (105.36–7) when on campaign, and 'put the philosopher Callisthenes to death' (105.37–8).

The contradiction between action and knowledge might not have surfaced so starkly had the speaker responded to the effeminacy charge by simply asserting poetry's ability to inspire great deeds. If he had gone straight, that is, from 'never was the Albion nation without poetry' to 'Poetry is the companion of the camps' (105.25). As it is, however the speaker's intervening argument—that poetry is, in addition, a source and supplier of learning—only draws attention to the underlying problem, which is that action can prove incompatible with knowledge if not positively hostile to it. For the great deeds that such poetry undoubtedly does inspire are exemplified above all in the ransacking and laying to waste of the knowledge and learning of other civilizations. This might be relatively easy to contemplate in the case of the classical heroes—Alexander inspired by Homer, or notable Roman soldiers and generals inspired by Ennius (including Fulvius and the three Scipios, the last two conquerors of 'Asia and Afric', respectively, 106.11–12)—and more difficult to do so in the case of enemy barbarians like the

Turks, Tartars (and quite possibly the Goths), similarly inspired by indigenous poets in whom they take no less delight. Nevertheless, in all cases the force that such epic-inspired Cyrus-types and their men exert over others is the same. As we saw in the case of Zopyrus and Abradatas, the way in which such military expansion looks is a matter of perspective and depends entirely on whether the 'action' in question—and the 'knowledge' it destroys—is seen from the point of view of the conquerors or their victims. Whether the Persians or the Babylonians, the Macedonians or the Persians, the Romans or the Asians and Africans, the Goths or the Greeks, however, the result is the same, and if conquest expands the remit of one civilization, then it usually does so at the expense of another (poetry evidently can be a force for ill if you happen to be on the losing side). By identifying poetry with action, therefore, and by giving the latter—in its rejection of learning and glorious destruction of it—the upper hand, the speaker pits one side of his argument against the other, effectively putting his twin benefits on a collision course in which the fruits of the one (empire) destroy the fruits of the other (learning). At war with itself, his defence naturally enough falters and collapses.

If the speaker's handling of the effeminacy charge destroys the credibility of his case, however, and does nothing for either the logic of his argument or the coherence of the *Defence* more generally, it nevertheless does not destroy—and is, indeed, entirely consistent with—the alternative argument that I have been tracing throughout Sidney's text: its other voice and the different ideas for poetry it dares to contemplate. This alternative registers, I think, in what keeps surfacing (despite the speaker's repeated attempts to repress it) as the fantasy of an *un*learned poetry: a poetry that is resistant to learning and to the instrumentalist model that would conceptualize it as a contribution to and accumulation of knowledge, as filling the national treasure-house and metaphorical chest, as taking naughtiness away and planting goodness in its place. From this perspective, the 'doctrine of ignorance' (105.16) that the speaker would reject—scornfully attributing it to the poet-haters—has a distinct appeal: it looks, when embodied in these highly active adherents, rather heroic and attractive. And that the *Defence*'s other voice might think so too is suggested by the quote from Horace that follows, which—while designed by the speaker to leave the poet-haters trembling in their boots—has, as noted earlier, a quite different effect. To the man who would think poetry ignorant, the speaker thunders, '*jubeo stultum esse libenter*' [I willingly tell him to remain a fool], but given the scenarios he presents of great warriors despising learning, and of the learned being unable to defend themselves against them, such ignorance or folly might not look so shameful after all. The speaker's attempt to brand the poet-haters as fools, therefore, backfires in much the same way as his insult that they are aiming a 'chainshot against all learning, or bookishness, as they commonly term it' (105.8–9) ends up getting slung back at him, Sidney clearly differentiating his own position here from those who might be horrified at such a prospect.[119] As elsewhere, moreover, the suppression of what Horace actually says ends up

---

[119] As Maslen (211) notes, 'bookish' was already being used as a disparaging term in the sixteenth century: see *OED* bookish *adj.* 1b.

speaking volumes: for, in the first place, his advice is that one should bid the object in question to be miserable ['*miserum*'], not foolish ['*stultum*'], and, in the second, the said object is a miser ['*avarus*'] and not someone who thinks that poetry might be unlearned.[120] The miser is miserable because he hordes his wealth instead of spending it, and he thus provides a conveniently negative portrait of capital accumulation—and of the profit-mindedness it exemplifies—at its worst. The speaker might try to pour his scorn on the foolish man, but Sidney seems altogether more sympathetic to the latter, and reserves *his* scorn, by contrast, for the avaricious man—the repressed hoarder—as his way of resisting the idea that the poet's job is dutifully to fill the nation's treasure-chest and libraries with golden poems written to order, their cultural and intellectual capital thereby contributing to the knowledge economy, and their moral and spiritual capital to individual salvation and the collective good.[121] If this constitutes the approved model of idealist poetics, then Sidney's poet would rather spend like there is no tomorrow: not as an exchange, not as a down payment on some future investment, not as a way of converting one kind of capital into another, but as pure expenditure, unredeemed, irredeemable, and thus destructive of that ideology, its 'civilized' values. The *Defence* and its idealist readers may attempt to repress this other voice and its alternatives—to cover up the contradictions within the official argument, to force knowledge and action (like *utile et dulce*) back together—but the project is destined to fail, for while the speaker (the defender of poetry) would support filling the national coffers with learned and bookish, valued and valuable poems, the poet (the writer of poetry) cannot bring himself to do so. His is a position of dissidence and dissent: he can't pay, won't pay.

If the speaker inadvertently presents himself as a Greek to the poetry-hating Goths, then one might say that his poet counterpart harbours an unconscious identification with the latter.[122] What the speaker's typically non-exemplary example seems to whisper, that is to say, is that on this occasion Sidney would, secretly, very much like to be a ravaging Goth to the speaker's learned, library-bound,

---

[120] Horace 1926, *Satires*, I.i.63, 103.

[121] Harington 1904 (208) makes the same connection, citing lines 68–70 of the same satire by Horace in order to illustrate the point that the 'couetous man' is the true enemy of poetry since he remains impervious to and unmoved by it (not realizing that the tale the poet tells of Tantalus is told of him), while foolish people—children at play, old men at the chimney corner—are, in their openness and receptiveness to poetry, altogether more friendlily disposed towards it. By this means, Harington refutes the 'great sinne that is layd to Poetrie', namely, that it pleases fools. In his book, as in Sidney's (and, arguably, in Horace's and Spenser's too), this is not a bad thing. By way of illustration, Harington cites the example of one 'Iustice *Randall* of London' who died leaving 'a thousand pounds of gold in a chest ful of old boots & shoes, yet was so miserable that at my Lord Maiors dinner they say he would put vp a widgen [wild duck] for his supper', i.e. was the most stingy of hosts. The fool's empty chest, by contrast, could never be accused of such a betrayal and, indeed, is likely to be empty because everything has been given away.

[122] Indeed, he has already confessed his own 'barbarousness' in loving the old unpolished 'song of Percy and Douglas' that typifies that 'unciuil age' (99.5, 6, 9). Not for the first time, therefore, Sidney ends up identifying with Gosson's position: the poet ironically at one with the poet-hater. Again, as at note 117, one might see this in terms of Gosson's own confused identification with anti-intellectual types: as, for example, in his praise for the Roman general, Gaius Marius, who similarly despised learning and took pride in never learning Greek, 'because he doubted the abuses of those Schooles, where Poets were euer the head Maisters' (*Schoole*, 80/A5ᵛ).

but defenceless Greek. This identification is the source of the disruptive, internal force that keeps scotching the speaker's best efforts at making a coherent defence: the plant, the infiltrator, the enemy within, that repeatedly gets the better of all his defensive designs. Such internal dissension is everywhere in Sidney's literary writings, and as Astrophil's warring wits result in nothing more than a confusion of mind, here too the battle between speaker and poet brings no victory for coherence, either of argument or identity.[123] That, however, may be precisely the point, and dealing the decisive blow that spells the defeat of 'logic'—where that entails a certain model of poetry—may, as far as the poet is concerned, be exactly the desired, the fantasized, if unconscious end. In the Goths' gleeful burning down of the library—or better still, in their decision to let it stand so that they might liquidate still more of its learned occupants—one might see a repressed but barely disguised wish: a schoolboy's fantasized retaliation against his schoolmasters. And, in their ransacking of the treasure-house of science, a poet's fantasized revenge against the pedagogical model of bankable poetry and all those who would defend and promote it, the speaker included.[124] Although Sidney would here be identifying with the conquerors rather than (as more normally) with their victims, his enmity in this case is directed against a despised and hated part of himself: against the official and public but false and alien voice that mounts a defence of poetry as accumulative and instrumentalist which, when push comes to shove, is what the poet in him detests above all else. Just as Astrophil 'to my selfe my selfe did give the blow', so the poet here does likewise.[125] I suggested earlier that to identify with the heroic, imperialist Cyrus-type—and to theorize the kind of poetry that produces more of the same—is to identify with an idealist, ideology-generating literature, and ultimately (whether consciously or otherwise) to promote professional interests and a defence of the literary critical discipline. This does not apply when identifying with the Goths, however, because—although their knowledge-destroying force is to all intents and purposes the same as that of Cyrus (or Alexander, or Fulvius, or the Scipios, and other such worthies)—*their* depredations bring home the fact that such territorial expansion is always destructive of civilization: just not always someone else's. In the Goths' case, that is, it powerfully registers that their action is directed against the knowledge bank (classical learning, 'memory') that the humanist pedagogues would do everything in their power to preserve. From the poet's point of view, the great advantage of identifying with the former is that it has the shock value of being, so far as the latter are concerned, *not*

---

[123] *AS* 34: 'Peace, foolish wit, with wit my wit is mard. / Thus write I while I doubt to write, and wreake / My harmes on Ink's poore losse, perhaps some find / *Stella*'s great powrs, that so confuse my mind.'

[124] Cf. Matz 2000 (60–3, 79–80) who sees Sidney as valiantly trying to combine pleasure with profit—in the glamorous figure of the chivalric warrior and the service he provides to the state—and thereby to defend courtly expenditure from Gosson's (implicitly middle-class) rebuke of its triviality and excess. Where Matz sees this attempted mediation as characteristically failing, however, leaving Sidney in a state of anxiety, I tend to see this failure as unconsciously motivated: as a massive parapraxis.

[125] *AS* 33; Sidney again reverting to what Astrophil calls 'selfe condemning me', *AS* 86.

ideal (there is little danger that idealist critics will identify with the anti-intellectual, library-burning, fund-cutting, resource-slashing barbarians).

The response to the effeminacy charge, therefore, is far from straightforward but no less symptomatic for that. By means of a strange kink in the argument, the very appeal to manliness that would appear, on the face of it, to be the most logical way of repudiating the charge—claiming that poetry is an art 'not of effeminateness, but of notable stirring of courage' (108.14–15)—perversely ends up, by means of the hyper-macho identification it invites, by siding with the enemy: with the poet-haters, with the destroyers of learning, with the heroically ignorant barbarians, with the splendid fools. If elsewhere Sidney identifies with the naughty pupil against his overbearing schoolmaster (with Icarus against Daedalus, with Cupid the 'wag' against 'Doctor *Cupid*'), then here the roles are reversed as he assumes the position of the towering, illiterate Goth against the cowering, learned Greek.[126] The rebelliousness is still the same, however, as is the overall masochistic scenario and its accompanying libidinal content. For—since Sidney is playing all the parts in this internal *mise-en-scène*—there is pleasure in all positions. Indeed, one might well say that it is here at last that Sidney finally succeeds in mediating opposing positions: in having it both ways, in having his cake and eating it too. A child is being beaten, so the classically masochistic feminine/effeminate position is certainly being occupied; *and*, on this occasion, that child happens to be the hated schoolmaster within: the compliant, obedient, and properly disciplined subject, the advertisement for the Tudor schoolroom and for a pedagogical, learned, studiously serious, right poetry that Sidney takes a wicked delight in repudiating (really, the school of abuse is not at all a bad name for it). Once again, therefore, the 'force of delight' gets the better of all the other forces in play. Like the wild untamed wits of a former uncivilized and preliterate age, Sidney is still able to set his heart's 'delight upon action' (105.2) and like the Turks, the Tartars, and the Goths, not to mention the Indians and the Welsh, to be 'delighted with poets' (105.28–9) too.

---

[126] For Cupid the 'wag', see *AS* 17, 46, and Other Poems 4, line 129; for 'Doctor *Cupid*', see *AS* 61. Cupid also appears as a naughty pupil in *AS* 11; and as a schoolmaster in *AS* 19. On the schoolroom as the place where these opposing figurations of Cupid appear most strikingly in Sidney's poetry, see Bates 2013 (186). Ascham's ideal schoolmaster seems implicitly to be the object of attack here. Ascham 1967 (145–6) wishes that—just as Virgil and Horace did not imitate the faults of their predecessors but rather followed the perfections of the Greeks—so 'we Englishmen likewise would acknowledge and understand rightfully our rude, beggarly rhyming, brought first into Italy by Goths and Huns when all good verses and all good learning too were destroyed by them, and after carried into France and Germany, and at last received into England by men of excellent wit indeed but of small learning and less judgement in that behalf. But now when men know the difference and have the examples both of the best and of the worst, surely to follow rather the Goths in rhyming than the Greeks in true versifying were even to eat acorns with swine when we may freely eat wheat bread amongst men'. While Ascham concedes that some English poets (including Chaucer, Surrey, and Wyatt) have managed rhyme reasonably well and 'gone as far, to their great praise, as the copy they followed could carry them', poets in general should nonetheless be 'directed to follow the best examples': i.e. they should avoid 'that barbarous and rude rhyming' in order to be 'counted, amongst men of learning and skill, more like unto the Grecians than unto the Gothians in handling of their verse'. As so often, Sidney chooses to follow the un-recommended, prodigal path.

III

Poetry Is Abused

The second strategy the speaker deploys in order to answer the charge that poetry abuses is that of reversal, although when he comes formally to refute the accusation in the *refutatio* it is this one, in fact, that he proposes first. Re-stating the allegation that poetry 'abuseth men's wit' (103.44), the speaker offers, by way of riposte, his own preposterous turn, which is to 'put the last words foremost, and not say that Poetry abuseth man's wit, but that man's wit abuseth Poetry' (104.16–17). This elegant turnaround—which switches poetry from the subject to the object position—is presented as something of a *coup de résistance*, the winning move that will foil the opposition: the decisive counterblow that will allow of no comeback and thus put the argument of abuse to rest once and for all. To take the assailant's strength and use it against them is, of course, a classic defensive manoeuvre, and, if successful, it stands to be doubly effective here given, first, the strength of the opposition—the authority of Plato, especially, but also the very vitriol of the antipoetic tradition which now promises to be turned against itself— and, second, the strength which that opposition imputes to poetry: for, as noted earlier, the *mysomousoi* invest poetry with a destructive power of virtually nuclear proportions, the ability, at the far end, to disrupt the operations of order, truth, and meaning and so to bring civilization as we know it to an end. By making poetry the victim rather than the perpetrator, the speaker's neat reversal puts subject and object in a direct correlation such that an inverse ratio obtains between the two. Poetry is as innocent as it is said to be guilty—as sinned against as it is said to be sinning—so the greater the charge against it, the more powerful the counter-attack. The reversal is striking for its telescoping of perspective, making it possible to see poetry from the other side and so to appear quite different from as charged. This tactic is similar to the '*Comparison* of contraries'—when 'Contraries are sometymes arranged togeither by payres one to one, as compare the ones impatience to the others myldnes, the ones impenitency wth the others submission, the ones humillity wth the others indignacon'—which John Hoskins saw as a signature Sidney device and which appears throughout Sidney's writings as a way of emphasizing a point or strengthening a case.[127] In the present situation, the more poetry is said to offend, the more it is in need of defence; the more vulnerable and defenceless poetry is, the more defensible; and the more

---

[127] Hoskins 1937 (135). Maslen (207) concurs that this passage is 'full of elaborate rhetorical figures (reminiscent of many passages in the two *Arcadias*)'.

defensible, the stronger the case.[128] On the strength of this strength, the speaker allows himself to make a number of concessions. These, admittedly, are not huge at first—the love that he would 'grant' (104.8, 10) poets write about is still restricted to the 'love of beauty' (104.8), that is, to the philosophical contemplation of the ideal—but as he grows in confidence he is prepared to give considerably more ground. By the end of the paragraph, he is willing to 'grant ... whatsoever [his opponents] will have granted, that not only love, but lust, but vanity, but (if they list) scurrility, possesseth many leaves of the poets' books' (104.12–15), so confident is he that no charge is so serious that his strategy of reversal will be unable to turn it to his own advantage. On this basis, he permits himself the triumphant conclusion that, 'in this their argument of abuse', his opponents have actually ended up by praising poetry—they 'prove the commendation' (104.43–4)—rather than denigrating it. They have, in effect, done his job for him.

This triumphalism notwithstanding, it remains to be seen just how effective this counter move really is: whether the speaker's self-confidence is well founded, and whether these are concessions he can afford to make. For the key question which this strategy of reversal poses is one of agency. In this new scenario, where poetry has been switched to the object position, who or what occupies the now vacated subject position? Who or what, that is to say, is abusing poetry? In order for the reversal argument to work, the subject or subjects that are abusing poetry need to match and equal the destructive agency attributed to poetry by the opposition. The candidate proposed, however—'man's wit' (104.17)—seems in the circumstances to be rather unsatisfactory: vague, unspecified, and de-particularized. How can man's wit abuse poetry in the same potentially annihilating way that poetry is said to undermine the social fabric and threaten life as we know it? The answer is unclear and one might be forgiven for suspecting something of a fudge. The situation calls, therefore, for a bit of probing, and one way to begin might be to say that the standing charge—that poetry 'abuseth men's wit, training it to wanton sinfulness and lustful love' (103.44–104.1)—does, at some level, make sense. The statement has a grammatical logic to it, at least, even if one might disagree with the proposition. In abusing men's wit, poetry has the power to lead them astray, to disrupt the processes of proper and orderly (re)production, to deconstruct the ideology that idealizes fullness, to evacuate the metaphysics of presence, and so ultimately to bring the *polis* to its knees. At this larger, macro-level of the argument, however, the speaker's simple reversal does not work: for while you can say that poetry abuses men's wit—that it has a negative impact on the city or commonwealth, a deleterious effect on society at large—you cannot so meaningfully say that society at large abuses poetry. For all the appearance of parity, what the speaker's reversal actually does is surreptitiously to *reduce* the charge: to shrink it down from

---

[128] The speaker similarly presents himself as a champion riding to the rescue of love—no less unfairly demeaned by the poetry-haters, in his view—and of which he declares that 'I would thou couldst as well defend thyself as thou canst offend others' (104.5–6).

the collective to the individual.[129] That he does this, in fact, is evident in the easy-to-miss and virtually unnoticed shift he executes from the plural to the singular: from the original charge—that poetry 'abuseth *men*'s wit' (103.44, my emphasis)—to his repetition of that charge and response to it: 'not . . . that Poetry abuseth *man*'s wit, but that *man*'s wit abuseth Poetry' (104.16–17, my emphasis). The latter makes sense because it limits the terms to individuals: you can say that maverick poets are responsible for abusing poetry in a way that you cannot say that people in general are responsible for abusing poetry.[130] Once you have established that it is such rogue artists who are to blame, you are on much firmer territory and can freely criticize those who act in such an irresponsible way accordingly. The destructive agency attributed to poetry by the *mysomousoi* is thereby safely attributed to the perverse and wilful agency of individual poets. It is *they* who occupy the villainous subject position, while poetry moves to the object position where, passive, prone, and victim-like, it need take no responsibility for what is done to it and is, therefore, able to preserve its fundamental goodness, beauty, and truth.

Clever as it is, however, the speaker's move remains for all that a disingenuous one, and although it reverses the terms of the argument (subject/object, abuser/abused) it does not succeed in reversing the argument itself. For the works which these maverick artists go on to produce are still judged by their effects: by the fact that they continue to act injuriously on those who read or see them. A theory of reception remains in evidence, that is to say—is still assumed—and although poetry might be passive under the new dispensation that does not mean it is inert. Poetry that has been 'abused' by such unscrupulous poets goes on to abuse its readership and audience just as much as it was accused of doing before:

> For I will not deny but that man's wit may make Poesy, which should be *eikastike*, which some learned have defined, 'figuring forth good things', to be *phantastike*, which doth contrariwise infect the fancy with unworthy objects; as the painter, that should give to the eye either some excellent perspective, or some fine picture, fit for building or fortification, or containing in it some notable example, as Abraham sacrificing his son Isaac, Judith killing Holofernes, David fighting with Goliath, may leave those, and please an ill-pleased eye with wanton shows of better hidden matters. (104.18–26)

---

[129] The same reduction is in evidence if one compares the speaker's and the poet-haters' respective opponents. While the latter are defending against *poetry* and the invidious, antisocial forces they attribute to it, the speaker is defending poetry against the *poet-haters*. As struggles go, defending poetry against its accusers is not on a par with defending the state against poetry, where the latter is perceived as a security threat to the former: the stakes are of an altogether lower order of magnitude. Plato is, admittedly, the big gun here, but all the same the speaker's defence devolves into a debate between writers and academics (poets, philosophers, historians)—it is not a matter for the state authorities, as, in being addressed to the Mayor of London, Gosson's is—and, for all its heat, this battle of the books entails a major scaling down of the conflict, a significant contraction of the theatre of war.

[130] Harington 1904 (209) has no hesitation on this front, declaring that 'where any scurrilitie and lewdnesse is founde, there Poetry doth not abuse vs, but writers haue abused Poetrie'. For Spenser, likewise, poetry on the subject of love should not be dismissed out of hand simply 'For fault of few that haue abusd the same': see Spenser 2007, *The Faerie Queene*, IV.Pro.2. Responsibility, that is to say, lies primarily with writers rather than readers. Cf. Webbe 1904 (252) for whom it is 'the abuse of the vsers' that is squarely to blame; and Ferguson 1983 (146–50) who ingeniously turns Sidney's argument about abusive writers into one about abusive readers.

It is clear from the transitive verbs the speaker employs that the works such artists produce are still capable of abusing those who consume them: they 'infect the fancy' and 'please an ill-pleased eye', as a subject works upon its objects. Like the painter who ought to provide some 'notable example' but ends up perversely doing the opposite, so the speaker (not for the first time) chooses an example that fails to do his bidding. It would be fair to say, then, that the strategy of reversal succeeds neither in turning the argument around nor in demolishing the opposition. Indeed, as the speaker himself admits—in another concessionary moment his argument can ill afford—he does 'not deny' the accusation but, rather, affirms it: poetry, the speaking picture, 'abuseth men's wit' as charged. A new formula is therefore called for, and this the speaker promptly produces as a revised and refined version of the original one: not that poetry does not abuse *because* it is abused but, rather, that poetry does not abuse *if* it is not abused:

> But what, shall the abuse of a thing make the right use odious? Nay truly, though I yield that Poesy may not only be abused, but that being abused, by the reason of his sweet charming force, it can do more hurt than any other army of words, yet shall it be so far from concluding that the abuse should give reproach to the abused, that contrariwise it is a good reason, that whatsoever, being abused, doth most harm, being rightly used (and upon the right use each thing conceiveth his title), doth most good.   (104.26–33)

By this means (although still conceding considerable ground), the speaker attempts to correct his wavering reversal strategy and put it back on track, cancelling one 'contrariwise' with another (104.20, 31) and so turning two wrongs back into a right.

The speaker thereby reaffirms his commitment to the language of 'rightness' that he has been maintaining since the beginning of the *Defence*, with his determination to show that in 'being rightly applied' (84.32) poetry will be justly esteemed; that 'so right a prince as Xenophon's Cyrus' (85.31–2) will invite emulation, so long as readers 'will learn aright why and how that maker made him' (85.42–3); that, so long as 'the poet do his part aright' (92.34), such figures as Cyrus will provide 'the right description of wisdom, valour, and justice' (95.27–8); that his concern is with 'right poets' (86.44) and the 'right describing note to know a poet by' (87.38–9), such that he thinks 'rightly' (100.34) that the poet deserves the laurel crown, and so on. The particular question of right *use*, moreover, has been in play since at least the second half of the *confirmatio*—in which the speaker had pledged to anatomize poetry's various kinds and genres so as to consider 'what faults may be found in the right use of them' (97.14), including 'the right use of Comedy' (98.24), failing, unsurprisingly, to find any—and it will go on to structure much of the *digressio* in which he looks at what happens where those various kinds and genres are *not* rightly used. There he laments that 'in neither [matter nor manner] we use Art or Imitation rightly' (110.5–6); that contemporary plays are therefore 'neither right tragedies, nor right comedies' (112.1–2) but only bastard tragi-comedies that achieve 'neither the admiration and commiseration, nor the right sportfulness' (112.5–6) and certainly 'no right comedy' (112.11); that in contemporary lyric 'we miss the right use of the material point of Poesy' (113.33–4); and that his admonitions are therefore designed with no other end in view than to bend contemporary poets back 'to the right use of both matter and manner' (115.12). None of this is very surprising, and neither would it be particularly exceptional, were it not for the fact that, as noted earlier, the word 'use' (noun and verb) did not have an exclusively positive sense: it could also connote the processes of using something up, of wearing it out, emptying it, exhausting it. In order to preserve 'use' for ideological purposes—to keep use positively useful, fruitful, and to minimize these possibilities of it depleting or running out—it therefore became necessary to distinguish the 'use' in question from any such potentially negative implications by clearly defining it as being of the 'right' kind. Thus, even Gosson is willing to allow for the 'right vse of auncient Poetrie'—defining it as having 'the notable exploytes of woorthy Captaines, the holesome councels of good fathers, and vertuous liues of predeces-sors set downe in numbers, and song to the Instrument at solemne feastes'—in order to differentiate this from the contemporary poetry and music that are his prime concern and that 'are nowe both abused' (82/A7ᵛ). Properly speaking, music should be 'vsed in battaile' in order to sound alarms rather than to 'tickle the eare' (82/A7ᵛ), while the mathematics of its frequencies, tones, and intervals signifies the underlying cosmological harmony (the music of the spheres) which the 'politike Lawes, in well gouerned common wealthes' are supposed to reflect, and which the ideal 'loue' (83/A8ᵛ) between king and subject, father and child, lord and slave, master and man ought to affirm. Rightly used, poetry and music thus perform a physically and socially curative function—whence their ancient connection with medicine, as embodied in the mythical centaur-poet Chiron, student of Apollo—whose model singing 'quencheth *Achiles* furye' (82/A7ᵛ) and repeated 'the famous enterprises of noble men' (83/A8ᵛ)—making him 'a wise man, a learned Poet, a skilful Musition', as well as a physician and 'a teacher of iustice, by shewing what Princes ought to doe' (83/B1). In Gosson's account, this ideal is clearly designed to stand in stark contrast to the scene he currently surveys, in which anyone looking for similar paragons of poetic virtue in contemporary London—trying to count 'how many *Chirons*... are heere'—might just as well do the sum in their head, since 'they were not' (84/B1ᵛ).

Since it is aspersions of this kind that Sidney's speaker is seeking to refute, it is understandable that he should try to reverse the charge and insist that the 'right use'—of which Gosson all but despairs—can easily be restored. It is simply a question of poetry 'being rightly used' and the problem will be solved, to the salvation both of poetry and his argument. Gosson is prepared to admit that poetry may not always or necessarily abuse and that it might sometimes be 'vsed with meane' (80/A5)—in moderation—as opposed to the excessive practice of the Syracusans who 'vsed such varietie of dishes in theyr banquets' (76/A1) as well as in their poetry, and with whose negative example he opens his pamphlet. He regards such restraint, however, as a rarity—poetry 'without vice' being like 'the *Phoenix* in *Arabia*' (79/A4ᵛ), a virtual impossibility, the exception that proves the rule—for 'these qualities [are] as harde to bee wel vsed when we haue them, as they are to be learned before wee get them' (80/A5). For Sidney's speaker, by contrast, it is the maverick artists who seem to be in the minority at this point—the rare birds—thereby minimizing the difficulty of eliminating or at least discounting the pernicious influence they have on the ideal presentation of their art. For all the speaker's unflagging determination to accentuate the positive, however, 'use' remains an unstable term, even when it is qualified as 'right'. Rebutting the charge and defending poetry against it thus turns out to be more complicated than first appeared, and the strategy of reversal—even in its refined form—to be incapable, finally, of solving the problem. As with the charge that poetry lies, here too the complexity arises from the need to negotiate the opposing term, but where, in that case, the inability to argue that poetry was true led to a dog-leg turn in the argument (yes, poetry lies, but lies are profitable and therefore true), in the present case, 'use' turns out to contain its opposing term—or at least its opposing sense—within its own semantic field. Sometimes 'use' has a positive sense and can connote a purposeful functionality, beneficial employment, instrumental application, and so on; but sometimes it also has a negative sense and can connote consumption (as comestibles are swallowed up, devoured) or deterioration, exhaustion (from the idea of habitual or customary practice—as in being 'used' to doing something—as a result of which clothes repeatedly worn, for example, can end up being worn out or destroyed), in which case 'use' comes rather closer to 'abuse' (using up, squandering, waste). The qualifier 'right' is designed to keep the two senses apart, but the very need for it suggests a weak point: an internal ambiguity if not contradiction within the word, a liability that the two senses might collapse into one (a curious feature of what Freud calls the antithetical meaning of primal words), that does nothing to strengthen the speaker's case.[131]

For his part, Gosson seems much more alert to this difficulty, returning to it at greater length in *Playes confuted in five actions* (1582)—the last and longest of his contributions to the antipoetic tradition and anti-theatrical debate—where he tries to hammer out the distinction between right use and wrong once and for all. In the First Action, for example, he takes this distinction as the basis for differentiating those things that Christian folk might legitimately take from the ancient world— which are 'reuealed vnto them by God, for necessary vses and the benefite of man' (155/B7ᵛ) and include things like ships, linen, various handicrafts, and other objects 'inuented for necessarie vses' (155/B8)—and those things that they must reject: which are 'inspyred by the Deuill' (155/B7ᵛ) and include things that are 'neither necessary nor beneficiall vnto man' (155/B8) like stage-plays. In the Third Action, he concedes that there is a 'true vse of Poetrie' (177/E5ᵛ), which is to imitate, more or less, what Sidney's speaker calls the 'inconceivable excellencies of God' (86.22–3), as in biblical poetry or drama.[132] It is in the Fourth Action,

---

[131] Freud (1910) and (1919). See also Derrida 1992 (73–82) on the anthropological and philological commonplace that operations that might be considered antithetical—such as giving and taking, buying and selling, owing and owning, or borrowing and lending—were anciently designated by single terms: referring to Benveniste 1971 (271–80) and Lévi-Strauss 1987 (45–50).

[132] Gosson is dealing here with the objection that Church Fathers (such as Gregory Naziancen) and contemporaries (such as George Buchanan) wrote religious dramas: 'As the beginning of poetrie in the bookes of Moses, & Dauid, was to sett downe good matter in numbers, that the sweetenesse of the one

however, that Gosson examines the question of right as opposed to wrong use the most closely. In the context of denying his position is an austerely puritanical one that would reject 'the vse of many creatures which God hath ordeined for the seruice of man' (189/F8ᵛ–G1), he insists that such 'may be vsed both for necessity, and for delight, so farre foorth as they are referred to that ende, for which they were made' (190/G1ᵛ). God has bestowed many things upon us that are either 'both necessary and delightsome' or 'only delightsome, nothing necessary' (although Gosson does not, interestingly, specify which category 'Treasure, as golde, siluer, pearle, bewetifull and rich stones' comes into), but the crucial point is that, either way, we 'vse them well, & by these transitorie benefits be led as it were by yᵉ hand, to a consideration of those benefits that are layde vp for vs in the life to come':

> We are placed as Pilgrimes in yᵉ flesh by which as by a iorney we must come to our own home, therefor passing by the earth, and by the flesh it is our duety (as trauelers) to be carefull to vse the earth, and the flesh, and the blessings of both, so; that they may further, not hinder the course we take in hande. (190/G1ᵛ)

Gosson is drawing here on St Paul's revision of the Aristotelian understanding of use—broadly, the sensible utilization of those things provided by nature that are of benefit to human life (such as the making of cloth from fleeces, for example)—so as to subordinate this to a higher, more spiritual end. Unlike their pagan counterparts, Christians are called upon to negotiate a tricky transition between the two. While on earth they may use the things of this world for the duration (properly and suitably, of course), but they must at the same time always keep their sights on the final goal, which is salvation. From the heavenly perspective of the latter, however, such earthly things will seem infinitely unimportant and dispensable—as having no real, fundamental use—and they are therefore to be treated accordingly. They may be used for the purposes of everyday life, that is, but only on the understanding (ideally) that they are spiritually redundant. Much of the ambiguity about when 'use' may be considered right or not is contained within this subtle Pauline doctrine which Gosson goes on to quote: 'Wherevpon *Paule* exhorteth vs to vse this worlde, as though wee vsed it not' (190/G1ᵛ–G2).[133] To Gosson's dismay, regardless of the fact that so much is at stake, this subtlety seems to be lost on his fellow countrymen whose behaviour is not only unconducive but positively detrimental to their salvation: 'howe vse we these blessings ... when they are riottously wasted vpon Comedies, which drawe vs all backe to a sinfull delight? howe vse wee the worlde as though wee vsed it not, when our studies are so fixed vpon the worlde?' (190/G2).

might cause the other to continue, and to bee the deeper imprinted in the mindes of men: So Naziancen and Bucchanan perceiuing the corruption of the Gentiles, to avoyde that which is euill, and yet keepe that which is good, according to the true vse of Poetrie, penned these bookes in numbers with interloqutions dialoguewise, as Plato and Tullie did their Philosophy, to be reade, not be played' (177/E5ᵛ).

[133] Referring to 1 Corinthians 7:31: 'And they that vse this worlde, [should be] as thogh they vsed it not' (Geneva Bible). Paul's views on right use were developed by Augustine in his distinction between use and enjoyment: see Augustine 1995, *De Doctrina Christiana*, 1.iii–iv. Cf. the concept of *usufructus*, note 80 above.

Although Sidney's speaker alludes to this Pauline doctrine in passing, referring only a couple of pages later to the Apostle's warning in Colossians against 'the abuse' (107.7) of philosophy—'Teaching you vaine speculations', as the Geneva gloss has it, 'as worshiping of Angels, of blinde ceremonies and beggerlie traditions: for now they haue none vse seeing Christ is come'—he does not, it has to be said, examine the matter with anything approaching Gosson's thoroughness.[134] Gosson's analysis, on the other hand, gives a good indication of how unstable the question of 'right use' could be—how easily it could be confused, in practice, with ordinary 'use' and thus, potentially, with 'abuse'—and the risks that might be entailed, therefore, in resting a defence of poetry upon it. One way of illustrating this instability might be to look at the trouble this word evidently caused translators of the Bible, for this appears with particular clarity in a passage (just a few verses later in Colossians) in which Paul is reiterating the point about the relative unimportance of worldly rules and regulations—including traditional religious observances—in the light of Christ's coming:

> Wherefore if ye *be* dead with Christ from the ordinances of the worlde, why, as thogh ye liued in the worlde, are ye burdened with traditions? *As*, Touche not, Taste not, Handel not. Which all perish with the vsing, *and are* after the commandements and doctrines of men.[135]

Prohibitions of this kind might continue to be observed as customary and accepted practice—and be 'used' in that sense—but, as man-made rituals, they serve no real purpose and ultimately come to nothing: that they 'all perish' with such use is suggestive of their irrelevance, their emptiness in spiritual terms.[136] The Geneva Bible's choice of the gerund 'vsing' here follows Tyndale, as Matthew's Bible did and as the Authorized Version would also do, while the Catholic Douai-Rheims translation would offer the variant 'vse'.[137] Coverdale, however, chose the verb 'abuse' to translate the same passage: 'All these thinges do hurte vnto men, because of the abuse of them, which abuse commeth onely of the commaundementes and doctrynes of men', and his version was followed, in turn, by both the Great Bible

---

[134] Referring to Colossians 2:8: 'Beware lest there be anie man that spoile you through philosophie, and vaine deceit, through the traditions of men, according to the rudiments of the worlde, and not after Christ' (Geneva Bible). The reference to Paul reinforces the preceding sentence in which the speaker—co-opting Plato as an ally rather than an enemy in poetry's cause—claims to 'honour philosophical instructions . . . so as they be not abused' (107.2–3). He thus sees philosophy as being, like poetry, capable both of abusing (as subject), and of being abused (as object), a point to which we shall return.

[135] Colossians 2:20–2, with a gloss adding: 'And apperteine nothing to the kingdome of God'; such things '*are of no value saue for the filling of the flesh*' (Geneva Bible, emphasis original).

[136] See *OED* use *v*. I.2.a.: 'to observe (a custom, a traditional practice or rule of conduct)'; using *n*. 1.a.: 'the action of making use of something, or the fact of being used' (current from the mid-fourteenth century), this quotation given as one of the citations.

[137] See: (1) Tyndale's Bible: 'which all perisshe with the vsynge of them and are after yᵉ commaundmentes and doctrine of men'; (2) Matthew's Bible: 'which all perisshe wyth the vsynge of them and are after the commaundmentes and doctrynes of men'; (3) Authorized Version: 'Which all are to perish with the vsing) after the commandements and doctrines of men'; and (4) Douai-Rheims Bible: 'which things are al vnto destruction by the very vse, according to the precepts and doctrines of men'.

and Cranmer's Bible, while the Bishop's Bible offered the variant 'abusing'.[138] Evidently 'using' something—in a way that was spiritually useless, pointless, hollow—could be deemed synonymous with 'abusing' it. In 1550 Coverdale's translation was 'conferred' with Tyndale's but his version nonetheless retained.[139] Going further back does not clarify matters. The Vulgate has '*quae sunt omnia in interitu ipso usu secundum praecepta et doctrinas hominum*', and Wycliffe follows suit with his 'whiche alle ben in to deth bi the ilke vss, aftir the comaundementis and the techingis of men'.[140] Erasmus, on the other hand, has '*abusu*': '*quae omnia ipso pereunt abusu, iuxta praecepta, & doctrinas hominum*'.[141] English translators, meanwhile, clearly felt able to cite Erasmus' '*abusu*' as the authority for either 'using' or 'abusing'.[142] As for the Pauline original, as set out in Erasmus' parallel Greek text, this does not clear the matter up either, since the verb employed—ἀποχράομαι, 'to use to the full, avail oneself of'—could also mean 'to abuse, misuse'.[143] While we are at it, it might also be worth mentioning that the passage from Corinthians, on which Gosson bases his lengthy disquisition on the difficult business of using the things of this world as if we were not doing so, reveals a similar uncertainty. For, while the majority of the Bible translations discussed above opt for the form of words that Gosson refers to—'they that vse this worlde, [should be] as thogh they vsed it not'—two, including the Authorized Version, have the following alternative:

[138] See: (1) Coverdale's Bible, followed by: (2) Great Bible: 'whych all perysshe thorow the very abuse: after the commaundments and doctrynes of men'; (3) Cranmer's Bible: 'whyche all perysh thorowe the verye abuse: after the commaundeme*n*ts and doctrines of men'; (4) Bishop's Bible: 'Which all be in corruption, in abusyng after the commaundementes and doctrines of men'. *OED* abuse *n*. 3 cites the Great Bible as the sole instance of 'abuse' in the sense of 'the process of using up or wearing out', although it clearly had wider currency, and may also be predated by a few years. This passage in Colossians is also cited by *OED* as the sole instance of 'abusing' being deployed in the sense of 'the action or process of using something up' (see abusing *n*. 2). *OED*'s citation (*a*1555) predates the Bishop's Bible, and is sourced from John Philpot's 'A Defence of the true and old authority of Christ's Church'—a manuscript translation of Celio Secundo Curione, *Pro vera et antiqua Ecclesiae Christi autoritate* (Basel, *c.*1546)—which refers to this passage: 'which all perish with the abusing of them, and are after the commandments and doctrines of men': see Philpot 1842 (419). Philpot (1516–55) was archdeacon of Winchester and a prominent Marian martyr.
[139] Coverdale's Bible 'conferred' with Tyndale's: 'All these thynges doo hurt vnto men, bycause of the abuse of theim, whiche abuse cometh onely of the co*m*mandementes and doctrines of men.'
[140] See: (1) Vulgate; (2) Wycliffe's Bible.　　[141] Erasmus, *Novum Instrumentum* (Basel, 1516).
[142] Thus, *The Newe Testament in Englyshe and in Latin of Erasmus translation* has 'whiche all peryshe with the vsynge of them and are after the commaundementes and doctrynes of men', with Erasmus' translation in parallel; while *The Newe Testament of our Sauiour Iesus Christ faithfully translated out of the Greeke* has 'Which al be in corruption, in abusing after the commandements and doctrines of men', with a marginal note referencing Erasmus' translation: 'Or, doo perish in abusing. Eras.'
[143] 'ἅ ἐστι πάντα εἰς φθορὰν τῇ ἀποχρήσει'. In his *Annotations on the New Testament* (1535) Erasmus justifies his translation of ἀποχρήσει by *abusu* here because it clarifies the sense of something being used up—consumed entirely with nothing remaining—as in the case of food and drink: '*Agit enim de cibo & potu, quae usu consumuntur, & in latrinam excernuntur. Nam iis proprie dicimur abuti, quae usu absumuntur*': see Erasmus 1993 (642). The primary sense of ἀποχράομαι was 'to use to the full, avail oneself of' (derived from ἀποχράω, 'to suffice, be sufficient, be enough'), but it also had the secondary sense of 'to abuse, misuse', as did Latin *abutor* (Liddell and Scott). In his own annotation on Colossians 2:22, Theodore Beza 1642 (609) comments: '*Erasmus vero τῇ ἀποχρήσει convertit abusu, recte quidem et ex iurisconsultorum distinctione, qui Abusum proprie in iis constituunt quorum usus in ipsa consumptione positus est. Usum tamen dicere malui, ut omnem ἀμφιβολίαν vitarem*'. I am most grateful to Paul Botley for bringing this to my attention and for his suggestion that here Beza 'connects use and abuse with Roman property law, and implies that this is in fact what Erasmus had in mind at this point' (private communication).

'they that vse this worlde, [be] as [though they are] not abusing it.'[144] Where one might have expected the opposite of 'use' to be 'abuse', in fact its antithesis turns out to be either 'not using' or 'not abusing'. The two words are to all intents and purposes interchangeable.[145]

As this brief survey would seem to suggest, therefore, the concept of right use is far from stable. Where 'use' could sometimes mean 'abuse' anyway (using something excessively to the point that it is all used up), and where 'right use'—intended to clarify the difference between the two—turns out on examination to do anything but, there is a case for saying that, in practical terms, abuse is all but inevitable. And this, more or less, is the regretful conclusion Gosson comes to, as he surveys the riotous scene of contemporary London before him. Sidney's speaker, meanwhile, seems minded to agree, for the strategic reduction of the antipoetic argument he had made at the outset now moves in the opposite direction. The destructive agency imputed to poetry by the poet-haters, that is to say, which the speaker had earlier sought to minimize by identifying it with a few rogue artists, here re-inflates and expands exponentially, not only infecting the fancy and pleasing the ill-pleased eye but doing 'more hurt than any other army of words' (104.29). From there, the possibility of abuse extends further still, going beyond poetry to invade every walk of life—medicine, law, religion, and (a couple of pages later) philosophy—and

---

[144] See: (1) Vulgate: '*et qui utuntur hoc mundo tamquam non utantur*'; (2) Wycliffe's Bible: 'and thei that vsen this world, as thei that vsen not'; (3) Erasmus' New Testament: '*qui utuntur mundo hoc, tanquam non utantur*'; (4) Tyndale's Bible: 'they that vse this worlde, be as though they vsed it not'. This formula is then repeated verbatim by: (5) Coverdale's Bible; (6) Matthews Bible; (7) Great Bible; (8) Cranmer's Bible; (9) the English New Testament in parallel with Erasmus' Latin translation; (10) Coverdale's Bible 'conferred' with Tyndale's translation; (11) Geneva Bible: (12) Bishop's Bible; and (13) Douai-Rheims Bible. The alternative formulation is found in the English New Testament translated from the Greek and in the Authorized Version, which has the same. Erasmus' thoughtful scholarship illustrates the crux particularly well. His choice of *utantur* here translates the Greek καταχράομαι which has the same complex range of senses as ἀποχράομαι, i.e. 'to make use of'; II.1. 'to use to the uttermost, use up, consume'; 2. 'to misuse, misapply, abuse' (Liddell and Scott). In the *Annotations on the New Testament*, however, he glosses '*tanquam non utantur*' with '*tanquam non abutentes*' to clarify that he is using the Greek word in its second sense (food and drink again providing an example of something that is completely consumed) as opposed to its first (something that is made use of, as in the wearing of clothes): see Erasmus 1990 (465).

[145] As an alternative opposing term, 'misuse' turns out to be no more stable, either. In I Corinthians 9, for example, Paul rather defensively insists that, although he might have received worldly benefits (board and lodging, for example) in return for preaching the gospel—and would have been entitled to do so—'neuertheles, we haue not vsed this power' (9.12), 'I haue vsed none of these things' (9.15) for 'I abuse not mine autoritie in the Gospel' (9.18) (Geneva Bible). This sequence (used/used/abuse) also appears in Coverdale's Bible, in Coverdale's Bible 'conferred' with Tyndale's, in Douai-Rheims, and in the Authorized Version. Tyndale's Bible, however, replaces 'abuse' with 'misuse'—'I misuse not myne auctorite'—and this sequence (used/used/misuse) appears in Matthew's Bible, the Great Bible, Cranmer's Bible, and the Bishop's Bible. The English New Testament in parallel with Erasmus' Latin text also has this sequence, employing it to translate Erasmus' '*non vsi fuimus*', '*nullo horum vsus fui*', and '*ne abutar*', as does the English New Testament translated from the Greek. Confusingly, however, Erasmus' *abutar* here translates a cognate of καταχράομαι which he had previously translated with *utantur* (see note 144). The Vulgate, similarly, has '*non usi sumus*', '*usus sum non*', and '*non abutar*', although Wycliffe's Bible—while translating *utor* with 'use' like everyone else ('we vsen not', 'Y vside noon of these thingis')—goes out on a limb by rendering *abutor* as the same: 'Y vse not my power in the gospel.' In sum, Paul's own practice of right use—of using/not using the things of this world—could equally be rendered in English as: not using them (Wycliffe), not abusing them (Coverdale, etc.), and not misusing them (Tyndale, etc.).

there is no holding back from the dire consequences such abuse is seen to have, not only on the individual but on the state:

> Do we not see the skill of Physic (the best rampire to our often-assaulted bodies), being abused, teach poison, the most violent destroyer? Doth not knowledge of Law, whose end is to even and right all things, being abused, grow the crooked fosterer of horrible injuries? Doth not (to go to the highest) God's word abused breed heresy, and His name abused become blasphemy? Truly a needle cannot do much hurt, and as truly (with leave of ladies be it spoken) it cannot do much good. With a sword thou mayest kill thy father, and with a sword thou mayest defend thy prince and country.
>
> (104.34–42)

Abuse is everywhere—endemic, ambient, omnipresent—and, by the same token, nowhere is safe: nothing, it seems, capable of withstanding the onslaught. Of course, the speaker is still holding out for the possibility of an ideal, defensible poetry: still resting his hopes on the policy of reversal and banking on his argument that 'whatsoever, being abused, doth most harm, being rightly used . . . doth most good' (104.31–3). In the circumstances, however, it becomes increasingly difficult for 'right use' to hold its own. The speaker's concessions have gone too far and stretched his argument to a point where it is hard to see how it can recover or how he might turn it round to his advantage after all. Abuse might be regretted and railed against, but evidently it cannot be helped. There is nothing for it. It happens anyway. Maverick artists 'may' (104.18, 25) do as they should not and abuse their art—and that art go on to abuse its recipients—but there is nothing anyone can do about it, any more than they can prevent the malpractice of rogue doctors, lawyers, believers, and philosophers. Having conceded this much, it becomes necessary for the speaker to revise his formula once again in order to produce a still more refined version than the last: namely, that poetry need not abuse *even though* it is abused. The problem with this formulation, however, is that the former scenario—the point at which poetry might be defended and commended—becomes an entirely theoretical one and the ideal of a true, right, non-abusive, and defensible poetry a concept so academic and hypothetical that it is in danger of being abstracted and rarefied out of existence.[146] Gosson was right: such ideal poetry is indeed a Phoenix in Arabia, it being 'impossible, or incredible, that no abuse should be learned where such lessons are taught, & such schooles [of abuse] mainteined' (79/A4ᵛ).

The speaker's strategy of reversal ends up, therefore, making a much weaker argument than his initial confidence had led us to believe; and that he becomes increasingly aware of this might be detected in the classic signs of an argument in disarray which appear here with a particular density. For, within a matter of fifteen

---

[146] See also Bronowski 1939 (30) who agrees that the quarrel between Gosson and Sidney 'hangs on the meaning which they give to the words, the right use'. For Gosson, the right use of poetry exists only as an unrealizable ideal. Since its actual production is necessarily mediated by the senses, poetry is open to abuse, cannot be unbound from its abuses, and is thus abusive in its very nature. For Bronowski, 'Sidney does not answer this charge at all. Tactically, he makes the most of what Gosson has allowed: that there is a right use of poetry, and that it is the abuses of poetry which are at fault . . . But if the right use is not an actual use, poetry cannot claim to be judged by it. For there is then no poem which is free from abuse' (31–2).

lines, we have three 'truly's (104.27, 39, 40), four rhetorical questions—'shall the abuse of a thing make the right use odious?' (104.26–7), 'Do we not see . . . ?' (104.34), 'Doth not . . . Doth not . . . ?' (104.36, 38)—and five examples that (in yielding so much ground to the opposition) fail to exemplify: poets who infect the fancy (104.18–21), painters who please an ill-pleased eye (104.21–6), doctors who poison (104.34–6), lawyers who injure (104.36–7), and false believers who breed heresy and who blaspheme (104.38–9). The speaker's attempt to wrest the strength of the opposition—and the strength they had imputed to poetry—in order to turn it against them, thus ends up rebounding against himself such that we find him yet again in what appears to be his perennial position: beating himself for spite, in the sense both of chastising and of defeating himself. The consequences for his defence—and for the *Defence* more generally—are predictable. Just as the 'skill of Physic'—supposedly 'the best rampire [rampart]' with which to defend 'our often-assaulted bodies'—proves helpless against abuse, so the speaker's body ends up being similarly assaulted, except this time by his own hand (this doctor does not know himself but only poisons himself, instead). And just as the sword with which one 'mayest defend thy prince and country' may just as easily 'kill thy father', so the speaker's defence of his own territory—poetry—proves equally unreliable, self-destructive, and self-defeating in the end.

The reason for this textual fluster, I suggest, is that under the auspices of the speaker's strategy of reversal there is, in fact, a completely different argument going on—a quite alternative case being made—and these familiar indications of a theoretical statement under strain suggest, as before, the intervention of a counter-voice that serves very effectively to sabotage the speaker's best efforts. The clue, I think, lies in the difference the speaker posits between poesy that is *eikastike* and that which is *phantastike*. For he uses this to draw out a clearly moralized distinction between what art 'should' do (104.18, 21)—which is to represent 'good' (104.19), 'excellent', 'fine', 'fit' (104.22) and exemplary things— and what art unfortunately 'may' do (104.18, 25), which is to represent 'unworthy' (104.21) and 'wanton' (104.25) things: a distinction he then maps onto that between 'right use' (104.27, 32) and 'abuse' (104.26, 30) respectively. However, when editors gloss *eikastike* as 'imitative', and *phantastike* as 'fanciful', 'dreamlike', 'imaginary'—the latter all used in a 'derogatory sense'—it becomes clearer, perhaps, that the distinction the speaker is really making here is that between *imitation* and *fiction*: where imitation is what I have been calling 'mimesis-plus' (that is, imitation not of the actual or real, but rather of the 'real', that is to say, the ideal 'realized': an art that makes things 'better' than Nature), and where fiction is another word for invention (creation *ab nihilo*, making things up, the fantastical, the counterfactual, the imaginative: an art that makes things 'anew').[147] The 'argument of abuse', in other words, is evidently being mapped directly onto the confrontation that lies at the very heart of the *Defence*, namely between an idealist poetics (*eikastike*) and an alternative, non-idealist poetics (*phantastike*) that is deemed hostile or inimical to it.

---

[147] Shepherd (202); Maslen (208). See also Bates 2007 (119–20) for an earlier discussion of this passage.

The speaker's return to another favourite analogy here—that between poets and painters—would seem to confirm this. Earlier discussions that distinguished between good painters and bad had identified the former as those who exemplify the idealist aesthetic—the 'excellent' painters (87.3) who depict what is 'fittest for the eye to see' (87.4) and fashion things 'to the best grace' (92.30–1)—as opposed to the 'meaner sort' (87.2) who depict merely what is 'set before them' (87.2–3). In the present discussion, likewise, paintings that depict 'excellent', 'fit', and exemplary subjects (scenes from the Bible, and so forth) are the visual equivalent of *eikastike* poetry. The latter's 'figuring forth good things' (104.19–20) echoes the approved model of imitation described earlier in the *propositio* as 'a representing, counterfeiting, or figuring forth . . . with this end, to teach and delight' (86.18–20), so that idealist aesthetics and poetics here come together and find their apotheosis in the 'speaking picture' (86.19; 90.42) that succeeds in manifesting the '*Idea* or foreconceit' (85.35) and in bodying forth the ideal in perceptual form. The opposite, by contrast—that which operates 'contrariwise' (104.20) and therefore deviates from the right and proper way—are paintings that 'please an ill-pleased eye with wanton shows' (104.25), the visual equivalent of *phantastike* poems that similarly 'infect the fancy with unworthy objects' (104.20–1). Admittedly, this is not quite the same charge as that levelled at the 'meaner painters', which was not that they depicted immoral subjects but rather that they failed to idealize what they represented, opting instead to reproduce verisimilar likenesses of their subjects, warts and all.[148] Nonetheless, the basic confrontation lying behind the analogy with the painters is the same, namely that between an idealist art, on the one hand, and a non-idealist art that questions, resists, challenges, opposes, destabilizes, and destroys, or at the very least offers a conceptual alternative to it, on the other. A number of things come to stand in for the latter—the actual, the realistic, the verisimilar, the fictional, the fantastic, the counterfactual, the 'wanton'—but these are all fairly interchangeable insofar as their polemical function is concerned: the part they play in the *Defence*'s underlying argument, that is, which is to signify anything that is not or is other to—which opposes and therefore 'abuses'—the ideal.

Since the speaker is trying his hardest to defend idealist poetics, it is not particularly surprising that he should continue against the odds to hold out for

---

[148] That the distinction between paintings that idealize their subjects and those that represent them accurately or realistically is not really one that lends itself to moralization—and that such moralization is therefore liable to deconstruction—is evident in the example the speaker provides of the 'perfect picture' (90.23, 25): that of an elephant or rhinoceros so 'well painted' (90.35) that the viewer could grasp the true nature of the creatures in question far more immediately and effectively than by receiving a merely 'wordish description' (90.27) of them. It is hard to discern how one might differentiate an ideal painting of a rhinoceros from an accurate and realistic one. The same weakness in the moralization argument appears a page or so later in the denigration of the painter who would paint 'Vespasian's picture right as he was' (92.24–5). While this is deemed better than a representation that is 'nothing resembling' (92.25), it is still subordinated to the representation that would idealize the notoriously ugly emperor (although the latter, presumably, would be 'nothing resembling' either), just as the feigned Cyrus and Aeneas in poetry are deemed to be better than the 'true Cyrus' (92.28) and 'right Aeneas' (92.29) who appear in the historical record. That accurate, realistic representation is described as 'right' or 'true', however—even if it is not ideal—suggests an intrinsic problem with the language of ideal rightness that tries to moralize it as wrong.

right use, nor that he should moralize the difference between imitative and fictive art. By the same token, it is not particularly strange that idealist editors should emphasize this as his aim, either, sourcing the distinction between art that makes likenesses (*eikastike*) and art that makes only appearances (*phantastike*) in Plato's *Sophist*, which similarly concludes that, as opposed to the former, the latter is, in their words, 'worthless', 'unworthy', and 'harmful'.[149] This evaluation is said to be compatible with Sidney's 'own literary theory', where the latter is assumed to be idealist and to assert 'the claims of the "real"' (the ideal 'realized', that is), as per the speaker's earlier assertions that poetry is 'not wholly imaginative' (85.38), and his denials that it presents things 'fantastically or falsely' (92.11).[150] Sidney's unwavering adherence to idealist poetics, however, is no longer something that can be serenely assumed. Indeed, this section of the *Defence* turns out, like so many others, to be the record of a battle between that ideal and its nemesis, and, for all the speaker's willed arguments to the contrary, to be no less of a losing one.[151] Instead, one might get a glimpse of Sidney's secret or unconscious identification with this vengeful attack on idealist poetics—and sympathy with its alternative—in the tautologous statement, not to be denied, that 'man's wit may make Poesy . . . to be *phantastike*' (104.18–20). That man's wit (the individual wit, the fertile wit, the quick wit, the freely ranging wit, the highest-flying wit, the infected and most definitely not erected wit) may make poesy—*may make making*—that is fictive, fantastical, imaginative, and inventive seems a pretty good definition of *poesis* to me.[152] Indeed, Sidney seems almost to have arrived at the position that poetry that does not abuse is not poetry. Moreover, for all its philosophical pedigree and moral righteousness, the idealist aesthetic proves powerless to resist this counterforce, remaining strangely defenceless against its attacks and obliged to 'yield' (104.27) to them. After the various refinements of his formula, the speaker's final position is that idealist art remains ideal only insofar as it may be *theorized* (since it cannot be practised) as such: an increasingly intangible, etherealized, and unrealizable conception of art

[149] Shepherd (202); Maslen (208). Distinguishing between art that is εἰκαστικήν and φανταστικήν, the interlocutors of Plato's dialogue find the latter to be ontologically empty (like dreams and day-dreams, shadows, reflections on water, or optical illusions): see Plato 1921, *Sophist* 235D–236C. Plato's words for this—or rather those of the Eleatic Stranger into whose mouth he puts them—are γοητεία, witchcraft, jugglery (e.g. 235A; 241B) and θαυματοποιέω, to do wonders, play jugglers' tricks (e.g. 235B; 268D).

[150] Shepherd (202).

[151] Just as the apparent antithesis between 'use' and 'abuse' exposes a weak point in the argument—since in practice they are on the same spectrum (to use to the full—to use up—to empty)—so here, while *eikastike* poetry is supposed to embody the ideal (the ideal behind appearances, truth within language, meaning within words, and so on), it necessarily shades into the realm of the *phantastike* or the purely imaginary since that ideal is, in practice, unrealizable. Again, the metaphysically full gives way to the ontologically empty.

[152] See also Puttenham 2007 (109) who gives a fairly robust defence of the 'fantastical', which in his view has been unfairly demeaned by the critics of poetry who insist on 'construing it to the worst side'. He does, however, distinguish between those who have 'disordered fantasies' and those whose fantasies are 'nothing disorderly' (109)—the *phantastici* and the *euphantasiote*, respectively—and makes sure to include 'all good poets' among the latter (110). While his position towards the fantastical is more generous than that of Sidney's speaker, therefore, Puttenham still holds out for the ideal to a degree, and in that respect goes less far than Sidney would.

that is in danger of disappearing into vanishingly fine smoke, and the moment, perhaps, to concede that a losing battle is finally a lost one.[153] By contrast, the challenging counterforce that resists this conception—and so 'abuses' it—proves, for its part, to be strangely irresistible. It cannot be denied. It has to be granted. And it will have its effects—deleterious, according to the speaker—quite regardless of any efforts he or his supporters might make to denounce or defend against it. This counterforce, however, is not, as the speaker would have it, a conquering army—its 'sweet charming force' doing 'more hurt than any other army of words'—since that is too redolent of his images of poets as masculinized, militarized, laurel-crowned, 'triumphing' and 'triumphant captains' (100.34; 108.18) who crush all before them in the name of the ideal and its ideology of value. Rather, this abusing counterforce is a more diffuse, invisible, almost airborne threat—as noted above, it is vague, unspecified, de-particularized, yet endemic, ambient, omnipresent—and, like the 'force of delight' (106.27–8), all the more overpowering for being so.

This, I suggest, is the real argument being made here, although 'real' is perhaps the wrong word since this counter-argument rather drifts like a cloud or floats like a disruptive ghost, haunting the speaker's official argument, emptying out its propositions, evacuating its confident claims, vaporizing its golden ideals, turning *l'auro* into *l'aura*—gold to airy thinness beat—and wafting off high into the atmosphere with a sense of relief (a breath of fresh air after all that attitudinizing) to the place it has wanted to be all along, which is the wholly imaginative, the thoroughly made up, the fantastical: the zodiac of the poet's own wit. If, therefore, we go back to the question posed at the beginning—where poetry is moved to the object position, who or what occupies the subject position; who or what is abusing poetry?—we might now answer that it is not some external body or extraneous force but, rather, poetry itself. Or, more specifically, that one kind of poetry (the fictive, the *phantastike*) acts against another kind of poetry (the imitative, the *eikastike*)—desiccates it, erodes it, and blows it away—as the alternative, non-idealist model of poetry sees off the idealist model very effectively. Poetry thus emerges as a split regime—as both subject and object—eternally self-divided, like so many of Sidney's avatars, and equally at war with itself: an outcome that returns us to the different positions, and relations between them, that I have been tracing throughout this book. For Gosson and the poet-haters, this internal split is an argument for abolishing poetry altogether. Riven in this way, poetry is not and never can be ideal. It can never manifest the '*Idea* or fore-conceit' because it is always at two removes (at least) away from it. Poetry thus undermines the tenets of idealist philosophy and the ideology that operates in its name, threatening the smooth operation and reproduction of that ideology in human society and civilization. Poetry abuses, end of story, and on those grounds it must be banished. For

---

[153] Bronowski 1939 might have been advised to do likewise, for—having shown that Sidney was unable to answer Gosson's charge of abuse (see note 146)—the critic redoubles his efforts to prove that Sidney defends idealist poetics nevertheless, revealing, in his very desperation to prove Sidney an idealist at all costs, the same signs of forcedness and strain that are evident in the speaker's argument. Cf. Sinfield 1992 (205) for whom this supposedly ideal synthesis in the *Defence* 'effects not a resolution, but a clash of rival absolutes'.

the speaker and other defenders of poetry, on the other hand, this is an argument for coming to poetry's rescue. The charge of abuse is denied or, as here, reversed. Poetry is abused, that much is granted, but ideally it is ideal (does not abuse) and on those grounds it must be defended. For Sidney, however, this is an argument for finding a new 'third' way between these two entrenched and equally unsatisfactory positions. For him, poetry that makes things 'anew' is preferable to poetry that claims to make things 'better', in the same way that fiction is preferable to imitation and the obviously false preferable to the supposedly true. Poetry that is *phantastike* gets the better of poetry that is *eikastike* and shows the latter's idealism to be pretty fantastical, anyway, just as 'use' turns out to be more or less the same as 'abuse', and the full chest on the way to being an empty one. Fantastical, fictive, abusive, 'wanton' poetry thereby offers an alternative to right 'use' and to the 'right' poetry supposed to exemplify it. An alternative to the officially sanctioned and approved model, enthusiastically espoused by the Protestant humanist culture of the day, that saw poetry as useful and fruitful, as delightfully teaching, as a force for good, as necessary and beneficial, as providing some quantifiable yield, as performing a valuable cultural service—which was to abstract value and to value things according to what they were worth and so to perpetuate that kind of thinking as not only right, proper, rational, reasonable, self-evident, and true, but as the only kind available—and as reproducing this thinking in the form of an infinite series of unthinking, self-reproducing Cyrus-types. Non-idealist poetry abuses such idealist poetics—deconstructs its ideology of profit and power, its determinations to be golden, to be rich—and on those grounds it must be written. Cue *Astrophil and Stella.*

The difference between these three positions comes down, ultimately, to the question of agency. For Gosson and the poet-haters, what poetry clearly abuses is 'men's wit'. He and they invest poetry with a power that supersedes all human intention and control, for it is not only innocent readers who stand to be duped and misled by it but, more worryingly, the most honest-to-goodness, well-trained, and well-meaning of writers. Even those who endeavour to 'plant goodness' (90.5) and who 'intend the winning of the mind from wickedness to virtue' (95.19–20) and nothing else can find their best efforts overturned by this most treacherous medium. For the speaker, who would deny poetry any agency independent of man's wit (like many such defenders, taking the power of art less seriously than its detractors), it is therefore easy enough to reverse the formula and say that 'man's wit abuseth Poetry'. Ideally, man's wit will wield poetry like a useful tool, bringing light to young minds, inspiring proto-Cyruses, and so forth—the pedagogic goal—but even when man's wit is behaving badly (infecting the fancy with unworthy objects, pleasing the eye with wanton shows), it is still in the ascendant: still in control, still the active subject abusing the passive object. And if that naughty poetry then goes on to abuse its readers and viewers, in turn, it is only those naughty poets who are to blame, not the poetry itself. For Sidney, by contrast, there is no doubt whatever about poetry's agency: about the power it exerts over everyone who reads it, but over its practitioners most of all. To the extent that he agrees that poetry can and does abuse—and thus occupy the subject position—Sidney finds himself in alliance with Gosson and the antipoetic tradition once again. Where he differs from them is that he perversely revels in that abuse. What Gosson fears and deplores, Sidney welcomes and celebrates—exults in, rejoices in—and puts lovingly into practice in his own art.

◯

Vestiges of the speaker's reversal strategy appear elsewhere in the *Defence*, most obviously in his 'not the art but the artificer' argument: another attempt to put the onus of failed or naughty art onto its wayward practitioners and so to deflect blame from the art itself. This argument—which culminates in the *digressio*—surfaces periodically throughout the text, although it fares no better in these places, unsurprisingly, than it does in the *refutatio*. Indeed, it tends to appear at particularly problematic or conflicted points within the speaker's defence, the first example appearing in his discussion of the *Utopia* where a major plank of his argument— namely, that poetry teaches better than philosophy—appears to slip for a moment, as he concedes that the latter might in fact have 'more force in teaching' (91.26) and thus behave 'more rightly' (91.27) than the former. That poetry can sometimes fail in its achievement is supported by a quote from Horace to the effect that no one likes poets to be anything but top-notch: '*Mediocribus esse poetis / non dii, non homines, non concessere columnae*' (91.30–1).[154] Even where such failure is the case, however, the speaker claims that it is 'not the fault of the art, but that by few men that art can be accomplished' (91.32–3). It was More's apparent failure to pull off the representation of an ideal commonwealth in the *Utopia*—setting out a state that was perfect or 'most absolute . . . not so absolutely' (91.24)—that prompts this reflection, for, where he 'erred, it was the fault of the man and not of the poet' (91.22–3). What the speaker seems to be implying here is that the idea (and the ideal) was a good one—and is not, therefore, to be critiqued in itself—but it just happened to be let down on this particular occasion by the failings of the individual writer. As discussed earlier, however, the *Utopia* is not concerned with representing an ideal, perfect, or 'absolute' commonwealth. Rather, More's text points to the absolutism that inexorably proceeds from such idealist thinking, through the ingenious device of making its vehicle—the money form—conspicuous by its absence. The example is cited in the context of poets' ability to steer princes toward virtuous action by means of their feigned representations: 'in the most excellent determination of goodness, what philosopher's counsel can so readily direct a prince' (91.18–19), the speaker asks, as the *Cyropaedia*, the *Aeneid*, or the *Utopia*? However, the fact that More failed, in the event, to direct his prince towards goodness—falling victim instead to the tyranny he exposed—makes it less obvious that the blame should lie squarely with him. If More's is a negative example, then it

---

[154] Quoting Horace 1926, *Ars Poetica*, lines 372–3: '*mediocribus esse poetis / non homines, non di, non concessere columnae*' [But that poets be of middling rank, neither men nor gods nor booksellers ever brooked], the speaker's only alteration being to put the gods before men. In fact, Horace admits a few lines earlier that there are faults he would gladly pardon—since things do not always go to plan and the occasional mistake can therefore be tolerated—it being repeated errors, and a lack of discernment and skill at which he draws the line.

is one of a number that are perversely followed in the *Defence*, regardless of the speaker's asseverations to the contrary. And, although the latter is still trying to use this example to distinguish great poetry from mediocre poets—ideal 'art' from the 'men' (91.32) who fail to accomplish it—what he in fact says in this case is that it was 'the fault of the man *and not of the poet*' (my emphasis). The distinction between the art and the artificer, that is, surreptitiously gives way to that between the artificer and the man, so as to put the latter in the dock but quietly to let the former off the hook. Whatever one might think of More (and space for confessional considerations may need to have been granted), the role of the naughty, resistant, nay-saying, and truth-speaking poet nonetheless remains in play and is, here, actually exonerated.

When the art/artificer argument crops up again it is at no less fraught a point in the speaker's deliberations: this time, the 'example' (93.11) he chooses to give (and inadvertently to make) of Zopyrus, Abradatas, and Sextus Tarquinius. Coming only a page or so after the reference to More, this forms a continuation of the argument that a 'feigned example hath as much force to teach as a true example' (93.9–10), the comparison with poetry now being weighed against history in order to demonstrate that here, too, nothing can so readily 'serve your prince' (93.21) as a poet's counsel. At the end of this highly problematic passage—in which the speaker effectively finds himself defending liars and rapists in the interests of absolute power—he concludes that whatever counsel the historian might present, 'that may the poet (if he list) with his imitation make his own, beautifying it both for further teaching, and more delighting, as it pleaseth him' (93.27–9). At this point, however, his mind goes strangely blank: 'Which if I be asked what poets have done so, as I might well name some, yet say I and say again, I speak of the art, and not of the artificer' (93.30–2). On the face of it, the repetition of this argument here seems odd—out of place—since, as far as the speaker is concerned, there is no failing artificer at this point who needs to be reprimanded and differentiated from the ideal art (on the contrary, he has drawn the example of Abradatas from his beloved Xenophon, that exemplar of exemplars of the right poet in the *Defence*).[155] And if it is this ideal art that he wants to exemplify—this poetry that so effectively advances the political and military ends of absolute rulers—then it seems even stranger that he should be unable to come up with any more such positive examples, especially as he 'might well name some'. Why doesn't he, then? You would think his argument was crying out for them. Instead, this blankness could be read symptomatically as an unconscious resistance to such 'ideal' art, a refusal to identify with its supposedly 'ideal' ends (perhaps using poetry for such ends itself constitutes an abuse). The same resistance might be read, incidentally, in that tellingly paren-thetical exemption-clause—that the poet might make such honest dissimulations

---

[155] Cf. Maslen (63) for whom the logic of the speaker's thinking here is that 'very few poets beside Xenophon have exploited their art to effective political or military ends', this being the reason he chooses to speak in general terms '"of the art, and not of the artificer" [93.31–2]'. Like other idealist critics, Maslen thus repeats rather than analyses the speaker's position: 'Poetry's status as the art of the fallen world means that its practice inevitably falls short of what it should be: but Sidney represents its shortcomings as the effect of pernicious outside influences.'

his own 'if he list' (93.27)—as if to say (*contra* the speaker), this particular poet does *not* in fact so list, and apologizing for tyranny does *not* 'pleaseth him'. In More's case, the poet who acts likewise surreptitiously goes unblamed. In this case, those poets who might serve the interests of a tyrannical regime and those who might fail to do so both go strategically unnamed: the speaker's sudden attack of forgetfulness conveniently allowing him to shroud the first in the obscurity they deserve and to leave the second—the aberrant, non-ideal, and noncompliant artificers—free to carry on at will.

Much the same dodging tactics are in evidence when the argument makes its next appearance: in the discussion of lyric that forms part of the anatomy of poetry's 'parts' in the second half of the *confirmatio*. The speaker's highly selective presentation of this form as the poetry of praise (restricting the object of that praise 'to the reward of virtue, to virtuous acts', 99.2), and his literal, narrowly academic definition of it as poetry sung to the lyre (restricting his examples to songs of praise for ancestors' valour, the kind of 'right vse' of poetry and music that Gosson had identified) have already been noted. As he proceeds, however, the speaker's attempt to praise this praise ends up tripping on its own faulty logic, unwittingly bringing him closer to the kind of tricksy mock encomium with which the *Defence* begins. If this battle poetry is so rousing when sung by such barbarous yet 'right soldierlike' (99.12) types as Welsh bards, Hungarians, and Lacedemonians, then how much better 'would it work', the speaker asks, if 'trimmed in the gorgeous eloquence of Pindar?' (99.9–10).[156] The rhetorical question then leads him to consider the problem that the things Pindar actually praised were not particularly praiseworthy—'victories of small moment, matters rather of sport than virtue' (99.18–19)—a difficulty he explains away by means of a now familiar argument: 'it was the fault of the poet, and not of the poetry' (99.20). The 'fault' (99.21), he assures us, lay rather with Greek culture in general, which 'set those toys at so high a price that Philip of Macedon reckoned a horserace won at Olympus [i.e. Olympia] among his three fearful felicities' (99.21–3).[157] Yet the problem, and the negative example supposed to exemplify it, is not to be so easily dismissed. For the illustrious father of Alexander the Great here provides a glimpse—much as Pugliano did—of an alternative economy, a different kind of 'reckoning', in which it is not, or not only, heroic, military, manly deeds (*vir*tuous action) that might be praised, but also things of relatively small account and personal value, matters of sport and pastime rather than of virtue: here a mere 'toy' that, on this occasion, is nonetheless held in very great price by another Philip, another non-exemplary lover of horses. The speaker

---

[156] That the blind poet who sings such songs (a generic type that goes back at least to Homer) might be identified specifically with the Welsh bards who were honoured earlier in the *narratio* (83.28–33) is suggested by the fact that he is described here as a 'crowder' (99.8). The crowd was a stringed instrument of ancient Celtic origin and associated with the Welsh (see *OED* crowd *n.*[1]a, derived from Welsh crwth).

[157] The other two felicities were a victory over the Illyrians and the birth of Alexander: see Plutarch 1926, *Lives: Alexander*, 666. The only poems of Pindar's that survived antiquity were the Epinician Odes that celebrated the victors of the Greek games, e.g. of boxing matches, foot races, horse races, chariot races, and mule-cart races.

thus finds himself in something of a fix. How is he able—when trying to praise praise-poetry—to praise poetry that praises apparently unpraiseworthy things? Pindar turns out to exemplify exactly this problem, for the speaker had started out by praising the Greek poet's 'gorgeous eloquence', and then recalled that he had used (abused, wasted?) the latter on comparatively trivial things.[158] Logically, the example of Pindar should be withdrawn—ideally, the entire reference should be scrubbed out—but it is not. Pindar is allowed to stand and the speaker to arrive at his characteristically triumphant conclusion as if nothing had happened and the problem had never materialized: 'But as the inimitable Pindar often did, so is that kind [i.e. lyric] most capable and most fit to awake the thoughts from the sleep of idleness, to embrace honourable enterprises' (99.23–5). This move is typical of the speaker's kettle-logic: if there were any failing it was not the poet's 'fault' so he is to be praised anyway. Yet an ambiguity remains and can be pinpointed in the phrase 'as the inimitable Pindar often did'. Editors gloss this as anticipatory—as if to say, 'as the inimitable Pindar often did awake thoughts to heroic action'—but it could also be read as retrospective: as if to say, 'as the inimitable Pindar often did praise unpraiseworthy, unworthy, non-worthwhile, small, sporting, toyful, and delightful things'.[159] The latter possibility leaves space, that is, for the kind of poetry that might do exactly that—regardless of bossy cultural demands that it produce more world-conquerors—and, indeed, it calls foul on the speaker's dubious attempt to strong-arm lyric into the services of epic activism. As with Pugliano, and as with More, Pindar proves another bad example that Sidney nonetheless chooses to follow.[160]

The last time the art/artificer argument gets wheeled out before the *digressio* is at the end of the *refutatio*, when the speaker attempts to wrest Plato away from the poet-haters so as to put the philosopher's strength to use (ideally) in his own cause. He proposes a parallel between St Paul, who 'setteth a watchword upon Philosophy,—indeed upon the abuse', and Plato, who does likewise 'upon the abuse, not upon Poetry' (107.6–8). Plato, that is, 'found fault that the poets of his time filled the world with wrong opinions of the gods, making light tales of that unspotted essence, and therefore would not have the youth depraved with such opinions' (107.8–11). The parallel, however, is a deceptive one. When Paul refers

---

[158] For Gosson there is no such ambiguity: Pindar is a straightforwardly negative example and the one with which he opens the *Schoole of Abuse*. As the Syracusans infamously 'vsed such varietie of dishes in theyr banquets', so Pindar was spoiled by a similar wealth of topics on which he might write poems, seeing 'so many turninges layde open to his feete, that hee knewe not which way to bende his pace'. While Gosson can commend those who, 'in banqueting', feed only on what 'doth nourish best', Pindar's example gives him licence to 'disprayse his methode in writing, which following the course of amarous Poets, dwelleth longest in those pointes, that profite least' (76/A1–A1ᵛ). One might read Astrophil's halting pace and wayward choice of an amarous subject for his own verse in *AS* 1 as a defiant response to Gosson's disapproval.

[159] Shepherd (192); Maslen (192).

[160] For Matz 2000 (82) Pindar's poetry provides the perfect template for Sidney, its combination of the heroic with the sportive or toyful neatly modelling the latter's desire to blend the ethos of the warrior with that of the courtier, or profit with pleasure: 'Sidney's aim is to resolve the clash between courtly and oppositional values, in order to claim the authority of both', although the final result is one of 'conflict rather than compromise' (83).

to the abuse of philosophy, he means that philosophy is doing the abusing: he is warning against the power pagan philosophy has to abuse Christian believers (its speculations now 'haue none vse seing Christ is come'). When Plato refers to the abuse of poetry, on the other hand, he means (according to the speaker) that poetry is being abused: he is warning against the power poets have to abuse poetry. In the first case, it is a system of thought that is threatening individuals (philosophy is in the subject position; believers in the object position); in the second, it is individuals that are threatening a system of thought (poets are in the subject position; poetry in the object position). In effect, the speaker is making exactly the same move identified earlier as characteristic of the reversal strategy: namely, using the appearance of parity to disguise the fact that a major reduction of the argument is actually going on, a scaling down from the collective to the individual so as to exonerate any failings in the former by shifting the blame onto fallible instances of the latter.[161] The speaker—who is still trying to defend idealist poetics—needs to show that, even though poetry was and is abused, it can nevertheless be ideal. To do this, he repeats the strategy he has tried before (although with little success)—of making the individual artificer take the rap so that the art itself might get off scot free—and then cheekily attributes it to Plato.[162] Minimized in this way, the latter's critique of poetry immediately becomes less difficult to negotiate, the big-gun reduced to a mere pistolet that is much easier to defend against. Plato's famous indictment was directed 'not in general of poets', we are assured, 'but only meant to drive out those wrong opinions of the Deity' (107.22, 24–5): a considerably smaller charge and one much more easily dealt with. Thus, the 'fault' that Plato is said to have found among his contemporary poets is not so very great after all. Poets were not responsible for *inventing* these stories of the gods or those wrong opinions about them. Such tales of the gods and their antics were out there already—as part of Greek culture—and were explicitly 'not taught' by the poets (107.14). Rather, poets merely 'did imitate those opinions already induced' (107.12–13), and 'followed [them] according to their nature of imitation' (107.15). Besides, those wrong opinions of the gods are not really so terrible. False gods, it turns out, are better than no gods at all: the superstitious 'dreams' (107.18) of the poets were better than nothing, and in making them poets 'truly . . . did much better in it than

---

[161] The difference is easy to miss because the speaker has introduced Paul's warning against the abuse of philosophy immediately after his own statement that he will 'honour philosophical instructions . . . so as they be not abused, which is likewise stretched to Poetry' (107.2–4). In this case, it is philosophy (as object) that stands to be abused or misinterpreted by individuals (as subject): see note 134. That is not in fact what Paul says, but the implication that it is typifies the speaker's determination to deny any systemic failure by shrinking the cause of the problem down to individual human failings. He is still trying to run the argument that it is not philosophy and poetry that abuse men's wit but man's wit that abuses philosophy and poetry.
[162] The speaker acts as though the charge that poets demean the gods constitutes the main plank of Plato's argument when, as noted earlier, it is—like the charge of wantonness—a mere secondary effect and subordinate to the main charge which is that poetry (being, like any representation, at several removes from the truth) is incapable of realizing the ideal. Where Shepherd (208–9) and Maslen (217–18) attribute this highly skewed reading of the *Republic* to Sidney—putting it in the context of medieval critiques of pagan philosophy—I attribute it, rather, to the speaker who acts (mistakenly, of course) as if such a misinterpretation will serve his turn.

the philosophers, who, shaking off superstition, brought in atheism' (107.19–21). Using this sleight of hand to reduce the charge, the speaker triumphantly allows himself to suggest that Plato is making the same argument as he is, and so to recruit the philosopher to his own cause: 'So as Plato, banishing the abuse, not the thing—not banishing it, but giving due honour unto it—shall be our patron and not our adversary' (107.30–2). Attributing one's own demonstrably weak argument to one's opponent in order to bring him down (or, better still, on side) really would be a diabolically clever ruse, were it not for the obvious objection, namely, that a weak argument is still a weak argument, and that what undermines the second will also undermine the first. It returns us, moreover, to the now familiar scenario of self-immolation—of a defence that deconstructs itself—as, one by one, propositions that have been central to the speaker's case get casually thrown out as dispensable and disproven. Out go the precedence argument (that poetry inaugurates culture), the *eikastike* argument (that poetry imitates the ideal), the pedagogic argument (that poetry teaches the truth and corrects errors), and the religious argument (that poetry is godly). And, in the dubious process of bringing Plato on side, the abuses that the latter would 'drive out' have been so minimized—so apologized for, so explained away—as to leave the way open for a poetry that does indeed tell 'light tales': that follows the wrong things (those wrong opinions already induced), that fashions false gods, and that observes superstitious dreams.[163]

By the time we reach the *digressio*, then, the speaker's curiously roundabout strategy—of defending a pure and unadulterated poetry by making an example of those who abuse it—has ended up pretty much doing exactly that: for what these rehearsals of the argument actually do is not so much provide a model of the theoretical ideal as showcase numerous examples of bad practice (or fail to provide examples of good practice where they might have done). If one of the editors of the *Defence* can claim that the art/artificer argument provides 'an ideal account of an idealizing poetry', then this can only be because the various iterations of it so far have been relatively scattered throughout the text, and because the faults of the poets in question, being for the most part played down, are relatively easy for the idealistically inclined reader to pass over.[164] It is much more difficult to do this in the case of the *digressio*, however, where the shortcomings of faulty artificers take centre stage and where their abject failure to realize the ideal in art becomes the focus of a lengthy, relentless, and unblinking discussion that nonetheless does little, arguably, to make the case for the latter. Indeed, the *digressio* has long registered as a problem among critics, anxious to explain what its extended survey of English poets

---

[163] Much of the complexity of the paragraph I have been analysing here derives from the fact that the split between critic (the speaker) and poet (Sidney) is also internal to Plato (at once philosopher and poet). The speaker abuses the argument of Plato-the-philosopher for his own purposes, but the effect is only to collapse his own (self-abuse being the order of the day). This collapse, however, allows Sidney to identify with Plato-the-poet: the figure he has 'ever esteemed most worthy of reverence, and with great reason: since of all philosophers he is the most poetical' (106.16–18). Plato-the-philosopher would attack poetry, but Plato-the-poet is not really on side. Sidney-the-critic (a.k.a. the speaker) would defend poetry, but Sidney-the-poet is not really on side.

[164] Alexander (lix).

whose work is very far from ideal—that is 'defectious' (110.34), 'faulty' (110.36), 'absurd' (111.13; 114.28), 'wrong' (112.18), guilty of 'great wants' (110.14) and 'gross absurdities' (112.1)—is doing in what otherwise purports to be a defence of idealist poetics. The difficulty has given rise to a range of explanations. At one end, the *digressio* is seen as being so incompatible with if not destructive of the idealist case mounted by the speaker as to be as the product of another 'voice' altogether, and to be, therefore—as its marginal status would seem to suggest—to all intents and purposes extraneous to, and thus detachable from, the main body of the *Defence*.[165] At the other, the *digressio* is seen as being central to the case for idealist poetics, its argument that poetry alone is capable of restoring the formerly heroic and national ideal of military activism from which England has catastrophically declined—and that the sorry state of contemporary English poetry so starkly symptomizes—playing out, in this re-enactment of the Fall, the text's essentially redemptive drama.[166] In both cases, the explanatory driver seems to be the need to maintain idealist poetics at all costs, the solutions offered—where that is imperilled—being either to cut the *digressio* off as belonging to a different treatise entirely, or to subject it to a characteristically dialectical 'turn' in which that which was thoroughly devalued gets to be revalued, the profitless to be profitable again, and stocks that were low to be high. There is, however, a third and in many ways simpler way of approaching this section of the *Defence*—one that has the advantage of seeing it as continuous with the earlier iterations of the art/artificer argument rather than as an afterthought or stand-alone discussion—and that is to consider what it actually does, as opposed to what it either tries or fails to do. For what the *digressio* does is offer an extended meditation on—and give considerable ground and discursive space to (without, of course, defending)—the alternative aesthetic of the un-ideal: indefensible, abusive, and abusing as it may be.[167]

---

[165] See e.g. Hardison 1972 (94): 'Sidney has abruptly turned from the Platonizing, idealizing tradition of humanist poetics to the critical and rationalistic poetic of neoclassicism that was gaining favor in Italy and France between 1560 and 1580.' The *digressio* thus belongs to a later development of Sidney's critical thinking and was 'interpolated' (98) into a treatise with which it was otherwise irreconcilable, the latter remaining unrevised at the time of his death. See also Helgerson 1976 (154): '[poetry] could neither be reconciled to the paternal notion of virtue, nor could it stand on its own as an alternative system of value. Sidney backed down . . . at the crucial moment, just when the attack turned against what he and his contemporaries actually wrote.'

[166] See e.g. Maslen (1–77), on whom this summary is largely based and who makes the case that the *digressio* is the 'core' if not the '*raison d'être*' (33) of the treatise and forms an 'integral part' (36) of it: much of this argument is repeated in Maslen 2003. See also Hadfield 1994 (143) for whom this section forms the central plank of Sidney's project to locate the identity of the English nation in its poetry—and specifically in Surrey, that noble progenitor of an aristocratic, military poetics—making the *digressio* 'the most useful part'. Both these readings see the *Defence* as proposing a notably masculinist model of poetry: see Maslen (12, 65, 71); and Hadfield 1994 (141, 143).

[167] The older 'disjunctive' readings of the *digressio* are nonetheless more compatible with this third way than those more inclusive ones that see it in redemptive terms. It is a relatively small matter, after all, to move from seeing the 'two voices' as existing at different phases in Sidney's life to seeing them as synchronous (as those of 'the speaker' and 'Sidney'). Similarly, not much is required to make the shift from Helgerson's claim that Sidney failed to make poetry 'stand on its own as an alternative system of value' to one that the *digressio* (like the examples of the art/artificer argument which anticipate it) *does* offer an alternative system: just one that values 'value' differently from the humanist poetics of profitability.

In the *digressio* proper, this abuse is presented, exactly as one would expect it to be, in terms of wantonness.[168] Not the 'wanton sinfulness' (103.44–104.1) and 'wanton shows' (104.25) that threaten to titillate readers or theatre-goers, inciting them to sexual immorality and vice—if anything, contemporary English poets are charged here with not being 'fiery' (113.27) or not showing their 'passions' (113.31) enough—but rather with wantonness as discussed above: namely, as shorthand for improper reproduction of any kind, 'abusive' because it endangers the legitimate, normal, 'useful' cycles of production and growth on which the household and the commonwealth depend. In this section of the *Defence*—which, as Maslen notes, 'unleashes a bewildering sequence of allusions to acts of sexual transgression' (67)—the various failings of English poets are repeatedly presented as forms of illegitimacy: bad genealogy, false issue, deviant succession.[169] The *Defence* proper had opened (in the first paragraph to follow the *exordium*) with an ideal model of production in which poets of the 'noblest nations and languages' (82.7) served as the 'deliverers of their knowledge to their posterity' (82.17–18), bequeathing their intellectual and cultural property to succeeding generations so as to preserve and increase it, just as good 'fathers in learning' (82.19) should. This *translatio studii* is presented as a proper succession (through the male line, of course) that extends from Greece to Rome to Italy to culminate triumphantly in England, whose model sons, Chaucer and Gower, 'others have followed' (82.28). By the time we get to the *digressio*, however, this orderly transfer of knowledge has irretrievably broken down, for now, it seems, those classical and Italian models are *not* being followed.[170] Rather, English sons are disobeying their literary fathers in a flagrant disregard for their heritage—'observing rules neither of honest civility nor of skilful Poetry' (110.29), flouting both 'Aristotle's precept and common reason' (110.38–9) and what 'Art hath taught, and all ancient examples justified' (111.13–14), not to mention 'the laws of Poesy' (111.21)—in order to go their own, stubborn, and independent way. This disturbance in the line of proper literary production ('use') is

[168] As Maslen (33) points out, the *digressio* constitutes an 'oration-within-an oration' and thus has its own mini-*narratio, propositio*, and *divisio* (this introductory section extending from 108.22 to 110.10 in this edition), leading to the main body of its argument or mini-*confirmatio*. For Maslen, the latter then extends continuously to the beginning of the *peroratio* (116.15). In my view, however, the *digressio* proper extends to the moment where it is named as such—'this digression' (115.7)—at which point a very approbatory discussion of the English language ensues which is not obviously consonant with the critical tone of the preceding pages and may, indeed, even be thought of as a mini-*refutatio*. The discussion in the present paragraph, therefore, refers to the section that extends from 110.11 to 115.4. I will be returning to the introductory sections of the *digressio* in the paragraphs that follow.

[169] In Maslen's redemptive reading, the same sexual transgression that signifies England's fall from grace becomes the means by which it might be restored to its former glory as a warlike nation—Venus' vigorous adultery with Mars metaphorically resulting in better issue than the homely quiet of her life as Vulcan's wife would have done—a circular argument, arguably (not to mention that of Edmund in *King Lear*), and one that I shall consider at greater length below.

[170] While Hadfield (1994) also sees the *digressio* as following on from this ideal genealogy of noble nations, his redemptive reading obliges him to minimize if not ignore its relentlessly negative tone and to single out the Earl of Surrey—whose lyrics are praised for testifying to his 'noble birth' and 'noble mind' (110.17)—as a model father/son who passes on the good name of English poetry in exemplary fashion and so preserves the literary lineage. This comes, however, at the expense of the numerous examples of illegitimate or improper (re)production that make up the bulk of the *digressio*.

presented, logically enough, as a disturbance in the line of proper sexual reproduction ('abuse'). In the case of stage-plays, for example—of which there is 'none so
much used in England' and none 'more pitifully abused' (113.14–15)—the failure
of contemporary playwrights is presented as a bastard child which, 'like an unman-
nerly daughter . . . causeth her mother Poesy's honesty to be called in question'
(113.15–17). In the case of oratory, likewise, Cicero correctly 'used' (114.12) such
figures as repetition, as indeed did his predecessors: Demosthenes, who 'with a rare
daintiness useth them' (114.19–20), and Antonius and Crassus who 'used [them] very
sparingly' (114.39). English writers, by contrast (and especially the learned, who
should know better), do 'generally use' them (114.39–40)—use them excessively,
that is—'using art to show art, and not to hide art' (115.3), as a result of which
they 'abuseth art' (115.4): a lapse in judgement that is also presented as an illegitimate
birth, such that the 'honey-flowing matron eloquence' (113.36) becomes a 'courtesan-
like painted affectation' (113.37) who spawns not good, native-born words but
rather 'monsters' (113.38), or 'strangers' (113.39) at best. Indeed, it is a classic sign
of such miscegenation that its productions should turn out to be grotesque hybrids—
'mingling kings and clowns' (112.2), for example, so as to produce not pure but
'mongrel' forms (112.6)—English writers neither following classical precedent where
it might allow for such things (as in Plautus' tragi-comedy, *Amphitrio*, for example)
nor, as above, exercising the ancients' characteristic moderation and restraint (where
the latter do mix forms they do so only 'very daintily', 112.10). Similarly, scenes that
can 'breed' (112.20) or 'breedeth' (112.38) mixed responses are only permissible
where such mingling meets a higher and so legitimate aim, as when scornful laughter is
'mixed with . . . that delightful teaching which is the end of Poesy' (112.42–3): a
discretion, again, rarely exercised by English writers of comedy.

   This reproductive free-for-all—and the mayhem that results—is more than
anticipated in the dense and highly problematic paragraphs that introduce the
digressio and that open with scenes of once model parenting and housekeeping now
thrown into unwonted disarray. Formerly a good 'mother' (108.24) who had
nurtured poets—her fruitful 'soil' (109.1) cultivating their laurels—England has
perversely 'grown so hard a stepmother' (108.24–5) as to deny them sustenance
and welcome. Initially, the blame for this state of affairs—in which a guiltless
poetry unaccountably finds itself abused—is directed firmly outwards. Where
previously the culprit occupying the subject position (who or what is abusing
poetry?) had been rather vague—'man's wit' (104.17)—here it is quite specific:
an external environment, as hostile as it is inhospitable, that is unmistakably to be
identified with one very particular woman. '*Musa, mihi causas memora, quo numine
laeso?*' (108.28), the speaker asks rhetorically, the invocation at the beginning of
the *Aeneid* allowing him very economically to implicate the irrational enmity of a
certain '*regina*' and to self-identify with the '*pietate virum*' who is not only her
undeserving victim but an epic hero and, as great-grandfather of Brutus, the
legendary founder of Britain, a cultural ancestor to boot.[171] The support for

---

[171] See Virgil 2001, *Aeneid*, I.8–11: '*Musa, mihi causas memora, quo numine laeso / quidve dolens
regina deum tot volvere casus / insignem pietate virum, tot adire labores / impulerit*' [Tell me, O Muse, the

poetry that is to be found among men—the countless 'kings, emperors, senators, great captains' (108.29–30), past and present, who were not only willing and able 'to favour' (108.31) and 'to read others' poesies' (108.40) but also 'to be poets' (108.31) and 'to poetize for others' reading' (108.41), making them exemplars of both patronage and practice—stands in stark contrast to this scene of female dereliction, and, at this stage in the argument, meets the poet-hero's needs in much the same way that Jupiter's ongoing support for Aeneas makes up for and ultimately overcomes Juno's condemnable and contemptible lack of it.[172] As the introduction to the *digressio* proceeds, however, these flattering and self-justifying identifications give way to alternative and altogether less wholesome genealogies, starting with the startling announcement that Poesy should be given 'great praise . . . which like Venus (but to better purpose) hath rather be troubled in the net with Mars than enjoy the homely quiet of Vulcan' (109.7–9). If the hero is hounded by the cruel and vindictive Juno—who amply fills the role of bad mother here—he is, of course, also cherished and supported by her great rival and his actual mother, Venus: except that this embarrassing allusion to her sexual escapades might put into question just how 'good' a mother she is. In the context of the *digressio*, the speaker's analogy is designed to support his case for a bellicose foreign policy and a heroic national poetry to match—war being better than peace, and epic adultery clearly justified if a means to that end—but, insofar as it casts aspersions on the mother's sexual probity, it also has the unfortunate effect of spotlighting the status of this son. Is he an Aeneas, the heroic son of a mighty goddess, or might he also perhaps, be a Cupid, the wanton son of an adulterous and promiscuous mother?[173] The speaker might seek to position himself as the first, but Astrophil will all too readily identify with the second: 'Desire', he says, 'so clings to my pure Love, that I / One from the other scarcely can descrie'.[174]

---

cause; wherein thwarted in will or wherefore angered, did the Queen of heaven drive a man, of goodness so wondrous, to traverse so many perils, to face so many toils]. In Maslen's reading, Sidney uses the *Defence* to put Elizabeth squarely in the frame, blaming the decline of heroism and heroic poetry in England on the quietism of her foreign policy: specifically, her reluctance to engage militarily with the Spanish in the Netherlands, as urged by the forward Protestants in her court led by Leicester. The presentation of Elizabeth as a bad housewife here contrasts with Gosson who, perhaps more diplomatically, praises her for 'filling her chests with the fruites of peace', and lays the blame instead on 'wee vnworthy seruants of so mild a Mistresse, vnnatural children of so good a mother, vnthankful subiects of so louing a prince, [who] wound her royall hart with abusing her lenitie, and stir *Iupiter* to anger': *Schoole* (96/C5ᵛ–C6).

[172] The speaker's invocation of male supporters lends itself to hyperbole: not only the unspecified 'thousand others' (108.30) and 'many' (108.37) mentioned here but also the 'whole sea of examples' (107.40) to whom he gestures a page or so earlier at the close of the *refutatio*: figures who are similarly represented as both 'favourers of poets' (107.41) and as poets themselves.

[173] In the *Aeneid*, Venus' support for one son takes the form of enlisting the support of the other, as she commissions Cupid—'*nate, meae vires, mea magna potentia, solus*' [Son, who is alone my strength, my mighty power] (I.664)—to enamour Dido on Aeneas' behalf, appealing to his brotherly concern: '*frater ut Aeneas pelago tuus omnia circum / litora iactetur odiis Iunonis acerbae, / nota tibi, et nostro doluisti saepe dolore*' [How your brother Aeneas is tossed on the sea about all coasts by bitter Juno's hate is known to you, and often have you grieved in our grief] (I.667–9).

[174] *AS* 72. On Astrophil's numerous identifications with Cupid, see Bates 2013 (183–8).

Things only get murkier as the argument proceeds, for in the fallen world of contemporary England the presumably chaste Muse of Virgil's invocation is now, it seems, tarred with the same brush: indeed, not only she but 'all the Muses [are] got with child to bring forth bastard poets' (109.17). The speaker might try to differentiate himself from the latter by classing himself among those '*Queis meliore luto finxit praecordia Titan*' [for whom the Titan (i.e. Prometheus) made hearts of better clay] (109.21), but in context this quotation from Juvenal is hardly resounding, and, besides, in what follows the 'I' identifies repeatedly (if apologetically) with these 'knights of the same order' (109.23):[175]

> But I that, before ever I durst aspire unto the dignity, am admitted into the company of the paper-blurrers, do find the very true cause of our wanting estimation is want of desert, taking upon us to be poets in despite of Pallas. Now wherein we want desert were a thankworthy labour to express; but if I knew, I should have mended myself. But I, as I never desired the title, so have I neglected the means to come by it. Only, overmastered by some thoughts, I yielded an inky tribute unto to them.
>
> (109.24–31)[176]

However much the speaker might claim to despise and deplore the poets of his generation, this other-speaking 'I' is self-confessedly one of them—a knight of their 'order' and member of their 'company'—their shared badge of dishonour being a willingness to write poetry 'in despite of Pallas', or '*invita Minervā*', as the *Ars Poetica* has it: an error, Horace says, that his honoured addressee would never commit but that characterizes the man who has no idea how to write poetry and yet dares to do so anyway simply because he belongs to the right class and is even rated at the fortune of a knight ['*census equestrem*'].[177] By including himself among those

---

[175] The speaker cites Juvenal 2004, *Satire* XIV.35. In context, the line refers to the worthy few whose moral probity enables them to reject the terrible examples set by their fathers, making them the exception that proves the rule: hardly a ringing endorsement for relations between ideal fathers and ideal sons: '*velocius et citius nos / corrumpunt vitiorum exempla domestica, magnis / cum subeant animos auctoribus. unus et alter / forsitan haec spernant iuvenes, quibus arte benigna / et meliore luto finxit praecordia Titan, / sed reliquos fugienda patrum vestigia ducunt / et monstrata diu veteris trahit orbita culpae*' [Bad examples in the home corrupt us more speedily and quickly, because they creep into our minds with powerful authority. One or other young man may reject this behaviour, if his heart is fashioned by the Titan with generous skill from a superior clay. But the rest are led along in the footprints of their fathers which they should avoid, and are dragged along in the track of an ancient fault which they've been shown for so long], lines 31–7.

[176] The answer to the hitherto inexplicable question of 'why' (108.24; 109.9) contemporary poetry should want estimation—the mysterious '*causa*' (108.28) demanded of Virgil's Muse—is finally located here, poets' irreverent disregard for learning being 'the very true cause'.

[177] See Horace 1926, *Ars Poetica*, lines 382–6: '*qui nescit versus tamen audet fingere. quidni? / liber et ingenuus, praesertim census equestrem / summam nummorum vitioque remotus ab omni. / Tu nihil invita dices faciesve Minervā; / id tibi iudicium est, ea mens*' [Yet the man who knows not how dares to frame verses. Why not? He is free, even free-born, nay, is rated at the fortune of a knight, and stands clear from every blemish. But you will say nothing and do nothing against Minerva's will; such is your judgement, such your good sense]. Maslen (226) describes 'knights of the same order' (109.23) as a 'puzzling phrase' and suggests that it might refer to George Gascoigne who often styled himself the 'Green Knight': see also Maslen 2003 (221). It seems more plausible that the 'knights' in question allude to Horace's *eques* (as van Dorsten agrees, 205) and that, having inadvertently come into the 'title' of poet himself, Sidney identifies with them (see Miller 1994 on the linked and changing fortunes of the *eques* and the lyric poet in the period of Catullus and Horace). This vexed question of title—whether it is the entitled who claim

who do exactly this, the 'I' admits himself to be just such a knight: not a right poet but a wrong one, not a good example but a bad. This reference, furthermore—which adds a rejection of Pallas to the existing scenario of hostility from Juno and favour from Venus—suggests another possible identification with a figure who is also very far from ideal (another brother, indeed): this time, Paris, great playboy of the western world, whose ill-judged Judgement was responsible for setting the entire crisis, in which Aeneas and Cupid both get caught up, in motion.

I suggested earlier that the *digressio* unfolds a scene of monstrous generation in which poet-sons give birth to their own mothers in a grotesque reversal of the natural order, for, as the 'I' assures us (in a voice I am increasingly inclined to attribute to Sidney), 'Exercise indeed we do, but that very fore-backwardly: for where we should exercise to know, we exercise as having known; and so is our brain delivered of much matter which never was begotten by knowledge' (110.1–4). This improper treatment of matter/*mater* constitutes, naturally enough, a form of abuse: there is 'matter to be expressed by words and words to express the matter' and 'in neither we use Art or Imitation rightly' (110.4–6). It also serves, of course, to re-state the poets' wilful rejection of Pallas. They do not receive knowledge from the goddess of wisdom and dutifully pass it on to the next generation, as good sons should, any more than Astrophil—who is equally impatient with 'step-dame Studie'—is 'great with child to speake' about anything that might have been begotten by learning.[178] Indeed, instead of choosing Pallas—the right mother for the conception and generation of learned poetry—contemporary poets evidently feel licensed to pick and choose whose sons they wish to be at will: 'Our matter is *quodlibet* [anything we like]' (110.6). Failing to exercise any discrimination in the matter, they behave as if anything and everything they say were suitable material for poetry, in this respect emulating Ovid, for whom, likewise, '*Quicquid conabar dicere, versus erit*' [whatever I tried to say turned into verse] (110.8). Unlike their Roman predecessor, English poets are said to do this 'wrongly' (110.7), but Ovid's

---

to be poets and whether they are entitled to do so—seems to be a matter of great concern in the *Defence*. The speaker claims that *vates* is 'so heavenly a title' (83.40) and 'maker' a 'high and incomparable . . . title' (84.39); that those skills which result in virtuous action 'have a most just title to be princes over all the rest' (88.32–3); and that the poet deserves 'to carry the title' (89.35–6) from the philosopher and historian. The speaker's motto might be 'upon the right use each thing conceiveth his title' (104.32–3). Since that 'right use' has proved to be somewhat unreliable, however, Sidney's take on title might be considered altogether more doubtful and self-deprecating. He claims to have 'slipped into the title of a poet' (81.26), again inadvertently; that 'the best title' for the poet-haters (with whom, disconcertingly, he identifies) is to be called 'good fools' (101.19–22, 20–1); that titles may be purely nominal, as when 'the reverend title of a bishop' (103.41–2) is applied to a chess-piece; and that readers should not, therefore (or is it should?) jest at 'the reverent title of a rhymer' (116.24) in the *peroratio*. The social fantasy of the '*libertino patre natus*' [son of a freedman]—the poet's self-description in Horace 1926, *Satires*, I.vi.6 and *Epistles*, I.xx.20—who suddenly becomes '*Herculea proles*' [an offspring of Hercules] (116.41, 42) through writing poetry would similarly seem to mock such pretentions. Might this be why Sidney appears not to have titled/entitled his treatise (Olney and Ponsonby being responsible for the alternative titles under which it first appeared in print): to foreground the question of its true or counterfeit status? On this question see also Derrida 1992 (83–7, 93–8). Sidney appears not to have entitled *Astrophil and Stella*, either: see Ringler, ed. 1962 (458).

[178] *AS* 1.

pun (*versus* is both 'verse' and 'turned') suggests that there is something inherently deviant about *any* poetry: that verse is necessarily turned—insofar as it turns aside from what is designated as the proper path, fails to be useful or to turn a profit—and that there is, therefore, something intrinsically perverse about writing it.[179] When, at the end of the *digressio*, Sidney claims that he has been 'acknowledging ourselves somewhat awry, [so that] we may bend to the right use both of matter and manner' (115.11–12), his statement of intent is, rather like Astrophil's ideal poem, indefinitely deferred, and—since there is no sign of that corrective return happening any time soon—the abuse is presumably set to continue.[180] For, given the choice of matter available to them, many if not most poets (including Sidney/ Astrophil) will—like Paris—opt to choose Venus, not Pallas, thus making lyric (logically) the place where 'we miss the right use of the material point of Poesy' (113.33–4). Where right and proper relations should obtain between sons and mothers—so as to ensure the continuity, legitimacy, and growth of learning down the generations in the prescribed fashion (much as poetry was the 'first nurse' that enabled men to feed afterwards on 'tougher knowledges', 82.8, 9–10)—they give way instead to scenes of a far more problematic nature in which hereditary lines are disturbed by preposterous births and extra-marital affairs, and where poetic pro- duction is confused by a cast not (or not only) of heroes and goddesses but also of step-mothers, half-brothers, adulteresses, and bastards.

Relations between sons and fathers, meanwhile, fare little better, and if, at the outset, innumerable male patrons and poetic progenitors are invoked reprovingly to fill the void left by England/Elizabeth's unmotherly behaviour (a whole host of Jupiters ready to come to the poet-hero's aid), this happy arrangement is not set to last. For it gives way, much as above, to an altogether more complex picture in which, alongside the approved models, the text floats quite alternative types of making and of maker, thereby opening up the possibility of identifications with figures who are, in that capacity, far from ideal. Initially, the model proposed is that

---

[179] Ovid 1924, *Tristia*, IV.x.26. Ovid is distinguishing between himself and an older brother (born only a year earlier and sharing a birthday, so virtually a twin) who was drawn to the useful art of oratory while he, Ovid, was to his father's chagrin helplessly drawn to the art of poetry: '*saepe pater dixit "studium quid inutile temptas?* / *Maeonides nullas ipse reliquit opes."* / *motus eram dictis, totoque Helicone relicto* / *scribere temptabam [conabar] verba soluta modis.* / *sponte sua carmen numeros veniebat ad aptos,* / *et quod temptabam scribere [dicere] versus erat*' [Often my father said, 'Why do you try a profitless pursuit? Even the Maeonian [i.e. Homer] left no wealth.' I was influenced by what he said and wholly forsaking Helicon I tried to write words freed from rhythm, yet all unbidden song would come upon befitting numbers and whatever I tried to write was verse], lines 21–6. See also *OED* verse *n.*: from Latin *versus*, a line or row, specifically a line of writing (so named from turning to begin another line); from *vertere*, to turn. As Frye 1985 (31) notes, 'in "verse," where we keep coming to the end of a line and then starting another, there is a germ of discontinuity. The more this sense of the discontinuous increases, the more closely we approach the lyrical area'.

[180] Cf. Maslen 2003 (230) whose redemptive reading obliges him to cast Sidney's identification with the bastard poets in the *Defence* (and with Pyrocles' libidinousness in the *Old Arcadia*) as 'a courageous gesture of political dissent, a bid for sexual and heroic fulfillment in a world where political leaders value personal safety and the satisfaction of their private desires over the higher national and religious interests they claim to serve'. This determination to redeem the fallen by legitimizing what is obviously illegitimate seems somewhat strained to me: it would be simpler to say that shooting awry is shooting awry and not a roundabout way of shooting straight: see Bates 2013 (126).

of the poet as a heroic self-maker whose success is put down entirely to the exercise of his own wit. English poets, the speaker assures us, 'certainly in wit ought to pass all other, since all only proceedeth from their wit, being indeed makers of themselves, not takers of others' (108.25–7). English poets possess a native and certainly not a borrowed wit and they owe (or ought to owe) their high poetic reputation to that: self-fashioning at its finest. Such wit, however, must be properly directed, as exemplified by the 'piercing wits' (108.36) of the Scottish playwright, George Buchanan—even for Gosson a model of the 'the true vse of Poetrie'—for, as Ascham warned, native wit alone is not enough.[181] Right poetry is in addition the product of education, industry, effort, and skill, and wit must therefore be trained to learn the rules of the trade, to copy worthy models, and to practise them repeatedly—'as the fertilest ground must be manured, so must the highest-flying wit have a Daedalus to guide him' (109.39–40)—the Cunning Artificer serving here as shorthand for these three requisites of a classical and contemporary rhetorical training, namely 'Art, Imitation, and Exercise' (109.42–3).[182] Left to its own devices, an untrained wit is a liability—worse, a danger to itself and to others—and, as right poetry emerges as the product of an ideal union between wit and application, so it increasingly becomes a matter of *techne*: of doing whatever is necessary to perform the art in question expertly and whatever, therefore, is 'artificial'. Excellence, that is, becomes expertise. To be an artificer, the artificer must follow the 'artificial rules' (109.43)—the rules of his art as laid down by the masters before him—at the risk, if he fails to do so, of producing a play that, like *Gorboduc*, is imagined 'inartificially' (110.40).[183] By implication, excellence—even the question of being a poet or not being one—comes down to the success or otherwise of mastering an art: technically, it is something that can be learned. Just as, in an earlier part of the *Defence*, the application and following of 'artificial rules' (85.11) is said to be the particular province of the rhetorician—this being the key to his success in persuasion—so, here, Cicero (undoubtedly a master in that art) is praised for his ability to do that 'artificially' (114.15) which men otherwise do naturally (express anger, for example). Those who really apply themselves—who acquire the skill-set and put it to good use (the ideal pupils of the Tudor education system)—can in theory make it to the top of their profession, making great art and making themselves in the process. In which case, the optimum model of the right poet—if that is defined as the self-made man, as the makers who are 'makers of themselves'—would be the orator: the figure who, as the speaker's proverb reminds us, is specifically 'made'—*orator fit* (109.38)—and not born. This, in other words,

---

[181] Gosson (177/E5ᵛ); Ascham 1967 (22–4).

[182] Daedalus deriving from δαιδάλλω, to work cunningly, deck or inlay with curious arts, to embellish. The ingenious inventions of this legendary craftsman were said to include animated statues and, of course, the great labyrinth at Crete.

[183] See also Scott 2013 (30): 'whatsoever is behoveful to this triple end is required in the poet inasmuch as he is a poet; whatsoever swerves from this end of delighting, and by delight of teaching and leading to goodness, that is not of the art but of the inartificialness of the undertaker, of the abuse or ignorance of the art.' Kennedy 2016 provides an exhaustive account of the poet as, by definition, a skilled craftsman and technician in the period.

is poetry as it would come to be promoted by Puttenham: an 'Art' (by dint of
the artificial rules which he outlines so assiduously and which anyone can learn)
of 'Poesy' (of making that is self-making at its best).

When Sidney's speaker later apologizes for 'this digression' (115.7), it is unclear
whether he is referring to the *digressio* as a whole or to his having strayed 'from
Poetry to Oratory' (115.5–6) (he has been preoccupied with the question of
eloquence, by that stage, for quite some time). The ambiguity works either way,
for, on the one hand, poetry and oratory are indeed closely related (the *digressio*
therefore forming a distinct unit that considers failures in the achievement of both),
and, on the other, they are quite different (the digression in question therefore
forming a distinct unit that considers one of them within the larger *digressio* as a
whole). However—while the orator might be the poet's brother if not near-twin—
Sidney (like Ovid) simply cannot help himself from swerving, from taking that
punning 'turn' away from oratory and towards verse: that turn for the worse that, in
opting for what is profitless (*inutile*), flouts every father's wish.[184] Indeed, the 'two
voices' of Sidney's *Defence* are particularly in evidence here: not, as Hardison would
have it, an idealist voice that belongs to one time and place being followed by a
critical voice that belongs to another, but, rather, an idealist voice (that of the
speaker) and a self-critical voice (that of Sidney) that, in these highly problematic
paragraphs that open the *digressio*, speak at the same time and over one another
as they try, like two very quarrelsome brothers, to battle it out. The twists and
turns of the argument (which is frankly all over the place here) can be measured in
the breathless to-and-fro between these two disputatious voices, as each tries to
make itself heard—'But . . . but . . . But . . . Yet . . . But . . . but' (109.24, 28, 39, 43;
110.1)—although Sidney's self-deprecating account of what naughty poets actually
do (all those 'buts') undoubtedly gains the upper hand over, if not drowns out, the
speaker's attempt to make the case for Daedalian instruction (that single 'yet'). And,
much as Astrophil similarly finds himself torn between two competing voices
('Come let me write, "And to what end?"'), so this dispute in the *Defence* also
comes down in the end to a battle of wits ('Peace, foolish wit, with wit my wit is
mard'), or, rather, to a battle between different kinds of wit.[185] For, ranged against
the hard, native 'wit' (108.25, 26) of the self-making, self-made, successful, well-
trained, and semi-professional English orator-poets (the speaker's team) stands
another, much more motley variety: the kind that belongs either to 'base men
with servile wits' (109.11) or to amateurs who are 'better content to suppress
the outflowing of their wit' (109.22), and for the simple reason that, while 'all
other knowledges lie ready for any that hath strength of wit; a poet no industry
can make' (109.36–7). The maker makes, that is, but unlike the practitioners
of 'other' sciences or arts—as so often, the decisive point of comparison—he
(or she) is not made. As opposed to the Orators, the Poets (supported and followed
by Sidney/Astrophil) reject the idea that—for the purposes of writing poetry at any

---

[184] See note 179.
[185] *AS* 34. See also Ascham 1967 (21): 'the quickest wits commonly may prove the best poets but
not the wisest orators.'

rate—'men's wit' can be directed, guided, taught, or trained in any way at all: unless, perhaps, it is a matter of 'training it to wanton sinfulness and lustful love' (103.44–104.1), exactly as their opponents charge. And along with this (now familiar) notion that poetry might actually be *un*learned goes another that also simply refuses to go away: the suggestion, that is, that poetry might be 'a divine gift, and no human skill' (109.35–6), the oracular outpouring of the high flying wit, and product of the heroic frenzy, inspiration, or 'genius' (109.37) of a poet who is no longer necessarily male or even masculine.[186] That this notion should resurface again despite numerous denials—the most recent being the speaker's assertion that Plato 'attributeth unto Poesy more than myself do, namely, to be a very inspiring of a divine force, far above man's wit' (107.36–8)—might be an argument for taking those denials as indications of a split within that 'myself' (or between Sidney and the speaker) rather than, as so often, for taking them at face value. For, as Sidney's proverb reminds us, the true poet is born—'*poeta nascitur*' (109.38–9)—and not made. Such a figure may, of course, be able to boast a 'noble birth' (110.17) as Surrey did, and so to identify with the poet-hero as a second Aeneas (the first English translator of the *Aeneid* being, indeed, a suitable candidate for this), but he might, equally, be of dubious birth and title: a 'bastard poet' (109.17) or knight of that order whose literary origins and productions can claim no such legitimacy, and who may identify instead—as Astrophil repeatedly does—with the latter's mischievous, dangerous, and supra-powerful half-brother, Cupid.

Alongside a figure like Daedalus, then, whose well-intended guidance Sidney and his fellow poets carelessly spurn—with neither his 'artificial rules nor imitative patterns, we much cumber ourselves withal' (109.43–110.1)—these paragraphs also make available two alternative figures who, while less obviously meeting with cultural approval, nonetheless enjoy, as master makers or craftsmen, equal if not greater mythic status. One of these is Prometheus—the Titan who 'made' (*finxit*) men's hearts from better clay, as the quotation from Juvenal obligingly reminds us (109.21)—and who was, indeed, credited with fashioning the first man and woman, bringing their clay forms to life with fire stolen from the gods, as well as with introducing fire to human beings and teaching them all sorts of other sciences and arts.[187] The other is the much-maligned Vulcan, cast here as the lame and cheated husband of Venus—her 'homely' (109.9) life with whom is contrasted most unfavourably with her very active and adulterous relationship with Mars— but who in myth and legend commanded deep respect as the great god of fire and of crafts. Far from the pusillanimous and faintly ridiculous character the speaker

---

[186] Ever irrepressible, this notion also reappears in the catch-all *peroratio* (by which stage any attempt at a reasoned argument on the part of the speaker has been gamely abandoned), where it is suggested that poets 'are so beloved of the gods that whatsoever they write proceeds of a divine fury' (116.34–5). As does the idea—ironic and not-so-ironic, paradoxical and not-so-paradoxical at the same time—that poetry is 'written darkly, lest by profane wits it should be abused' (116.33–4), which by no means rules out the possibility that it *is* so abused.

[187] *finxit* perfect of *fingere*, to form, fashion, mould; of mental or speech acts, to imagine, suppose, fabricate, invent (whence English 'fiction' and 'figment'). Prometheus ('Forethought', from προμηθής, forethinking, provident, cautious) is to be differentiated from his careless brother, Epimetheus ('Afterthought').

would paint him, Vulcan—like his Greek counterpart, Hephaistos—is the supreme artificer. It is his ingenuity and not his cuckoldry that is exemplified by the strong yet invisible net he makes of bronze—its links thinner than the finest thread or a spider's web—and with which he captures and shames the adulterous pair. In Ovid's rendering of the story, it is Venus and Mars who are the object of the gods' derision, not Vulcan, and when Venus takes her revenge it is not on her husband (whom she implicitly respects) but rather on the Sun, whose all-seeing eye had revealed her infidelity to him in the first place.[188] It is in order to forge a new definition of the artificer, I suggest—as one who, when it comes down to it, might *not* follow 'artificial rules'—that the text insouciantly introduces Prometheus and Vulcan here. They may be incidental to the speaker's argument—passing references that otherwise invite little scrutiny—but (and perhaps for that very reason) they are, arguably, central to Sidney's. Central, that is, to the 'other', alternative, unofficial, and quite possibly unconscious argument that the text is making: for a quite different kind of maker, one who chooses to follow his own flights of fancy wherever they may lead (even if that is downwards), whose 'wit may make Poesy, which should be *eikastike* ... be *phantastike*' (104.18–19, 20), and whom these mythic identifications make it possible to imagine or at least render visible. If so, it is no accident that both figures are associated with fire, with falling, and with a resistance to (and certainly a lack of support from) figures in authority.[189] Where Daedalus had been a father-figure against whom Sidney and his fellow poets rebel, Prometheus and Hephaistos/Vulcan are rebellious or vengeful figures with whom they—or rather 'we' (109.43; 110.1, 2, 6)—might identify.[190] Prometheus brings Zeus' anger and punishment down upon himself as a result of giving mankind fire, and, when he refuses to divulge the secret about Thetis (whom Zeus wishes to marry but whose son is destined to be more powerful than his father), he is thrown, still defiant, into the abyss. Hephaistos falls earthwards from the sky, cast out from Olympus either by his father (Zeus) for taking his mother's side in a dispute, or by the latter (Hera) for being born lame, entrapping her on a magic throne, in turn, by

---

[188] See Ovid 1916, *Metamorphoses*, IV.171–92.

[189] See Cooper 1565, under 'Prométheus' and 'Vulcanus'. The two figures are repeatedly connected. Both are associated with the creation of the first woman (Pandora) who was either fashioned by Prometheus himself or by Hephaistos (at Zeus' command) to punish Prometheus for one of his characteristic deceptions (tricking the gods into thinking that men offer them the tastiest portions of meat in their sacrifices, when in fact they keep these for themselves). In the latter case, Prometheus refuses the proffered 'gift' of the chaos-causing Pandora but, in spite of his warnings, his reckless brother accepts it, with predictable results. In *Prometheus Bound*, Zeus commands (a reluctant) Hephaistos to nail Prometheus to a rock in punishment for giving fire to mankind.

[190] Indeed, Daedalus' supposedly benign role as father and teacher is belied by the story of his fateful nephew and pupil, Talos. Instead of instructing the latter, Daedalus becomes envious of his native wit—this bright boy turns out to be an artificer in his own right, inventing the saw and the mathematical compasses—and so hurls him from the Acropolis, making it look like an accident. Metamorphosed into a partridge (*perdix*), Talos reappears to reproach his uncle at the very point when the latter is burying Icarus, another victim of a fatal fall: see Ovid 1916, *Metamorphoses*, VIII.236–59. Given the choice, Sidney and his fellow poets identify with those who fall rather than with those who push. For Astrophil's identification with Prometheus—'him who first stale downe the fire'—see *AS* 14.

way of revenge.[191] A master of metalwork, who uses volcanoes as his forge, the great blacksmith god brings forth from the fire the most beautiful objects, his many artefacts including not only the invisible net that entraps Venus and Mars—and Achilles' shield, of course—but also the chariot of the Sun which, in another story of a fatal filial flight and fall, the latter's reckless son Phaeton brings (along with its horses) crashing down to earth.[192]

The speaker's strategy of reversal thus proves something of a liability, for in the name of defending an ideal—what poetry might theoretically look like in its un-abused state—he ends up by demonstrating that poetry is always and everywhere abused: something this part of the text does not seem to be very apologetic about, or not nearly apologetic enough. Not the least reason for this turn of events is Sidney's repeated self-identification—especially in the opening and closing paragraphs of the *digressio*—with those who have fallen or gone 'awry' (115.11). He could easily have avoided this had he wanted to: by ensuring, for example, that the speaker refer to the abusing poets in question only in the third person so that his self-justificatory ire might be directed clearly at them. Since Sidney does not do this, however, he ends up by giving an extended survey of the damned—amongst whose number he counts himself—rather than, as the speaker had intended, giving a picture of the heaven from which they fall. In place of determinedly redemptive readings of the *digressio*, therefore, I would like to suggest that here, if not in the *Defence* as a whole, these multiple falls are not necessarily there to be made good. Sometimes a fall from grace is a fall from grace and not a *felix culpa* that enables fatherly forgiveness and a return to the fold. Take, for instance, the strange comparison that is designed to illustrate the degree to which these un-ideal poets have lapsed:

> And so as Epaminondas is said, with the honour of his virtue to have made an office, by his exercising it, which before was contemptible, to become highly respected, so these, no more but setting their names to it, by their own disgracefulness disgrace the most graceful Poesy. (109.13–16)

---

[191] Might this congenital condition of Hephaistos/Vulcan be alluded to in Sidney's account of the fact that 'we . . . walk so stumblingly' (110.13–14), describing the way he and his contemporaries fail to follow Chaucer's lead? Astrophil's first words, after all, 'came halting forth' (*AS* 1), and lameness is a recurrent motif in Sidney's life and art: see Bates 2007 (56–60).

[192] See Ovid 1916, *Metamorphoses*, II.106–10. In *Achilles shield* (1598), George Chapman presents Hephaistos' creation of Achilles' shield as a synecdoche of Homer's art: 'nothing can be imagined more full of soule and humaine extraction: for what is here prefigurde by our miraculous Artist, but the vniuersall world, which being so spatious and almost vnmeasurable, one circlet of a Shield representes and imbraceth?' (A2). Homer's poetry, moreover, is specifically presented as the product of inspiration—'this more then Artificiall and no lesse then *Diuine Rapture*' (A2), '*Homers* Poems were writ from a free furie, an absolute & full soule' (A2ᵛ)—and not of imitation and learning. Learning— and especially learned detractors of Homer such as the 'soule-blind Scalliger' (A3ᵛ)—comes in for some spectacular detraction of its own for misunderstanding the Greek poet so completely. Chapman could not have influenced Sidney, of course, but the latter may have influenced him. The claim for poetry's superiority over philosophy in his closing poem, for example, may echo the *Defence*: 'Yet where high *Poesies* natiue habite shines, / From whose reflections flow eternall lines: / *Philosophy* retirde to darkest caues / She can discouer' (D3ᵛ).

The reference relates to an anecdote in Plutarch in which the great Theban general is, 'through envy and as an insult', appointed to a position that involves 'supervision of the alleys for the removal of dung and the draining off of water in the streets', but turns the insult on its head by performing his duties with such an exemplary public diligence that he converts this once lowly position into one of 'great consideration and dignity': thereby demonstrating that the man distinguishes the office, not the office the man.[193] In stark contrast, English writers appoint themselves poets when they have no business doing so and thereby bring the once high office of Poet into disrepute. This is a good example of the '*Comparison* of contraries' being used for emphasis, Epaminondas' striking reversal of low to high being a measure of just how far English poets have moved in the opposite direction. It is also a good example of the device being used to turn the strength of one's opponents against them, for Plutarch's anecdote appears in the midst of a discussion about how best to deal with abusive speech, which is precisely *not* to trade insults (considered unstatesmanlike) but rather to return them whence they came with the lightest of touch: 'Retorts which turn his own words back upon the speaker are especially good in this way. For just as things which are thrown and return to the thrower seem to do this because they are driven back by some force and firmness of that against which they are thrown, so that which is spoken seems through the force and intellect of him who has been abused to turn back upon those who uttered the abuse.'[194] As noted above, however, this strategy can also prove a dangerous one, and *has* proved as much in the case of Sidney's speaker, who repeatedly finds the abuse he would deflect rebounding upon himself. And so it proves here, for within a sentence Sidney is identifying with these reprobates: he too is 'wanting estimation' (109.26) and 'desert' (109.26, 27), just like them, and is not very 'inclinable' (109.33) to do anything about it. If the comparison with Epaminondas is meant to show how low English poets have fallen—and the comparison of contraries to show that they have fallen to the very lowest—then that is where they remain. If there is any rebound, it is not upwards towards redemption and the light—as Wyatt 'from mine error / Am plunged up, as horse out of the mire / With stroke of spur'—but rather backwards or sideways: against the speaker, and anyone else who might hope for such a thing or insist that the *Defence* delivers it.[195] In the eyes of their elders and betters, the prodigal poets waste their time and their talent prodigiously—the very *digressio* which inquires as to why this should be the case is itself 'but a little more lost time' (108.23)—and they therefore quite rightly

---

[193] See Plutarch 2004, *Moralia*, 'Precepts of Statecraft', 811B. The role of such officials has been compared with that of the *koprologoi* (i.e. private waste contractors) of Athens: see Owens 1983 (49).

[194] See Plutarch 2004, *Moralia*, 'Precepts of Statecraft', 810E–F. Epaminondas is also cited here, this time for an exemplary put-down: when Callistratus (an Athenian orator and statesman) reproached the Thebans and the Argives on the grounds that Oedipus had killed his father and Orestes had killed his mother, Epaminondas retorted: 'When we had driven out the doers of those deeds, you took them in.'

[195] From Wyatt 1978, 'Paraphrase of the Penitential Psalms', Psalm 38, lines 333–5. See Bates 2007 (10–11) for an earlier discussion of this passage and of the redemptive reading of it in Greenblatt 1980 (123). Harington's metamorphosis of Ajax ('A Iakes')—'in plaine English a shiting place'—would seem to play on just this dilemma: see Harington 1596 (A6ᵛ, A2ᵛ).

belong where their greatest detractors put them: amongst the garbage-men, the sewage-sweepers, the waste-collectors, the swine.[196] Like the poems they produce, they are deemed nothing—empty of value—to be expelled from the common-wealth as dung is removed from its streets. Their great refusal condemns them to the refuse heap. They are the lowest of the low: from the 'earth' and 'soil' (109.1) that once grew poets' laurels, to the '*meliore luto*' (109.21) from which they might have been made, to the 'fertilest ground [that] must be manured' (109.39–40), they descend lower still until they merge with the ordure itself, the ultimate in abjection. And yet, like Astrophil, it is here they choose to remain: if 'Desire / Doth plunge my wel-form'd soule even in the mire / Of sinfull thoughts, which do in ruine end . . . Then Love is sinne, and let me sinfull be'.[197]

   Poetry is abused. A statement of fact, regrettable to some, but so be it. And as the *digressio* constitutes a lengthy disquisition to that effect—its efforts to argue the contrary proving counterproductive—so it plays host to a host of other wayward identifications that are by now all too familiar. Since he has 'run so long a career in this matter' (108.22), the speaker begins, he resolves to carry on in much the same manner before he brings himself to 'a full stop' (108.23): his riding metaphor serving not only to introduce the *digressio* but to cast it as a continuation of the course the *Defence* has been on since the beginning. A short gallop at full speed at the end of which the rider brings his horse to a complete stop, a 'career' represented the ultimate test of a horseman's skill: a manoeuvre that was indicative of extraor-dinary ability and promise—in the case of Alexander, for example—and that contemporary courtesy books singled out for praise.[198] All the more pronounced, therefore, is the shortfall of the man whose otherwise 'well chosen course in virtue' gives way instead to a 'slacking of the main career you had so notably begun': Pyrocles (the renegade in question) being by no means the only character in Sidney's writings whose failure to control his passions is figured as a failure to

---

[196] For Helgerson 1976 (27) the prodigal 'wastes not money, but time, wit, and learning, goods that should be spent in some way "beneficial unto the commonweal" and "profitable to himself"': as Astrophil wastes his talents, for example, in *AS* 18.

[197] *AS* 14; confirming Gosson's charge that poets, in the 'maner of swine . . . forsake the fayre fieldes, and wallow in the myre', *Schoole* (76/A1ᵛ), and anticipating the base matter and base materialism of Bataille's theorizations that, as Stoekl, ed. 1985 (xv) notes, 'cannot be reduced to systems of scientific or political mastery' nor be '*reappropriated* in the progressive dialectic' (xvi, emphasis original).

[198] For Alexander, see Plutarch 1579 (PPP3): '[Alexander] put [the horse] to his full career . . . Philip at the first with feare beholding his sonnes agility, least he should take some hurt, said neuer a word: but when he saw him redily turne the horse at the end of his career, in a brauery for that he had done . . . [he] fell a weeping for ioy. And when Alexander was lighted from the horse, he sayd vnto him kissing his head: O sonne, thou must needes haue a realme that is meete for thee, for MACEDON will not hold thee.' For courtesy books, see Guevara 1568 (X6): 'it is very fitt, and lawfull for yong courtiers . . . to ryde a horse well to manedge and geeue him his carere well'; and della Casa 1576 (O1ᵛ): 'as in horses you see it: which by nature would be euer wilde, but yᵗ their ryder makes them tame, and withal, after a sorte, redy & very well paced. For many of them would haue a hard trot, but that the rider makes them haue an easier pace. And some he doth teache to stand still, to galopp, to treade the ringe, and do the carreere: And they learne to doe it all well you see.' See *OED* career *n*. 2a, although these examples antedate the earliest citation (1591). Sidney appears to have been the first to use the word to refer to the ground on which the gallop is run, as at a tournament: see *OED* career *n*. 1a, citing *NA* (396).

control his horse.[199] That such a figure should appear in the *Defence*, therefore, is no cause for surprise, nor the fact that the course his career takes should go 'awry' (115.11) or that he should be 'pounded for straying' (115.5), or even end up '*in pistrinum*' (98.20). The speaker lampoons the bastard poets who, apparently in a similar hurry, 'do post over the banks of Helicon' (109.18) in endless relays: not only making their own readers 'more weary than post-horses' (109.19) (more weary than themselves, that is, presumably because they are in a desperate race to keep up), but also marking the distance between their own poor nags and the soaring Pegasus, from whose hoof the fountain of the Muses—more properly named Hippocrene—was said to have been struck.[200] These posting 'knights' (109.23) no more live up to the chivalric ideal than Pyrocles does, and yet in the next sentence it is with these that Sidney identifies: 'our' (109.26) rejection of Pallas being also, quite possibly, a rejection of the reverential attitude towards the Muses' spring which the goddess of learning had displayed.[201] For Sidney and his fellow poets, by contrast, 'Poesy must not be drawn by the ears' (109.33–4), as if it were a stubborn horse to be chivvied by its keeper, or a recalcitrant schoolboy by such a schoolmistress, for that matter. Instead, 'it must be gently led' (109.34).[202] As if to water, perhaps: except there is always the possibility that it might not drink from the specified stream (Astrophil's didn't, after all, 'Study-ing inventions fine... Oft turning others' leaves, to see if thence would flow / Some fresh and fruitfull showers upon my sunne-burn'd braine. / But words came

---

[199] *OA* (13); see Bates 2013 (205–8, 229–36) on Astrophil, Amphialus, and Philisides as comic and tragic examples of the knight whose failures in mounted combat symptomize his moral failings. The word 'career' could also be applied to the course the sun or a star takes through the heavens (see *OED* career *n.* 3a), a slowing or deviation of which would constitute a cosmological catastrophe, as in the case of Phaeton's wild ride: see Ovid 1916, *Metamorphoses*, II.171–7, 208–9.

[200] Literally 'fountain of the horse' [Ἵππου κρήνη]. The 'banks of Helicon' (109.18) conflates the spring with the mountain from which it flows. In *AS* 74 Sidney refers to it as '*Aganippe* well', i.e. the spring of the gentle (ἀγανός) horse. To post was 'to travel with relays of horses, originally as a courier or bearer of letters' (current from the early sixteenth century); see *OED* post *v. intr.* I.1.

[201] Minerva visits the fountain as a tourist: '*fama novi fontis nostras pervenit ad aures, / dura Medusaei quem praepetis ungula rupit. / is mihi causa viae; volui mirabile factum / cernere*' [The fame of a new spring has reached my ears, which broke out under the hard hoof of the winged horse of Medusa. This is the cause of my journey: I wished to see the marvellous thing]: see Ovid 1916, *Metamorphoses*, V.256–9.

[202] An allusion, perhaps, to the gentle methods newly popularized by the rediscovery of Xenophon's works on horse-training. Although Xenophon has little time for the 'disobedient horse', the techniques he recommends nonetheless aim at cooperation rather than compulsion, advising the rider to 'direct [his horse] to go by the most gentle aids', for example, and to 'let him begin at a very slow pace and increase the speed with the same gentle help'. The secret to success is to 'cause the horse to do the very things in which he himself delights and takes the greatest pleasure', and therefore 'you should not deal hardly with him as though you were forcing him to work, but coax him'. 'For what a horse does under constraint... he does without understanding, and with no more grace than a dancer would show if he was whipped and goaded... No, a horse must make the most graceful and brilliant appearance in all respects of his own will with the help of aids': see Xenophon 1925, *Cavalry Commander*, I.3, and *Art of Horsemanship*, III.6; IX.3; X.3, 13; XI.6. When all goes well, 'no action of man bears a closer resemblance to flying': *Cavalry Commander*, IV.6; and, as Cyrus says, 'if I become a horseman I shall be a man on wings': see Xenophon 1914, *Cyropaedia*, IV.iii.15. See LeGuin 2005 (177) on the way Xenophon's humane approach 'marks a turning point... in basic European understandings of how power and command work upon selfhood'; also Raber 2013 (86–92).

halting forth').[203] And so, 'rather it must lead' (109.34): the horse Poesy leading its rider-poet, and the latter—operating 'fore-backwardly' (110.2) here as in everything else—thus voting with his halting feet and opting for the wrong kind of following for the umpteenth time.[204] Poets, the speaker laments, 'are almost in as good reputation as the mountebanks at Venice' (109.5–6). But these notoriously voluble salesmen, charlatans as they may seem, nonetheless bear an uncanny resemblance to another Italian discourser—another peddler of nonsense who shows the way towards Utopia—and who sets the entire 'career' that is the *Defence* in motion, quite simply because it is his non-exemplary example that Sidney elects to follow in the first place, in despite of very determined efforts to make him do otherwise. The fertileness of this master's wit is never in question and is manured by his own originality—a positively Augean commodity—rather than by any Daedalian guidance or schoolmasterly instruction. And it is this figure, I suggest, that—albeit from the margins and between the lines of the text—is really carrying the *Defence*. The horseman who is loudly proclaimed a bad, faulty, or indecorous poet: like Pugliano, or the 'knights of the same order', and behind them the despised *eques* of Horace. The horse-man with whom the latter opens his own defence of poetry as the epitome of poetic indecorum: and an anti-type, perhaps, of Chiron, the ideal centaur-poet whose like (Gosson mourns) is no longer extant.[205] The horse-lover who cherishes toys and esteems matters

---

[203] *AS* 1. Elsewhere, Astrophil takes his halting metre from his 'trampling horses feet', *AS* 84: see Prescott 2005 (42), and Bates 2007 (56–7).

[204] See Boehrer 2005 (94) on the way 'the horse comes to be identified most persistently with figures of social abjection such as the woman, the child, the base-born, the ethnic Other' in the period: a phenomenon he attributes to the decline of aristocratic chivalry which militated against the horse being used as 'an emblem of aristocratic triumphalism' (101). Boehrer cites satirical and tragic figures in Shakespeare to illustrate his argument but—in embracing this image of self-sabotage in his own work—Sidney may perhaps have shown the way.

[205] See *Schoole* (82/A7ᵛ; 83–4/A8ᵛ–B1ᵛ). Although a centaur, Chiron differed dramatically from the normal type insofar as he was wise, learned, skilled, and kind: e.g. he sacrificed his immortality so that Prometheus might live, and at his death was transformed by Zeus into the constellation Sagittarius. Since for Gosson and for Sidney this atypically ideal centaur emphatically no longer exists—and indeed represents the absence and impossibility of such an ideal—it is as if the centaur reverts to the nature more typical of its breed here to figure the poet who is not ideal and in whom the horse's body assumes priority over the man's head, the passions over reason. For an extended discussion of the way Chiron represents the possibilities of such categorical collapse in Renaissance texts, see Raber 2013 (75–101). In Dante, Chiron is leader of the centaurs whose job it is to guard the tyrants in Hell (see Dante 2004, *Inferno*, XII.55–99): their biform nature lends itself to this peculiarly dual role as the enforcers of infernal punishment. In Ovid's version of the myth, Chiron's daughter Ocyrhoë is transformed into a horse when, 'not satisfied to have learnt her father's art' (i.e. medicine), she instead 'sang prophecy' [*fatorum arcana canebat*] and feeling the 'prophetic madness' [*vaticinos furores*] in her soul, predicts that he will exchange his immortality for that of the infant Aesculapius whom he fosters and raises. In losing her humanity, Ocyrhoë pays a high price for her oracular outpouring—'Not worth the cost were those arts [*non fuerant artes tanti*] which have brought down the wrath of heaven upon me'—and she complains that she is 'turning into a mare, my kindred shape' [*in equam cognataque corpora vertor*], even though her father is only half horse, half man. This 'new wonder gave her a new name as well' [*nomen quoque monstra dedere*], for she was also known as Melanippe (black mare) or Euippe (good mare), and was transformed by Zeus into the constellation Pegasus: see Ovid 1916, *Metamorphoses*, II.638–40, 659–60, 663, 675. In this mythic backstory, Chiron's absence or reversion to type mobilizes, perhaps, the identification with the figure of the rapturous female seer and poet to which Sidney seems strangely and recurrently drawn.

rather of sport than of virtue: like Philip Sidney, or like Philip of Macedon, and a poet such as Pindar who praises him. Or even, at the end of this line, the horse that is beloved: the alter ego whom, in a moment of self-love, Sidney almost wishes himself on the opening page, and to whom Astrophil—once 'A horsman to my horse'—also reverts: now 'a horse to *Love*'.[206] A horse like the Trojan horse, worshiped and brought into the city whose civilization it promptly destroys, or like the post-horses of the bastard poets, or like Folly's happily illiterate horse, or Agrippa's discreet ass, or the Bath keeper's ass who contents himself with the smell of the smoke, or Ascham's Italianate Englishman—the awry-transformed traveller who is a horse when he flies to Italy and an ass when he returns.[207] A horse like 'Pacolet's horse' (111.28) who, not bounded by gravity or geography, can like the imagination fly anywhere in the world, or like Pegasus, or the horses of the Sun, or the horses of the soul, or the horses of the doomed Achilles who are capable of tears and of speech.[208] A horse whose characteristic movement is careering, stumbling, halting, trampling, swerving, straying, flinging, flying, falling: but always leading.

∝

This might be thought preposterous, and technically it is: an example of that 'disordered speech when ye misplace your words or clauses and set that before which should be behind', as Puttenham defines *hysteron proteron* or, in its more homely English articulation, 'the cart before the horse'.[209] As a rhetorical trope, he grants, this is tolerable enough 'if it be not too much used' (253). But to put the horse before the rider (more absurd still), and to do so not as a mere device but as the substance of your argument—as an acknowledgement that this is how the real poet actually succeeds—and to do so repeatedly (and in your own poetry, to boot): this really does amount to an abuse. Indeed, to someone who has devoted his own enterprise to pulling the poet 'first from the cart to the school, and from thence to the court' (378), it is the most retrograde step imaginable, as if the ambitious self-maker—should he ever make it to court—were to find when he got there that

---

[206] *AS* 49. In defiance of Platonic prescription in the *Phaedrus*—and like Gosson's colt that 'flinges about' (101/D3)—Astrophil also declines to tame his 'coltish gyres' in *AS* 21: 'gyres' being glossed by Prescott 2005 (26) as 'a colt's swerves as it shies'. As Raber 2013 (85) notes, even idealized representations of man-horse relations—e.g. the description of the mounted Musidorus as 'centaur-like' because he was of 'one piece with the horse', *NA* (153)—are prone to such 'boundary collapse', thereby opening up possibilities for a human–animal eroticism that might be described as 'profoundly queer'.

[207] Erasmus 1549 (F3); Agrippa 1569 (Bbb1); Gosson, 'An Apologie' (132/M1ᵛ); Ascham 1967 (66).

[208] In the late medieval romance, *Valentyne and Orson*, an enchanter named Pacolet creates a magical wooden horse that, at the turn of a pin, can go 'thorughe the ayre more faster than ony byrde coude flee' and transport him wherever in the world he wishes to go: see Watson 1555 (Aa4). Sidney's speaker invokes it when mocking English stage-plays for making similar geographical leaps. For Pegasus and the horses of the Sun see Ovid 1916, *Metamorphoses*, V.262 and II.153–5; for the horses of the soul, see Plato 1914, *Phaedrus*, 246A–247C; for Achilles' horses, see Homer 1925, *Iliad*, XVII.426–8; XIX.399–417 (like Ocyrhoë, they too predict their master's death).

[209] Puttenham 2007 (253).

the courtly maker he aspires to be is unaccountably moving in the opposite direction. For all that, however, Sidney's reversal is not quite as preposterous as it seems. For the faults his speaker seeks to disparage are precisely those that would put English poetry on a whole new footing and go on, in time, to put it on the map. At the end of the *digressio* the speaker's critique of what contemporary poets have been doing—especially with the English language—gives way to a celebration of the latter's flexibility and range. The qualities of mixture and miscegenation, earlier condemned for polluting the poetic inheritance, are now—in the case of a decidedly mongrel 'mother-tongue' (115.20) which is descended from quite divergent language clans—admitted to be the very key to its success: 'I know some will say it is a mingled language', Sidney concedes, 'And why not so much the better, taking the best of both the other?' (115.14–15).[210] This cheerful acceptance of hybridization—and the fertility to which it gives rise as a bastard mother breeds bastard poets, and vice versa—becomes an occasion not for shame but for pride: 'our tongue is most fit to honour Poesy, and to be honoured by Poesy' (116.19–20). In the development of a literary vernacular (that great project of the sixteenth century, even if it only appeared as much in hindsight), the most innovative writers would turn out to be those who looked to and made the most of this mixed heritage. Who, in the experience of their own 'barbarous' distance from the classical tongues, took to heart the essence of what the ancients had taught about style, namely, that it lay precisely in a departure from the rule, the rules—in barbarizing, defamiliarizing, making an exception, making strange—literariness being, in its very deviation from common usage, a form of abuse.[211] In the speaker's survey of the contemporary scene, two very recent productions stand out for their linguistic aberration: the hyper-ornate diction of *Euphues* (1578) and its spin-offs—its obsessive use of alliterative similitudes being condemned as 'absurd' (114.28)—and the archaisms of *The Shepheardes Calender* (1579): the 'old rustic language' being the one aspect of this otherwise exemplary text that he 'dare not allow' (110.19–20). In both cases, however, the parading of a self-consciously not to say provokingly affected style proved to be an enabling strategy, as Lyly and Spenser were to forge a distinctively English poetry precisely by making their language seem—in being at variance from and so alien, foreign, and unfamiliar to itself—*literary*.[212] The literature that would come to characterize the period

[210] I am inclined to agree with van Dorsten (208) and Alexander (357) that this refers to the language's roots in Anglo-Saxon and Norman French, rather than—as Shepherd (231–2) and Maslen (248) suggest—to Latin and Greek, although, as Alexander notes, it does not exclude the abundant presence in English of classical loan-words. Skretkowicz 1998 (4) finds Sidney's argument here 'calculatingly perverse' in its marked deviation from the nationalism of Henri Estienne, du Bellay, etc. which stressed the purity of the French language: Sidney, by contrast, 'contrarily argues that English is a language even better suited to poetry precisely because it is not pure'.

[211] See Nicholson 2014 (62): 'The near identity between rhetorical ornamentation and rhetorical abuse . . . produces a constant anxiety over the desirable and dangerous effects of language that departs from ordinary usage.'

[212] See ibid. (15): 'the writers credited with accomplishing the most in and for the mother tongue were those who underscored its freaks, fissures, and indecorums.' Lyly and Spenser provide case histories in support of Nicholson's argument, although she continues to read the *Defence* as promoting an idealist poetics. See also Blank 1996.

did so, by and large, by making just such unexpected, unorthodox, even counter-intuitive moves: by taking liberties—the high-flying liberties of conceit proper to the poet—even if that ran the gauntlet and risked being met with the charge of abuse. It was far from certain at the time, no doubt, that their gamble would pay off or that such an off-beat intimation would ever prove correct. And that remains the speaker's bet. In his critique of English drama, likewise, he holds to his position that—in flouting the 'rules' (110.29)—contemporary playwrights were similarly aberrant and thus destined to fail: not able, at that stage, to foresee a playwright who would do everything that he, the speaker, continues to condemn as a pitiful abuse. A playwright who would regularly require his viewers to imagine the stage 'a garden', 'a cave', 'a rock' that wrecks ships (111.3, 6, 4); to see in 'four swords and bucklers' (111.7–8) two mighty monarchies at war; to accept that the story of an entire generation might be told 'in two hours' space' (111.12), thus turning the accomplishment of many years into an hourglass; to agree that 'min-gling kings and clowns' (112.2) was something that a playwright might do. The speaker lost the bet, and Sidney—with his preposterous case for a poet and a poesy that might not be ideal—ended up by winning it. Which is not to accord him any undue prescience but rather to put him where he belongs: among the poets of his generation, the makers who were feeling their way towards a new and distinctive English literature by following dubious masters and going down unobvious, unsigned, and disallowed paths. The struggles, self-doubts, and stubborn determinations that are registered in the *Defence* do not speak directly for the members of this generation but they may have spoken to them and to those who came after. They may have suggested, hinted, enabled, encour-aged, and inspired: to be vindicated in time by the course—the career—that only literary history would determine.

Bibliography

ABBREVIATIONS

CamQ	*Cambridge Quarterly*
Comp Lit	*Comparative Literature*
CQ	*Classical Quarterly*
EiC	*Essays in Criticism*
ELH	*English Literary History*
ELR	*English Literary Renaissance*
ESC	*English Studies in Canada*
HJ	*Historical Journal*
JMRS	*Journal of Medieval and Renaissance Studies*
JWCI	*Journal of the Warburg and Courtauld Institutes*
MLN	*Modern Language Notes*
MLQ	*Modern Language Quarterly*
MLR	*Modern Language Review*
NLH	*New Literary History*
NQ	*Notes and Queries*
PLL	*Papers on Language and Literature*
PMLA	*Publications of the Modern Language Association of America*
PS	*Prose Studies*
RES	*Review of English Studies*
RL	*Religion and Literature*
RP	*Renaissance Papers*
RQ	*Renaissance Quarterly*
RS	*Renaissance Studies*
SCJ	*Sixteenth Century Journal*
SEL	*Studies in English Literature, 1500–1900*
SJ	*Sidney Journal*
SLI	*Studies in the Literary Imagination*
SP	*Studies in Philology*
YJBM	*Yale Journal of Biology and Medicine*

PRIMARY TEXTS

Agrippa, Henry Cornelius *De incertitudine et vanitate scientiarum atque artium declamatio invectiva* (Cologne, 1527).

Agrippa, Henry Cornelius *Henrie Cornelius Agrippa, of the vanitie and vncertaintie of artes and sciences,* trans. J. Sandford (London, 1569).

Anon *Rhetorica ad Herennium*, trans. Harry Caplan (Cambridge, MA: Harvard University Press, 1954).

Aristotle *Art of Rhetoric*, trans. J. H. Freese (Cambridge, MA: Harvard University Press, 1926).

Aristotle *The Nicomachean Ethics*, trans. H. Rackham (Cambridge, MA: Harvard University Press, 1926).

Aristotle *Politics*, trans. H. Rackham (Cambridge, MA: Harvard University Press, 1932).

Aristotle *Metaphysics*, trans. Hugh Tredennick and G. Cyril Armstrong, 2 vols. (Cambridge, MA: Harvard University Press, 1933–35).

Aristotle *Poetics; Longinus, On The Sublime; Demetrius, On Style*, trans. Stephen Halliwell et al. (Cambridge, MA: Harvard University Press, 1995).

Ascham, Roger *Toxophilus the schole of shootinge contayned in tvvo bookes. To all gentlemen and yomen of Englande, pleasaunte for theyr pastyme to rede, and profitable for theyr use to folow, both in war and peace* (London, 1545).

Ascham, Roger *The Schoolmaster* (1570), ed. Lawrence V. Ryan (Ithaca: Cornell University Press, 1967).

Augustine *De Doctrina Christiana*, ed. and trans. R. P. H. Green (Oxford: Clarendon Press, 1995).

Beza, Theodore *Jesu Christi Domini Nostri Novum Testamentum . . . ejusdem Theod. Bezae Annotationes* (Cambridge, 1642).

Bibles

Vulgate <http://vulgate.org/>.

Wycliffe's Bible *The Holy Bible, Containing the Old and New Testaments, with the Apocryphal Books, in the Earliest English Versions made from the Latin Vulgate by John Wycliffe and his Followers*, ed. Josiah Forshall and Frederic Madden, 4 vols. (Oxford: Oxford University Press, 1850).

Erasmus' New Testament *Novum Instrumentum* (Basel, 1516).

Tyndale's Bible [*The Newe Testament*] [*dylygently corrected by W. Tindale: fynesshed M.D. and xxxv*] (Antwerp, 1535?).

Coverdale's Bible *Biblia the Bible, that is, the holy Scripture of the Olde and New Testament, faithfully and truly translated out of Douche and Latyn in to Englishe* (Cologne?, 1535).

Matthew's Bible *The Byble which is all the holy Scripture: in whych are contayned the Olde and Newe Testament truly and purely translated into Englysh by Thomas Matthew* [pseudonym for John Rogers] (Antwerp, 1537).

Great Bible *The Byble in Englyshe that is to saye the content of all the holy scrypture, both of ye olde and newe testament, truly translated after the veryte of the Hebrue and Greke textes, by ye dylygent studye of dyuerse excellent learned men, expert in the forsayde tonges* (Paris, 1539).

Cranmer's Bible *The Byble in Englyshe that is to saye the content of al the holy scrypture, both of ye olde, and newe testament, with a prologe therinto, made by the reuerende father in God, Thomas archbysshop of Cantorbury* (London, 1540).

English/Erasmus parallel text *The Newe Testament in Englyshe and in Latin of Erasmus translation. Nouum Testamentum Anglice et Latine* (London, 1549).

Coverdale's Bible 'conferred' with Tyndale's *The Newe Testament. Translated by Myles Couerdale, an[d] conferred with W. Tyndales translation* (London, 1550).

Geneva Bible *The Bible and Holy Scriptures conteyned in the Olde and Newe Testament. Translated according to the Ebrue and Greke, and conferred with the best translations in diuers langues. With moste profitable annotations vpon all the hard places, and other things of great importance as may appeare in the epistle to the reader* (Geneva, 1560).

Bishop's Bible *The. holie. Bible conteynyng the olde Testament and the newe* (London, 1568).

New Testament translated from Greek *The Newe Testament of our Sauiour Iesus Christ faithfully translated out of the Greeke, with the notes and expositions of the darke places therein* (London, 1579).

Douai-Rheims Bible *The Nevv Testament of Iesus Christ, translated faithfully into English, out of the authentical Latin, according to the best corrected copies of the same, diligently conferred* vvith the Greeke and other editions in diuers languages; vvith arguments of bookes and chapters, annotations, and other necessarie helpes, for the better vnderstanding of the text, and specially for the discouerie of the corruptions of diuers late translations, and for cleering the controuersies in religion, of these daies (Rheims, 1582).

Authorized Version *The Holy Bible conteyning the Old Testament, and the New: newly translated out of the originall tongues: & with the former translations diligently compared and reuised, by his Maiesties speciall co[m]mandement* (London, 1611).

Boccaccio, Giovanni *Boccaccio on Poetry: Being the Preface and the Fourteenth and Fifteenth Books of Boccaccio's* Genealogia Deorum Gentilium, ed. and trans. Charles G. Osgood (Princeton: Princeton University Press, 1930).

Calvin, John *The institution of Christian religion, vvrytten in Latine by maister Ihon Caluin, and translated into Englysh according to the authors last edition*, trans. Thomas Norton (London, 1561).

Camerarius, Philip *Operae horarum succisivarum sive meditationes historicae* (Nuremberg, 1591).

Campano, Giannantonio *Opera* (Rome, 1495).

Caracciolo, Pasqual *La Gloria del Cavallo* (Venice, 1566).

Chapman, George *Achilles shield Translated as the other seuen bookes of Homer, out of his eighteenth booke of Iliades* (London, 1598).

Chaucer, Geoffrey *The Riverside Chaucer*, ed. Larry D. Benson (Oxford: Oxford University Press, 3rd edn., 1987).

Cicero *On Duties* [*De Officiis*], trans. Walter Miller (Cambridge, MA: Harvard University Press, 1913).

Cicero *Tusculan Disputations*, trans. J. E. King (Cambridge, MA: Harvard University Press, 1927).

Cooper, Thomas *Thesaurus linguae Romanae & Britannicae . . . Accessit dictionarium historicum et poëticum propria vocabula virorum, mulierum, sectarum, populorum, urbium, montium, & caeterorum locorum complectens, & in his iucundissimas & omnium cognitione dignissimas historias* (London, 1565).

Corte, Claudio *II Cavallarizzo* (Venice, 1562).

Curione, Celio Secundo *Pro vera et antiqua Ecclesiae Christi autoritate* (Basel, *c*.1546).

Cuspinianus, Joannes *De Caesaribus atque imperatoribus Romanis, opus insigne* (Basel, 1561).

Dante Alighieri *Dante Alighieri's Divine Comedy*, ed. and trans. Mark Musa, 6 vols. (Bloomington: Indiana University Press, 1996–2004).

della Casa, Giovanni *Galateo of Maister Iohn Della Casa, Archebishop of Beneuenta. Or rather, A treatise of the manners and behauiours, it behoueth a man to vse and eschewe, in his familiar conuersation*, trans. Robert Peterson (London, 1576).

Dethick, Henry *Oratio in laudem poëseos* (*c*.1572–76), in *Latin Treatises on Poetry from Renaissance England*, ed. Binns (1999).

Elyot, Thomas *The boke named the gouernour* (London, 1531).

Elyot, Thomas *Of the knowleg whiche maketh a wise man* (London, 1533).

Elyot, Thomas *The castel of helth corrected and in some places augmented* (London, 1541a).

Elyot, Thomas *The image of gouernance compiled of the actes and sentences notable, of the moste noble Emperour Alexander Seuerus, late translated out of Greke into Englyshe* (London, 1541b).

Erasmus, Desiderius *Apophthegmes that is to saie, prompte, quicke, wittie and sentencious saiynges, of certain emperours, kynges, capitaines, philosophiers and oratours, aswell Grekes, as Romaines, bothe veraye pleasaunt & profitable to reade, partely for all maner of persones, [&] especially gentlemen*, trans. Nicholas Udall (London, 1542).

Erasmus, Desiderius *The praise of folie. Moriae encomium a booke made in latine by that great clerke Erasmus Roterodame*, trans. Sir Thomas Chaloner (London, 1549).

Erasmus, Desiderius *Erasmus' Annotations on the New Testament: Acts—Romans—I and II Corinthians* [1535], ed. Anne Reeve and M. A. Screech (Leiden: Brill, 1990).

Erasmus, Desiderius *Erasmus' Annotations on the New Testament: Galatians to the Apocalypse* [1535], ed. Anne Reeve, intr. M. A. Screech (Leiden: Brill, 1993).

Estienne, Robert *Dictionarium, seu Latinae linguae thesaurus* (Paris, 1543).

Gosson, Stephen *The s[c]hoole of abuse, conteining a plesaunt inuectiue against poets, pipers, plaiers, iesters, and such like caterpillers of a commonwelth; setting vp the flagge of defiance to their mischieuous exercise, & ouerthrowing their bulwarkes, by prophane writers, naturall reason, and common experience* (London, 1579).

Gosson, Stephen *The ephemerides of Phialo . . . And a short apologie of the Schoole of abuse, against poets, pipers, players, & their excusers* (London, 1579a).

Gosson, Stephen *Playes confuted in fiue actions prouing that they are not to be suffred in a Christian common weale, by the waye both the cauils of Thomas Lodge, and the play of playes, written in their defence, and other obiections of players frendes, are truely set downe and directlye aunsweared* (London, 1582).

Gosson, Stephen all of the above in *Markets of Bawdrie: The Dramatic Criticism of Stephen Gosson*, ed. Kinney (1974).

Greville, Fulke 'A Dedication to Sir Philip Sidney', in *The Prose Works of Fulke Greville, Lord Brooke*, ed. John Gouws (Oxford: Clarendon Press, 1986).

Grisone, Federigo *Degli Ordine del Cavalcare* (Naples, 1550).

Guevara, Antonio de *The dial of princes, compiled by the reuerend father in God, Don Antony of Gueuara, Byshop of Guadix, preacher, and chronicler to Charles the fifte, late of that name Emperour*, trans. Thomas North (London, 1568).

Harington, John *A new discourse of a stale subiect, called The metamorphosis of Aiax vvritten by Misacmos to his friend and cosin Philostilpnos* (London, 1596).

Harington, John 'A Briefe Apologie of Poetrie' (1591), in *Elizabethan Critical Essays*, ed. Smith (1904).

Harrison, William *An historicall description of the Iland of Britaine*, in Holinshed, ed. (London, 1587).

Herodotus *The Persian Wars*, trans. A. D. Godley, 4 vols. (Cambridge, MA: Harvard University Press, 1920–25).

Heron, Haly *A newe discourse of morall philosophie, entituled, The kayes of counsaile* (London, 1579).

Holinshed, Raphael et al., eds. *The first and second volumes of Chronicles comprising 1 The description and historie of England, 2 The description and historie of Ireland, 3 The description and historie of Scotland* (London, 1587).

Homer *Iliad*, trans. A. T. Murray, revised William F. Wyatt, 2 vols. (Cambridge, MA: Harvard University Press, 1924–25).

Horace *Satires. Epistles. The Art of Poetry [Ars Poetica]*, trans. H. Rushton Fairclough (Cambridge, MA: Harvard University Press, 1926).

Horace *Odes and Epodes*, ed. and trans. Niall Rudd (Cambridge, MA: Harvard University Press, 2004).

Hoskins, John 'Direccions For Speech and Style' (1599), in *The Life, Letters, and Writings of John Hoskyns, 1566–1638*, ed. Louise Brown Osborn (New Haven: Yale University Press, 1937).

Isidore of Seville *The Etymologies of Isidore of Seville*, trans. Stephen A. Barney et al. (Cambridge: Cambridge University Press, 2006).

Justinus, Marcus Junianus *Thabridgment of the histories of Trogus Pompeius, collected and wrytten in the Laten tonge, by the famous historiographer Iustine*, trans. Arthur Golding (London, 1564).

Juvenal *Satires, in Juvenal and Persius*, trans. Susanna Morton Braund (Cambridge, MA: Harvard University Press, 2004).

Lépez de Gómara, Francisco *The pleasant historie of the conquest of the VVeast India, now called new Spayne atchieued by the vvorthy prince Hernando Cortes Marques of the valley of Huaxacac*, trans. T. N (London 1578).

Livy *History of Rome*, trans. B. O. Foster, Evan T. Sage, Alfred Cary Schlesinger et al., 14 vols. (Cambridge, MA: Harvard University Press, 1919–59).

Lodge, Thomas [*A Defence of Poetry*] (1579), in *Elizabethan Critical Essays*, ed. Smith (1904).

Marlowe, Christopher *The Collected Poems of Christopher Marlowe*, ed. Patrick Cheney and Brian J. Striar (New York: Oxford University Press, 2006).

Milton, John *Paradise Lost*, ed. Alastair Fowler (Harlow: Pearson Longman, 2nd edn., 2007).

Moffet, Thomas *Nobilis: Or a View of the Life and Death of a Sidney*, ed. Virgil B. Heltzel and Hoyt H. Hudson (San Marino: Huntington Library, 1940).

More, Thomas *A dyaloge of syr Thomas More knyghte . . . Wherin be treated dyuers maters, as of the veneration & worshyp of ymages & relyques, prayng to sayntys, & goyng on pylgrymage* (London, 1529).

More, Thomas *A fruteful, and pleasaunt worke of the beste state of a publyque weale, and of the newe yle called Vtopia*, trans. Ralph Robinson (London, 1551).

More, Thomas *Utopia*, in *The Complete Works of St Thomas More*, vol. 4, ed. Edward Surtz, S. J. and J. H. Hexter (New Haven: Yale University Press, 1965a).

More, Thomas *Utopia*, trans. Paul Turner (Harmondsworth: Penguin 1965b).

More, Thomas *Utopia: Latin Text and English Translation*, ed. and trans. George M. Logan, Robert M. Adams, and Clarence H. Miller (Cambridge: Cambridge University Press, 1995).

Mornay, Philippe de, seigneur du Plessis-Marly *A vvoorke concerning the trewnesse of the Christian religion . . . Begunne to be translated into English by Sir Philip Sidney Knight, and at his request finished by Arthur Golding* (London, 1587).

Ovid *Metamorphoses*, trans. Frank Justus Miller, revised G. P. Gould, 2 vols. (Cambridge, MA: Harvard University Press, 1916).

Ovid *Tristia. Ex Ponto*, trans. A. L. Wheeler, revised G. P. Gould (Cambridge, MA: Harvard University Press, 1924).

Ovid *The Art of Love [Ars Amatoria], and Other Poems* [including *Remedia Amoris*], trans. J. H. Mozley, revised G. P. Gould (Cambridge, MA: Harvard University Press, 1929).

Pace, Richard *De Fructu qui ex Doctrina Percipitur* (1517), ed. and trans. Frank Manley and Richard S. Sylvester (New York: Renaissance Society of America, 1967).

Petrarch, Francesco *Petrarch's Lyric Poems: The* Rime sparse *and Other Lyrics*, ed. and trans. Robert M. Durling (Cambridge, MA: Harvard University Press, 1976).

Petrarch, Francesco *Invectives*, ed. and trans. David Marsh (Cambridge, MA: Harvard University Press, 2003).

Philpot, John *The Examinations and Writings of John Philpot*, ed. Robert Eden (Cambridge: Cambridge University Press, 1842).

Plato *Euthyphro. Apology. Crito. Phaedo. Phaedrus*, trans. Harold North Fowler (Cambridge, MA: Harvard University Press, 1914).

Plato *Theaetetus. Sophist*, trans. Harold North Fowler (Cambridge, MA: Harvard University Press, 1921).

Plato *Laches. Protagoras. Meno. Euthydemus*, trans. W. R. M. Lamb (Cambridge, MA: Harvard University Press, 1924).

Plato *Lysis. Symposium. Gorgias*, trans. W. R. M. Lamb (Cambridge, MA: Harvard University Press, 1925).

Plato *Laws*, trans. R. G. Bury, 2 vols. (Cambridge, MA: Harvard University Press, 1926).

Plato *Republic*, trans. Chris Emlyn-Jones and William Preddy, 2 vols. (Cambridge, MA: Harvard University Press, 2013).

Plutarch *The liues of the noble Grecians and Romanes, compared together by that graue learned philosopher and historiographer, Plutarke of Chaeronea*, trans. Thomas North (London, 1579).

Plutarch *Lives*, trans. Bernadotte Perrin, 11 vols. (Cambridge, MA: Harvard University Press, 1914–26).

Plutarch *Moralia*, trans. Frank Cole Babbitt et al., 16 vols. (Cambridge, MA: Harvard University Press, 1927–2004).

Puttenham, George *The Art of English Poesy* [1589] *by George Puttenham*, ed. Frank Whigham and Wayne A. Rebhorn (Ithaca: Cornell University Press, 2007).

Quintilian *The Orator's Education* [*Institutio oratoria*], trans. Donald A. Russell, 5 vols. (Cambridge, MA: Harvard University Press, 2002).

Scaliger, Julius Caesar *Select Translations from Scaliger's Poetics*, ed. and trans. Frederick Morgan Padelford (New Haven: Yale University Press, 1905).

Scott, William *The Model of Poesy* (1599), ed. Gavin Alexander (Cambridge: Cambridge University Press, 2013).

Scott, William *The Model of Poesy* Original spelling version available at <http://www.cambridge.org/gb/academic/subjects/literature/renaissance-and-early-modern-literature/model-poesy?format=HB#resources>.

Seneca *The lamentable tragedie of Oedipus the sonne of Laius Kyng of Thebes out of Seneca*, trans. Alexander Neville (London, 1563).

Seneca *Seneca his tenne tragedies, translated into Englysh*, trans. Thomas Newton (London, 1581).

Shakespeare, William *The Riverside Shakespeare*, ed. G. Blakemore Evans et al. (Boston: Houghton Mifflin, 2nd edn., 1997).

Sidney, Philip *An apologie for poetrie. VVritten by the right noble, vertuous, and learned, Sir Phillip Sidney, Knight* ... Printed for Henry Olney (London, 1595).

Sidney, Philip *The defence of poesie by Sir Phillip Sidney* ... Printed for VVilliam Ponsonby (London, 1595).

Sidney, Philip 'An Apology for Poetry', in *Elizabethan Critical Essays*, ed. Smith (1904).

Sidney, Philip *The Poems of Sir Philip Sidney*, ed. W. A. Ringler, Jr (Oxford: Clarendon Press, 1962).

Sidney, Philip *An Apology for Poetry, or The Defence of Poesy*, ed. Geoffrey Shepherd (Manchester: Manchester University Press, 2nd edn., 1973).

Sidney, Philip *The Countess of Pembroke's Arcadia (The Old Arcadia)*, ed. Jean Robertson (Oxford: Clarendon Press, 1973).

Sidney, Philip *A Defence of Poetry*, ed. van Dorsten, in *Miscellaneous Prose of Sir Philip Sidney*, ed. Duncan-Jones and van Dorsten (1973).

Sidney, Philip *Miscellaneous Prose of Sir Philip Sidney*, ed. Katherine Duncan-Jones and Jan van Dorsten (Oxford: Clarendon Press, 1973).

Sidney, Philip *The Countess of Pembroke's Arcadia (the New Arcadia)*, ed. Victor Skretkowicz (Oxford: Clarendon Press, 1987).

Sidney, Philip 'The Defence of Poesy', in *The Oxford Authors: Sir Philip Sidney*, ed. Duncan-Jones (1989).

Sidney, Philip *An Apology for Poetry, or The Defence of Poesy*, ed. R. W. Maslen (Manchester: University of Manchester Press, 3rd edn., 2002).

Sidney, Philip *The Defence of Poesy*, in *Sidney's 'The Defence of Poesy' and Selected Renaissance Literary Criticism*, ed. Gavin Alexander (Harmondsworth: Penguin, 2004).

Sidney, Philip *The Correspondence of Sir Philip Sidney*, ed. Roger Kuin, 2 vols. (Oxford: Clarendon Press, 2012).

Smith, G. Gregory, ed. *Elizabethan Critical Essays*, 2 vols. (Oxford: Oxford University Press, 1904).

Solon 'Fragments', in *Greek Elegiac Poetry From the Seventh to the Fifth Centuries BC*, trans. Douglas E. Gerber (Cambridge, MA: Harvard University Press, 1999).

Spenser, Edmund *The Shepheardes Calender* (1579), in *The Yale Edition of the Shorter Poems of Edmund Spenser*, ed. William A. Oram et al. (New Haven: Yale University Press, 1989).

Spenser, Edmund *The Faerie Queene*, ed. A. C. Hamilton et al. (Harlow: Pearson Longman, revised 2nd edn., 2007).

Spenser, Edmund and Gabriel Harvey *Three proper, and wittie, familiar letters: lately passed betvveene tvvo vniuersitie men: touching the earthquake in Aprill last, and our English refourmed versifying With the preface of a wellwiller to them both* (London, 1580).

Suetonius *Lives of the Caesars*, trans. J. C. Rolfe, 2 vols. (Cambridge, MA: Harvard University Press, 1914).

Temple, William *William Temple's* Analysis *of Sir Philip Sidney's* Apology for Poetry, ed. and trans. John Webster (Binghamton, NY: Medieval and Renaissance Texts and Studies, 1984).

Virgil *Eclogues, Georgics, Aeneid*, trans. H. Rushton Fairclough, revised G. P. Goold, 2 vols. (Cambridge, MA: Harvard University Press, revised edition, 1999–2001).

Vives, Juan Luis *On Education*, trans. Foster Watson (Cambridge: Cambridge University Press, 1913).

Watson, Henry, trans. *The hystory of the two valyaunte brethren Valentyne and Orson, sonnes vnto the Emperour of Grece* (London, 1555).

Webbe, William *A Discourse of English Poetrie* (1586), in *Elizabethan Critical Essays*, ed. Smith (1904).

Wilde, Oscar *Oscar Wilde: The Major Works*, ed. Isobel Murray (Oxford: Oxford University Press, 1989).

Wills, Richard *De re poetica* (1573), ed. and trans. A. D. S. Fowler (Oxford: Blackwell, 1958).

Wilson, Thomas *The arte of rhetorique for the vse of all suche as are studious of eloquence, sette forth in English* (London, 1553).

Wyatt, Thomas *Sir Thomas Wyatt: The Complete Poems*, ed. R. A. Rebholz (Harmondsworth: Penguin, 1978).

Xenophon *Cyropaedia*, trans. Walter Miller, 2 vols. (Cambridge, MA: Harvard University Press, 1914).

Xenophon *Hiero. Agesilaus. Constitution of the Lacedaemonians. Ways and Means. Cavalry Commander. Art of Horsemanship. On Hunting. Constitution of the Athenians*, trans. E. C. Marchant and G. W. Bowersock (Cambridge, MA: Harvard University Press, 1925).

Xenophon *Memorabilia, Oeconomicus, Symposium, Apology*, trans. E. C. Marchant and O. J. Todd, revised Jeffrey Henderson (Cambridge, MA: Harvard University Press, 2013).

SECONDARY TEXTS

Adamson, Sylvia, Gavin Alexander, and Katrin Ettenhuber, eds. *Renaissance Figures of Speech* (Cambridge: Cambridge University Press, 2007).

Adorno, Theodor W. *Minima Moralia: Reflections from Damaged Life*, trans. E. F. N. Jephcott (London: Verso, 2005).

Alexander, Gavin, ed. *Sidney's 'The Defence of Poesy' and Selected Renaissance Literary Criticism* (Harmondsworth: Penguin, 2004).

Alexander, Gavin, ed. *The Model of Poesy* (Cambridge: Cambridge University Press, 2013).

Allen, M. J. B., Dominic Baker-Smith, and Arthur F. Kinney, eds. *Sir Philip Sidney's Achievements* (New York: AMS Press, 1990).

Alsop, J. D. 'Sir Philip Sidney's Tax Debts, 1585–1586', *NQ* 44.4 (1997): 470–1.

Anderson, Judith H. *Translating Investments: Metaphor and the Dynamic of Cultural Change in Tudor-Stuart England* (New York: Fordham University Press, 2005).

Arendt, Hannah *The Human Condition* (Chicago: University of Chicago Press, 1958).

Barish, Jonas *The Antitheatrical Prejudice* (Berkeley: University of California Press, 1981).

Barker, Arthur E. 'An Apology for the Study of Renaissance Poetry', in *Literary Views: Critical and Historical Essays*, ed. Camden (1964), 15–43.

Barnes, Catherine 'The Hidden Persuader: The Complex Speaking Voice of Sidney's *Defence of Poetry*', *PMLA* 86.3 (1971): 422–7.

Barthes, Roland *The Pleasure of the Text*, trans. Richard Miller (Oxford: Blackwell, 1975).

Bataille, Georges *Visions of Excess: Selected Writings, 1927–1939*, ed. and trans. Allan Stoekl et al. (Minneapolis: University of Minnesota Press, 1985).

Bates, Catherine 'Much Ado About Nothing: The Contents of Jonson's *Forrest*', *EiC* 42.1 (1992): 24–35.

Bates, Catherine *Play in A Godless World: The Theory and Practice of Play in Shakespeare, Nietzsche, and Freud* (London: Open Gate Press, 1999).

Bates, Catherine 'Astrophil and the Manic Wit of the Abject Male', *SEL* 41.1 (2001): 1–24.

Bates, Catherine *Masculinity, Gender and Identity in the English Renaissance Lyric* (Cambridge: Cambridge University Press, 2007).

Bates, Catherine *Masculinity and the Hunt: Wyatt to Spenser* (Oxford: Clarendon Press, 2013).

Bates, Catherine 'Pamela's Purse: The Price of Romance in Sidney's *Arcadia*', in *Romance Writing in English Literature*, ed. Stanivukovic (Montreal: McGill-Queens University Press, forthcoming).

Benveniste, Emile *Problems in General Linguistics*, trans. Mary Elizabeth Meek (Coral Gables, FL: University of Miami Press, 1971).

Bergvall, Åke *The 'Enabling of Judgement': Sir Philip Sidney and the Education of the Reader* (Stockholm: Almqvist, 1989).

Bergvall, Åke 'Reason in Luther, Calvin, and Sidney', *SCJ* 23.1 (1992): 115–27.

Berger, Harry, Jr *Second World and Green World: Studies in Renaissance Fiction-Making*, ed. John Patrick Lynch (Berkeley; University of California Press, 1988).

Berry, Edward *The Making of Sir Philip Sidney* (Toronto: University of Toronto Press, 1998).

Bersani, Leo *The Freudian Body: Psychoanalysis and Art* (New York: Columbia University Press, 1986).

Bersani, Leo *The Culture of Redemption* (Cambridge, MA: Harvard University Press, 1990).

Binns, J. W. 'Henry Dethick's in Praise of Poetry: the First Appearance in Print of an Elizabethan Treatise', *Library* 30.3 (1975): 199–216.

Binns, J. W., ed. *Latin Treatises on Poetry from Renaissance England* (Carbondale, IL: Southern Illinois University Press, 1999).

Blank, Paula *Broken English: Dialects and the Politics of Language in Renaissance Writings* (London: Routledge, 1996).

Blasing, Mutlu Konuk *Lyric Poetry: The Pain and the Pleasure of Words* (Princeton: Princeton University Press, 2007).

Blood, Susan 'The Poetics of Expenditure', *MLN* 117 (2002): 836–57.

Boehrer, Bruce 'Shakespeare and the Social Devaluation of the Horse', in *The Culture of the Horse*, ed. Raber and Tucker (2005), 91–111.

Booth, Wayne C. *A Rhetoric of Irony* (Chicago: University of Chicago Press, 1974).

Borris, Kenneth *Allegory and Epic in English Renaissance Literature* (Cambridge: Cambridge University Press, 2000).

Bourdieu, Pierre *Distinction: A Social Critique of the Judgement of Taste*, trans. Richard Nice, intr. Tony Bennett (London: Routledge and Kegan Paul, 1984).

Braden, Gordon *Petrarchan Love and the Continental Renaissance* (New Haven: Yale University Press, 1999).

Brink, C. O. *Horace on Poetry: The 'Ars Poetica'* (Cambridge: Cambridge University Press, 1971).

Brljak, Vladimir *Allegory and Modernity in English Literature, c.1575–1675* (unpublished PhD thesis, University of Warwick, 2015).

Bronowski, J. *The Poet's Defence* (Cambridge: Cambridge University Press, 1939).

Bruster, Douglas *Drama and the Market in the Age of Shakespeare* (Cambridge: Cambridge University Press, 1992).

Burke, Kenneth *A Rhetoric of Motives* (New York: Prentice-Hall, 1950).

Camden, Carroll, ed. *Literary Views: Critical and Historical Essays* (Chicago: University of Chicago Press, 1964).

Challis, C. E. *The Tudor Coinage* (Manchester: Manchester University Press, 1978).

Cheney, Patrick *Marlowe's Republican Authorship: Lucan, Liberty, and the Sublime* (Basingstoke: Palgrave Macmillan, 2009).

Cheney, Patrick *English Authorship and the Early Modern Sublime: Spenser, Marlowe, Shakespeare, Jonson* (Cambridge: Cambridge University Press, 2017).

Colie, Rosalie L. *Paradoxia Epidemica: The Renaissance Tradition of Paradox* (Princeton: Princeton University Press, 1966).

Connell, Dorothy *Sir Philip Sidney: The Maker's Mind* (Oxford: Clarendon Press, 1977).

Coogan, Robert M. 'The Triumph of Reason: Sidney's *Defense* and Aristotle's *Rhetoric*', *PLL* 17 (1981): 255–70.

Correll, Barbara 'Symbolic Economies and Zero-Sum Erotics: Donne's "Sapho to Philaenis"', *ELH* 62.3 (1995): 487–507.

Correll, Barbara 'Scene Stealers: Autolycus, *The Winter's Tale*, and Economic Criticism', in *Money and the Age of Shakespeare: Essays in New Economic Criticism*, ed. Woodbridge (2003), 53–66.

Correll, Barbara 'Terms of "Indearment": Lyric and General Economy in Shakespeare and Donne', *ELH* 75.2 (2008): 241–62.

Costelloe, Timothy M., ed. *The Sublime: From Antiquity to the Present* (Cambridge: Cambridge University Press, 2012).

Craig, D. H. 'A Hybrid Growth: Sidney's Theory of Poetry in *An Apology for Poetry*', *ELR* 10.2 (1980): 183–201.

Crewe, Jonathan *Unredeemed Rhetoric: Thomas Nashe and the Scandal of Authorship* (Baltimore: Johns Hopkins University Press, 1982).

Crewe, Jonathan *Hidden Designs: The Critical Profession and Renaissance Literature* (London: Methuen, 1986).

Crewe, Jonathan *Trials of Authorship: Anterior Forms and Poetic Reconstruction from Wyatt to Shakespeare* (Berkeley: University of California Press, 1990).

Curtright, Travis 'Sidney's *Defense of Poetry*: Ethos and the Ideas', *Ben Jonson Journal* 10 (2003): 101–15.

Danielson, Dennis R. 'Sidney, Greville, and the Metaphysics of "Naughtinesse"', *ESC* 10.3 (1984): 265–77.

de Man, Paul 'Excuses (Confessions)', in *Allegories of Reading: Figural Language in Rousseau, Nietzsche, Rilke, and Proust* (New Haven: Yale University Press, 1979), 278–301.

de Man, Paul 'The Rhetoric of Temporality', in *Blindness and Insight: Essays in the Rhetoric of Contemporary Criticism* (Minneapolis: University of Minnesota Press, revised 2nd edn., 1983), 187–228.

De Neef, A. Leigh 'Rereading Sidney's *Apology*', *JMRS* 10.2 (1980): 155–91.

Deng, Stephen *Coinage and State Formation in Early Modern English Literature* (New York: Palgrave Macmillan, 2011).

Derrida, Jacques *Of Grammatology,* trans. Gayatri Chakravorty Spivak (Baltimore: Johns Hopkins University Press, 1976).

Derrida, Jacques *Writing and Difference*, trans. Alan Bass (Chicago: University of Chicago Press, 1978).

Derrida, Jacques *Given Time: I. Counterfeit Money*, trans. Peggy Kamuf (Chicago: University of Chicago Press, 1992).

Devereux, James A., S. J. 'The Meaning of Delight in Sidney's *Defence of Poesy*', *SLI* 15.1 (1982): 85–97.

Dickson, Lynne 'Sidney's Grotesque Muse: Fictional Excess and the Feminine in the *Arcadias*', *RP* (1992): 41–55.

Doherty, M. J. *The Mistress-Knowledge: Sir Philip Sidney's* Defence of Poesie *and Literary Architectonics in the English Renaissance* (Nashville: Vanderbilt University Press, 1991).

Dolan, Frances 'Taking the Pencil out of God's Hand: Art, Nature, and the Face-Painting Debate in Early Modern England', *PMLA* 108.2 (1993): 224–39.

Dollimore, Jonathan *Radical Tragedy: Religion, Ideology and Power in the Drama of Shakespeare and his Contemporaries* (Basingstoke: Palgrave Macmillan, 3rd edn., 2004).

Donaldson, Ian *The Rapes of Lucretia: A Myth and its Transformations* (Oxford: Oxford University Press, 1982).

Duncan-Jones, Katherine 'Sidney's Anacreontics', *RES* 36.142 (1985): 226–8.

Duncan-Jones, Katherine, ed. *The Oxford Authors: Sir Philip Sidney* (Oxford: Oxford University Press, 1989).

Duncan-Jones, Katherine *Sir Philip Sidney: Courtier Poet* (New Haven: Yale University Press, 1991).

Duncan-Jones, Katherine and Jan van Dorsten, eds. *Miscellaneous Prose of Sir Philip Sidney* (Oxford: Clarendon Press, 1973).

Dundas, Judith *Sidney and Junius on Poetry and Painting: From the Margins to the Center* (Newark: University of Delaware Press, 2007).

Eden, Kathy *Hermeneutics and the Rhetorical Tradition: Chapters in the Ancient Legacy and Its Humanist Reception* (New Haven: Yale University Press, 1997).

Edwards, Peter, Karl A. E. Enenkel, and Elspeth Graham, eds. *The Horse as Cultural Icon: The Real and the Symbolic Horse in the Early Modern World* (Leiden: Brill, 2012).

Ellinghausen, Laurie *Labor and Writing in Early Modern England, 1567–1667* (Aldershot: Ashgate, 2008).

Elliott, John R., Alan H. Nelson, Alexandra F. Johnston, and Diana Wyatt, eds. *Records of Early English Drama: Oxford*, 2 vols. (Toronto: University of Toronto Press, 2004).

Enterline, Lynn *The Tears of Narcissus: Melancholia and Masculinity in Early Modern Writing* (Stanford: Stanford University Press, 1995).

Enterline, Lynn *Shakespeare's Schoolroom: Rhetoric, Discipline, Emotion* (Philadelphia: University of Pennsylvania Press, 2012).

Evans, Scott D. 'A "Divine Consideration": *Utopia* in Sidney's *Defence of Poetry*', *Moreana* 33.125 (1996): 7–29.

Farley-Hills, David 'Sidney and Poetic Madness', *NQ* 38.1 (1991): 24–6.

Ferguson, Margaret *Trials of Desire: Renaissance Defenses of Poetry* (New Haven: Yale University Press, 1983).

Fineman, Joel *Shakespeare's Perjured Eye: The Invention of Poetic Subjectivity in the Sonnets* (Berkeley: University of California Press, 1986).

Finkelstein, Andrea *The Grammar of Profit: The Price Revolution in Intellectual Context* (Leiden: Brill, 2006).

Fischer, Sandra K. *Econolingua: A Glossary of Coins and Economic Language in Renaissance Drama* (Newark: University of Delaware Press, 1985).

Fisher, Will 'Queer Money', *ELH* 66.1 (1999): 1–23.

Fraser, Russell *The War Against Poetry* (Princeton: Princeton University Press, 1970).

Freccero, John 'The Fig Tree and the Laurel: Petrarch's Poetics', in *Literary Theory/ Renaissance Texts*, ed. Parker and Quint (1986), 20–32.

Freud, Sigmund *The Standard Edition of the Complete Psychological Works of Sigmund Freud*, ed. and trans. James Strachey, 24 vols. (London: Hogarth Press, 1960), hereafter *SE*.

Freud, Sigmund *The Interpretation of Dreams* (1900), *SE* 4–5.

Freud, Sigmund *Jokes and Their Relation to the Unconscious* (1905), *SE* 8.

Freud, Sigmund 'The Antithetical Meaning of Primal Words' (1910), *SE* 11.155–61.

Freud, Sigmund 'The "Uncanny"' (1919), *SE* 17.219–56.

Freud, Sigmund *Beyond the Pleasure Principle* (1920), *SE* 18.7–64.

Freud, Sigmund *The Ego and the Id* (1923), *SE* 19.3–66.

Freud, Sigmund 'The Economic Problem of Masochism' (1924), *SE* 19.159–70.

Frye, Northrop 'Approaching Lyric', in *Lyric Poetry: Beyond New Criticism*, ed. Hošek and Parker (1985), 31–7.

Gallop, Jane 'Precocious *Jouissance*: Roland Barthes, Amatory Maladjustment, and Emotion', *NLH* 43.3 (2012): 565–82.

Giddens, Anthony *Central Problems in Social Theory: Action, Structure and Contradiction in Social Analysis* (London: Macmillan, 1979).

Goldberg, Jonathan *Writing Matter: From the Hands of the English Renaissance* (Stanford: Stanford University Press, 1990).

Goodrich, Peter *Law in the Courts of Love: Literature and Other Minor Jurisprudences* (London: Routledge, 1996).

Goodrich, Peter 'Gay Science and Law', in *Rhetoric and Law in Early Modern Europe*, ed. Kahn and Hutson (2001), 95–124.

Goux, Jean-Joseph *Symbolic Economies: After Marx and Freud*, trans. Jennifer Curtiss Gage (Ithaca: Cornell University Press, 1990).

Grayling, A. C. *The Age of Genius: The Seventeenth Century and the Birth of the Modern Mind* (London: Bloomsbury, 2016).

Greenblatt, Stephen *Renaissance Self-Fashioning from More to Shakespeare* (Chicago: University of Chicago Press, 1980).

Greene, Roland *Unrequited Conquests: Love and Empire in the Colonial Americas* (Chicago: University of Chicago Press, 1999).

Greene, Roland 'Resistance in Process: On the semantics of early modern prose fiction', *PS* 32.2 (2010): 101–9.

Greene, Thomas M. *The Light in Troy: Imitation and Discovery in Renaissance Poetry* (New Haven: Yale University Press, 1982).

Greene, Thomas M. 'Pitiful thrivers: failed husbandry in the Sonnets', in *Shakespeare and the Question of Theory*, ed. Parker and Hartman (1985), 230–44.

Guillory, John *Cultural Capital: The Problem of Literary Canon Formation* (Chicago: University of Chicago Press, 1993).

Guy-Bray, Stephen *Against Reproduction: Where Renaissance Texts Come From* (Toronto: University of Toronto Press, 2009).

Hadfield, Andrew *Literature, Politics and National Identity: Reformation to Renaissance* (Cambridge: Cambridge University Press, 1994).

Hager, Alan *Dazzling Images: The Masks of Sir Philip Sidney* (Newark: University of Delaware Press, 1991).

Halpern, Richard *The Poetics of Primitive Accumulation: English Renaissance Culture and the Genealogy of Capital* (Ithaca: Cornell University Press, 1991).

Hamilton, A. C. 'Sidney and Agrippa', *RES* n.s. 7.26 (1956): 151–7.

Hamilton, A. C. *Sir Philip Sidney: A Study of His Life and Works* (Cambridge: Cambridge University Press, 1977).

Hamilton, A. C. 'Sidney's Humanism', in *Sir Philip Sidney's Achievements*, ed. Allen, Baker-Smith, and Kinney (1990), 109–16.

Hamlin, Hannibal *Psalm Culture and Early Modern English Literature* (Cambridge: Cambridge University Press, 2004).

Hardison, O. B., Jr 'The Two Voices of Sidney's *Apology for Poetry*', *ELR* 2.2 (1972): 83–99.

Hassell, James Woodrow, Jr *Middle French Proverbs, Sentences, and Proverbial Phrases* (Toronto: Pontifical Institute of Mediaeval Studies, 1982).

Hawkes, David *Idols of the Marketplace: Idolatry and Commodity Fetishism in English Literature, 1580–1680* (New York: Palgrave, 2001).

Hawkes, David *The Culture of Usury in Renaissance England* (New York: Palgrave Macmillan, 2010).

Hawkes, David *Shakespeare and Economic Theory* (London: Bloomsbury, 2015).

Heinzelman, Kurt *The Economics of the Imagination* (Amherst, MA: University of Massachusetts Press, 1980).

Helgerson, Richard *The Elizabethan Prodigals* (Berkeley: University of California Press, 1976).

Heninger, S. K., Jr 'Speaking Pictures: Sidney's Rapprochement Between Poetry and Painting', in *Sir Philip Sidney and the Interpretation of Renaissance Culture*, ed. Waller and Moore (1984), 3–16.

Heninger, S. K., Jr *Sidney and Spenser: The Poet as Maker* (University Park: Pennsylvania State University Press, 1989).

Herman, Peter C. *Squitter-wits and Muse-haters: Sidney, Spenser, Milton and Renaissance Antipoetic Sentiment* (Detroit: Wayne State University Press, 1996).

Herrick, Marvin T. *The Fusion of Horatian and Aristotelian Literary Criticism, 1531–1555* (Urbana: University of Illinois Press, 1946).

Höltgen, K. J. 'Why Are There No Wolves in England? Philip Camerarius and a German Version of Sidney's Table Talk', *Anglia* 99 (1981): 60–82.

Hošek, Chaviva and Patricia Parker, eds. *Lyric Poetry: Beyond New Criticism* (Ithaca: Cornell University Press, 1985).

Hulse, Clark 'Tudor aesthetics', in *The Cambridge Companion to English Literature, 1500–1600*, ed. Kinney (2000), 29–63.

Hunt, John 'Allusive Coherence in Sidney's *Apology for Poetry*', *SEL* 27.1 (1987): 1–16.

Hutson, Lorna *The Invention of Suspicion: Law and Mimesis in Shakespeare and Renaissance Drama* (Oxford: Oxford University Press, 2007).

James, Susan *Passion and Action: The Emotions in Seventeenth-Century Philosophy* (Oxford: Oxford University Press, 1997).

Jameson, Fredric *The Political Unconscious: Narrative as a Socially Symbolic Act* (London: Methuen, 1981).

Jameson, Fredric *Postmodernism, or, The Cultural Logic of Late Capitalism* (London: Verso, 1991).

Jameson, Fredric *Archaeologies of the Future: The Desire Called Utopia and Other Science Fictions* (London: Verso, 2005).

Jefferson, Ann *Genius in France: An Idea and Its Uses* (Princeton: Princeton University Press, 2014).

Kahn, Victoria and Lorna Hutson, eds. *Rhetoric and Law in Early Modern Europe* (New Haven: Yale University Press, 2001).

Kennedy, William J. *The Site of Petrarchism: Early Modern National Sentiment in Italy, France, and England* (Baltimore: Johns Hopkins University Press, 2003).

Kennedy, William J. *Petrarchism at Work: Contextual Economies in the Age of Shakespeare* (Ithaca: Cornell University Press, 2016).

Kierkegaard, Søren *The Concept of Irony, with Continual Reference to Socrates*, ed. and trans. Howard V. Hong and Edna H. Hong (Princeton: Princeton University Press, 1989).

Kinney, Arthur F. 'Parody and Its Implications in Sydney's *Defense of Poesie*', *SEL* 12.1 (1972): 1–19.

Kinney, Arthur F., ed. *Markets of Bawdrie: The Dramatic Criticism of Stephen Gosson*, (Salzburg: Salzburg Studies in English Literature, 1974).

Kinney, Arthur F., ed. *The Cambridge Companion to English Literature, 1500–1600* (Cambridge: Cambridge University Press, 2000).

Kinney, Arthur F. 'A Poetics of Romance', *SJ* 26.2 (2008): 1–16.

Lacan, Jacques *Écrits: The First Complete Edition in English*, trans. Bruce Fink, with Hélöise Fink and Russell Grigg (New York: W. W. Norton, 2002).

Lamb, Mary Ellen 'Apologizing for Pleasure in Sidney's *Apology for Poetry*: The Nurse of Abuse Meets the Tudor Grammar School', *Criticism* 36.4 (1994): 499–519.

Landreth, David *The Face of Mammon: The Matter of Money in English Renaissance Literature* (Oxford: Oxford University Press, 2012).

Langer, Ullrich *Lyric in the Renaissance: From Petrarch to Montaigne* (Cambridge: Cambridge University Press, 2015).

Lazarus, Micha 'Sidney's Greek *Poetics*', *SP* 112.3 (2015a): 504–36.

Lazarus, Micha 'Greek literacy in sixteenth-century England', *RS* 29.3 (2015b): 433–58.

Lazarus, Micha 'Poetry and Horseplay in Sidney's *Defence of Poesie*', *JWCI* 79 (2016): forthcoming.

LeGuin, Elisabeth 'Man and Horse in Harmony', in *The Culture of the Horse*, ed. Raber and Tucker (2005), 175–96.

Lehnhof, Kent R. 'Profeminism in Philip Sidney's *Apologie for Poetrie*', *SEL* 48.1 (2008): 23–43.

Leinwand, Theodore B. *Theatre, Finance and Society in Early Modern England* (Cambridge: Cambridge University Press, 1999).

Levao, Ronald *Renaissance Minds and Their Fictions: Cusanus, Sidney, Shakespeare* (Berkeley: University of California Press, 1985).

Levao, Ronald '*Shakespeare's Perjured Eye: The Invention of Poetic Subjectivity in the Sonnets*, by Joel Fineman; *Such Is My Love: A Study of Shakespeare's Sonnets*, by Joseph Pequigney' (review article), *RQ* 40.4 (1987): 814–19.

Lévi-Strauss, Claude *Introduction to the Work of Marcel Mauss*, trans. Felicity Baker (London: Routledge and Kegan Paul, 1987).

Lewis, C. S. *Studies in Words* (Cambridge: Cambridge University Press, 2nd edn., 1967).

Loewenstein, Joseph 'Sidney's Truant Pen', *MLQ* 46.2 (1985): 128–42.

Low, Anthony *The Reinvention of Love: Poetry, Politics and Culture from Sidney to Milton* (Cambridge: Cambridge University Press, 1993).

Mannoni, Octave 'I Know Well, but All the Same...', trans. G. M. Goshgarian, in *Perversion and the Social Relation*, ed. Rothenberg, Foster, and Žižek (2003), 68–92.

Marshall, Cynthia *The Shattering of the Self: Violence, Subjectivity, and Early Modern Texts* (Baltimore: Johns Hopkins University Press, 2002).

Maslen, R. W., ed. *An Apology for Poetry, or The Defence of Poesy* (Manchester: University of Manchester Press, 3rd edn., 2002).

Maslen, R. W. 'Sidney, Gascoigne, and the "Bastard Poets"', in *Prose Fiction and Early Modern Sexualities in England, 1570–1640*, ed. Relihan and Stanivukovic (2003), 215–33.

Marx, Karl *Early Writings*, ed. and trans. T. B. Bottomore (London: C. A. Watts & Co., 1963).

Matz, Robert *Defending Literature in Early Modern England: Renaissance Literary Theory in Social Context* (Cambridge: Cambridge University Press, 2000).

Mayhew, Nicholas *Sterling: The History of a Currency* (Harmondsworth: Penguin, 1999).

McIntyre, John P., S. J. 'Sidney's "Golden World"', *Comp Lit* 14.4 (1962): 356–65.

McMahon, Darrin M. *Divine Fury: A History of Genius* (New York: Basic Books, 2013).

Miller, Anthony, 'Sidney's *Apology for Poetry* and Plutarch's *Moralia*', *ELR* 17.3 (1987): 259–76.

Miller, Jacqueline T. 'The Passion Signified: Imitation and the Construction of Emotions in Sidney and Wroth', *Criticism* 43.4 (2001): 407–21.

Miller, Paul Allen *Lyric Texts and Lyric Consciousness: The Birth of a Genre from Archaic Greece to Augustan Rome* (London: Routledge, 1994).

Moore, Michael D. 'Genre of Genre: Sidney and Defences of Poetry', *Florilegium* 16 (1999): 147–54.

Moore, Roger E. 'Sir Philip Sidney's Defense of Prophesying', *SEL* 50.1 (2010): 35–62.

Muldrew, Craig *The Economy of Obligation: The Culture of Credit and Social Relations in Early Modern England* (Basingstoke: Macmillan, 1998).

Myrick, Kenneth Orne *Sir Philip Sidney as Literary Craftsman* (Cambridge, MA: Harvard University Press, 1935).

Nelson, Alan H., ed. *Records of Early English Drama: Cambridge*, 2 vols. (Toronto: University of Toronto Press, 1989).

Nelson, Eric 'Greek Nonsense in More's *Utopia*', *HJ* 44.4 (2001): 889–917.

Nicholson, Catherine *Uncommon Tongues: Eloquence and Eccentricity in the English Renaissance* (Philadelphia: University of Pennsylvania Press, 2014).

Nietzsche, Friedrich *The Birth of Tragedy*, trans. Douglas Smith (Oxford: Oxford University Press, 2000).

Owens, E. J. 'The Koprologoi at Athens in the Fifth and Fourth Centuries B.C.', *CQ* 33.1 (1983): 44–50.

Parker, Patricia, 'Hysteron proteron: or the preposterous', in *Renaissance Figures of Speech*, ed. Adamson, Alexander, and Ettenhuber (2007), 133–45.

Parker, Patricia and Geoffrey Hartman, eds. *Shakespeare and the Question of Theory* (Baltimore: Johns Hopkins University Press, 1985).

Parker, Patricia and David Quint, eds. *Literary Theory/Renaissance Texts* (Baltimore: Johns Hopkins University Press, 1986).

Perry, Nandra '*Imitatio* and Identity: Thomas Rogers, Philip Sidney, and the Protestant Self', *ELR* 35.3 (2005): 365–406.

Prendergast, Maria Teresa Micaela *Renaissance Fantasies: The Gendering of Aesthetics in Early Modern Fiction* (Kent, OH: Kent State University Press, 1999).

Prescott, Anne Lake 'King David as "Right Poet": Sidney and the Psalmist', *ELR* 19.2 (1989): 131–51.

Prescott, Anne Lake 'Tracing Astrophil's "Coltish Gyres": Sidney and the Horses of Desire', *RP* (2005): 25–42.

Quint, David *Epic and Empire: Politics and Generic Form from Virgil to Milton* (Princeton: Princeton University Press, 1993).

Raber, Karen *Animal Bodies, Renaissance Culture* (Philadelphia: University of Pennsylvania Press, 2013).

Raber, Karen and Treva J. Tucker, eds. *The Culture of the Horse: Status, Discipline, and Identity in the Early Modern World* (Basingstoke: Palgrave Macmillan, 2005).

Raiger, Michael 'Sidney's Defense of Plato', *RL* 30.2 (1998): 21–57.

Raitiere, Martin 'The Unity of Sidney's *Apology for Poetry*', *SEL* 21.1 (1981): 37–58.

Refini, Eugenio 'Longinus and Poetic Imagination in Late Renaissance Literary Theory', in *Translations of the Sublime*, ed. van Eck et al. (2012), 33–53.

Reisner, Noam 'The Paradox of Mimesis in Sidney's *Defence of Poesie* and Marlowe's *Doctor Faustus*', *CamQ* 39.4 (2010): 331–49.

Relihan, Constance C. and Goran V. Stanivukovic, eds. *Prose Fiction and Early Modern Sexualities in England, 1570–1640* (Basingstoke: Palgrave Macmillan, 2003).

Ringler, William A., Jr, ed. John Rainolds, *Oratio in laudem artis poeticae (c.1572)*, trans. Walter Allen, Jr (Princeton: Princeton University Press, 1940).

Ringler, William A., Jr, ed. *The Poems of Sir Philip Sidney* (Oxford: Clarendon Press, 1962).

Robertson, D. W., Jr *A Preface to Chaucer: Studies in Medieval Perspectives* (Princeton: Princeton University Press, 1962).

Robinson, Forrest G. *The Shape of Things Known: Sidney's Apology in Its Philosophical Tradition* (Cambridge, MA: Harvard University Press, 1972).

Roche, Thomas P., Jr *Petrarch and the English Sonnet Sequences* (New York: AMS Press, 1989).

Rothenberg, Molly Anne, Dennis Foster, and Slavoj Žižek, eds. *Perversion and the Social Relation* (Durham, NC: Duke University Press, 2003).

Rudenstine, Neil L. *Sidney's Poetic Development* (Cambridge, MA: Harvard University Press, 1967).

Salman, Phillips 'Instruction and Delight in Medieval and Renaissance Criticism', *RQ* 32.3 (1979): 303–32.

Saunders, Ben *Desiring Donne: Poetry, Sexuality, Interpretation* (Cambridge, MA: Harvard University Press, 2006).

Scanlon, James J. 'Sidney's *Astrophil and Stella*: "See what it is to Love" Sensually!' *SEL* 16.1 (1976): 65–74.

Schiffer, James, ed. *Shakespeare's Sonnets: Critical Essays* (New York: Garland, 1999).

Schoeck, R. J., ed. *Acta Conventus Neo-Latini Bononiensis* (Binghamton, NY: Medieval and Renaissance Texts and Studies, 1985).

Sedgwick, Eve Kosofsky *Between Men: English Literature and Male Homosocial Desire* (New York: Columbia University Press, 1985).

Sedley, David L. *Sublimity and Skepticism in Montaigne and Milton* (Ann Arbor: University of Michigan Press, 2005).

Sekora, John *Luxury: The Concept in Western Thought, from Eden to Smollett* (Baltimore: Johns Hopkins University Press, 1977).

Shell, Marc *The Economy of Literature* (Baltimore: Johns Hopkins University Press, 1978).

Shell, Marc *Money, Language, and Thought: Literary and Philosophic Economies from the Medieval to the Modern Era* (Baltimore: Johns Hopkins University Press, 1982).

Shepherd, Geoffrey, ed. *An Apology for Poetry, or The Defence of Poesy* (Manchester: Manchester University Press, 2nd edn., 1973).

Shuger, Debora 'Castigating Livy: The Rape of Lucretia and *The Old Arcadia*', *RQ* 51.2 (1998): 526–48.

Sinfield, Alan 'The Cultural Politics of the *Defence of Poetry*', in *Sir Philip Sidney and the Interpretation of Renaissance Culture*, ed. Waller and Moore (1984), 124–43.

Sinfield, Alan *Faultlines: Cultural Materialism and the Politics of Dissident Reading* (Oxford: Clarendon Press, 1992).

Singer, Julie *Blindness and Therapy in Late Medieval French and Italian Poetry* (Woodbridge: D. S. Brewer, 2011).

Singer, Kurt '*Oikonomia*: An Inquiry into Beginnings of Economic Thought and Language', *Kyklos* 11 (1958): 29–57.

Skretkowicz, Victor 'Sidney's *Defence of Poetry*, Henri Estienne, and Huguenot Nationalist Satire', *SJ* 16.1 (1998): 3–24.

Socolow, Elizabeth Anne 'Letting Loose the Horses: Sir Philip Sidney's Exordium to *The Defence of Poesie*', in *The Horse as Cultural Icon*, ed. Edwards, Enenkel, and Graham (2012), 121–42.

Spufford, Peter *Money and its Use in Medieval Europe* (Cambridge: Cambridge University Press, 1988).

Stanivukovic, Goran, ed., *Romance Writing in English Literature* (Montreal: McGill-Queens University Press, forthcoming).

Steinvorth, Ulrich *Rethinking the Western Understanding of the Self* (Cambridge: Cambridge University Press, 2009).

Stillman, Robert E. *Sidney's Poetic Justice: The Old Arcadia, Its Eclogues, and Renaissance Pastoral Traditions* (Lewisburg, PA: Bucknell University Press, 1986).

Stillman, Robert E. *Philip Sidney and the Poetics of Renaissance Cosmopolitanism* (Farnham: Ashgate, 2008).

Stillman, Robert E. 'Fictionalizing Philippism in Sidney's *Arcadia*: Economy, Virtuous Pagans, and Early Modern Poetics', *SJ* 27.2 (2009): 13–37.

Stoekl, Allan, ed. and trans. Georges Bataille, *Visions of Excess: Selected Writings, 1927–1939* (Minneapolis: University of Minnesota Press, 1985).

Stone, Lawrence *The Crisis of the Aristocracy, 1558–1641* (Oxford: Clarendon Press, 1965).

Stone, Lawrence *Family and Fortune: Studies in Aristocratic Finance in the Sixteenth and Seventeenth Centuries* (Oxford: Clarendon Press, 1973).

Strier, Richard *Resistant Structures: Particularity, Radicalism, and Renaissance Texts* (Berkeley: University of California Press, 1995).

Strier, Richard *The Unrepentant Renaissance: From Petrarch to Shakespeare to Milton* (Chicago: University of Chicago Press, 2011).

Tilley, Morris Palmer, *A Dictionary of the Proverbs in England in the Sixteenth and Seventeenth Centuries* (Ann Arbor, MI: University of Michigan Press, 1950).

Tilmouth, Christopher *Passion's Triumph over Reason: A History of the Moral Imagination from Spenser to Rochester* (Oxford: Oxford University Press, 2007).

Traub, Valerie 'Sex without Issue: Sodomy, Reproduction, and Signification in Shakespeare's Sonnets', in *Shakespeare's Sonnets: Critical Essays*, ed. Schiffer (1999), 431–52.

Trone, George A. '"You Lie Like a Doctor!": Petrarch's Attack on Medicine', *YJBM* 70.2 (1997): 183–90.

Ulreich, John C., Jr '"The Poets Only Deliver": Sidney's Conception of *Mimesis*', *SLI* 15.1 (1982): 67–84.

van Dorsten, Jan, ed. *A Defence of Poetry*, in *Miscellaneous Prose of Sir Philip Sidney*, ed. Duncan-Jones and van Dorsten (Oxford: Clarendon Press, 1973).

van Eck, Caroline, Stijn Bussels, Maarten Delbeke, and Jürgen Pieters, eds. *Translations of the Sublime: The Early Modern Reception and Dissemination of Longinus' 'Peri Hupsous' in Rhetoric, Visual Arts, Architecture and the Theatre* (Leiden: Brill, 2012).

Waller, Gary F. '"This Matching of Contraries": Bruno, Calvin and the Sidney Circle', *Neophilologus* 56.3 (1972): 331–43.

Waller, Gary F. and Michael D. Moore, eds. *Sir Philip Sidney and the Interpretation of Renaissance Culture* (London: Croom Helm, 1984).

Warley, Christopher *Sonnet Sequences and Social Distinction in Renaissance England* (Cambridge: Cambridge University Press, 2005).

Warley, Christopher *Reading Class Through Shakespeare, Donne, and Milton* (Cambridge: Cambridge University Press, 2014).

Weber, Max *The Protestant Ethic and the Spirit of Capitalism*, trans. Talcott Parsons, intr. Anthony Giddens (London: Routledge, 2001).

Webster, John, ed. and trans. *William Temple's* Analysis *of Sir Philip Sidney's* Apology for Poetry (Binghamton, NY: Medieval and Renaissance Texts and Studies, 1984).

Webster, John 'Temple's Neo-Latin Commentary on Sidney's *Apology*: Two Strategies for a Defense', in *Acta Conventus Neo-Latini Bononiensis*, ed. Schoeck (1985), 317–24.

Weiner, Andrew D. *Sir Philip Sidney and the Poetics of Protestantism: A Study of Contexts* (Minneapolis: University of Minnesota Press, 1978).

Weiner, Andrew D. 'Sidney, Protestantism, and Literary Critics: Reflections on Some Recent Criticism of *The Defence of Poetry*', in *Sir Philip Sidney's Achievements*, ed. Allen, Baker-Smith, and Kinney (1990), 117–26.

Williams, James A. 'Erected Wit and Effeminate Repose: Philip Sidney's Postures of Reader-Response', *MLR* 104.3 (2009): 640–58.

Williams, Raymond *Problems in Materialism and Culture: Selected Essays* (London: Verso, 1980).

Wilson, N. G. 'The Name Hythlodaeus', *Moreana* 29.110 (1992): 33.

Winston, Jessica 'Seneca in Early Elizabethan England', *RQ* 59.1 (2006): 29–58.

Wolfley, Lawrence C. 'Sidney's visual-didactic poetic: some complexities and limitations', *JMRS* 6 (1976): 217–41.

Woodbridge, Linda, ed. *Money and the Age of Shakespeare: Essays in New Economic Criticism* (New York: Palgrave Macmillan, 2003).

Woodmansee, Martha and Mark Osteen, eds. *The New Economic Criticism: Studies at the Intersection of Literature and Economics* (London: Routledge, 1999).

Woudhuysen, H. R. *Sir Philip Sidney and the Circulation of Manuscripts, 1558–1640* (Oxford: Clarendon Press, 1996).

Wrightson, Keith *Earthly Necessities: Economic Lives in Early Modern Britain, 1470–1750* (New Haven: Yale University Press, 2000).

Zim, Rivkah *English Metrical Psalms: Poetry as Praise and Prayer, 1535–1601* (Cambridge: Cambridge University Press, 1987).

Žižek, Slavoj *The Sublime Object of Ideology* (London: Verso, 1989).

Žižek, Slavoj *For They Know Not What They Do: Enjoyment as a Political Factor* (London: Verso, 1991).

Index

Abradatas 86, 125–7, 148–9, 229, 250
Adorno, Theodor 60n, 146n
Aeneas 34, 46, 47, 118, 123, 142n, 204, 223, 245n, 258, 260, 264
  see also Virgil, *Aeneid*
Agrippa, Henry Cornelius 50–2, 55–6, 57n, 83, 86, 92, 93n, 94n, 95n, 104n, 120, 121n, 126–7, 134, 136–7, 142, 149, 170, 173, 271
  The vanitie and vncertaintie of artes and sciences [*De incertitudine et vanitate scientiarum atque artium*] 19n, 50, 61n, 83, 86, 95n, 96n, 104n, 120, 126n, 127, 142, 149, 151n, 169n, 170, 191n
Agrippa, Menenius 23, 71, 144n, 199–202, 221n
Alexander, Gavin x, xiv, 15n, 17n, 20n, 49n, 85n, 106n, 125n, 127n, 147n, 198n, 254n, 272n
Alexander the Great 121, 128n, 186n, 228, 231, 251, 268
Alexander Pheraeus 50n, 128n, 221n
Alsop, J. D. 56n
Amphion 14, 152
Anderson, Judith 35n, 38n, 39n, 55n
Apollo 96n, 237
Arendt, Hannah 165n
Aristotle 4n, 17, 25n, 38n, 44, 46, 59n, 60n, 83, 91n, 103–10, 120n, 146n, 147, 164n, 189n, 191n, 207–8, 221, 222n, 228, 239, 256
  Art of Rhetoric 105n, 158n, 208n
  Metaphysics 60n, 83n
  Nicomachean Ethics 103n, 223n
  Poetics, 103–10, 208n
  Politics 152n
Ascham, Roger 4, 10, 158n, 160–2, 166, 224, 232n, 262, 271
  The Schoolmaster 107n, 159n, 160–2, 166n, 172n, 224n, 232n, 263n, 271n
  Toxophilus 4n
ass 50, 61n, 137, 162n, 186, 271
  see also horse
Augustine 17n, 143n, 154n, 191n, 198–9, 239n
Authorized Version, *see* Bible

Bacon, Francis xii, 145–6n
Barish, Jonas 79n
Barker, Arthur 134n, 148n
Barnes, Catherine 9n, 157n
Barthes, Roland xi, 213
Bataille, Georges xi, 60n, 70, 74, 218–19, 268n

Bates, Catherine xiii, 17n, 18n, 102n, 124n, 131n, 140n, 154n, 158n, 159n, 174n, 216n, 219n, 221n, 232n, 244n, 258n, 261n, 266n, 267n, 269n, 270n
Benveniste, Emile 238n
Berger, Harry 173n
Bergvall, Åke 118n, 119n, 122n, 154n, 157n
Berry, Edward 10n, 25n, 158n, 159n
Bersani, Leo 102n, 144n
Beza, Theodore 241n
Bible 97n, 121n, 240–2, 245
  Geneva Bible 91n, 196n, 239n, 240–2
  Binns, J. W. 99n
Bishop's Bible, *see* Bible
Blank, Paula 5n, 272n
Blasing, Mutlu Konuk 89n
Blood, Susan 219n
Boccaccio, Giovanni 5, 17, 60n
Boehrer, Bruce 270n
Booth, Wayne 136n
Borris, Kenneth 94n
Botley, Paul xiv, 241n
Bourdieu, Pierre 212n
Braden, Gordon 116n
Brink, C. O. 210n, 211n
Brljak, Vladimir xiv, 94n
Bronowski, Jacob 93n, 97n, 109, 118n, 119n, 243n, 247n
Bruno, Giordano 17n
Bruster, Douglas 185n
Buchanan, George 238n, 262
Burke, Kenneth 72n

Calvin, John 16n, 121n
Camerarius, Philip 49n
Campano, Giannantonio 151n
capital vii, 4, 24n, 25n, 26, 34, 40, 45, 49, 52, 54, 62, 63, 64, 69–70, 73, 84, 101, 112, 115, 119n, 132, 151, 153, 158, 162, 165, 166, 168, 169, 186, 197, 212, 213, 218, 230
capitalism x, xi, 4n, 27n, 28, 29, 32n, 41, 43, 53, 54n, 55, 56, 60–3, 65, 69, 70, 71, 77n, 79, 112, 141n, 150, 169, 191n
Caracciolo, Pasqual 161n
Challis, C. E. 36n, 38n, 132n
Chapman, George 172n, 266n
Chaucer, Geoffrey 5, 17, 21, 164n, 181, 232n, 256, 266n
Cheney, Patrick xiii, 172n
Chiron 73, 237, 270
Cicero 3, 87, 148n, 227n, 257, 262
  On Duties [*De Officiis*] 5n
  Tusculan Disputations 3n, 206n

class viii–ix, 4n, 17, 19, 21n, 22n, 23–4, 25n, 26–7, 34, 52–3, 56, 69, 98, 129n, 161, 165, 168n, 174n, 188, 209, 211, 231n, 259–60
Colie, Rosalie 91n, 134n, 140n
comparison of contraries 233, 267
Connell, Dorothy 134n, 136n
Coogan, Robert 10n
Cooper, Thomas 5n, 96n, 265n
Correll, Barbara 28n, 33n, 65n, 152n, 153n, 191n
Corte, Claudio 161n
Costelloe, Timothy 172n
Coverdale's Bible, *see* Bible
Coverdale's Bible 'conferred' with Tyndale's, *see* Bible
Craig, D. H. 9n
Cranmer's Bible, *see* Bible
Crewe, Jonathan xi, xii n, 16n, 63–5, 67, 101, 102n, 134n, 158n, 163–4n, 208n
Cupid 180n, 232, 258, 260, 264
Curtright, Travis 105n
Cuspinianus, Joannes 166n
Cyrus 41, 44n, 46, 47, 86, 95, 106, 108, 112, 119, 120, 121, 122, 123, 125, 126n, 127, 128, 142, 201n, 215, 229, 231, 236, 245n, 248, 269n
see also Sidney, *Defence*, 'many Cyruses'

Daedalus 59n, 164n, 217, 232, 262, 264, 265
Danielson, Dennis 199
Dante Alighieri 5, 17, 21n, 116, 128, 270n
David 15–16, 50n, 96, 223, 235
see also Psalms
de Man, Paul 134, 136
De Neef, A. Leigh 9n
della Casa, Giovanni 268n
Deng, Stephen 36n, 38n, 69n
Denny, Edward 5n, 227
Derrida, Jacques xi, 55n, 60n, 61, 70n, 133n, 136n, 151n, 160n, 170n, 174n, 186n, 238n, 260n
Dethick, Henry 10, 99n
Devereux, James 208n
Dickson, Lynne 100n, 124n, 142n, 154n
Dido 123n, 204, 222, 223, 258n
see also Virgil, *Aeneid*
Doherty, M. J. 120n, 157n, 208n
Dolan, Frances 106n, 124n, 144n
Dollimore, Jonathan 77n, 145n, 174n, 182n
Donaldson, Ian 129n
Donne, John vii, x, 49n, 65n, 119n, 153n
Douai-Rheims Bible, *see* Bible
Duncan-Jones, Katherine 31n, 37n, 49n, 56n, 125n, 134n, 140n
Dundas, Judith 147n, 172n

Eden, Kathy 136n
Elizabeth I 20–1, 36n, 72, 100, 102n, 150n, 188, 189, 257–8, 258n, 261
Ellinghausen, Laurie 22n, 65n

Elliott, John 111n
Elyot, Thomas 4, 10, 24, 85, 172n, 195, 198n
The boke named the gouernour 85, 195, 198n
Enterline, Lynn 75n, 140n, 219n, 222, 223
Epaminondas 121, 266–7
Epimenides 91, 92, 113, 174
Erasmus, Desiderius 4, 51, 52, 55, 56, 60, 61, 70, 134, 136, 137, 173, 241, 242
Annotations on the New Testament 241n, 242n
Novum Instrumentum, *see* Bible
The praise of folie [Moriae encomium] 50, 51, 57, 60n, 64, 134, 169n, 271n
see also folly, fool's gold
Estienne, Robert 5n, 272n
Evans, Scott 48n, 49n

Farley-Hills, David 17n
Ferguson, Margaret 9n, 24n, 50n, 57n, 70–2, 92n, 100n, 105n, 109n, 116n, 119n, 125n, 134, 136n, 140n, 150n, 157n, 168n, 202n, 208n, 235n
fetishism vii, 29, 30, 34, 38, 39–41, 43, 46, 47, 50, 53–6, 60–1, 63, 69, 74n, 79, 101n, 110, 112, 114–16, 137, 143–4, 145, 151
Fineman, Joel 65n, 72n, 105n, 107n, 108n, 109n, 120n, 124n, 134n, 140n, 159n, 162–3, 166, 207n
Finkelstein, Andrea 4n, 23n, 189n, 190n
Fischer, Sandra 148n, 197n
Fisher, Will 151n, 186n
folly xii, 13, 14, 17, 57–60, 61, 68, 73n, 74, 78n, 84n, 85, 87, 88, 90, 95n, 134–5, 136, 147, 164n, 169, 170, 172, 205, 211, 229–30, 231n, 232, 260n, 263
see also Erasmus, *The praise of folie*
fool's gold 60, 151, 169
Fraser, Russell 4n, 25n, 27n, 187–8
Freccero, John 17n, 91–2, 154
Freud, Sigmund 10, 57, 66–8, 70–1, 216, 219, 223n, 238
'The Antithetical Meaning of Primal Words' 238n
Beyond the Pleasure Principle 66–8, 70–1
'The Economic Problem of Masochism' 66, 67n, 216
The Ego and the Id 68n
The Interpretation of Dreams 142n
Jokes and Their Relation to the Unconscious 57n, 141n
'The "Uncanny"' 238n
Frye, Northrop 261n
furor poeticus 16–17n, 26, 79n, 119n, 172n, 216, 223n, 264, 270n
see also *jouissance*, oracles, Sibyl, sublime

Gallop, Jane 213n
Gascoigne, George vii, 65n, 111n, 158n, 259n
Giddens, Anthony 118n
Goldberg, Jonathan 115n
Goodrich, Peter 100n

Gosson, Stephen viii, 3–5, 9, 18–19, 22–4, 27, 50–5, 57, 72–9, 83, 84, 86, 93–8, 101, 113n, 114, 119n, 122, 123n, 135, 138, 141, 148n, 149, 169n, 179–93, 199n, 206, 211, 224, 225, 227n, 230n, 231n, 235n, 237–43, 247–9, 251, 252n, 258n, 262, 270
  An apologie of the Schoole of abuse 23n, 72n, 74n, 77n, 84, 94n, 96n, 185, 186, 187n, 192n, 193n, 271n
  Playes confuted in fiue actions 22n, 77n, 78n, 93n, 96n, 179n, 180, 184, 185n, 186, 189n, 190n, 192n, 193n, 238–41
  The schoole of abuse 3–5, 18–19, 22–4, 50–5, 72–9, 83, 84, 86, 93–8, 114, 148n, 149, 179–93, 199n, 206, 211, 224n, 227n, 230n, 235n, 237, 251, 252n, 258n, 262, 268n, 270n, 271n
Goux, Jean-Joseph vii, xi, 28n, 29n, 33–4, 35n, 38n, 40, 60–1, 63n, 70, 110n, 115–16, 118n, 119n, 129n, 143n, 155
Gower, John 5, 17, 164n, 256
Grayling, A. C. 172n
Great Bible, *see* Bible
Greenblatt, Stephen xi, 69, 267n
Greene, Roland 37n, 212n
Greene, Thomas 107n, 152n
Greville, Fulke 23n, 37n, 76n, 132n, 140n
  'A Dedication to Sir Philip Sidney' 37n, 76n, 132n, 140n
Grisone, Federigo 161n
Guevara, Antonio de 268n
Guillory, John 208n
Guy-Bray, Stephen 145n
Gyges 7, 15n, 29, 30, 32, 40, 155, 174

Hadfield, Andrew 5n, 12n, 64n, 255n, 256n
Hager, Alan 9n, 100n, 134n, 135n, 136n, 139n, 157n, 161n
Halpern, Richard 23n, 41n, 62–3, 65, 68–70, 71, 74, 75n, 162n, 174n, 217, 218, 219n, 221
Hamilton, A. C. 10n, 50n, 92n, 118n, 134n, 136n
Hamlin, Hannibal 196n
Hardison, O. B. 9–10, 255n, 263
Harington, Sir John 20n, 51n, 84n, 86, 92n, 94n, 95–6n, 100, 101, 123n, 156, 173, 181, 195, 211n, 230n, 235n
  'A Briefe Apologie of Poetrie' 20n, 51n, 84n, 86, 92n, 94n, 95–6n, 100, 121n, 156, 182n, 195n, 205–6n, 211n, 230n, 235n
  The metamorphosis of Aiax 94n, 173, 267n
Harrison, William 36
Harvey, Gabriel 36n, 211n
Hassell, James Woodrow 96n
Hawkes, David 39n, 185n, 191n
Hegel, Georg Wilhelm Friedrich 33, 118n, 136n
Heinzelman, Kurt 53n, 167n

Helgerson, Richard vii, viii, 122n, 134n, 136n, 208n, 255n, 268n
Heninger, S. K. 104n, 106n, 108n, 109, 143n, 157n
Hephaistos 265–6
  see also Vulcan
Hera 265–6
  see also Juno
Hercules 121, 218, 260n
Herman, Peter 24n, 54n, 157n
Herodotus 18, 125, 164n, 220
heroic frenzy, see *furor poeticus*
Heron, Haly 161n
Herrick, Marvin 108n
Holinshed, Raphael 36n
Höltgen, K. J. 49n
Homer 6, 21n, 29, 59n, 73, 190, 204–5, 228, 251n, 261n, 266n, 271n
Horace 3–4, 44, 46, 58–9, 108–9, 110, 204, 205–6, 209–11, 218, 224, 229, 232n, 249, 259–60, 270
  Odes 23n
  Satires, 58 229, 230n, 260n
  Epistles 59n, 204, 205n, 210n, 260n
    The Art of Poetry [*Ars Poetica*] 58n, 108n, 109, 163n, 205–6, 210–11, 218, 224, 249, 259–60, 270
horse 60n, 74, 117, 159n, 160, 161, 162, 164, 167, 180, 206, 210, 222, 224, 251, 266, 267, 268–71
  see also ass
horseman 163, 166, 172, 173n, 223, 224, 268, 269n, 270
horsemanship 5, 113, 158n, 159–61, 166, 170, 172n, 223, 269n
Hoskins, John 233
Hulse, Clark 44n, 65n
Hunt, John 9n, 139n, 158n
Hutson, Lorna 13n
hysteron proteron, see preposterous, the

Icarus 217, 221, 232, 265n
Isidore of Seville 217n

James, Susan 75n, 207
Jameson, Fredric xi, 10n, 31, 48n, 61n, 69n, 70n, 141n, 142n
Jefferson, Ann 172n
jouissance 48n, 213–14, 216, 217, 218–19
  see also *furor poeticus*, oracles, Sibyl, sublime
Juno 142n, 258, 260
  see also Hera
Jupiter 142n, 190, 258, 261
  see also Zeus
Justinus, Marcus Junianus 106n, 125, 126n
Juvenal 259, 264

Kennedy, William 12n, 25n, 262n
Kierkegaard, Søren 136n
Kinney, Arthur 3n, 17n, 54n, 75n, 93n, 97n, 227n

labour 19, 20n, 22–7, 30, 31, 34, 44–5, 62, 74, 75n, 84, 98, 115, 117, 124, 145n, 153n, 159, 165n, 172n, 186, 190, 196, 200–1, 223, 224, 259
Lacan, Jacques xi, 68n, 141n, 150n
Lamb, Mary Ellen 75n, 122n, 124n, 155n, 174n, 219n
Landreth, David 4n, 5n, 24n, 28n, 31n, 34n, 36n, 38n, 54n, 58n, 63n, 65n, 69n, 148n, 154n, 167n
Langer, Ullrich 146n, 172n
Lazarus, Micha xiii, 108n, 163n
LeGuin, Elisabeth 269n
Lehnhof, Kent 124n
Leinwand, Theodore 27n, 53n, 61n, 63n
Lépez de Gómara, Francisco 77n
Levao, Ronald 9n, 88n, 122n, 134n, 140n, 141n, 142n, 143n, 153n, 154n, 157n
Lévi-Strauss, Claude 238n
Lewis, C. S. 19n, 25n
Livy 129, 200n
Lodge, Thomas 10
[*A Defence of Poetry*] 94n, 172n, 179n, 188n
Loewenstein, Joseph 102n
Low, Anthony 25n, 65n
Lucretia 50n, 129, 147, 149, 150
Lyly, John 65n, 272

McIntyre, John 108n
McMahon, Darrin 172n
Mammon 167n
Mannoni, Octave 112n
Marius, Gaius 127n, 193, 230n
Marlowe, Christopher vii, 65n, 75
Mars 256n, 258, 264, 265, 266
Marshall, Cynthia 102n, 216n
Marx, Karl 28, 61, 63n
Maslen, R. W. 3n, 6, 15n, 16n, 20n, 21n, 23n, 24n, 25n, 31n, 49n, 50n, 51, 54n, 59n, 65n, 88, 100n, 106n, 122n, 125n, 126, 127n, 140n, 159n, 160, 161n, 165, 166n, 169n, 173n, 197, 198n, 203n, 221–2, 225n, 229n, 233n, 244n, 246n, 250n, 252n, 253n, 255n, 256, 258n, 259n, 261n, 272n
masochism viii, xii, 58n, 64, 66–8, 70, 71, 96n, 101–2, 172, 215–16, 232
Matthew's Bible, *see* Bible
Matz, Robert 24n, 62–3, 69n, 70n, 100n, 155, 159, 173n, 194n, 202n, 205n, 208–12, 218, 231n, 252n
Mayhew, Nicholas 36n
Medea 75, 158, 164n, 214n
Midas 40
Miller, Anthony 139n
Miller, Jacqueline 107n
Miller, Paul Allen 259n
Milton, John 65n, 119n, 199n

Minerva 58n, 259, 269n
  see also Pallas
Moffet, Thomas 140n
money form vii, 28–31, 34, 37–40, 54n, 57, 79, 112, 114, 115–16, 119n, 128, 132, 137, 139, 143, 145, 152, 155, 187, 212, 249
  see also Sidney, *Defence*, 'golden' world
money thought viii, 28–30, 32, 33, 35, 39–43, 46–8, 54–5, 57, 60–1, 68, 69n, 79, 101n, 122, 141, 143–4, 150, 164n, 166–7, 174–5
Moore, Michael 208n
Moore, Roger 17n
More, George 49n
More, Thomas 31n, 48–50, 57, 60, 61, 64, 69–70, 79, 114, 134, 136–40, 150, 173, 201, 249–50, 251, 252
  A dyaloge of syr Thomas More knyghte 113n
  Utopia ix, xii, 31, 39, 46, 47–50, 52, 56, 57, 61n, 64, 68–70, 74, 136–40, 141n, 142–3, 145, 147, 152, 155, 162, 169, 174n, 259–60, 270
Mornay, Philippe de, seigneur du Plessis-Marly 128n, 198–9
Muldrew, Craig 113n
Myrick, Kenneth 21n, 100n, 139n, 157n

Nashe, Thomas vii, 65, 134n, 163–4n, 173
Nelson, Alan 111n
Nelson, Eric 162n
Neoplatonism 17n, 103, 119n, 172n
Newe Testament in Englyshe and in Latin of Erasmus translation, *see* Bible
Nicholson, Catherine 65n, 75n, 272n
Nietzsche, Friedrich 61, 63n, 118n, 174n

Ocyrhoë 270n, 271n
OED 16n, 18n, 19n, 21n, 25n, 31n, 36n, 49n, 113n, 123n, 132n, 133n, 148n, 160n, 173n, 192n, 196n, 197n, 198n, 211n, 215n, 229n, 240n, 241n, 251n, 261n, 268n, 269n
Oedipus 111, 151–2, 267n
Olney, Henry 6, 23n, 31n, 59n
oracles 14–17, 43, 44, 91–2, 154, 172n, 174n, 216–17, 223, 264, 270n
  see also furor poeticus, *jouissance*, Sibyl, sublime
Orpheus 14
Ovid 34n, 56–7, 75, 76n, 184, 260–1, 263, 265–6, 270n
  The Art of Love [*Ars Amatoria*] 56–7
  Metamorphoses 32n, 34n, 75, 168n, 265–6, 269n, 270n, 271n
  Remedia Amoris 59n
  Tristia 260–1
Owens, E. J. 267n

Pace, Richard 161n
Pallas 58, 124, 259–61, 269
  see also Minerva

paradox ix, 41, 50–3, 55–7, 59n, 60, 67, 70, 72,
88, 91–2, 98–100, 103, 110, 134–41,
144n, 146, 150, 157–8, 169, 173, 212,
216n, 218, 264n
see also wit
Paris 260, 261
Parker, Dorothy 222n
Parker, Patricia 83n
passions 12n, 16n, 48n, 61n, 75n, 90, 100,
123–4, 147n, 153n, 158, 164n,
169, 171, 180n, 204, 205, 207–8,
210, 216–17, 220, 222–4, 256,
268–9, 270n
Pegasus 269, 270n, 271
Perry, Nandra 119n
Petrarch, Francesco 5, 15n, 17, 21n, 91,
116–17n, 154, 166
Rime sparse 158n, 166
Invectives 96n
Petrarchism 64, 67, 96n
Phaeton 217, 224, 266, 269n
Philip of Macedon 73n, 251, 268n, 271
Philpot, John 241n
Pindar 73, 251–2, 271
Plato vii, 4, 5–8, 11, 15n, 25n, 29–30, 32,
33, 33–4, 38n, 40–4, 46, 53, 54, 72,
73, 74, 77n, 78–9, 91, 92, 103, 108–10,
115, 123, 143n, 150n, 152, 155–6,
165, 174, 187, 188, 193n, 204, 216,
223, 233, 235n, 239n, 240n, 252–4,
255n, 264
Laws 73n
Lysis 174n
Meno 165n
Phaedrus 46n, 224n, 271n
Protagoras 165n
Republic 4, 7, 11, 29–30, 41, 73, 91, 110n,
152, 156, 161n, 165n, 174n, 182n, 188,
191n, 205n, 253
Sophist 246
Symposium 135n
Theaetetus 174n
Plutarch 6n, 44, 46, 154, 197n, 267
Lives 200n, 251n, 268n
Moralia 86n, 108n, 186n, 267
Ponsonby, William 6, 31, 59n, 92n, 181,
196n, 260n
Prendergast, Maria Teresa 124n
preposterous, the 83, 132, 157, 233, 261,
271–2, 273
Prescott, Anne Lake 15n, 270n, 271n
Prometheus 259, 264, 265–6, 270n
Psalms 15–17, 164n, 196, 223, 267n
see also David
Pugliano, John Pietro 5, 44n, 78n, 157–75,
215n, 217, 251, 252, 270
Puttenham, George 14n, 20n, 65, 150n,
159, 172n, 194n, 207n, 208, 246n,
263, 271

Quint, David 212n
Quintilian 55n, 157n, 198n

Raber, Karen 172n, 269n, 270n, 271n
Raiger, Michael 108n
Raitiere, Martin 9n
Refini, Eugenio 16n, 172n
Reisner, Noam 103n, 107n, 109, 139n
Rhetorica ad Herennium 157n
Rich, Lady Penelope 25n, 39, 100n, 101n
Ringler, William A. 99n, 260n
Robertson, D. W. 154n
Robinson, Forrest 46n, 108n
Robinson, Ralph 49n
Roche, Thomas 117n, 147n
Rudenstine, Neil 62n

St Paul 91, 113, 239–40, 241, 252–3
Acts 113n
Colossians 240, 241n
Corinthians 113n, 239–40, 241, 242n
Titus 91n, 113n
Salman, Phillips 222n
Saunders, Ben x, xi
Scaliger, Julius Caesar 10, 14n, 21–2, 42n, 109,
118–19, 226n
Scanlon, James 147n
Scott, William 47n, 58n, 103n, 105n, 147n,
148n, 197n, 198n, 204n, 207n, 216n,
262n
Sedgwick, Eve Kosofsky 42n
Sedley, David 172n
Sekora, John 162n
Seneca 111n
Shakespeare, William vii, 27n, 38–9n, 62–3,
65n, 70, 119n, 146, 148n, 150, 173,
270n, 273
Edward III, 163n
Henry V, 38n, 163n
King Lear 23, 62–3, 69, 70n, 168n, 170,
256n
Merchant of Venice 53n, 58n, 63n
Sonnets ix, 123–4n, 134n, 140n, 146, 152n,
153n, 163, 168n
Timon of Athens 53n
Shell, Marc vii, 22, 28–30, 32n, 33, 35,
40, 79, 115, 136n, 152, 155, 165n,
172n
Shepherd, Geoffrey 14n, 15n, 16n, 20n, 31n,
49n, 57, 93n, 102n, 106n, 108n, 118n,
119n, 125n, 127n, 154n, 159n, 161n,
173n, 198n, 207, 217, 244n, 246n,
252n, 253n, 272n
Shuger, Debora 129n
Sibyl 15, 43, 131, 144n, 171, 172n, 223n
see also *furor poeticus, jouissance*, oracles,
sublime
Sidney Herbert, Mary, Countess of
Pembroke 100, 155n, 196n

Sidney, Philip
  Astrophil and Stella x, 25n, 26, 39, 58, 59n,
    65, 85, 90, 100n, 101, 119n, 123n,
    133–4, 140, 146n, 147, 153, 158n,
    162n, 163, 167n, 219, 221, 223, 231,
    248, 252n, 258, 260, 261, 263, 264,
    265n, 266n, 268, 269–70, 271
  Correspondence 5n, 8n, 10n, 12n, 20–1, 40n,
    41n, 42n, 104n, 155n, 161n, 162n,
    165n, 223n, 227n
  The Defence of Poesy
    exordium 5, 99, 157–75, 256
    narratio 5–8, 9, 11–28, 30–32, 34–43, 44,
      45, 46, 89, 91, 99, 100n, 103, 107,
      109–10, 131, 138, 195, 216, 225, 226,
      228, 251n
    propositio 41, 44, 99, 103, 107, 108, 110,
      111–12, 138, 147, 245
    divisio 44, 99, 103, 107, 110, 196
    confirmatio 23, 44–6, 99, 103–14, 116n,
      124–9, 147–8, 196–7, 201–5, 220–4,
      236, 251–2
    refutatio 44, 50–9, 83–102, 103,
      110, 113–14, 181–3, 193–4, 195,
      197–8, 220, 224–32, 233–49,
      252–4, 258n
    digressio 46, 58, 76, 83, 123n, 203–4,
      216n, 217n, 236–7, 249, 252, 254–72
    peroratio 46, 59–60, 61n, 98, 113n, 139,
      256n, 260n, 264n
    following xi, 5, 17–18, 20, 21, 75n, 89,
      107n, 108, 113, 117, 120, 122, 157–8,
      161, 164, 168, 169, 172, 174, 196,
      232n, 250, 252–4, 256, 262, 265, 266n,
      270, 273
    'golden' world ix, 7, 12, 30–2, 33, 34–40,
      50, 56, 60, 62, 71, 107, 109n, 110,
      112–14, 116, 118, 119n, 128–9,
      132, 137, 144, 155, 164n, 167n,
      171, 230, 247
      see also money form
    'if' 8, 46, 58, 78, 84–5, 122–4, 151–2,
      157n, 163, 168, 196, 203, 204, 216,
      220–1n, 223, 250–1
    'many Cyruses' viii, 41, 86, 106, 107, 112,
      119, 120, 122, 127, 142, 152, 162, 171,
      201n, 224, 225, 248
      see also Cyrus
    'the simple Indians' 11–12, 31–2, 34–5,
      39, 56, 57, 61, 64, 78n, 107n, 164n,
      172n, 174n, 215n, 226n, 228, 232
    'Thebes' 38–9, 41, 85, 110–11,
      151–2, 155
    'title' 13, 15, 16, 17, 19, 20n, 21, 22–3,
      24, 25, 26, 30, 43, 44, 57–8, 85, 91,
      116, 236, 259–60, 264
    'truly' 6, 7, 8, 14, 16, 46, 50, 77n, 88, 105,
      118, 122–3, 125, 138, 154–5, 203, 204,
      228, 236, 243, 253–4
  The Lady of May 59n, 100

The Old Arcadia 13n, 23n, 62n, 100, 123n,
    128, 153, 155n, 198n, 204, 217, 261n,
    268–9
The New Arcadia 24n, 43n, 76n, 140n, 142,
    154n, 204n, 217, 268n
Sidney, Robert 8, 41n, 100n, 104, 155n,
    160–1, 161–2n, 165n, 223n, 227
Sinfield, Alan 24n, 116–18, 121–2, 247n
Singer, Julie 96n
Singer, Kurt 189n
Skretkowicz, Victor 272n
Smith, G. Gregory 15n
Socolow, Elizabeth Anne 158n, 159n
Solon 7, 83, 91n, 92
Spenser, Edmund vii, 23, 27n, 31n, 34n, 64,
    65, 79, 83, 119n, 141, 150, 167n, 172n,
    174n, 183, 211, 230n, 235n, 272
  The Faerie Queene 31n, 119n, 141n, 235n
  The Shepheardes Calender 172n, 174n, 272
  Three proper, and wittie, familiar letters 23, 211
Spufford, Peter 27n, 31n, 36
Steinvorth, Ulrich 75n
Stillman, Robert 43n, 71n, 104n, 108n, 118n,
    119n, 122n, 136n, 153n, 154n, 158n,
    208n
Stoekl, Allan 74n, 268n
Stone, Lawrence 26–7n
Strier, Richard xi, 57n, 64n, 212n
sublime xii, 16n, 124, 153n, 172n, 217
  see also furor poeticus, jouissance, oracles, Sibyl
Suetonius 127n
Surrey, Henry Howard, Earl of 20n, 63–4, 67,
    168n, 170, 232n, 255n, 256n, 264

Talos 265n
Tarquinius, Sextus 129, 148, 149, 155, 250
Temple, William 93–4n, 100, 102, 165
third way 54–6, 150, 152–3n, 158–9, 182–3,
    247–9, 255
Tilley, Morris Palmer 96n, 222n
Tilmouth, Christopher 123n, 206n, 207n, 222n
Traub, Valerie 152n
Trone, George 96n
Tyndale's Bible, *see* Bible

Ulreich, John 9n

Valentyne and Orson 271n
van Dorsten, Jan 15n, 16n, 31n, 47n, 49n,
    106n, 125n, 127n, 139n, 159n, 259n,
    272n
Venus 184n, 185n, 256n, 258, 260, 261, 264,
    265, 266
Virgil 13, 14, 21n, 34, 47, 59n, 133, 142, 164n,
    222, 232n, 259
  Aeneid 34, 39n, 47, 78n, 142n, 222, 223,
    249, 257–8n, 259n, 264
  see also Aeneas, Dido
  Eclogues 32n
Vives, Juan Luis 7n

Vulcan 256n, 258, 264–6
  see also Hephaistos
Vulgate, *see* Bible

Waller, Gary 17n
Warley, Christopher 25n, 27n, 53n, 140n, 168n
Webbe, William 172n, 235n
Weber, Max viii, 43n
Webster, John 93n, 97n
Weiner, Andrew 43n
Wilde, Oscar 144n, 152
Williams, James 24n, 54n, 100n, 122n, 124n
Williams, Raymond 121n
Wills, Richard 10, 99n
Wilson, N. G. 162n
Wilson, Thomas 47n, 157n
Winston, Jessica 111n
wit 10n, 46, 50–2, 55, 85, 101, 139–41, 158
  see also paradox
Wolfley, Lawrence 120n, 122n, 124n

Woodmansee, Martha 35n
Wotton, Edward 159, 160, 161n, 165, 167, 168, 170
Woudhuysen, H. R. 23n, 24n, 100n, 140n
Wrightson, Keith 36n
Wyatt, Thomas 232n, 267
Wycliffe's Bible, *see* Bible

Xenophon 47, 106, 112, 120, 125, 236, 250
  Art of Horsemanship 172n, 269n
  Cavalry Commander 172n, 269n
  Cyropaedia 47, 106, 112, 120, 125, 236, 250, 269n
  Symposium 184n

Zeus 265, 270n
  see also Jupiter
Zim, Rivkah 196n
Žižek, Slavoj 112n
Zopyrus 86, 125, 126, 127, 148, 149, 229, 250